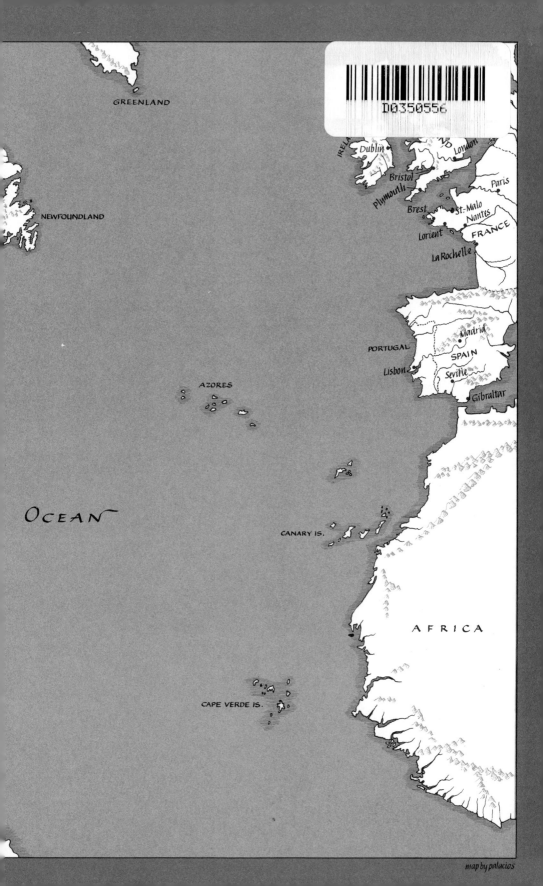

GREENLAND

NEWFOUNDLAND

IRELA

Dublin

Bristol

Plymouth

Brest

Lorient

La Rochelle

London

Paris

St.-Malo
Nantes

FRANCE

PORTUGAL

Madrid

SPAIN

Seville

Lisbon

Gibraltar

AZORES

CANARY IS.

OCEAN

AFRICA

CAPE VERDE IS.

map by palacios

IN DEFENSE OF THE PUBLIC LIBERTY

OTHER BOOKS BY SAMUEL B. GRIFFITH II

IN DEFENSE OF THE PUBLIC LIBERTY

BRITAIN, AMERICA, AND THE STRUGGLE
FOR INDEPENDENCE—FROM 1760
TO THE SURRENDER AT YORKTOWN IN 1781

SAMUEL B. GRIFFITH II

DOUBLEDAY & COMPANY, INC., GARDEN CITY, NEW YORK
1976

Library of Congress Cataloging in Publication Data

Griffith, Samuel B

    In defense of the public liberty.

    Bibliography: p. 698.
      1. United States—History—Revolution, 1775–
1783. 2. United States—History—Revolution, 1775–
1783—Causes. I. Title.
E208.G83   973.3
ISBN 0-385-02541-6
Library of Congress Catalog Card Number 73–9159

    Excerpts from *The Letters of King George III*, edited by Bonamy Dobrée, 1935. Published by Cassell & Co., Ltd.
    Excerpts from *The Correspondence of King George the Third from 1760 to 1783*, edited by the Honourable Sir John Fortescue, 1928. Published by Macmillan Publishers, Ltd. Reprinted by permission of Curtis Brown, Ltd.
    Excerpts from *Diary of Frederick Mackenzie, Giving a Daily Narrative of His Military Service as an Officer of the Regiment of Royal Welch Fusiliers During the Years 1775–1781 in Massachusetts, Rhode Island, and New York*, 2 vols., Cambridge, Mass.: Harvard University Press. Copyright © 1930, 1958 by the President and Fellows of Harvard College; excerpts from *The Diary and Autobiography of John Adams*, edited by L. H. Butterfield, Cambridge, Mass.: The Belknap Press of Harvard University Press, copyright © 1961 by the Massachusetts Historical Society. Both reprinted by permission of Harvard University Press.
    Excerpts from *The Political Journal of George Bubb Dodington*, edited by John Carswell and L. A. Drabble. Copyright © Oxford University Press, 1965. Reprinted by permission of Oxford University Press.
    Excerpts from *Horace Walpole's Correspondence with Sir Horace Mann*, edited by W. S. Lewis, 1967; excerpts from *The American Rebellion*, edited by William B. Willcox, 1954; excerpts from *The Correspondence of General Thomas Gage with the Secretaries of State and with the War Office and the Treasury, 1763–1775*, edited by Clarence E. Carter, 1933. All reprinted by permission of Yale University Press.
    Excerpts from *American Journal of Ambrose Serle*, edited by Edward H. Tatum, 1940. Reprinted by permission of Henry E. Huntington Library and Art Gallery.
    Excerpts from *The Life and Letters of John Paul Jones*, by Anne de Koven. Copyright 1913 by Anne de Koven. Reprinted by permission of Charles Scribner's Sons.
    Excerpts from *Letters of Members of the Continental Congress*, Volumes I–VIII. Reprinted by permission of the Carnegie Institute of Washington.
    Excerpts from *The Last Journals of Horace Walpole During the Reign of King George III*, edited by A. Francis Steuart. Reprinted by permission of The Bodley Head, 1910.
    Excerpts from *The Private Papers of John, Earl of Sandwich, First Lord of the Admiralty, 1771–1782*, published in 1932. Reprinted by permission of the Navy Records Society.
    Excerpts from *Letters from America by William Eddis*, edited by Aubrey C. Land. Reprinted by permission of Harvard University Press.
    Excerpts from *The Barham Papers*, edited by Sir J. K. Laughton, and *Naval Songs and Ballads*, by C. H. Firth. Reprinted by permission of the Navy Records Society.
    Excerpts from *The Papers of Thomas Jefferson*, edited by Julian P. Boyd. Reprinted by permission of Princeton University Press.
    Excerpts from *The Spirit of 'Seventy-six*, edited by H. S. Commager and R. B. Morris. Reprinted by permission of Bobbs-Merrill.
    Excerpts from *The Writings of Samuel Adams*, edited by H. A. Cushing. Reprinted by permission of G. P. Putnam's.
    Excerpts from *Political and Military Episodes in the Latter Half of the Eighteenth Century, Derived from the Life and Correspondence of John Burgoyne*, by E. B. de Fonblanque. Reprinted by permission of Macmillan of London.
    Excerpts from *The Letters of Philip Dormer Stanhope, 4th Earl of Chesterfield*, edited by Bonamy Dobrée. Reprinted by permission of The Viking Press.
    Excerpts from *The Writings of Benjamin Franklin*, edited by A. H. Smyth. Reprinted by permission of Macmillan Company of New York.

to B.

PREFACE

George William Frederick, third King of the Hanover line and the first to be born a Briton, was crowned in Westminster Abbey on September 22, 1761. The young sovereign came to a mighty inheritance. In North America his red-coated soldiers stood at Michilimackinac, Detroit, Fort Pitt, Fort Niagara, Montreal, Ticonderoga, Quebec, Halifax, New York, Pensacola, Mobile, Bermuda, and the Bahamas. In the Caribbean they guarded Jamaica and the lesser Sugar Islands. At Gibraltar they controlled the entrance to the Mediterranean; at Minorca, the trade routes to the Levant. They had destroyed French ambitions in India and were soon to be supreme in the Western Hemisphere at Havana; in the Eastern, at Manila. The King's ships cruised the oceans of the world unchallenged and British merchantmen sailed everywhere unmolested.

Few indeed (and perhaps least of all His Majesty's loyal subjects in the thirteen American colonies) could have anticipated that the ceremony on that day heralded any condition other than a generation of tranquillity, increasing prosperity, and a further strengthening of the relationship that tied the colonists to the mother country. But this happy state of affairs was not to be realized, for within a few years the bonds that men on both sides of the Atlantic thought so secure were to be progressively loosened and finally cut.

The American Revolution was not a revolution as we have come to understand that term. In the words of those who led the struggle one finds no indication of intent to dismantle the existing social structure, no assertion that ills could be cured by turning society upside down, no yearning for an omniscient and omnipotent Caesar or a republican Cromwell. What they sought to achieve, and did achieve, was the acknowledged right to govern themselves as they saw fit, free of dictation by a remote king, a ministry, and a parliament whose mandates they were expected, while in a dependent state, to obey.

The purpose of this book is to attempt to place the American struggle for independence in the context of the period in which it took place. To do this in an appropriately objective and comprehensive manner requires first that one accord to developments of policy and strategy in Great Britain and France more attention than these generally receive, and second that one allow the actors to speak, to the greatest degree possible consistent with relevance, to the subject of the historic drama in which they took part. My thesis in this latter respect is that selective use of apposite quotations is to be preferred to a presumptuous indulgence in unfounded speculation as to what the actors may have thought or felt.

SAMUEL B. GRIFFITH II

Norcross Lodge
Mount Vernon, Maine
March 1976

ACKNOWLEDGMENTS

The major problem faced by anyone who attempts to compress a story as diffuse and complicated as the American struggle for independence into a single volume is not so much what to put in the book as what to leave out of it. This exercise in discrimination is the ultimate responsibility of the writer, who must anticipate the certainty that views of many of those who read his book will not be identical with his own.

Members of my family have been most helpful, as have been my friends Lester and Barbara Tuchman, Robert B. Asprey, Vice-admiral Edwin B. Hooper, Brian B. Burland, Saville T. Clark, Robert D. Heinl, John Shy, Arlene Kleeb Shy, J. W. P. Frost, Joan Saunders, K. G. Davies, Sir Berkeley Gage, Viscount Gage, KCVO, Sir Malcolm Henderson, Brigadier General Edwin H. Simmons, and Major General James D. Lunt.

No research effort can be carried through without the sympathetic assistance of the dedicated people who staff the libraries, and I wish particularly to express my gratitude to Marcus A. McCorison and Mary Brown at the American Antiquarian Society; Howard H. Peckham, John Dann, and Douglas Marshall at the William L. Clements Library; Thomas S. Adams and Richard Boulind at the John Carter Brown Library; James P. Gregory and Sue Gillies at the New-York Historical Society; Joyce Boulind at the Rhode Island Historical Society; Arthur Monke, Mary H. Hughes, and A. Laura McCourt at the Bowdoin College Library; Egon Weiss, Robert E. Schnare, and Marie Capps at the West Point Library; Earl R. Schwass and Anne A. Hardy at the U. S. Naval War College Library; Gerald E. Morris and Thomas L. Gaffney at the Maine Historical Society; John J. Auman at the Fort Ticonderoga Museum; Donald T. Gibbs and Judy E. Hilliard at the Newport Redwood Library; and John Luzader, Historical Division, U. S. National Park Service.

During two years spent in research in England, I utilized the resources of the Public Record Office, the London Library, the Defense Library, the Codrington Library (All Souls), and the Rhodes House Library, and am greatly indebted to the many people who gave of their time to dig out documents and books long out of print.

I wish to thank my editor at Doubleday, Stewart Richardson. "Sandy" has given me constant support and encouragement. I am indebted also to Susan Schwartz and Bill Betts at Doubleday, and to Rafael Palacios for the maps. Finally, I suspect this book would never have been completed had it not been for my sister, Jane Rettew, who typed and typed and typed.

CONTENTS

Book VII
THE COMMON CAUSE

LIST OF MAPS

Illustrations follow pages 126, 270, 438, and 582.

IN DEFENSE OF THE PUBLIC LIBERTY

BOOK I

Most Troublesome and Boisterous Times

🦋 1

A Patriot King

In the late afternoon of October 25, 1760, Londoners learned that George II, King of Great Britain and Ireland and Elector of Hanover, had died that morning and that they had a new King, his twenty-two-year-old grandson.* Few of his loyal subjects knew anything about the character and temperament of George William Frederick, who came to the throne as George III, during whose long reign Great Britain was to lose one empire and gain another.

The young King's father, Frederick Prince of Wales, had died in March 1751, when George was thirteen. Some months previously, Frederick had given his two elder sons a separate establishment in Savile House and had appointed the Earl of Harcourt governor of the household and the Bishop of Norwich preceptor. As such, the bishop was responsible for the education of the two young princes. The governor and the preceptor soon fell into a dispute regarding the political views of the tutors, particularly those ascribed to George Scott, who, some alleged, had been inculcating his young charges with doctrines of monarchical absolutism and arbitrary prerogative. The immediate result of the quarrel was that Harcourt and Norwich were replaced by the Earl of Waldegrave and the Bishop of Peterborough.

* George II had collapsed in his water closet and died a few hours later.

The relationship between Prince George and Waldegrave was formal and unsympathetic. The Prince was resolute, but exceedingly obstinate; he would "seldom do wrong except when he mistakes wrong for right . . . Whenever he is displeased, his anger does not break out with heat and violence; but he becomes sullen and silent and retires to his closet; not to compose his mind by study and contemplation, but merely to indulge the melancholy enjoyment of his own ill humor."[1]

George's early curriculum consisted of daily instruction in the English, German, and French languages, with a smattering of Latin; history, arithmetic, algebra, and some elementary chemistry. The program was rounded out with music, dancing, fencing, and riding lessons. Sunday mornings and evenings were reserved for worship and religious instruction. This demanding routine, which allowed the prince and his younger brother the Duke of York very little time to indulge in normal recreations and pleasures enjoyed by every growing boy, is enough to account for occasional lack of response and fits of sullenness.

George's widowed mother, Augusta of Saxe-Gotha, had shielded him during adolescence and young manhood from the pleasures and vices of London society. He knew nothing of what went on outside Leicester House, where his mother lived and where, until given his own household, he was immured. The princess would not permit him to associate with his contemporaries; she was "averse to the young people from the excessive bad education they had and the bad examples they gave."[2] She wanted her son to see more company, but "who among the young people was fit?" Although she often wished George "had acquaintance older than himself" she allowed him neither a liberal education nor an expanded social life. As a result, the lonely young man, so Waldegrave wrote, was "uncommonly full of princely prejudices, contracted in the nursery and improved by the society of bed-chamber women and pages of the back stairs."[3]

His grandfather, aging, indolent, lecherous, and delighted to be rid of Frederick, whom he always regarded as an incompetent clown and had taken considerable trouble to humiliate at every possible opportunity, paid no attention to the upbringing of the heir apparent. The King, amused with his German mistress, was civil to his widowed daughter-in-law and, according to her testimony, kind to her children, whom he rarely saw.

George loved and respected his mother: from her and the gossipy circle of her friends and ladies in waiting he repeatedly heard how his grandparents had habitually insulted and mistreated his father. "Monster," "villain," "coward," and "wretch" were some of the least opprobrious terms the King and Queen Caroline had used when describing their son, the heir to the throne. Mention of Frederick's name reduced the King to apoplectic rage, and the Queen was heard to say that she wished her son in hell, a fate Her Majesty obviously deemed far too good for him. George thus naturally enough conceived an intense dislike for "the old K," whom he thought selfish, mean, arbitrary, and stupid; for the arrogant William Pitt, Principal Secretary of State for the Northern Department, who led the powerful Whig bloc in the House of Commons; and for Thomas Pelham-Hollis, Duke of Newcastle, the First Lord of the Treasury. Pitt controlled policy; Newcastle the preferments, pensions, and places that were translated into obligatory votes in both Lords and Commons.†

Waldegrave, who had ample opportunity to observe these two gentlemen, acknowledged that Pitt was a man of genius. Although courageous, he was imperious, impatient of contradiction, violent, and implacable. "Under the mask of patriotism," Waldegrave sensed "the despotic spirit of a tyrant."[4] Very few people who knew Newcastle had anything good to say about him. Most judged him, as did the earl, as inordinately ambitious, jealous, irresolute, unreliable, and evasive. The duke attempted to please all his petitioners and ended by pleasing none. Prince George had determined that after his accession he would rid himself of this pair at the first opportunity.

George had not traveled in England or anywhere else. He knew nothing of his land. He was a stranger to the character and aspirations of the people he would rule, as he was to the nature and structure of the extensive empire he would be called upon to govern. He needed a surrogate father, a sophisticated man in whom he could confide, to advise and guide him. Some years earlier his mother had chosen John Stuart, Third Earl of Bute, a Scots courtier for long his mother's close friend and confidant, to be his mentor.

Bute, a handsome and immensely wealthy nobleman who cherished political ambitions, was honestly devoted to George. He was a shallow man; vain, pompous, theatrical, and sententious, and inclined to deal in high-sounding platitudes. George's father, who knew Bute well, described him as "a fine, showy man, who would make an excellent ambassador in a court where there was no business." He had no experience in the vicious world of British factional politics. That he was the young King's favorite did not make him popular with the tough schemers envious of his privileged position and secret influence and fearful of what might happen to them when he came to power, as it was evident he would.

Even worse in the eyes of the earl's growing army of detractors was that he was a Scot and hence, by definition, crafty, designing, and possibly a Jacobite. Gossips in government circles, London drawing rooms,

---

† The "Northern Department" included the Low Countries, the Germanic States, Prussia, the Scandinavian countries, and Russia. The "Southern Department" included France, Spain, Portugal, the Mediterranean, the Italian principalities, and the transatlantic colonies in North America and the Caribbean.

and coffeehouses speculated openly that Bute's relationship with George's mother had been something more than merely friendly. That the earl was ever the princess dowager's bedfellow may be doubted, but at the time many believed he had been. The King had long been aware that "the Favourite's" name was scandalously linked to his mother's. George's reaction was that these malicious attacks were equally directed at him, and assured his "dearest friend" of his continuing affection and loyal support.

Political machinations began a few moments after the fact of George II's death was made public. George Bubb Dodington, who for years had been a hanger-on at Leicester House and was a close friend of both Princess Augusta and the Earl of Bute, whose star was now obviously in the ascendant, indefatigably sought recognition and reward for his loyalty. He could deliver three seats in the House of Commons—or possibly four, if he got the peerage he thought he deserved.‡ He and dozens of others seeking royal favor bombarded Bute mercilessly with letters, crowded his antechambers from morning till night; pressed him with offers of political help, invitations to dine, and much unwanted advice.

Those who had been out of favor for years were clamoring for spoils. The Whigs had gorged themselves for far too long. They should be swept from office—all of them, from the highest to the lowest. And the ambitious Earl of Bute, the only person who enjoyed the full confidence of the King, was the man who when he came to power could wield the broom and "recover the Monarchy from the inveterate usurpations of Oligarchy." The ultimate fate of the Pitt-Newcastle administration was not in doubt. The question tormenting those out of office was "When?"

Dodington sent Bute an anonymous and unpublished poem:

> Quoth Newcastle to Pitt,
> 'Tis vain to dispute,
> If we'd quarrel in Quiet,
> We must make room for Bute:
> Quote Pitt to his Grace,
> To bring that about,
> I fear, my dear Lord,
> Either you or I must turn out,
> Not at all quoth the Duke,
> I meant no such Thing,
> To make room for us all,
> We must turn out the King.
> If that's all your scheme,
> Quote the Earl, by my troth,
> I should stick to my Master,
> And turn ye out, Both.[5]

‡ He did deliver and was created Baron Melcombe.

His Majesty addressed his assembled Lords and Commons for the first time on November 18, 1760. The King declared that he gloried "in the name of Briton," implored the blessings of heaven on his reign, announced that he proposed to encourage piety, religion, and virtue, to reward merit and to strengthen and defend the British Constitution and the rights and liberties of his loyal subjects. The speech was well received in Parliament, as it was in America. John Adams thought these sentiments "worthy of a King—a Patriot King."[6]

Later, Edmund Burke would write: "His Majesty came to the throne of these Kingdoms with more advantages than any of his predecessors since the revolution [of 1688]. . . . His Majesty came, indeed, to the inheritance of a mighty war; but, victorious in every part of the globe, peace was always in his power, not to negotiate, but to dictate." The fleets and armies directed by Pitt, George II's great war minister, had "carried the glory, the power, the commerce of England to a height unknown even to this renowned nation in the times of its greatest prosperity." George II left his throne "resting on the true and only true foundations of all national and all regal greatness; affection at home, reputation abroad, trust in allies; terror in rival nations."[7] His successor's loyal subjects in Great Britain and across the Atlantic shared the hope that he would enjoy a long, happy, peaceful, and prosperous reign.

The King's ambition was to rid politics of factional quarrels and to create a nonpartisan coalition. This was precisely what followers of Newcastle; the Grenville brothers, whose younger sister had married Pitt; the Marquis of Rockingham; and John Russell, Fourth Duke of Bedford, leader of the "Bloomsbury Gang," did not want. Each faction aspired to enjoyment of exclusive power and was reluctant to compromise, either on men or on measures. Thus there could be no simple solution to replacing the Pitt-Newcastle administration with one more amenable to the wishes of the King and his adviser.

Both the young King and Bute were anxious to end the Seven Years' War, which was forcing England toward bankruptcy; to terminate as soon as possible the subsidy of £670,000 a year paid to secure the good will and doubtful alliance of Frederick the Great of Prussia; and, to free Great Britain from continental complications and the vast expenses these entailed, to somehow manage to extricate her from the entangling responsibility to march to the defense of the Electorate of Hanover. Bute felt (according to Dodington) that defending Hanover "would ruin this country without defending that." His Majesty should "no longer expose his regal dominions to such hardships for fruitless attempts to defend his electoral ones."

A power struggle was obviously imminent, but it would be one between factions rather than parties, for there were as yet no parties.

There were men in politics who identified themselves, or whose supporters and antagonists did, as "Whigs" or "Tories." But what sentiments and convictions distinguished a Whig from a Tory? Aspirants for local office concerned themselves exclusively with local affairs and bore no distinctive political label; candidates for seats in the House of Commons were not instructed by their constituents and rarely offered electors any choice of programs. Whigs generally upheld the right of religious dissent; Tories supported the Established Church. Whigs tended to favor London banking, mercantile, and shipping interests; Tories, those of the country gentlemen. Again in general (and generalizations about English politics in this period cannot be avoided), Whigs were dedicated to maintaining the unchallengeable supremacy of Parliament; Tories, usually, to maintaining the prerogatives of the crown. The split extended to the universities: Cambridge was Whig; Oxford, Tory.

Soame Jenyns, who never attained cabinet rank but was in the midst of the political broils characteristic of the period, wrote that he had "diligently inquired" as to the cause of the "disease" of factional dissension. Had this arisen from cleavages in political principles or opinions? "On the strictest examination," Jenyns found no such fundamental differences to exist. All thirsted for office and the power, privileges, and loot that went with it. He saw many parties, but could not discern a single political principle to which any steadfastly adhered: "They are neither Whigs nor Tories, Monarchy-men nor Republicans, High-church nor Low-church, Hanoverians nor Jacobites: they have all acted alternatively on all these principles as they have served a present occasion but have adhered to none of them, nor even pretended to profess them; they have all been ready to support government, whenever they have enjoyed the administration of it; and almost all as ready to subvert it, whenever they were excluded."[8] Indeed, he suggested sarcastically that ministers might as well be chosen by a lottery, for should this method be adopted "a wise, just and virtuous prince" would no longer have to suffer knaves, profligates, and fools in high office.

The King was not interested in labels; he wanted what he described as a "broad-bottomed" administration composed of men he could trust, and in March 1761 persuaded Lord Holderness to step out as Secretary of State for the Northern Department and appointed the Earl of Bute to that office.** Pitt, a Principal Secretary of State and the King's First Minister, acquiesced to this arrangement, which he realized—as did everybody else—boded no good for him.

In the same month, George III dissolved the Parliament elected in 1754, and his ministers made ready for a general election. The young King, resolved to provide an example of virtue, decreed that the Treasury would provide no public money to support candidates favored by

** Lord Holderness was bought off with a pension of £4,000 a year for life.

Administration. This novel and preposterous idea reduced the Duke of Newcastle to tears. How, pray, could he be expected to manage elections in doubtful constituencies unless electors were suitably wined, dined, and otherwise entertained? As polling took place in the shire towns and boroughs and there only, many electors who must ride or post from their estates and farms expected to be reimbursed their expenses in hard cash. Newcastle, an accomplished political manipulator, managed to provide this commodity in 1761 as efficiently as he had in previous elections, and as things turned out, the duke need not have worried. Bute, who had forecast a "King's Parliament," was accurate; many electors cast their votes for men they felt they could trust to support their King.

The King had imagined himself to be in love with Lady Sarah Lennox, the sixteen-year-old sister of the Duke of Richmond, but Lady Sarah's affections were elsewhere engaged, and she responded to His Majesty's cautiously tentative advances with elusive politeness. As usual, George appealed for advice to his "dearest friend" and confidant, who viewed the possible union with dismay. Although Sarah was of noble family, she was not royal. Further (and of material interest to Bute), all her male relations held questionable political views, which is to say they all disliked him. The earl promptly informed the King that this most unbecoming alliance would never do. George replied in a humble letter. If Bute decreed he could not woo the woman of his choice, he would bed the woman his "dearest friend" selected.

Bute had already sent scouts to Germany to find a Protestant princess suitable if not in looks at least in bloodlines and temperament. Half a dozen were on the market. Of the three finalists in this regal tournament, the scouts reported one to be ugly and fat, a second equally ugly, ill tempered, and possibly insane, and a third, Charlotte of Mecklenburg-Strelitz, merely ugly. Charlotte, who has been described as "repulsive" and "hideous," may not have deserved these adjectives, but even the most flattering portraits reveal that she was a singularly homely young woman. Happily, she was said to be "amiable." With the King's choice thus limited, negotiations for Charlotte's hand were initiated, and on July 8, 1761, the court announced the engagement. A dual coronation was set for September 22.

George III has often been depicted as a gross dullard, which he was not. Even before he ascended the throne, his "dearest friend," a man of impeccable artistic taste, had encouraged his predilection to collect objects of elegance and beauty. (Although the prospective Queen satisfied neither of these criteria, she was an accomplished musician.) The moment the King got control of some money, he began to collect. His first major acquisition was a group of 150 drawings and 50 paintings by Canaletto, bought for him in Italy by Bute's younger brother. The young

King did not confine himself to acquiring pictures; he had already formed an impressive collection of medals, and when his purchasing agents exhausted this field, he turned to maps, books, clocks, watches, and musical and astronomical instruments. He had the financial means to buy what he wanted and the discrimination to select the best. His collections attest an uncommon degree of artistic sensitivity.

Bute's entrance on the political stage set off a running battle in the Cabinet. Reflecting the desire of the King, the earl urged termination of the war with France. Great Britain had battered the French to their knees, taken Canada and Guadeloupe, ejected them from India, and was in a position to demand and enforce highly favorable terms. Her mighty navy could not be challenged on the seas. Pitt knew he held the whip in his hand. He hated the French and was reluctant to negotiate. The royal standard flew over the battlements of Quebec; he wished next to drive France from her West Indian Sugar Islands and to break her power as a maritime nation.

Bute thought the First Minister's lust for conquest unreasonable and insatiable, an opinion confirmed when Pitt proposed that Great Britain declare war on Spain, attack the Philippines and Cuba, and waylay a great Spanish treasure fleet just then leaving South America. The Cabinet refused to sanction his projects, and on October 5, 1761, he resigned. Lord Temple, his brother-in-law, was the only one who followed him. Although the King gave Bute credit for driving Pitt out, other members of the Cabinet had been equally adamant in opposing an extension of hostilities and had made it clear to Pitt that they would no longer support him.

With the departure of Pitt, peace could be made, and the Duke of Bedford was instructed to proceed to Paris to conduct preliminary negotiations. Pitt's injured feelings were assuaged with a generous annuity of £3,000 for three "lives" and his wife was created Baroness of Chatham, or, as London wits chose to describe her, "Baroness of Cheat 'em." No doubt the King felt this a resonable ransom to pay to rid his confidential councils of a "snake in the grass." His Majesty's next target was Pitt's long-time cohort, that wily manipulator the Duke of Newcastle.

A week after George III ascended the throne, John Adams, B.A., Harvard, 1755, bachelor, and attorney at law in Braintree, Massachusetts, celebrated his twenty-sixth birthday. Adams was not pleased with the way he had spent the preceding year, and on November 14, 1760, wrote in his diary: "Most of my Time has been spent in Rambling and Dissipation. Riding, and Walking, Smoking Pipes and Spending Evenings consume a vast Proportion of my Time, and the Cares and Anxieties of Business, damp my Ardor and scatter my Attention." The Puritan in him thought it was "high Time for a Reformation, both in the man and the Lawyer."[8]

Actually, John wasted little time either in dissipation or in idle conversation. He was sociable and temperate and enjoyed a glass or two of madeira and a pipe with friends; he sought the company of attractive young ladies, inevitably closely chaperoned by a mother, a maiden aunt, or an unmarried elder sister. He probably disapproved of the old New England custom of bundling, and discreetly did not record that he practiced it. He was an accomplished Latin scholar and found time to read the classical literature. He was inquisitive about everything—hydraulics, earthquakes, mathematics, and farming in all its varied aspects. Most importantly, he was interested in the human beings he had to deal with in his practice of law and those he learned to know as he was gradually and reluctantly drawn into Boston politics. But his profession absorbed most of his energies, and despite his self-criticism he was assiduous in his studies and cultivated his growing practice.

He was much inclined to moralize. The ostentatious display of affluence and luxury in Boston's artificial society irritated him quite as much as it did his puritanical and pious cousin Samuel Adams. The gentry were clothed in silks, velvets, and laces; their glassed chariots, built by the best London coachmakers, clattered through the streets, splattering pedestrians with mud and filth. Their houses were full of expensive furniture; their buffets gleamed with burnished plate; their tables were loaded with delicacies; their cellars stocked with rare and expensive wines; their haughty daughters "blazed in the rich Vestments of Princesses." But the country people, who wore threadbare homespun and bent their backs in the fields from dawn to sunset, ate salt pork and had nothing to drink but "Cyder and Small Beer." This was an exaggeration. Most Massachusetts farmers lived very well. No madeira, turtle, lobster, or laces, but fresh beef, lamb, pork, chicken, milk, eggs, cheese, bread, butter, and a varied assortment of fresh fruits and vegetables including apples, plums, peaches, strawberries, asparagus, and lettuces. Nor were they working themselves into early graves to pay taxes, as John alleged.

Taverns and dramshops provided another constant irritant. These had "systematically and scandalously multiplied" in Braintree and neighboring towns: ". . . like so many boxes of Pandora they are hourly scattering plagues of every kind, natural, moral and political." Much tavern talk was indeed political. In the evenings, small groups of men locally influential gathered to discuss and select candidates for office in Braintree, just as similar groups did in Boston. John drafted a series of letters he proposed to send to a Boston paper detailing the evils spawned in dramshops. If he submitted any, none was published.

Adams was quite as critical of himself as he was of rich Bostonians and habitués of Braintree's traverns. He suffered spells of despondency;

at times his life seemed to be utterly without meaning; at others he buried himself in books on law. When bored with legal studies, as he often was, he rode or walked the quiet countryside. Perhaps, at heart, John Adams was a farmer. Certainly he was not yet a "political man," nor was he eager to question the nature of the system under which he and almost two million white Americans lived. He and they were loyal to the crown, shared a profound respect for Parliament, and venerated the Constitution which guaranteed them the inherent and inalienable rights all freeborn Englishmen enjoyed. The system they accepted was soon to receive its first serious challenge.

2

A Contest Appears to Be Opened

Because England's ultimate security and the defense of her overseas empire depended on the Royal Navy, and because maritime commerce was the veritable lifeblood of her economy, the first duty of every government was to maintain an effective naval establishment and to encourage the expansion of seaborne trade. This trade was systematically regulated by the Navigation Acts, which supporters of the mercantilist system professed to believe assured equal economic benefits to the mother country and her overseas colonies. Actually, the principal purpose of the sacrosanct laws of trade was, as they well knew, to protect Great Britain's flourishing commercial monopoly and to guarantee huge profits to her manufacturers, traders, merchants, and bankers.

The system was designed to ensure that the colonies provide a flow of raw materials to the mother country and in return receive from her processed goods. It was therefore necessary to discourage or prohibit colonial development of any industrial capability that might challenge British producers. And as it was equally necessary to exclude foreigners from competition in burgeoning colonial markets, the Navigation Acts provided that all freight must move in ships of British registry built in British or colonial yards. The master and 75 per cent of the complement must be citizens of Great Britain or of the colonies. All foreign manufactures destined for the transatlantic colonies passed en route through British ports where they were off-loaded and where H. M. Customs levied duties sufficiently heavy to make them noncompetitive in America. Successive Parliaments had enacted further rigid laws to control American exportation and importation. Americans could export to countries other than Britain agricultural products not "enumerated," or forbidden. They were permitted to import wines, fruit, and olive oil from Britain's ally Portugal and the Portuguese islands, from Spain, and from Italy provided duty was paid at destination. This was the extent of the freedom they enjoyed in their commercial dealings with nations other than Great Britain.

Americans traded legally and directly with British colonies in the West Indies and illegally with French, Spanish, Danish, and Dutch colonies. From New England and the middle colonies they exported lumber, barrel staves, horses and other livestock, grain, flour, and "trash" fish, a staple in the diet of Negro slaves. In exchange, they took "hard money," sugar, rum, and molasses. They had most unpatriotically, but to their great financial advantage, continued to trade with the French islands during the Seven Years' War. This behavior had understandably outraged Pitt, his cabinet colleagues, the mercantile community, members of Parliament, and English country gentlemen, but during hostilities the government, otherwise engaged, had done nothing to get the situation under control.

Before Whitehall had opportunity to take corrective action, a case that was to have a profound effect on Great Britain's relationship with her American colonies came before the Superior Court of Massachusetts Bay Colony, Chief Justice Stephen Sewall presiding. The case had to do with the legality of "Writs of Assistance." When granted by inferior courts on application by His Majesty's commissioners of customs, writs authorized customs officers to use general warrants to conduct searches for goods suspected to have been smuggled, and directed sheriffs and constables to assist the officers in such searches. Specific search warrants were not required. Justice Sewall realized that he had to handle an explosive package and set arguments for the term of February 1761. Many years later, John Adams wrote that the purpose of the Writs was to enable officers of the customs to call upon sheriffs "to aid them in breaking open houses, stores, shops, bales, trunks, chests, casks, packages of all sorts, to search for goods, wares and merchandize which had been imported against the prohibitions, or without paying the taxes imposed by certain acts of Parliament, called the Acts of Trade."

His Majesty's Customs had good reason to ask for Writs of Assistance. Bostonians were consummate smugglers, as were their brethren in Rhode Island, Connecticut, New York, Pennsylvania, and Maryland. When, for example, a ship arrived with a cargo of wines, normal procedure in Boston and other ports was for the captain, the owners of the ship, and the consignees to falsify the manifest and bribe the customs officers to render a false return. This routine was sanctified by long-established precedent; as far as Boston merchants were concerned, it was a way of life. When William Paxton, the recently arrived commissioner of customs, made it clear that he proposed to enforce the laws and put an end to habitual conspirational nullification of the Acts of Trade, leading merchants immediately squalled that writs were illegal and unconstitutional, and announced they would sue the commissioners.

The case was argued in February—but not before a Superior Court over which Chief Justice Sewall presided. He had died, and Governor Francis Bernard, conveniently forgetting a promise made by his predecessor to Colonel James Otis, an eminent attorney, had appointed Lieutenant Governor Thomas Hutchinson to fill the vacant seat. Hutchinson, a native of Massachusetts, a Harvard graduate, a rich merchant, an inflexible conservative and an accomplished nepotist who had placed half a dozen relatives in lucrative jobs, had no particular qualification to sit as chief justice of the Superior Court. That he was concurrently lieutenant governor and judge of probate might have suggested to Bernard and to him that this additional appointment with its inherent probabilities of conflict was, if not an obvious impropriety, at least politically inadvisable. But Hutchinson, alert to grasp at any lucrative position that came his way, accepted the offer.

Colonel Otis was shocked at Bernard's duplicity; his son, James Otis, Jr., the most brilliant young lawyer in Massachusetts, enraged. "Jemmy" Otis was a mercurial man easily roused to violent anger. In Hutchinson's appointment to the seat earlier promised his father, he saw clear evidence of a "job," and he determined to exact a due measure of retribution. Although "Jemmy" was a Whig, he had for a time been an Advocate of the Court of Vice-admiralty, a position he had recently resigned because he said he could not in good conscience argue in support of Writs of Assistance. He was now free to take the opposite position and was anxious to do so. A group of merchants retained him and Oxenbridge Thatcher to plead in their behalf.

John Adams was one of a score of lawyers who heard the arguments, and in his *Autobiography* described Otis when this brilliant young lawyer was at the height of his powers: "This Gentlmans reputation as a Scholar, a Lawyer, a Reasoner, and a Man of Spirit was then very high . . . by far the most able, manly and commanding Character of his age at the Bar."[1] In this case Otis distinguished himself. The crux of the matter, as he saw it, was the legality of general warrants. After several days of argument the court rose, and in judicial conclave decided to request instructions from His Majesty's attorney general. The justices then suspended the case until they could hear from London.*

Adams was deeply affected by this experience. He had come from Braintree to Boston planning to take copious notes, but "I was much more attentive to the Information and the Eloquence of the Speakers, than to my minutes, and too much allarmed at the prospect that was opened before me, to care much about writing a report of the Controversy." He continued:

> The Views of the English Government towards the Collonies and the Views of the Collonies towards the English Government, from the first of our History to that time, appeared to me to have been directly in Opposition to each other, and were now by the imprudence of Administration, brought to a Collision. England proud of its power and holding Us in Contempt would never give up its pretentions. The Americans devoutly attached to their Liberties, would never submit, at least without an entire devastation of their Country and a general destruction of their Lives. A Contest appeared to me to be opened, to which I could foresee no End, and which would render my Life a Burden and Property, Industry and every Thing insecure. There was no Alternative left, but to take the Side, which appeared to be just. to march intrepidly forward in the right path, to trust in providence for the Protection of Truth and right, and to die with a good Conscience and a decent grace, if that Tryal should become indispensible.[2]

War with Spain, which Pitt had urged and for which he had made plans and preparations before he was forced to resign, broke out on January 4, 1762, after confirmation of rumors that France and Spain had recently agreed to an offensive and defensive alliance.† Britain struck immediately in the West Indies; one after another, French islands fell. The string of conquests, to which Havana and Manila would later be added, greatly enhanced the Duke of Bedford's bargaining position in Paris. Britain was everywhere supreme.

While his generals and admirals were winning victories in the West Indies and the Orient, the King continued to wage his personal political campaign. His Majesty's object was to replace Newcastle with "a man void of his dirty arts," and informed Bute that he was the chosen man. Early in May Newcastle resigned and Bute became First Lord of the Treasury and the King's First Minister. The earl had yearned for position and power, but he was worried, and had good reason to be, for he was

---

* Six months later the justices were advised by the attorney general that general warrants issued for the purpose of enforcement of the Acts of Navigation were legal instruments.

† This was a renewal of the treaty known as the Family Compact.

completely lacking in political experience and was not competent to direct the government.

This particular appointment was then (as it has been since) the subject of much debate. Although at the time no one challenged the King's right to name Bute as his First Minister, many questioned his political perspicacity in doing so. Bute had many enemies and no powerful political "connexion." Saving the "King's Friends" and forty-odd members from Scotland, the earl commanded no loyal and responsive squadron in the House of Commons. He dared not enter the city, where a mob had hissed him and threatened to overturn his coach, and where a jack boot adorned with a petticoat had been burned.‡ Such public demonstrations of antipathy to his chosen First Minister and of contempt for his mother afflicted the King and served only to strengthen his determination to support the man he had selected.

Although Bute enjoyed the unqualified confidence of his royal master, he could not exorcise the image of his illustrious predecessor from the memories of thousands of Londoners who stubbornly greeted the name of William Pitt with huzzas and hissed that of John Stuart, Earl of Bute. Bute did not seek to gain the measure of popularity the "venerated Mr. Pitt" had won; he was aware such efforts would be futile. But he was also aware that he had no public support and that a measure of such support was necessary to bolster his administration. Accordingly, he determined to establish a weekly to compete with the antiadministration *Monitor,* and chose Tobias Smollett to edit it. The first issue of Smollett's *Briton* evoked an immediate journalistic response. On June 5, 1762, John Wilkes and his friend Charles Churchill, a dissolute young poet who had accompanied him in assorted amatory adventures, brought out the first number of *The North Briton.*

Wilkes had sat for five years for Aylesbury in the House of Commons, where he had consistently voted as he was told and had done nothing to distinguish himself. He was an intimate of Pitt's wealthy, arrogant, and autocratic brother-in-law, Earl Temple; he had been elected a Fellow of the Royal Society; was a member of the Sublime Society of Beef Steaks and of Sir Francis Dashwood's notorious Hell Fire Club, a secret fraternity whose "brothers" gathered at Medmenham where they reputedly conducted Black Masses and indulged in a variety of sexual orgies. Legally separated from his wife, Wilkes enjoyed all the sex he could possibly use in London and Bath, and there is no reason to suppose he had to travel to Medmenham for that purpose. He did, however, spend considerable time in Buckinghamshire, where Earl Temple was lord lieutenant and Wilkes the hospitable, witty, and hard-drinking colonel of militia.

Wilkes's reputation as a staunch supporter of Pitt and an outspoken

‡ The jack boot and the petticoat symbolized Bute's association with the Dowager Princess of Wales.

opponent of the preliminary terms of peace being negotiated by Bute's emissary, the Duke of Bedford, assured him and his partners support of Pittites, City merchants, and all antagonists of the Favourite, including Temple, who provided funds necessary to launch the enterprise. Wilkes may not have won a following on the floor of the House; he would very soon gain one through his anonymous articles in *The North Briton,* which he planned to use as the medium for a relentless attack on the Earl of Bute, his administration, and his policies. He knew he would be treading on dangerous ground, for Bute had recently moved to suppress *The Monitor,* which had incurred ministerial wrath, and in the first issue of *The North Briton* Wilkes revealed a strategy carefully calculated not only to protect himself and his journal from the powers of government and the courts, but to appeal to those who detested the First Minister and disliked all his works.

For these reasons, Wilkes devoted his first article to liberty of the press:

> The *liberty of the press* is the birthright of a BRITON, and is justly esteemed the firmest bulwark of this country. It has been the terror of all bad ministers; for their dark and dangerous designs, or their weakness, inability and duplicity have thus been detected and shewn to the public, generally in too strong and just colours for them long to bear up against the odium of mankind. Can we then be surpriz'd that so various and infinite acts have been employed, at one time entirely to set aside, at another to take off the force and blunt the edge, of this most sacred weapon, given for the defence of truth and liberty? A wicked and corrupt administration must naturally dread this appeal to the world; . . . every method will then be try'd and all arts put in practice to check the spread of knowledge and enquiry . . .[3]

This was, of course, an indirect arraignment of Bute and an attack on his known intent to suppress *The Monitor.* Wilkes astutely protected his flanks with judiciously phrased compliments to a ruler who "had not known disgrace" and whose only fault was misplaced confidence "in an insolent, weak and treacherous minister" whose conduct of the war since the late lamented departure of Mr. Pitt had been "infamously" languid.

Thus in the initial issue of *The North Briton,* which would be read from Boston in Massachusetts to Charleston in South Carolina with the same consuming interest as in City coffeehouses, Wilkes struck on themes that appealed to Whigs on both sides of the Atlantic. First, he had declared freedom of the press an inherent and inviolable right to be enjoyed by every Englishman; second, the name of a young, inexperienced, well-meaning, and amiable King should not be associated with the acts of duplicitous and corrupt ministers who for their own evil purposes deceived and misinformed their royal master, and finally, laurels of the recent conquests should rightfully grace the brow of Mr. Pitt. Americans did not need reminders from John Wilkes to impress upon them the evident fact that a free press was a fundamental guarantee of liberty, or to enhance in their eyes the stature of Mr. Pitt. But they found the careful distinction Wilkes had drawn between a righteous and benevolent monarch and his depraved ministers of singular propaganda value, and would ring the changes on this subject until 1775.

Although Administration affected to pay little attention to the relatively mild attacks that appeared every week in *The Monitor* or to the more venomous articles in *The North Briton*, Bute and his colleagues had reason to be worried, for the first order of business when Parliament met in late November was to debate on terms of preliminaries of the peace, which both journals vehemently opposed. From Bute's point of view, it was obviously desirable to close these scurrilous and seditious weeklies before debates opened, and early in November 1762, Lord Halifax, Principal Secretary of State for the Southern Department, issued a warrant for the arrest of Arthur Beardmore, alleged to be the author or printer of several "Very seditious papers," to wit, various numbers of *The Monitor*, which contained "gross and scandalous reflections and invectives, upon his Majesty's Government, and upon both Houses of Parliament." This threat did not dismay Wilkes, who in the next issue of *The North Briton* boasted he would never tamely give up the struggle nor allow himself to be intimidated "by the menaces of a wicked minister."

When debates began on the peace preliminaries, the editors of *The North Briton* chose a new tack, one designed to identify the ministry as a Tory faction devoted to placating France, dividing the people, and sowing discord. From "Tory" to "Jacobite" was an obvious progression. As Wilkes would have it, the Earl of Bute and William Murray, Lord Mansfield, both Scots, and hence by Whig definition "Jacobites," had driven Pitt and the friends of liberty from offices which they had then proceeded to staff with their corrupt sycophants. And lest there be any lingering misconception of what Tories believed, Wilkes made it clear that they were maintainers of the detested doctrines of arbitrary power, passive obedience, and nonresistance.

Henry Fox, who had enriched himself as paymaster of the forces (an office later to be enjoyed by Richard Rigby, a coarse and clever henchman of the Duke of Bedford), was chosen to see the preliminaries of the peace safely through the lower House. Fox knew how to handle men as avaricious as he, and with the full and open support of the King and unlimited access to the Treasury, was easily able to rally the support needed. With the Treaty of Paris signed in February 1763, Bute withdrew his subsidies to Tobias Smollett and Arthur Murphy, and *The Briton* and *Auditor* closed down. The demise of *The North Briton's* two competitors would probably have quieted any polemicist but Wilkes, who from week to week continued his attacks on Bute and his ministers. Many of the articles he and Churchill wrote during this period might have been deemed actionable, but the ministers were wary and took no action.

During some of this time Wilkes was in Paris, but when he heard that Bute was shortly to quit office he hurried home and arrived in London on April 11, 1763, to learn that the Favourite had resigned three days earlier and that George Grenville was the new First Minister. The earl's retirement was not entirely unexpected; since early December he had been begging the King to allow him to resign his seals. Bute was out of his element; the political waters were too deep and too rough, their currents and sudden furies too unpredictable. He complained of constant pressure and tension; disorder of the bowels; headaches; insomnia. But the King urged him to stay, for who could succeed him? His Majesty had no faith in the "abandoned men" who held high office or were ambitious to attain it. He distrusted the lot: Pitt, Fox, Grenville, Bedford, Halifax. Finally, in March 1763, he reluctantly acquiesced to Bute's repeated entreaties to retire within the month. That the Earl of Bute had retired from public employment signified nothing to Wilkes, who in an anonymous handbill asserted that the new First Minister was no more than Bute's odious tool and that the detested Scot would continue to exercise his malign influence.

Bute was succeeded by a triumvirate consisting of George Grenville as First Lord of the Treasury and Chancellor of the Exchequer, the Earl of Halifax as Secretary of State for the Northern Department, and the Earl of Egremont as Secretary of State for the Southern Department. None of these men commanded great wealth, and although all three enjoyed the support of powerful "connexion," none had any significant personal following in the House of Commons. Halifax, an intolerant aristocrat who had earlier been president of the Board of Trade and Plantations, was an able politician who detested the Americans and had some ideas of his own as to how they should be treated. Suffice it to say that these ideas were not exactly liberal. Egremont had no qualities to recommend him for high position. Grenville, who led the ministerial forces in the House of Commons, devoted his energies to finance; he did not pose as an expert on either foreign or colonial affairs, and was happy to leave the conduct of these to Halifax and Egremont. This trio had a limited power base, and those who had consistently opposed Bute smelled a conspiracy. From behind the curtain the Favourite would pipe the tunes and pull the strings while his puppets danced. Such was prevailing opinion in gentlemen's clubs, as it was in the City and in London drawing rooms and coffeehouses.

Horace Walpole of Strawberry Hill, a member of the House of Com-

mons who enjoyed excellent social and political connections and had a
fairly good idea of what was going on in London society, in ministers'
drawing rooms, and in Whitehall, wrote his friend Horace Mann in
Florence that though Bute was nominally out of office he was still "as
much minister as ever." Bute's unpopularity had rubbed off on all his associates; Walpole thought the Grenville ministry "a general joke . . . I
had ever thought this would be a turbulent reign, and nothing has happened to make me alter my opinion." Walpole was even a better prophet
than he imagined himself to be.°°

For the next two weeks, as Wilkes assessed the situation, *The North
Briton* did not appear. Parliament would rise on April 19 after the King
delivered his customary speech from the throne. This policy speech, as
everyone knew, was habitually written by the ministry, and Wilkes
waited anxiously to hear what words the "wretched" ministers who had
supported the "infamous" peace would put in His Majesty's mouth. Apparently, George Grenville had given his brother Earl Temple a copy on
April 18, and there is reason to believe that Pitt, Temple, and Wilkes
discussed the speech the night before it was to be delivered in Parliament. Wilkes immediately hastened from Stowe to London to prepare
the articles that would appear in *The North Briton's* celebrated issue
Number 45, on April 23, 1763.

Wilkes made it abundantly clear that his attack on the King's speech
was not aimed at a prince possessed of "many great and amiable qualities" but at his advisers. The speech, "the most abandoned instance of
ministerial effrontery ever attempted to be imposed upon mankind,"
could, he wrote, find no parallel "in the annals of this country." He went
on to assail the ignominious terms of peace negotiated by Bedford and
attacked the Earl of Bute and his "tools" who had destroyed the spirit of
concord and liberty.†† Bute, said Wilkes, had attempted to enlarge the
royal prerogative, and through his creatures in office would establish a
corrupt and arbitrary despotism. Wilkes closed Number 45 with these
words:

°° Horace Mann (later Sir Horace Mann, K.B.) was envoy extraordinary and
minister plenipotentiary to the Court of Florence. Horace Walpole (1717–97),
fourth son of Sir Robert Walpole (later First Earl of Orford), was educated at Eton
and King's College, Cambridge. In 1741 he was elected a member of Parliament
from Callington, Cornwall, and later represented Castle Rising and Lynn. In 1757 he
purchased a "shooting box" on the Thames near Twickenham. This was to become
his celebrated and beloved "Strawberry Hill." He resigned his seat in Parliament in
May 1767, and thereafter devoted himself to writing. His voluminous correspondence
has been impeccably edited at Yale University under the direction of W. S. Lewis.

†† Although the allegation has never been proved, many thought Bedford was
bribed. Visitors to Woburn have seen the banquet setting, said to have cost £ 18,000,
that Louis XV gave to the Duchess of Bedford. As no one has ever accused the duchess of being a chaste woman, the King may have presented this gift for services she
rendered rather than for those rendered by the duke.

The *prerogative* of the crown is to exert the constitutional powers entrusted to it in a way, not of blind favour and partiality, but of wisdom and judgement. This is the spirit of our constitution. The people too have their *prerogative,* and, I hope, the fine words of DRYDEN will be engraved in our hearts.

Freedom is the English subject's Prerogative.[4]

His Majesty was outraged. He had not only been represented as a mere puppet who mouthed the words ministers had given him to speak, but as a sovereign lacking in both wisdom and judgment who had bestowed his favors blindly and partially. Finally, and perhaps most galling, he had been implicitly accused of seeking to destroy the constitution he continually asserted he revered and had sworn to uphold. George III had overlooked the slurs Wilkes had cast upon the Stuarts from whom he was descended and the scandalous innuendoes linking Bute with his beloved mother, but Number 45 was more than he proposed to tolerate. He summoned Grenville and directed him to submit the offensive paper to Attorney General Charles Yorke and Solicitor General Sir Fletcher Norton for consideration and, if possible, for immediate prosecution of the author of these infamous and seditious libels.

Three days after Number 45 appeared, Yorke and Norton gave their opinion that a charge of seditious libel should be brought against the anonymous editors and the publishers and printers, and Grenville directed his two Secretaries of State to act. Halifax and Egremont immediately drew up a warrant and dispatched their messengers to find and arrest the publishers and the printers. These two gentlemen, George Kearsley and Richard Balfe, were duly apprehended and brought before Halifax, who during a rigorous examination elicited the fact that Wilkes had written the offensive articles. The messengers, armed with the same general warrant they had used to arrest Kearsley and Balfe, proceeded to 13 Great George Street, where they found Wilkes.

Wilkes, who feared that his parliamentary immunity did not protect him from arrest on the charge of seditious libel, harangued the messengers for several hours and was sufficiently persuasive to convince them to allow a delay until the following day. Early the next morning he went to Balfe's printing shop, set up a ladder, broke through a second-story window, and entered the shop, where he destroyed the manuscript of Number 45 and the proof of Number 46 and muddled the typesetting. He then returned to Great George Street, agreed to submit to arrest, and appeared before Halifax and Egremont. After an exchange of insults, the secretaries ordered him committed to the Tower. There he was held in close confinement until May 3, when Earl Temple secured his release on a writ of habeas corpus.

Proceeding in style to Westminster, Wilkes was cheered and huzzaed en route by crowds of his admirers. Standing at the bar of the Court of Common Pleas, he pled parliamentary immunity, and Chief Justice Charles Pratt adjourned the court until May 6, when he handed down the opinion that Wilkes did indeed enjoy immunity from arrest on the charge brought. The case was dismissed and Wilkes was discharged.

When he left the courtroom as a free man, he became the idol of the City of London. A crowd wildly cheering "Wilkes and Liberty" escorted him to his lodgings in Great George Street. He then proceeded to sue Halifax and Egremont for false arrest and charged them with having ordered his apartment burglarized while he had been held in the Tower. Although these episodes increased Wilkes's popularity in London, they added fuel to the King's anger, and for the better part of the next six months His Majesty devoted himself to waging a personal vendetta against the editor of Number 45 of *The North Briton.*

During the proceedings against Wilkes, Chief Justice Pratt had pondered the legal problems raised by arrests made under the authority of general warrants, and had several times adverted to this question. Finally on July 6, 1763, in an opinion that must be regarded as one of the most significant in the history of development of English constitutional law, Pratt declared the general warrants issued by Halifax and Egremont illegal, null, and void.‡‡

Wilkes, who no doubt imagined he was out of the woods, embarked on a triumphal progress to Aylesbury, where his constituents accorded him a tumultuous greeting and where he was sumptuously entertained, as he was at Stowe by his patron Lord Temple. In August he embarked at Dover to visit his daughter Polly, who was attending a convent school in Paris. He wrote Temple that enthusiastic crowds had everywhere acclaimed him with cries of "Wilkes and Liberty."

Wilkes returned from Paris in high spirits and immediately announced he would publish a collection of all issues of *The North Briton.* He also planned to publish for limited circulation an *Essay on Woman,* an obscene parody of Pope's *Essay on Man,* which he dedicated to one of London's most popular ladies of easy virtue. After making these arrangements, he departed again for Paris, secure in the belief that he would shortly be able to cause further embarrassment to the ministry.

The King was determined to chastise Wilkes for *lèse-majesté;* neither he nor his ministers had any intention of allowing this insolent and licentious troublemaker to escape deserved punishment. Unfortunately for Wilkes, one of his printers was induced to give or sell a proof copy of the *Essay* to Charles Jenkinson, then solicitor to the Treasury. This soon

‡‡ Parliament did not declare general warrants illegal for several years after Chief Justice Pratt's decision.

found its way to the hands of John Montagu, Fourth Earl of Sandwich, a onetime member of the Medmenham brotherhood, who had recently become a Secretary of State.* For reasons not wholly clear, Sandwich was determined to destroy his erstwhile friend, and when Parliament assembled on November 15, 1763, he rose in the House of Lords and with obvious enjoyment read aloud the bawdy poem. The noble lords promptly unanimously resolved the *Essay* to be "a most scandalous, impious and obscene libel"; Earl Temple, who professed to be shocked, made no attempt to exculpate his drinking companion and protégé.† On the same day the Commons resolved that *North Briton* Number 45 constituted "a false, scandalous and malicious libel" and ordered it to be burned by the common hangman.

Events moved rapidly. On November 16 Wilkes was seriously wounded in a duel with Samuel Martin, who many believed had been prevailed upon to call him out. Wilkes was carried to his house in Great George Street, where for five weeks he recuperated. The resolves of both Houses and the highly questionable motivation of Martin, who for some time before the duel had been engaging in pistol practice, evoked considerable sympathy for Wilkes. Indeed, the hangman and the sheriff, attacked by a mob when they attempted to consign Number 45 to the flames, were forced to beat a precipitate retreat, their mission unaccomplished. The House of Commons now ordered Wilkes to appear before the bar to vindicate himself. The ministry chose to ignore statements of reputable surgeons that he was physically unable to appear as ordered; the House was adamant, and Wilkes, sensing that he would be shown no mercy, fled secretly to exile in France. On January 20, 1764, the House voted that he be expelled. Although no one questioned the prerogative of the House to expel a member who had committed a felony or been found guilty of treason, there are grounds for believing the action taken on this day was unconstitutional.

Recent events may have gained Wilkes support in the City but certainly gained him none in St. James's Palace or in Whitehall. He had insulted the King and ridiculed his chosen ministers, whom he had described as corrupt wretches and despotic tools intent on subverting English liberties. In the eyes of members of the establishment he was a dangerous man, an incendiary demagogue who at any cost must be silenced.

But to Americans, as to many thousands of Englishmen, John Wilkes

---

* The Earl of Egremont died in September 1763. Halifax took his place at the Southern Department and Sandwich was given the Northern Department.

† The *Essay* was no more lubricous than much of the pornographic poetry of the period, but in notes Wilkes had written there were several obscene references to Bishop Warburton; these appear to have provided the basis for the action taken by the peers. Still, as the *Essay* had not been published or circulated, it is difficult to see how it could have constituted a libel.

had become the symbol of struggle against those in positions of power whose fixed purpose, so they believed, was to curtail their liberties and deprive them of their constitutional rights. In England and her transatlantic colonies "Wilkes and Liberty" soon became a popular slogan and the toast most frequently proposed.

℀ 3

A Most Pernicious Measure

Before Pitt left office in October 1761, he had decided to keep Canada and return Guadeloupe to France. Aside from the treasures of fish and furs, which they had not exploited to the extent they might have, the French had derived little profit from Canada. Most Frenchmen preferred tropical islands to a freezing waste covered for nine months with ice and snow where vicious arctic winds tore the skin from one's face. Pitt's choice seemed eminently logical to Benjamin Franklin, agent in London for the proprietary colony of Pennsylvania, who shared the minister's imperial vision.

Pitt's opponents held that removal of the French menace from the northern and western borders of the Atlantic colonies would inevitably encourage the Americans to act more independently. But Franklin thought otherwise. In his opinion, union of the American colonies to oppose the mother country was not "merely improbable" but impossible "without the most grievous tyranny and oppression . . . while the government is mild and just, while important civil and religious rights are secure such subjects will be dutiful and obedient."[1]

Both Pitt and Franklin argued that acquisition of Canada would round out a continental imperium which with passage of time and rapid growth of a fecund population would provide a constantly increasing flow of raw materials to the mother country and an ever-expanding market for British products. This burgeoning trade would in turn strengthen the merchant marine and assure Britain's continued domination of the seas. Here the minister was appealing directly not only to manufacturers, but also to powerful banking, insurance, trading, and shipping interests which for years had dictated British commercial policy. The decision was accepted by Lord Bute's ministry, and by terms of the treaty signed on February 10, 1763, which formally ended hostilities, France transferred sovereignty over Canada (or "Québec") to Great Britain. France also surrendered all claims to lands east of the Mississippi River.

Although the factional press vilified Bute and his opponents excoriated the treaty, most Britons, who after seven years of war longed for peace, were pleased. The King's personal popularity was not diminished but enhanced. Benjamin Franklin did not fear that faction would overpower "the virtuous young king." On the contrary, his opinion was that His Majesty's virtue and the consciousness of his sincere intentions to make his people happy would "give him firmness and steadiness in his measures and in support of the honest friends he has chosen to serve him, and when that firmness is fully perceived, faction will dissolve and be dissipated like a morning fog before the rising sun. . . ."[2] Franklin was an astute political observer but in this assessment he perhaps allowed his emotions to cloud his judgment. As he was soon to perceive, the young King's "firmness" did nothing to dissolve factional strife, but served rather to exacerbate it.

When Grenville and his colleagues took office, they inherited the intricate problem of how best to organize and administer the newly acquired American empire. Was emigration from the seaboard colonies to this wilderness to be encouraged, tolerated, or prohibited? Obviously, if uninhabited forests were to be cleared and the wilderness to become the agricultural empire Pitt dreamed of, settlers would have to be encouraged by financial bounties and grants of land. What sort of administration should be established in the new provinces? Should these be royal colonies, or should their charters be similar to those of Connecticut and Rhode Island, whose citizens enjoyed the rare privilege of electing their own assemblies and governors? And how was the area to be policed and the security of settlers assured during the period before effective governments could be established? Already droves of speculators hungry to get their hands on trans-Appalachian lands had formed stock companies in both Great Britain and America and developed grandiose schemes to promote migration to the rich country west of the mountain barrier. The situation demanded immediate attention.

The man Grenville selected to find a solution was William Petty, Earl of Shelburne. Although Shelburne's contemporaries expressed differing opinions of his political reliability and effectiveness, all agreed that he was a sensible and industrious "man of parts," imaginative, studious, and thorough, and one not disposed to leap to conclusions. When he became president of the Board of Trade and Plantations in April 1763, Shelburne immediately immersed himself in the stupendous task of collecting available maps and collating all information relevant to the vast territory so recently surrendered by France.

This primeval wilderness, where there were as yet only isolated settlements, was the domain of the Indians, whose forefathers had been lords of it for centuries. There virgin forests teemed with game; streams and rivers flowing clear provided inexhaustible harvests of beaver, otter, and fish. The Indians tolerated trappers, and despite their well-earned reputation for unmitigated chicanery, welcomed traders, who in exchange for fine peltry and deer hides offered muskets and powder and ball ammunition; blankets, kettles, mirrors, and gaudy costume jewelry; shovels, picks, axes, knives, and tomahawks made of the best British steel; and rum—gallons and gallons of rum. But they wanted no white settlers. They knew their brothers to the east had been robbed of their ancestral lands, reduced to beggary, and finally destroyed by mendacious white interlopers. Nor did trappers whose way of life and livelihood depended on preservation of the wilderness welcome an invasion of land-hungry immigrants.

And Shelburne had to consider the claims of colonies to lands extending to the Mississippi or even to the remote and unknown "South Seas." Already there was increasing pressure on the frontier; bold spirits had crossed the mountains, bought land from Indians, cleared it, and started to farm. Indian leaders who for many years had enjoyed good relations with the French, distrusted, disliked, and feared the English, and General Sir Jeffrey Amherst, His Majesty's commander in chief in America, had done nothing to allay their well-founded apprehensions. Amherst, contemptuous of the Indians, had ceased giving them the customary gifts and had done little to control either greedy traders or the drift of settlers into their hunting grounds.

In the great Indian uprising of 1763, hundreds of these settlers had been kidnapped, murdered, and scalped; those fortunate enough to escape had fled to safety east of the mountains. But with Pontiac's "Conspiracy" crushed and the flames ignited by this ephemeral alliance extinguished, those who had been driven from their cabins returned to the ruins and to the scorched earth. And in the seaboard colonies thousands waited anxiously to move with their families to a virgin area where they could begin a new life.

By midsummer, Shelburne was ready to present to the Cabinet a draft of a royal proclamation designed to establish new governments in the ceded territories and to control further settlement in the forested empire reaching from the Appalachians to the Mississippi. But before he was able to do so, reports of Pontiac's uprising had produced their effect in London and his draft gathered dust in Grenville's office. When Shelburne's paper was finally discussed at cabinet level, his carefully considered plans in respect to meticulous surveys of the areas to be made available for regulated and gradual settlement and those to be marked off as Indian hunting preserves were deemed no longer appropriate. But the Indians must be assured that their rights were recognized and would be protected. Emigration must be stopped and a clearly recognizable line, beyond which settlers could not pass, must be drawn immediately.

The changes proposed did not meet with Shelburne's approval. He resigned, and on September 9, 1763, Wills Hill, Earl of Hillsborough, took his place at the Board of Trade. Many of his contemporaries thought him indolent, arrogant, and dogmatic. He had no more than a cursory knowledge of the problem that had engrossed Shelburne's attention, and while he adopted portions of his predecessor's plan, he made several important modifications. His draft, approved by the Cabinet, was issued as a royal proclamation on October 7.

The proclamation established three new governments in North America: Quebec, East Florida, and West Florida. In general, the boundary beyond which settlers could not trespass followed the Appalachian watershed and would embrace all the territory formerly claimed by France lying west of the mountains. The entire area to the Mississippi was to be preserved as Indian hunting grounds. Emigrants who had settled there (now the states of Ohio, West Virginia, Indiana, Illinois, Kentucky, Tennessee, Alabama, and Mississippi) were to withdraw immediately, and on pain of suffering royal displeasure, His Majesty's "loving subjects" were for the future prohibited to make there "any purchases or settlements whatever" or to take possession of any land without royal "leave and license for that purpose first obtained." Indian superintendents, one for the north and one for the south, would control trade. All traders would be required to have licenses; in the future all trading would be conducted under the immediate supervision of deputy superintendents for Indian affairs at posts established for the purpose.

Although traders paid little attention to the royal ukase, which they well knew could not possibly be enforced, the proclamation generated considerable heat in America. Several colonial assemblies claimed their charter rights had been violated; speculators who had anticipated a financial harvest were incensed, and prospective emigrants, who felt they were entitled to move where they pleased to improve their livelihood, outraged. Thus Grenville's first effort to consolidate the empire Pitt's genius had won provoked nothing but ill feeling in America.

The Proclamation of 1763 was the first step in a larger program designed to impose more effective centralized control over Britain's huge American empire. Although the Grenville government did not anticipate an immediate resurgence of Bourbon power, the always restless Indians posed a latent threat to border settlements, and as colonial governments were reluctant to provide protection, the responsibility fell inescapably on the mother country. Even before formation of the Indian confederation, Grenville had decided that ten thousand troops, stationed at the discretion of the commander in chief in America, would be needed.* This measure evoked immediate hostility in the colonies, where radicals asserted that a Redcoat "standing army" was to be deployed, not, as Administration alleged, to protect settlers from Indian raiding parties, but rather to intimidate His Majesty's loyal, dutiful, and affectionate subjects, who considered the troops to be as undesirable as they were unnecessary. Critics of the policy, including Franklin, had pointed out that small garrisons stationed in widely separated wilderness outposts could not possibly prevent sudden Indian incursions. Regular troops could not cope with Indians in the forest; for these operations, "Rangers" were needed.† This may not have been as readily apparent to ministers in London as it was to Americans living in scattered settlements on the fringes of civilization.

Grenville soon gave the King's affectionate subjects reason for further complaint when in the spring of 1764 he informed colonial agents in London that His Majesty's government expected the Americans to contribute a reasonable share to defray in part the expenses of maintaining the King's army stationed there. He pointed out that the principal mission of the Redcoats spread thinly over the vast territory recently acquired was to protect the colonists, and thought their share of the funds required might be most easily and painlessly raised by imposition of a stamp tax. This, he explained, would be a tax on legal documents of all descriptions, including liquor licenses for taverns and wineshops, diplomas granted by any college, newspapers, almanacs, pamphlets, calendars, playing cards, and dice. The minister indicated he would not introduce the measure, which he and his colleagues considered unexceptionable, if colonial legislatures preferred to raise the money by some other means, and suggested the agents communicate his intentions to the assemblies they represented. Dr. Franklin, His Majesty's deputy postmaster general for North America, who had but recently returned to London, voiced mild objections to the tax, but neither he nor any other

---

* Of these, sixteen battalions (7,500 enlisted) would be stationed on the continent, the remainder in the West Indies.

† Rangers, used effectively during the Seven Years' War, had been disbanded in 1761.

colonial agent seemed to be unduly worried at the prospect. Although they were reasonably sure the colonies would not respond favorably to Mr. Grenville's proposals, they did not apprehend that a stamp act would raise a clamor.

While these discussions were going on, Grenville brought in two bills that provoked immediate protests in America. One of these, the Currency Act, declared that heretofore negotiable bills of credit, which every colony had been issuing for years and were the normal medium of exchange, would no longer be considered legal tender in settlement of any public transaction. Quite naturally this would tend to make such tender unacceptable in satisfaction of any private transaction. The Currency Act was a most impolitic piece of legislation, and for several reasons. First, very little specie circulated freely in the colonies, where a significant amount of trading was done by barter. In Maryland and Virginia debts and wages were often paid in tobacco or in notes that could be exchanged for tobacco. In the Carolinas rice provided security for similar notes. Merchants who could get their hands on "hard money" hoarded it to pay customs duties and to satisfy their London accounts. Second, Grenville's tinkering with the working of a rather complicated but satisfactory financial system with which he was totally unfamiliar tended to exacerbate the deepening depression that had settled in shortly after the War for Empire ended.‡ Finally, the colonists suspected the minister's purpose was to drain them of specie and reduce them to beggary to the ultimate benefit of British traders and merchants.

Grenville's Sugar Act lowered the duty on sugar and molasses from the British West Indian Islands. The purpose was to make these products more nearly competitive with sugar and molasses habitually run in illegally from Dutch, Danish, French, and Spanish Sugar Islands. The better to enforce this act, Grenville proposed to reorganize H. M. Customs in America from top to bottom. Customs personnel who had places in America but lived in England and hired deputies to discharge their duties overseas were ordered to proceed to their posts at once. Additionally, officers of the Royal Navy in American waters, directed to assist in enforcing the Acts of Navigation, were required "to act in the capacity of the meanest revenue officers." Naval officers were empowered to board and search any ship they suspected of carrying contraband. If contraband were found, they were authorized to seize her and order her owners and master to appear before a court of vice-admiralty, where a judge would decide the issue. Condemnation of ships carrying illegal cargoes was a lucrative business. Those who had taken a ship were liberally rewarded, and the commissioner and governor enjoyed a share of the proceeds. The system offered manifold opportunities for bribery and corruption, and a relatively small proportion of the cash generated by con-

‡ The Seven Years' War, or, as it was known in America, the French and Indian War.

demnation reached the royal Treasury. The trading community conceived all those associated with His Majesty's Customs to be enemies whose designs were to be thwarted whenever and however possible.

The New York Assembly learned with "Concern and Surprize" of Grenville's intent to persuade Parliament "to impose Taxes upon the Subjects *here* by Laws to be passed *there*." They conceived that this "Innovation" would "reduce the Colony to absolute Ruin." The right of taxation was exclusively vested, the Assembly continued, "in the inhabitants of every free state, or in their duly chosen representatives." Should taxes be otherwise imposed, there could "be no Liberty, no Happiness, no Security." No man could be deprived of his property "at the Pleasure of another." Such a procedure, they alleged, was manifestly unjust and an evident transgression of a "natural right." This invocation of "laws of nature" transcending laws of man was to become a constant theme in colonial remonstrances and petitions.

All those familiar with the philosophical concept of "natural laws" accepted that they were compatible with the universal order revealed by Isaac Newton, were in harmony with the laws of God, of Nature, or of a Divine Providence, and were rational, just, discoverable, and applicable to the human condition. Most educated Americans of the late eighteenth century, including Samuel Adams, George Mason, John Adams, Richard Bland, Benjamin Franklin, Richard Henry Lee, Thomas Jefferson, and George Washington, were familiar with John Locke's assertion that reason, "the common rule and measure God hath given to mankind," should teach all men not to harm others in enjoyment of their lives, health, liberty, or possessions. To these men it seemed apparent that despotism and tyranny in any form were contrary to "right reason," as were laws whose effect would be to deprive men of liberty, happiness, and security of their persons and property. Thus, if Parliament enacted such laws, resistance was morally justified. The Assembly of the province of New York had sent a warning signal to London. No one there paid it the slightest attention.

The Sugar Act, designed to raise a revenue, raised instead a storm of protest and catalyzed amorphous political opinion. Before this time, the appellations "Whig" and "Tory" had rarely been used in America. But "all on a sudden," as Thomas Hutchinson wrote, "the officers of the crown, and such as were for keeping up their authority, were branded with the name tories, always the term of reproach; their opposers assuming the name of whiggs."**

** Hutchinson said that the Massachusetts people were, in general, "of the principles of the ancient whiggs; attached to the revolution [the "Glorious Revolution" of 1688] and to the succession of the crown in the house of Hanover" (Thomas Hutchinson, *The History of the Colony and Province of Massachusetts Bay*, Vol. III, p. 75). Tories, or "Jacobites," had supported the Stuarts. The appellation "Tory" had thus become, as he wrote, "a term of reproach."

In January 1765 George III, afflicted with a persistent chest cold, a hacking cough, and severe stomach cramps, took to his bed. He could not rest comfortably; his temperature fluctuated; his pulse rate was dangerously high. During the following three months he suffered recurrent attacks with similar symptoms. Court physicians, unable to diagnose the malady, resorted to a course of potions, pills, purgings, bleedings, blisterings, and cuppings. The King, blessed with a strong constitution, survived the unpleasant and debilitating treatment. But he knew, as did those close to him, that he had been critically ill and that another such attack might carry him off, and in April informed the House of Lords of his wish to provide for a regent assisted by a council to function in the event of his death and during the minority of his infant son.††

In a moment of inattention at an audience hurriedly arranged, the King had allowed George Montagu Dunk, Second Earl of Halifax, and the Earl of Sandwich, his Principal Secretaries of State, to persuade him that his mother was not technically a member of the royal family, and hence not eligible to act as regent or to sit on the council. The name of the Dowager Princess Augusta was therefore stricken from the bill to the delight of all those who feared that should the young King die Bute would return to power. During the debates, which were lengthy, confusing, and frequently tactless, Princess Augusta's name was restored. The episode, which embarrassed the King and deeply offended his mother, confirmed His Majesty's determination to turn out Grenville and his insolent colleagues.

Indeed, the King could not abide his First Minister, whose pedantic dissertations bored him nearly to distraction. In long and tiring interviews in the Closet, the King fell into the habit of consulting his watch frequently, but this clear signal that the royal patience was exhausted never registered with the loquacious First Lord of the Treasury. In a memorandum composed about this time, the King wrote of the ministers: "Whenever Opposition allarm'd them, they were very attentive to Me; but whenever releas'd from that their sole ideas were how to get the Mastery of the Closet‡‡; no Office fell vacant of ever so little value, or in the Department of any other person that they did not claim it & declar'd if not comply'd with they would not serve. . . ."[3] His Majesty could endure much, but drew the line at egregious political blackmail. Riots of thousands of unemployed weavers who attacked the Duke of Bedford's mansion and laid siege to the House of Lords hastened the King's decision to rid himself of Grenville.

†† Grenville announced that the King was suffering from a severe bronchial affliction. It has been presumed that this illness was the second attack of the rare disease known as porphyria, a metabolic disturbance which later led to his insanity. This thesis has not been established. None of George III's hundreds of descendants is known to have suffered from this hereditary disease.

‡‡ The King's private drawing room.

That he sent his royal uncle, the Duke of Cumberland, to parley with Newcastle, a man he despised, and with Pitt, one he feared would reduce him to "a sypher," reflects the degree of the King's frustration and the prevailing state of political chaos. Pitt, always a most difficult man, finally agreed to form a ministry on condition that his brother-in-law Earl Temple, George Grenville's elder brother and senior member of the Grenville clan, would come in. Temple said he would. Then, suddenly, everything fell apart. Grenville, who had no intention of being run out of office and publicly humiliated, persuaded his brother to forsake Pitt and join forces with him. The King's emissaries found Pitt adamant; he would not attempt to form an administration without Temple, and Temple was no longer willing to co-operate.

Having thus neatly disposed of the "Master of Hayes," Grenville and Bedford were now, or so they thought, in an unassailable position, and in an audience presented His Majesty with a set of humiliating ultimata, to which the enraged King was forced to acquiesce. Finally, they demanded that he would at once cease all political intercourse, personal or by correspondence, with Lord Bute. The King agreed, but could swallow no more insolence from Grenville and sent for Pitt.

Again lengthy interviews came to nothing. Pitt, too, presented demands: European policy must be reversed; the subsidy to Frederick of Prussia must be resumed, his friendship cultivated, and an alliance with him negotiated. And there must be another purge; all those Pitt found objectionable must be dismissed from office. The King had taken enough bullying; he did not propose to take more from Mr. Pitt; he would not betray his friends, and "the ramming of Austria deeper with France & kindling a new war by unnecessary alliances are things I can neither answer to my God nor to my conscience." George III, at twenty-seven already a scarred veteran of the political wars, would not bend. Pitt, his advice rejected, returned to Hayes to wrap his legs in black velvet and nurse his gout and his injured ego.

Colonial responses to Grenville's suggestion that their assemblies contribute a reasonable proportion of the funds needed to support the King's forces in America had reached London and were uniformly negative. The colonists, so they averred, were well able to take care of themselves, and as red-coated soldiers were quite unnecessary, they did not propose to contribute anything to maintain the King's troops. Petitions expressing colonial objections had been sent to London; several pamphlets had been circulated, and although sentiment in America ran strongly against the bill, a number of respected men discreetly supported it. In 1764 American sentiment had not yet been mobilized, and disagreement did not give way to radical demonstrations, turbulent mobs, and violence.

In February 1765 the bill slid through Parliament with very little opposition. An exchange between Charles Townshend, a brilliant speaker who supported the measure, and Colonel Isaac Barré, who opposed, enlivened an otherwise dull debate. The act was fully justified, Townshend asserted, for the Americans were "children planted by our care, nourished by our indulgence, protected by our arms." Barré, who had served with Americans during the Seven Years' War, was quick to respond: "They planted by your care?" he asked angrily. "No. Your oppressions planted them in America. They nurtured by your indulgence? They grew by your neglect of them." He attacked Great Britain's policies as misguided and described Americans who resisted them as "Sons of Liberty." The colonel's impassioned reply evoked feeble applause and won no votes. The bill passed a final reading without a division; administration majorities in both Houses were overwhelming. The act, to become effective on the first day of November 1765, aroused little interest in London and occasioned practically no comment in the press.

Dr. Franklin thought the Americans would accept the duties levied and suggested to Jared Ingersoll of Connecticut, then in London, that he apply for the position of provincial stamp distributor, one that would entail very little work and would be rewarded with a generous annual stipend of £300. In Virginia, Richard Henry Lee applied for the job. Lieutenant Governor Hutchinson, who had a better feeling for the situation than did Franklin, Ingersoll, or Lee, thought the proposed Stamp Tax was impolitic and was sure it would be resisted. In official and private letters, he urged that it be dropped.

The doctor had certainly misjudged the mood and probable reaction of his countrymen, for when news arrived that Grenville's scheme to pick their pockets had become law it generated an immediate uproar: "Clamor, Tumults and Plots" in Virginia, New York, Massachusetts, Connecticut, and even (as Major General Thomas Gage, His Majesty's commander in chief in America whose headquarters were in New York, reported) "in the little turbulent colony of Rhode Island."

Virginia was the first colony to express unequivocal opposition to the Stamp Act. At Williamsburg on May 30, 1765, the House of Burgesses resolved "That the General Assembly of this Colony has the only and sole exclusive right and power to lay taxes and impositions upon the inhabitants of this colony," and that the loyal inhabitants of Virginia were "not bound to yield obedience to any law or ordinance whatever, designed to impose any taxation whatsoever upon them other than the laws or ordinances of the General Assembly aforesaid." A final resolve, submitted by Patrick Henry, declared that any person who maintained the right of any legislative body other than the General Assembly to lay taxes on Virginians should be deemed an enemy to the colony.* The Virginia Re-

---

* This resolve was expunged from the record, but not before the "Resolves" as originally passed had been sent from Williamsburg to Philadelphia.

solves were widely circulated, and as Gage wrote Conway, "gave the Signal for a general outcry over the continent." When the Resolves reached Boston, Samuel Adams, the fiery radical who presided over the powerful Whig Caucus Club, decided the time had come when Americans who wished to defend their liberties should do something more than talk. For years Adams had been churning out vitriolic and frequently distorted and slanderous attacks on Governor Francis Bernard, Lieutenant Governor Hutchinson, Chief Justice Peter Oliver and his brother Andrew, secretary of the colony, to whom the lieutenant governor was related by marriage, and their wealthy and aristocratic supporters. Peter Oliver described Adams as a man of "serpentine cunning" who would stop at nothing to gain his ends.

Although Sam Adams's power base was the Caucus Club, he could rely for faithful support on other clandestine clubs and caucuses such as the North End Club, the Middle District Caucus, the Long Room Club, and the South End Caucus. These Boston clubs and caucuses were the seed beds of the Sons of Liberty, the organization that would generate colonial resistance to the Stamp Act and so contribute decisively to hastening the ultimate union of the thirteen colonies. Some of the leading "Sons," including Thomas Chase, partner in Chase and Speackman's rum distillery, had formed a small, closely knit ultraradical group known as the Loyall Nine, whose members met frequently in a room on the second floor of the distillery to eat, drink, and plot the discomfiture of Bernard and Hutchinson. This was an appropriate meeting place; from the windows they could gaze at Liberty Tree, a majestic oak planted a century and a quarter earlier. Whether the "Sons" derived inspiration from contemplation of Liberty Tree, from the exhortations of the "serpentine" Mr. Adams, or, as Tories alleged, from the rum distilled by Mr. Chase has not been resolved, but in early August 1765, at a series of meetings called by Adams, plans were made to act.

The target selected was Andrew Oliver, who had been named stamp distributor for Massachusetts, and who was then engaged in superintending construction of a frame building near the docks for his office and stamp depository. The plan was to intimidate Oliver, pull down his depository, and force his resignation. The date was set for August 14. On that morning, Oliver's effigy was seen hanging from the limb of a tree on Boylston Street. The sheriffs were afraid to remove it.

In the evening a crowd gathered, cut down the effigy, and carried it to the Town-house, where the governor and Council (including Oliver) were sitting. The mob then marched to the docks and in short order pulled down Oliver's newly erected frame building. The next stop was the stamp distributor's home. The mob broke all the windows, tore down the fences, demolished the gardens, and smashed the furniture on the ground floor. On Fort Hill, thousands cheered and sang as they con-

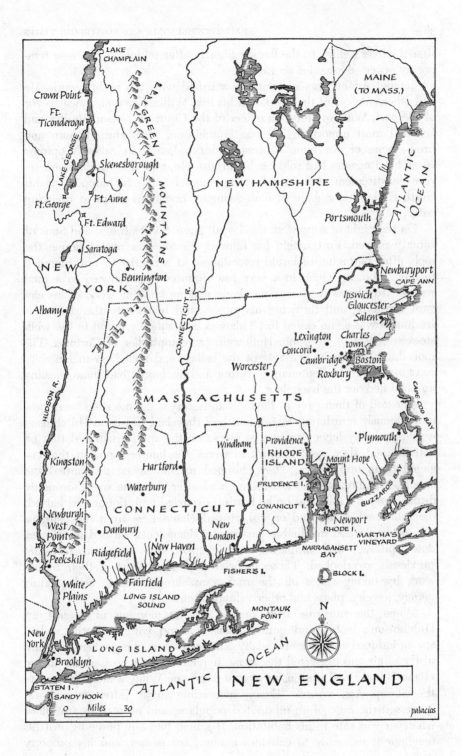

LAKE
CHAMPLAIN

MAINE
(TO MASS.)

Crown Point
Ft.
Ticonderoga

LAKE GEORGE

GREEN MOUNTAINS

Skenesborough

Ft. Anne

Ft. George

Ft. Edward

NEW HAMPSHIRE

Saratoga

Portsmouth

NEW

YORK

Bennington

Albany

CONNECTICUT R.

ATLANTIC OCEAN

Newburyport
CAPE ANN
Ipswich
Gloucester
Salem

Lexington
Concord
Cambridge
Roxbury

Charles
town
Boston

Worcester

M A S S A C H U S E T T S

CAPE COD BAY

HUDSON R.

Windham

Providence
RHODE
ISLAND

Plymouth

Kingston

Hartford

Mount Hope

Waterbury

PRUDENCE I.

CONANICUT I.

C O N N E C T I C U T

BUZZARDS BAY

Newburgh
West
Point

Danbury

New
London

Newport
RHODE I.

MARTHA'S
VINEYARD

Peekskill

Ridgefield

New Haven

NARRAGANSETT
BAY

White
Plains

Fairfield

FISHERS I.

BLOCK I.

LONG ISLAND
SOUND

MONTAUK
POINT

N

New
York

Brooklyn

LONG ISLAND

ATLANTIC

OCEAN

STATEN I.

SANDY HOOK

0   Miles   30

NEW ENGLAND

palacios

signed Oliver's effigy to the flames. Shortly after midnight, peace—a temporary peace—descended on Boston.

Samuel Adams was not entirely satisfied with the night's work. He had other enemies of the people on his list: William Paxton, the surveyor of the port; William Story, an officer of the Court of Vice-admiralty; and last and most important, Thomas Hutchinson, Massachusetts-born and bred—"bone of our bone"—Harvard-educated, and in Adams's opinion an archtraitor who had sold his birthright. He, said Adams, deserved severe chastisement. Adams called on Samuel Swift for support of his North End Boys, a gang of club-swinging hoodlums adept at breaking pates.

On the night of August 26 the Loyall Nine, Swift's thugs, and Sons of Liberty moved. Fortunately for himself, Paxton was not at home; the mob, after partaking of liquid refreshment at a nearby tavern, marched to Story's house, which in a very few minutes they reduced to a total wreck. After breaking Story's windows, making kindling wood of his elegant furniture, and throwing his papers and books into the street, refreshment was again called for. This was conveniently found in the well-stocked cellars of Benjamin Hallowell, Jr., comptroller of Customs. The mob drank down the contents of the cellars and reeled on to Hutchinson's mansion. The lieutenant governor and his family had some warning and had fled out the back door.

Cheated of their prey at Paxton's and Story's, the mobsters were now in a viciously murderous mood, and had they laid hands on Hutchinson would probably have torn him to pieces on the spot. Frustrated that he had escaped, they went to work to wreck the house, a project that engaged them until dawn. They chopped up the floors, dismantled the cupola, broke open the wine cellars, and after everyone was thoroughly drunk, stove in casks and broke bottles. Frenzied with liquor and hatred, they smashed dishes and crystal, ripped chandeliers from the ceilings, tore up books and invaluable papers and documents, slashed mattresses, down pillows, and draperies, and chopped up pieces of furniture previously overlooked. Those inebriated patriots finished their night's work by taking slates off the roof, ransacking bureaus, and stealing money, jewelry, plate, and other valuable items.

When the sun rose over Boston on the morning of August 27, Hutchinson's looted and gutted mansion stood witness to the violent spasm induced and encouraged by Samuel Adams, who, when he heard of the affair and inspected the scene, hypocritically expressed his horror. His mob had ruled Boston for twelve days; one Whig, a man opposed to the Stamp Act, wrote: "Every succeeding night [after August 14] witnessed the rage of an infatuated populace, and no man in any office whatever was safe in his habitation. If a man had any pique against his neighbor it was only to call him a few hard names, and his property would certainly be destroyed, his house pulled down, and his life be in jeopardy."

In Newport, Rhode Island, "Liberty Boys" first looted and then pulled down the houses of two prominent Tories who had advocated the stamp tax. The owners, happy to escape with their lives, abandoned their possessions to the drunken mob and sought refuge in Providence. As "Sons" moved into action from Boston to Annapolis, those who had accepted commissions to distribute stamped paper began to have second thoughts. Jared Ingersoll of Connecticut, waylaid as he rode toward Hartford and threatened by a mob armed with muskets and clubs, resigned. In Annapolis, "Sons" burned the stamp distributor's office and hanged him in effigy. With Gage's Redcoats at hand, prudent New Yorkers restrained those inclined to violent action.

Encouragement to all "lovers of liberty" filled newspapers and flowed from pulpits. Printers worked at their presses from morning till night running off remonstrances, petitions, handbills, and pamphlets. Effigies of Grenville, Bute, and the deposed stamp distributors swung from limbs of trees in dozens of towns to the wild applause of less genteel members of the populace. But calmer voices were being heard and tumult and violence gradually subsided.

Gage feared the worst and in a letter to Major General Robert Monckton, former governor of New York, wrote that he daily anticipated the arrival of Sir Henry Moore, who could share with him the burden: "The sooner Sir Henry Moore arrives the better, tho he will find his hands full, and will enter upon Government in most troublesome and boisterous Times. *The Province never declared their Sentiments of Independency so openly before* and they *state their Grievances,* (if in reality they have any) in *such away,* that I do not see how it will be possible *to relieve them.* They push matters so closely to the Point, that the Subject seems to be whether they are Independent states, or Colonys dependent on Great Britain." At the time Gage wrote this letter, very few responsible persons in the colonies were thinking of independence save as a remote and unlikely possibility, and none had publicly advocated it.

Neither Gage nor any other crown official made a determined effort to analyze the state of opinion in the colonies or to discover whether alleged grievances were justifiable or were specious, as indeed many were. He and his colleagues, who fed on rumors, were prejudiced and badly informed, and their biased and often inflammatory reports and private letters tended only to encourage latent animosities in St. James's Palace, Whitehall, and Westminster. British civil officials stationed in the colonies regarded themselves as members of a socially and culturally superior caste and associated only with Americans whose wealth and position they deemed acceptable and whose political opinions coincided with their own. In their eyes, the rest were no better than "ignorant mechanicks"; a rude, troublesome, and disloyal rabble. Those they haughtily described as "the rabble" regarded them as arrogant and corrupt pensioners, ministerial pimps, and avaricious parasites.

Daniel Dulany of Maryland, a young scholar at Eton when Pitt was there, had gone on to Clare College, Cambridge, and had read law at the Temple. Dulany was a lawyer much respected in his province. He believed the Stamp Act unconstitutional, and in an essay entitled "Considerations on the Propriety of Imposing Taxes in the British Colonies for the purpose of raising a Revenue by Act of Parliament" demolished the theory, popular in England, that the colonies were "virtually represented" in Parliament. This was "a mere cob-web, spread to catch the unwary, and intangle the weak." He drew a distinction between taxes imposed on the colonists without their consent for the sole purpose of raising a revenue, and duties imposed for the regulation of trade. He categorically denied Parliament's right to impose any internal taxes, but upheld the right to regulate imperial trade by imposition of duties. His pamphlet had considerable effect in the colonies and in England, where it was reprinted several times.

The Massachusetts House of Representatives, justly alarmed by the violent scenes in Boston during August, had issued a call to similar assemblies to send delegates to New York in October to debate the tax issue and recommend a uniform plan of action to which all would adhere. Twenty-eight delegates from nine colonies—all except Virginia, Georgia, North Carolina, and New Hampshire—gathered in New York during early October 1765. Timothy Ruggles of Massachusetts, "a friend to Government," was chosen to preside.

Gage did not know what would come of this assembly and wrote Major General Henry Seymour Conway that delegates were of "various characters and opinions, but it's to be feared in general that the Spirit of Democracy is strong amongst them." He then came to the heart of the matter: "The Question is not of the inexpediency of the Stamp Act, or of the inability of the Colony's to pay the Tax, but that it is unconstitutional, and contrary to their Rights, Supporting the Independency of the Province and not subject to the Legislative Power of Great Britain." The general was cautiously optimistic; he hoped the gathering would produce "a Modest, decent and proper Address." Still, as James Otis, Samuel Adams's unstable and unpredictable running mate, was present, anything could happen.

After almost two weeks of apparently well regulated and temperate discussion, the Congress produced an address to His Majesty, petitions to both Lords and Commons, and thirteen resolves. In these, delegates asserted the undoubted right of all Englishmen to suffer no taxes to be imposed on them "but with their own consent, given personally or by their Representatives." Parliament had no constitutional right "to grant to His

Majesty the property of the Colonists." This was too radical for several gentlemen including the president, who returned to Massachusetts to receive a stinging reprimand from the House of Representatives. His colleague from New Jersey was hung in effigy. The symbolic importance of this gathering was fully appreciated in England where the innovation produced shock waves of apprehension, and in America, where it aroused speculation that rights might be successfully asserted and maintained if all would unite.

As the Congress was breaking up, a ship bearing stamped paper for New York arrived at Sandy Hook; the packages were delivered to Lieutenant Governor Cadwallader Colden. A mob immediately surrounded his fortified mansion. Gage had thoughtfully sent a battery of three-pounders and a company of the Royal American Regiment to provide protection. But what to do with the stamped paper? Colden wanted to be rid of it but could find no one to take it. The captain of one of His Majesty's ships of war lying in the North River would not touch it.

New York was on the verge of open rebellion, and Gage's few troops could not cope with mobs whose ranks were daily swelling as armed men poured in from the countryside. But moderates were able to dissuade the more violent from provoking a confrontation with the Redcoats. Both sides allowed the situation to drift along; business faltered, then came to a dead halt. Merchants in New York, and in every colony, pressured to sign "Non-importation" agreements, were busy writing their correspondents in London to cancel orders and to ship no goods of any description until the Stamp Act was repealed. Such an embargo would create hardship in America, but it was the language London traders understood.

While Samuel Adams and his radical henchmen were planning strategy and tactics to be employed to nullify the Stamp Act, the King was engaged in yet another attempt to rid himself of George Grenville and thoroughly obnoxious colleagues. As before, his agent in these complicated maneuverings was his respected uncle, the Duke of Cumberland. Pitt could not be induced to serve except under his own terms, and in desperation Cumberland had approached Charles Watson Wentworth, Second Marquis of Rockingham, a young, wealthy, indolent, urbane, and influential Whig nobleman allied to the Duke of Newcastle. Rockingham agreed to form a ministry. The marquis did not demand too much and the King apparently did not expect too much, for almost anyone—even should his ministry include the slippery Duke of Newcastle—would be more pleasing to him than was "Mr Greenville." On July 10, 1765, the marquis kissed hands and accepted seals as First Lord of the Treasury.

The new First Minister was a peer; he sat in the House of Lords; he could exercise no personal control over his supporters in the Commons.

There he was forced to depend on the cautious and indecisive General Conway, Principal Secretary of State for the Southern Department (which included the transatlantic colonies) and William Dowdeswell, Chancellor of the Exchequer, a man of "shining talents and inflexible virtue" and a country gentleman highly respected by all who knew him, to carry through his policies. The marquis had recently invited Edmund Burke to be his secretary, and five months later Burke, winner of a by-election at Wendover in Buckinghamshire, took his seat in the House. Burke, a fine orator and a man of exceptional intelligence and management ability, would shortly become leader of the Rockingham Whigs in the Commons. But it would require more than Conway's unimpeachable honesty and amiability, Dowdeswell's undeniable political talents and personal virtues, and Burke's oratorical skills to glue together Rockingham's administration. Pitt, ambitious to return to office under his own terms, dissociated himself from the marquis and let it be known that he would not align himself with a ministry he thought not deserving of public confidence. The Grenvilles, the Bedfords, and friends of Lord Bute closed ranks in opposition.

In late December 1765 the Earl of Chesterfield wrote his son to wish him joy of the holiday season and to convey the latest political news. The "great object" at the next meeting of Parliament would be debate on repeal of the Stamp Act, "which our Colonists absolutely refuse to pay." Rockingham's administration was "for some indulgence and forebearance to those forward children . . . the opposition are for taking vigorous, as they call them, but I call them violent, measures." The earl had never seen "a forward child mended by whipping, and I would not have the mother country become a stepmother."[4]

Chesterfield was unable to give an exact account of the state of affairs, "for no man living . . . knows what it is; it varies not only daily, but hourly. Most people think . . . the date of the present ministers is pretty near out. . . ." He thought the act "a most pernicious measure" which would severely affect British trade and manufactures, and wrote his friend Lord Dartmouth to express his "horror of the Stamp Act." He wrote in similar terms to the Duke of Newcastle: "The absurdity of that Act equals, if possible, the mischief of it, by asserting a right which you know you cannot exert." No sensible person could balance a revenue of £80,000 per annum, "which you cannot get neither, with the loss of at least one million a year in your trade and manufactures."[5] The Rockingham ministry seemed to be tottering; conjecture was rampant. Pitt's name was on everyone's lips, but Chesterfield doubted he would come in; most ministers, thinking of the fate of the horse who called a man to assist him, were firmly opposed to any deals with Mr. Pitt.

During the holidays the Cabinet met to consider tactics. Several ministers opposed repeal, but Rockingham, Newcastle, the Duke of Graf-

ceased to pursue his policy of stubborn isolation and joined Rockingham's administration, history may have taken a different turn. But the "Master of Hayes" put forward his customary demands: unchallenged control of policy and appointments. These the marquis had no choice but to reject.

News that Parliament had repealed the Stamp Act arrived in America in mid-May and immediately evoked universal rejoicing. Crowds thronged the streets; church bells pealed gaily from dawn till dark; cannon roared; militia companies paraded and fired salutes as their drums rattled and fifes shrieked triumphantly. Taverns and dramshops did a rousing business; in the evenings Boston Whigs illuminated their homes. In his diary, John Adams wrote that the entire province "was in a Rapture." From New York, Gage reported that "Rejoicings on this Occasion have been remarkably great . . . Nothing of Consequence seems at present to be Apprehended in most of the Provinces." Finally, perhaps, colonial governors and the King's commander in chief in America would enjoy a period of restful calm.

In Cambridge, the Reverend Nathaniel Appleton could not restrain himself until the following Sunday, and summoned his flock to the First Church on Tuesday, May 20, to listen to a thanksgiving sermon dedicated to "The Right Honorable William Pitt, Esq: All the Friends of Virtue and Patrons of Freedom." God had intervened to turn mourning into dancing by raising up such wise and able men as the Duke of Grafton, Rockingham, Lord Camden, General Conway, William Dowdeswell, and Colonel Isaac Barré, "all great and worthy patriots." Surely, God had chosen "the excellent Mr. Pitt, that grand patron of true virtue" to be "the deliverer of these British colonies from captivity and slavery."

Mr. Appleton's sermon was justly applauded and immediately printed in the Boston *Gazette*. His was but one of scores of similar thanksgiving sermons. Many were published in the press, and at least half a dozen of the more notable (including Mr. Appleton's) circulated widely as pamphlets. Although over the years the power of the pulpit had gradually decayed, it was still significant, and nowhere more so than in Boston. Appleton and his brothers of the cloth (with the exception of some Church of England pastors) had been in the forefront of resistance to "that grievous and bitter Act," and at its repeal had reason to rejoice.

One of the few in Boston who did not join in the happy celebrations was Samuel Adams, the man more responsible than any other for mustering American opposition to the Stamp Act. He had read the Declaratory Act with care, and thought he knew what it portended. As he correctly surmised, Administration had not come to repeal in a graceful way, but had been forced to it by pressure of the embargo that had aroused British banking, mercantile, and trading interests. Although Samuel Adams was a pious man, he never for a minute entertained the delusion that the hand of God had rested even momentarily on the heads of Mr. Pitt, the Marquis of Rockingham, or the Duke of Grafton.

But the atmosphere in the colonies in May 1766 was not conducive to reasoned consideration of the implications of the Declaratory Act or to speculation as to what taxes, duties, and other measures of control a ministry which might succeed that led by the amiable marquis would attempt to impose. While Bostonians appreciated Samuel Adams's previous efforts, they were not inclined to listen to his gloomy speculations.

⅘ 4

A Farmer in Pennsylvania

In mid-July, Chesterfield reported "great bustles at Court, and a great change of persons is certainly very near." He thought Pitt would be at the head of a new ministry within the week. Bute, who still had considerable influence in the Closet, was urging the King to summon Pitt, and during the last days of July "the curtain was at last drawn." Pitt agreed to form a ministry and took the Privy Seal. In exchange for his services he demanded the right to name his ministers and, for himself, an earldom. George III had no recourse. He complied, and Mr. Pitt became Earl of Chatham. Chesterfield wrote his son: "The joke here is, he has had a fall upstairs."

Those who followed affairs closely, as Chesterfield did, realized that the "Great Commoner" had made a gross political blunder. His enemies rejoiced; his friends, including Chesterfield, were dumbfounded, for "he is now certainly only Earl of Chatham. . . . Such an event, I believe, was never read nor heard of. To withdraw, in the fullness of his powers, and in the utmost gratification of his ambition, from the House of Commons (which procured him his power and which alone could insure it to him), and to go into that Hospital of Incurables, the House of Lords, is a measure so unaccountable, that nothing but proof positive could have made me believe it; but true it is." Chesterfield prophesied that the new earl would enjoy his dignity, if not the odium he had brought on himself. Certainly he had lost "the greatest part of his popularity, especially in the City."[1] How long this administration would last no one could guess.

That Chatham was in failing health was a secret poorly kept. The earl was in no condition to conduct great affairs. In a hot August, his solicitor was summoned to Hayes. He found the First Minister seated under a shade tree, conversing with Lady Chatham. The earl, pale and emaciated, was obviously an ill man. He seemed bewildered, despondent, and dejected, and expressed no hope he could return to the political scene. Leadership devolved upon his First Lord of the Treasury, the inexperienced Duke of Grafton, a very rich young man addicted to the turf and to his beautiful mistress, Nancy Parsons. The duke was not too attentive to business; his detractors said he had fled to his country estate to seek "rural entertainment, lolling in the arms of a faded beauty," and described him in verse as a "horse jockey" and his mistress as a whore.

Grafton was a poor judge of men; it was he who had induced Chatham to take the ambitious, high-spirited, unstable, and witty Charles Townshend into the ministry as Chancellor of the Exchequer. Townshend, known in London clubs and coffeehouses as "Champagne Charley," was one of many who thought Rockingham's American policy too lenient, that repeal of the Stamp Act had been a colossal blunder, and that measures to reduce the insubordinate colonials to a proper state of dutiful subjection and to extract some revenue in the process were in order. Accordingly, in the spring of 1767 he introduced bills designed to effect both purposes.

Townshend's revenue bill levied duties on glass, lead, painters' colors, paper, and tea. The colonists could not manufacture the first four items in any quantity and were forbidden to purchase them elsewhere than from England. Tea could legally be imported only from England. The monies collected were to be used for the purpose of "defraying the charge for the administration of justice and support of civil government . . . and further defraying the expense of defending, protecting and securing the said dominions." A board of five customs commissioners charged with ensuring strict compliance with the act was to be established in Boston, as was a new and revitalized Court of Vice-admiralty, whose judges were empowered to hear charges brought by the commissioners against those alleged to have violated Revenue Acts. As Townshend was reasonably sure no one suspected of smuggling would be found guilty by a jury composed of his peers of the vicinage, admiralty judges were given authority to determine guilt or innocence. As even Townshend must have known, this was certain to be viewed in America as a distinct violation of a fundamental right.

There is good reason to believe that Chatham was unaware of the nature of Townshend's proposals. The earl, whose chronic gout had become progressively more incapacitating and whose mental lapses and periods of despondency more frequent, had secluded himself in the country and adamantly refused to receive anyone. In the columns of *The Chronicle*, "Junius" described him as "a lunatic with a crutch." He gave no guidance to the patchwork administration over which he nominally presided, and only after the King had personally intervened would he agree to a brief consultation with his colleague the Duke of Grafton. His Majesty would permit no discussion of Chatham's ailments; he deemed it essential to maintain the appearance of a united ministry under the earl's firm control.

But Chatham either could not or perhaps would not take charge, and his ineffectual administration drifted aimlessly. Most political observers allowed it very little time: "The Ministers seemed to proceed with little attention to their nominal leader, whom in their turn they accused of deserting them, and of either refusing his council when he was able to give it, or on insisting on a direction in administration, when by his infirmities he was no longer able to support it."[2] Chesterfield thought the earl would soon quit either his post or the world: ". . . he sees nobody and nobody sees him . . . here is at present an interregnum. We must soon see what order will be produced from this chaos." In efforts to strengthen a sinking administration, Grafton negotiated with the Bedfords, the Grenvilles, and the Rockinghams. None of the factional leaders would commit himself.

Townshend's bills experienced no difficulty in the House of Commons, where the Rockinghams could muster only feeble opposition. Edmund Burke prophesied that Great Britain would never see a single shilling from America, and that when news of the acts reached the colonies it would throw the people "into despair." Burke was not entirely correct. The Townshend Acts would evoke not despair, but indignation.

Grafton, bereft of Chatham's advice and guidance, was threatening to resign, and Secretary Conway, the not too effective administration leader in the House of Commons, announced his wish to retire, as did Lord Chancellor Camden. The King, again afflicted with a ministry on the verge of collapse, faced the situation with his customary determination, and on May 31, 1767, wrote Chatham: "My firmness is not dismaed by these unpleasant appearances; for from the Hour You entered into Office, I have uniformly relied on Your firmness to act in defiance to that faction wh. has never appeared to the height it now does. . . . Tho Your Relations [the Grenvilles] the Bedfords and the Rockinghams are joined with the intention to storm my Closet . . . be firm & You will find me amply ready to take as active a part as the hour seems to require, Tho none of my Ministry stand by Me, I cannot truckle."[3]

Shortly after passage of the acts that aroused the wrath of the failing Earl of Chatham and would evoke a storm of protest in America, Townshend succumbed to an attack of a virulent fever. His demise, unlamented on the other side of the Atlantic, left open the office of the Exchequer. After some ministerial bumbling and calculated dithering by Lord North, to whom Chatham had offered the seals, North accepted, and on October 7, 1767, kissed hands as Chancellor. Several weeks later, General Conway relinquished his position as leader of the House of Commons and Lord North took over. At this time, too, North was given the cabinet seat Chatham had denied Townshend. This mark of confidence in North's ability and probity did not pass unnoticed in political circles.

Frederick Lord North, eldest son of the Seventh Baron North, had been elected in 1754 to the House of Commons from Banbury, Oxfordshire.* As the thirteen qualified voters from Banbury were safely in his father's pocket, the election had posed no problem. North was well endowed by birth, family connection, and education to pursue a career in politics. A godfather was Frederick, Prince of Wales, for whom he was named; his mother, who died in 1734 when he was two years old, was a sister of the Earl of Halifax; his first stepmother was the widow of Viscount Lewisham. Her son William Legge, who inherited that title, would become Second Earl of Dartmouth.

North had been sent to Eton, where he was not a particularly good scholar but where he made a favorable impression on both masters and boys. He went on to Trinity College, Oxford. The family's home, Wroxton Abbey, was owned by Trinity, and the college had benefited from the generosity of Frederick's forebears. Although Frederick devoted little time to drinking, gambling, wenching, and roistering, he was pleasant, witty, a graceful dancer, and popular among his fellow undergraduates. He left behind him no record of academic accomplishment. After Trinity, he and his stepbrother, who had acquired a local reputation for abstemiousness and piety, had together enjoyed a grand tour of the Continent, then the obligatory culmination of every young patrician's education.

Two years after he took his seat in the House of Commons, North married. He was twenty-four years old, with a career before him. Already, he had been favorably noticed by Newcastle, but not until 1759 was he given a position. In June of that year he was appointed a junior lord of the Treasury at a yearly salary of £1,400. North, inclined to be indolent, found this employment not too onerous. He was respected by his Treasury colleagues and was making a reputation as an able debater in the House. When George Grenville's ministry fell in 1765, Lord

---

* His father was created Earl of Guilford in 1752, at which time he assumed the courtesy title of Lord North.

North resigned. He refused to serve in Rockingham's faltering administration, which he correctly estimated to be an ephemeral one. With Chatham's return to power North had accepted a joint paymastership.†
Henry Fox had made the Paymaster's office a gold mine from which he had extracted hundreds of thousands of pounds, but Lord North had from it nothing but his salary.

Lord North was thirty-five when he became Chancellor of the Exchequer and leader in the House of Commons. He had voted for the Stamp Act, against its repeal, and for the Townshend duties. He was generally considered to be one of the group known as "King's Friends." His Majesty, who followed political developments with diligent attention, was impressed with Lord North's loyalty, his fundamental conservatism; his opposition to any compromise with the Americans; his ability to influence his colleagues in the House of Commons, and perhaps above all, his amiable pliancy.

A change in cabinet structure previously much discussed and one that for several years had obviously been desirable, was finally made in January 1768, when the office of Principal Secretary of State for the Colonies was created. Henceforth, responsibility for conduct of American affairs would repose in the less than sympathetic hands of the Earl of Hillsborough rather than in those of Lord Shelburne, whose Southern Department had been radically reduced in scope by the amputation of the transatlantic colonies.

On Monday, December 14, 1767, Benjamin Edes and John Gill, publishers of the Boston *Gazette*, a radical Whig weekly, organ of the Sons of Liberty, and the platform from which Samuel Adams under an assortment of pseudonyms regularly and vindictively chastised Governor Francis Bernard, Lieutenant Governor Thomas Hutchinson, the ministry, Parliament, and all Tories in Boston and elsewhere, printed a letter from "A Farmer in Pennsylvania to the inhabitants of the British colonies." This they copied from the Philadelphia *Chronicle*, where it first appeared. The "Farmer" was John Dickinson, who had been a delegate to the Stamp Act Congress. His twelve letters ran sequentially in eleven of the twenty-three weekly newspapers then published in America. Eight other papers printed one or more letters, so that coverage, although in general limited to the weekly press in Philadelphia, New York, and New England, extended to Williamsburg, Virginia, and Savannah, Georgia.

Dickinson, a country gentleman of considerable means, addressed his letters to his "Beloved Countrymen" and began the first: "I am a farmer, settled after a variety of fortunes, near the banks of the river Delaware in the province of Pennsylvania . . . my farm is small, my servants are few and good; I have a little money at interest; I wish for no more, and with

† Joint paymaster of the forces.

a contented, grateful mind I am compleating the number of days allotted
to me by divine goodness." The Farmer spent much time in his library;
the Latin classics, especially Tacitus, were favorite reading; his few chosen friends were "gentlemen of ability and learning." His life was quiet; a
man, said he, may be "as happy without bustle as with it." In this bucolic
ambiance Dickinson found opportunity to reflect on the dangers threatening his beloved country. Times were troublous; some "late transactions
. . . of the utmost importance" impelled him "to request the attention of
the public."[4]

One of the "late transactions" to which the Farmer referred related to
a demand made by Lieutenant General Thomas Gage that the New York
Legislature appropriate money to provide candles, firewood, salt, pepper,
and vinegar for Redcoats stationed in the city.‡ The legislators considered that as the general's demand constituted a form of "internal" taxation, it was clear violation of charter rights, and refused to appropriate
the small amount necessary to meet Gage's modest request. Dickinson
supported the position taken by the Legislature; if the British had the
right to requisition *anything* for the troops, they had the right to requisition *everything*: ". . . in short, to lay any burden they please upon us."

Lord Shelburne wrote the governor, Sir Henry Moore, that the King
was displeased and ordered Moore to direct the Legislature to reconsider. The New Yorkers refused. Parliament replied with an act suspending the recalcitrant Legislature. This raised a storm of protest; the Farmer
considered the act unwarranted, probably illegal, prejudicial to American liberties, and "justly alarming," for by it Parliament had deprived the
people of New York of their inherent and charter rights to make laws to
govern themselves. Dickinson's argument was simple and impossible to
confute: "If they may be legally deprived . . . of the privilege of making
laws, why may they not with equal reason, be deprived of every other
privilege?" He described this arbitrary assertion of authority as "a dreadful stroke" and called on the colonies to unite, for the cause of one was
the cause of all. He believed that "firm, modest exertion of a free spirit"
would bring the ministry to see the error of its ways and conduce to
speedy redress.

He turned next to the Townshend Acts, which he ascribed to "the sordid arts of intriguing men" whose "pestilential ambition" would alienate
the colonists and induce civil discord. In his opinion, the acts deserved
the bitterest curses of posterity and should be opposed by all legal
means. The Farmer did not question Parliament's constitutional authority
to regulate trade, but as Daniel Dulany had done, he challenged the asserted right to levy duties for the purpose of raising a revenue. The language of the preamble to the acts was precise and the threat to American

‡ Provision of certain of these items was called for by annual act of Parliament.
Heretofore, no objection had been raised in any colony to providing them.

liberties imminent, for the revenues raised were to be used to pay the salaries of royal governors, lieutenant governors, colonial secretaries, judges, and other crown officials. Heretofore all such salaries had been paid with monies appropriated by colonial legislatures in accordance with authority granted and guaranteed by royal charters. A plethora of new offices would soon be created to satisfy the rapacity of ministerial favorites and absentee "pimps." Revenue squeezed out of Americans would ultimately support a horde of ravenous pensioners who would reside in England and make paltry allowances to the corrupt and incompetent "cooks" they would deputize to do the work locally. Ireland provided a frightening example.

If colonial legislatures were no longer to be allowed to appropriate money to sustain the civil authority, what was their function to be? Perhaps they would be permitted to pass laws for "the yoking of pigs" or the "pounding of stray cattle." And what of the administration of justice? In England, judges held their seats on the bench "during good behavior." It was now proposed that judges in America hold their appointments "at pleasure." With judges totally dependent on the crown, and supported by a standing army, "What inumerable acts of injustice may not be committed, and how fatally may the principle of liberty be sapped, by a succession of judges *utterly independent of the people.*"

The Farmer called upon his fellow Americans to rouse themselves: ". . . behold the ruin hanging over your heads. If you ONCE admit that Great Britain may lay duties on her exportations to us *for the purpose of levying money on us,*" she would proceed to lay duties on all articles she supplied "and the tragedy of *American* liberty is finished. . . . Can the Parliament legally *take money out of our pockets* WITHOUT OUR CONSENT? If they can, our boasted liberty is but

> *Vox et Praeterae nihil*
> (A voice, and nothing else.)"

Dickinson anticipated reaction from the timid and the conservative. Some would think Great Britain too powerful to oppose and resistance futile; others would fear the letters would generate "riots and tumults." To those who questioned his intent, the Farmer had a ready answer: "The meaning [of the letters] is to convince the people of these colonies that they are at this moment exposed to the most imminent dangers, and to persuade them immediately, vigorously and unanimously to exert themselves, in the most firm but most peaceful manner, for obtaining relief."

Was force ultimately warranted to obtain this relief? Yes, for when an "inveterate resolution" is apparent "to annihilate the liberties of the governed, the English history affords frequent examples of resistance by force." But force was not as yet justified, and Dickinson urged his countrymen to pursue constitutional methods. He wished with all his heart to preserve the relationship between Great Britain and America, and could not bear the thought of his country "Torn from the body to which we are united by religion, liberty, laws, affections, relations, language and commerce. . . ."

Dickinson had correspondents in London. He knew what line the ministry would take:

> The people of Great Britain will be told and have been told that they are sinking under an immense debt; that great part has been contracted in defending the colonies, that *these* are so ungrateful and undutiful that they will not contribute one mite to its payment, nor even to the support of the army now kept up for their defence, protection and security; that they are rolling in wealth and are of so bad and republican a spirit, that they are aiming at independence; that the only way to retain them in obedience is to keep a strict watch over them, and to draw off part of their riches in *taxes*, and that every burden laid upon *them* is taking off so much from *Great Britain*. These assertions will be generally believed. . . .

These assertions were indeed continually made by the ministry and its supporters, in the subsidized press, and in speeches in Lords and Commons, and were generally believed.

The theme of the last two of the twelve letters was colonial unity and firm but nonviolent resistance to all encroachments. Under no circumstances should Americans supinely acquiesce. This would set a dangerous precedent and invite progressive erosion of their liberties. The Farmer exhorted his fellow countrymen "to instantly and firmly oppose" the duties laid by the Townshend Acts: ". . . this opposition can never be effectual unless it is the united effort of these provinces."

In a Boston town meeting on March 14, 1768, the citizens voted unanimously to express the thanks of the Town "to the ingenious Author of a course of letters published in Philadelphia and in this place signed A FARMER," and appointed a committee including Samuel Adams, Dr. Benjamin Church, and John Hancock to draft a letter of appreciation. Apparently Adams composed the epistle, which begins " 'Tis to YOU, worthy Sir! that AMERICA is obliged for a most seasonable, sensible, loyal and vigorous Vindication of her Rights and Liberties."

Several days previously, Sons of Liberty in almost every city and town in America had gathered to celebrate the second anniversary of repeal of the Stamp Act. The Boston Sons assembled at Liberty Tree and proceeded in an impressive cavalcade to the outskirts of the city where they enjoyed a buffet and drained their glasses in the usual toasts to "Liberty," John Wilkes, William Pitt, and the Marquis of Rockingham. In

New York, Sons gathered at elegant "Turtle feasts" at Mr. Jones's and Mr. Gardin's taverns, where they and their guests first ate their way through a fine dinner and then drank their way through a series of toasts, of which the symbolic twelfth was "To the ingenious and patriotic author of the Farmer's letters." A "Band of Music" and "curious fireworks" provided entertainment for the enthusiastic public. The Sons sent the remains of their banquet to prisoners in the jail, "with a suitable amount of liquor." Apparently there were no unseemly disturbances: "Everything was conducted with proper Decorum."

Letters extolling the Famer's perspicacity and patriotism poured in to every newspaper that had published his letters. They were read, studied, quoted, and discussed in fashionable drawing rooms as they were in dramshops and town meetings from Boston to Savannah, and were dissected and analyzed by the men who formed public opinion. The Farmer had challenged Parliament's supremacy and provided abundant intellectual ammunition for Americans determined to preserve their liberties against further encroachment.

Whig members of the Massachusetts House of Representatives had not needed the Farmer's letters to stir them to action. In early January 1768, Samuel Adams, clerk of the House, the man Hutchinson described as "the Grand Incendiary," had drafted a circular letter calling for united opposition to the Townshend Acts. By an overwhelming vote the House had approved. Adams sent copies of the circular to the Boston *Gazette*, to principal towns in Massachusetts, to speakers of other colonial assemblies, and mailed some to the Bay Colony's London agents. Responses were immediate and enthusiastic, and were promptly printed in the *Gazette*.

Possibly Dickinson's temperate and reasoned letters had a calming effect, for April and May 1768 were relatively tranquil months. Gage appeared to be wholly absorbed in direction of Indian affairs, which as usual he reported in meticulous detail. In Boston Sam Adams wielded his quill with accustomed acerbity, but Sons of Liberty were quiet and Chase's North End roughnecks confined their activities to their own pitch. Still, the ever present possibility of destructive mob action hung ominously over the town. His Majesty's commissioners of Customs lived from one day to the next in fear of their lives. They and everyone else knew that any incident, however trivial, might trigger violence.

Wilkes had recently returned from his exile on the Continent ambitious to regain a seat in the House of Commons from which he felt he had been illegally expelled, and decided to stand for the City, where he commanded a substantial following. On March 10, 1768, he had become a member of the Joiners Guild, "and took the cloathing of the Company on him accordingly." Having thus qualified as a member of the London livery, Wilkes presented himself to the voters in a moderate speech which his supporters noisily acclaimed. But as polling progressed, it was apparent that their hero was not doing as well as expected, for of some 20,000 votes cast for seven candidates, Wilkes received only 1,247. This electoral disaster would have discouraged anyone but Wilkes, who calmly announced that he proposed to stand for a seat then vacant in the county of Middlesex.

On the first day of polling Wilkes arrived at the Brentford hustings followed by a train of 250 coaches crammed with devoted adherents who wore blue cockades and carried lettered cards proclaiming their dedication to "Wilkes and Liberty." Polling was peaceful; Wilkes was returned. In London, mobs chalked "No. 45" on doors, walls, and coaches, pulled the Austrian ambassador from his chariot, chalked "45" on the soles of his shoes, and otherwise celebrated the victory in Middlesex by parading London "from east to west, obliging everybody to illuminate and breaking the windows of such as did not do it immediately." For three nights mobs armed with copious supplies of bricks roamed the city smashing windows and lamps. To his credit, Wilkes did everything he could to control the enthusiasm of his riotous followers.

Although Wilkes was legally an outlaw, the government hesitated to move against him, and while timid ministers dithered, Wilkes resolved their dilemma by surrendering voluntarily. He was promptly committed to King's Bench Prison to await trial on the charge of seditious libel. A mob soon gathered; the mood was ugly, and leaders who announced their intent to pull down the prison were only dissuaded from doing so when the distinguished prisoner appeared and urged the crowd to disperse. Wilkes's behavior in the circumstances rehabilitated him to a measurable degree in the eyes of many moderates, including Grafton and Newcastle, but did nothing to change the King's opinion.

His Majesty provided Lord North, who was at first reluctant to force this issue, with a letter expressing his fixed determination to drive Wilkes from the political scene: "The expulsion of Mr. Wilkes appears to be very essential, and must be effected." Although His Majesty thought expulsion "essential," some members of Parliament believed it would be unconstitutional. Wilkes had been convicted of libel and blasphemy, not of a felony. The government was faced with an extremely delicate and potentially dangerous situation. Parliament was to open on May 10; the King feared that anarchy would ensue and directed Viscount Weymouth to take necessary steps to suppress rioters: "Bloodshed is not what I delight in, but it seems to me the only way of restoring due obedience of the laws." This, a written order to a Secretary of State, gave Weymouth regal authority to order troops to fire on rioters.

Several days later the King's apprehensions were justified when a great concourse of coal-heavers and seamen striking for higher wages, weavers, Thames watermen, dockers, apprentices, and idle spectators assembled in the vicinity of the prison. Some said the crowd exceeded twenty thousand. Foot and Horse Guards were called out; the presence of the troops infuriated the mob, and as brickbats flew and tension rose, the troops fired. During this and subsequent confrontations, a dozen persons were killed and several score injured. The affray of May 10, known in history as the Massacre of St. George's Fields, ignited riots in every part of the metropolis. The King hastened to St. James's Palace to encourage his timorous ministers, issued orders to call more troops to London, and personally directed their deployment. Magistrates read the Riot Act to no avail, and the troops had but little effect on rioters roaring "Wilkes and Liberty," as volleys of brickbats smashed glass from one end of town to the other. For a week during May 1768, anarchy reigned in the British capital.

While mobs ravaged London, Bernard and Hutchinson, who lived from one dawn to the next in apprehension of an incident that would raise mobs in Boston, enjoyed a welcome period of tranquillity. This was shattered on June 10, when a boarding party from His Majesty's frigate *Romney* seized John Hancock's sloop *Liberty*, then lying at his wharf laden with two hundred barrels of whale oil and twenty barrels of tar, fully provisioned and ready for sea. She had not yet been cleared for departure. *Liberty* had arrived a month earlier from Madeira and discharged a cargo of wine. There is substantial evidence that a considerable amount of this madeira had been put ashore without payment of duty.

Hancock was a wealthy and influential man. He was active politically; he was captain of the Boston Cadet Company and had contributed to keep Sam Adams afloat and the Sons of Liberty handsomely supplied with cash. His enmity toward Governor Bernard, Lieutenant Governor Hutchinson, the Oliver brothers, and the customs commissioners, whom he, with other Boston merchants, regarded as a pack of nepotists and scheming rascals, was well known and fully reciprocated. The commissioners, who had been waiting for an opportune moment to seize one of his ships, acted on June 10, when they ordered *Liberty* towed into the bay and anchored under the guns of *Romney*.

Within the hour a belligerent crowd had gathered on the wharf. This seems to have been spontaneous; for once, neither Sam Adams nor Sons of Liberty were involved. Several customs officials unlucky enough to be caught on the streets were beaten. Offices and residences of the defenseless commissioners were the next targets. The mob moved on them, broke the windows, terrorized the commissioners' wives and children, and concluded the evening's work by carrying off the collector's "pleasure boat," hacking it to pieces, and making a bonfire of it. The next night the commissioners and their families fled to H.M.S. *Romney*. Here Paxton composed an urgent letter to Lord Hillsborough: "Unless we have immediately two or three regiments, 'tis the opinion of all the friends to government that Boston will be in open rebellion."

Governor Bernard had realized for some time that another crisis was in the making, and had earlier asked General Gage to send troops to Boston to maintain public order and protect His Majesty's commissioners of Customs in the execution of their duties. The commissioners, now thoroughly intimidated, had good reason for fear for their lives and the safety of their families. Bernard knew, Hutchinson knew, and they knew that a word from the "Grand Incendiary," his aide William Molineux, leaders of the Loyall Nine, or Benjamin Edes would raise a murderous mob.

Finally convinced that the situation in Boston was rapidly reaching the point when a spark could initiate a conflagration, Gage had dispatched an aide-de-camp to confer with the governor, and had ordered Lieutenant Colonel William Dalrymple at Halifax to embark the 14th and 29th Foot and sail at once to Boston. At the same time he informed Hillsborough that although New York was tranquil, reports of the "Outrageous Behavior, the licentious and daring Menaces and Seditious Spirit of the People of all Degrees in Boston" were truly alarming, and warned the secretary to expect a flood of "Petitions, Memorials, Remonstrances, etc.," objecting to duties levied by the Townshend Acts, and to be prepared to hear that all colonial assemblies would support Massachusetts. Worried that the presence of troops would further inflame the Bostonians, Gage wrote the secretary that while he reposed great confidence in Colonel Dalrymple's "Prudence, Resolution and Integrity," he had recommended "very great Circumspection in his Conduct and the strictest Discipline among the Troops."

The *Liberty* episode happened to coincide with reports that Gage had ordered two regiments from Halifax to Boston. These rumors enraged Sam Adams and the radicals and induced profound apprehension in moderate breasts. All feared having in their midst a "Standing Army," a "most ready engine in the hands of despotism," and believed with Mercy Otis Warren, sister of "Jemmy" Otis and wife of James Warren, a radical Whig, that to station troops in any community would establish "a revolution in manners," corrupt morals, propagate "every species of vice, and degrade the human character."

Instructions Bernard received at this time from Hillsborough were not designed to lessen mounting tensions. In these, the secretary wrote that the King had seen the Massachusetts circular and considered it factious, inflammatory, and subversive, and added his opinion that it constituted a "flagitious attempt to disturb the Publick Peace." Governors were to prevail upon their assemblies to treat the circular "with the Contempt it deserves." It was "the King's pleasure" that Governor Bernard direct the Massachusetts House promptly to rescind these seditious resolves.

On June 21, 1768, Bernard transmitted Hillsborough's letter to the House, with the comment that His Majesty considered the circular to be an attempt to create "unwarrantable combinations" and to excite "an unjustifiable opposition to the constitutional authority of Parliament." There ensued a week of rude sparring, during which the governor threatened to dissolve the House. Before he could do so, the House, on the last day of June, voted by a count of 92 to 17 not to rescind. The governor promptly dissolved the General Court.

This vote, which directly challenged the King, Parliament, Hillsborough, and Bernard, was greeted in Massachusetts and elsewhere with manifestations of joy. As bells rang and cannon boomed, effigies of Hillsborough were hanged and consigned to the flames. With notice of the vote, the legislators sent Bernard a letter stating that the House had been actuated "by a conscientious . . . clear and determined sense of Duty to God, to our King, our Country, and to our latest Posterity," and most ardently wished and humbly prayed that the governor, in his future conduct, would be influenced by the same principles.

The "Glorious Ninety-two" were everywhere acclaimed and toasted; the "Seventeen Slaves" execrated. The spirit of determination to resist was not confined to Boston. In all the colonies "the mean, abject wretches" who had voted to rescind were castigated and cursed. Hillsborough's intemperate letter did more to promote colonial union than had the Massachusetts circular.

Most Bostonians, including some of the more vociferous Sons of Liberty, had not believed troops would be sent to occupy their city, and confirmation of reports that two regiments were preparing to embark at Halifax produced confusion and consternation in the ranks of the radical Whig leadership. Samuel Adams advocated armed resistance to a landing of troops, but the arguments of colleagues endowed with more equable temperaments prevailed. They could not, however, prevent him from calling a town meeting, which after much debate resolved to request Governor Bernard to summon the General Court to consult on "the dread calamity" impending. The governor refused. Sam Adams and his more radical colleagues then decided to summon a convention to meet in Boston. Delegates from dozens of towns gathered at Faneuil Hall on September 22, but Adams soon discovered that their sentiments did not accord with his. They elected Thomas Cushing, a moderate Whig, as speaker. Cushing urged them to proceed cautiously and prudently, and this was precisely what they did. Practically all delegates from the Massachusetts hinterland had been instructed by their towns not to support illegal or unconstitutional measures advocated by Boston demagogues. "Jemmy" Otis, who perhaps sensed the temper of the delegates, restrained himself. Indeed, he did not even attend some of the sessions, which were conducted with decorum. Delegates would unite in a petition to the crown, but firmly refused to sanction ordering militia to Boston. Bernard's reaction to this assemblage was impolitic, as usual. Instead of ignoring the gathering, he branded it as "illegal" and ordered the delegates to disperse. Experience might have suggested to the governor that his order would be ignored.

Sam Adams, never one to let an opportunity slip, flayed Bernard in his best manner and urged the people to take up arms. He was not supported in the convention, but did deliver an impassioned harangue to a crowd the Sons of Liberty had collected. One who was present described him as trembling and agitated: "We will not submit to any tax," he shouted. "We will take up arms . . . we are free, and want no king."

Several days after the convention disbanded, Redcoats from Halifax disembarked and Colonel Dalrymple led his long column through the streets of the city. Mercy Warren witnessed the event, and later wrote:

> The American war may be dated from the hostile parade of this day; a day which marks with infamy the councils of Britain. At this period the inhabitants of the colonies almost universally breathed an unshaken loyalty to the King of England, and the strongest attachment to a country whence they derived their origin. Thus was the astonishment of the whole province excited, when to the grief and consternation of the town of Boston several regiments were landed, and marched sword in hand through the principal streets of their city, then in profound peace.[5]

John Adams, who had moved from Braintree and was practicing law in Boston, lived on Brattle Square where Redcoats paraded every morning: "Their very Appearance in Boston was a strong proof to me that the determination of Great Britain to subjugate Us, was too deep and inveterate ever to be altered by Us: For everything We could do was Misrepresented and Nothing We could say was credited."

When Gage learned that a provincial convention had met, he wrote Hillsborough (September 26, 1768) that all eyes in New York were turned toward Boston. He had ordered a detachment of the New York garrison, plus a field train of ten pieces of artillery, to be prepared to embark on a moment's notice. But "Sedition is catching"; he had to protect the military stores in New York. The general correctly opined that the Americans were encouraged by activities of those in England who opposed the government, or, to advance their own selfish interests, were willing to betray those of their country. Further,

The News of the Tumults and Insurrections which have happened in London and Dublin, and in general every Circumstance,
which can involve the Mother Country in Difficulty and Distress,
is received by the Factions in America as Events favorable to their
Designs of Independency. Hoping that Confusion and Division at
home, will render any Designs in Government to oppose their
Schemes, ineffectual.

His Majesty's commander in chief in America was fast losing
confidence in the will of the British Government to take vigorous action, and closed this long letter to the secretary with the following
advice:

> . . . I know of nothing that can so effectually quell the Spirit of
> Sedition, which has so long and so greatly prevailed here, and
> bring the People back to a Sense of their Duty, as Speedy, vigor
> ous and unanimous measures taken in England to suppress it.
> Whereby the Americans shall plainly perceive, that it is the gen
> eral and determined Sense of the British Nation, resolutely to sup
> port and Maintain their Rights, and to reduce [the Americans] to
> their Constitutional Dependence on the Mother Country.[6]

Bernard now had the troops he had secretly requested to maintain
the King's peace in Boston, but he had made no effort to prepare proper
billets for them. The 29th Foot encamped on the Common; the 14th slept
on straw pallets laid in the floors of Faneuil Hall and the Town House.
This was no more than a temporary solution, for winter was approaching. Decent accommodations must be found, and quickly. Very
few householders were inclined to provide hospitality, and despite urgent pleas from the governor and Colonel Dalrymple, the Council
remained stubbornly unconcerned. The town had not asked for troops;
Bernard had. Arrangements for quartering were clearly his responsibility.

Bernard, balked and frustrated, begged Gage to hasten to Boston to
resolve the billeting problem. The commander in chief arrived on October 15, met with the Council, and prevailed upon the members to turn
over a building in a sad state of repair. Now an unexpected contretemps
developed: The poor people living in the dilapidated structure refused to
move. Bernard dispatched his lieutenant governor to the scene to order
them out. After listening to Hutchinson's harangue, their spokesman declared that they had taken legal advice and proposed to remain unless
evicted by force. Troops were called to encircle the building; the tenants
reviled them and stayed where they were. Suitable billeting space was
found and troops living under canvas struck their tents. Gage reported to
Hillsborough that the affair had "only served to shew, a most obstinate
Spirit of Opposition to every measure of Government."

But the general was cautiously optimistic; he hoped "that things being in a more quiet State than they were, the violent Temper of the People will abate in a little time, and their Minds be more composed. . . . The Town has been under a kind of Democratical Despotism for a considerable time, and it has not been safe for People to act or Speak contrary to the Sentiments of the ruling Demagogues; and Surprizing as it may Appear, those Fears are not yet annihilated." In closing this report Gage wrote: "From what has been said, your Lordship will conclude there is no Government in Boston. There is in Truth very little at present. . . ."[7] With two regiments bedded down for the winter, the customs commissioners and their families returned to town from Castle William, where for some months they had been living in isolation and discomfort.

During November the 64th and 65th regiments of foot arrived from Ireland, and Commodore Samuel Hood came in from Halifax. Transport *Raven,* carrying Colonel Alexander Mackay and three companies of foot, blown off course, wound up at Nevis in the West Indies. Lieutenant Colonel William Dalrymple was to be senior British officer in Boston for some time. Dalrymple, a sensible officer with some appreciation of the political situation, assured Gage he would keep his troops in hand. Before he sailed for New York on November 24, Gage felt able to report that the arrival of Redcoat regulars had done much to curb "the Licentious and Seditious Spirit, which has so long prevailed in this Place . . . and it appears very Necessary for His Majesty's Service that both his land and Sea forces should be strong in North America for some time to come."[8]

Such reports and recommendations from the King's officers in America were not designed to encourage a spirit of moderation in either St. James's or Whitehall, and Shelburne, who had consistently advocated such a policy, found himself isolated in the Cabinet. He and Grafton were not on speaking terms; his attitude found little favor with the King and even less with the belligerent Bedford clique. Convinced that Shelburne was unreliable, if not indeed disloyal, His Majesty encouraged Grafton to dismiss him. In early October 1768 Shelburne gave up the seals of office, and Thomas Thynne, Third Viscount Weymouth, a member of "the Bloomsbury Gang" best known for his addiction to the bottle, kissed hands as Secretary of State for the Southern Department. Chatham, who had earlier learned of the plans to dump Shelburne, resigned. Grafton retained the office of First Lord of the Treasury and became First Minister. The duke's was the seventh ministry in eight years.

Nearly 3,000 British officers and soldiers were now billeted in Boston, and although in general they behaved themselves, their presence grew daily more obnoxious. No man or woman could move on any street without encountering ubiquitous Redcoats; after dusk, citizens were challenged as they walked from their offices or places of work to their homes and lodgings. Those who crossed by ferry to Charlestown or entered and left town by Boston Neck were stopped, searched, questioned, and otherwise harassed. Fights broke out in taverns and dramshops. Many Redcoats deserted; one was caught, tried, and shot; a dozen were publicly whipped on the Common.

Bostonians who witnessed the execution and the whippings were appalled at the brutality of the proceedings, and soon began reviling soldiers as "Bloody Backs" and "Lobster Backs." Sam Adams and his friends, ever diligent to create animosity, cooked up scurrilous and slanderous stories and magnified every incident, however insignificant. Each day several of Dalrymple's men were haled before magistrates to answer manufactured charges of misbehavior. As winter closed down on Boston, tension inexorably mounted. But it was contained. Despite virulent attacks in the Boston *Gazette* and constant heckling from town rowdies eager to foment trouble, the King's soldiers comported themselves well. During a long winter Boston was peaceful.

Londoners were less fortunate than their fellow subjects in the town of Boston, for the winter and spring of 1769 were marked in the British capital by political turmoil, demonstrations, and rioting. Parliament assembled on January 19 to be confronted with a variety of pressing problems, among them the straitened financial condition of the East India Company, the late disturbances in America, the King's Civil List, and last, and in the King's opinion perhaps the most important, the status of John Wilkes.

George III was not a man who indulged in emotional outbursts, but apparently mere mention of Wilkes's name was sufficient to induce them. The King had somehow managed to convince himself that his crown would be in jeopardy should Wilkes be allowed to take the seat to which the voters of Middlesex had elected him, and had earlier expressed his opinion that the expulsion of Wilkes from the House of Commons was "most essential." On February 2, 1769, Wilkes was expelled. The King was delighted; Wilkes, he was convinced, would now sink into deserved oblivion.

But the effect of the expulsion was precisely the opposite, for "his popularity increased in proportion to his difficulties; and his persecution, as it was termed, and generally understood, raised him new friends in every quarter." The voters of Middlesex promptly re-elected him; the House as promptly declared the election void. He was for a second time elected; again the House declared the election void, and writs were issued for a third. These ridiculous proceedings provoked Horace Walpole to write that there were still people "so wild and blind as not to see that every triumph against him is followed by mortification and disgrace."[9]

The ministry now prevailed upon Colonel Henry Lawes Luttrell, M.P., whose animus toward Wilkes was a matter of common knowledge, to give up his seat for Bossiney in Cornwall and to stand against Wilkes in Middlesex. Luttrell agreed to do so; on April 13, 1769, he was submerged in a four-to-one landslide. The ministry next proceeded to a measure probably unconstitutional and patently absurd: On April 15 the House declared that Luttrell should have been elected, and seated him. Outraged voters in Middlesex replied by castigating the "evil minded persons" who had imposed upon the King "notions and opinions of the most dangerous and pernicious tendency."

In a loyal petition they listed thirty-two "grievances" and added that policies of "evil counsellors," injurious to the liberties of freeborn Englishmen, had produced justified apprehensions in America similar to those prevalent at home. Walpole wrote Horace Mann that the House of Commons had "done nothing but flounder from one blunder to another" and that the seating of Luttrell was "a new egg laid for riots and clamours." He continued to be amazed that the ministry did not prefer "the safe, amicable and honourable method of governing the people as they like to be governed, to the invidious and restless task of governing them contrary to their inclinations."[10]

A veritable torrent of remonstrances and petitions poured into London from dozens of counties, cities, and towns whose freeholders realized that if the expressed will of Middlesex electors could be so easily thwarted and their votes nullified, so, too, could their own. John Wilkes in King's Bench Prison doubtless derived considerable pleasure from the events of this spring.

In May 1769 rumors circulated that Gage had ordered two regiments to be evacuated from Boston. Equally welcome was the news that Governor Francis Bernard had been ordered to return to England to report on the situation in the Bay province. Bernard, who had been trying to escape for some time, could not possibly have been as delighted as were the Bostonians, and when in late July he sailed for England in H.M.S. *Rippon*, the citizens rejoiced. Bells pealed and bonfires fed by effigies of the most thoroughly unpopular man who had ever set foot in the town of Boston illumined the night skies. In the next issue of the *Gazette*, Sam Adams bade polite farewell to the former governor; Boston was finally free of "a Scourge to this Province, a Curse to North America, and a Plague on the whole Empire of Britain."

In late September, Sam Adams got his hands on copies of letters Bernard, Gage, Commodore Hood, and customs commissioners had written to London, and at a town meeting on Wednesday, October 4, it was decided to prepare and publish for order of the town "An APPEAL to the WORLD, or a VINDICATION of the Town of Boston from Many False and Malicious Aspersions." Shortly thereafter, Edes and Gill published the document (probably written by Samuel Adams with help from his cousin John) together with resolutions passed unanimously at Town Meeting. This influential pamphlet, which circulated in all the colonies, intensified the growing distrust of royal officials, who, so many Americans were now convinced, were engaged in an evil conspiracy to oppress them and deprive them of their liberties.

Parliament assembled in November. The King dwelled at length on the situation in Boston, and declared the town to be "in a state of disobedience to all law and government." In addresses of thanks for the royal message, Lords and Commons expressed their willingness to consider just complaints, but asserted their determination "to maintain the supreme authority of the British legislature over every part of the British empire." It soon became evident that consideration of alleged grievances did not extend to an investigation into the conduct of the King's servants in America. Rather, the House of Commons was in a mood to support all crown officials however arbitrary, inept, corrupt, or unpopular, and to take vigorous measures to suppress tumult and enforce obedience.

As a first step, the House declared proceedings of the town meeting of September 12, 1768, "illegal, unconstitutional, and calculated to excite sedition and insurrection," and described the call for the provincial convention that had assembled ten days later as "subversive, and evidently manifesting a design . . . to set up a new and unconstitutional authority independent of the Crown." The elections held in almost one hundred towns and villages in the Bay Colony were described as "daring insults" to His Majesty's authority, and "audacious usurpations of the powers of government." The House requested the governor of Massachusetts Bay to provide a full report on the activities of Bostonians who might be guilty of treason or misprisions of treason, to arrest them forthwith, and send them to England for trial.

This inflammatory language precipitated bitter debate. Opposition speakers declared that the army of customs officers sent to America had made themselves as odious to the inhabitants as were the duties they were supposed to collect. Another army, sent to assist them, was "still more odious and much more dangerous." They condemned the plan to bring Americans to England to stand trial as unjust, absurd, unconstitutional, and impracticable. There is reason to believe that the ministry had designed the provocative proposal to intimidate, for it must have been apparent even to such arrogant and inflexible conservatives as the Bedfords that any attempt to arrest men of the standing of James Otis, Samuel Adams, John Hancock, and James Warren, and to transport them to England to stand trial for treason, with conviction and the gallows inevitable, would evoke armed resistance.

The Grafton ministry now came under a searing attack from the anonymous "Junius," described by his enraged targets as "a wicked and incendiary writer" and "the high priest of envy, malice and all unchari-tablness." His vitriolic articles in the *Public Advertiser* are unequaled in the annals of journalism. "Junius" (who has never been identified) had surveyed the state of affairs in Great Britain and had found the situation altogether deplorable: "We are governed by councils, from which a rea-sonable man can expect no remedy but poison; no relief but death. And, he continued:

> If by the immediate interposition of Providence it were possi-
> ble for us to escape a crisis so full of terror and despair, posterity
> will not believe the history of the present times. They will either
> conclude, that our distresses were imaginary, or that we had the
> good fortune to be governed by men of acknowledged integrity
> and wisdom: they will not believe it possible that their ancestors
> could have survived, or recovered, from so desperate a condition,
> while a Duke of Grafton was prime minister, a Lord North chan-
> cellor of the exchequer, a Weymouth and a Hillsborough secre-
> taries of state, a Granby commander in chief, and a Mansfield
> chief criminal judge of the kingdom.[11]

Concerted colonial reaction to the Townshend Acts induced the Duke of Grafton to urge the Cabinet to support repeal. He was opposed by the Bedford clique whose members asserted the proposal would affront the dignity of Parliament and impair the principle of its right to tax America. After considerable wrangling, Grafton agreed to a compromise in which all duties except that on tea would be annulled. But his defeat in the Cabinet presaged his downfall, and the King began a diplomatic search for a new First Minister.

Opposition had now a clear opportunity to capitalize on the evident weakness of the Grafton administration, but as usual failed to get to-gether, and early January 1770 found the duke still clinging to office. His position grew daily more precarious and he could do nothing to strengthen it. Chatham unexpectedly and ostentatiously withdrew his support by attacking the ministry in a speech in the Lords. This last defection was too much for Grafton, who informed His Majesty he was unable to continue. The King, fighting for time, was desperately casting about for a successor. His choice was severely limited; Chatham, Gren-ville, and Rockingham were alike impossible.

On the evening of January 22 he summoned Lord North to Queen's House. The discussion was satisfactory, and on the following morning the King wrote: "After Seeing you last night I saw Lord Weymouth, who by My Direction will wait upon You with Lord Gower this morning to press You in the strongest Manner to accept the Office of First Commissioner of the Treasury. . . ." That Gower and Weymouth consented to add their weight to the King's plea suggests that the Bedfords felt they had nothing to fear from North. They were right.

Junius commemorated Grafton's departure from office in the following words:

> Retire, then, my lord, and hide your blushes from the world; for with such a load of shame, even black may change its colour. A mind such as yours, in the solitary hours of domestic enjoyment, may still find topics of consolation. You may find it in the memory of violated friendship; in the afflictions of an accomplished prince whom you have disgraced and deserted; and in the agitations of a great country, driven, by your counsels, to the brink of destruction.[12]

Lord North kissed hands on February 10, 1770, accepted seals as First Lord of the Treasury and became the King's First Minister. He took office under unusual circumstances. He inherited Grafton's Cabinet; he had been given no authority to select the men who were to be his colleagues, and it was generally believed he would be tolerated by the Bedfords only until they wished to get rid of him. North's appointment evoked neither rejoicing nor despair. To most, he was not objectionable. The country, torn by the seemingly endless disputes over the parliamentary status of John Wilkes, was sick of parades, petitions, demonstrations, strikes, remonstrances, riots, broken heads, and broken glass, and wanted more than anything else a period of calm and restoration of political stability. Lord North, an amiable and placid man loyal to the King, and himself a country gentleman, seemed to promise this.

As Chancellor of the Exchequer, North had clearly demonstrated his grasp of intricate budgetary matters; as leader of the House of Commons he had proven himself able in debate. He lacked Chatham's eloquent fire, Colonel Barré's impassioned vehemence, and Burke's cold, analytic skill, but he was a man of ready wit who could summon an apposite quotation, and who neither indulged himself nor agitated the House with forensic fireworks. In all, a man of moderation. So, many in America conceived him to be.

Bostonians had done everything they could think of to have the hated troops removed. The selectmen had petitioned the British commander to take them out of town and barrack them on Castle Island. He replied he had no authority to do this, but would confine them to quarters during an approaching election. The town deemed his response unsatisfactory.

The Redcoats must be withdrawn. The House of Representatives had also petitioned the governor to no avail; Hutchinson insisted he could not order the troops to be withdrawn. This was a blatant lie, and the citizens of Boston knew it was. In letter after letter to the *Gazette,* Sam Adams dwelled on the "aggravated tyranny" imposed on Boston: "Was not an army of placemen and pensioners sufficient, who would eat us up as they eat bread, but an array of soldiers must be stationed in our very bowels." What had happened to destroy Magna Carta and the Bill of Rights? His fellow townsmen, he wrote, were finally reduced to a dreadful alternative: *"To resist this Tyranny, or Submit to chains."*

Adams signalized the advent of 1770 with an attack on acting Governor Hutchinson's maladministration and another on his sons, who had announced their intent to break the nonimportation agreement. These offspring of *"An Unnatural Parent"* had forgotten, as had their father, "the first principles of virtue" and were wounding their own country "in the very heart." Then the implied threat: They should not think they could continue with impunity to affront their countrymen.** Actually, the embargo to which they and other merchants had agreed had expired on December 31, 1769; the Hutchinsons were not the only traders in town who unlocked their warehouses on New Year's Day, 1770.

"Nonimportation" had forced many small merchants into bankruptcy. Prospective customers, for long deprived of wares, were avid to purchase. Numbers who in the beginning had supported the embargo were now weary of it, and, one may suspect, equally weary of Samuel Adams and his unceasing propaganda. But he, his radical colleagues, the Loyall Nine, and Sons of Liberty were determined that merchants who would not voluntarily conform to their edicts would be forced to do so, and necessary orders were passed to Will Molineux to alert his gangs of ruffians. Hutchinson, his sons, and a handful of Tory merchants, sensing that violent action was imminent, capitulated. The situation in Boston was now one of fragile armed truce, a truce soon to be shattered. During two weeks in mid-February gangs of rioters smashed windows of shops whose owners stubbornly refused to comply with Adams's mandates.

Everyone in Boston knew who was pulling the strings. Although the "Grand Incendiary" has never been directly linked to this wave of destructive violence, the conclusion that he played a major role in instigating it is inescapable. One killing occurred; an eleven-year-old boy, Christopher Sider, died of wounds received when Ebenezer Richardson, believed to be a customs informer, fired into a mob assembled in front of his house. Unaccountably, he was not dragged to the street and hanged from the nearest tree, but was arrested and held for trial.††

** Both letters appeared in the Boston *Gazette* of January 8, 1770. The first was signed VINDEX, the second DETERMINATUS.

†† Richardson was convicted of murder, received a royal pardon, and left Boston.

The boy's death provided the Sons of Liberty an unexpected opportunity, and they made arrangements for a massive public funeral. John Adams arrived in Boston at dusk on February 26 as mourners were assembling at Liberty Tree. He found "a vast Collection of People . . . a Vast Number of Boys walked before the Coffin, a vast Number of Women and Men after it, and a number of Carriages. My Eyes never beheld such a funeral."[13] The propaganda value of this unfortunate episode was incalculable, and radicals made the most of it.

As Gage later reported to Hillsborough, government was "at an end" in Boston. Things were slightly better in New York, but Sons of Liberty there had lately inflamed the people against the Redcoats, and the soldiers were "so sowered, as to become alarming, and to require uncommon Care to restrain them from Excess. But thro' the Diligence of the Civil and Military Powers, Harmony and good Order was soon restored." New Yorkers were accustomed to a British garrison; King's troops had been in the city for years.

⚴ 5

Quarrells, Rencounters and Combats

Boston was locked in a deep cold winter; streets were treacherous, the bay frozen with eight inches of ice. Those who did not have to leave their homes to work or to buy food clung to warm firesides. British sentries stamped frostbitten feet and shivered in their boxes. On Friday, Saturday, and Sunday in the first week of March townsmen and soldiers tangled in a series of brawls. Threats and invective were succeeded by fisticuffs, snowballs, chunks of ice, and finally, clubs. Lieutenant Governor Hutchinson, Lieutenant Colonel Dalrymple, and most citizens were alarmed. They had good reason to be, for when night came, brawlers ruled the streets. Rumors spread that a bloody affray could not for long be avoided. Soldiers and townspeople expected one. Hutchinson refused to order the troops to be withdrawn to Castle Island; the sheriffs could not control bands of rioters, and Samuel Adams and Will Molineux, who could have, would not. British officers and soldiers knew that an infuriated mob armed with muskets, axes, and clubs could murder them all.

Monday, March 5, 1770, brought the confrontation most Bostonians had dreaded and Dalrymple's Redcoats had for some time expected. Several versions of the events of this night are available; Gage's report to Hillsborough has the twin virtues of being reasonably objective and relatively brief. Although the general based his description on official reports from Hutchinson and Dalrymple, he also had before him assorted affidavits from eyewitnesses and American versions of the "Horrid Massacre" as published in Boston papers.* In his dispatch to the Secretary of State, His Majesty's commander in chief in America observed that as events had run their course on that fatal night "there were Faults on both sides."[1]

Circumstantial evidence suggests that advocates of violent action chose to bring the riots of the preceding three days to a bloody culmination on March 5, for after darkness fell on that night, gangs armed with staves and cudgels appeared at various locations, including Boston Neck, remote from the scene of the confrontation that would develop in King Street. Those who planned the operation were unsure just where the major action would be, but had sent one group of rowdies to King Street to insult, harass, and provoke the sentry stationed there. The young private soldier sent for help, and Captain Charles Preston of the 29th Foot, who was "Captain of the Day," marched with a squad of a corporal and six men to his relief. While the captain and his column, slipping and sliding on the narrow iced streets, moved to the scene, clamorous bells began insistently signaling "Fire" and the male populace poured into the streets, some armed with cudgels, a few carrying leather buckets. No one discovered who was responsible for this false alarm.

At the sentry post in King Street the atmosphere was lethal, and as Preston's Redcoats lined up before the sentry box they had good reason to fear for their lives, for the situation was rapidly passing beyond possibility of control. The courageous young captain took post in front of his squad and attempted to parley with the mob, whose members cursed and reviled him and the soldiers, pelted them with chunks of ice, stones torn from the street, bricks, and snowballs. The mob, possibly one hundred men and boys rapidly growing, repeatedly challenged the soldiers to fire. As Preston continued to talk, one Redcoat, struck by a brickbat, stumbled, dropped his musket in the snow, picked it up, and fired at random. At least five of his comrades then fired once or twice at point-blank range.† Eleven rioters fell; five died.‡ The mob dispersed. Captain Pres-

---

* Supported by ninety-six affidavits, some of which were falsely sworn.

† Paul Revere's famous print shows the British soldiers in line, firing a volley, apparently on orders of Captain Preston, who is shown with raised sword, as if giving the command to fire. In fact, the captain had taken his position in front of the soldiers; he did not at any time unsheathe his sword, nor did he give the command to fire.

‡ The dead included Crispus Attucks, a Negro from the Bahamas who lived in Framingham and was present under an assumed name. Attucks arrived on the scene with a band of twenty sailors, all armed with two-foot bludgeons.

ton and eight soldiers surrendered to the authorities and were jailed to await trial.

John Adams (who would later successfully defend Preston) reflected that night on the state of affairs that had produced the tragic climax on King Street:

> Endeavours had been systematically pursued for many Months by certain busy Characters, to excite Quarrells, Rencounters and Combats single or compound in the night between the Inhabitants of the lower Class and the Soldiers, and at all Risques to inkindle an immortal hatred between them. I suspected that this was the Explosion, which had been intentionally wrought up by designing Men, who knew what they were aiming at better than the Instrument employed. If these poor Tools should be prosecuted for any of their illegal Conduct, they must be punished. If the Soldiers in self-defense should kill any of them they must be Tryed, and if Truth was respected and the Law prevailed must be acquitted. . . . The real and full Intentions of the British Government and Nation were not yet developed: and We knew not whether the Town would be supported by the Country: whether Province would be supported by even our neighboring States; nor whether New England would be supported by the Continent. These were my Meditations in the night.[2]

The next morning he accepted a retainer of one guinea to defend Captain Preston and the British soldiers.

While John Adams was discussing Preston's case with James Forrest, who had come to his office to engage him to lead the defense of the captain and his grenadiers, now under heavy guard in the town jail, his cousin Sam was conducting a mass meeting at Faneuil Hall, where some 3,000 angry Bostonians had assembled. The unanimous sense of the meeting was that the troops must be withdrawn from the town, and withdrawn at once, for, so the resolution read: ". . . nothing can rationally be expected to restore the peace of the town and prevent further blood and carnage but the immediate removal of the troops." A committee of three carried the resolution to Hutchinson. Despite the urging of most of his councilors, the lieutenant governor refused to comply, and added that those who wished to drive the King's troops from Boston were guilty of high treason. Finally, at Dalrymple's suggestion, Hutchinson agreed that the colonel might order the 29th to Castle William. This response did not suit Samuel Adams, nor the citizens gathered at Faneuil Hall. Both regiments must go, and go without further delay.

Although Hutchinson was not then aware of the fact, express riders had already left with pleas to neighboring towns to muster their militiamen and to prepare them to move on Boston at a moment's notice.

Ten thousand men, armed and accoutered, their hearts set to avenge the blood staining the snow and ice on King Street, could arrive within twenty-four hours and another ten thousand during the following day. When this news was conveyed to him during the afternoon, Hutchinson's determination began to crumble, and when his brother-in-law Andrew Oliver, secretary of the colony, told him directly that he must either order the troops out at once or "quit the government," he gave way. Will Molineux, belligerent leader of the Boston Sons of Liberty and Sam Adams's friend and adviser, led the Redcoat columns to the docks. The crowds lining the route of march watched in silence. In late afternoon, March 11, 1770, the last detachment of His Majesty's troops left for Castle William.

During the next few months, prosecution and defense maneuvered. For once, John Adams found himself in complete agreement with Hutchinson: both wanted to buy time; time for passions to calm; time for outraged Bostonians to come gradually to a more temperate view, as John was certain they would. In this, he was opposed in the Whig press and from the pulpit. Sam Adams wanted to hurry the trial; he demanded "an eye for an eye and a tooth for a tooth" and he did not propose to wait all summer for the eyes and the teeth. A new gallows had been erected. Sam wanted it used. Boston clergymen howling for blood invoked the prophets and called on the Lord God of Hosts to intervene.

On April 17, 1770, John Wilkes posted a bond for good behavior and was released from King's Bench Prison. His confinement had been something less than onerous. He received streams of visitors of both sexes and gifts of food and wine, so that he was able to set a good table. While Wilkes was thus languishing in prison, his partisans had been active in forming the Society of the Supporters of the Bill of Rights. Under the aggressive leadership of John Horne, the society attracted a number of influential men who were ready and able to contribute to the support of John Wilkes as well as to any cause that might conceivably lead to urgently needed electoral and parliamentary reforms. From these benefactors, Horne collected enough to clear Wilkes of an indebtedness of nearly £20,000 and to provide him with an annuity of £1,000 for several years.

The birth of the society was not the only indication that a growing number of urban middle-class Englishmen were dissatisfied with things as they were and wanted to move by constitutional methods toward a more open and democratic political system. This was precisely what the King, most members of the ruling aristocracy, and the country gentlemen did not want, and when George Grenville moved in the Commons for an accounting of disbursements under the King's Civil List, this motion, vigorously opposed by Lord North, failed as did other demands for legislation to declare placemen and pensioners ineligible to sit in the House of Commons. As nearly half the members of the House were receiving bounties, such motions were inevitably shouted down and overwhelmingly rejected. Many both in and out of Parliament believed seven years too long a time between elections, and petitions were sent up to Westminster urging triennial rather than septennial parliaments. Unfortunately, what sympathy the Bill of Rights Society could muster and what influence it might possibly have exerted on developing a program of electoral and other reforms was nullified by the violent behavior of London mobs, whose members, carrying cudgels and throwing paving stones, threatened ministers and members of Parliament, overturned carriages, and shattered windows to cries of "Wilkes and Liberty."

Some in both Lords and Commons felt that the expulsion of Wilkes had been illegal, and shortly after the hero of the London mobs emerged from King's Bench Prison, Chatham so moved. The motion was defeated. In the Commons, Lord North was constantly called upon to defend the ministry's avowed policy to deny Wilkes his seat. Neither the King nor his First Minister behaved in this affair with any perspicacity, for so long as Wilkes could be cast in the role of a man martyred by a stubborn King and a ministry clearly amenable to his every wish, Wilkes's supporters could raise a mob almost at will. What is surprising is that there was not a great deal more indiscriminate violence than there was.

The Wilkes affair had not absorbed Lord North's entire attention. He had persuaded Parliament to repeal all duties imposed by the Townshend Acts save that on tea, which did not produce even enough revenue to pay for the expense of collecting it. The preamble to the acts was not repealed.** Thus, monies collected from the tea impost were to be used to help defray the expenses of civil government and to support Redcoat garrisons in America. That the tax on tea for the purposes asserted was a silly measure was recognized by some at the time. But the King was insistent. The tax not only symbolized the constitutional supremacy of Parliament, but would free senior royal officials in America from financial dependence on colonial assemblies.

Late in the summer of 1770, Great Britain came perilously close to a war with Spain, when the Spanish governor of Buenos Aires forced the surrender of the small British garrison at Port Egremont in the Falkland Islands and raised the Spanish flag. North was in the country when the news arrived in London, and Viscount Weymouth, Secretary of State for the Southern Department, an inexperienced and muddleheaded diplomat, dispatched a tactless and bellicose note to Madrid. This note could not possibly have been sent without the King's specific approval. North hastened to London; he was horrified to learn of Weymouth's action

** Franklin described the preamble as "odious."

and by a series of adroit diplomatic maneuvers managed to calm the storm the indiscreet secretary had raised. In thus averting a totally unnecessary war, Lord North appeared at his best in a carefully reasoned and conciliatory speech in the Commons. Madrid disavowed the action of its governor, and the crisis subsided.††

Captain Preston appeared in the dock on October 28. Evidence for the prosecution and defense was presented. Attorneys for the crown and John Adams summed up. The case went to the jury. Preston, acquitted, left for Castle William a free man.‡‡ The grenadiers were brought to trial a month later. Five were acquitted; two, convicted of manslaughter, pled benefit of clergy* and escaped with a branding on the thumb. All except Captain Preston thanked John Adams. Most Bostonians, happy to have done with the affair, were anxious to forget it.

Samuel Adams was not one to forget or to forgive. Indeed, he simply refused to accept the verdicts of the juries, and in the columns of the Boston *Gazette*, over the signature VINDEX, presented his own biased and distorted interpretation of the evidence adduced. Citizens of Boston, weary of altercations and turmoil, paid little attention to these effusions, but did elect both Samuel and his cousin John to the Massachusetts House of Representatives as members of the four-man "Boston Seat."

The death of George Grenville on November 13, 1770, and of the Duke of Bedford in January 1771 removed two factional leaders from the political scene, and the resignation of Admiral Sir Edward Hawke, one of the "great captains" of the War for Empire, left the Admiralty vacant. This important position was given to John Montagu, Fourth Earl of Sandwich, the betrayer of Wilkes and a notorious jobber described by a contemporary as

> Too infamous to have a friend,
> Too bad for bad men to commend.

This was one of Lord North's least happy appointments.

The First Minister next sought to buy the services of Alexander Wedderburn, a lawyer of undeniable talent, a fine speaker, and a man of no political morals whatever, and offered to make him Solicitor General. Wedderburn was a fit running mate for Edward Thurlow, a long-time member of "the Bloomsbury Gang," who was appointed Attorney General. Thurlow was tough-minded, profane, and bellicose; few dared cross

†† No doubt because Louis XV of France refused to aid Spain should she provoke England to hostilities.

‡‡ When he arrived in England and retired from the army, Preston was paid expenses and given a life pension of £200 p.a.

* A literate man could so plead.

him. He and the Solicitor General were not on speaking terms save in their necessary official intercourse. North completed his Cabinet with the apppointment of Henry Bathurst, a former judge of the Court of Common Pleas, as Lord Chancellor. Bathurst, created Baron Apsley, was possibly the worst Lord Chancellor in English history.†

Although Governor Hutchinson reported the citizens of Massachusetts calm and contented, Samuel Adams, never at a loss for issues, spilled vast amounts of ink developing new ones or raking over old ones.‡ In January 1772 he wrote Henry Marchant, agent in London for Rhode Island, lamenting the collapse of his cherished nonimportation plan, a failure entirely due (so he asserted) to the machinations of merchants "under the Court Influence." He assured Marchant that citizens of the Bay Colony, where "absolute Despotism appears to be making large Strides with barefaced Impudence," were by no means reconciled to ministerial policies. Nor would they be so long as the ministers continued to take money out of their pockets and use it to maintain a governor dependent upon ministerial largess who would "always yield obedience to their Instructions," to station ships of war in the harbor, and to garrison "the Capital fortress" (Castle William) with "a standing Army." Bostonians had ceased drinking fine British teas, and contented themselves with inferior brands smuggled in from Holland.

Although one Tory printer who had incurred the wrath of the Grand Incendiary had been literally run out of town, another continued to publish the Massachusetts *Gazette*, in which articles supporting Parliament's "irresistible, absolute, uncontrolled authority" had appeared. Under the pseudonym "Candidus," Adams belabored the author of these, who signed himself "Chronus." Adams summoned Vattel, Montesquieu, Lord Coke, John Locke, Magna Carta, and the Pennsylvania Farmer to buttress his arguments. If, as the great Mr. Locke had unequivocally asserted, one of the principal functions of governments instituted by men was to protect each in enjoyment of the property he had acquired by his skill and toil, how came it that the British Parliament could arrogate to itself the authority to take money from the Americans? "Chronus" held

---

† As of midsummer, 1771, leading members of the Cabinet were:

First Lord of the Treasury and Chancellor of the Exchequer	Lord North
Lord President of the Council	Earl Gower
Secretary of State, Northern Department	Earl of Suffolk
Secretary of State, Southern Department	Earl of Rochford
Secretary of State, American Colonies	Earl of Hillsborough
First Lord of the Admiralty	Earl of Sandwich
Lord Chancellor	Baron Apsley
Lord Keeper of the Privy Seal	Duke of Grafton

‡ Hutchinson took the oath of office as governor of Massachusetts on March 14, 1771.

that the King, Lords, and Commons of Great Britain formed "the supreme Legislatures of the British dominions." But, said Adams, the American colonies were a separate dominion, and: "It is certainly more concordant with the great law of nature and reason, which the most powerful nation may not violate and *cannot alter*, to suppose that the Colonies are separate, independent *and free*, then to suppose that they *must* be one with Great-Britain *and slaves*."[3] Adams had previously hinted at independence; in his answers to "Chronus" he took a further step. But he was not yet ready to urge it.

Adams was an astute politician; he spent hours every day visiting shops, coffeehouses, taverns, ropewalks, docks, warehouses, and building yards, where he talked freely with everyone. He knew that the great majority of his fellow Americans were not yet ready to entertain the notion of independence. Those who advocated separation from Great Britain, said "Chronus," were "pretended patriots," "intemperate politicians," and "men of no property" whose sole purpose was "perpetually keeping up the ball of contention." Adams paid little attention to these attacks, which did nothing to damage his personal popularity or to lessen his determination. He soon made his position clear: He was fighting for the independence of the American colonies.

During the spring of 1772 his country cousin John found time to reflect on the state of the colonies. Notes he prepared for an "Oration" he had been invited to deliver on election day in Braintree show his thoughts at that time:

> What is the Tendency of the late Innovations? The Severity, the Cruelty of the late Revenue Laws, and the Terrors of the formidable Engine, contrived to execute them, the Court of Admiralty? Is not the natural and necessary Tendency of these Innovations, to introduce dark Intrigues, Insincerity, Simulation, Bribery and Perjury, among Customs house officers, Merchants, Masters, Mariners, and their Servants?
>
> What is the Tendency, what has been the Effect of introducing a standing Army into our Metropolis? Have we not seen horrid Rancour, furious Violence, infernal Cruelty, shocking Impiety and Profanation, and shameless abandoned Debauchery. . . ?[4]**

Liberty was always in danger, for the only maxim of a free government ought to be "to trust no man living with Power to endanger the public Liberty."[5]

Having disposed of "Chronus," Samuel returned to his favorite target, Governor Thomas Hutchinson, who with characteristic obstinacy

---

** The citizens of Boston had not seen "a horrid Rancour, furious Violence, infernal Cruelty, shocking Impiety and Profanation, and shameless abandoned Debauchery," as John alleged. The British troops were on the whole well behaved.

persisted in his refusal to move the General Court from its temporary seat at Harvard College back to its traditional seat in Boston. This, the House of Representatives asserted, was a great "grievance." Hutchinson, determined to humble the legislature, paid no attention to these remonstrances, nor did the citizens of Boston appear to do so. The General Court continued to sit at Harvard College.

In August 1772 the "psalm-singing" Earl of Dartmouth succeeded the Earl of Hillsborough as Principal Secretary of State for America. Hillsborough left office, said Samuel Adams, "with the curses . . . of the better part of the Colonials." But the recent Secretary of State was not the most "inveterate" conspirator: "There are others on this Side of the Atlantick who have been more assiduous in plotting the Ruin of our Liberties than even he." Adams did not expect too much from Dartmouth, nor did Gage, who wrote Hillsborough he regretted his departure from office; his firmness in dealing with the colonies had raised him "in the esteem of the World" and had earned "the applause of every honest man." The "World" of Thomas Gage and the Earl of Hillsborough was not the world of the Adams cousins and of a growing number of their compatriots.

Some weeks previously, the revenue schooner *Gaspee* had run aground in Narragansett Bay south of Providence, Rhode Island.†† A party had boarded her, wounded her commander, Lieutenant William Duddington, R.N., taken off all portable articles of value, ordered the crew ashore, and set her afire. The schooner burned. The affair of the *Gaspee* was the first problem to face Dartmouth when he took office. He described the seizure, plundering, and burning of the King's revenue schooner as a "daring Act of Violence" and instructed Gage to send troops to Rhode Island to assist "in the suppression of any Riots or Insurrections and for preserving the Peace within the colony." (There were neither riots nor insurrection, and no troops were sent.) The secretary also recommended that a royal commission be convened in Newport to investigate the affair.

Sandwich directed Rear Admiral of the Blue John Montagu, commander in chief in American waters, then based in Boston, to assist the royal commissioners. Montagu thought those who had destroyed the *Gaspee* would never be brought to justice and that nothing would come of the inquiry. According to John Adams, Montagu was a coarse and vulgar man, whose "continual Language is cursing and damning and God damning, 'my wife's d——d A-se is so broad that she and I can't sit in a chariot together'—this the Nature of the Beast and the common Language of the Man." That Montagu's principal functions were to seize smugglers and to protect revenue officers and assist them in enforcing

†† In Providence River.

the Acts of Trade were sufficient reasons to arouse the animosity of the Bostonians, who in their turn cursed and damned him.

The commission to inquire into the destruction of the *Gaspee* was empowered to offer a reward of £500 for the arrest of any participants, who were then to be delivered to Admiral Montagu and sent to England for trial. That suspects were to be transported beyond the seas to stand trial and to be hanged in chains if found guilty raised an immediate clamor, and not only in Rhode Island. This, so colonial newspapers unanimously asserted, was tyrannical, despotic, and indicated the intent of the ministers to deprive the colonists of due process of law and reduce them to a condition of abject slavery.

In late October, Samuel Adams was given an opportunity to sharpen his quill when he learned that salaries of crown-appointed judges in America who would hold their commissions at the King's pleasure rather than during good behavior were thenceforth paid from revenues collected in America.‡‡ In a series of letters Adams wrote to Elbridge Gerry he gave an intimation of the ideas he and his colleagues were then discussing. "This country must shake off their intollerable burdens at all Events. Every day strengthens our oppressors and weakens us. If each Town would declare its Sense in these Matters I am persuaded our Enemies would not have it in their power to divide us in wh[h] they have all along shown their dexterity. Pray use your Influence with Salem and other Towns." In the last of these letters he called for "a free Communication with each Town." Some people, too timid, were not convinced that sentiment in rural Massachusetts necessarily coincided with that in the metropolis. But Adams was confident the country towns could be brought to support Boston "and when once it appears beyond Contradiction, that we are united in Sentiments there will be a Confidence in each other, and a plan of Opposition will be easily formed, and executed with Spirit."[6]

These letters contain the first hints of the plan for concerted colonial action Samuel Adams and his closest friends, including James Warren, "Jemmy" Otis, Dr. Benjamin Church, and Thomas Young, had been secretly discussing for some time. All were aware of the efficacy of "Committees of Correspondence" earlier developed by dissenting churchmen in New England in their successful battle against establishment of an Anglican episcopacy in America. Jonathan Mayhew, the foremost Congregational pastor in Boston, who had colonial liberty much in his mind and heart and had led this war of sermons and pamphlets, suggested to Otis that similar local committees could be valuable instruments in the political struggle. Samuel Adams and his colleagues agreed. But as such an organization would be an innovation, they decided to move cau-

‡‡ Hillsborough was responsible for this.

tiously. Many towns remote from Boston were essentially conservative and did not trust radical Whigs in the metropolis.

A strategy needed to be devised, and happily an issue was at hand. For some months the salary granted Governor Hutchinson by the Provincial Assembly had been supplemented by a royal stipend, and it now became known that the lieutenant governor, the justices of the Superior Court, and both the attorney general and solicitor general were also to receive generous grants from the crown. A Boston town meeting requested the governor to convene the General Court to inquire into the matter. This was a neat trap, and Hutchinson promptly fell into it, as Sam Adams had been sure he would. He refused to convene the General Court. Adams immediately called for another town meeting, and after attacking Hutchinson for accepting the King's bounty, moved that a Committee of Correspondence consisting of twenty-one members be appointed. The motion passed unanimously. On this day the Boston Committee of Correspondence was born.

Samuel Adams, John Hancock, the Warren brothers, and other leading radical Whigs were putting pressure on John Adams to forsake rural Braintree and return to Boston. He did so in late November 1772, but firmly resolved he would "remember Temperance, Exercise, and Peace of Mind. Above all things I must avoid Politicks, Political Clubbs, Town Meetings, General Court, etc, etc, etc." When John returned to Boston he found himself immediately immersed in Boston politics, in writing letters to the *Gazette,* and in the secret transactions of assorted political "Clubbs."

The Boston Committee of Correspondence moved into action by naming three subcommittees, the first to prepare a list of "Rights," a second, "Infringements" of those rights, and the third, "A letter of Correspondence with the other Towns."[7] The "Rights," their "Infringements," and the "Letter of Correspondence" written in direct and forceful prose, were promptly printed, bound in pamphlet form, and distributed to some six hundred prominent Whigs in every town in Massachusetts.

Hutchinson's first reaction was to ridicule the effort as absurd and futile. He would soon revise his opinion, for contrary to his expectations dozens of towns elected committees to correspond with each other and with Boston. Thomas Young had earlier prognosticated that the program would be successful and would make Tory heads "reel." He was a good prophet. Samuel Adams wrote James Otis, "As there is no measure which tends more to disconcert the Designs of the enemies of the public liberty than the raising Committees of Correspondence in the several towns throughout the Province, it is not to be wondered at that the whole strength of their opposition is aimed against it."[8]

In his *History of the Colony and Province of Massachusetts Bay,* Thomas Hutchinson would write: ". . . the appointing a committee to correspond with alike committee of the assembly of each other colony, whose business should be to obtain intelligence of all acts of the British parliament, and all proceedings of administration affecting the colonies, and reciprocally to communicate the same, seems to have laid the foundation of that union of the colonies, which was afterwards bound or secured by the establishment of a general congress, as a supreme authority over the whole."[9] As John Adams would correctly describe them, the committees were a mighty engine.

As Committees of Correspondences proliferated in Massachusetts and her neighboring colonies, Hutchinson and his friends realized that something had to be done to counterbalance their growing influence. But they were at a loss as to appropriate steps to be taken. The governor addressed the General Court in mid-February and again in early March and announced that the "late proceedings" were displeasing to the King, unwarranted, and of a dangerous nature and tendency. In a reply written by Samuel Adams the House asserted the indisputable right of the people to assemble to discuss their grievances, to petition for their redress, and for committees to communicate. Admiral Montagu reported to Sandwich that Boston was "managed by the select men and mob by what is called a town meeting." These miscreants, said the admiral, had "set the whole province in a flame." Towns throughout the province of Massachusetts Bay were agreeing with the resolutions taken in Boston town meetings: "In short, they are almost ripe for independence."

Samuel Adams, who was doing all he could to hasten separation from the mother country, would have agreed with the admiral. In mid-February, he had drafted a letter from the House of Representatives to Governor Hutchinson objecting to the King's decision to allow royal salaries to justices of the Superior Court. The House conceived "that no Judge, who has a due regard to justice, or even to his own character, would choose to be placed under an undue bias as they must be under, in the opinion of this House, by accepting of, and becoming dependent for their salaries upon the Crown." And the letter continued,

> When we consider the many attempts that have been made, effectually to render null and void those clauses in our charter, upon which the freedom of our constitution depends, we should be lost to all public feeling, should we not manifest a just resentment. We are more and more convinced, that it had been the design of administration, totally to subvert the constitution, and introduce an arbitrary government into this province; and we cannot wonder that the Apprehensions of the people are thoroughly awakened.[10]

The House waited in vain to receive Hutchinson's assurances that the justices would "utterly refuse ever to accept of support, in a manner so

justly obnoxious," so repugnant to the charter, and so "utterly inconsistent with the safety of the rights, liberties and properties of the people." Hutchinson would have needed half a dozen able propagandists
and an equal number of scriveners to keep up with the literary output of
Samuel Adams.

Adams was not too happy with Dartmouth's appointment, and in
April 1773 wrote Arthur Lee: "I wish I could hear more of Lord D to
qualify him for his high office, than merely that he is a *good* Man.
Goodness I confess is an essential, tho to rare a Qualification of a
Minister of State. . . . Without a Greatness of Mind adequate to the Importance of his Station, I fear he may be embarrassed by his present
Connections."[11] At about the same time he wrote Richard Henry Lee,
Arthur's brother in Virginia: "The Colonies are all embarked in the same
bottom. The liberties of all alike invaded by the same haughty Powers."
Candid and frequent communication was essential so that "the Fire of
true Patriotism will at length spread throughout the Continent." He
urged Lee to encourage immediate establishment of Committees of Correspondence in Virginia "to promote that General Union upon which the
Security of the Whole depends."[*][12]

The society known as the Sons of Liberty was soon to be active in
every colony and the Boston chapter led the way. The members were
"spirited men . . . determined to resist the oppressive edicts of the British Ministry, and to sustain and support each other in their effort to rescue the town and country from the thraldom of tyrannic power." Although the association was supposed to be clandestine, everyone in
Boston knew that Dr. Joseph Warren, his brother James, John Hancock,
John and Samuel Adams, James Bowdoin, Paul Revere, and Dr. Benjamin Church were among the most active members.

Other clubs and caucuses met in secret, usually in private rooms in
such taverns as the Salutation and the Green Dragon, where members of
the North End Club, led by Joseph and James Warren and the Adams
cousins gathered frequently to drink madeira and debate measures they
thought necessary to arouse and unite the people to oppose the policies
of the ministry as interpreted by Governor Hutchinson. As leading
members of the "Sons" were usually members of local Committees of
Correspondence, they were able decisively to mold public opinion. These
were the "conspirators" who in the opinion of ministers had deluded the
people.

The most active member of the North End Club was Samuel Adams,

---

[*] A month before Adams wrote R. H. Lee, the Virginia House of Burgesses had
resolved (March 12, 1773) to establish an eleven-man committee for intercolonial
inquiry and correspondence. The resolutions were sent to assemblies in all the other
colonies together with a letter urging each to form a similar committee. Such committees were soon found at that level in every colony. But the idea of pervasive local
networks was developed by Samuel Adams.

"the Torch of Liberty," a powerfully persuasive writer and an indefatigable advocate of independence (a word he did not yet venture to use in his voluminous correspondence). Paul Revere, by trade a silversmith, printer, and engraver, was well able "to rally a caucus." Indeed, Sam Adams depended much on Revere, "the great leader of the mechanics," to influence that large body of craftsmen and artificers.

Shortly before the Boston Committee of Correspondence was established, Dr. Benjamin Franklin, agent in London for the Massachusetts House of Representatives, had come into possession of letters written some years previously by Hutchinson, Andrew Oliver, and Paxton to Thomas Whateley, a member of Parliament and formerly secretary to George Grenville. The doctor had sent the letters to Thomas Cushing, speaker of the House of Representatives, with the caution that although they might be privately read they were not to be published.†

Cushing realized immediately that the letters contained material that if made public would damage Governor Hutchinson's credibility severely. His decision to hold the letters for the time being but to circulate rumors of their contents was calculated to arouse the apprehensions of the Bostonians. Rumor begat rumor, and soon the whole town was talking of little else. Cushing had given the letters to John Adams shortly after they arrived in Boston. But as Franklin had explicitly stated they were not to be printed, John was unable to see how to make any public use of them. His diary entry of March 22, 1773, describes his reaction: "These curious Projectors and Speculators in Politicks will ruin this Country—cool, thinking, deliberate Villains[s], malicious and vindictive, as well as ambitious and avaricious."

On June 2, 1773, Samuel Adams asked that the gallery of the House of Representatives be cleared and rose to read the letters. The contents of several were sufficiently indiscreet, for both Hutchinson and the secretary of the colony had suggested that the only way to restore due subordination in the town of Boston was by an abridgment of liberties. They would scarcely have recommended such action to a man known to have considerable influence unless they believed he would advocate measures sufficiently severe to ensure unquestioning obedience of Bostonians to any further acts of Parliament.

Having heard the letters read and debated their import, the House resolved, by a vote of 101 to 5, "that the design and tendency" of them was "to subvert the Constitution and introduce arbitrary power into the province." A few days later, Adams wrote Arthur Lee: "I think there is now a full discovery of a combination of persons who have been the

† Franklin pointed out that publication of the letters would make it difficult for him to get his hands on similar materials, as those who possessed sensitive letters and documents would be "put upon their guard."

principal movers, in all the disturbances, misery, and bloodshed which has befallen this unhappy country."[13] The House consigned the letters to a Committee of the Whole for consideration; while deliberations proceeded in secret, Adams again wrote R. H. Lee. He thought it evident that "a plan for the ruin of American Liberty" had been hatched by a few designing men "governed by Avarice and a Lust of Power."[14]

On June 23, 1773, the House adopted a humble petition to the King's Most Excellent Majesty. After a recitation of complaints against Hutchinson and Oliver, the petitioners humbly prayed that the King would be graciously pleased to remove these officials "from their posts in this Government and place such good and faithful men in their stead as Your Majesty in your great wisdom shall think fit."[15] The petition was dispatched to Franklin, who delivered it to Lord Dartmouth. His Majesty was not graciously pleased to remove Hutchinson and Oliver "from Government." Nor would he direct an inquiry into the complaints lodged against them.

For some time the King, his First Minister, and both Houses of Parliament had been almost totally engrossed in an effort to alleviate financial difficulties of the East India Company, which was on the verge of collapse. The company had survived peculation and corruption on a truly majestic scale and was now staggering toward inevitable bankruptcy.‡ Lord North introduced several bills to salvage the company. His tea bill would allow the company to export tea from England to America duty-free, but subject to a duty of three pence per pound when landed in America. As the Americans were annually consuming an average of six million pounds of tea, the noble lord, who held a fairly large block of East India stock, as did his friend the Earl of Sandwich, anticipated that revenues would defray the expenses of the King's civil government in America and pay a reasonable proportion of the costs of supporting His Majesty's forces stationed there. And as the company's high-quality Soochong and Hysong teas would undersell the less fragrant teas smuggled in from Holland, the system projected would be more effective in putting an end to this illegal trade than were the King's revenue ships.

The tea bill alarmed Franklin, who had followed debates in the House of Commons, and he wrote Cushing: "It was thought at the Beginning of the Session that the American duty on Tea would be taken off. But now the wise scheme is to take off so much Duty here as will make Tea cheaper in America than Foreigners can supply us, and to confine the Duty there to keep up the exercise of the Right." The ministry, he

‡ Lord Clive had returned from India with a huge personal fortune and a vast collection of jewels he had wrung from native princes. The King thought Clive's "rapine" inexcusable.

went on, had no idea that people could act "from any other Principle but that of Interest" and believed that a duty of three pence per pound would be "sufficient to overcome all the Patriotism in Americans."[16]

The Tea Act became law on May 10, 1773, but almost six months elapsed before Americans paid it more than cursory attention. When they did, Whigs in Philadelphia and New York took the lead. Boston Town Meeting followed on November 5 with a series of resolutions declaring the tariff of three pence per pound to be an unconstitutional tax; that "a virtuous and steady opposition to the Ministerial Plan of governing America, is absolutely necessary to preserve even the shadow of Liberty and is a duty which every Freeman in America owes to his Country, to himself and to his Posterity," and finally, that any person who should directly or indirectly countenance this illegal attempt, or "in any wise aid or abet it" would be considered "an Enemy to America."[17] The Committee of Correspondence saw to it that these resolves were immediately circulated in Massachusetts and sent by courier to other colonial capitals. A few days later, Samuel Adams wrote Arthur Lee that while he could not foresee events, he could assure him his next letter would not be "upon a trifling subject."[18]

Although public pressure had forced tea consignees appointed by the East India Company in Philadelphia, New York, and Charleston to resign, those in Boston, including Governor Hutchinson's two sons, had refused to do so. By this time public meetings and daily articles in the press from Boston to Savannah had aroused every colony. On November 11, 1773, the Boston *Evening Post* carried an article urging opposition to the landing of tea:

> The duty is absolutely to be paid in America for the purpose of raising a revenue to support improper officers in America. . . . Are the Americans such blockheads as to care whether it be a red hot poker or a hot red poker which they are to swallow, provided Lord North forces them to swallow one of the two. . . . Surely, the people will unanimously agree to send the Tea to the place from whence it came or to a worse place. . . .[19]

On Sunday, November 28, 1773, the *Dartmouth,* first of four tea ships scheduled for Boston, arrived in the harbor and tied up at Griffin's Wharf. The Committee of Correspondence immediately ordered an armed guard to the dock to prevent any tea from being unloaded. On the following day, a mass meeting resolved that "the tea should be returned to the place whence it came." Governor Hutchinson ordered the five thousand Bostonians to disperse. The response was hoots, jeers, and prolonged hissing.

On the afternoon of December 15, three heavily guarded tea ships lay

alongside Griffin's Wharf.** Within thirty-six hours, unless duties were
paid, His Majesty's customs commissioners would seize the ships and
their cargoes. Wednesday and Thursday, December 15 and 16, 1773,
were critical days in Boston. On Thursday, thousands of Bostonians
gathered in Old South Church. The governor, who could have ordered
the ships out of the harbor, was totally distracted and refused to act. He
fled to his country estate in Milton. When one of the tea consignees sent
to Milton to make a final plea returned to Old South with the report that
Hutchinson would do nothing, Samuel Adams, who had anticipated the
governor's reaction, rose and after quieting the assemblage said: "This
meeting can do nothing more to save the country." These words were apparently an agreed signal, for the cries immediately arose: "Boston Harbor a Teapot tonight"; "Hurrah for Griffins Wharf"; "The Mohawks are
Come."[20] Samuel Adams's "Mohawks," their faces blackened, their ordinary clothing concealed by blankets, were ready. Each man carried a
tomahawk or an ax. Before midnight they had split open and dumped
the contents of 342 chests of tea worth £18,000 into Boston Harbor. No
other cargo was damaged.

On December 17, 1773, John Adams wrote in his diary: "Last Night
3 Cargoes of Bohea Tea were emptied into the Sea. . . . This is the most
magnificent Movement of all. There is a Dignity, a Majesty, a Sublimity
in this last Effort of the Patriots, that I greatly admire. The People
should never rise without doing something to be remembered, something
notable And striking. This Destruction of the Tea is so bold, so firm, in-
tripid and inflexible, and it must have so important Consequences, and so
lasting, that I can't but consider it as an Epocha in History."[21]

** *Dartmouth, Eleanor,* and *Beaver. William* went aground off Cape Cod. The
tea was salvaged by a few "patriots," who were able to sell it off at vast profit.

BOOK II

Lyons and Lambs

⚜ 1

A Nest of Locusts; A Focus of Tumult

The court observed New Year's Day, 1774, as a "high Festival." At St. James's, George III and Queen Charlotte received the compliments of foreign ambassadors, lords spiritual and temporal, admirals, generals, lesser nobility, and the gentry. Knights companions of the Garter, Thistle, and Bath appeared in the collars of their several orders. In public apartments ladies of fashion moving with gliding grace (they could not risk disturbing mountainous coiffeurs) paused at gilded mirrors to survey their gowns, jewels, and extravagant plumage before being presented to Their Majesties.

Following the reception, children of the Chapel Royal sang an ode composed for the occasion by the poet laureate and set to music by the master of the King's Band of Musicians. The laureate, in forgettable verse, recounted the chilling tale of the tyrant Xerxes, who impelled by pride and vain ambition, brought desolation to multitudes. Not so Britain's King, who, although his mighty fleets would "hurl just thunders on insulting foes," would ever "guard the World's Repose."

The theatrical season was in full swing: the Theatre Royal announced the forthcoming production of *Love in a Village* plus an exciting "Musical Entertainment"; His Majesty's Company at Drury Lane was playing

A *School for Wives* to the applause of packed houses; at Covent Garden, *Richard III* was sold out. Almack, proprietor of the celebrated gambling house, promised a dozen Assemblies for the pleasure of the nobility and gentry, and the Pantheon had scheduled twelve Grand Concerts "with Refreshments of Tea, Coffee, Cakes, Orgeat, Capillaire, Lemonade and Jellies."*

Lady subscribers to a series of Bach concerts presented their compliments to "Gentlemen Subscribers solicitous of Exhibiting their Persons at the Expence of Politeness and Good Manners" and requested they confine *entre-acte* preening and posturings to the side aisles, where "Ladies will still submit to the Risk of having their Ruffles, Laces and Trimmings demolished by the Gentlemen's Swords."

Many of these ladies and gentlemen were rich in manorial estates, town houses, furniture, pictures, crystal, plate, and jewels, but suffered from a shortage of ready cash. Moneylenders who offered this commodity in any amount at wounding interest rates to temporarily impecunious "Persons of Distinction" flourished. So did the gambling houses, where a single rouleau was worth £50 and where as much as £10,000 often depended on the turn of a card.†

Gambling was a mania. Nabobs who had amassed fortunes in India, wealthy West Indian planters who had come home to buy seats in the House of Commons, shipping tycoons, City bankers and stock-jobbing 'Change speculators rubbed shoulders at Brooks and Almacks from midnight to dawn, jostling noble lords and wealthy country gentlemen for places at the table. Here, too, were the inveterate gamblers: "Gentleman Johnny" Burgoyne, a member of Parliament, a cavalry major general, an amateur dramatist, poet manqué, and a royal favorite whose wife Lady Charlotte, a daughter of the Earl of Derby, was very rich; Charles James Fox, already a man to mark in the House of Commons, a wild young plunger who had gone through several fortunes; the Earl of Sandwich, First Lord of the Admiralty, clutching his rouleaux in one hand and in the other the delicacy named for him.

During the first week of the new year members of Parliament converged on the capital. In town houses servants removed dust covers from furniture, unrolled carpets, washed windows, waxed floors, and polished plate. The ladies made ready for a gay season. Seamstresses, jewelers, staymakers, and hairdressers rushed breathless from one great house to another to meet demanding schedules.

For the royal couple, one season was much like any other. They took

---

* *Orgeat:* a drink made from almonds, sugar, and a solution of orange flowers. *Capillaire:* a syrup flavored with orange flower water. Boswell reported that Dr. Johnson, during his drinking days, habitually poured capillaire into his after-dinner port.

† A *rouleau:* a "chip." These were of different shapes and colors which indicated values. £10,000 at that time would now be equivalent to a sum approximately twenty to twenty-five times as much.

no part in the gaieties, follies, and extravagances of London society. The King lived unostentatiously and frugally in a world circumscribed by habitual regularity and rigid protocol. He detested idleness, abhorred gambling and drunkenness, and viewed the sexual promiscuity of the aristocracy as degrading and sinful. He never took a mistress, but tolerated those among his confidential servants, notably the Earl of Sandwich, who had. George III was a temperate and pious man, which may account for his affection for the Earl of Dartmouth, Principal Secretary of State for the colonies and President of the Board of Trade and Frederick, Lord North, his First Minister, First Lord of the Treasury, and Chancellor of the Exchequer, whose private lives were exemplary.

When the court was at St. James's, the King rose before seven, rode for an hour or two in the adjacent parks, and returned to a breakfast of buttered toast and tea. In this exercises as in all else, the King was methodical. Often his companions were young officers of the Horse Guards, routed out of bed at dawn. Sometimes, he asked more distinguished gentlemen to ride with him. One favorite was John Burgoyne.

George III, a man of many and varied interests, attended personally to masses of official and private correspondence. He spent long hours at his writing desk drafting letters and making fair copies. He prided himself on his ability to transact business punctually; habitually, at the bottom of letters he meticulously set down his location, the date, and the precise time, as:

QUEEN'S HOUSE
Jany 10th 1774
$\underline{22 \ p \ \overset{m}{} \ 10}$ P.M.‡

m t

He was intensely interested in the progress of bills through the House of Commons, and required Lord North to provide him with lists of speakers pro and con administration measures, and of those who in divisions in Lords and Commons supported and opposed with indications of how placemen and pensioners voted. He was equally concerned with elections and brought patronage and influence to bear to assure the choice of a man he could count on as a "King's Friend."

While many privately derided the King's religious habits and described him as a pious hypocrite, the truth is that George was a profound believer in the doctrines of Christianity as interpreted by the Established (Anglican) Church. The King prayed and read his Bible daily, and was more familiar with the Book of Common Prayer than were most of his clergy. He devoted considerable time to Church appointments; he selected and named the archbishops, bishops, deans, canons, and many prebendaries. Most noblemen and many country gentlemen disposed of

‡ The King resided in Queen's House (formerly Buckingham House) on the site of the present Buckingham Palace. His offices were in St. James's.

Church livings; those who supported Administration were not likely to select a vicar who did not. Crown influence over the ecclesiastical establishment was pervasive.

George had an abiding love for the navy; everything connected with it fascinated him. He insisted on examining basic drawings and advanced designs, and when a model of a new class was built he had it sent to him. He followed the progress of naval construction and armament and frequently to the discomfiture of his First Lord of the Admiralty demanded current reports of naval recruiting and assorted activities in the dockyards. He knew the location and condition of every rated ship in the navy from three-decker *Royal George* of one hundred guns and a complement of about 1,000 to *Kingfisher* of fourteen guns and 125 men.

His Majesty may never have fancied himself standing on the quarterdeck of his flagship while her destructive broadsides shattered the hulls of an enemy line of battle, but he could and did imagine himself in the role of a "Warrior King" at the head of a victorious army. The martial tradition in his family was strong; his great-grandfather, his grandfather, and his uncle the Duke of Cumberland had commanded troops in combat. He thus naturally devoted considerable attention to military affairs, and not least to promotions. Colonelcies of British regiments were his to bestow and to rescind, as were all appointments to flag and general officer rank.** He kept his eye on the sale of commissions by senior officers and on transfers from one regiment to another, a common practice to avoid arduous or unpleasant duty. Viscount Barrington, an able and industrious Secretary at War, did not dare meddle with any matters affecting senior officer personnel.

His Majesty visited military encampments when opportunity offered. He loved to watch parades, reviews, maneuvers, sham battles, and even such mundane ceremonials as changing of the guard. On these occasions he was usually accompanied by his senior military adviser, Major General Edward Harvey, adjutant general of the British Army, a competent professional soldier. Unfortunately there was later to be very little indication that His Majesty paid attention to Harvey's sensible advice.

The King was not a great reader—indeed his duties allowed him little time to read anything other than newspapers—but he built up his private library and assisted those who contributed to the advancement of learning and literature. Dr. Johnson was but one of a number of intellectual pensioners.

George III had a real bent for agriculture and would have been a progressive and prosperous farmer on his own acreage had his duties permitted him time for this indulgence. He knew a great deal more

---

** Some colonelcies were purely honorary and carried an annual stipend. The King appointed to these, as he did to active colonelcies in the Guards or regiments of the line.

about cattle, pig, and sheep breeding, drainage, crop rotation, composting, and fertilization than did most of the great landowners and squires, whose methods were on the whole traditional and inefficient. At a later period he contributed to farming journals under the pseudonym of "Farmer George."

In political terms he was a dogmatic and inflexible conservative; in his own words: "a great enemy to innovation . . . wise nations [he once wrote Lord North] have stuck scrupulously to their antient Customs." He could not understand why some people wanted to alter "every rule our Ancestors have left us." He was hurt that some of his countrymen had forsaken the established Anglican communion to embrace dissenting creeds and that others had cast off "every [religious] restraint."

Sir William Wraxall, who knew something of the routine of the court and of the King's character, wrote that George III passed his days "either in the severe and exemplary discharge of his *public* duties of every description, or in the bosom of his family amidst *domestic* sources of amusement." He "neither frequented Masquerades, or ever engaged at Play, nor protracted the Hours of Convivial Enjoyment, nor passed his evenings in society calculated to unbend his mind from the fatigues of Business and the vexations of State." The young King was contemptuous of the splendors, frivolities, and vanities that distinguished most contemporary courts: ". . . rarely did he join in any scene of public amusement, if we except the diversion of the Theatre." Still more rarely did he entertain the great nobles: ". . . his repasts, private, short and temperate, never led to the slightest excess." Court etiquette did, however, demand that he appear at certain royal functions. At these he was dignified but approachable, and left the assemblages for his private apartments at the earliest possible moment. His Majesty, although a great talker, was not an attentive listener. He was willing to accept change and development in practically every field but in the ecclesiastical and civil establishments. These were sacrosanct. He was a staunch supporter of the mercantile system, of the unchallengeable supremacy of Parliament, an unwavering defender of the royal prerogative and of the Constitution as he interpreted it.

On Saturday, January 8, Dr. Benjamin Franklin, agent in London for the Assembly of the Province of Massachusetts Bay, the Proprietary of Pennsylvania, the Royal Colony of Georgia, and His Majesty's deputy postmaster general for North America, received a summons to appear before the Privy Council on the Tuesday following. Solicitor General Alexander Wedderburn notified the doctor that he would then be expected to sustain the plea of the Massachusetts Legislature that His Majesty would be graciously pleased to remove Governor Thomas Hutchinson from office.

The doctor requested a delay of three weeks, alleging he needed so much time to get his papers in order and engage and instruct a solicitor. His request was granted; he was ordered to appear on January 29. He engaged John Dunning and John Lee, both eminent in their profession, as counsel for the Massachusetts Assembly, to which body he had sent Bernard's, Hutchinson's, and Oliver's letters under a seal of secrecy. Technically, the case was between Hutchinson, Oliver, and the Massachusetts Assembly, actually, it was the Crown vs. Dr. Franklin.

Franklin's acknowledgment in *The Public Advertiser* just before Christmas that he alone was "the person responsible for procuring the letters [written earlier by Hutchinson and Oliver] and transmitting them to Boston" had provided Administration with the opportunity publicly to defame and humiliate him, and this was precisely what Wedderburn planned to do. News of the forthcoming "trial" threw London drawing rooms and coffee shops into a furor of speculation, rumor, and gossip. Friends of Administration gloated at the prospect of Wedderburn laying low the cunning old intriguer, who had recently become something more than just a thorn in their sides.

Parliament assembled on Thursday, January 13, 1774, to hear the King's "most gracious speech," which was unusually brief. His Majesty did not mention America; according to the latest dispatches received in London the situation there appeared to be relatively tranquil; no one had reason to believe that additional troops would be required to maintain order in the colonies. Indeed, only a few days later Lord North assured the House of Commons that reductions in His Majesty's land and sea forces could safely be made. Accordingly, appropriations to support the Royal Navy in 1774 provided for only 15,600 seamen and 4,400 marines; land forces on the English establishment were cut to an over-all strength of slightly more than 18,000. The King was not particularly pleased with these reductions, but preferred them to an increase in the land tax, a measure vigorously opposed by the country gentry upon whose favor Administration relied.

A few days after these bills passed the House, disconcerting news arrived from the other side of the Atlantic. In Boston "a number of resolute men (dressed like Mohawks or Indians)" had emptied 342 chests of tea into the harbor; in Philadelphia a handbill informed Delaware pilots that ship *Polly*, laden with tea, was in the bay and warned them that "Tar and Feathers will be his Portion, who pilots her into this Harbour."†† In

†† Captain Ayres, master of *Polly*, was warned in the same broadside that he had been sent from London "on a diabolical service" and that if he brought *Polly* to Philadelphia he "would run such a Gauntlet" as would induce him in his "last Moments" most heartily to curse those who had made him "the Dupe of their Avarace and Ambition. What think you Captain, of a Halter around your Neck—ten gallons of liquid Tar decanted over your Pate—with the Feathers of a dozen wild Geese laid over that to enliven your Appearance?" Captain Ayres did not bring *Polly* to Philadelphia.

New York, "Mohawks" distributed notices warning any who accepted a consignment of tea to expect "an unwelcome visit in which they shall be treated as they deserve." Colonial officials reported the political climate far from tranquil; radicals in port cities inspired by Sons of Liberty were in a rebellious mood; a potentially explosive situation was rapidly developing.

On Saturday January 29, members of the Privy Council assembled at the "Cockpit" in Whitehall to enjoy the public scalping of the eminent Dr. Franklin. The proceedings on that occasion were reported by one present, and are recorded in Franklin's memoirs:

> The matter being a complaint from the Massachusetts Assembly, their counsel (Dunning and Lee) were first heard, of course. Mr. Wedderburn was very long and laborious, and indecently acrimonious in his answers. Instead of justifying his clients (Bernard, Hutchinson and Oliver) or vindicating their conduct in the administration (of Massachusetts Bay) which was the matter complained of, Mr. Wedderburn bent the whole force of his discourse, which was an inflammatory invective, against Dr. Franklin, who sat, with calm equanimity, an auditor of this injudicious and indecorous course of proceeding.[1]

Letters written by Hutchinson, in which he had urged abrogation of charter rights the colonists had enjoyed for a century and a half, were read. They provided conclusive evidence that the Massachusetts Assembly had been justified in petitioning for his removal. The Lords of the Privy Council did not, however, arrive at the verdict supported by the evidence. Rather, they reported their opinion to His Majesty that the petition was "groundless, vexatious and scandalous, and calculated only for the seditious purpose of keeping up a spirit of clamor and discontent in the said province."[2] The humble petition begging that Hutchinson be removed was dismissed. So was Franklin from his office of deputy postmaster general. Wedderburn had taken another stride toward the peerage that was the consuming object of his ambition.

Several days later, the King received Major General Thomas Gage, commander in chief of His Majesty's forces in North America, then on home leave, in the Closet. The general had requested an audience to inform his royal master of his "readiness to return at a day's notice, if the conduct of the Colonies should induce the directing coercive measures." The King found Gage much to his liking: "an honest determined man." The general assured His Majesty the rebellious Bostonians would "be Lyons, whilst we are Lambs; but if we take the resolute part they will undoubtedly prove very meek."[3] This advice confirmed the King's opinion that the Americans were pusillanimous cowards and he directed

Gage to meet with Lord North and convey his ideas "as to the mode of compelling Boston to submit."

Thomas Gage, married to an American from New Jersey, had spent most of his adult life in the colonies. In 1755 he had distinguished himself as commander of the advance guard in Major General Edward Braddock's disastrous expedition to drive the French from Fort Duquesne (now Pittsburgh, Pennsylvania) at the confluence of the Allegheny and Monongahela rivers. Braddock, a courageous but a choleric, dogmatic officer, was not inclined to take advice from anyone, least of all from a young colonel of Virginia militia, a volunteer aide named George Washington.‡‡ His column had been ambushed and disgracefully defeated. The general, mortally wounded, had been carried from the field and his body interred in an unmarked grave as the Redcoats threw down their muskets and fled before the howling Indians.

Behavior of the Provincials had been less than spectacular, and Gage managed to persuade himself that their ill discipline, or as he chose to see it, their cowardice, rather than the stupidity of a British major general, had been the proximate cause of the debacle. But his later experience in the colonies had provided ample testimony that Americans were not inclined to submit supinely to measures they conceived nullified their rights. In many letters to Barrington, Conway, Shelburne, Hillsborough, and Dartmouth he had stated precisely this opinion. Still, he told his lord and master what he (correctly) thought the King wanted to hear.

George III may have been ignorant of the American character but he divined the trend: ". . . independence is their object"; one "this Country can never submit to," for should the American colonies succeed in cutting their ties of dependence, the British West Indies, the invaluable Sugar Islands, would inevitably become dependent upon *them;* Ireland would follow, and then "this Island would be a poor Island indeed, for reduced in Her Trade Merchants would retire with their Wealth to Climates more to their Advantage and Shoales of Manufacturers would leave this country for the New Empire."

Cabinet opinion held that ringleaders in the Tea Party and those who had planned it must be brought before the bar of justice; they had not only destroyed a cargo of tea worth £18,000 but defied the law, and, as both the King and his ministers saw the case, violently challenged the sovereignty of Parliament. The King described the act as "quite subversive of the obedience which a colony owes to its mother country." But this was beside the point, as the tea thrown overboard was the property not of the British Government, but of a private monopoly, the East India Company, whose shareholders—many of whom were of the parlia-

‡‡ Washington urged Braddock to allow the Virginians to fight as they knew how to fight. But Braddock refused to accommodate his tactics to an unfamiliar enemy, a new terrain, and a new situation.

mentary majority—stood to profit considerably if the company could unload on the Americans some seventeen million pounds of tea then in its warehouses.

It is difficult to believe that no responsible person in Administration knew of the company's plan to ship the tea, and that none knew how the cargoes were to be handled on arrival. Yet William Knox, undersecretary to Lord Dartmouth, states unequivocally that Dartmouth's office knew nothing: "When the tea was sent out by the E. I. Co. to America in 1773, no communication of the project was made to the American Secretary, nor any orders, or even notices, sent respecting it but when the account of its destruction at Boston arrived the ministers appeared determined to act with extraordinary vigour." Lord Dartmouth apparently pressed his colleagues in an effort (Knox said) "to exculpate himself for having formerly moved the repeal of the Stamp Act."* The government would have to do *something*. The immediate question in ministerial councils was what.

At this particular moment, the subversive and violent behavior of his subjects in Boston did not monopolize the King's attention, nor that of his First Minister. Both were distracted by an uproar in the House of Commons generated by publication by Henry Woodfall in his notorious *Public Advertiser* of a letter allegedly libeling the speaker. The King jumped to the conclusion that Wilkes was the author. Brought before the Commons, Woodfall stated that the author was John Horne. This minuscule tempest raged for several days, and is of interest in the context of the American struggle for independence only because it produced an important defection from Lord North's well-ordered ranks. The deserter was Charles James Fox.

Fox, then twenty-five years old, was the second son of the immensely wealthy Lord Holland, who had accumulated a fortune as paymaster of the forces, and was possibly one of the most permissive parents in history. Lord Holland had encouraged his sons, Stephen and Charles, to live precisely as they wished, and during most of an exciting life, Charles did just that. Volatile, erudite, witty, a compulsive gambler and a favorite with the ladies, he was generally conceded to be the most brilliant debater in the House. Fox never prepared a speech, but when he rose members could be assured of a devastating display of intellectual fireworks. Edmund Burke's carefully reasoned and overly long disquisitions often lulled his colleagues (and sometimes emptied the House), but even the somnolent First Minister did not doze when Fox cast his magic spell.

He was at this time a junior lord of the Treasury. He had previously incurred royal displeasure; his speeches during debates in the case of Woodfall and Horne aroused the King's anger, and on February 16 His

* In the House of Lords. (Knox Papers.)

Majesty wrote Lord North that Fox had "so thoroughly cast off every principle of common honour and honesty that he must become as contemptible as he is odious; and I hope you will let him know you are not insensible of his conduct toward you." A few days later, the First Minister let Fox know: "Sir—His Majesty has thought proper to order a new Commission of Treasury to be made out, in which I do not see your name. North."⁴ From this day, Charles Fox was in opposition. There was no doubt that he would eventually join the faction nominally led by the Marquis of Rockingham.

Having damped down the controversy aroused by Horne and Woodfall and injudiciously sacked Fox, the ministry was now free to deal with the more distant but equally troublesome and obnoxious Bostonians. The first thought that occurred to Lord North was to remove the seat of colonial government from Boston to Salem. In light of the festering situation this was not a bad idea. The Cabinet then considered how to deal with the offenders, and Dartmouth queried Attorney General Thurlow and Solicitor General Wedderburn for an opinion as to whether the crime of high treason had been committed, and if so, by whom. How could the government proceed against those involved? Thurlow and Wedderburn interrogated several people who had been in Boston at the time, and mulled over the problem for four or five days. Finally, after persistent prodding from the American secretary, they sent him an opinion that the crime of high treason had been committed and named half a dozen Bostonians, including Samuel and John Adams, John Hancock, Cushing, Dr. Joseph Warren and his brother James, together with anonymous members of the Committee of Correspondence, who might possibly be charged.

Government attorneys next questioned others recently arrived from Boston who may have had some knowledge of the affair and took depositions. Thurlow and his colleague were astute lawyers, and as they picked over the testimony, reached the conclusion that the charge could not be proved. Dartmouth was all for stern measures and asked that the Cabinet meet in his office. His undersecretaries awaited the result of deliberations in an outer room. As Thurlow and Wedderburn left the secretary's sanctum, the two undersecretaries, Thomas Pownall and William Knox, rose.† "'Well' cried Pownall, 'Is it done.' 'No' answered Thurlow, 'Nothing is done. Don't you see,' added he, 'that they want to throw the whole responsibility of the business on the Solicitor General and me, and who would be such damned fools as to risk themselves for such shiten fellows as these. Now, if it was George Grenville who was so damned obstinate

---

† Pownall had been governor of Massachusetts Bay from August 1757 until November 1759. He was then appointed "to the more lucrative and less irksome" position of governor of South Carolina. He returned to England in 1760 and resigned his office. He was known at this time as sympathetic to American objections to taxation and had predicted that the colonists would oppose such measures with arms.

that he would go to hell with you before he would desert you, there would be some sense in it.'" ‡ Thurlow and Wedderburn left the outer office and slammed the door. The project to arrest the ringleaders in Massachusetts and bring them to trial in England was dropped, much to Dartmouth's chagrin. Thus, on the last day of February 1774, with legal recourse deemed impracticable, Administration was precisely where it had been on the first day of the month. Executive action by an order in council or by royal proclamation was thought to be inappropriate.

In the meantime, the ministry had not been idle, and on March 7 Lord North laid before Parliament a mass of reports and documents collected by the King's servants in Boston. These consisted of newspaper accounts of the Tea Party, together with inflammatory handbills and other material patently of a treasonable and seditious nature. The King's message was then read. His Majesty declared that the proceedings at Boston were as outrageous as they were unwarranted, and asked his loyal Lords and Commons to take such steps as they considered necessary to put an immediate stop to the disorders and to consider what further regulations and permanent provisions were necessary for enforcement of the laws "and the just dependence of the Colonies upon the Crown and Parliament of Great Britain."[5]

Copies of handbills that had been plastered all over Boston in January reached London in early March. Their message was not one to encourage the ministry to a moderate policy. The bills warned the tea consignees, described as "odious miscrents and detestable tools to the ministry and the governor," not to dare show their faces in the city, where they would receive "a reception as such vile ingrates deserve." The bills were signed "Joyce, Chairman of the Committee for tarring and feathering."[6]

All public and private reports reflected a situation in Massachusetts verging on open rebellion: ". . . no person employed by Government could in any act, however common or legal, fulfill the duties of his office or station without its being immediately exclaimed against by the licentious, as an infringement of their liberties." Most of those in Government felt Parliament must act, for only Parliament "was capable of re-establishing tranquility among those turbulent people, and of bringing order out of confusion."[7]

While Parliament considered the King's message and members studied the papers provided, the ministry launched a well-orchestrated campaign in the subsidized press. This was aimed primarily at the mercantile, shipping, and banking communities, for their support was seen as vital if a united front were to be successfully formed. Accordingly, daily papers and periodicals were "systematically filled with writings painting

‡ William Knox Papers, William L. Clements Library.

in the strongest colours, and in particular urging the impossibility of the future existence of any trade to America if this flagrant outrage on commerce should go unpunished." The First Minister described the Tea Party variously as "an insult"; "an unparalleled outrage"; "a heinous act which called for severe and exemplary punishment"; and announced he had plans "for a thorough reformation."[8] The climate of opinion was in general highly favorable to such a project.

On Monday, March 14, a petition drawn by William Bollan, agent for the Council of Massachusetts Bay, was read in the House. This related that the ancestors of the Bostonians had overcome "difficulties, perils and hardships inexpressible and innumerable" to raise "the King's American Empire out of a dreary and dangerous wilderness"; that their efforts and those of generations of their descendants had brought a tremendous increase to British commerce and shipping, and had added to the dignity and strength of the Empire. The Acta Regia of Queen Elizabeth and her successors had guaranteed the colonists "perpetual enjoyment of their public liberties"; they believed these were now threatened. Bollan prayed, therefore, to be allowed to plead their case. The House was in no mood to listen to a harangue devoted to a familiar and tiresome catalogue of complaints of violated rights. The King's message had made clear his intent and that of his ministry to put an end once and for all to fruitless transoceanic wrangling, to assert Great Britain's supremacy, and to bring the Bostonians to a proper state of dependent subordination. The speaker ordered the petition to lie on the table.

Lord North now rose to ask leave to bring in a bill drawn by Thurlow and Wedderburn to remove the commissioners of Customs from Boston and close the port on the first day of June to all shipping except that carrying fuel, provisions, or supplies to His Majesty's forces. In introducing his bill, the noble lord said that for seven years Boston had been "the focus of tumult and the originator of all colonial disturbances." His administration intended to put an end to these uproars and "secure the just dependence" of the colonies. The port was to remain closed until "complete satisfaction" had been made to the East India Company for the loss of its tea and royal officials reimbursed for damage done by rioters to their homes and offices. And even then "the Crown . . . will not be obliged to restore the custom house unless His Majesty is thoroughly convinced that the laws of this country will be better observed in the harbor of Boston for the future."[9]

This condition, which prescribed a probation of indeterminate duration, made perfectly clear the intent of the King and his ministers to punish Boston most severely. For the port was the heart of Boston's economy. Closure of the port would directly affect not only seafarers and fishermen, but the broad community of factors, brokers, bankers, warehousemen, longshoremen, ship chandlers, merchants, tavern keepers, and shipwrights whose livelihood totally depended on shipping. Boston's eighteen thousand inhabitants would suffer, too, as they would be deprived of woolens and linens and such common household articles as needles, pins, and ironware. The more affluent would be unable to procure silks, gloves, and lace for their ladies; expensive coats, hats, and waistcoats for themselves; or wines, fresh tropical fruits, and olive oil. The act was designed to deal a mortal blow to one of the first cities in America.

Mr. Dowdeswell rose to observe that the proposed measure was, *ex post facto,* mischievous and discriminatory. Why could not the Bostonians be heard in their own defense before the ministry laid upon them this wrongful punishment? Colonel Isaac Barré, a long-time friend of America, supported Lord North. He thought the Bostonians deserved the "moderate" punishment the First Minister designed.

A second reading of the bill a week later provoked lively debate. Rose Fuller, former chief justice of Jamaica and a staunch supporter of the colonists' position, prophesied that the Bostonians would certainly not pay the East India Company for the tea; that the bill would generate a colonial confederacy; and that troops would be needed. Lord North answered him: "Now is our time to stand out, to defy them—to proceed . . . without fear . . . we are in earnest, we will proceed with firmness and vigour . . . we mean to punish them . . . to assert our rights." He refuted Fuller's assertion that troops would be required: "four or five frigates would do the business." The noble Lord did not expect the other colonies "to take fire."

He was temperately supported until Mr. Van rose to say that the offenses of the Americans were "flagitious . . . the town of Boston ought to be knocked about their ears and destroyed. *Delenda est Carthago . . .* you will never meet with proper obedience to the laws of this country until you have destroyed that nest of locusts." Barré had reconsidered; he thought the bill "a vengeful step . . . keep your hands out of the pockets of the Americans and they will be obedient subjects."[10]

The bill was scheduled for a third and final reading on March 25. By this time Opposition had managed to pull itself together sufficiently to make a concerted effort to stop it. A petition from Americans living in London asserted "the rights of natural justice and the common law of England" as inalienable. Elementary rules of justice prescribed that no man could be condemned unheard, and as the trespass alleged (the Tea Party) was committed by persons unknown, it was unreasonable to punish innocent citizens of Boston and the Bay Colony. The bill would establish a precedent by which any body of men in America could be punished for the transgressions of an unidentified few. How, in these circumstances, could the colonists hope to enjoy security? This rigorous and arbitrary punishment would alienate the affection of the Americans. "To prevent the dissolution of that love, harmony and confidence between the two countries which was their mutual blessing and support" the signers beseeched the House not to pass the bill.

Fox attempted with no success to have various offensive provisions stricken. Dowdeswell, too, opposed. He described the proposition as "totally unjust and unfair." The ministry was punishing British merchants and shippers quite as severely as it was the Bostonians. Should the House persist in such childish folly, it would soon "inflame all America . . . you will by and by have your hands fully employed." Would the minister address himself to the reasonable petition just read and answer it?

In Edmund Burke's breast the proposed measure, hastened through the House without due attention either to its intrinsic importance or its probable effects, induced "heart-felt sorrow." The House had even refused to hear Mr. Bollan speak in behalf of Massachusetts Bay. Were the Bostonians not entitled to a day in court? The subsidized press was "tarring and feathering" all who dared oppose the bill, which he excoriated as both unjust and imprudent: ". . . the consequences will be dreadful and I am afraid destructive; you will draw a foreign force upon you at a time when you little expect it; I will not say where that will end . . . but think, I conjure you, of the consequences."

George Johnstone, a captain in the Royal Navy who had spent some time in America as governor of West Florida, described the measure as cruel and coercive; the "abortion of an indecisive mind . . . incapable of comprehending the chain of consequences which must result" from its passage. Instead of quieting disturbances in Boston, it would produce "a General Confederation" and mutual hostilities, which "most probably will end in a GENERAL REVOLT."[11] The ministry did not propose to waste time answering these arguments; Lord North commanded an overwhelming majority and the bill passed without a division.°°

As the port bill reached its last reading in the House of Lords, Americans resident in London, including Benjamin Franklin, Arthur Lee, Edward Bancroft, and Thomas Pinkney, drew two humble petitions, one addressed to the King's Most Excellent Majesty, the other to "the Right Honourable, the Lords Spiritual and Temporal in Parliament assembled." In these, they averred the measure was "calculated to condemn and punish" the Bostonians without a hearing, and that its enactment would establish a precedent to deprive Americans of their rights under law. Neither the petitions nor efforts by Lords Rockingham, Camden, and Shelburne availed to amend the bill, much less to stop it.

The King watched the progress of the measure with satisfaction and

°° This bill (14 Geo III, c. 19) was the first of the "Intolerable Acts." The others that followed were the Massachusetts Government Act (14 Geo III, c. 45), the Administration of Justice Act (14 Geo III, c. 39), and the Quartering Act (14 Geo III, c. 54). These acts are printed in *English Historical Documents*, Vol. IX, *American Colonial Documents, to 1776*, pp. 779–84.

expressed his pleasure to Lord North in a brief note on March 21. Two days later, he wrote his First Minister: ". . . the feebleness and futility of the opposition of the Port Bill shews the rectitude of the Measure." This remark perfectly illuminates the King's character: As long as Administration had a voting majority, God was manifestly on his side.

A great many of the King's loyal subjects agreed with him. Among those who had fled London to avoid the pneumonic season was Henry Ellis, former governor of Georgia, and one of William Knox's intimate friends. On March 22 he wrote Knox from the Mediterranean coast, where he was hoping to recover his health, damaged by "the smoak, the fogges, and cold, humid air" of London. He was suffering from a variety of afflictions, including "a sore throat, deafness in the ear, and sharp sciatic pains," but still able to hold a quill in arthritic fingers long enough to inform Knox that he by no means thought the situation past retrieving "for we know the real inability of the Americans to make any effectual resistance to any coercive method which might be employed to compell their obedience. For far too long the Colonists had been permitted with impunity to give scope to their insolent licentiousness." This opinion reflected the attitude of most supporters of Administration.

The First Minister did not wait for automatic royal assent to his port bill to bring in a measure entitled "For the Better Regulating the Government of the Province of Massachusetts Bay." In introducing this, his lordship said his intent was to remove power from the hands of the "democratic part," which had demonstrated a uniform contempt for the laws; he therefore proposed that the royal governor should be empowered "to appoint the officers throughout the whole civil authority," including members of the Provincial Council, always heretofore chosen by the lower House in accordance with the Charter. Town meetings were to be held but once a year and were to confine their deliberations exclusively to matters of local interest. Sheriffs appointed by the governor would hereafter empanel juries. The noble lord was sure gentlemen present would agree that town meetings and similar assemblies should be brought under some degree of control.

Lord George Germain rose to applaud the First Minister's proposals. Although worthy of approbation, he considered them too mild. Lord George would not have "men of a mercantile cast" assembling in town meetings "debating about political matters." In Massachusetts the government had been usurped by "a tumultuous and riotous rabble, who ought, if they had the least prudence, to follow their mercantile employment and not trouble themselves with politics and government, which they do not understand." The popularly elected assembly was "a downright clog" upon all the proceedings of government; the existing jury system perverted justice and led to "the most palpable enormities." The First Minister thanked the noble lord for contributions "worthy of a great mind"; the wise counsels of men of such rare abilities as his lordship's would assist in restoring peace and happiness in the colonies.

Precisely what arrangements had been made with Germain were not then known, but those who followed political developments sensed a job. Germain's price was reputed to be reinstatement in the army, from which some years earlier he had been ignominiously dismissed, plus a lucrative post. The Administration could not accede to the former demand, but did promise Lord George a position of power. Germain, as he was later to prove, was endowed with neither a great mind nor superior abilities, but his views accurately reflected those of the King, the "King's Friends," the ministry, and most of the lords spiritual and temporal, who held the Americans to be a fractious, litigious, cowardly lot, and would have agreed with Dr. Johnson's description of them as "a race of convicts who ought to be thankful for anything we allow them short of hanging."

The Massachusetts government bill was read the first time on April 15, and the second a week later. Again Opposition was slow in working out a line to be followed and mobilizing the shock troops. Dowdeswell vigorously opposed the minister's program: The further his measures went, the worse they were. The Bostonians, he said, had "laboured with unwearied industry and flourished" under a democratic charter which "breathes the spirit of liberty." This charter the minister now proposed to destroy in a petulant and obstinate effort to establish "a most ridiculous superiority." Sir George Savile prophesied that abrogation of charter rights, without hearing the case of the Bostonians, would result "in bloodshed and strife." General Henry Seymour Conway concurred; he pointed out that the House was, in effect, talking about the charter rights of "all America." He said: "We are the aggressors and innovators, and not the Colonies. We have irritated and forced laws upon them for these six or seven years last past. . . . These Acts respecting America will involve this country and its Ministers in Misfortunes, and I wish I may not add, in ruin."

The First Minister challenged those who opposed his plan to regulate the government of Massachusetts Bay: "The Americans have tarred and feathered your subjects, plundered your merchants, burnt your ships, denied all obedience to your laws and authority . . . political necessity urges this measure; if this is not the proper method, shew me any other which is preferable, and I will postpone it." Opposition could show him no other, or, at least, no other the First Minister considered appropriate.

Possibly a program could in time be developed, but Thomas Pownall, one of the few men in Parliament qualified to speak to the subject, believed that proposed by the minister could not possibly ameliorate the situation, but would inevitably exacerbate it: "The measure which you are pursuing will be resisted . . . by a regular united system . . . I told this House, it is now four years past, that the People of America would resist the tax which lay then upon them . . . I tell you now, that they will resist the measures now pursued in a more vigorous way." He described the functioning of Committees of Correspondence; prognosticated that a colonial congress would be called, and "should matters ever come to arms, you will hear of other officers than those appointed by your Governors."

On May 2, at the third and final reading of the bill, Opposition made a final effort. Sir George Savile presented a petition drawn by "several Natives of America." The petitioners had studied both this bill and the Port Act "with astonishment and grief"; they apprehended "the horrid outrages of military oppression" and "the desolation of civil commotions" should the government attempt to enforce them. The tendency of these two bills, so the petitioners asserted, was "to reduce their countrymen to the dreadful alternative of being totally enslaved or compelled into a contest the most shocking and unnatural, with the Parent State which has ever been the object of their veneration and their love."[12]

John Dunning accused the minister of imposing "a system of tyranny." He offered neither peace nor an olive branch: "it is war, severe revenge, and hatred, against our own subjects. We are now come to that fatal dilemma—'Resist and we will cut your throats; submit, and we will tax you'—such is the reward of obedience." He asserted that the measures already adopted and those now proposed would "disunite the affection of the Americans" and instead of promoting peace, order, and obedience would produce "nothing but clamour, discontent and rebellion."

Colonel Barré followed: "The question now before us is, whether we will chuse to bring over the affections of all our Colonies by lenient measures, or to wage war with them?" Boston would not be alone in her resistance: ". . . you will very soon have the rest of [the] Colonies on your back." He vigorously condemned the bill: "A law that shocks Equity is Reason's murderer." The people would turn out: ". . . a set of sturdy rebels . . . therefore, let me advise you to desist." Conway had heard much talk of an olive branch, but where was it? He said he was unable to find it. Fox pulled together Opposition's arguments as he posed the fundamental question: "Whether America is to be governed by a force or management?" If Massachusetts were to be deprived of her charter, "for God's sake let it be taken away by law and not by legislative coercion." Burke had no hope he could convince the House of its error, but red-coated soldiers, and they would be needed, could never govern America.

Rigby and Lord George Germain spoke in support of the measure and advocated use of what force was necessary. The paymaster of the forces wasted few words: "I say stand and deliver, to the Americans." Obviously, it did not occur to Rigby that the colonists might see this argot of the highwayman as appropriate. Lord George asserted America was in a state "of anarchy and confusion" and that crown officers there were intimidated by "a lawless rabble." If the Americans would give up, Great Britain might condescend to negotiate.[13]

Lord North was not to be moved from his course by Cassandras in either Lords or Commons. Burke had earlier touched a chord that may have aroused some misgivings—the possibility of a third-party (French) intervention—but if the First Minister harbored any such apprehensions he was careful to conceal them. The bill passed by an overwhelming majority and was sent on to the Lords.

As debates in the upper House were not then taken down, there exists only a fragmentary record of what was said either for or against the bill, which sailed through with no trouble. A number of Opposition lords including Rockingham, Portland and Richmond, drew up a "Dissent" to be recorded in the *Journal*. In this they asserted that the measure was substantially unjust and tended to annihilate the powers of the popularly elected Assembly as it increased those of the crown. The bill not only put the lives, liberties, and properties of the King's subjects at the disposal of a royal governor and his hand-picked Council, but destroyed invaluable rights the people had enjoyed for well over a hundred years. They declared the punitive nature of the bill to be "unexampled in the records of Parliament" and objected strenuously but ineffectually to its arbitrary provisions, as well as to the precipitate manner in which Administration had pushed it through. These objections did not deter Lord North, whose fixed determination, and that of his royal master, was to beat the Bostonians to their knees.

To this end he brought in a third bill, which he described as an integral and necessary part of his plan to restore order and tranquillity in Massachusetts. This, "For the Impartial Administration of Justice," provided that any crown officer—including members of the armed forces—who might be charged with murder or other capital crime while acting to suppress riots or disturbances, could be tried in another colony, or at the discretion of the royal governor, be sent to England.†† Lord North described the bill as not unfair or vindictive, but temperate and necessary. His lordship was certain it would be efficacious. The government, determined to enforce the law, would no longer tolerate "the least degree of disobedience." Ringleaders in the recent mischievous disturbances would, he hoped, soon be apprehended, speedily brought to trial, and appropriately punished. General Gage was being sent out as governor vice Hutchinson, who was to sail to England "to report." Gage would command means adequate "to prevent the first rise of disobedience." The government would continue, as always, to observe "a perfect innocence and a conscientious avoidance of the breech of any laws."

This proved to be too much for Colonel Barré:

†† Known in America as "the Murder Bill."

> Sir, I am sorry to say that this is declamation, unbecoming the character and place of him who utters it. In what moment have you been quiet? Has not your Government for many years past been a series of irritating and offensive measures, without policy, principle, or moderation? Have not your troops and your ships made a vain and insulting parade in their streets and in their harbors? It has seemed to be your study to irritate and inflame them. You have stimulated discontents into disaffection, and you are now goading that disaffection into rebellion.[14]

He predicted that when the "banners of rebellion were spread in America" Great Britain would be undone. He would resist to the utmost "the phrenzy" of the ministers, who, rather than an olive branch, were sending a naked sword.

Various gentlemen supported Lord North. Lord Carmarthen, a reliable but not a particularly percipient "King's Friend," asked how much longer Great Britain would be required to endure the behavior of the Americans: "For what purpose were they suffered to go to that country," he asked, "unless the profit of their labor should return to their masters here?" Mr. Van, who had previously recommended destroying Boston, now suggested the entire country be burned out.

Alderman Sawbridge, in opposition, was quite as vehement as Mr. Van. The bill was "pernicious"; "ridiculous"; "cruel." The minister meant to enslave the Americans and given the opportunity would enslave the English. The alderman hoped the Americans would resist these destructive bills: ". . . if they do not, they are the most abject slaves that ever the earth produced, and nothing the Minister can do is base enough for them."[15]

On May 18, when the bill was to be read in the Lords for the third time, Mr. Bollan again presented a brief petition and asked to be heard. His request was rejected. Rockingham spoke "with all the insight and authority of an able statesman," but to no avail. The bill passed by a majority of four to one. Two days later His Majesty gave royal assent.

Lord North next brought in a bill that authorized commanding officers in North America to requisition billeting space for troops, and to take over uninhabited structures in areas where no barracks were immediately available. Chatham made one of his infrequent appearances in the House of Lords in late May to oppose the bill at its third reading.‡‡ Chatham's speech was short and charged with emotion. He proposed to vote against the Quartering Act; he castigated the Port Act as so "diametrically opposite to the fundamental principles of sound policy, that individuals possessed of common understanding, must be astonished at such proceedings." He charged the Administration with purposely irritating

‡‡ Walpole described him as "a comedian even to his dress, to excuse his late absence by visible tokens of the gout, had his legs wrapped in black velvet boots."[16]

the Americans "to be revenged on them for the victory they gained by the repeal of the Stamp Act." He closed with an appeal: "My Lords, I am an old man, and would advise the Noble Lords in office to adopt a more gentle mode of governing *America;* for the day is not far distant when *America* may vie with these Kingdoms, not only in arms, but in arts also."[17]

One final bill was to add fuel to the flames induced by the Coercive Acts. This was the Quebec Act, framed by Major General Guy Carleton, governor of Quebec. The bill guaranteed French residents of Canada (who numbered nearly 120,000 as compared with fewer than 1,000 British) free enjoyment of their religion, prescribed that they would be subject to the French rather than the British legal code, and confirmed the seignorial rights of aristocratic landowners. They, and priests whose right to tithe was written into law, were naturally pleased. *Habitants* were not exactly happy.

New England preachers attacked the Quebec Act as a wicked design to thrust Popery down American throats. An editor of the *Pennsylvania Packet* wrote: "We may live to see our churches converted in mass houses, and lands plundered of tythes for the support of Popish Clergy; the Inquisition may erect her standard in Pennsylvania and the city of Philadelphia may yet experience the carnage of a St. Bartholomew's day."[18] This was inflammatory nonsense, but many fanatic antipapists and gullible Dissenters believed it.

Another provision of the act was calculated to arouse resistance. This was the extension of the borders of the province of Quebec southward to the Ohio River to embrace the present states of Ohio, Indiana, Illinois, and most of Michigan. Feeling was particularly strong in Virginia, where Washington and other wealthy gentry including Lord Dunmore, the royal governor, were involved in speculative land schemes. English and American speculators in western lands and those who professed to fear the extension of "Popish tyranny" would not be alone in objecting to the Quebec Act. Connecticut, Massachusetts, and Virginia conceived that the act alienated certain rights granted by charter; frontiersmen saw in it an attempt to close the wilderness to exploration, hunting, trapping, and settlement and to convey this vast forested area to Canadian trappers as an exclusive preserve from which they would be barred. Thus while in England the Quebec Act was generally applauded, the colonists saw it as a malicious attempt to prevent exploitation of the rich lands west of the Appalachians and to confine them to the Atlantic seaboard.

As Lord North's Coercive Acts passed through Lords and Commons and received royal assent, leaders in Boston were busy. Samuel Adams plied his quill vigorously; he wrote Franklin that people of the Bay Colony would not "be contented with a partial and temporary relief" nor "be amused with Court promises while they see not the least relaxation of Grievances." Activities of the Committees of Correspondence had "wonderfully enlightened and animated" the entire province: "They are united in sentiment and their opposition to unconstitutional Measures of Government is become systematical, for Colony communicates freely with Colony. There is a common Affection."[19] He could not foresee the measures "an injudicious Ministry" would propose; anything might be expected: ". . . it will be wise for us to ready *for all events*. . . . It is our duty at all Hazards to preserve the Publick Liberty. Righteous Heaven will graciously smile on every manly and rational Attempt to secure the best of all his Gifts to man, from the ravishing Hand of Lawless & brutal Power."[20] Adams realized a nation was struggling to be born. He saw himself as the midwife.

Sons of Liberty in New York, eager to emulate their patriotic brethren in Boston, had been anxiously awaiting the arrival of a ship freighted with tea, and when they learned on April 18 that *Nancy* was off Sandy Hook with a cargo of the "detestable herb" they made ready to receive her. But thanks to the discretion of Lieutenant Governor Cadwallader Colden and Captain Lockyer of *Nancy*, the "Mohawks" were denied their tea party.* *Nancy* departed, her cargo intact. Four days later "Mohawks" had their opportunity when a second ship arrived. Her captain, more determined than Lockyer, decided to land his tea. The "Mohawks" decided he would not, boarded his ship, and threw the tea into the North River.

After an interval of three weeks a public meeting was called at the Exchange to elect a Committee of Correspondence. Among those chosen were men whose names are today familiar to New Yorkers: a Bache, two Livingstons, a Randall, John Jay, a De Lancey, a Goelet, a Beekman. Towns and villages in upper New York quickly followed the example set by the metropolis, and a network of local committees began to function. But the city was conservative and inclined to move cautiously.

Not so the committee in Boston, where Samuel Adams, John Hancock, Dr. Warren, and their colleagues were anxious to challenge Great Britain. They soon found opportunity to do so. On May 10, copies of the Port Act arrived; three days later Adams dispatched Paul Revere with a circular letter to Committees of Correspondence in Rhode Island, Connecticut, New York, New Jersey, and Philadelphia, reporting receipt of the act, and reaction of the Boston town meeting: "The Town of Boston is now Suffering the Stroke of Vengeance in the Common Cause of America." He hoped Bostonians would sustain the blow "with a becoming fortitude, and that the Effects of this cruel Act, intended to intimidate and subdue the Spirits of all America will by the joynt Efforts of all

---

* Governor Tryon was in England on leave. He, no doubt, would have ordered the tea to be landed.

be frustrated." Boston needed help: "This Town singly will not be able to support the Cause under so severe a Tryal."[21]

Several days later the new captain general and governor in chief of His Majesty's colony in Massachusetts Bay arrived in H.M.S. *Lively,* which cast anchor off Castle William. Hutchinson briefed his successor and confirmed Gage's opinion that if he acted the "Lyon" the colonists would be "Lambs." The history of the next few months suggests that organized "Lambs" may cope successfully in the political arena with unorganized "Lyons." The colonists were rapidly mastering a basic tool of revolutionary action: the creation of extralegal bodies, some overt, some clandestine, capable of moving in political and psychological fields, and of carrying the people with them.

On May 10 Louis XV died of smallpox. The heir to Le Roi Soleil was sixty-four and had reigned for fifty-nine years. Neither his personal qualities nor his policies had endeared him to his impoverished and discontented subjects; as a sovereign he had been a royal disaster. During his reign Pitt had dismembered the rotting French colonial empire; at Paris the Duc de Choiseul-Praslin, with trembling hand and eyes glazed with tears, had signed a treaty that reduced his master's proud state, once the most respected in Europe, to inglorious impotence. Few in France mourned the passing of Louis XV; all welcomed the accession of his grandson, the twenty-two-year-old Dauphin, who came to the throne as Louis XVI.

Louis XV's death did not create much of a stir in Whitehall, where his youthful successor, believed to lack political acumen, was judged to be immature, unsophisticated, and in bondage to his Austrian wife Marie Antoinette, a daughter of the Empress Maria Theresa, and a young woman reported to be abandoned to extravagance, gaiety, and frivolity. Most would have agreed with Sir William Wraxall's unflattering estimate: ". . . though young, Louis possessed neither the Graces, the activity, nor the elasticity of mind, usually characteristic of Youth. Heavy, inert, inclined to corpulency and destitute of all aptitude for any exercises of the body except Hunting . . . His manners were shy; a natural result of his neglected Education."[22] Madame Du Barry described him as *"Le Gros garçon, mal élevé."*

The young man was shortly to show that he had both more energy and more political sense than Lord North thought. His first move was to exile Madame Du Barry; his next, to appoint a man he trusted, the aging Count de Maurepas, as *chef du cabinet* and private secretary and install him in an apartment at Versailles just above the royal study. He then rid himself of his grandfather's inane Foreign Minister, the Duc d'Aiguillon, who had held office at the pleasure of Du Barry. This clearing of the decks should have suggested to ministers in London that a reorientation of French foreign policy, characterized since the disastrous peace of 1763 by a supine passivity, was to be expected.

In Versailles, Conrad Alexandre Gérard, permanent Secretary General in the Ministry of Foreign Affairs, watched developments in America with perceptive attention. In June he concluded that the situation in the colonies was in delicate tension, and wrote Charles Jean Garnier, the King's chargé d'affaires in London: "We are nearing the moment when the fate of the Bostonians will be sealed; General Gage will need much talent, wisdom and patience if he is to manage to quiet the unrest and insubordination afflicting almost all the British colonies." M. Gérard (as he was later to be known in America) busied himself during June assembling data to brief the new Foreign Minister, Comte de Vergennes, expected to arrive from the embassy in Stockholm in July.

Vergennes did not pretend to be an expert on Great Britain's colonial problem, but he was receptive, objective, and prudent. His fixed idea was that his country needed, above all, European peace, and that French policy must be based on a firm alliance with his master's Spanish uncle, Charles III. His first measures on taking over the ministry were designed to assure a close working understanding with the Queen's mother, Empress Maria Theresa, and to cement the Madrid-Versailles relationship. These were essential preliminaries to a modification of diplomacy by which he hoped to regain for France her lost primacy in the affairs of Europe, and again to challenge England on the seas.

Many years later he dictated a private memorandum for the King in which he described his feelings as he took office in July 1774. At the Peace of Paris, England had struck France to her knees, deprived her of her possessions and commerce in India, Canada, Louisiana, and Africa, humiliated her in the eyes of the European nations, and debased her by arrogantly stationing a British commissioner at Dunkirk to oversee destruction of its defenses and ensure that they would not be rebuilt. "General opinion was that France no longer had strength or resources; envy [of France] . . . had degenerated into a kind of contempt; the cabinet of Versailles lost all prestige and influence abroad; having once been the center of all great affairs, it became a passive spectator; no one sought its advice; its approval or disapproval no longer mattered. In other words, France, the most powerful nation in Europe, had become an absolute nonentity; it had lost the support of its allies and the regard of other nations. Such were our sad and humiliating circumstances when Your Majesty came to the throne."[23]

The treaty, he continued, "contains the harshest as well as the most unfair stipulations, and . . . the Court of London, when circumstances enabled it to lay them down, well knew that we should observe them only so long as we were unable to shake them off." Such, he observed, must have been the feelings of British and French negotiators alike, and such were his. France could no longer continue to endure the embarassing humiliations inflicted on her; she must rise again. "These important truths" were "engraved" upon his heart when he was called to office. And because of these same truths, Vergennes at once fixed his attention on "that oppressed nation" across the Atlantic. The Americans, encouraged and assisted by France, could be the means of humbling the arrogant and detested English.

✂ 2

All America Is in a Flame

In a letter of instruction Dartmouth handed Gage a few days before the general sailed to take up his new responsibilities, he wrote that the King had conferred on his chosen governor unlimited powers to deal with "every opposition." Should "the madness of the people" make it necessary, Gage was to employ his troops "with effect." The secretary directed him to induce compliance "by mild and gentle persuasion" if possible, but reminded him that His Majesty's dignity required the "full and complete submission of the town of Boston." He ordered Gage to establish his seat of government at Salem; to make every effort to apprehend the "ringleaders and abettors" of the riotous proceedings of November and December, and to remove from the Council those who had encouraged opposition to the laws.[1] He was to show no leniency to those who persisted in advocating disobedience. When the Bostonians acknowledged their manifold wickednesses and humbly submitted, His Majesty would consider exercising royal clemency.

The appointment of one of the most senior generals in the British Army to the concurrent posts of commander in chief in America and royal governor of Massachusetts Bay was a major political blunder. Possibly this would ease some administrative problems, as it was no doubt designed to do, but it was bound to inflame American animosity. The colonists were inheritors of the British antipathy to standing armies and governors in red coats. Established tradition in both Britain and America was that the military must be subservient to civil authority. The King now chose deliberately to flout this custom. The appointment confirmed American opinion that an evil ministry was determined to suppress their constitutional liberties, by force of arms and "enslave" them step by step.

Bostonians were delighted to see the last of Governor Hutchinson, whose private letters urging alterations in the Charter of Massachusetts Bay and other measures designed to curtail what they conceived to be their established liberties had enraged them. His reputation as an avaricious nepotist was well deserved. One brother-in-law, Andrew Oliver, had been lieutenant governor; a bill of impeachment had been brought against a second, Chief Justice Peter Oliver. Two of five merchants to whom the East India Company had given tea monopolies in December 1773 were his sons, another a nephew, and the other two close family friends. Nepotism was a way of life in the late eighteenth century; the Bostonians indulged in it themselves but objected to the governor's outrageous favoritism, which would make the chosen consignees very rich indeed. After Hutchinson sailed, he was hanged and burned in effigy in dozens of towns in New England.

On the day the governor arrived, the Boston Committee of Correspondence drew up a circular letter that was to have a critical effect in promoting unification. Although the Port Act had been directed only at Boston, it presaged similar action against any colony that refused to surrender "sacred rights and liberties into the hands of an infamous ministry." *All* must therefore unite in the common cause. Would her sister colonies support Massachusetts Bay? Would they at once suspend all trade with Great Britain? Answer by the bearer was immediately desired by those who signed the manifesto "Your friends and fellow countrymen." The circular letter was at once printed, and dispatch riders, their saddlebags bulging, set off with it to the north, west, and south.

Samuel Adams wrote Arthur Lee in London that he had received a copy of the act: "For flagrant injustice and barbarity one might search in vain among the archives of *Constantinople* to find a match for it." Adams thought the citizens well able to ensure their safety, which "does not consist in a servile compliance with the ignominious terms of this barbarous edict." He was sure the other colonies would rally to the support of Boston and that a united America would "gloriously defeat" the designs of her common enemy.[2]

Even while couriers were riding with their seditious cargo, Gage was compiling his first report to Lord Dartmouth. He wrote that the Port Act had "staggered the most Presumptuous" and hoped to find the situation calmer and "the Assembly in better temper" after they had removed to

Salem.[3] During the following week the Assembly presented Gage with a petition calling for an "Extraordinary Day of Humiliation." The governor, convinced this "was only to give an opportunity for Sedition to flow from the Pulpits," rejected the petition. He was well aware of the ability of Dissenting pastors to intoxicate their flocks by political philippics clothed in biblical phraseology.*

The Connecticut General Assembly acted immediately and vigorously. After declaring themselves dutiful and faithful subjects of His Majesty King George the Third, the assemblymen resolved "that the late Act of Parliament inflicting pains and penalties on the town of Boston, by blocking up their harbor, is a precedent justly alarming to the British colonies in America, and wholly inconsistent with, and subversive of, their constitutional rights and liberties," and "that the apprehending and carrying persons beyond the sea to be tried" was "unconstitutional and subversive of the liberties and rights of the free subjects of this colony." Finally, they unanimously resolved that it was "the indispensable duty which we owe to our king, our country, ourselves, and our posterity, by all lawful means in our power to maintain, defend and preserve these our rights and liberties, and to transmit [them] entire and inviolate to the latest generation—and that it is our fixed determination and unalterable resolution faithfully to discharge this our duty."[4]

New York was more wary. Here the merchants, generally conservative, made an effort to keep the whole business out of the hands of what Gouverneur Morris called the "mobility"—unlettered and radically inclined artisans, day laborers, longshoremen, and petty tradesmen. Morris exemplified the colonial merchant aristocrat: well born, well educated, rich. Neither he nor many other members of his class felt an abiding loyalty to George III. But they were loyal to the system His Majesty personified and naturally wished to preserve it. In a word, they wanted above all to avoid a social revolution which would inevitably deprive them of position and wealth and the power these assured.

Morris wrote his opinions quite frankly to John Penn: The great danger was that "lower orders of mankind," who were no better than sheep, had been aroused by their self-appointed "Shepherds" and were now "grown dangerous to the gentry." How to keep them down was the prob-

* Congregational clergymen in New England and particularly in Massachusetts played a decisive role in whipping up a spirit of resistance to the Coercive Acts, and they had little competition, for the established Church had made little headway east of the Hudson. The few Anglican priests ministered to sparse congregations in the larger towns, where many of their communicants held crown offices, or were dependent on trading connections with the mother country. Congregationalists had for long suspected the Anglicans of attempting to establish in the colonies an Episcopal see responsible to the Archbishop of Canterbury, and had spent considerable time and energy fighting those who promoted the idea, which was no longer even a remote possibility. The fact did not deter parsons from calling down hell-fire and damnation on the Established Church, and castigating the Episcopacy as an enemy of freedom and liberty.

lem; they had formed committees to correspond with other colonies; convened popular assemblies, and bullied printers; it had become impossible to curb them. The mob had begun "to think and reason. Poor reptiles! It is with them a vernal morning; they are struggling to cast off their winters slough, they bask in the sunshine, and at noon, they will bite, depend upon it. The gentry begin to fear this." Soon, unless their leaders were curbed, mobs would assume control. Then, "farewell aristocracy . . . we shall be under the worst of all possible dominions; we shall be under the domination of a riotous mob."[5]

While he and other New York oligarchs sympathized with Boston's plight and condoled with their sister city's "unexampled distress," they did not propose to do much about it. A committee of fifty-one, elected to draft a reply to Boston's plea, suggested that "a congress of deputies" from all the colonies assemble without delay to consider measures.

Paul Revere rode into Philadelphia on May 19 with copies of the Port Act and the Boston committee's circular letter in his saddlebags. The conservative citizens of Benjamin Franklin's city, never prone to act hastily, might have sat on their hands had not Charles Thomson, Joseph Reed, Thomas Mifflin, and other leaders of the more radical element forced them to action. On the following day a committee was formed, and a reply, moderate in tone, drafted. Next, the members approved a resolution that declared closure of the Port of Boston "unconstitutional," "oppressive," and "dangerous" to the liberties of the colonists, and called for a "congress of deputies" to assemble for the purpose of "re-establishing peace and harmony . . . on a constitutional foundation." A subscription was planned to help relieve the suffering inhabitants of Boston, and "a large and respectable committee" of forty-three named. Many members of this group would distinguish themselves in the cause of American independence.

News from Boston arrived in Annapolis, the capital of Maryland, on May 23; at a public meeting two days later citizens present expressed their opinion that as Boston was "suffering in the common cause of America," it was "incumbent on every colony to unite in effectual measures" to force repeal of the Port Act. They decided, therefore, "to put an immediate stop to all exports to Great Britain" and "after a short day" to cease all imports. Radicals attempted to influence the mercantile community by enjoining "gentlemen of the law" to bring no suits for recovery of debts owed to any inhabitant of Great Britain. This bit of chicanery did not appeal to honest Annapolitans.

William Eddis, a respected resident who concurrently held three fairly well paid positions, wrote his English sister-in-law on May 28: "All America is in a flame." Citizens of Annapolis had "caught the general contagion." He anticipated with horror "the most dreadful consequences." Several days later, he subscribed to a protest drawn up by "the most respectable inhabitants" disapproving a resolution that called for nonpayment of debts due English merchants. With emotions running high and tempers on edge, it would indeed have been dangerous openly to take a stand against other resolves which were "too popular . . . to admit of opposition."[6] The "iniquitous resolution," he wrote, would not have been carried had moderates "thought it safe or prudent to appear in support of their sentiments." But in Annapolis, as elsewhere, conservatives were unorganized and timorous; the radical minority disciplined, well led, and by no means averse to using intimidation and directed violence. Eddis and his friends and men and women of their station in life from Portsmouth to Savannah hoped somehow to placate this "mobility"; they earnestly believed reconciliation with Great Britain possible.

In Williamsburg, older members of the House of Burgesses were inclined to temporize, but some of their less conservative juniors were not. This group, including Patrick Henry, Richard Henry Lee, and Thomas Jefferson, decided the Burgesses "must boldly take an unequivocal stand in the line with Massachusetts," and that the most effective way to arouse their fellow Virginians "from the lethargy into which they had fallen" was a resolution designating a day for fasting and prayer. Jefferson and his colleagues "rummaged over for the revolutionary precedents . . . and cooked up a resolution," which he drew.[7] This declared that the House, filled with alarm and apprehension by the "hostile Invasion of the City of Boston," had fixed the first day of June (when the Port Act would take effect) as "a day of Fasting, Humiliation and Prayer, devoutly to implore the divine Interposition," not only to give the Virginians "one Heart and one Mind firmly to oppose . . . every Injury to *American* rights," but to inspire the King and Parliament, whose recent policy was "pregnant with Ruin," with "Wisdom, Moderation and Justice."

The Burgesses passed the resolve unanimously and ordered it printed. By the evening of May 24, expresses were galloping to Norfolk, Petersburg, Richmond, Fredericksburg, and Alexandria with copies. The royal governor, John Murray, Fourth Earl of Dunmore, read the handbills at breakfast the following morning. The clear implication that His Majesty and Parliament sadly lacked the qualities of "Wisdom, Moderation and Justice" enraged the governor and impelled him to summon the Burgesses to meet at once. This must have been the shortest session on record; his lordship, holding in hand the seditious document, dissolved the House.

The Burgesses reacted immediately; within twenty-four hours Jefferson and several others drew up a paper entitled "An Association, Signed by 89 Members of the Late House of Burgesses." Although not a call to arms, the "Association" was a summons to united political action. Not only had Great Britain disregarded "dutiful applications" for redress of grievances; her King and Parliament had also "pressed for reducing the

inhabitants of British America to slavery by subjecting them to the payment of taxes imposed without the consent of the people or their representatives." The "Associators," including Peyton Randolph, Richard
Bland, Edmund Pendleton, George Washington, Thomas Jefferson,
Richard Henry and Francis Lightfoot Lee, Patrick Henry, and Thomas
Nelson, Jr., called upon all Americans to boycott East India Company
products (except saltpeter and spices).

And as they conceived an attack on one colony an attack on all British America, they urged "the expediency of appointing deputies from the
several colonies . . . to meet in general congress." Although this was not
the first call for a congress, it was perhaps the most important, for those
who signed were respected leaders in a rich and powerful colony: well-
educated, well-to-do gentlemen versed in the law. The Virginia Committee of Correspondence met the following day and transmitted copies of
the resolve by courier to similar committees in the sister colonies.[8]

On the first day of June 1774, the Port of Boston was closed; a
week later, Gage convened the General Court at Salem. Instead of discussing measures of conciliation, as the governor had anticipated, the
House of Representatives, "deeply affected with the unhappy differences
which have long subsisted and are encreasing between Great Britain and
the American colonies," resolved that a general meeting of delegates from
all colonies was necessary "to consult upon the present state of the
Colonies and the miseries to which they are and must be reduced . . . to
deliberate and determine on wise and proper measures" to be recommended "for establishment of their rights and liberties, civil and religious, and the restoration of union and harmony between Great Britain
and the Colonies, most ardently desired by all good men."[9]

The representatives then elected James Bowdoin, Thomas Cushing,
John Adams, Samuel Adams, and Robert Treat Paine to attend a general
congress which they suggested meet in Philadelphia on the first day of
September, and directed Cushing, speaker of the House, to notify the
other colonies of the tenor of the resolves. They then proceeded to draw
up a statement assailing the ministry's plan to impose "arbitrary rule" on
America, and finally voted an embargo on all goods from Great Britain.
When news of these proceedings reached the governor, he sent an emissary to dissolve the House. His effort proved ineffectual. The legislators
had taken the precaution of locking and barring the doors. Gage's frustrated secretary nailed the governor's proclamation to the door and departed.

King George and his ministers would describe the resolutions of the
Massachusetts House and other popular colonial assemblies as seditious
and treasonable and the congress they unanimously agreed to convene as
an illegal gathering. But no colony was to give its elected delegates

specific powers other than to consult, to deliberate, and with their colleagues to formulate and recommend "prudent and lawful measures" to
obtain redress of grievances.

Captain William Evelyn of the King's Own Regiment of Foot landed
in Boston on June 10. His first letter home, written some three weeks
later, suggests that his colleagues in the Officers' Mess had thoroughly in-
doctrinated him: ". . . we have no apprehensions from the very great
number in this province. . . . for though upon paper they are the
bravest fellows in the world, yet in reality I believe there does not exist
so great a set of rascals and poltroons."[10] The Whigs—"the Liberty Boys,
the tarring and feathering gentlemen"—were responsible, he wrote, for
the disorders of "a most villainous mob." What worried Evelyn even
more than the treasonable actions of Boston Whigs was "the unsteadiness
of the English government" and "the intrigues of a disaffected faction at
home." Bostonians deserved "the scourge . . . for they are a most execrable set of villains." But he was enjoying the climate, and the regimental
mess steward was taking good care of them: "Plenty of turtle, pine-ap-
ples and Madeira."[11]

When Evelyn spoke of "the unsteadiness of the English government,"
he was undoubtedly referring to waverings of General Gage, whose esti-
mates of the political situation varied almost from week to week. Lord
North's administration *had* followed a consistent policy; one designed to
force the Bay Colony to submit. To officers in Boston, it appeared that
Gage, the designated executor, was at fault. Evelyn was on firmer ground
when he ascribed a share of the difficulties the general was encountering
to intrigues of partisan factions determined to drive Lord North's administration from the seats of power and privilege. Speeches of opposition
leaders in Lords and Commons were sent to America by fast sailers, immediately reprinted in handbills and newspapers, and discussed in every
tavern.

In June, Vice-admiral of the White Samuel Graves arrived in Boston
and assumed command of the British fleet in North American waters.
Graves had very little to work with: one fifty-gun ship, four frigates, and
sixteen sloops and schooners. He immediately asked for three ships of the
line and they were promised. The admiral's orders were not exactly precise. The nature of the command relationship between him and Gage
and his mission in support of the army was stated in ambiguous terms.
Otherwise, he was to annoy the rebellious province, awe the refractory,
restrain colonial trade, and protect friends of government. He was also to
maintain watch on the St. Lawrence, Florida, and the Bahama Islands.
Graves could not possibly have managed to carry out these orders with
twice the number of ships allotted, even had he been able to maintain

three fourths of them on station. The Admiralty had given him tasks greatly exceeding his limited capabilities, a fact that no doubt contributed to his boorish behavior and intemperate cholers. His first report to Sandwich contained the discouraging news that desertion from the troops ashore "was considerable, but more so from the Navy."

Boston was now swarming with red-coated soldiers; the 4th (King's Own) and 43rd regiments were encamped on the Common. Gage issued regulations that made passage over Boston Neck difficult. The colonists considered his behavior arbitrary and threatening, and prepared for the worst. Militia and their "minutemen" drilled daily on every village green.† After its historic session at Salem, the Assembly had moved to the more politically salubrious climate of Cambridge, where it voted itself a "Provincial Congress," passed a bill to raise a militia force of 12,000 and named Artemas Ward and Jedediah Preble "Generals."

In Massachusetts the machinery of royal government was disintegrating; Gage was beleaguered in Boston; his writs ran only as far as the tips of his soldiers' bayonets. Throughout the province law courts closed; no juries could be empaneled as no one dared accept a sheriff's summons; no writs could be served, no wills probated. In Worcester a mob of three or four thousand closed the court and forced the judges to walk, caps in hand, between ranks of armed men. Gage considered sending troops to keep the court open but had second thoughts, and reported to Dartmouth that "popular Fury was never greater in this Province than at present." Boston was the seat of the trouble; "the Demagogues" there trusted their safety "in the long Forbearance of Government." The governor wrote that the infection had spread to Connecticut, where there was great alarm "in the alteration of their charter." However, the 59th Foot had arrived from Halifax and encamped near Salem; the Welch Fusiliers were en route from New York; and Gage thought he would be able to handle the situation in Massachusetts and Connecticut. He did not "apprehend any Assistance would be given by the other colonies."[12]

The general expressed a conviction held by the ministry in London, and indeed by many Americans: that the colonies, parochial and jealous of one another, could not conceivably bring themselves to unite on any agreed course of action. Hutchinson, when chief justice of Massachusetts, had compared them to a bundle of "separated sticks" which might easily be broken, for, he said, "no two colonies think alike; there is no uniformity of measures." Events of the spring and summer of 1774 seemed to confirm his view. Virginians and Pennsylvanians were fighting in Westmoreland County in the Proprietary. Lord Dunmore's agent, an Irish adventurer named Connolly, had stirred up the Indians and taken over Fort Pitt, which he impudently renamed Fort Dunmore. All in that area was

† One fourth of each militia company were "minutemen," i.e., the best marksmen and the most agile; these were subject to immediate call.

"desolation and distress." Scores of farm families had left their homes and fled to Lancaster for safety. New York and New Hampshire were wrangling over the "Grants," those lands including the Green Mountains, the forests, and rich valleys on the eastern shore of Lake Champlain. Pennsylvania and Connecticut were at swords' points over a piece of territory within the boundaries of the former province but claimed by the Yankees because (so they alleged) their charter entitled them to a belt of land stretching to the Pacific Ocean.

Private letters from London written in early April reached New York five weeks later. One, from a London Whig to his American correspondent, was reprinted on the reverse of a widely distributed broadsheet deeply edged in mourning, which carried the text of the Boston Port Act. This was widely circulated, widely read and discussed, and generally approved, probably because its content confirmed American suspicions that Administration was plotting to destroy their liberties. The Londoner expressed his "most anxious and deep concern . . . of the bitter things that are meditated against *America*, and through her, against England herself. . . . A plan of despotism and arbitrary power has incessantly been pursued during the present reign . . . an absolute, arbitrary government has infinite charms for a multitude of haughty, luxurious parasites and flatterers, that ever surround a throne, and hope to share it in tyranizing over the people." The King and those surrounding him schemed (so the Londoner wrote) to engross all power. In his opinion, most members of the House of Commons were "corrupt ministerial tools" who voted as they were directed; he thought the Lords little better. The severe measures contemplated would not be restricted to Boston, "but depend upon it, if they succeed against Boston, the like measures will be extended to every colony in America. They only begin with Boston, hoping the other colonies will not interfere. But you are all to be visited in turn, and devoured one after another. . . . Depend upon it, every Colony is to be subdued into a slavish obedience to tyranical impositions of Great Britain. Nothing less will suffice; nothing less is intended."[13]

Scores of similar letters supporting the American position were published in Boston, Philadelphia, Baltimore, Annapolis, Charleston, and anywhere else there happened to be a Whig printer. The question of authenticity troubled neither the printers nor their readers. Flaming missives from "A Gentleman in Bristol" (or Plymouth, or Portsmouth, or London) were said to arrive in every ship, together with assorted pamphlets extolling the American stand against "despotism" and "tyranny." Some of these anonymous letters were authentic; others were probably concocted locally. Pamphlets originally published in London (where many were) and sent to the colonies were reprinted if the point of view was pro-American.

The question that cannot now be satisfactorily resolved is the degree of impact they made on the colonists. Certainly they conveyed the impression—as their publication was designed to do—that the colonial position met with considerable sympathy in the mother country. Actually at this time American optimism was ill founded, for the vast majority of people of position and influence in England were completely in favor of administration policy. The colonists were hearing one side of the story. The colonial press was not free. If a printer published anything that offended the Sons of Liberty, his press would be smashed, his type confiscated, his windows broken, his shop closed, and he and his family terrorized.

One can get today a feeling of the common emotion in the colonies during late May, June, and July 1774 by reading the voluminous files of Committees of Correspondence assembled by Peter Force. These show that letters were passing constantly, indeed almost daily, between the committee in Boston and towns in Connecticut, Rhode Island, New Hampshire, New York, Maryland, Pennsylvania, Delaware, and Virginia. Practically all the resolutions (and there were scores) asserted loyalty and allegiance to the King, castigated the designs of a corrupt ministry and a managed Parliament, and pledged assistance to Boston. In Farmington, Connecticut, a copy of the Port Act was consigned to the flames by the common hangman, and the names of ministerial "pimps and parasites who dared advise their master to such detestable measures" damned to eternity.[14]

Daily, Sam Adams talked to friends in Boston and attended secret meetings and discussions. At night he wrote letters, vigorous, spirited, and animated with his fierce zeal for colonial liberty. He saw his duty clear. With him there would be no compromise, no trimming: "We live in an important Period and have a post to maintain to desert which would be an unpardonable Crime and would entail upon us the Curses of posterity." He thought Lord North "infatuated"; the minister's malicious and tyrannical policies seemed designed to unite the colonies, and would inevitably accelerate "that Independency she so much dreads."[15] Letters went off by every post and express to Charles Thomson in Philadelphia; Silas Deane in Wethersfield, Connecticut; Richard Henry Lee in Virginia; Christopher Gadsden in South Carolina; and assorted Committees of Correspondence.

But the man his colleagues described as "the Torch of Liberty" and the Tories as "the Grand Incendiary" did not have everything his own way in Boston. A substantial segment of the community vigorously opposed the radical resolutions he maneuvered through town meetings and the Committee of Correspondence of which he was the moving spirit. On June 29, some members of the mercantile community gathered to sign a protest against the "Solemn League and Covenant" which called for an association to enforce a complete embargo on British goods. The protestors described the covenant as "a base, wicked and illegal measure, calculated to distress and ruin many merchants, shopkeepers and others in this metropolis." Such "associations" would create "unhappy divisions in towns and in families . . . and introduce almost every species of evil that we have not yet felt." The 129 citizens who signed this protest were courageous men. Few of their descendants may be found today in Massachusetts.

It was perhaps these men's misfortune that Lieutenant General Thomas Gage reacted in the same manner; he at once issued a proclamation describing the Solemn League and Covenant as an "unlawful instrument" and the circular letter that accompanied it as "scandalous, traitorous and seditious" and "calculated to inflame the minds of the people." This "unwarrantable, hostile and traitorous combination," so Gage announced, was dangerous, alarming, criminal, and unprecedented. Any persons who adhered to such an agreement might be considered "as the declared and open enemies of the King, Parliament, and Kingdom of Great Britain."[16] He called upon magistrates and other crown officers to "apprehend and secure for trial" those who joined the "illegal" association. A proclamation phrased in such threatening tenor could not possibly moderate the situation, and as Gage had no means to enforce his mandates, even in such nearby towns as Charlestown, Roxbury, and Cambridge, was worse than useless. His Majesty's general, engaged in a psychological game in which he held few cards, had drawn a distinct line between the King's loyal subjects and the refractory radical leaders and their followers, and played directly into their hands.

Donations of all sorts were now pouring into Boston; Sam Adams acknowledged them, thanked the donors, and exhorted them to organize and resist. The committee formed to distribute food to the needy was swamped; from Marblehead came cash, a barrel of olive oil, eleven cartloads of fresh-caught fish with more promised; from Farmington in Connecticut, three hundred bushels of rye and Indian corn; from South Carolina, two hundred barrels of rice; from dozens of small towns in Massachusetts and Connecticut, hundreds of bushels of grain; from Virginia, generous cash donations. To Adams and his fellow members of the Committee of Correspondence, it was "a great satisfaction . . . to find the Continent so united in opinion," so ready to support the town of Boston "now suffering for the common liberties of America."[17] But the continent was by no means "united in opinion." New York, New Jersey, Pennsylvania, and the Lower Counties upon Delaware did not respond to pleas from Boston with the spontaneity and generosity their sisters to the north and south had done. Thirteen colonies "united in opinion" was Sam Adams's dream. It was, as yet, a dream.

In early July Boston conservatives confronted radicals at a town meeting. Some shippers, merchants, and factors wanted to pay the East India Company for the tea and get the port opened; radicals would have no such cowardly backsliding. But Gage was optimistic that the force he had in hand—six regiments, something over 3,000 officers and men— would awe the Bostonians. He wrote Dartmouth there was now "open opposition" to the rebellious faction that he would "cherish and support" those who were loyal and obedient.

Arrival of the 5th and 38th regiments did not abate the unrest. Rather, the augmented Redcoat presence raised the temperature, and not only in Massachusetts. To the south, colonies began to seethe. Opposition gained adherents; town meetings and ad hoc gatherings drew up countless resolutions; radical journalists and pamphleteers flayed the ministry unceasingly. One American wrote he would heartily join in "a humble and dutiful petition to the throne, provided there was the most distant hope of success. But have we not tried this already? Have we not addressed the Lords and remonstrated to the Commons? And to what end? Did they deign to look at our petitions? Does it not appear, as clear as the sun in its meridian brightness, that there is a regular, systematic plan formed to fix the right and practice of taxation upon us? Does not the uniform conduct of Parliament for some years past confirm this? . . . Is there anything to be expected from petitioning after this? Is not the attack upon the liberty and property of the people of Boston before restitution of the loss of the India Company was demanded, a plain and self-evident proof of what they are aiming at? Do not the subsequent bills (now I dare say acts), for depriving the Massachusetts Bay of its charter . . . convince us that the administration is determined to stop at nothing to carry its point? Ought we not, then, to put our virtue and fortitude to the severest test?"

Several weeks later the same gentleman wrote his opinion that conduct of the Bostonians could not justify the rigor of the measures taken. As there was no necessity for the series of oppressive acts, they constituted "self-evident proofs of a fixed and uniform plan" to levy internal taxes on the colonies. Gage was behaving more like a "Turkish bashaw" than an English governor. Had not his conduct since arriving in Boston "exhibited an unexampled testimony of the most despotic system of tyranny, that was ever practised in a free government?" The author of these words was not a revolutionary pamphleteer, but George Washington.[18]

Shortly after he wrote the letters in which he expressed his sentiments so clearly and his determination to resist so emphatically, Washington met with George Mason and other prominent "Freeholders and Inhabitants" of Fairfax County at the courthouse in Alexandria, Virginia, where on July 18 they drew up the celebrated "Fairfax County Resolutions." They are of singular importance, for the political philosophy expressed in them was to have a profound effect in shaping American thought during the next two increasingly tumultuous years.

The signers first asserted that their ancestors who settled Virginia brought with them the civil constitution and form of government of England; that their rights under these had been confirmed by royal charter; and that they were by the laws of nature and of nations entitled to all "the priveleges, immunities and advantages" enjoyed by His Majesty's subjects who lived within his realm.

The second article is worth quoting in full:

> Resolved, That the most important and valuable part of the *British* Constitution, upon which its very existence depends, is the fundamental principle of the people's being governed by no laws to which they have not given their consent by Representatives, freely chosen by themselves, who are affected by the laws they enact equally with their constituents, to whom they are accountable, and whose burthens they share, in which consists the safety and happiness of the community; for if this part of the Constitution was taken away, or materially altered, the Government must degenerate into an absolute and despotick monarchy, or a tyrannical aristocracy, and the freedom of the people be annihilated.[19]

As Americans could not be represented in the British Parliament, it followed that Parliament could enact no laws governing them except such as regulated trade. These, their ancestors had obeyed, as they would continue to do. But Parliament's assumption of the right to make laws to govern the people of the colonies, and particularly to extort money from them in the form of taxation without their consent, was "diametrically contrary" to the first principles of the revered British Constitution: ". . . totally incompatible with the privileges of a free people and the natural rights of mankind, will render our own Legislatures merely Nominal and nugatory, and is calculated to return us from a state of freedom and happiness to slavery and misery."[20] These resolves were widely circulated and generally approved. Thousands of Americans soon to be known as "Patriots" adhered to the covenant. Others refused to do so. Their lot would become increasingly difficult and finally intolerable.

℀ 3

Blows Must Decide

Parliament rose after hearing an address from the King on June 22. Toward the end of the month, ex-Governor Hutchinson arrived in the capital; on the first day of July Lord Dartmouth escorted him to St. James's Palace where His Majesty received them in the Closet. Later that day, Hutchinson made a diary record of the interview. The King was much interested in the leaders of the rebellious Bostonians: the Adams cousins, Dr. Benjamin Church, Warren, Bowdoin, Cushing. Hutchinson described Samuel Adams as having "a great pretended zeal for liberty, and a most inflexible natural temper." He told the King the Port Act had arrived in Boston just before he left, and was "extremely alarming to the people."

His Majesty did not pursue the subject; he seemed more anxious to discuss the attitude of the Dissenting (Congregational) clergy. He then asked about appointments to the Provincial Council. Hutchinson replied the people would find the appointment of Episcopalians "disagreeable." The King questioned his ex-governor acutely on such matters as population increase, immigration, and agriculture, in which he evinced particular interest. Writing to Gage several days later, Hutchinson observed that the King's knowledge of so many facts astonished him. In this protracted interview there was no discussion of the state of public feeling in the Bay

1. George Washington: "The Atlas of America and the God of the Army"

2. King George III

3. Earl of Bute

4. William Pitt, Earl of Chatham

5. Lord Grenville

6. Frederick Guilford, Lord North

7. John Montagu, Earl of Sandwich

8. Lord George Germain

9. William Legge, Earl of Dartmouth

10. Earl of Shelburne

11. John Wilkes

12. Marquis of Rockingham

14. Edmund Burke

13. Charles James Fox

15. Lieutenant General Thomas Gage   16. General Sir William Howe, K.B.

17. General Sir Henry Clinton, K.B.

18. Vice-admiral Viscount Richard Howe

19. Lieutenant General the Honourable John Burgoyne

20. Major General Sir Guy Carleton, K.B.

Colony, although Hutchinson was well aware that most of his fellow citizens would resist, and with arms if necessary, abrogation of political rights their ancestors had enjoyed and which they considered inviolable.

In a note to Lord North, the King told him he had received Hutchinson, who "ownes the Boston Port Bill was the only wise and effectual method that could have been suggested for bringing them to a speedy submission, and that the change in the legislature will be a means of establishing some government in that province which till now has been one of anarchy."[1] Hutchinson never admitted that he had made such statements. In the long letter he wrote to Gage, giving details of the interview, he said: "In the course of conversation, the King asked me how the late Acts of Parliament were received at Boston? I answered that when I left Boston I had heard only of one, that for shutting of the Port, which was to take place the day I came away! That I had heard, since my arrival, that another act had been passed, which I had not seen, nor had I been able to obtain a particular account of it. That the first act was exceedingly severe, I did not presume to say. . . ."[2]* This statement seems conclusively to rule out the possibility of a royal misunderstanding and suggests that the King was deceiving his First Minister, which Lord North no doubt discovered during his private interview with Hutchinson. The King was not averse to calculated deceit if it served to strengthen Lord North's determination.

The detailed communiqués Gage dispatched to Lord Dartmouth with commendable regularity made little impression on the King, whose correspondence with Lord North during June, July, and August indicates that he was more interested in doling out sinecures and pensions to the deserving than in the state of affairs in America. Early in September he received an address from Philadelphia Quakers asserting their loyalty to the throne but sadly "omitting declaration of their submission to the mother-country, . . . the dye is now cast, the Colonies must either submit or triumph. I do not wish to come to severer measures, but we must not retreat. By coolness and unremitted pursuit of the measures that have been adopted I trust they will come to submit."[3] "Submit" was the King's favorite verb.

The statesman who had created the empire George III had inherited, and who desired above all else to preserve it, was more flexible than his royal master, and toward the end of August, Chatham, sequestered at Hayes by a debilitating attack of gout, sent for Franklin. The doctor, who had never met this "truly great man," was escorted to Hayes by Lord Stanhope. The earl received him "with abundant civility . . . enquired particularly into the situation of affairs in America . . . and expressed great regard and esteem for the people of that country." Franklin

---

* He was now wholly dependent on the royal bounty and could not afford to express an opinion so diametrically opposed to the King's.

"lamented the ruin which seemed inpending" and hoped that "if his Lordship, with the other great and wise men of the British nation would unite and exert themselves," the empire might yet "be rescued out of the mangling hands of the present set of blundering ministers" and "union and harmony" restored.

Chatham agreed he earnestly desired harmonious relations, but expressed fear the colonies sought "an independent state." Franklin assured him this was not the case, "that having more than once travelled almost from one end of the continent to the other, and kept a great variety of company, eating, drinking, and conversing with them freely, I never had heard in any conversation from any person, drunk or sober, the least expression of a wish for separation." The earl was delighted to hear this. What the dissembling doctor neglected to tell his host was that he had done his extensive traveling in the colonies some years earlier. Franklin's statement reflected attitudes prevalent in that happier time, and he must have considered it justified if it served to gain the earl's support. The agreeable visit terminated with an exchange of compliments and an invitation to the doctor to visit Hayes again. Franklin was "very sensible of the honor" and assured his lordship that he ". . . should reap great advantages and improvement from his instructive conversation."[4]

Horace Walpole spent early September at Strawberry Hill indulging himself in pessimistic ruminations, "almost desponding of the liberty of this country, from the abandoned profligacy and indifference of every higher order of men, and from the great strides which the Court, grown presumptuous on such passive obedience, had lately taken. I saw no chance of a free spirit arising, unless in America, and the accounts from thence did not make me sanguine."[5]

Knox's friend Henry Ellis had forsaken the Côte d'Azur for Spa, where he was "employing every method" for the preservation of his health. Life at this watering place was pleasant; the tables at the *hôtels* of the Prince de Guéménée and the Bishop of Narbonne left nothing to be desired. The only cloud on Ellis's horizon was far across the Atlantic: "I wish the Bostonians were at the D—L, for they are likely to be a continuous plague to us. I have, however, no apprehensions from their power, nor yet from their courage. We know their weakness as well as their want of bravery. I think no measures could be better calculated to bring them to reason than those adopted by Government."†

About this time the King and his First Minister were planning to dissolve Parliament on October 1 and issue Writs of Election for a new one to assemble on November 29. His Majesty hoped the election would "fill the House with more gentlemen of landed property." This was the group he could count on to support his American policy. Walpole learned on

† The Coercive Acts. Letters from Ellis to Knox in William Knox Papers, William L. Clements Library.

September 27 of the secret decision. He did not doubt his intelligence, and thought the reasons were: "1st. Very arbitrary measures to be taken against America. 2nd. The pressing cry of the King's debts. . . . 3rd. A probability of war with France. . . ."[6] Walpole wrote Sir Horace Mann that the new Parliament "must be wiser than any of its predecessors if it can remedy what the last two of them have done. In short, all North America is in a flame, and I don't see whatever the future measures shall be, but they will be new barrels of oil."[7]

Dr. Samuel Johnson's pamphlet "The Patriot" had recently been published. Walpole described the eminent lexicographer, whose violent anti-American tendencies were well known, as a "venal champion of the Court" who, "according to the practice of renegades," was "most virulent." Dr. Shebbeare, another pensioned writer, also wielded a poisoned pen; Walpole described his piece, which called for the proscription of "all lovers of liberty and the Constitution . . . and the Americans," one of the most "outrageous and profligate libels" ever penned.[8]

The idea that a congress of delegates from all colonies must soon assemble to define their rights, discuss common grievances, and seek means of redress speedily gained momentum during an exciting summer. No one individual or particular group may be given credit for the concept; the seed had been germinating for more than a year, and Franklin had been assiduously cultivating it from London. Indeed, in July 1773, he had written Thomas Cushing: "the strength of an empire depends not only on the *union* of its parts, but on their *readiness* for united exertion of their common force." In this letter Franklin hinted his opinion—soon to become a conviction—that war between Britain and her American colonies was a possibility, and urged that a "GENERAL CONGRESS" assemble without delay to make "a full and solemn *assertion and declaration of their* RIGHTS. . . . Such a step, I imagine, will bring the dispute to a crisis." And if it did, "all the world will allow that our proceeding has been honorable."[9]

By August, the colonies had agreed a general congress would convene in Philadelphia on Monday, September 5, 1774, and during the month there was much political activity as delegates were chosen. Those from Massachusetts—John and Samuel Adams, Thomas Cushing, John Hancock, and Robert Treat Paine—left Boston on August 10 in great style.‡ The entourage, accompanied by many mounted well-wishers, drove by the Common, where Gage's Redcoat regiments were encamped, "being in a coach and four, preceded by two white servants well mounted and armed, with four blacks behind in livery, two on horseback and two footmen."[10] Gage must have been tempted to arrest them, put them aboard

‡ James Bowdoin was elected, but was ill, and did not go to Philadelphia.

a ship, and send them off to Halifax. A general with more courage might have done so.

John Adams reported his arrival in Philadelphia on August 29 "dirty, dusty and fatigued." The trip from Boston had been a triumphant progress. The Massachusetts delegates were met outside the city by a distinguished company and Adams was escorted to "the most genteel tavern in America" to refresh himself. The following day he was introduced to a number of Philadelphians, including Charles Thomson, whom he described as the "Sam Adams of Philadelphia, the life of the cause of liberty." On Saturday he met Richard Henry Lee of the Virginia delegation, who announced his position for repeal of all revenue laws, the four "Intolerable Acts," and the Quebec Act. "He thinks we should inform His Majesty that we can never be happy while Lords Bute, Mansfield and North are his confidants and counsellors."[11] Adams passed that sticky afternoon in William Barrell's cool store, where he "drank punch and eat dried smoked sprats."

Silas Deane, from Connecticut, was in town, too, and wrote his wife the city was "full of people from abroad" and all the lodgings "full or taken up." On Saturday, Deane met the Virginians, and was impressed, as indeed he should have been, for the delegates from the Old Dominion were Richard Bland, Benjamin Harrison, Patrick Henry, Thomas Jefferson, Edmund Pendleton, Peyton Randolph, and George Washington. All appeared to be "men of importance . . . sociable, sensible and spirited." Everyone, Deane wrote, was "in high spirits, if it is possible to be really so when the eyes of millions are upon us, and who consider themselves and their posterity interested in our conduct." Deane was impressed by the spirit of unanimity that prevailed as the delegates prepared to face the task before them, "as arduous and of as great consequence as ever man undertook and engaged in."

Philadelphia was festive; bells rang all day Saturday to welcome those riding or posting in from North and South Carolina, Massachusetts, New Hampshire, Rhode Island, Connecticut, Virginia, New Jersey, New York, Delaware, and Maryland. That night the city served an elegant supper. Richard Henry Lee had been drinking burgundy all afternoon. His sentiments were "very high" (i.e., radical). He would not allow Lord North to have great abilities; "he had seen no symptoms of them; his whole administration had been blunder." As for the Opposition, Lee dismissed it as hopeless: "feeble and incompetent." Much wine was consumed, and after the cloth was drawn, many "sentiments" were proposed, among them a toast to which all responded with cheers: "A constitutional death to the Lords Bute, Mansfield and North."**

Still, the evening before the delegates met for the first time, Joseph

---

** Lord Bute had long since suffered his "constitutional death."

Galloway, a rich and influential Pennsylvania conservative, was able to write his young friend William Franklin, illegitimate son of the celebrated doctor and royal governor of New Jersey, that his colleagues were moderate men, fully aware of "all the consequences which may attend rash and imprudent measures."

On the following morning, the delegates assembled at Smith's Tavern and walked to Carpenters' Hall, which by a majority vote they deemed "suitably commodious." They wasted no time getting down to business. Peyton Randolph was elected to the chair with the "stile" of president. Randolph seemed "designed by nature" for the office: "Of an affable, open and majestic deportment, large in size, though not out of proportion," he commanded "respect and esteem." Charles Thomson of Philadelphia, "a gentleman of Family, Fortune and Character," was elected secretary. Delegates read their commissions, and Randolph called the Congress to order. A delegate from New York immediately rose to move that a committee be appointed to draw up rules for procedure. Edward Rutledge of South Carolina averred that this would be "a waste of time . . . every gentleman [is] acquainted with the usage of the House of Commons."

The all-important question of how the colonies were to vote, one much debated during the preceding week at coffeehouses and taverns over breakfasts, dinners, and suppers, would arise the following day, and that night John Adams committed his thoughts to his diary:

> If we vote by colonies, this method will be liable to great inequality and injustice, for five small colonies with one hundred thousand people in each may outvote four large ones each of five hundred thousand inhabitants. If we vote by the poll, some colonies have more than their proportion of members, and others have less. If we vote by interests, it will be attended by insuperable difficulties to ascertain the true importance of each colony. Is the weight of a colony to be ascertained by the number of inhabitants merely, or by the amount of their trade, the quality of their exports and imports, or by any compound ratio of both? This will lead us into such a field of controversy as will greatly perplex us.[12]

Delegates assembled on Tuesday morning to debate this perplexing question. Patrick Henry urged that votes be weighted in accordance with the number of inhabitants in a colony; its opulence; the volume of its exports and imports. This would have required statistical data that did not exist and could not possibly be collected. After much discussion, Henry rose to retract his motion and to declare that the colonies were now "in a state of nature"; that government "was dissolved" and that no distinction between colonies existed. He closed this speech with an explosive statement: "I am not a Virginian, but an American." This proud declaration induced the delegates to stop haggling and to resolve unanimously that each colony would have one vote.

Having settled this, Congress considered a proposal that the proceedings of the morrow be opened with a prayer. As there were several deists and agnostics among those present, to say nothing of Congregationalists, Presbyterians, Anglicans, and Baptists, this might have posed a problem. The knot was cut by Samuel Adams who proposed that the Reverend Jacob Duché, a local Anglican priest, handle the situation. On Wednesday Mr. Duché did so, and in commendably eloquent fashion. He read the Psalter for the seventh day (Psalm 35), which begins:

> Plead thou my cause, O Lord, with them that strive with me: and fight thou against them that fight against me.
> Lay hand upon the shield and buckler: and stand up to help me.
> Bring forth the spear, and stop the way against them that persecute me: say unto my soul, I am thy salvation.

and then delivered a prayer "worth riding a hundred miles to hear."

After a week of close association both in Carpenters' Hall and "out of doors," delegates were beginning to assess one another, and the inevitable polarization of radicals and moderates was taking shape. This was not specifically sectional. Silas Deane wrote his wife that Christopher Gadsden of South Carolina left all New England Sons of Liberty far behind, "for he is for taking up his firelock and marching direct to Boston." The Rutledge brothers, John and Edward, were equally zealous in the cause of liberty. And John Adams wrote Abigail: "There is in the Congress a collection of the greatest men upon this continent in point of ability, virtues and fortunes. The magnanimity and public spirit which I see here make me blush for the sordid, venal herd which I have seen in my own Province!"

Silas Deane provides sketches of Washington and Patrick Henry: "Col. Washington is nearly as tall as Col. Fitch [Washington stood over six feet] and almost as hard a countenance; yet with a very young look, and an easy soldier-like air and gesture." He was "a tolerable speaker in public . . . who speaks very modestly and in cool but determined style and accent." Patrick Henry was "the completest speaker" Deane had ever heard, with a musical voice and an easy eloquent style. "Colonel Lee is said to be his rival in eloquence and in Virginia and to the southward they are styled the *Demosthenes* and *Cicero* of America. God grant they may not, like them, plead in vain for the Liberties of their Country."[13]

John Adams found "Young Rutledge" from South Carolina "sprightly but not deep. He has the most indistinct, inarticulate way of speaking. Speaks through his nose." Caesar Rodney, from Delaware, "is the oddest looking man in the World—quite tall, thin and slender as a reed—pale—

his face is not bigger than a large apple, yet there is sense and fire, spirit, wit and humour in his countenance." Dickinson, the "Pennsylvania Farmer," was "a shadow," "pale and ashen," and also "slender as a reed."[14]

Delegates had slowly become aware their proceedings were the focus of attention from Boston to Savannah, and that the thirteen colonies huddled along the Atlantic seaboard were but the eastern fringe of a vast continent stretching interminably west, past the Alleghenies, past the confluence of the great rivers at Fort Pitt to the Mississippi—and far beyond. Patrick Henry's avowal had awakened them. They were beginning to realize they were Americans—a different breed. They professed themselves to be "His Majesty's dutiful and loyal subjects," but in the phraseology of the Virginia Convention, they thought it "an indispensable duty which we owe to our country, ourselves, and latest posterity" to guard against "such dangerous and extensive mischiefs" as the "Intolerable Acts."

Congress appointed two committees, one to define the rights of the colonists, to list "the several instances in which these rights are violated or infringed," and to recommend means of redress; the other to "take a view of all those acts of the British Parliament which affect our Trade and Manufactures." John Adams was a member of the first, which on September 9 "agreed to found our rights upon the laws of Nature, the principles of the English Constitution, and charters and compacts; [and] ordered a Sub-Committee to draw up a Statement of Rights."††

The Congress moved tediously, but it did move—"slow as snails," John wrote Abigail. At this time there was no evident inclination for separation from Great Britain, nor were any attacks made on the King. The more radical delegates reserved their venom for Lord North and his colleagues, and that was rarely expressed on the floor, where deliberations proceeded with decorum. Most members would have agreed with James Duane of New York that "the great object of this Congress" should be "a firm Union between the Parent State and her Colonies."

Much business was done "out of doors"—before and during dinner, and after the cloth was drawn when decanters of port and madeira began to circulate. John wrote Abigail the pace was wearing: "I shall be killed with kindness in this place. We go to Congress at nine and there we stay, most earnestly engaged in debates upon the most abstruse mysteries of state until three in the afternoon; then we adjourn and feast upon ten thousand delicacies, and sit drinking Madeira, Claret, and Burgundy till six or seven and then go home fatigued to death with business, company and care. Yet I hold it out surprisingly." He was thirty-nine years old, and despite his occasional grumbling he was obviously enjoy-

†† It appears that John Rutledge and Samuel Ward were other members of this subcommittee.

ing it all. John's complaints of the tedium of business and the "perpetual round of feasting" were unlikely to have made much of an impression on his "Portia."‡‡

Shortly after he left her, Abigail wrote she longed to have him "on the stage of action." Braintree was quiet; "Portia" found time for reading and reflection. She doubted that any state, deprived of its liberties, could regain them without bloodshed, and quoted Polybius to the effect that nothing was more shameful and pernicious than peace "purchased at the price of Liberty." A week later she wrote that Boston was the scene of "perturbation, anxiety and distress." Why had she not heard from him? Mr. Sam Adams had written his son and Mr. Cushing his lady. Colonel Brattle's behavior had enraged and exasperated the people, who would expend their accumulated wrath upon him could they but lay hands on him. He had fled "not only to Boston, but into the camp for safety." The drought was severe; the cows were not giving the milk they should.

There may have been a shortage of liquid refreshment in Braintree, but there was plenty in Philadelphia. If the entertainment the "Honourable Delegates" enjoyed on September 16 is a criterion, John had some reason to be "fatigued to death," and, as well, to be occasionally inebriated. At three that afternoon they assembled at the City Tavern, where they took a few glasses, and then proceeded to the State House where they were received by their hosts, "the gentlemen of Philadelphia" and a very large company composed of "the Clergy, such genteel strangers as happened to be in Town, and a number of respectable citizens, making the whole near five hundred." Unfortunately this particular menu is not preserved, but after dinner thirty-two toasts were offered, beginning with "The King," "The Queen," and "The Duke of Gloucester," and ending with "General Conway," "Doctor Franklin," and "Mr. Hancock." Halfway along this alcoholic trail the delegates drank to: "May the Cloud which hangs over *Great Britain* and the colonies bust only on the heads of the present Ministry," and "May no man enjoy freedom who has not the spirit to defend it." Lord Chatham, the Marquis of Rockingham, John Wilkes, Mr. Burke, and the City of London were not forgotten.*

On the following morning the delegates, some probably suffering the affliction now described as a hangover, met to consider the resolves forwarded for their approbation by Suffolk County, Massachusetts. The preamble, a flaming attack on "a licentious Minister" who, dagger in hand, proposed to impose his arbitrary will, was followed by an appeal to patriots to resist this "parracide" and his tyrannous edicts so that posterity would acknowledge their virtue and "the torrent of panegyrists

‡‡ She signed many of her letters to him "Portia."
* In his diary for September 8, Adams records "a most sinful feast again!" this time at Mr. Powell's. "Everything which could delight the eye or allure the taste . . . creams, jellies, sweet meats of various sorts, 20 sorts of tarts, fools, trifles, floating island, whipped Sillabubs, etc., Parmesan cheese, punch, wine, porter, beer, etc., etc."

will roll our reputation to that latest period when the stream of time shall be absorbed in the abyss of eternity." The tenor of the nineteen resolutions was totally uncompromising and violently aggressive. The King was indeed acknowledged as "rightful Sovereign" to whom allegiance was owed, but in the next breath appeared a direct challenge to this sovereignty: "That no obedience is due from this Province . . . to the Acts above mentioned [the Coercive Acts] . . . [and] that they be rejected as the attempts of a wicked Administration to enslave America." Those who publicly supported the acts and had accepted membership on General Gage's hand-picked council were designated as "obstinate and incorrigible enemies of America."[15]

The citizens of Suffolk County ardently desired "harmony and union" but not until Gage and his throng of "military executioners" were withdrawn from Boston and the "wicked and oppressive measures" of Lord North's administration repealed. While awaiting these happy events, they would "withhold all commercial intercourse with Great Britain, Ireland, and the West Indies"; elect a Provincial Congress; embark on a full-scale campaign of civil disobedience to all edicts or orders given by law officers holding crown appointments, and purge the militia of officers named by Hutchinson or his successor.†[16] After protracted secret debate, the delegates unanimously approved the Suffolk Resolves.

By the end of September, Congress had been in session for four weeks, and delegates who ate, drank, talked, and worked daily with one another had formed opinions of the capabilities and temperaments of their colleagues. On September 29, John Adams wrote a friend that never had the world seen such an assembly as that gathered in Philadelphia: "Here are fortune, abilities, learning, eloquence, acuteness, equal to any I have ever met with in my life. Here is a diversity of religions, educations, manners, interests, such as it would seem almost impossible to unite in one plan of conduct. Each question is discussed with a moderation, an acuteness and a minuteness equal to that of Queen Elizabeth's privy council." To him, debates over minutiae seemed interminable, but he was aware of the necessity for them. Despite the high opinion he had expressed of the attainments of his colleagues, he warned his Massachusetts friends not to count on any immediate help from the Congress.[17]

The moderates, he reported, were "fixed against hostilities and rupture except they should become absolutely necessary, and this necessity they do not yet see. They dread the thought of an action, because it would make a wound which would never be healed; it would fix and establish a rancor which would descend to the latest generations; it would render all hopes of a reconciliation with Great Britain desperate; it would light up the flames of war, perhaps through the whole continent,

† The militia had already been purged.

that might rage for twenty years, and end in the subduction of America as likely as in her liberation."[18]

But even moderates agreed that some of Gage's activities were unnecessarily provocative, and on October 11 Congress addressed a letter to the general charging him with attempting to precipitate armed conflict by fortifying the town of Boston, cutting its communication with the hinterland, and allowing his troops to inflict assorted "Indignities" upon the peace-loving citizens: "These Enormities committed by a standing Army, in our opinion unlawfully posted there in time of Peace, are irritating in the greatest Degree, and if not remedied, will endanger the involving all America in the Horrors of a civil War! Your Situation Sir is extremely critical." Far more critical than the governor seemed to realize.

A few days later Samuel Adams wrote Thomas Young in Boston that he had advised "our Friends to provide themselves without Delay with Arms & Ammunition, get well instructed in the military Art, embody themselves & prepare a complete Set of Rules that they may be ready in case they are called to defend themselves against the violent Attacks of Despotism." The "Grand Incendiary" was determined that America would not lie "prostrate" at the feet of an iniquitous minister.

On October 14 Congress approved by unanimous vote a document entitled "Declarations and Resolves." In this, the delegates set forth the "Rights" of the inhabitants of the colonies of Great Britain in North America. These "Rights" derived from "the immutable laws of nature, the principles of the English constitution," and "the several charters and compacts," and included:

(1) the exclusive right to dispose of their own lives, liberty and property,
(2) enjoyment of all the freedom and immunities of natural-born Englishmen,
(3) the right to participate in their own legislative councils,
(4) the right to trial by jury of their "peers of the vicinage," and
(5) the right "peaceably to assemble" to consider their grievances, and to petition the King.

The Congress resolved also that "the keeping a standing army in these colonies, in times of peace, without the consent" of the legislature concerned was illegal, and appointments made by the King to provincial councils unconstitutional, dangerous, and destructive of freedom in America. Congress then listed the acts deemed to be in direct violation of the colonists' constitutional rights and finally resolved unanimously that:

1. Effective the first day of December 1774, there was to be no importation into British America, from Great Britain or Ireland, "of any goods, wares or merchandize whatsoever."

2. The colonies would forthwith enter into nonimportation, nonconsumption, and nonexportation associations.

3. Addresses to the people of Great Britain and the Province of Quebec, and a memorial to the inhabitants of British America would be prepared.

4. A loyal address to His Majesty would be drawn.

As Silas Deane had written, "the eyes of millions" were on Philadelphia. All America, rich and poor, high and lowly, merchants and bankers, tradesmen, "mechanicks," farmers, and ministers of the Gospel alike awaited the result of the deliberations in Philadelphia "with the utmost impatience."

Sons of Liberty, who planned and directed mob violence, were not given to waiting. On October 15, these "frantic zealots," on discovering that the brig *Peggy Stewart* had arrived in Annapolis with 2,320 pounds of tea aboard, determined to take action; they forced the owner of the brig and the importers publicly to admit they had "committed a most daring insult" and an "act of the most pernicious tendency" to American liberties by importing "the detestable article" which, under duress, the consignees promised to consign to the flames. The ship's owners were ordered to run her aground and burn her to the water's edge.

John Adams's "best friend" wrote him from Braintree in mid-October that she had spent many anxious hours since he drove off to Philadelphia: "the threatening aspect of our public affairs, the complicated distress of this province, the anxious and perplexed business in which you are engaged have all conspired to agitate my bosom with fear and apprehensions." She thought the curtain was just being drawn; "only the first scene of the infernal plot disclosed." She despaired of the ostentation still exhibited by ladies and gentlemen in their dress and ornamentation. As for herself, she would encourage simplicity: "I will seek wool and flax, and work willingly with my hands; and, indeed, there is occasion for all our industry and economy."[19] In these trying times "Portia" provided constant loyal and thoughtful support to John.‡

In Philadelphia, he and others, working in committees, prepared drafts of the addresses and memorials and a "Humble Petition" to the King. The latter recited the manifold grievances suffered by the colonies, including the stationing of a standing army without the consent of provincial legislatures; the multiplication of "new, oppressive and expensive offices"; and the "injurious" dissolution of duly elected colonial assemblies. These and a variety of other afflictions had caused His Majesty's loyal subjects to "fly to the foot of his Throne and implore his clemency for protection against them." The delegates asserted their loyalty in the most solemn terms: "We ask but for Peace, Liberty and

‡ Abigail was an accomplished woman, but could not make pins, and asked John to send her some of the best imported variety.

Safety. We wish not a diminution of the prerogative, nor do we solicit the grant of any new right in our favour. Your Royal authority over us, and our connection with *Great Britain,* we shall always carefully and zealously endeavour to support and maintain."[20] This appeal, couched in temperate language, was sent off on October 26. Copies for all colonial agents were sent at the same time to Dr. Franklin.

Several days later, delegates met at the City Tavern, where the House of Representatives of the Province of Pennsylvania afforded "a most elegant entertainment." Among the sentiments offered was "May the sword of the parent never be stained with the blood of her children." In this mood the First Continental Congress broke up; by the last day of October, delegates were bound to their homes, some few, perhaps, optimistic that before they were to gather again in early May 1775 the break with the mother country would be healed.

But, in fact, the radicals had won; the course was set. Galloway's plan for political union with Great Britain, defeated by only one vote, had been irrevocably lost. Radicals saw to it that the motion, and the vote on it, were expunged from the Journals of Congress. So early did our forefathers begin to rewrite American history.

The nonimportation resolves and creation of associations to enforce them constituted a clear declaration of enmity to Parliament's measures, an equally clear determination to nullify them, and a direct constitutional challenge that neither the ministry nor its subservient Parliament could possibly avoid. The "Loyal Address" was thrown in as a sop to the conservatives. As Governor George Johnstone had earlier predicted, the Coercive Acts had "raised a general confederacy." Although the Americans, still parochial, did not realize it at the time, the resolutions taken by the Continental Congress marked a momentous historical watershed. For there in Philadelphia the first seeds of a distinctive American nationalism germinated.

In mid-September Gage wrote Dartmouth that "the Country People are exercising in Arms in this Province, Connecticut, and Rhode Island, and getting Magazines of Arms and Ammunition in the Country, and such Artillery as they can procure good and bad. They threaten to attack the troops in Boston."[21] The general reported that since his arrival he had done all he could do to get government on a firm footing and enforce the laws. But "the arrival of the late Acts overset the whole and the Flame burst out in all parts at once beyond the Conception of every Body." The disease was "so universal there is no knowing Where to apply a Remedy."[22]

Gage was now attempting to build barracks to house his troops, but there was little progress; gangs were "burning the Straw and sinking Boats with Bricks . . . and overturning the Wood Carts." He kept his troops in hand. But more, many more, were needed. Carleton embarked the 10th and 52nd regiments at Quebec; the 47th was en route from New York. Several days after Congress adjourned, Gage wrote a long letter to the Secretary of State. He was, he said, "not a little chagrinned that my Endeavours to serve His Majesty have not met with better success," but

> Nobody here or at home could have conceived, that the Acts, made for the Massachusetts Bay, could have created such a Ferment throughout the Continent, and united the whole into one common Cause, or that the Country People could have been raised to such a pitch of Phrenzy. . . .[23]

And, he went on,

> If Force is to be used at length, it must be a considerable one, and Foreign Troops must be hired, for to begin with Small Numbers will encourage Resistance, and not terrify, and will in the End cost more Blood and Treasure.

In an earlier private letter to Lord Barrington, Secretary at War and a personal friend, Gage had been more direct.** After reporting that nothing was going on "but Preparations for War and Threats to take Arms . . . and to overwhelm us with forty or fifty Thousand Men," the general made a specific recommendation: ". . . if you would get the better of America in all your Disputes, you must conquer her, and to do that effectually, to prevent further Bickerings, you should have an Army near twenty Thousand Strong composed of Regulars, a large Body of good Irregulars, such as the German Huntsmen, picked Canadians, etc, and three or four Regiments of Light Horse, these exclusive of a good and sufficient Field Artillery."[24] Here Gage showed his appreciation that if war came—and the tenor of the letter suggests he thought it inevitable—a powerful balanced force would be required. His mention of "irregulars" including Jägers (who were armed with rifled guns) and Canadians suggests he was not quite the military conservative habitually pictured.††

On chilly October nights most British troops in Boston were still under canvas on the Common. "The good people of this place have done everything in their power to prevent our getting quarters, and to distress us by forbidding all labourers and artificers to work for us; by hindering the merchants to supply us with blankets, tools, or materials of any kind, by burning the straw provided in the country for the troops [for bedding] and threatening to stop all provisions coming to the market." But this type of resistance was not entirely effectual: ". . . money (for which

---

** Correspondence marked "Private" was not published in *The Gazette*.

†† Gage had in fact organized the first light infantry regiment in the British Army in 1757–58. The regiment (the 80th) was disbanded in 1763.

these holy men would sell the Kingdom of Heaven) defeats their charita-
ble intentions."[25] And it did; the King's guineas could buy anything
officers or their men wanted, including female favors.

In late October, the 10th and 52nd arrived from Canada, and Major
General Frederick Haldimand, with the 42nd and part of the 18th, came
in from New York. The 65th was en route from Halifax. Boston was
swamped with Redcoats. The more radical citizens did everything conceivable to annoy, insult, and harass the troops short of actually attacking them; terrorists apparently threatened to assassinate senior British
officers. Gage's younger officers were panting for action; to them it
seemed absurd to continue "to suffer the treason and rebellion of these
villians to go unpunished." Their only fear was that the colonists would
"avail themselves of the clemency and generosity of the English, and by
some abject submission evade the chastisement due to unexampled villainy, and which we are so impatiently waiting to inflict."[26]

By November the entire province was in arms; "This whole country is
in a state of actual open rebellion; there is not a man from sixteen to
sixty, nay, to a hundred years old, who is not armed and obliged to attend at stated times to train."[27] Treason and naked rebellion were not
confined to Massachusetts, or even New England. In the middle and
southern colonies men were arming, militia units forming, powder and
ball ammunition being collected and hidden.

Gage reported in early November that the Continental Congress held
in Philadelphia "will not have come to such determinations as you will
approve of at home. In Massachusetts "the Chiefs seem to me to want to
push Matters as far as they can." Both Massachusetts and Connecticut
were preparing for a shooting war, and he admonished the Secretary at
War: ". . . if you will resist and not yield, that Resistance should be
effectual at the Beginning. If you think ten Thousand men sufficient,
send Twenty, if one Million is thought enough, give two; you will save
both Blood and Treasure in the End."[28]

His Majesty's commander in chief in America and royal governor of
Massachusetts Bay Colony was now face to face with revolution. He and
his officers realized this, as did the King, who on November 18 wrote his
First Minister he was "not sorry" that the line of conduct to be pursued
was "now chalked out . . . the New England Governments are in a State
of Rebellion; blows must decide whether they are to be subject to this
Country or independent." The following day he gave Lord North another
injection of royal determination; the colonists were "ripe for mischief
. . . we must either master them, or totally leave them to themselves and
treat them as Aliens." The wavering First Minister had somewhat belatedly suggested that commissioners be sent to the colonies to examine
into the disputes. The King put a stop to this pacific nonsense: ". . . this
looks like the Mother Country being more afraid of the Colonies and I

cannot think it likely to make them reasonable; I do not want to drive them to despair but to Submission."[29]

Some Englishmen presumed that Lord North's American policy would be a major issue in the election of the new Parliament. But it was not. The limited electorate was totally indifferent to the crisis building across the Atlantic. Since 1765 the colonial problem had received considerable attention of both Houses of Parliament, but it no longer aroused the same passion as previously. The subject had literally been talked to death. Many assumed the measures Administration had jammed through the last session with but little opposition would suffice to chasten the recalcitrant Americans. Others believed they would eventually simply grow tired of frenetic disturbances, riots, and chaos and decide to calm down and behave themselves. Administration poured money into questionable constituencies; there were no startling upsets. Wilkes was again elected from Middlesex in a walkover; the ministry, thoroughly beaten and humiliated on this particular issue, silently acknowledged defeat.

On Wednesday, November 30, the new Parliament assembled. His Majesty, suitably attired for the occasion, adorned with his crown and regal ornaments, and attended by high officers of state, delivered a short speech from the throne. It gave him much concern, he announced, to have to inform his loyal Lords and Commons "that a most daring spirit of resistance and disobedience to the law still unhappily prevails in the Province of the Massachusetts Bay, and has in divers parts of it broke forth in fresh violences of a very criminal nature." The other colonies had "countenanced and encouraged" these unlawful proceedings, but the members might depend upon His Majesty's "firm and steadfast resolution" to uphold the supreme authority of Parliament over all his dominions.

In the Commons, Hillsborough moved the "humble Address," which provoked heated debate. The address passed in both Houses, but nine Opposition lords signed a "Protest" alleging that the ministry had pushed its arbitrary measures through the last Parliament without allowing time for "full information, mature deliberation and temperate enquiry." The minister's "unfortunate system," hurriedly and imprudently concocted, had been "pursued with so little temper, consistence, or foresight" that they had thought it would have been abandoned. But the ministry proposed to pursue its fatal and mischievous measures. The noble lords who signed the protest made it clear they did not desire to be associated with such proceedings, "which may precipitate our country into all the calamities of a civil war."[30] The policy of coercion was reaffirmed in both Houses by overwhelming majorities, and members departed for their homes to enjoy the holidays.

News that "Certain Persons" who flagitiously styled themselves "Delegates of several of His Majesty's Colonies" had presumed to meet in Philadelphia during September and October reached London before Christmas. Dartmouth immediately wrote Gage to communicate the King's displeasure that such an unwarrantable and presumptuous assemblage had been held. He directed the general to use his "utmost endeavours" to prevent the election of delegates to the Congress scheduled to assemble in Philadelphia on May 10, and to "exhort all Persons to desist from such an unjustifiable Proceeding, which cannot but be highly displeasing to the King."[31]

Although this was not the most appropriate moment to present to His Majesty the Humble Petition from "Certain Persons" who had assembled in Philadelphia, Franklin, Arthur Lee, and William Bollan waited upon Dartmouth on December 21. He received them politely. "The Secretary of State, after a Day's Perusal (during which a Council was held) told us it was a decent and proper Petition, and cheerfully undertook to present it to his Majesty, who, he afterwards assured us, was pleased to receive it very graciously, and to promise to lay it, as soon as they met, before his two Houses of Parliament."

The packet that brought the Humble Petition also brought copies of the Suffolk Resolves and of Congress' "Declaration and Resolves" of October 14. The uncompromising tenor of these documents indicated quite clearly that the colonists would fight unless Great Britain retracted. Three thousand Redcoats in Boston and half a dozen frigates in the harbor would not suffice to intimidate the rebellious Americans.

At the same time, "a gentleman in Philadelphia" sent seasonal greetings to a London friend, a member of the House of Commons, to disabuse him of the conviction then current in ministerial circles that the Americans would not fight. "Nothing but the total repeal of the acts of parliament of which we complain can prevent a civil war in America. Our opposition has now risen to desperation. It would be easy to allay a storm in the ocean by a single word as to subdue the free spirit of Americans without a total redress of their grievances. May a spirit of wisdom descend at last upon our Ministry and rescue the British Empire from destruction." The Philadelphian was not optimistic that the ministry would hear the Christmas message of peace on earth and good will to men. Two days later, he added a postscript: "There cannot be a greater error than to suppose that the present commotions in America are owing to the acts of demogogues. . . . It is to no purpose to attempt to destroy the opposition to the omnipotence of parliament by taking off our Hancocks, Adams, and Dickinsons. Ten thousand patriots of the same stamp stand ready to fill their place."[32] This American was no fiery radical; he was loyal to the King and "trembled" at the thought of separation from the mother country. He was one of dozens who wrote to alert friends that the public temper in the colonies was ready for a trial at arms; if it came to that, "blows must decide."

☙ 4

To Scourge Them with Rods of Iron

As Boston radicals and red-coated officers rang in the new year at midnight on December 31, 1774, General Gage found some reason for cautious optimism, and in early January reported to Dartmouth that tempers had cooled. Boston Tories assured him over the madeira that "if a respectable Force is seen in the Field, the most obnoxious of the leaders seized, and a pardon proclaimed for all other's . . . Government will come off Victorious. . . ."[1]

The "most obnoxious" of those who kept the people in a "phrenzy" was Samuel Adams, described by a Pennsylvania colleague in the first Congress as not "remarkable for brilliant abilities" but "equal to most men in popular intrigue and the management of a faction. He eats little, drinks little, sleeps little, and thinks much, and is most decisive and indefatigable in the pursuit of his objects." The British saw him as an unprincipled and ambitious rabble-rouser who played upon the emotions of the people to gain his ends: "a man of ordinary birth and desperate fortune, who by his abilities and talent for factious intrigue, has made himself of some consequence, whose political existence depends upon the continuance of the present dispute, and who must sink into insignificancy and beggary the moment it ceases."[2]

The young British captain who wrote these words was not unaware of the underlying causes of the ferment in America, for, he said, they were "to be found in the nature of mankind and that it proceeds from a new nation, feeling itself wealthy, populous and strong; and being impatient of restraint, [they] are struggling to throw off that dependency that is so irksome to them."[3] This was a more thoughtful appreciation of the situation in the colonies than was current at ministerial level.

On the first day of February 1775, elected deputies of the several towns and districts in Massachusetts Bay assembled at Cambridge and after unanimously electing John Hancock as president and Benjamin Lincoln as secretary, invited the Reverend Dr. Appleton, pastor of the First Church, to provide the necessary spiritual guidance. When Appleton finished his pleas to the Lord God of Hosts, the deputies resolved that "In consideration of the coldness of the season and that the Congress sit in a house without fire, Members who incline thereto may sit with their Hats on."

Information that certain of their less patriotic fellow citizens, anxious to line their pockets with His Majesty's golden guineas, were supplying Gage with timber, boards, straw, bricks, canvas, tent poles, and carts angered the deputies, who promptly resolved that any engaged in this traffic should "be held in the highest detestation and deemed inveterate enemies to *America,* and ought to be prevented and opposed by all reasonable means whatever." They urged those determined to preserve their freedoms and to pass them "inviolate to posterity" to make every preparation for defense against "a set of men who, through depravity of mind, and cruelty of disposition," were determined to reduce America "to a state of misery." During the first two weeks of February, deputies met daily to attend to business relating to perfecting the defenses of the province. None of the published resolves confirmed General Gage's optimistic report to Lord Dartmouth of January 18.[4]

In New Hampshire, royal authority had collapsed. The people had seized four cannon from Fort William and Mary on the Piscataqua River and burned a large quanitity of tea in Portsmouth. Governor John Wentworth wrote Gage that the magistrates he had lately appointed could not apprehend those who had made off with the cannon, nor keep them securely in jail should they be able to find and arrest them. He asked for two regiments to keep order. Gage could not spare two regiments, or even two companies. He sent an officer to inquire into the situation, and the admiral dispatched a frigate and a sloop to the scene.

But on the whole, His Majesty's commander in chief in North America and royal governor of Massachusetts Bay passed a relatively quiet winter in Boston. That hostilities did not erupt was due largely to his tact. The radical element, spurred on by Sons of Liberty, provided the sparks required to ignite the powder train, but Gage handled their provocations with consummate skill. The nocturnal activities of his younger officers frequently embarrassed the general. They assembled to "game and drink"; occasionally, in alcoholic exuberance, they attacked the town watch. Their behavior dishonored the services and resulted in "Quarrels and Riots." This was but one of Gage's numerous problems. Bostonians were buying New England rum for Redcoats who frequented taverns; great numbers were daily intoxicated; some were induced to desert and others to sell arms and ammunition. The punishment for this last offense was literally death: five hundred lashes.

No love was lost between the unwelcome British troops and their inhospitable hosts. Captain Evelyn had nothing but contempt for the "lower orders" in Boston: "utterly devoid of every sentiment of truth or common honesty; [they] possess no other human qualities but such as are the shame and reproach of humanity." They had perpetrated "many horrid villainies"; "Fire and Sword" should be let loose among them. Evelyn thought with reason that there was "a very large party in our favour," and other "thousands" inclining toward Britain who would not "openly declare themselves from an apprehension that Government may leave them in the lurch." He observed that "those gentlemen who have declared on our side are men of the best property in this country."[5]

But even in Boston the cleavage was by no means as clear-cut as Evelyn seemed to think; many men of good family, education, and substance took their stand with the Adams cousins, Bowdoin, Hancock, Robert Paine, Cushing, Dr. Benjamin Church, and the Warrens. One such wrote to London that although his town was "suffering amazing distress," he and other Bostonians were yet "determined to endure as much as human nature can, rather than betray America and posterity." He described Gage's army as "sickly, and extremely addicted to desertion. . . . Do you think such an army would march through our woods and thickets and country villages to cut the throats of honest people contending for liberty."[6]

Gage was now convinced his Redcoats were going to have to fight, and issued orders for intensive training and patrolling. He ordered target practice: soldiers fired from dockside at floating bobbing silhouettes cut from thin boards. Detachments marched regularly into the surrounding countryside. At the general's headquarters, there was a pervasive feeling that orders for action must come soon from London, and when they did, British regulars would teach rebellious Americans a lesson they would not soon forget. Captain Evelyn and his colleagues were anxiously waiting "to scourge them with rods of iron."

Major General Frederick Haldimand, now Gage's second-in-command as he had earlier been in New York, kept very much in the background. During this exciting period in the history of Boston, his name rarely appears. But he kept his eyes open: "It is useless to hope to recover the

New England provinces by any kind of accommodation. They tend toward independence. The evil is great and only a violent remedy can cure it." He thought the Sons of Liberty, assiduous in training people in the use of arms, one source of the "evil"; their abettors were incendiary "Presbyterian [Congregational] priests . . . the most dangerous of all human beings."[7] Students at Harvard College, classed by Tories with Yale as a "Seminary of sedition," were radical and riotous.

On March 22, deputies to the Massachusetts Congress assembled to hear reports of the doings of General Gage and his Redcoats. These were not calculated to allay their apprehensions that the governor planned aggressive action. With good reason, deputies thought Concord a more secure site than Cambridge for future deliberations, "especially as by the latest advice from *Great Britain* we have undoubted reason for jealousy, that our implacable enemies are unremitting in their endeavours, by fraud and artifice, as well as by open force, to subjugate the people."* They urged citizens "to be ready to oppose with firmness and resolution, at the utmost hazard, every attempt for that purpose."[8]

Chatham, who, despite his infirmities of mind and body, was planning a return to the political scene, invited Franklin to Hayes to give him a report on the doings of the First Continental Congress. The doctor accepted with alacrity, sent the earl a copy of the congressional petition to the King, and went to Hayes the day after Christmas. (There is no record that he took a copy of the Suffolk Resolves.) Chatham received him "with an affectionate kind of respect that from so great a man was extremely engaging." The earl had read the petition and expressed his admiration for the Congress, which, he said, had acted with moderation and wisdom. Indeed, to Franklin's delight, he declared Congress "the most honorable assembly of statesmen since those of the ancient Greeks and Romans, in the most virtuous times." In the course of a long conversation, the doctor put the idea into the earl's head that reconciliation was certainly still possible, provided that as a preliminary step Gage and his Redcoats were withdrawn from Boston. Chatham agreed with his visitor that this measure would clearly evidence Britain's desire for accommodation.[9]

Franklin's dealings with Chatham at this time and the advice he gave "the Great Commoner" raise the question of his motives. The doctor was well advised as to prevalent feeling both in Administration and in America, and certainly knew the gesture he proposed would be totally unacceptable to the ministry and would not conduce to the orderly re-establishment of royal government in Massachusetts, but would probably have the opposite effect, for it would be interpreted in America as a sign of weakness and would thus increase the influence of the radicals.

---

* "Jealousy": fear; apprehension.

Franklin was an eminently practical man and his recommendation must be seen for what it probably was: a splitting maneuver. Chatham's name still carried great weight. He was the idol of the City of London, the one man, many still thought, capable of bringing the errant colonies back to the imperial fold. He was still a useful ally.

Franklin had other irons in the fire. Among members of Parliament anxiously seeking reconciliation were Vice-admiral Richard Viscount Howe and his younger brother William, a senior major general. Admiral Howe thought it a good idea to discuss American affairs with Franklin. He wished to arrange some sort of cover for these conversations, for to meet openly with a representative of the rebellious citizens of Massachusetts would be most indiscreet for a senior serving officer and a member of Parliament. His sister Lady Caroline solved the problem; she invited Franklin to visit her to play chess. The admiral was present at these encounters, during which little attention was devoted to the chessboard and much to discussion of measures that might serve as a basis for reconciliation. Although Franklin later sent the admiral a memorandum, nothing came of the sessions other than to arouse in the doctor's breast a real admiration for his hostess. He was always easy game for charming and intelligent women, as they were for him.

On January 20 Parliament assembled. During the preceding month members had full opportunity to study a variety of official documents and letters dealing with American affairs. These papers were on the table when Chatham rose to speak in the Lords. Present with other invited visitors was his guest, Dr. Benjamin Franklin. Chatham addressed a crowded House. He led off by castigating the acts passed during the preceding session as "violent, precipitate and vindictive," and described the Americans as an "injured, unhappy, traduced people." The ministry had succeeded in uniting a continent. All they had to show as the fruit of their unjust measures was an impotent general and a dishonored army. Great Britain was staggering to ruin; Chatham felt it his duty to rescue her Sovereign from "the misadvice of his present Ministers." Affairs in America must be settled, and quickly settled; the crisis was urgent and pressing. He continued: "I will not desert for a moment the conduct of this weighty business from the first to the last, unless nailed to my bed by the extremity of sickness: I will give it unremitting attention; I will knock at the door of this sleeping and confounded Ministry, and rouse them to a sense of their imminent danger."

Chatham contended the Americans owed obedience "in a limited degree . . . to our Ordinances of Trade and Navigation." But Parliament had no right to deprive them of their property by levying internal taxes. Commercial restraints they would recognize; taxation for revenue, never. Their resistance, he asserted, was as necessary as it was just; Parliamentary declarations of omnipotence were vain; the "imperious doctrines of the necessity of submission . . . equally impotent to convince or to enslave." This was "Tyranny . . . intollerable to British subjects." Troops sent to enforce this thralldom were "penned up—pining in inglorious inactivity." They were in a most unworthy situation "and to render the folly equal to the disgrace, they are an army of irritation and vexation." They must be withdrawn. And withdrawn at once, before the first, "the unexpiable drop of blood is shed in an impious war with a people contending in the great cause of publick liberty." He would never permit a son of his, nor anyone he could influence, to "draw his sword upon his fellow subjects."

The ministry's measures, he said, were irritating the colonies to unappeasable rancour. If war came, the cause was already lost, for how could England hope for more than "temporary and local submission"? The Americans, animated by a "glorious spirit of Whiggism," preferred "Poverty with liberty to golden chains and sordid affluence" and "would die in defense of their rights as men—as freemen." And, he reminded their lordships, their cause would be aided by the "congenial flame" glowing in the breast of every Whig in England. All attempts to impose servitude upon such a people, and to establish despotism over "such a mighty Continental *Nation* must be vain, must be futile."

Great Britain would be forced to retract: ". . . let us retreat whilst we can, not when we must. I say we must necessarily undo these violent and repressive Acts; *they must be repealed;* I pledge myself for it, that you will in the end repeal them; I stake my reputation on it; I will consent to be taken for an idiot if they are not finally repealed." He urged his noble colleagues to take the first step to re-establish "concord, peace and happiness" for, if they did not, and the King's ministers continued "in misadvising and misleading" him, he could affirm that they would make the crown not worth the wearing. "I shall not say that the King is betrayed; but I will pronounce that the Kingdom is undone." He then moved that "an humble Address" be presented, advising and beseeching His Majesty, as a first step toward reconciliation and to allay ferments and discords, to order General Gage to remove the troops from Boston.

Suffolk rose. He condemned Chatham's speech as improper and divisive. Parliament must be obeyed. He excoriated the proceedings of the late Congress, defended the policy of coercion, and asserted that any concessions would be "to the last degree impolitick, pusilanimous and absurd." He spoke as a member of an administration determined to pursue "the object of subduing the refractory, rebellious *Americans*," and avowed its resolution "to enforce obedience by arms."

Camden spoke in support of Chatham, as did Shelburne, who asserted that the First Minister and four or five colleagues had arrayed themselves in opposition to the people of an entire continent; he could only describe their policy of attempting to coerce the Americans into a state of servile submission as mad, unjust, and infatuated. Richmond and Rockingham added their pleas and were answered in forceful terms by noble lords who opposed. The motion went down to overwhelming defeat by a vote of 68 to 18.[10]

Several days later Chatham sent Franklin a transcript of the motion, copies of which the doctor promptly sent off to Boston and Philadelphia. He then wrote Lord Stanhope to thank him and Chatham for their courtesies, and in his note added: "Dr. F. is filled with admiration of that truly great man. He has seen in the course of life, sometimes eloquence without wisdom, and often wisdom without eloquence; in the present instance he sees both united, and both as he thinks, in the highest degree possible."[11]

Lord North had laid the petition from Congress before both Houses. In the Commons, so Franklin wrote Charles Thomson, "It came down among a great Heap of letters of Intelligence from Governors and officers in America, Newspapers, Pamphlets, Handbills, etc., from that Country, the last on the list, and was laid upon the Table with them, undistinguished by any particular Recommendation of it to the Notice of either House; and I do not find that it has had any further notice taken of it as yet. . . ." Indeed, no notice of it was to be taken, although Franklin, Lee, and Bollan petitioned that it be read. Administration obviously did not wish the document read aloud; a motion to do so was overwhelmed, 218 to 67.[12] Hutchinson, who was in the gallery, felt the ministry's course was firmly set: The government would concede nothing. If his emotions were torn by conflicting loyalties, he did not allow it to become evident.

Franklin went to Hayes again on January 27. During the preceding week, the earl had drafted a bill that he hoped would effect a reconciliation. In this, Chatham proposed repeal of all acts of Parliament the colonists deemed offensive. But the bill also asserted the unchallengeable sovereignty of the British legislature in all matters exclusive of internal taxation, which was to be reserved to elected colonial assemblies. Franklin would later state that he made no substantive suggestions.

The earl visited him in London two days later. Chatham's "equipage" waited at the doctor's door "for near two hours," and as this day happened to be a Sunday, attracted a concourse of the curious. Franklin was not the humble man devoid of vanity depicted in American legend. Quite the contrary, as many episodes in his career (including this one) testify: "Such a visit from so great a man, on so important a business, flattered not a little my vanity"—particularly as the visit took place exactly one year to the day after the ministry "had taken so much pains" to disgrace him at the Cockpit.[13] In a few hours all London knew "the Great Commoner" was conferring with the American philosopher. The subject was Chatham's "Plan for Reconciliation," which he proposed to offer in the House of Lords on the following Wednesday, the first day of February.

Franklin devoted Monday to preparing "Notes for a Discourse with Lord Chatham on his Plan" and carried them to Hayes on Tuesday. There he and the earl spent four hours going over the "Plan" but the doctor "found his lordship so full and diffuse in supporting every particular" he could say only that no progress was made. On the following day he again went to the House of Lords as Chatham's guest to hear the earl introduce his "Provisional Act for settling the Troubles in *America* and for asserting the supreme legislative authority and superintending power of *Great Britain* over the Colonies." Members of Administration and Opposition "drawn up in martial array" awaited "the signal to engage in a contest . . . in which ruin and destruction must be the inevitable consequence to both parties."[14]

The bill was read. It asserted the indubitable authority of Parliament "to bind the people of the *British* colonies in *America* in all matters touching the general weal of the whole Dominion of the Imperial Crown." Here Chatham specifically cited acts to regulate trade, which he deemed beyond the competency of any colony. His bill provided that no troops would be stationed within any colony without its consent, nor would any internal tax be levied except by vote of provincial assemblies. Other concessions would be made; the Coercive Acts passed during the previous session were to be repealed, and the inviolability of charters guaranteed.

Sandwich was on his feet before the clerk who had read the bill had time to sit down. The concessions proposed made no sense; the Americans "had formed the most traitorous and hostile intentions"; they were "not disputing about words, but about realities" and were in a state of rebellion. He moved to reject the bill. Earl Gower, Lord President of the Council, "rose in great heat" to condemn the bill. Great Britain must assert and if necessary enforce her "legislative supremecy entire and undiminished." A most unparliamentary altercation now ensued; when quiet was finally restored, Gower declared "in the most unreserved terms" that the Americans must be reduced to submission.

The House was silent as Chatham rose to reply. He declared he could easily demonstrate that ministerial conduct in respect to America had been "one continued series of weakness, temerity, despotism, ignorance, futility, negligence, blundering and the most notorious servility, incapacity and corruption." The ministers were aware, he said, that if his bill were to pass it would annihilate their power, deprive them of their emoluments, and at once reduce them "to that state of insignificance for which God and nature" had designed them.

Gower again rose to assert that Chatham was attempting "to influence the people both here and in America." He was content, he said, "to perish in the ruins" but was determined not to concede any rights to the Americans. Sandwich's motion was put to the vote. Chatham's bill was rejected by a vote of 61 to 32. Five dukes voted with the minority.[15]†

It is all too easy to condemn the Lord President, Sandwich, Lord North, Rigby, Wedderburn, Germain, and the many other advocates of coercion as shortsighted, obstinate reactionaries. But this conclusion takes no account of many potent traditional concepts that influenced their attitudes toward America.

First, and perhaps most important, they saw the prerogatives of the crown and the dignity of Parliament to be at stake. Edmund Burke believed that Parliament had the constitutional right to tax the colonists; with him, as with many members of the minority, the question was simply the expediency of attempting to do so. They felt the colonies should contribute to expenses of the Empire, and were willing to have them do it on a voluntary basis. But all members, including Burke, upheld the principle of Parliament's supreme authority.

Had anyone at this time suggested that John and Samuel Adams, John Hancock, and Patrick Henry, for example, be brought to England to discuss with ministers the relationship that should exist between the mother country and her rebellious colonies, he would have been regarded as demented. Parents did not confer with obstinate and recalcitrant children. They chastised them. Any adolescent who attempted to assert a position of equality with adults would have been looked upon as singularly deluded and sadly in need of correction. Nor would the political mores of the time have countenanced a meeting, on a basis of equality, of the King's "confidential servants" with colonists. This idea would have been dismissed as ludicrous. Gentlemen did not marry their mistresses, nor did superior beings parley with their social inferiors. Colonists were inferior beings; they were supposed to take orders, not give them. The parent-child relationship as between Great Britain and her American colonies was a concept that to a great degree dictated the reaction of the British Establishment to the behavior of the Americans. When George III referred to England as "the Mother Country," as he so frequently did, he meant the term in its literal sense.

Traditional mercantilist thought also exercised a profound influence on political behavior. Lord Townshend expressed this succinctly in the Lords during debate on Chatham's motion to withdraw the troops from Boston. He pointed out that Congress, in condemning the Navigation Acts, had clearly shown that American views were not confined to the redress of grievances real or imagined, but were "immediately directed to the overthrow of that great palladium of *British* commerce, the Act of Navigation." Was "that great commercial system on which the strength and prosperity of *Great Britain,* and the mutual interests of both coun-

† One of these was the Duke of Cumberland, the King's uncle.

tries vitally depended" to be destroyed "to gratify the foolishly ambitious temper of a turbulent ungrateful people"?[16]

Chatham had knocked on the door, but he had knocked in vain. Actually, the earl's proposals would not have been acceptable to radicals in America, for the preamble to his bill expressly asserted the supreme legislative authority and superintending power of Parliament. The vote on Chatham's motion gave the King "infinite satisfaction." "Nothing," he wrote, "can be more calculated to bring the Americans to a due submission" than this "very handsome majority."[17]

One may ask why George III thought the Americans were to be influenced by "very handsome" ministerial majorities in a Parliament they believed, with reason, to be managed and corrupt. But the King was convinced his wishes, and the acts of the new Parliament he and his ministers had taken considerable pains to pack, would ultimately prevail. For the King, American rejection of the supreme authority of the crown in Parliament, an authority he had pledged his word to uphold when he took the coronation oath, had been—and would continue to be—a severe emotional experience. Americans and their disloyal behavior were to him totally incomprehensible.

The King was not alone. His First Minister, Frederick, Lord North, did not understand them either, and made no particular effort to do so. Lord North was not a violent man. He was a born temporizer and an incurable procrastinator who tended to mislay letters and papers, leave secret dispatches in his water closet, forget appointments, and doze during debates in the House of Commons. Lord North did not consider himself to be "Prime Minister," nor would he ever permit members of his family or his friends to address him or refer to him by that title. But he was the King's First Minister and he did not, as a First Minister during a time of national crisis should have done, try to exercise influence over the Cabinet. Far less did he attempt to control and direct it.

Lord North was not the domineering, driving man Pitt had been. His natural good humor, his hesitancy, his invariable courtesy, always prevented him from being the King's First Minister in more than name. Indeed, his temperament was almost the opposite of Pitt's: North was placid, tolerant, subject to fits of irresolution, and inclined to forgive mistakes. Rather than force an issue, he sought a compromise. The Cabinet rarely functioned as a corporate body, and the First Minister frequently refused to accept responsibility for acts of its individual members, each of whom ran his department almost entirely as he pleased. North ran his own—the Treasury—efficiently, and did not meddle with those of his colleagues, all of whom had access to the Closet.

Lord North was a gentleman, popular in society and in the House of Commons. He was known in London as an engaging host and in the House as a witty speaker, whose "jocose levity" frequently amused the members as much as it irritated Horace Walpole. "The Noble Lord in the Blue Ribband" (the Garter)‡ was not inclined to take anything too seriously. During a debate at a somewhat later date, T. Townsend, attacking administration policy, said: "Happen what will, the noble Lord is ready with his joke. Amidst the Calamities of War and the Ruin of the Country, while the State of public Affairs renders every other Person serious, he is prepared to treat Events the most distressing, as Subjects of Merriment, of Gaiety and of Repartee! Such is his luxuriant Fancy, and sportive Elasticity of Character."[18] It was precisely this "sportive Elasticity of Character" that enabled Lord North to ride out tempests in the House of Commons.

He was not a gambler but was an engaging host who did his fair share of social drinking. Once, when he was said to be confined to bed with a severe cold, His Majesty reminded him that the only cure for his affliction was "WATER and ABSTINENCE." No one could hate Lord North, but many held him in contempt for the reason that he refused to function as First Minister.

The noble lord shared the conviction with others of his class that American behavior was irrational, insupportable, and merited severe chastisement, but his speeches in support of the punitive measures he introduced were temperate. He was not given to ranting and raving, and was at his best when he presented the annual budget in speeches that evoked even Horace Walpole's reluctant admiration. He may have been a vacillating and weak man, and history testifies he was a misguided one, but perhaps he did not deserve to be the prime target of American abuse and execration unto the third and fourth generations.

Few of the governing oligarchy, composed of nobles, prelates, heads of county families, wealthy merchants, shipowners, East Indian nabobs, bankers, and retired West Indies planters, many of whom sat in Parliament, felt any sympathy for the Americans, an inferior order whose ordained position was one of servile subordination. Peers of the realm and bishops who sat in the House of Lords were even less disposed than their colleagues in the lower House seriously to entertain the various addresses, remonstrances, and petitions that flowed across the Atlantic in a steady stream. The bishops, who held their dioceses and their revenues by virtue of royal appointment, were with the possible exception of the Scots the most reactionary group in Parliament. Only the Bishop of Saint Asaph ventured to speak consistently in support of the American position.

Not all members of this exclusive ruling class were as vehement in their denunciation of the colonists as the Earl of Sandwich, North's First

‡ On June 18, 1772, the King invested Lord North a Knight of the Garter, a rare distinction for a member of the House of Commons. Several months later he was unanimously elected chancellor of Oxford University.

Lord of the Admiralty, "a politician of evil reputation and an inveterate jobber." He was also an inveterate enemy of the Americans. There were indeed a great many of them, but "Suppose the Colonies do abound in men, what does that signify? They are raw, undisciplined, cowardly men. I wish instead of forty or fifty thousand of these *brave* fellows, they would produce in the field at least two hundred thousand, the more the better, the easier would be the conquest; if they did not run away, they would starve themselves into compliance with our measures."[19] These sentiments were shared by the bellicose Lord Mansfield; Richard Rigby, a man as intemperate in speech as in his consumption of brandy who held the lucrative office of paymaster of the forces; Earl Gower, Lord President of the Council; Lord George Germain, soon to be brought into the Cabinet as Principal Secretary of State for America; Attorney General Edward Thurlow and his colleague Solicitor General Alexander Wedderburn, who had insulted Franklin at their confrontation in the Cockpit.

These gentlemen had some reason to be arrogant. Britain had humbled France in the Seven Years' War; her navy commanded the seas; her ambassadors were accorded precedence in every European court; her great merchant fleets were scattered over every ocean; her lucrative export-import trade exceeded that of all continental Europe combined. Her woolens and linens were unequaled; her craftsmen and artisans produced silverware, furniture, and utensils of the highest quality.

A society on the whole politically stable assured its citizens freedoms as yet undreamed of in the Germanic states, Russia, and the Hapsburg and Bourbon empires. An essentially free press flourished, as did more serious literature—history, poetry, the drama. Progressive landowners were beginning to apply new methods to increase agricultural production; great attention was being paid to breeding of horses, cattle, sheep, and hogs. Industrial and craft processes were constantly improving.

Perhaps most important was the undeniable fact that the people of Great Britain were governed by law, not by the whim of a despot, his mistresses, and their sycophants. True, penalties for many crimes were barbarous, but even murderers, highwaymen, rapists, and coiners were tried by a jury. Britain's legislative and judicial institutions were everywhere respected, and not least in America.

The men who with their King "gloried in the name of Briton" were not the evil creatures American propaganda represented them to be. But they were quite incapable of comprehending the American position in any other way than as a distinct threat to the established order. In their eyes, the Americans were determined "Levellers": an ill-bred, crude, vulgar, litigious, obstinate lot who had forgotten their place and must forcefully be reminded of it, lest the example they set be emulated closer to home.

In attempting across a gulf of two hundred years to assess the motivations of the aristocratic oligarchs who then ruled Great Britain, one must remember that they were the products of a rich, privileged, stratified, and essentially parochial society, a society quite ready to tolerate amusing eccentricities and profligacy at the gaming table or in the bedroom, but one that would react instinctively to any dynamic challenge to its political, economic, and social prerogatives. This challenge had now been posed.

The British command in America was not ready to meet it, nor was there in London a leader competent to fashion realistic policies. General Burgoyne had suggested a civilian "viceroy" for America, whose office would combine supreme political authority with military command. The general was well ahead of his time; such an arrangement would have diminished the royal prerogative George III was at all costs determined to maintain. Nor with a timid First Minister in power was this solution politically practicable. Pitt might possibly have shoved this unsavory medicine down the King's throat. But only possibly. The suggestion received no serious consideration in Whitehall.

The problem facing the British naval commander in chief in North American waters was cogently argued in the Boston *Gazette* in early April. Graves's squadron, when assembled (which it never was), would have been imposing: "But let us consider—How many ships are there to blockade Boston harbour?—How many ships can Britain spare to carry on this humane and political war, the object of which is a peppercorn? Let her send all the ships she has round her island.—What if her ill-natured neighbors, France and Spain, should strike a blow in their absence?—In order to judge what they could all do, when they arrived here, we should consider what they are all able to do round the island of Great Britain. We know that the utmost vigilance and exaction, added to all the terrors of sanguinary laws are not sufficient to prevent continual smuggling into their own island"—were there not along the coast of America "fifty bays, harbours, creeks and inlets" to each one in Britain? If the Royal Navy could not stop wholesale smuggling at home, how could it possibly stop the importation of arms and ammunition into America?[20]

Since 1763 successive administrations had allowed the naval establishment to run down. Many ships were in need of extensive refitting; most in commission were undermanned. To provide a force adequate to impose and maintain an effective blockade would take time, and there was no time. With the exception of Dartmouth, who favored a strategy of blockade, no member of the Cabinet conceived that the colonists could possibly resist the might of the British Army. Major General Edward Harvey and Viscount Barrington both opposed commitment of the army; Harvey told the King the army would be dribbled away in the vast expanse of America.**

A correspondent who signed himself "Americanus. A British Freeholder" wrote the London *Chronicle* his opinion that a land war in America must be futile: "A continent in extent not less that 1500 miles, covered with a numerous and hardy people, armed and accustomed to the use of arms to a critical dexterity cannot be brought to submit . . . but by repeated defeats, and almost a total annihilation." The topography imposed insuperable problems: "The face of the Country, interspersed with forests and rivers, mountains, and mighty lakes will always afford numberless asylums. . . ." Communication must be by sea, for there were no roads. And how were the ranks of the army "thinned down" in battle to be replenished? To hope to recruit in America was a delusion, and to ship replacements from Britain expensive and time-consuming.

"Americanus" was one of the few who apprehended the possibility that a continental war might develop from seeds of rebellion in a single small city. But the Cabinet did not choose to deal with future imponderables. The situation in Massachusetts Bay demanded action, and the decision taken, to use Gage's troops immediately and aggressively, was approved by the King.

** Neither of these gentlemen was a member of the Cabinet.

✄ 5

An Affair that Happened on the 19th Inst.

Major Thomas Pitcairn, the senior marine ashore in Boston, agreed with his friend Captain Evelyn; in a letter to Lord Sandwich on February 14 he wrote: ". . . vigorous measures at present would soon put an end to this rebellion. The deluded people are made believe that they are invincible. . . . When this army is ordered to act against them, they will soon be convinced that they are very insignificant when opposed to regular troops."[1] Pitcairn had frequently led strong patrols for a distance of six or seven miles into the countryside. The people, unresponsive and surly, watched the Redcoats warily and cursed them, but avoided confrontations.

There was constant friction between the general in his Boston headquarters and the admiral aboard his flagship in the harbor. One source of this trouble was Major Pitcairn and his battalion of marines. The major, irritated with Admiral Graves's conduct, wrote their common superior, the First Lord: "The Admiral distresses me much." The point in dispute was not unusual—under whose command *were* the marines? Graves insisted they belonged to him, but Pitcairn had received specific orders from the Admiralty Board to report to General Gage, which he had done to the extreme annoyance of the admiral.

Apparently Pitcairn's marines were no sooner ashore than they headed for the nearest tavern.* The major reported to Sandwich that they were a drunken lot and that he was required to sleep in barracks to stop all-night drinking bouts. Pitcairn was having "a disagreeable time of it." Soldiers, sailors, and marines could not, it seemed, be effectively denied "that pernicious rum . . . the rum is so cheap that it debauches both army and navy. Depend on it my Lord, that it will destroy more of us than the Yankies will."[2]

In late February, Gage sent an expedition under Lieutenant Colonel Alexander Leslie by sea to Marblehead to seize half a dozen brass cannon reported to be hidden at Salem. The local militia assembled with arms in hand and faced Leslie and his Redcoats, but there was no violence. The colonel, considerably outnumbered and impressed with the evident determination of the provincials, decided not to march on Salem; he embarked his men and returned to Boston without the cannon.

Leslie's abortive excursion engendered an enormous increase in the militia in Massachusetts. No precise record of the number of men on the rolls exists, but there must have been at least fifteen to twenty thousand. Most were armed; the great majority with muskets, a few with Pennsylvania rifles. The youngest and most active were organized in small detachments of "minutemen." The militia drilled regularly. Many towns had "a deserter from His Majesty's forces by way of a drill sergeant."[3]

The colonel's foray to Marblehead inspired other activities in the province. Secret committees in almost every New England town observed activities of "ministerial tools and Jacobites"; levied contributions and collected powder and ball ammunition. Any person who refused to co-operate was publicly branded "an enemy to America." To be so marked invited mob action. Most reached for their purses.

In Boston, Gage shut down the radical press, and where the Americans could do so, they closed Tory print shops.† Colonial journalists and pamphleteers demonstrated that they could be every bit as virulent and scurrilous as their London cousins. "Pensioned prostitutes" of the crown in Massachusetts had formed an infamous cabal "to subjugate and enslave" the people; these "hirelings" were assisted in their evil designs "by odious and wicked traitors," who in support of "bad governors and an abandoned ministry" constantly represented the friends of liberty to be but "a small, insignificant, divided faction." Fortunately, the designs of these malignant men were "perfectly kenned" by even the most shortsighted; their "impudent and injurious" allegation that those who opposed British punitive measures sought independence was a malicious falsehood.[4]

* Habits of marines have apparently not changed greatly in the last two hundred years.

† In New York, James Rivington published a Tory journal, *The Royal Gazette*, the only such outside occupied Boston.

Controlled mob action was now occurring almost daily in Massachusetts. Sons of Liberty who managed these "spontaneous" affairs were
careful not to allow action to get too far out of hand; there was no
wholesale rioting, looting, or burning. Specific targets—known supporters
of government—were waylaid, heckled, insulted, and threatened. Their
fences were torn down; their windowpanes smashed; their farm buildings demolished; their livestock driven off; their families grossly intimidated. But there was no personal physical violence. No one was beaten,
maimed, or killed.

Incidents were reported in Taunton, Worcester, Freetown, Cambridge, Hardwick, Salem, Plymouth, Springfield, and Bridgewater.
Sheriffs of Essex and Sussex counties—including the respected Colonel
Saltonstall—were obliged to seek refuge in Boston. Scores of "Non-As-
sociators" subject to "intolerable threats and insolent treatment" abandoned their homes, stores, and farms and sought the protection afforded
by British bayonets. Many of these men, only a few months previously
esteemed in their communities, were educated and well-to-do, but as
supporters of parliamentary edicts, were no longer tolerated. Sam
Adams, the principal creator of this revolutionary situation, understood
discriminate terror and applied it.

A British diarist in Boston recorded March 6, 1775, as a "warm day"
by the Fahrenheit thermometer. Before the day was over, an emotional
scale would have recorded "hot," for at eleven o'clock, Dr. Joseph Warren, robed in a "Ciceronian toga," ascended the pulpit in Old South
Meeting and delivered the annual oration commemorating the affray
known in America as the Boston Massacre. "An immense concourse" of
people assembled, including "the most violent fellows in town," among
them, John Hancock, John and Samuel Adams, and Dr. Benjamin
Church. Warren spoke in less inflammatory terms than had been anticipated and was interrupted only by "a few hisses from some of the [Brit-
ish] officers." When he left the pulpit, Samuel Adams rose to remind the
people that an oration would be delivered on the fifth of March of the
next year to commemorate the "Horrid Massacre" in King Street. Some
officers hissed him; others cried out "Oh! Fie! Oh! Fie!" The exclamations
were mistaken for "Fire! Fire!" and a near panic ensued. This crisis was
successfully surmounted, though "the towns people certainly expected a
Riot," as "almost every man had a short stick or bludgeon, in his hand."
They had arrived prepared; they anticipated British officers would become incensed at Warren's expected caustic animadversions on the military and would attempt to lay hands "on some of the party." This "would
have been the signal for Battle. It is certain both sides were ripe for it,
and a single blow would have occasioned the commencement of hostilities."[5] Gage, indeed, expected a riot of monumental proportions. He kept
troops under arms and ordered officers to sleep in barracks with their

men. But on this day he again let slip an opportunity to arrest the entire Massachusetts rebel leadership.

Two days later a countryman was apprehended attempting to purchase a musket from a soldier. Other men of the regiment seized the American, applied a coat of tar and feathers, and paraded him through the town, an act of violence that enraged General Gage, though it was slight recompense for similar treatment dozens of Loyalists had suffered at the hands of Boston mobs.

Major Pitcairn wrote Lord Sandwich: "I am satisfied that one active campaign, a smart action, and burning two or three of their towns, will set everything to rights. Nothing now, I am afraid, but this will ever convince those foolish bad people that England is in earnest."[6] Sandwich forwarded this letter to the King, who, in his reply, praised the major's conduct, and agreed with his opinion "that when once those rebels have felt a smart blow, they will submit; and no situation can ever change my fixed resolution, either to bring the colonies to a due obedience to the legislature of the mother country or to cast them off!"[7] Dartmouth had a more realistic picture of the situation than did the King, but even he thought the outrages Gage reported were "merely the Acts of a tumultous Rabble, without any Appearance of general Concert"; he was confident that if the general would take more vigorous measures he could get the situation in hand. To this end, Dartmouth informed him that seven hundred marines, three regiments of infantry, each at establishment strength of five hundred, and a regiment of light dragoons would soon arrive in Boston. The secretary hoped the augmentation would enable Gage "to take a more active and determined part" and suggested it might be a good idea for him to precipitate hostilities by arresting and imprisoning "the principal actors and abettors in the Provincial Congress," as this would "surely be better that the conflict should be brought on upon such ground than in a riper state of Rebellion." He anticipated that the reaction, if any, would be that "of a rude Rabble" and that a small force, "if put to the Test," would enjoy more probability of success than would a larger force later, after the Americans had gathered resources and made plans to act in concert.

In this detailed letter of instruction, the secretary made it clear that the King and his ministers expected Gage to exert himself to defend His Majesty's dignity, to support the Constitution, and to "restore the Vigour of Government." But on the other hand, Dartmouth reminded the general his conduct must be governed to a great extent by his own "Judgement and Discretion."[8] In this letter the secretary did not suggest that Gage's "Discretion" extended to discussion of conciliatory measures; indeed, any such conversations on the local level would have been idle. The general's clear duty was to enforce the acts of Parliament approved by the King, not to argue with treasonable and rebellious men. Dartmouth did not send the letter to America immediately because he wanted first to get the promised reinforcements on the way.

At this late hour Lord North persuaded his royal master that possibility of preventing an effective colonial union still existed if concessions sufficient to induce one or more colonies to desert their sisters and return to the parental fold were made. Accordingly, on February 20 he offered a motion providing that no duty, tax, or assessment would be levied on any colony that would agree to contribute its proportionate share "to the common defence . . . the support of the civil government and the administration of justice."

The proposal aroused a storm of opposition from die-hards on the Treasury benches which "seemed to totter." Momentarily, it appeared that Lord North's hitherto irresistible phalanx was about to split wide open. But the First Minister, aided by Sir Gilbert Elliot, rallied the troops. Even Rigby, "whose coarse zeal and impudent servility could not be repressed," kept quiet, slipped the notes he had made into his pocket, and voted, as usual, with the "King's Friends." The motion was carried.

North's splitting strategy might have borne fruit a year earlier had he thought to try it. But what might have been practical in February 1774 was not relevant in February 1775. His Majesty, however, seemed to regard the move as a master stroke, and wrote the First Minister that as it would put an end to Congress, "it certainly will have a good effect in this country, and I should hope in at least some of the Colonies."[9] The King, his First Minister, and members of the Cabinet were all aware of the nature of Dartmouth's latest directive to General Gage: to take immediate forceful action to put down the rebellion, a course of action not exactly compatible with the pacific resolution Lord North had moved. Several days later the King, who had repeatedly signified his intention of using force on whatever scale was necessary, wrote: "The more I revolve in my mind the line adopted in the American affairs, the more I am convinced of the rectitude, the candour, and becoming firmness, and if properly attended to, must be crowned with success."[10]

The First Minister's unexpected move roused Burke to possibly his supreme effort; on March 22 he rose in the Commons to deliver his celebrated speech "On Conciliation." Burke believed there remained a chance that a reasoned review of the situation would convince members of the need for accommodation. Otherwise the colonies would be incurably alienated. Burke stated his proposition simply: "Peace." As the stronger party, Britain should take the initiative; she could offer concessions with no impairment of her honor, and such measures as she took to conciliate her colonies must inevitably be to her great financial advantage. Burke established this thesis by a detailed analysis of the tremendous growth in colonial trade with the mother country during some fifty years. Here he was touching the key. Trade was Britain's lifeblood. Her growing commerce with the American colonies was the "envy of the world."

He next described the growth in agriculture in America, and the remarkable enterprise of New Englanders in fishing and whaling: "Whilst we follow them among the tumbling mountains of ice, and behold them penetrating into the deepest frozen recesses of Hudson's Bay and Davis' Straits, whilst we are looking for them beneath our Artic Circle, we hear that they have pierced into the opposite region of polar cold, that they are at the antipodes, and engaged under the frozen serpent of the south." Every sea was vexed by their skill and industry.[11]

How, he asked, had the North American colonies achieved this position? Surely their own toil had contributed, but so had a wise and salutary neglect of their conduct and affairs. Britain had not attempted to squeeze them in a mold, but had let them go on their own way. He dilated on the temper of the Americans of their love of liberty, of their pleasure in participating directly in local government, of the generally high standard (as compared to that of Great Britain, high indeed) of their education; of the contribution religious differences had made to encouragement of the characteristic free spirit which animated them:

> The temper and character which prevail in our colonies are, I am afraid, unalterable by any human art. We cannot, I fear, falsify the pedigree of this fierce people, and persuade them that they are not sprung from a nation in whose veins the blood of freedom circulates. . . . An Englishman is the unfittest person on earth to argue another Englishman into Slavery.

Study of the law, to which so many barristers in New England devoted themselves, had, he admitted, made the colonists unusually disputatious and litigious. But this study had also rendered them "acute, inquisitive, dexterous, prompt in attack, ready in defence, full of resources." Hence, they anticipated the evils of repressive government: "They augur misgovernment at a distance and snuff the approach of tyranny in every tainted breeze."

Burke closed his three-hour speech with an urgent appeal: "Magnanimity in politics is not seldom the truest wisdom and a great Empire and little minds go ill together."[12] He called upon his colleagues to elevate their minds "to the greatness of that trust to which the order of Providence has called us" and urged the House to "lay the first stone of the temple of peace."

A few days after Burke's speech, David Hartley rose to "sift out" some of the allegations made against the colonists: "We hear of nothing now but the protection which we have given to them; of the immense expense incurred on their account. We are told that they have done nothing for themselves; that they pay no taxes; in short, everything is asserted about *America* to serve the present turn without the least regard for truth." He then summarized in detail the contributions the Americans had made during the War for Empire. They had "turned the success of the war at both ends of the line"; they had fought with British regulars "in *Nova Scotia* and in the *Floridas*, at *Havana* and *Martinique*. During the preceding war, they were at the seige of *Carthagena* but what was Carthagena to them?" They had taken Louisbourg—"as mettled an enterprize as any in our history"—only to see it restored to the French. They had been zealous, courageous, and persevering:

> Whenever Great Britain has declared war they have taken their part. They were engaged in King William's Wars, and Queen Anne's, even in their infancy. . . . They have been engaged in more than one expedition to Canada, ever foremost to partake of honour and danger with the mother country. Well, sir, what have we done for them? Have we conquered the country for them from the *Indians?* Have we cleared it? Have we made it habitable? What have we done for them? I believe precisely nothing at all. . . . What Towns have we built for them? What deserts have we cleared?‡

Now that they had struggled through their difficulties and were beginning to hold up their heads, the ministry, "without the least regard to truth," charged them with ingratitude. He added that if the Americans could not see the tendency of Administration's policy they were surely "insane," but Britons were being "more insane and blind" if unable to see what "the sovereignty, property and possessions of *North America*, with every military and despotic power, vested solely in the King's hands," augured for their own liberties.

He then faced Lord North. "The eyes of all this country and America, too, are turned toward the Noble Lord, as the ostensible and responsible Minister, to receive his final determination as to the measures which are to decide the safety or ruin of this Empire. The ways of peace are still before him." The noble lord replied briefly: It was not consistent with British "dignity" and "superiority" to recede.[18] Hartley's motion to repeal the Coercive Acts was buried under an avalanche of ministerial votes.

Horace Walpole watched these proceedings with cynical detachment, and in late March wrote Sir Horace Mann: "The Houses go on fulminating against America—we shall see whether their edicts are regarded, or rather their troops and generals." The possibility of war with the colonies aroused no apprehensions: Society devoted itself "to profusion, extravagance and pleasure—Heroism is not at all in fashion. Cincinnatus will be found at the hazard table and Camillus at a ball. . . . Our young ladies are covered with more plumes than any nation that has no other cover-

‡ Desert: an uninhabited wilderness.

ing." Fortunes were made and lost in a night at Almacks, where Charles Fox, since the recent death of his father and mother, had left a proportion of his cash inheritance. "The first people of fashion are going to act plays. . . . The summer is to open with a masquerade on the Thames. I am glad the American enthusiasts are so far off; I don't think we should be a match for them."[14]

In Virginia, "enthusiasts" had been busy; most no longer cherished hope for redress of grievances, or for that conciliation for which Burke and Hartley had so powerfully pled. Two days after Burke spoke, leaders of the colony gathered in St. John's Church in Richmond, ostensibly to discuss the resolutions adopted by the Congress. The meeting proceeded with parliamentary decorum under the eye of President Peyton Randolph until Patrick Henry rose to move immediate enrollment of an independent militia. The moderates' instinctive opposition to this motion as unnecessarily provocative, if not indeed treasonable, lit off Henry's oratorical fires; he replied with the impassioned speech that ends:

> Gentlemen may cry peace, peace, but there is no peace. The war is actually begun! The next gales that sweep from the north will bring to our ears the clash of resounding arms. Our brethren are already in the field! Why stand we here idle? What is it that the gentlemen wish? What would they have? Is life so dear, or peace so sweet, as to be purchased at the price of chains and slavery? Forbid it, Almighty God! I know not what course others may take, but as for me, give me liberty, or give me death."[15]**

Many gentlemen present felt the situation did not merit such histrionics. They did, however, vote to recommend to each county to raise a company of infantry and a troop of horse. They also elected a slate of delegates to attend the Congress scheduled to meet on May 10 in Philadelphia. Dunmore hastily issued a proclamation prohibiting any such procedure. This served only to arouse contemptuous amusement.

The lord mayor, aldermen, and livery of London, in regalia of office, and accompanied by the sheriffs, carried an "Address, Remonstrance and Petition" to St. James's on April 10. In this they expressed their "Abhorrence" of the oppressive measures applied against their fellow subjects in America. The petitioners were persuaded, so they alleged, that the ministry's measures "originate in the secret advice of men who are enemies equal to your Majesty's Title and the Liberties of your People; that your Majesty's Ministers carry them into execution by the same fatal Corruption which has enabled them to wound the Peace and violate the Consti-

---

** Are these words actually those of Patrick Henry, or those of his biographer, William Wirt? There is no way of knowing!

tution of this Country." These wicked men were "poisoning the fountain of public security" and transforming Parliament, the bastion of the people's liberties, into a formidable instrument of arbitrary power; their purpose was to establish a despotic rule "over all America." The King received this document with the "utmost astonishment." How, he inquired, could any loyal subject encourage the "rebellious disposition" of the Americans?[16]

This remonstrance expressed in most decided terms the belief, widely held on both sides of the Atlantic, that a secret and sinister cabal, whose members were invariably said to include Lords Bute and Mansfield, was busy conniving to enhance the power of "Prerogative" at the expense of the people's guaranteed liberties. No evidence has been adduced that any such group of conspiring Machiavels existed but in the imagination of the Americans and their supporters in Great Britain.†† This belief was even shared by some peers of the realm, as it was by Londoners who formed a clandestine Committee of Correspondence and surreptitiously struck off hundreds of handbills attacking "the present arbitrary ministry and their attempt to subvert the Constitution." The "ruinous consequences" of their policies would be visited not only on the Americans but ultimately equally on the English. As the colonies had not yet been declared in a state of rebellion, the propaganda was not treasonable; the government could take no action against the authors of these diatribes, who were careful to stay within the bounds of technical legality.

Dartmouth dispatched a copy of his secret letter of instruction to Gage about February 24. The general received it in his Boston headquarters on April 14. Two days later H.M.S. *Falcon* arrived with the original.‡‡ Gage now knew exactly what the ministry expected of him. He did not procrastinate, and on April 18, at 8 P.M., he sent for his regimental commanders and ordered them to have their grenadier and light infantry companies "on the beach near the Magazine Guard at 10 o'Clock . . . with one day's provisions and without knapsacks." The troops were to proceed in small batches, quietly, and to be prepared to embark immediately on arrival of the boats at the designated beach. But Admiral Graves's boats did not all arrive at the appointed time, and several precious hours elapsed before the flotilla was ready to move with

†† Lord Bute had not been confidentially associated with the King for at least eight years.

‡‡ It is important to note that the commander in chief's letters to Dartmouth and Barrington were normally not received at Whitehall offices for some six weeks after the general dispatched them; their replies usually required seven or eight weeks, since at least another week was added for administrative handling and paper work. Thus, Gage could not have had Whitehall's reaction to events he had reported in late August until early in December. Some round-trip mail packets made better time, of course, but some also made poorer due to adverse Atlantic weather. Time is a crucial factor in war, and in the war soon to begin, it was on the side of the Americans.

nine companies of grenadiers, eight of light infantry, and four of marines, a total of twenty-one companies. As the average strength of these was 32 men, some 672 rank and file, plus officers, sergeants, drummers, fifers, and medical orderlies must have set out on this night.

Lieutenant Colonel Francis Smith, almost too corpulent to sit a saddle, was in command; Major Pitcairn of the marines, second-in-command. Smith, indolent and slow-moving, was an obstinate dullard; why Gage ever selected him to lead this particular foray is one of the questions imposed by history. Lord Percy, an audacious and courageous young brigadier, was available. But Gage chose Smith.

The general and the admiral had planned that the movement be made secretly. Both were aware that agents of the Committee of Safety in Boston were reporting all suspicious activity. But security broke down. There have been many speculations as to the identity of the persons who might have passed information of the scheduled operation to the Americans. Indeed, the loyalty of Gage's own beloved wife was later to be challenged. To be sure, there may have been an informer. But no informer was needed to apprise the Americans, whose espionage net in Boston was efficient, that an early movement was projected.

By midafternoon on April 18, "it was pretty generally known," as Mackenzie's diary entry for that date testifies, that the British planned a large-scale movement by water that night. Many boats were already at the selected embarkation points; sailors who manned them were drinking and talking in the taverns. It was even quite possible to adduce a likely objective for the expedition: Concord, where Gage knew cannon and powder were stored, where the illegal Assembly had met, and where John Hancock and Samuel Adams, the two most wanted men, were thought to be.*

Legend has it that Paul Revere responded to lantern signals shown in the tower of the Old North Church to indicate the British were moving by sea, then took horse to alert the countryside, as did his friend and colleague, William Dawes.† Thus news that the Redcoats were on the way in force preceded them, and before the advance guard reached Lexington, insistently clamorous church bells, drums, bonfires, and musket shots had awakened everyone within a radius of twenty miles of the little town.

Colonel Smith was initially two hours behind schedule; he lost another because his men had been required to fight their way thigh-deep across tidal creeks which, had Graves's boats been on time, they could have walked through without wetting their calves. He had perforce to

---

* Hancock spending the night with his mistress, or so it was commonly believed at the time.

† Revere was taken by a British patrol and with a pistol put to his head, told all he knew—which was considerable. He never reached Lexington.

push the troops hard. When they arrived in Lexington at daybreak, they were tired, thirsty, and hungry. There, at the village green, seventy-seven militiamen stood in ragged ranks. They too were tired—their commander, Captain John Parker, had routed them out of warm beds shortly after midnight.

Pitcairn, commanding the advance party of the British column, rode toward the Americans and called out: "Disperse, ye Rebels! Lay down your arms and disperse." Parker ordered his men to file off—not, as legend has it, to stand—and the men began moving toward a stone wall on the right flank of the British column. As Pitcairn later reported to Gage: "The Light Infantry, observing this, ran after them. I instantly called to the Soldiers not to Fire, but to surround and disarm them . . . Some of the Rebels who had jumped over the Wall Fired Four or Five Shott at the Soldiers." Scattered firing began; within minutes the first Americans to give their lives in defense of the public liberty lay bleeding to death on the edge of the village green.

The British took up the march to Concord, which they reached without serious interruption. There they seized two bridges. At both, militiamen were posted, but no shots were exchanged. Outside the town, Redcoat detachments found and destroyed several cannon, some ammunition, and a few barrels of flour. When they returned, light infantry posted at the bridges began to retire on order. Suddenly, shots were exchanged at North Bridge,‡ and both sides suffered a few casualties.

With his assigned mission accomplished, Colonel Smith began his withdrawal toward Lexington. An orderly retirement rapidly became a retreat and soon a near rout, for the ranks received galling close-range fire from militiamen hidden behind boulders, trees, and stone fences lining the road. The Americans were fighting Indian fashion—and they were better marksmen than the Indians.

Early on the morning of the nineteenth, Gage had prudently ordered Brigadier General Lord Percy's brigade with two six-pounders attached to march to Lexington to support Smith's column. As Percy's advance guard approached the town, they heard firing and distinguished grenadiers and light infantry falling back in disarray. Percy covered the retirement, and shortly after three o'clock in the afternoon pulled in his flanking companies and took up the retreat to Boston.

Lieutenant Frederick Mackenzie, adjutant of the Royal Welch Fusiliers, who marched for seven miles in the rear guard, told the story in his diary:

> As the Country for many miles round Boston and in the neighborhood of Lexington and Concord, had by this time had notice of what was doing, as well as by the firing, as from expresses

‡ "The rude bridge that arched the flood."

which had been [sent] from Boston and the adjacent places in all directions, numbers of armed men on foot and on horseback were continually coming from all parts guided by the fire, and before the Column had advanced a mile on the road, we were fired at from all quarters, but particularly from the houses on the roadside and the Adjacent Stone Walls. Several of the Troops were killed and wounded in this way, and the Soldiers were so enraged at the suffering from an unseen Enemy that they forced open many of the houses from which the fire proceeded and put to death all those found in them. . . . As the Troops drew near to Cambridge the number and fire of the Rebels encreased, and altho they did not shew themselves openly in a body in any part, except on a road in our rear, our men threw away their fire very inconsiderately and without being sure of its effect.[17]

The British found continental tactics of no avail against an enemy who fought this way. The Redcoats, disciplined to face an enemy they could see, could not well be expected to charge in ordered ranks with fixed bayonets against impalpable shadows flitting from tree to tree in roadside apple orchards. Nor would British steel have much effect against individual skirmishers who lay on their stomachs or knelt to fire through chinks in stone walls.

On this day, American farmers dealt a blow to the thesis that massed infantry could always settle the issue with the bayonet. But the success of the Provincials on April 19 engendered the dangerous myth that the highly individualistic militiaman, untrained in orthodox combat techniques and contemptuous of authority and discipline, could cope with regulars in a battlefield situation. This myth was a long time dying.

Percy fell back via Charlestown Neck; until he gained that haven at about 7 P.M. his column was subject to "incessant irregular fire from all points" which increased in volume and accuracy. He brought in 17 officers and 167 enlisted wounded, many mortally. The British suffered 273 casualties, the Americans 93.

On the following day Lieutenant Mackenzie confided to his diary a critique of this botched affray: "I believe the fact is, that General Gage was not only much deceived with respect to the quantity of the Military Stores said to be collected at Concord, but had no conception the Rebels would have opposed the King's troops in the manner they did. But the temper of the people, the preparations they had been making all the winter to oppose the troops should they move out of Boston with hostile intentions, and above all their declared resolution to do so, made it evident to most persons, that opposition would be made."[18] The lieutenant also criticized security, and observed that Colonel Smith was a poor choice to command an expedition of this sort.

Mackenzie apparently saw or heard of a confidential report Percy had made to Gage, in which the earl was critical of the men's conduct: "tho they behaved with much courage and spirit, [they] shewed great inattention and neglect to the Commands of their Officers." Some, it seems, had left the ranks "to plunder and pillage." Gage at once issued an order prohibiting this "under pain of death." The general naturally omitted these items, which reflected seriously on himself, from his rather cryptic report to Dartmouth, in which he observed that the countryside had "assembled in Arms with Surprising Expedition"; that the rebels had surrounded Boston; were "getting up artillery" and "threatening an Attack."[19]

He wrote Viscount Barrington on the same day: "I have now nothing to trouble your Lordship with, but of an Affair that happened here on the 19th Inst." In this missive he reported that a "Body of Men" had opened fire on Lieutenant Colonel Smith's column as it approached Concord. After leaving Concord "the Troops . . . were Attacked from all Quarters . . . and they were so Fatigued with their March, that it was with difficulty they could keep out their Flanking Partys . . . so that they were at length, a good deal pressed." Brigadier Lord Percy's relief column had saved the day. But there had been a fight for the "Space of Fifteen Miles," the troops "receiving fire from every Hill, Fence, House, Barn, and his Lordship kept the Enemy off and brought the Troops to Charles Town."[20]

Gage immediately tightened discipline. "From all the measures which have been taken since the 19th Inst. it appears that the General is apprehensive the Rebels will make some desperate attempt in the town." He ordered officers "to lie in barracks with the men." Both officers and men were "to lie dressed in their tents, and ready to turn out on the shortest notice." The men slept with arms beside them. Mackenzie thought "The Duty at this time . . . very severe upon the Troops."[21]

Evelyn, who had marched out with Lord Percy's relief column, wrote his father of "the little fracas . . . between us and the Yankey scoundrels." He admitted British losses were heavy; this was because the rebels would not stand and fight. The militia had converged on Boston; the city was "absolutely invested with many thousand men"; the country was in arms, and supplies of provisions cut off. General Gage was expecting reinforcements; Evelyn plaintively wrote: "I wish they were arrived."

News that the Americans had faced Redcoat regulars at Lexington, and at relatively small cost had hurt them seriously, was traveling fast. On "Wednesday Morning near 10 of the Clock," as Pitcairn's advance guard approached Concord, Joseph Palmer, a member of the Massachusetts Committee of Secrecy, drew up a brief account of the morning's action, addressed it "To All Friends of American Liberty," and handed it to Israel Bissell, one of the committee's couriers, with instructions to "alarm the Country quite to Connecticut."

If ever a ride deserved a poet, Bissell's did. Fortunately, the record exists. He galloped to Worcester, where his spent and lathered horse dropped dead. There he spent the night. At dawn Thursday he saddled up and set off for "Connecticutt," stopping at every town and village to have Palmer's alert read, copied, and endorsed, to refresh himself, and to change horses when necessary. By seven in the evening he was in New London. He left at midnight, went on to Lyme, to Saybrook, to Guilford, to Branford, and to New Haven, where he spent the night after nearly twenty hours in the saddle. Saturday he slept. On Sunday, April 23, at about noon, he rode into New York, reported to the Committee of Safety, took a meal, crossed the Hudson, and galloped to Brunswick, New Jersey, where he arrived shortly after midnight. He reached Princeton at dawn, Trenton at nine, crossed the Delaware, and was in Philadelphia for supper.[22] By this time thousands of Massachusetts militiamen were converging on Cambridge. The reinforcements Captain Evelyn wished for were going to be needed.

It is impossible to try to establish the sequence of events that occurred on the village green at Lexington on that Wednesday morning in April so long ago. Even at the time, no two tales were precisely the same; the one woven into American legend is substantially this: "At Lexington, 6 miles below Concord, a Company of Militia, of about 100 men, mustered near the Meeting House; the Troops came in sight of them just before Sun-rise; and running within a few rods of them, the Commanding Officer accosted the militia in Words to this Effect:—'Disperse you Rebels —Damn you, throw down your Arms and disperse.' Upon which the Troops huzza'd, and immediately one or two officers discharged their Pistols."[23] This was not the way Pitcairn had reported the affair to Gage.

It is a reasonable conjecture that Sam Adams planned a violent confrontation on April 19. He of course knew that a few score militiamen— all that Parker could muster—could not stand up to British light infantry, grenadiers, and marines. That did not interest him. What did was that American blood must be shed. Concord was as good a place as any to start it flowing.**

The Massachusetts Congress, well aware that in a propaganda battle the first blow is decisive, acted at once to ensure that American accounts of "the 19th Inst." reached London before Gage's official dispatches. Members hurriedly interviewed a number of participants of the skirmishes at Lexington and Concord, took their affidavits, and prepared "An Address to the Inhabitants of Great Britain." The Congress chartered a sloop lying at Salem and entrusted the dispatches to her captain

** This is an unpopular hypothesis, and I readily admit there is no documentation to support it. Nevertheless, it remains a reasonable conjecture.

who, after a speedy passage, arrived in London on May 28. "The advice was immediately dispersed, while the Government remained without any intelligence. Stocks immediately fell."[24]

"Thus," Walpole wrote, "was the civil war begun and a victory the first fruits of it on the side of the Americans, whom Lord Sandwich had had the folly and rashness to proclaim coward."[25]

BOOK III

Imbarked on a
Tempestuous Ocean

1

A Kind of Destiny

The day after the British retreat from Concord, Majors General William Howe, the Honourable John Burgoyne, and Henry Clinton, all members of the House of Commons, embarked in His Majesty's frigate *Cerberus* for Boston. That Cerberus was the name of the three-headed dog that according to Greek mythology guarded the portals of Hades was not overlooked by colonial wits; one commemorated the passage thus:

> Behold the Cerberus
> The ocean plough
> Her precious cargo
> Burgoyne, Clinton, Howe,
> Bow Wow Wow!

The King had desired his three generals be allotted a special equipment allowance "as they have behaved so properly and are so poor" and wrote Lord North to direct Barrington to allow each £500. This example of royal generosity irked Gage, who had never received such consideration and had paid for his "chariot" out of his own pocket.

Howe was a competent and ambitious professional soldier. He had served in America under Major General Wolfe during the War for Empire, and, as a junior colonel, had led the storming party of twenty-four men who scaled the forbidding cliffs from the narrow shingle below Quebec to the Plains of Abraham. He was one of Wolfe's few favorites, and deserved to be. He was an advocate of light infantry; at the King's explicit direction, Howe had set up a camp at Salisbury and organized, drilled, and trained seven companies. Light infantrymen, sturdy and agile, served with the grenadiers of each regiment as "flanking companies" on the march, and in combat were assigned missions and posts deemed dangerous and demanding.

Howe had revived the idea that "flanking companies" of a number of regiments (usually five or six) could be temporarily withdrawn from their parent organizations and formed into separate elite battalions. By 1774 this system had been generally adopted in the British Army; the "flank companies" of Gage's regiments comprised the major part of the column that marched to Concord on April 19 under the command of Colonel Francis Smith and Major Pitcairn. As a senior permanent major general, Howe naturally anticipated he would eventually succeed Gage as commander in chief in America. All he had to do was await the day.

Henry Clinton, recently widowed, was thirty-seven years old when he arrived in Boston. His father, an admiral, had served for seven years as royal governor of New York. His uncle, the Earl of Lincoln, had married into the powerful Pelham family; the eldest son of this union, who became Duke of Newcastle, was Clinton's first cousin. The general's aristocratic connections were impeccable; his early record as an officer, distinguished. During the Seven Years' War, when aide-de-camp to the Prince of Brunswick, he was cited for gallantry; in 1763, when the war ended, he was a twenty-five-year-old colonel, but one with very little command experience.

When he returned to England, he was given several boring assignments and then began to dabble in politics. In 1772 he was elected to Parliament from a constituency controlled by Newcastle. During this decade of peace Clinton made some effort to improve himself in his chosen profession. He was shy and inclined to conceal his natural diffidence by stubborn assertiveness, a dichotomy bound to lead to personality clashes with his seniors, his naval colleagues, and his subordinates.*

Burgoyne had not particularly wanted to go to America as an unassigned major general, where he would be a "cypher," or at best get "a small brigade" with no responsibilities other than "to see that the soldiers boiled their kettles regularly." His two companions and both Major General Guy Carleton, governor of Canada, and Haldimand were senior to him; in these circumstances he saw no chance of getting the independent command he so ardently desired. Further, his adored wife, "dearest

---

* He described himself as "a shy bitch."

Charlotte . . . the tenderest, the faithfullest, the most amiable companion and friend that ever man was blessed with," was in poor health. He did not wish to linger in Boston.

But he had employed his last week in London to good advantage. The King was fond of Burgoyne; they often rode together; there appeared to be an intimate relationship, and before the general sailed, the King directed Lord North to see him and to have "a full conversation" as "he feels a little hurt at not having been enough let into the views of Government, and if he remains at Boston he may be able to suggest what falls in conversation to the Commander-in-Chief, which may prove of great utility."[1] This arrangement reflects unfavorably on the King's character, as it does disagreeably on that of "Gentleman Johnny." Possibly in exchange for Burgoyne's agreement to do a little high-level informing, the King approved his request to return to England the following winter "during the time the troops cannot be employed."

While H.M.S. *Cerberus* ploughed the Atlantic, several imaginative Connecticut militia officers worked out a plan to take by surprise the British fort at Ticonderoga at the southern end of Lake Champlain. During the Seven Years' War, British and French alike considered Ticonderoga to be the strategic key to control of the northern country. After Major General James Abercrombie had sustained a thoroughly humiliating defeat in his attempt to take the fort in July 1758, an army of British and colonials under General Jeffrey Amherst had forced the French to withdraw and raised the royal standard.

Since that time the British had spent very little money on maintenance. A small caretaker garrison, idle and bored, stood guard over the deteriorating remains. Bastions were crumbling, roofs leaking, and doors rotting and sagging from rusting hinges. The armament still in place included upwards of one hundred cannon of various types ranging from six- to twenty-four-pounders, a large number of swivel guns, some mortars, several score barrels of powder, and ten tons of musket balls.

A small group of Connecticut men determined to take the fort, and in April went to Berkshire, Massachusetts, to enlist volunteers. There they encountered Benedict Arnold, a colonel of militia, who had been contemplating the same object. With his help they collected fifty volunteers, armed them, and proceeded to Bennington, where Colonel Ethan Allen joined with a hundred "Green Mountain Boys" from the Hampshire Grants (now Vermont). Allen refused to serve under Arnold, but agreed he could accompany the expedition as an observer.

Allen halted his column some ten miles from Ticonderoga and dispatched Captain Noah Phelps to make a reconnaissance of the target. The captain, a discreet man, proceeded to Ticonderoga and ingratiated himself with several officers of the garrison who were indulging in a drinking party at a nearby tavern. On the following day he went to the fort to be shaved; after he had been barbered he called on the commanding officer, Captain William de la Place, who welcomed him and showed him around. Phelps observed that the ramparts were dilapidated. The captain agreed they were indeed, and added that, much worse, all his powder was damp. Phelps did not wait to hear more. He politely took his leave and returned to the rendezvous set by Allen, who marched the force over forest trails to Ticonderoga. En route, Allen detached a small group to Skenesborough (now Whitehall, N.Y.) to arrest Major Philip Skene, the principal Tory in the vicinity. Before dawn on May 10, Allen (as he was to tell the tale) demanded surrender of the fort "in the name of the Great Jehovah and the Continental Congress." Captain de la Place, routed out of bed in his nightcap, excused himself to dress, and obliged.

The Massachusetts Committee of Safety had given Arnold a commission as colonel in the Massachusetts militia and had ordered him "to take the King's Vessel on the Lake," sloop *Betsy*, at St. Johns on the Richelieu River. Arnold did not wait while a few cannon were being mounted on Skene's forty-foot sloop (rechristened *Liberty*), but set off immediately in a large bateau. *Liberty* overtook him on May 17 and was becalmed thirty miles from the target. Again Arnold put his men to the oars. They rowed all night, and early the next morning surprised the unsuspecting garrison of fourteen at St. Johns, seized *Betsy* and four bateaux, and took off for Ticonderoga. This exploit, executed with the vigor that was to distinguish Arnold, gave the Americans undisputed control of Lake Champlain.

Arnold and Allen now resumed their interrupted feuding. Each equally conceited and ambitious for fame claimed command and neither would give an inch. Arnold was unnecessarily arrogant and obnoxious, and when news of his misbehavior reached the ears of his Massachusetts sponsors, they dispatched a committee to investigate. The committee, empowered to discharge Arnold from his command, did so, but not before he had resigned and departed the scene of his late triumph in a profane dudgeon.

The seizure of Ticonderoga considerably embarrassed Congress. The colonists could not convincingly sustain the role of injured party while groups of aggressive militiamen took over His Majesty's undermanned military installations. The delegates thereupon hit on the scarcely novel idea of excusing Allen's brash action by accusing the ministry of planning "a cruel invasion" from Quebec. They thoughtfully directed that cannon and stores be removed from the site, and ordered exact inventories to ensure "that they may be safely returned, when the restoration of the former harmony between Great Britain and her colonies, so ardently wished for by the latter," had been achieved. Finally, Congress expressed its pious disapproval of colonial excursions into Canada.

The three generals landed at Boston on May 25, and Howe, the senior, delivered a Letter of Instruction from Lord Dartmouth to Gage. In this, the secretary observed that as "Acts of Treason and Rebellion" had continued "with impunity," Administration had decided to augment the forces in America. He directed Gage to seize all military stores, equipment, and cannon deposited in royal magazines, or known to have been secreted by the rebels. But even with the newly arrived reinforcements Gage did not have the capability of mounting a serious operation into an aroused and armed countryside. Indeed, he would have had a real fight on his hands had he tried to force his way out of beleaguered Boston.

Dartmouth also authorized the royal governor to issue a proclamation offering sizable rewards for the apprehension of the rebel leaders, and promising His Majesty's gracious pardon to all who would surrender their arms and subscribe to an oath of allegiance to the crown. The letter contained another directive of particular interest, authorizing the enlistment of two corps of Loyalists, one in Canada and upper New York and one in the hill country of the Carolinas, where there were many emigrant Highland Scots.

As he had anticipated, Burgoyne was given an insignificant job, and on June 14 wrote Adjutant General Harvey lamenting the "ill success" of the foray to Concord, which he blamed on Gage's mismanagement and the ineptitude and "want of capacity" of the various staff departments. "Short of the interposition of a miracle" he saw no chance the colonies could be pacified in 1775. Nor did the commanding general, who two days earlier had written Lord Barrington urging the Administration to muster every resource, including Indians and Negros: "Nothing is to be neglected of which we can avail ourselves. Hannovarians, Hessians, perhaps Russians May be hired. . . ."[2] In the same letter he reported he had been forced to declare martial law and added that he could wait no longer for promised reinforcements, but "must Attempt some of the Rebels Posts without more delay."

Reports of the affair that happened on April 19 reached London in late May; John Pownall wrote his colleague William Knox, who was taking the waters at Spa, that the news "had little or no effect, either to create apprehension or disturb public Credit." He added that general opinion in Administration was "the dye is cast, and more mischief will follow." Indeed, "mischief" very soon followed, for in the next week members of the Constitutional Society resolved to raise a subscription of £100 "To be applied to the Relief of the Widows, Orphans and Aged Parents of our beloved American fellow-subjects, who faithful to the character of Englishmen, preferring Death to Slavery were, for that

Reason only, inhumanly Murdered by the King's Troops at or near Lexington and Concord." The sum was quickly subscribed and John Horne
paid it into Dr. Franklin's account. The resolution appeared in the press
several days later; Lord Suffolk immediately asked the crown's legal advisers for an opinion. Thurlow and Wedderburn replied that the resolution constituted a seditious libel and Suffolk signified the King's pleasure
that Thurlow forthwith commence prosecution.[3]

At this point the King, who had refused to receive on the throne another petition from the City, let it be known he was heartily sick of
addresses, remonstrances, and petitions from the lord mayor, aldermen,
and livery, who, on receipt of this news, promptly drew up a resolution
(June 24) declaring that those who had advised His Majesty to this
course were enemies of the "Constitutional Rights" of the people.[4] They
then determined to present their latest "Address, Remonstrance and Petition" in the most formal manner possible, and directed the sheriffs and
the remembrancer "to wait on his Majesty on Monday next to know his
Royal Will and Pleasure." This they did; the King reiterated his determination to receive no more such communications on the throne.

The lord mayor summoned the aldermen, who mulled over this during the next week. Finally, on July 4, they adopted half a dozen
discreetly belligerent resolutions and ordered the town clerk, one
William Rix, to have attested copies made and delivered to the "Publick
Papers." The resolutions were duly printed in *The Public Advertiser* on
July 6. This contumacious behavior enraged the King, who directed
Suffolk to act. The secretary as usual passed the chore to the crown's
overworked legal advisers, who some three weeks later advised him that
neither the lord mayor nor any alderman could be summoned, but that
Rix and the printer of *The Public Advertiser* could be charged with
publishing a seditious libel. This did not please His Majesty, who was
after bigger game than a town clerk and an obscure printer. If those who
opposed his policy could do nothing else, they would at least clog the
offices of a Principal Secretary of State, the Attorney General, and the
Solicitor General with reams of paper work.

While the British were cooped up in Boston, members of Congress in
Philadelphia debated the problems of how best to organize provincial
governments to supplant disintegrating royal administrations. John
Adams wrote later that this question then lay with great weight on his
mind: "for from the beginning I always expected we should have more
difficulty and danger in our attempts to govern ourselves, and in our negotiations and connections with foreign powers, than from all the fleets
and armies of Great Britain." But the sword had been drawn; Adams
urged Congress to throw away the scabbard, and "to call forth every energy and resource of the country." Although "as fond of Reconciliation

. . . as any man," he thought it now but a remote possibility: "I think, that if we consider the Education of the Sovereign, and that the Lords, the Commons, the Electors, the Army, the Navy, the officers of Excise, Customs, etc., have been now for many years gradually trained and disciplined by Corruption to the System of the Court, We shall be convinced that the Cancer is too deeply rooted and too far Spread to be cured by anything short of cutting it entire."[5] He advocated holding a sword in one hand and an olive branch in the other: "to proceed with Warlike Measures and Conciliatory Measures *Pari Passu*."

John was working long hours in humid Philadelphia; Abigail worried about his health; he was not to forget that his body was "so infirm as to require the tenderest care and nursing." In the Bay Colony the future was ominous; everyone lived "in continual expectation of alarms." Gage would soon take "desperate steps"; she hourly expected the seacoast to be ravaged and she and young Johnny "driven away from our yet quiet cottage."

One of the "Warlike Measures" absorbing the attention of Congress was the appointment of a general to command the American forces encamped near Roxbury. The question had been discussed "out of doors," and on June 14 was raised on the floor. Washington, approached informally, was not yet persuaded to accept; although "deeply impressed with the importance of that honourable trust" he was diffident of his own superior abilities. His nomination on the following day was an inspired political move. He was a respected leader in Virginia; his election would automatically identify that rich and populous colony and her sisters to the south with the cause of New England. Second, and equally important, he was a wealthy aristocrat, a patrician landholder, one who would draw influential waverers into the revolutionary fold. His military experience during the War for Empire was of course an important qualification for the "high office" to which he was elected on June 15, 1775, "by the unanimous voice of all America." As "Captain-General and Commander-in-Chief of all forces raised and to be raised in the common cause" his responsibilities would be immense, a fact he well realized.

He accepted the appointment on June 16, and two days later wrote Martha at Mt. Vernon: "You may believe me, my dear Patsy, when I assure you in the most solemn manner that so far from seeking this appointment, I have used every endeavor in my power to avoid it, not only from my unwillingness to part from you and the family, but from a consciousness of its being a trust too great for my capacity. . . . But as it has been a kind of destiny that has thrown me upon this service, I shall hope that my undertaking it is designed to answer some good purpose."

In a letter to his friend Burwell Bassett, he said: "I am now Imbarked on a tempestuous Ocean, from whence, perhaps, no friendly harbor is to be found."[6] The commander in chief could not then have even imagined how tempestuous his passage was to be on the ocean of war and politics. But his belief that he had been summoned by "a kind of destiny" would sustain him through many storms.

On the day Washington was appointed, Congress secretly adopted the Massachusetts troops, as well as those guarding the Highlands of the Hudson, and authorized the immediate enlistment of ten companies of riflemen at a strength of sixty-eight men per company. As the British were to learn, these were "the finest Marksmen in the world" who did "Execution with their Rifle Guns at an Amazing Distance." The next morning, Congress elected Artemas Ward, Charles Lee, Philip Schuyler, and Israel Putnam as major generals, and Horatio Gates as adjutant general.

John Adams wrote James Warren that nothing had given him "more Torment than the Scuffle we have had in appointing the General Officers. . . . Dismal Bugbears were raised . . . Prejudices enough among the weak, and fears enough among the timid, as well as other obstacles from the Cunning." But he had the commander in chief he wanted, and on June 17 wrote Abigail: "I can now inform you that the Congress have made choice of the modest and virtuous, the amiable, generous and brave George Washington, Esquire, to be General of the American army, and that he is to repair, as soon as possible, to the camp before Boston. This appointment will have a great effect in cementing and securing the Union of these colonies . . . the liberties of America depend on him, in a great degree."[7] John Hancock signed Washington's commission on June 19.

Jonathan Boucher, the fiery, courageous, hard-drinking Anglican rector of St. Anne's in Annapolis, Maryland, who spent less time in his parish than he did riding to hounds, had known Washington and provided a reasonably objective assessment of the Virginia militia colonel: "I know Washington well and can say of him what I can of few of his Confreres, that I believe him to be an honest Man. In the Military Line . . . his merit can be considerable." Boucher judged that Washington could atone for professional shortcomings by coolness and caution, but in battle might be "confounded by Strategems; in a regular Action he may by his Steadiness and extreme Care acquit himself well, but against the manoevers of Art, I am satisfied he is defenceless."

It was indeed fortunate the liberties of America were not to depend on some of the others. Charles Lee, a former British regular lieutenant colonel and sometime flamboyant soldier of fortune who had sold his commission and purchased land in Virginia, was conceited, brash, devious, and arrogant. Sir Horace Mann, Walpole's correspondent in Florence, who had known Lee, described him as "a furious, upstart hero . . . [who had] perverted the great parts he was possessed of into the rankest malice that the most indecent terms could express against every individual who differed with him in politics." Mann thought him "a scheming politician" who had cast his lot with the rebels to make himself conspicuous.[8] But Lee was an experienced officer with an impressive record, and his claim to high rank was vigorously and successfully supported when selections were made.

Artemas Ward was an amiable and benevolent amateur soldier who had fought in the War for Empire; Israel Putnam an honest, tough Indian fighter who could lay a good ambush but had no conception of how to handle any body of men larger than a company. Schuyler, a wealthy and politically powerful Hudson Valley patroon from Albany, was an intelligent and cultivated man with some military experience, who might prove himself a competent general officer. His appointment was purely political. Horatio Gates, another former British officer who had sold his commission and bought land in Virginia, was a capable martinet, a good administrator, and a conscientious quill-driver, well suited by temperament to the responsible staff position allotted him. Several of the brigadiers appointed by Congress, notably Nathanael Greene and Richard Montgomery (the latter also late of His Majesty's service), were younger officers of promise.

Several days before Hancock signed the most important commission in American history, a bloody battle was fought near Boston. The genesis of Bunker Hill goes back to May 12, when the Massachusetts Committee of Safety resolved that "a strong redoubt" should be raised there. From this position cannon could interdict approaches to Charlestown and the mouth of the Mystic River. The committee, which must have had a well-placed informer in Gage's headquarters, had learned that he contemplated seizing Bunker Hill and Dorchester Heights, and directed Ward to forestall him. Apparently Ward's Council of War concluded that nothing could be done about Dorchester Heights, but decided to occupy and fortify the hills overlooking Charlestown. Shortage of powder, ball ammunition, cannon, cannonballs, and engineer tools influenced this decision.

Ward gave the job to Colonel William Prescott, a tall, blue-eyed, muscular man who concealed his thinning brown hair with a gray wig. The colonel, long known as a determined opponent of British policy and an advocate of American liberty, accepted the assignment with alacrity. During the early evening of June 16 Prescott assembled three understrength regiments, part of another, one lone engineer, and a wagonload of shovels, picks, mattocks, and axes at Cambridge.† As nothing relating to command was put on paper, it is not clear how General Israel Putnam got into the picture, but he did. The orders given by the committee, presumably on Ward's recommendation, explicitly designated the objective as Bunker Hill. For some unknown reason, Putnam, who was senior officer present, prevailed on Prescott to raise the redoubt on adja-

† Normally, a "regiment" numbered about five hundred rank and file.

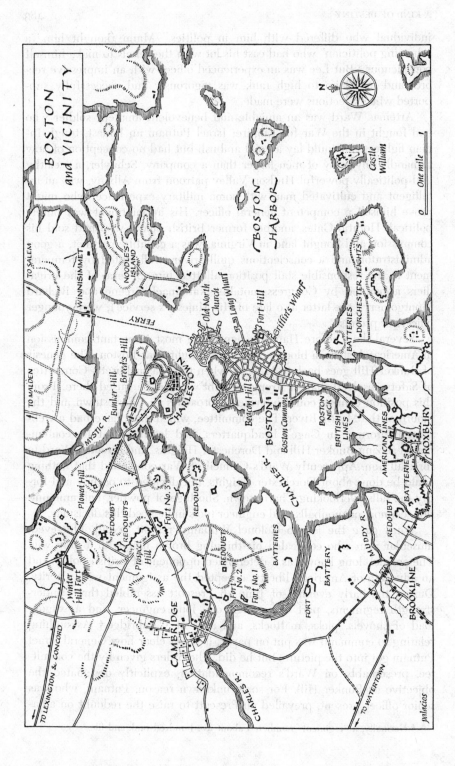

BOSTON and VICINITY

N

BOSTON HARBOR

Castle William

0   One mile

TO SALEM

WINNISIMMET

NOODLES ISLAND

FERRY

DORCHESTER HEIGHTS

BATTERIES

TO MALDEN

Bunker Hill

Breed's Hill

MYSTIC R.

CHARLESTOWN

Old North Church

Long Wharf

Griffin's Wharf

Fort Hill

Beacon Hill

BOSTON

Boston Common

Boston Neck

BRITISH LINES

AMERICAN LINES

ROXBURY

BATTERIES

REDOUBT

MUDDY R.

FORT

BATTERY

CHARLES R.

BROOKLINE

TO WATERTOWN

CAMBRIDGE

CHARLES R.

TO LEXINGTON & CONCORD

Winter Hill Fort

Plowed Hill

Prospect Hill

REDOUBTS

REDOUBT

Fort No. 3

Fort No. 2

Fort No. 1

REDOUBT

BATTERIES

palacios

cent lower Breed's Hill. From midnight to dawn the men moved dirt. Shortly after sunrise, guns of H.M.S. *Lively* signaled the alarm. Soon *Falcon* and other ships were firing. Admiral Graves's guns made a great deal of noise but had little effect on the hill where dirt was flying.

Gage immediately summoned a Council of War; at this meeting Clinton proposed that he embark a battalion, proceed at once toward the Mystic River, and land in the American rear while Howe attacked from the front. Howe rejected this plan; he wanted to await the rising tide and land in force on the beach in front of the position, where beyond musket range, he could form up his ranks and launch an orthodox assault. Clinton wanted to avoid a frontal attack and thought a six- or seven-hour delay quite unnecessary and potentially dangerous. But as he later wrote, he was "not attended to." Gage approved Howe's plan; Brigadier General Robert Pigot's brigade was to land behind Howe, move rapidly to the left, and attack from that direction.

The Redcoats, heavily encumbered with packs containing three days' rations and a variety of other items suitable for a protracted field operation, began landing on a rising tide shortly after 2 P.M. Admiral Graves's ships covered them by a continuous cannonade; Charlestown was set afire by hot shot as the first wave of regulars disembarked and waded ashore. Behind them came wave after wave of boats. "The sun was shining in meridian splendor and the scarlet uniforms, the glistening armor [gorgets worn by the officers?], the brazen artillery, the regular movement of the boats, the flashes of fire and the belching of smoke formed a spectacle brilliant and imposing." The grenadiers landed at Moulton's Point, formed up, dressed ranks, were issued a ration of grog, and stood easy.

When Howe, surrounded by aides and attended by his servant (whose function was to keep the general supplied with wine), gave the order to advance, the Redcoats marched slowly and methodically up the slope. They stopped every few yards to dress ranks. The hill was ready for haying; there were several wooden fences and stone walls to negotiate; the thermometer stood at 90° or 91°; a light breeze wafted across the bay from south-southwest. The Redcoats were sweating.‡

Howe had expected to open his artillery to support the advance; he had asked for six-pound cannonballs, and was sent twelve-pounders: "The wretched blunder of the oversized balls sprung from the dotage of an officer of rank who spends his whole time in dallying with the schoolmaster's daughter." There was no effective artillery preparation. The advance was exhausting, but on they went.

‡ The British complained of the heat, and this time with reason. The faint breeze afforded little relief. The Redcoats wore heavy woolen uniforms, and in the first two assaults carried in addition to their muskets and ammunition, packs weighing fifty to sixty pounds.

In the redoubt, officers and sergeants talked to their men in hushed voices: "Fire low"; "Aim at the waist bands"; "Shoot the officers"; "Wait until you see the whites of their eyes"; "Aim at the handsome coats"; "Aim at the commanders." The Americans held fire until the British were less than fifteen rods from the redoubt. Then, suddenly, within ninety seconds, three successive sheets of flame blazed from the parapets. The Redcoats faltered, turned, and stumbled down the hill to the safety of the beach. Again they tried; again they were driven back.

Howe called for reinforcements. These duly arrived, disembarked, and ascended the dreadful hill. Major Pitcairn, who had written to the First Lord of the Admiralty in mid-February that "the deluded people" believed they were invincible but would "soon be convinced that they are very insignificant when opposed to regular troops," was one of hundreds who fell mortally wounded in the bloody grass. He died cradled lovingly in the arms of his son, a lieutenant of marines. Burgoyne witnessed the battle from the side of Boston, and later described it as "one of the greatest scenes of war that can be conceived . . . Howe's corps, ascending the hill in the face of intrenchments, and in a very disadvantageous ground, was much engaged."

The Americans, too, were being reinforced. The admiral's ships and floating batteries kept firing furiously; Charlestown was blazing; church steeples crashed in fountains of flame. Burgoyne reflected that a defeat would mean "a final loss to the British empire in America." This thought "made the whole a picture [and] a complication of horrour and importance beyond anything that ever came to my lot to be witness to."[9] Shortly before 5 P.M. the Redcoats, in a third assault, took the position, and Burgoyne was able to write, "The day ended with glory." It was glory dearly bought.

Rarely had a victorious force suffered such proportionately heavy losses as the British did in two hours on that sultry afternoon. If Howe landed with 2,400 rank and file, his casualty rate was almost exactly 44 per cent. A rate of half this figure (particularly when one remembers that officers and sergeants suffered even more heavily than did the rank and file) would wreck a modern regiment.

Gage reported 1,054 casualties, of whom 226 were killed on the shambles of the slopes. Many later succumbed to severe wounds inflicted at short range by musket balls almost three quarters of an inch in diameter. Some bled to death in boats as they were being taken back to Boston; many others died shortly after in hospital. Some lingered after excruciatingly painful amputations to die in agony. Bunker Hill did not shatter Gage's army but it did crack his morale. And to the general who returned to Boston, his breeches soaked with blood, the battle had done something, too. For on the slope Howe experienced "*a Moment that I never felt before.*" American casualties totaled 441, including Dr. Joseph

Warren, who had laid aside his mortar and pestle to participate. The doctor died wearing his red silk waistcoat.

It is surprising that Howe proposed this unimaginative battle plan.** Clinton had objected strenuously, but Gage persisted in his decision. Bunker Hill cost Gage about one fifth of his force; several more such "victories" would ruin the British Army in America. The colonials, who could summon more militia, could make up losses in three or four days; the British required as many months.

If only because they had taken ground, the British could claim a victory. So Lord Rawdon of the grenadiers reported the result of the battle. He estimated the American force as 6,000, and wrote "they should have kept off five times our number . . . the men advanced with infinite spirit."†† But American eyewitnesses claimed to have seen British officers driving their men forward to the disastrous second, and successful third, assaults with the points of their swords.

The stubborn valor of British officers and men was not equaled by the tactical skill of their field commander, who did, however, give a more objective account of the battle than had the young and inexperienced Lord Rawdon. In his report to the adjutant general, Howe described the action as "an unhappy day—I freely confess to you, when I look to the consequences of it, in the loss of so many brave Officers, I do it with horror—The Success is too dearly bought." Howe did not favor another effort: "We must not risk the endangering the loss of Boston." To attack the rebels in their entrenchments would be an expensive and fruitless undertaking: "The intentions of these Wretches are to fortify every Post in our way; wait to be attacked at every One . . . destroying as many of us as they can. . . ."[10] The clear implication is that this was a most ungentlemanly way to fight.

Howe's contempt for the Americans, his inexcusable failure to make even a superficial reconnaissance and to modify his tactics after the first unsuccessful assault, had led to the needless sacrifice of superb British regiments. Admiral Graves had control of the waters in Boston Harbor and could have landed troops at any spot. The tactics on this day were dictated by the determination to demonstrate unequivocally the invincibility of British arms. But something had happened on the way to the top of a hill.

Rain fell gently all Sunday, and British cannon in Boston ceased firing on American positions in Cambridge and Roxbury. Everyone feared the British would attack the thin lines. Abigail wrote John: "It is expected they will come out over the Neck tonight and a dreadful battle must ensue. Almighty God! cover the heads of our Countrymen and be a

---

** Or did Gage propose the plan? The record is not precise.

†† Actually, something fewer than 1,500, and not equal in numbers to the attacking force.

shield to our dear friends." Americans in the lines, apprehensive and fearful, awaited the assault they believed imminent.

But Gage had no intention of going out over the Neck. Quite the contrary. He feared the Yankees would pour in over the Neck and from their whaleboats and slaughter his Redcoats. The patriots in Boston would rise, fire the town, burn his headquarters, and string up every Tory they could find. He ordered night patrols, directed his troops to sleep on their arms, and to be prepared to respond to an immediate summons.

Several days after this bloody fight, Burgoyne wrote his friend Lord Rochford, Secretary of State for the Southern Department, that the engagement was inevitable, for had the rebels emplaced cannon on the eminence, both His Majesty's fleet and army would have been ignominiously "kicked out of America." He did not explain why Gage could not have occupied the heights earlier without a battle. But he gave the Americans full marks: "The defence was well conceived and obstinately maintained; the retreat was no flight; it was even covered with bravery and military skill." To the British, he was less complimentary: "The zeal and intrepidity of the officers . . . was ill-seconded by the private men. Discipline, not to say courage, was wanting."[11]

This was the biggest story colonial printers had ever got their hands on, and they made the most of it. In Hartford the *Courant,* in the mistaken belief that Connecticut's own beloved hero, Israel Putnam, had been in command, described him as the general "whose undaunted courage and martial abilities strike terror through all the hosts of Midianites." The panegyrist, carried away by his own rhetoric, declared that Putnam was "formed to work wonders in the sight of those uncircumcised Philistines at Boston and Bunker Hill who attempt to ravage this country and defy the armies of the living God." Accounts in other journals were only slightly less bombastic.‡‡

Certainly New Englanders expected that their great fight would inspire their sisters to the south to arouse themselves. But no general explosion of anti-British feeling followed on the news of Bunker Hill. Although the battle had drawn a distinct line between patriots and Loyalists and forced neutralists to declare themselves, most colonists were not yet ready to accept the arbitrament of a bloody civil war.

For months the ministry had been prodding Gage to do something. But what could he do now? He could not withdraw by sea—no transports were available. He could not afford again to attack the entrenched Americans, for even if he drove them from one position they would fall back and occupy another. And, Burgoyne wrote, if Gage broke into the countryside he would not find a "single sheep or an ounce of flour." Fur-

‡‡ Another Yankee newspaper summarized the general's situation after Bunker Hill boastfully when it observed that Gage's army could be divided into three parts: one-third underground, one-third aboveground, and the remaining third in hospital.

ther, the army had no train to support such an operation; Gage had no horses, oxen, carts, wagons, or drivers. And, he continued, the greatest failure was intelligence: "We are ignorant not only of what passes in Congress, but want spies for the hill half a mile off." He admitted Gage's situation was one "in which Caesar might have failed," and although he judged the King's general in America to be benevolent and humane, he was neither an energetic nor a resourceful commander: "an incompetent General." He dismissed Graves in three words: "an apathetic Admiral."

Burgoyne then turned to a consideration of what offensive action "Our present small Force will permit to be taken this Season" and concluded that after expected reinforcements arrived, an expedition of some 2,200 could be put together and sent off to raid coastal towns in Rhode Island, Connecticut, and Long Island. These descents would terrify the colonists; Rhode Island and Connecticut would certainly demand immediate return of their militia encamped before Boston. At least a few towns could be burned, their inhabitants driven off, and sheep, cattle, grain, and hay collected. Burgoyne suggested this idea to Gage; the governor, still in a state of shock, was in no mood to entertain it.

Gentleman Johnny then presented his ideas of how to "do the business in one Campaign" and urged a major effort on the line of the Hudson River both from the side of New York and from Canada. In the South, Indians and Negro slaves could be raised and armed to co-operate with regulars; at the same time, "a numerous Fleet" could "sweep the whole coast."[12] Burgoyne discounted Loyalist potential and events were to prove him right in doing so. Fruitless pursuit of this will-o'-the-wisp would later have a pernicious effect on British strategic planning and conduct of operations in America.

Gage followed up his first reports with a private letter to Dartmouth on June 25. In this he gave the secretary an objective assessment of American strengths. "The Tryals we have had shew that the Rebels are not the despicable Rabble two many have supposed them to be, and I find it owing to a Military Spirit encouraged among them for a few years past, joined with an uncommon degree of Zeal and Enthousiasm." As to their tactics: "Wherever they find Cover, they make a good Stand, and the Country, naturally Strong, affords it them, and they are taught to assist in its Natural Strength by Art, for they entrench and raise Batterys."[13] He reported the rebels working feverishly to complete the circumvallation of Boston: ". . . they have fortifyed all the Passes and Heights round this Town from Dorchester to Medford on Mystick."

The commander in chief again warned Dartmouth that the "Conquest of America would not be easy" and could be expected only "by Time and Perseverance, and Strong Armys attacking it in various Quarters." On the following day, he wrote Barrington his opinion that the Americans were "spirited up by a Rage and Enthusiasm as great as ever People were possessed of, and you must proceed in earnest or give the Business up. A small body Acting in one Spot will not avail. You must have large Armys making Divertions on different sides; to divide their force. The loss we have sustained is greater than we can bear, Small Army's cant afford such losses. . . ." In Boston, he said, "we are taking the bull by the horns . . . I wish this cursed place was burned."[14]

Opinion in ministerial and parliamentary circles held that Boston was the focus of sedition and treason and that the rebellious sentiments of her inflamed people were shared only in adjacent New England colonies. Gage attempted to dispel this delusion; he assured Dartmouth that in most provinces "all Powers both Legislative and executive, are lodged in the Hands of Congresses and Committees, and the People's Minds kept So heated and inflamed that they are always ripe for everything that is extravagant. Truth is kept from them, and they are too full of Prejudice to believe it if it's laid before them, and so blind and bigotted that they can't see they have exchanged Liberty for Tyranny."[15] Obviously, General Gage and the Adams cousins had differing definitions of the words "liberty" and "tyranny." This estimate was, however, essentially correct, for although the colonies were as yet not united, they had formed a common front in determination to resist further encroachments of the crown and Parliament on their Charter rights and infringements of what they conceived to be their liberties as British subjects. In the process the structure of royal government in America, with the exception of precarious enclaves in Boston and New York, had disintegrated. The colonists had not demolished it, but had simply ceased to pay the slightest attention to it, and were attempting to establish their own local authorities in its place.

In almost every respect the resolutions adopted in the various colonial assemblies were identical in content, and for the most part in language. One important common feature was the expressed intent to achieve economic self-sufficiency. This of course meant that Navigation Acts and other acts restricting colonial trade were dead letters. The inhabitants of all colonies were urged to practice economy and frugality, to eschew ostentation, and to give up cards, dicing, horse racing, and cockfighting. Most made some attempt to ensure financial stability by imposing some sort of commodity price control. These clear signals that the Americans were preparing for a protracted resistance, and war—if it came to that—were not read in Whitehall.

Administration had a difficult time convincing skeptics that Bunker Hill had been anything other than a near disaster. Walpole thought the announced "success" at best a "very equivocal" one: ". . . the conqueror lost three to one more than the vanquished. The last do not pique themselves upon modern good breeding, but level only at the officers, of whom they have slain a vast number. We are a little disappointed indeed at their fighting at all which was not in our calculation. . . . Well! We had better have gone on robbing the Indies; it was more lucrative trade."[16] Here Walpole got to the heart of the matter. The British had not expected the Americans to fight.

Bunker Hill called for an immediate assessment of strategy now to be pursued. But no such assessment was made. Knox urged Dartmouth to order Gage to withdraw from Boston as soon as shipping could be provided, and to mount an attack against Georgia and South Carolina, where he believed Loyalist influence to be strong. He pointed out that Redcoats had to arrive in force and remain long enough to get the Loyalists organized and armed. The suggestion was discussed at cabinet meetings and was approved in principle.

On June 23, Generals Washington, Lee, and Schuyler set off for Cambridge; two days later they arrived at "Colonel Lispenard's seat," about a mile above New York City. In the city they received a tumultuous reception. Coincidentally, Governor William Tryon had on that day returned from London, but tactfully did not land until the festivities in honor of Washington were concluded and he and his colleagues safely out of town. Tryon "was conducted to the house of the Hon. Hugh Wallace, Esq. by an immense number of the principal people. . . ."[17] Some who greeted the governor had acclaimed the American generals a few hours earlier.

Before he left New York for Cambridge the commander in chief directed Schuyler to assume command of the Northern Department with headquarters at Albany; to "keep a watchful Eye upon Governor Tryon" and to arrest and detain him should the royal governor take any action to rouse the Tories, or to impede recruitment of militia. He was "in like manner" to watch carefully "the Movements of the Indian Agent," Colonel Guy Johnson, who had succeeded Sir William Johnson in that critical position. The general then found time to get off his first letter to the president of Congress asking that powder be expeditiously forwarded to New York: The city had sent one thousand pounds to Cambridge and was now "almost destitute of that necessary article."

Washington, Lee, Gates, and Joseph Reed, the general's secretary, arrived in Cambridge on July 2 and moved into the house Samuel Langdon, president of Harvard College, hospitably offered. The following day Washington assumed command of the American troops investing Boston. It would be stretching military terminology to an unwarrantable degree to state that he took command of an "army." Most officers and their fellow militiamen who had elected them to be captains or lieutenants had enrolled to meet a temporary emergency, and none expected to serve more than three months. They had not thought to be away from their families, their farms, their shops, or their workbenches for long. Many left camp and went home for brief visits when the spirit moved them; when sows were about to farrow or cows to calve, or when summoned to attend to pressing business. General Ward, with little success, had attempted to bring a degree of order out of this chaotic situation by instituting a generous system of furloughs. The result was that scarcely more than half the Massachusetts contingent was to be found in the lines before Boston at any one time. The other half was at home or traveling to and fro.

A strong contingent from Connecticut had arrived at Cambridge in early May. This corps of two brigades, organized by the Connecticut Assembly immediately after Lexington-Concord, was commanded by Joseph Spencer and Israel Putnam. Men were enlisted for seven months from May 1. Each was to provide a blanket, a knapsack, his clothing, and a musket. The Assembly set the strength of the militia at 6,000; fixed all rates of pay; appropriated money for three thousand stand of arms, powder, ball ammunition, flints, tentage, spades, picks, and axes. Each regiment of ten companies of one hundred men was assigned an adjutant, a quartermaster, a chaplain, and a surgeon with two mates. The Assembly appointed all officers and assigned them directly to the several regiments and companies, and thus departed from the system generally in vogue in other colonies, where company officers were elected by the rank and file. The measure was not popular, but was a step in the right direction, one unfortunately not emulated elsewhere.

Connecticut militiamen were quite as untutored as their brethren from Massachusetts in all but the rudiments of infantry drill. To march in a column of fours to music provided by a fifer and a drummer and to maintain dress in ranks or alignment in files would have been rated an achievement reflecting great credit on the drill sergeant. Of complex unit evolutions for deployment into battle formation, officers and men were equally ignorant. One of the first problems Washington encountered at Cambridge was that no standard manual for drill existed. Most senior militia officers were familiar with Bland's *Treatise of Military Discipline*, published in 1727, or with several plagiarized versions, but these were hard to come by. In the spring of 1775, shortly before Lexington and Concord, Lieutenant Timothy Pickering of the Massachusetts militia set himself the task of writing a new manual to govern infantry drill. His tract was published in July and he presented a copy to Washington. Pickering's manual would serve the Continental Army and militia well until a more professional work appeared. At the time, few men were competent to produce anything better. Lee, Gates, or Montgomery, all formerly King's officers, could have, but their duties kept them fully occupied.

The army was not organized in any sense of the word. Rather, it was a loose agglomeration of volunteer detachments from almost every town and village in the four New England colonies: a true "people's army." There was no supply system; most items required in field service were totally lacking. Vegetables, flour, meat, and milk were collected from the countryside on a haphazard basis, and no central authority was responsible for their equitable distribution. There was no tentage and very little planking for the erection of even primitive shacks. Fortunate officers and men slept in private homes, churches, barns, stables, or the buildings of Harvard College. Others slept on straw under any shelter they could manage to put together from boards and odd pieces of sailcloth and sacking. No medical services had been organized, nor was there a paymaster's department. Sanitation was execrable. The army was practically immobile. The only horses were those owned by men who had ridden them to Cambridge. Some militia detachments had arrived with one or two ox carts or wagons; saving these, there was no transport. The army had few cannon and practically no cannon balls.

Officers and men were dressed as they had come, some in rough farm clothes, petty tradesmen and artisans in homespun, others in tattered, greasy tow or buckskin hunting shirts. Few had other shoes or stockings than those they stood in. Officers were distinguished as to rank by vari-colored ribbons. The commander in chief purchased one, and quite properly entered the charge in his expense account. This, "a light blue Ribband," he wore "across his breast between his Coat and Waistcoat." Major generals were to wear "broad Purple Ribbands," and brigadiers, "Pink Ribbands." Field officers would wear "red or pink colour'd cockades in their Hatts."

Blankets were scarce, but most men carried powder horns and some ball ammunition and flints in leather pouches. Some had brought leathern bottles filled with the standard New England drink—rich, strong, black West Indies rum. Militiamen barbers arrived with their tonsorial equipment; British officers in Boston were contemptuously amused to read that one of "Mr. Washington's Captains," in civil life a barber, did a thriving business in the rebel camp. They would have been equally entertained to learn that several majors kept taverns, and that among the captains and subalterns there could be found blacksmiths, harness makers, gunsmiths, carpenters, and masons. In every sense of the word, this was a democratic army—too democratic, as Washington was shortly to discover.

At the commander in chief's urging, Congress soon created departments to take responsibility for essential matters: a quartermaster general, a commissary general of stores, a commissary of artillery, a muster master general, a paymaster general and deputy, and a chief engineer with two assistants. The common problem was that neither the commander in chief nor any of the appointees had any money. The officer who needed cash and needed it badly was the paymaster general. The average volunteer had been willing to hazard his life at Lexington, at Concord, and in the redoubt at Bunker Hill, but unless he could count on being decently fed and regularly paid he was not at all eager to sit in the lines around Boston for an indefinite period while weeds choked his crops or his small business or trade ran down to ultimate ruin. On June 22 Congress resolved on an issue of $2 million in "bills of credit." This was the first of many such unsecured emissions, but it solved the immediate crisis.

Military discipline, as it was known in the British Army (which the press of the time invariably referred to as "the Ministerial Troops" or "the Regulars"), did not exist. Officers were loath to order their fellow villagers and friends to undertake dangerous assignments or unwelcome jobs and perforce depended on exhortation, persuasion, or cajolery. The men had enrolled as individuals and demanded to be respected and treated as such. All were free and equal—wasn't that precisely what this fight was about? Their highly developed idiosyncratic individualism, their profound sense of democratic egalitarianism, had already shaped American life and society, and would continue to do so, but could scarcely be tolerated by a general charged with the task of creating an army.

Fortunately for the cause of America, Washington refused to put up with nonsense from either his officers or the rank and file. He began at once to issue regulatory General Orders and they thence forward poured out of his headquarters in a steady stream. Nothing was too minute to engage his attention. Major derelictions of duty and absence from camp without leave were punished immediately and severely, in accordance with the rules and regulations for the governance of the Continental Army adopted by Congress on June 30. Courts-martial sat continuously. Flogging was prescribed for serious offenses, and other severe punishments were inflicted. But the commander in chief, who had served with such men against the French and Indians, respected them and made allowance for their shortcomings. His essential humanity inclined him to pardon many who acknowledged their faults and promised to mend their ways.

No system of regular reports existed when Washington assumed command. General Ward never had more than a vague idea how many effective officers or men he had present; how many men were armed or with what; how much powder was in store, the number or caliber of the cannon or the cannon balls.* Washington at once demanded returns of all descriptions. He formed a committee of doctors to report on medical and hospital facilities; forbade profane cursing and swearing; ordered "punc-

---

* Actually cannon and cannonballs were not classified in terms of "calibers," but in terms of the weight of shot; i.e., an "eighteen-pounder" fired a ball weighing eighteen pounds.

tual attendance on divine Service"; demanded an immediate inventory of all types of tools, tentage, and canvas; directed that "Necessaries" be filled in weekly and new ones dug; that streets be swept, camp areas policed, and trash and garbage burned daily; that officers inspect the kitchens and the food served at every meal. In sum, as he wrote Richard Henry Lee, the army was "in an exceedingly dangerous situation" and not only because the British were actually then almost equal in numbers (or so he thought), but also because the abuses in the army were "considerable, and the new modelling of it, in the face of an enemy from whom we every hour expect an attack is exceedingly difficult and dangerous."[18]

Three problems dwarfed any others. The first was "a dearth of public spirit"; the second, parochial jealousies and maneuvering for rank and position in the officer corps; and the last, supplies and equipment. The general would in time instill spirit into the American Army, but he was to be afflicted with dissensions in the officer corps for many months, and not until the last months of the war was the grave problem of supply to be even partially solved. His troubles with the officers arose from the fact that their primary loyalties were to the "country"—the colony—they came from; there was as yet no sense of unity, no sense that now they were all Americans and members of a *Continental* Army. And until that conception could take hold, sectional bickering would persist. Washington wrote he had never before witnessed such "fertility in all the low arts to obtain advantages of one kind or another." But he was endowed with seemingly infinite patience; only in private letters did he express his frustrations and disappointments.

But this army was not exactly a rabble. A significant number of the Massachusetts and Connecticut men who manned the lines around Boston had previous experience of camp life and had received a modicum of military training in the field. All were familiar with the muskets they carried to camp. From 1758 to 1760 almost 11,000 Provincials had served with the British Army in North America. Some 7,700 militia, of whom almost half were from Massachusetts, had participated in Amherst's campaign of 1759–60 down Champlain to Montreal and in concurrent operations against Fort Niagara. Seven hundred Rangers were with Major General James Wolfe at Quebec, and over 4,000 men from Pennsylvania, Virginia, Maryland, and North Carolina marched to Fort Duquesne with John Forbes in November 1758.

As is usual, experienced American officers—of whom there were few indeed—did not esteem militiamen highly, nor would the Continental troops respect them. As bushfighters they performed well, for these operations gave full scope to their peculiar individualism. But the citizen temporarily under arms resented regimentation and discipline. The professional's "home" might be the army; the citizen-soldier's was elsewhere.

They were troublesome, often insubordinate men who consistently shirked unpleasant routine duties when they could.

When the first shots were fired at Lexington and Concord, many of these men were in their late thirties or early and middle forties. They were family men. Their reaction to the threat posed by the British was to leave the plough in the furrow as Israel Putnam had done, pick up a musket, bullet pouch, and powder horn, roll a blanket, kiss their wives and children, and set off for Boston for a few weeks. This "rabble in arms" was motivated, and there was a layer of experience. The potential existed. Washington's letters show, despite his disappointments and frustrations at Cambridge (and later), that while he recognized and deplored the too-evident weaknesses of the human material, he appreciated the latent possibilities. He knew he could "new-model" the army, but he needed time.

Charles Lee, who at Washington's behest spent ten to twelve hours a day in the saddle visiting every unit in the lines, was hopeful. There was much fault to be found, but "Upon my Soul the material here (I mean the private men) are admirable [?]—had they proper uniforms, arms and proper officers their zeal, youth, bodily strength, good humor and dexter-[ity] would make 'em an invincible army." He thought the young officers would do very well with a little time, but called on God to liberate the army from "the old big wigs." The engineers were useless—"not a single man of 'em" was capable of constructing a simple oven.

During the first weeks of July Washington devoted the few hours he could spare from the pressure of daily demands to drawing up plans for reorganization of the Continental Army into three Grand Divisions, of the Right, the Left, and the Corps de Réserve, to be commanded respectively by Major Generals Ward, Charles Lee, and Israel Putnam. The general disposed the three Grand Divisions roughly as follows:

Right Wing: The line DORCHESTER–ROXBURY–BROOKLINE–MOUTH of the CHARLES RIVER.
Corps de Réserve: Covering CAMBRIDGE.
Left Wing: North of CAMBRIDGE, with the left flank resting on the MYSTIC RIVER.

Washington did not have nearly enough cannon to support his extensive lines. He deployed what he had effectively, with particular attention to covering the approach to the center of his position via the Charles.

The reorganization progressed smoothly; on July 28 Washington wrote Schuyler: "Our Army is in good Health, and Spirits, well supplied with all kinds of Provisions. The Situation of the Enemy is directly the Reverse, and we have Reason to think Desertions will be very great. Four have come out within the last twenty-four hours." The commander in chief was gaining confidence daily, and soon again wrote Schuyler:

". . . we mend every Day, and I flatter myself that in a little time we shall work up these raw materials into good stuff."[19] He reported about 16,000 present, including 1,000 sick, and estimated Gage's force at some 12,000.†

Washington's stern disciplinary measures were bearing fruit. He cracked down on officers who were in the habit of taking leave without authority to visit their homes: "Such irregularity . . . may be productive of the worst of consequences." Hereafter, he announced in a General Order, those who so absented themselves "may depend upon being punished with the utmost severity." Since he had assumed command, general courts-martial had cashiered three colonels and half a dozen subalterns. These were all Massachusetts men; the people of that province had acquired a reputation the general thought they by no means deserved: "I daresay the men would fight very well (if properly Officered) although they are an exceeding dirty and nasty people; had they been properly conducted at Bunker's Hill . . . the Regulars would have met with a shameful defeat."[20] He thought many of the Massachusetts officers unreliable dilatory schemers who were mulcting the men of their rations, who would not exert themselves, and were possessed of "an unaccountable kind of stupidity." They devoted their time to currying favor with the men who had chosen them: "inattentive to everything but their Interest."[21] Fortunately, these indiscreet observations did not find their way back to New England.

In this summer of 1775 the dissenting clergy, in the pulpits and in the camps, played a most important role in crystallizing opinion in the colonies and particularly in the army. Washington, Putnam, and other generals at Cambridge were well aware of the profound influence the clergy could exert on the minds and emotions of untutored militiamen. Congress had suggested that Sunday, July 20, be observed as a day of fasting and solemn devotion; the troops spent several hours listening to hortatory addresses, as indeed they did every Sunday and on every ceremonial occasion. The pastors may not have been highly educated, but most could movingly call down hell-fire and damnation on the hosts of the wicked, then commanded in Boston by the Devil's acolyte, General Thomas Gage.

These men of the cloth might well have devoted some time and effort to awakening a spirit of selfless devotion to the cause among the officers, in most of whom the quality of leadership was conspicuous by its absence. Many senior officers had a ridiculously inflated conception of

† Strength reports prepared by Adjutant General Horatio Gates showed 1,119 officers, 1,768 noncommissioned officers, and 15,082 rank and file, of whom approximately 13,000 were present and fit for duty. Of the total rank and file, 10,000 were from Massachusetts; 2,333 from Connecticut; 1,664 from New Hampshire; and 1,085 from Rhode Island. To the over-all figure, some 500 fifers and drummers could be added.

their martial abilities. Several militia brigadiers simply walked out when Congress did not accord them ranks commensurate with those they deemed their station in life merited. Congress had ranked one, Joseph Spencer, number 5 on the list; for some reason, he thought he should have been ranked as a major general, and indicated his dissatisfaction by departing without a by-your-leave. His behavior shocked Congress. Silas Deane wrote his wife on July 20 that Spencer had "acted a part inconsistent with the character either of a soldier, a patriot, or even of a common gentleman."[22]

Washington did not bother to write Spencer, but did write to Brigadier General John Thomas, who had sent up a letter of resignation: ". . . surely every post ought to be deemed honorable in which a Man can serve his Country. What matter of triumph will it afford our enemies, that in less than one month, a spirit of Discord should shew itself in the highest ranks of our Army, not to be distinguished by anything less than a total desertion of Duty." The commander in chief urged Thomas to stifle the dictates of resentment, and banish from his mind "anger and disappointment."[23] Thomas recalled his request. Much of Washington's valuable time was taken up with attempting to placate vain or ambitious men, whose abilities frequently did not warrant his attention. But he needed them.

Dartmouth was not pleased with Gage's reports: "[his] Dispatches contain literally nothing. . . ." But the government had other means of acquiring the sensitive information Gage was unable to provide. A senior artillery officer just returned from Boston called on Pownall early in September, and the undersecretary wrote his colleague, again taking the waters at Bath, of the "Unfavourable report of the State of our Army, diminishing every day by disease and beginning to lose men by desertions. Of the state of the Rebells Army or of their situation and designs," Gage knew nothing.

A subordinate, possibly Clinton or Burgoyne, had proposed crossing the Mystic suddenly in an attempt to pull the Americans out of their entrenchments, but "The General did not think it would succeed, or if it did and victory was the consequence, it would not much mend our situation."

☒ 2

Oh! Mad, Mad England!

Washington's adversary commanded a professional army. The character, structure, and tactical doctrine of His Majesty's Army penned in the town of Boston conformed in every fundamental respect to British and continental military tradition. Gage's officers were reasonably competent, and by prevailing standards the troops they commanded were well trained. The army was rigidly disciplined and well equipped. In every respect it differed radically from the heterogeneous military detachments manning the lines from Dorchester to the Mystic.

The British officer corps resembled an exclusive gentlemen's club. Young men of Anglican families who enjoyed influential "connexion" bought their way into the select circle. If plentifully endowed with cash, a politically powerful family, and friends who would bring influence to bear, they could often purchase a commission in a guards regiment whose officers automatically outranked their colleagues in the less prestigious regiments of foot. Except for those who became artillerymen and engineers, none had even the most rudimentary professional schooling. Roman Catholics and Dissenters could not aspire to commissions in the forces.

Many who succeeded in getting commissions were younger sons of noble houses or of aristocratic county families, who after attending one of the great public schools had completed their education with the almost mandatory tour of the Continent, where they spent much of their time gambling, dancing, drinking, and whoring. One officer on the staff of Prince Frederick of Brunswick, who had ample opportunity to observe the British in Germany during the Seven Years' War, described the officers as insouciant; they "did not trouble their heads about the service, and with few exceptions understand nothing whatever about it; and this goes on from the ensign to the general. . . . To all this is added a quite natural arrogance which tempts them to despise the enemy as well as the danger."

The attitude of junior officers may be explained in part by the fact that the inflexible battle tactics of the times offered them very little opportunity to display individual initiative, nor did their seniors encourage them to do so. At the lower echelons, the profession did not demand competence in a wide variety of military skills, and given the system of promotion, there was very little incentive for a young officer to try to improve himself. In the British Army of the late eighteenth century, promotion in time of peace was rarely made on merit. Rather, progress up the ladder depended on birth, "connexion," money, and influence. Even well-born young men who lacked friends in high places could not get very far along; the most many such could hope for was to retire as a major or lieutenant colonel on half pay.

When an officer desired to leave one of His Majesty's regiments for more congenial or lucrative employment, he sold his commission. If, for example, a major left his regiment for civilian life on a half-pay status, a vacancy in grade was created. This was offered to the senior captain, who ordinarily bought it if he could raise the cash. If he could not, the vacant commission was offered to the next senior captain. Not for many years would there be a common army list, from which officers would be selected for promotion on the basis of proven merit.

Several other factors complicated the purchase system and tended to demoralize the officer corps. One of these was transfers from one regiment to another; a second, the privilege accorded guards officers of buying into a regiment of foot at a higher rank than they held in the guards. The system seemed designed to ensure stagnation and to inhibit progress of competent officers of lower and middle grades, however highly motivated and qualified.

Practically all generals and admirals, and many colonels and royal navy captains, enjoyed sinecures revokable at the King's pleasure, that did not require their presence and could be administered by an underpaid deputy on the spot. But money, though desirable to support a way of life commensurate with one's station in society, could not necessarily secure a high command. The complaint that one had "no friends" was common enough. To protect their sinecures, active generals and admirals who sat in the House of Commons had to toe the line. The ministry could generally rely on this bloc to support its measures, for as assignment of senior generals and flag officers of the navy was a royal prerogative, no ambitious officer would have dared vote consistently against Administration.

Officers expected to live well in the field and did. There was little romantic nonsense; sleeping under the stars rolled in a blanket did not appeal and was not necessary. Regimental baggage trains made generous allowances for mess equipment, wines, tentage, and furniture. In Europe it was by no means unusual for officers' wives or mistresses, complete with ladies' maids and wardrobes, to accompany them on campaign. The army commissary provided basic subsistence for them. Officers and their ladies could not, however, be expected to be happy with army rations; they all carried delicacies and arranged for periodic replenishments to be sent by families and caterers at home. Many placed standing orders with wine merchants for casks and cases of port, claret, champagne, and madeira to be sent forward at regular intervals. The system encumbered the trains, created logistics problems of monumental proportions, and interfered with strategic and tactical mobility.

The life of an enlisted man in the British Army, unless he had the rare good fortune to be selected as a headquarters orderly or an officer's servant, was grim to say the least. Punishment for infraction of minor rules of discipline was arbitrary and brutal. For major infractions, barbarous sentences of hundreds of lashes were usual. Promotion was very slow and pay absurdly low. Little opportunity existed to rise from the ranks. But the rank and file shared one of the officers' privileges. They, too, were allowed their women. Four, six, or eight per company, battery, or squadron was normal. Some of these women were married to soldiers; others, who were expected to perform their sexual chores, tended the sick and wounded and did cooking and washing. Women and their children were subsisted by the commissary.

A "private man" in the British Army was a thoroughly trained automaton. He was not supposed to think for himself, and rarely did. In approach to battle, in deployment, in the advance toward his enemy, he was trained to follow specific drills and specific commands, as he was in loading and firing his heavy musket. Ultimate reliance was in the bayonet at close quarters; in closing with the steel British infantrymen had no equals. Their problem during the bloody retreat from Lexington-Concord was simply that the Americans would not wait to be bayoneted. Most were illiterate, politically unconscious and unmotivated, and had no conception why they had been transported across three thousand miles of stormy ocean to kill people against whom they bore no grudge.

But they were professionals. The King's soldiers took the King's shilling and did what was demanded of them.

All was far from well in Boston. Toward the end of July, Gage reported the rebels taking "very great pains to starve the Troops and the Friends of Government in Boston, for no article necessary for the Support of Life is Suffered to be Sent there from any of the Provinces from New Hampshire to South Carolina."[1] Americans crewing Nantucket whaleboats constantly patrolled the nearby coastline, seized numerous fishermen suspected of supplying the British, and impounded their boats and catches. Mess stewards no longer served turtle and pineapple.

Gage did not criticize Admiral Graves's obvious lack of activity except by inference, but his subalterns did, and in strong language. Repeated insults had been offered to "the honour of the British flag"; too many, indeed, to relate—so wrote Captain Evelyn, his arrogance chastened to a degree by his experience at Bunker Hill. "The Yankee fishermen in their whaleboats have repeatedly drove off the stock, and set fire to the houses on islands, under the guns of the fleet. They have killed a midshipman . . . and destroyed the sloop he commanded. They have burned the lighthouse at the entrance of the harbour, killed Lieutenant Colthurst (who commanded thirty Marines), some of his men, and took the rest prisoners."[2]

While these sea-borne guerrillas carried on their depredations in the harbor and set up a quasi blockade of Boston, Admiral Graves continued to bicker and feud with the general. When Graves failed to carry out his mission in a small combined operation planned by General Clinton, Evelyn wrote: "The truth is, there is no good understanding between him and the General, and he endeavours to counteract the General whenever he is concerned. Every man both in the army and navy wishes him recalled, as the service must always suffer when there is such disagreement betwixt the leaders."[3] It is reasonable to surmise the captain was reflecting opinions current in the regimental mess.

Reports that Gage and Graves were no longer on speaking terms had reached London, and prompted Sandwich to write the admiral. The First Lord hoped rumors of disagreement were without foundation, but cautioned Graves that if he gave his enemies just cause for criticism "the most disagreeable consequences both public and private will happen." The admonition had no noticeable effect on the admiral's behavior. William Eden begged Sandwich to relieve a "corrupt Admiral without any shadow of capacity," but Sandwich took care to shield his friend, who had important political "connexions."

Graves was quite as unpopular with his own captains and the Boston Tories as he was around the general's headquarters. Three of the admiral's nephews were serving under him in Boston and a fourth was on the way. Their records in the Royal Navy were by no means commensurate with the billets he assigned them. In two instances he favored his kinsmen to the detriment of close relations of two of his captains, behavior not calculated to improve morale afloat. Ashore, his wife and Mrs. Gage were involved in a running fight to establish an unchallenged position as social arbiter. Graves had participated in a public fist fight with a leading Boston Tory, an unseemly affair which turned the tightly knit Loyalist community solidly against him. Vice-admiral of the White Samuel Graves was not a well-loved man in Boston.

Graves's manning problem was daily becoming more acute. He appealed to Rear Admiral Robert Duff at Halifax for assistance: "Besides the common losses by Sickness and by Desertions which have lately much prevailed, we have been unfortunate in having a great many good men taken prisoners by the rebels, and some killed and wounded." Commerce had evaporated; there were no more merchant ships from which Graves could impress seamen, and thus little prospect that he could replace men lost; "The King's Authority is entirely at an End throughout the Continent, except in Canada, Nova Scotia and the Floridas . . . I believe by this time not a Ship on the Coast can get supplies, or refreshments of any kind but what are taken by Force or Strategem. . . . Already we have received Supplies from England, and our sole reliance for Provisions must be from thence."

Captain Evelyn's contempt for the Americans had given way to frustrated rage. The British, he wrote, must steel themselves, and lay aside that "false humanity towards these wretches which has hitherto been so destructive to us. They must . . . permit us to restore to them the dominion of the country by laying it waste and almost extirpating the present rebelious race."[4]

It is not too difficult to understand the feelings of this young company commander who had seen several dozen friends and messmates killed or terribly maimed on June 17. Hundreds of British troops lay wounded in improvised hospitals with no proper surgical attention and no prospect of nursing care. There, Evelyn wrote, they were dying every day. General Gage could do little to ameliorate their sufferings. Even to provide patients the wholesome diet needed for recuperation was daily becoming more difficult. Admiral Graves, who dined well aboard his flagship, was not disposed to exert himself or to hazard His Majesty's ships on foraging expeditions; the troops, beleaguered by land and sea, could get few fresh provisions.* If officers were dining on salt pork and peas, heaven only knows what rations enlisted men subsisted on. Occasionally, the captain was fortunate enough to be invited to "a good dinner among the great people"—Lord Percy, General Clinton. Such invita-

---

* The adjacent waters abounded with fish and lobsters. Curiously, the British never made an organized effort to capitalize on this source.

tions were all too infrequent. He had not yet had "the honour" of meeting General Burgoyne.

Shortly after his arrival, Gentleman Johnny, who thought little of Gage's unadorned literary style, had relieved the general of the onerous responsibility of writing proclamations and had drawn up a bombastic address to "the infatuated multitudes" who, fallen under the spell of "incendiaries and traitors," had rebelled against constituted authority. The British, who did not "bear the sword in vain," were now forced to inflict "the fulness of chastisement." The misguided few participating in the "preposterous parade" outside Boston might enjoy the King's mercy if they laid down their arms and surrendered the two most nefarious malefactors, Samuel Adams and John Hancock. Burgoyne's announcement excited much mirth and impelled the Massachusetts Committee of Safety to issue a counterblast calling upon the British to turn over General Gage and Admiral Graves.

Reinforcements Gage received during July more than compensated for losses sustained on June 17, and London obviously expected action. The general claimed he had not enough troops "to secure the Town and other Posts, and move out with the Remainder in Force Sufficient to Subdue the Country."[5] There was indeed no possibility of subduing the country, but he could have made an effort to break through the American lines, spread destruction in the American camp, and possibly destroy Washington's army. The rebels' line of circumvallation was slightly over twelve miles in length. With Graves in control of the harbor waters and with an overwhelming weight of artillery at his disposal, Gage could have selected a point for a disruptive attack co-ordinated with distracting efforts. This, in fact, was precisely what Washington anticipated—and feared—the British general would do. But Gage would not hazard such an effort. The bloody road from Concord and an afternoon on a hill had produced their effects.

In mid-July, Gage's return showed British strength in Boston standing at over 7,200 rank and file in regiments of the line, plus officers, sergeants, drummers, fifers, two battalions of marines, and two companies of artillery. During the next ten days, fresh drafts aggregating 1,000 men disembarked; by the end of the month, Gage's total strength was well over 9,000. He seemed incapable of making a major decision and contented himself with occasionally cannonading Washington's positions and mounting petty patrol actions designed to annoy and harass the Americans, who labored unceasingly by day and night to strengthen their defenses. As July slipped into August, his chances of pushing home a successful attack diminished daily.

Major General Charles Lee, once a lieutenant colonel in His Majesty's service, did not think much of Gage's army, largely composed, he wrote, "of the most debauched weaver's 'prentices, the scum of the Irish Roman Catholics who desert upon every occasion, and a few, very few Scotch who are not strong enough to carry packs." Those who had seen something of the troops in Boston judged them "very defective in size and apparently in strength." The Redcoats might know all "the tricks of the Parade" and could acquit themselves "tolerably in puerile reviews . . . the tinsel and shew of war." To be sure, Regulars were "well dressed and . . . well powdered" and were masters of the manual exercise. But powdered hair neatly clubbed was no criterion of their ability to fight. In Lee's opinion, the yeomanry of America enjoyed "infinite advantage" because they were accustomed to the use of arms and were experts in handling "instruments necessary for all military works, such as spades, pickaxes, hatchets, etc." Lee then proceeded to blast the British officer corps: They did not study the art or science of war; their competence extended to "mounting guard once or twice a week" or preparing a review.

Just as armed truce prevailed in Boston, so it did generally elsewhere along the Atlantic seaboard. This brittle state of affairs had been rudely shattered in early June at Machias, a coastal town in the present state of Maine. Gage needed lumber for pallets and tent floors, and Ichabod Jones, a Machias Tory then in Boston, offered to supply him. Jones arrived at Machias and stated he would exchange provisions for lumber. While he dickered with the merchants, H.M.S. *Margaretta*, an armed schooner, escorting two sloops to transport the lumber, lay in the harbor. The townspeople voted to accept Jones's proposition and trading began. At this point, local Sons of Liberty intervened and an uproar ensued. Jones fled to the woods; the midshipman commanding the expedition to *Margaretta*.

The Yankees, determined to take the schooner which had made sail and was under way, pursued her, lay alongside, boarded her, killed the midshipman and several of the crew, and hauled down His Majesty's colors. The Americans hailed this first naval encounter of the war as a good augury. The fishermen responsible for the capture now had a three-vessel "navy" and appealed to the Massachusetts Provincial Assembly for recognition. For some reason, the Assembly—no doubt for press of other business considered more important—did not act until the middle of August. Then, by resolution, delegates voted to commission Jeremiah O'Brien "Commander of the Armed Schooner Diligent . . . now lying in the harbour at Machias."†

There were several other naval contretemps. Rebels took two British survey vessels on the Maine coast together with another about to load

† The town can thus rightfully lay claim to being one of the birthplaces of the United States Navy.

mast and spar timbers. In Narragansett Bay, Abraham Whipple's two small ships disputed mastery of local waters with Captain James Wallace, R.N., commanding H.M.S. *Rose*. Wallace had a working arrangement with citizens of Newport, who promised to keep him supplied with beef, lamb, pork, chickens, and fresh provisions if he would observe a truce and keep his sailors in hand when on shore leave. This the captain was quite willing to do. Washington, apprised of the conduct of the Newporters, condemned it in strong terms but found it impossible to put a stop to their trade with the enemy. Here a matter of principle was involved: If he sent a battalion to Newport, he would have to send one to each of two dozen coastal towns. He then and later resisted all such requests. He was determined to maintain the integrity of the army.

At about this time, he also decided to step into the naval picture and put coastal activities on an organized and controlled basis. He therefore created his own "Continental" Navy as a "detachment" of the army, and named Captain Nicholas Broughton of Glover's Marblehead regiment to command its lone vessel, schooner *Hannah*, which the general paid to have fitted out. The consistent successes of the assorted "navies" did much to convince Congress to support and encourage maritime efforts.

Delegates fully appreciated that the colonies could not challenge British supremacy on the seas, but colonial sailors were experienced and competent; all they needed to irritate, harass, and stab the British were shallow-draft fast craft, lightly armed. With this type of ship they could outsail and capture clumsy transports and victualers and elude larger British vessels which outgunned them but could not pursue them into unfamiliar bays and inlets without fear of grounding on uncharted bars and reefs.

While there had been considerable informal discussion of the need for a navy, Congress did nothing until early October, when delegates from Rhode Island submitted a resolution calling for ships to be constructed, outfitted, and manned at Continental expense. On October 7 this was debated on the floor. Samuel Chase of Maryland thought it "the maddest Ides in the World, to think of building an American Fleet. . . . We should mortgage the whole Continent." This statement produced considerable wrangling. A motion to appoint a committee failed, and discussion of the subject was put off for a week. On October 13, "after some debate," Congress resolved that two "swift sailing" vessels, each armed with "ten carriage guns, and a proportionable number of swivals," and each with a crew of eighty, "be fitted with all possible despatch." A committee consisting of Silas Deane, John Langdon, and Christopher Gadsden was appointed to prepare an estimate of expenses and "contract with proper persons" for building and fitting out.

Four weeks later Congress authorized the formation of the first and second battalions of American marines, each to consist of such officers and men "as are good seamen, or so acquainted with maritime affairs as to be able to serve to advantage by sea when required."

The King's cause in America was not prospering. Gage received disquieting reports from Carleton: The governor had no money and fewer than 1,000 regulars; Indians in Canada had not responded to his blandishments and were noncommittal; *habitants* aloof and not to be trusted. Gage urged Whitehall to reinforce Canada at once with 4,000 men and send Carleton "large quantities of Indian goods." In reply to this plea, Dartmouth informed the governor that the King relied on the loyalty of his Canadian subjects to repel the rebels, and suggested Carleton could easily raise 3,000 stalwart French Canadians to defend the province of Quebec. On July 12 the secretary wrote that H.M.S. *Lizard* was convoying a storeship to Quebec with arms for these 3,000. Two weeks after *Lizard* and the storeship sailed, he directed Carleton to raise a total of 6,000. The governor could not possibly raise 6,000, or 3,000, or even 1,000; he exerted himself and raised about 300, in whom he reposed no confidence.

From Annapolis, William Eddis wrote to London of the "calamitous" situation in Maryland. Government was "almost totally annihilated and power transferred to the multitude. Speech is become dangerous; letters are intercepted; confidences betrayed; and every measure evidently tends to the most fatal extremities." Seven militia companies drilled daily in Baltimore; two were exercising in Annapolis. Most Marylanders were armed, "almost every hat is decorated with a cocade; and the churlish drum and fife are the only music of the times." Eddis had suffered no bodily harm, but was in a state of depression and despair, as were his fellow Tories in other provinces. "It seems but yesterday that I considered my situation as permanent. Every flattering prospect appeared before me. Happy in my family, in my connections, in my circumstances, cherished and supported by a patron able and anxious to promote my interest. Alas! my brother, how cruelly is the scene reversed!"[6]

In Virginia the royal governor, fearful for his life, hastily betook himself to the safety of H.M.S. *Fowey*, anchored in the James River. Lord William Campbell, royal governor of South Carolina, had fled Charleston and installed himself in H.M.S. *Tamar*, appropriately lying in Rebellion Roads. From this haven he corresponded with a "General Committee" headed by Henry Laurens. The committee assured his lordship that he would be welcomed in Charleston should he desire to return. Lord William considered an invitation from this source presumptuous and replied that he had no intention of setting foot in Charleston until he could "support the King's authority." If he was not then aware of the fact, he would shortly discover that the King's authority in South Carolina was no more than fictive.

Josiah Martin, governor of North Carolina, was waterborne in His Majesty's sloop of war *Cruzier* anchored in the Cape Fear River. From his cramped abode he went through the motions of exercising an authority he no longer possessed. A "popular Assembly, unknown to the laws and constitution," was now functioning in his province. Dunmore did something more than lament "the unnatural and unhappy contest" and managed to make a considerable nuisance of himself. His behavior served only to confirm Virginians in their determination to be rid of him. In Maryland, Robert Eden, a respected and popular governor, remained quietly and safely in Annapolis. Unlike his three colleagues to the south who (one may suspect) were writing for the record, Eden refused to exacerbate the situation.

At Philadelphia the mood was optimistic. In mid-June a letter arrived from Colonel Benedict Arnold urging an immediate invasion of Canada. Arnold wrote he had every reason to believe French Canadians and some Indians would take up the hatchet against Carleton. His idea was that a force of about 2,000 could do the job. He wanted no "Green Mountain Boys"—certainly not if they were to be commanded by the volatile and unreliable Ethan Allen. He would establish a base at Isle aux Noix, use a few men to mask the little forts at St. Johns and Chambly, and lead the remainder to Montreal. To take the city would be no problem; the Americans had friends there who would open the gates the moment they appeared. Then on to Quebec. He volunteered to take command: "I will undertake it, and, with the smiles of Heaven, answer for the success of it.

Toward the end of June, Congress resolved to authorize an expedition to be commanded by General Schuyler "to Take or Destroy all Vessells, Boats or Floating Batteries prepared by Governor Carleton on or near the waters of the Lakes, and to Take possession of St. Johns and Montreal if he finds it practicable, and not Disagreeable to the Canadians." This directive, signed by John Hancock and dispatched to Schuyler by express, enjoined the general to make necessary preparations without delay. That the projected invasion would add a new dimension to the existing situation apparently did not occur to members of Congress; indeed, most thought the Americans would be welcomed. "The Canadians absolutely refuse to join Carleton, and the Indians assure us that they will observe a strict neutrality. Thus we seem to be well secured in the north against ministerial madness."[7] Hancock, however, had second thoughts, and cautioned Schuyler to proceed to Montreal and Quebec only if circumstances seemed to favor such action.

During the following week, delegates busied themselves preparing a "Declaration on Taking Arms," an "Address to the People of Great Britain," a "Loyal Petition" to the King, and addresses to the people of

Jamaica and Ireland. Jefferson and John Dickinson wrote the first, a catalogue of the oppressive acts of Parliament, an indictment of the ministry, and an attack on General Gage. The Americans, so the declaration alleged, were reduced to the alternative of unconditional submission to the tyranny of irresponsible ministers, or resistance by force. "The latter is our choice. . . . *The Arms we have been compelled by our Enemies to assume, we will, in defiance of every Hazard, with unabating Firmness and Perseverance, employ for the preservation of our Liberties,* being with one Mind resolved to die Freemen rather than live Slaves."[8]

Dickinson wrote the "Loyal Petition," approved on July 5, which according to Jefferson was "an indulgence to Mr. Dickinson. . . . The disgust at this humility was general." The wording of the petition makes clear the attitude of many Americans, who were convinced that not the King, but his ministry, was "the fatal source" from which "the unhappy differences" between Great Britain and her colonies flowed. The ministers (not the King) had practiced an "irksome variety of artifices," had attempted to intimidate the colonists, and had inflicted upon them numerous "unavailing severities." His Majesty's ministers, persevering in these ill-judged and impolitic measures, had opened hostilities designed to compel the "still faithful colonists" who earnestly desired to stop the further "effusion of blood" and avert "the impending calamities that threaten the British Empire," to take up arms in self-defense.

The King's "dutiful" subjects submitted their humble petition with the utmost deference in the hope His Majesty would not "ascribe any seeming deviation from linguistic reverence to reprehensible intention," but rather to the imperative necessity for "preservation [of colonial rights] against those artful and cruel enemies" who were abusing the royal confidence for the purpose of destroying them.

They asserted their inviolable attachment to the King's "person, family and government" and solemnly assured him they most ardently desired restoration of harmony and establishment of concord on so firm a basis as "to perpetuate its blessings, uninterrupted by future dissensions." They beseeched the King to interpose his royal authority and influence to relieve them from the fears induced by the practices of an evil set of ministers, to the end that "a happy and permanent reconciliation" might be assured, and that he would enjoy a long and prosperous reign.[9] The "humble Petition," suitably engrossed and duly signed, was entrusted to Richard Penn of the proprietary family for delivery to Lord Dartmouth, whose duty it would be to present it to His Majesty.

In a postscript to one of his frequent letters to James Warren, John Adams saw "a strange oscillation between love and hatred, between War and Peace—Preparation for War and Negotiations for Peace. We must have a Petition to the King and a delicate Proposal of Negotiation, etc. . . . We can't avoid it. Discord and total Disunion would be the certain Effect of a resolute Refusal to petition and negotiate." Adams was certain that while the petition would effect nothing, it might buy time, a commodity sorely needed. His sole purpose was to promote independence; sadly, "the colonies are not yet ripe for it."[10]

Delegates from Georgia arrived in mid-July with a welcome gift—140 barrels of the King's powder. All thirteen colonies were now represented in the Congress, which had sat every day since May 10. Although tempers were a bit frayed, support of Washington was unanimous and delegates hastened to grant his requests. Many, notably John Adams and Dr. Franklin, felt that the most pressing political problem was confederation; Franklin had submitted draft articles shortly after Congress assembled, but no strong sentiment for this move had yet developed.

To many Americans, the eminent doctor was an enigma, and Abigail wrote John asking for a character sketch. He responded in late July: "Franklin has been very constant in his attendance on Congress from the beginning. His conduct has been composed and grave, and, in the opinion of many gentlemen, very reserved. . . . He does not hesitate at our boldest measures, but rather seems to think us too irresolute and backward." Franklin rarely spoke, and did not take the lead: "he is however a great and good man."[11] Not so, in Adams's opinion, was John Dickinson, "the Pennsylvania Farmer," a gentleman of "great Fortune and piddling Genius" wedded to the cause of reconciliation, who delayed proceedings to such an extent, so Adams wrote James Warren, that he had "given a Silly cast to our Whole Doings." He entrusted this most indiscreet letter to a young man going to Boston. Taken by the British, the traveler was made to disgorge everything in his luggage. The letters were promptly forwarded to Gage, who immediately published them. Thereafter, Dickinson publicly snubbed Adams.

John Adams was an accomplished politician who took care of his Massachusetts friends. He wrote Warren that Congress was about to name a paymaster general, and that if "this office of vast importance" were not "filled with a Gentleman, whose Family, Fortune, Education, Abilities and Integrity, are equal to its Dignity," it would not be *his* fault. A few days later, Warren was appointed. It is interesting to observe that Adams gave precedence to Warren's social position, his ancestry, and his money, rather than to his "Education, Abilities and Integrity."

In letters to family and friends, members expressed the hope that Congress would recess for a few weeks to avoid the "sickly season" in Philadelphia. Appointments of general officers in the army had been threshed out and money provided to Generals Washington and Schuyler; commissioners named to treat with the Indians in the Northern, Middle, and Southern Departments; a post office established; a "Director General and Chief Physician" of the Continental Army appointed; and a salary of twenty dollars per month authorized for chaplains ministering to the spiritual needs of Washington's army. Above all, the "capital object of powder" had been attended to. On August 2, 1775, Congress adjourned to meet again on September 5.

Delegates may have thought they had dealt satisfactorily with "the capital object" of ensuring adequate supplies of powder, flints, and lead, but the commander in chief did not, and wrote urgently to the governors of Rhode Island and Connecticut and the New Hampshire Committee of Safety to forward any they could find. No amount, however small, was "beneath Notice. . . . every Hour in our present situation is Critical." On August 4, in a long letter to Hancock, he reported an alarming shortage of powder and ball; he had only nine cartridges per man: "I need not enlarge on our melancholy Situation it is sufficient to say that the existence of the Army and Salvation of the Country depend upon something being done for our relief both speedy and effectual and that our Situation be kept a profound Secret."[12] During the next two weeks affairs improved: He had 184 barrels of powder, but still not enough for "30 Musket Cartridges a Man."

The crucial shortage arose from the fact that there were no manufacturies in America capable of producing high-quality gunpowder in any quantity. Not only were supplies meager, but a large proportion forwarded to the army was unreliable. Nor were there any arsenals in North America capable of producing rifles, pistols, muskets, cannon, gun carriages, or mortars. Rifles were made by Pennsylvania gunsmiths, most of them Germans whose fathers had brought to America the art and the tools. But rifle making in Lancaster and other towns in the province was a small-scale craft, and all the expert gunsmiths together could not turn out more than a very few a day. Pennsylvania and Virginia riflemen cherished their rare and expensive weapons above all other possessions.

Of cannon there were none other than those earlier seized at Ticonderoga, or taken from various small forts and royal magazines. Had the New Hampshire militia earlier been somewhat more ambitious and energetic, Washington would have had at Cambridge a respectable "park" of artillery, for at Fort William and Mary there were forty-five large cannon the rebels had neglected to seize and haul away. Graves dispatched H.M.S. *Scarborough* to Portsmouth in June to pick up these guns.

Cannon balls could be laboriously cast, but there were few furnaces, and pig iron was as yet a scarce commodity. Congress wrestled with this problem, but with no particular success. Bullets for muskets and rifles were manufactured by householders who had bullet molds—when they could get the lead. One or two molds might be found in most towns and villages, but Washington's requests for several hundred thousand rounds of ball ammunition, sufficient to supply fifty per man, could not possibly be met for weeks or even months.

Washington thus constantly wondered at Gage's inactivity. The British general did not know the "profound Secret" and consistently overestimated Washington's capabilities and underestimated his own. But Washington had made an accurate assessment of Gage's character: He felt he had "nothing more to fear from the *Enemy*, provided we can keep men to their duty." This was the rub: Most of the men at Cambridge had been born and bred on farms and were constitutionally averse to being regimented, counted, and mustered for daily drills, parades, or working parties. Actually, few indeed had a clear idea of just what their duty was.

With the drudgery of daily pick and shovel work tapering off, the troops were enjoying "New Cyder." The general prohibited this beverage, and threatened all purveyors of "Cyder," pernicious to health and "productive of the body flux," that their casks would be "stove in" if they brought the liquor into camp. His sense of propriety was shocked, too, to learn "that many Men, lost to all sense of decency and common modesty," were bathing naked "near the Bridge in Cambridge . . . whilst Passengers and even Ladies of the first fashion" were passing over it.[13]

The morals of the army were not above reproach. Although chaplains labored manfully to abate the "profane cursing" characteristic of any army, they were not too successful, as some officers were apparently unable to give any order unaccompanied by a shattering string of oaths. Nor was the army remarkable for sobriety. When the troops could lay their hands on enough rum for a drinking bout, they got drunk. Officers expected to drink reasonable amounts of punch, claret, and madeira every day, and usually did. Gambling, which later became something of a problem, was not a usual pastime in New England, and as the army was on its home ground, sexual activities were restrained. Washington was not a prig, but he was distressed at what he considered unnecessary cursing and excessive drinking, and in General Orders reminded the army that Articles of War recently adopted by the Congress forbade profane cursing, swearing, and drunkenness. He added that he expected "punctual attendance on divine Service to implore the blessings of Heaven" on the Cause. His attitude to organized religion may have been ambivalent, but his profound belief in a beneficent Deity was not.

The commander in chief had been in Cambridge for two months and had devoted his days and the greater part of many nights to what he sometimes considered a fruitless effort to create an army capable of defending American liberties. He was often frustrated, despondent, and frequently angry. In a personal letter to Richard Henry Lee, he unburdened himself: "There has been so many great, and capital errors, and abuses to rectify—so many examples to make—and so little Inclination in the officers of inferior Rank to contribute their aid to accomplish this work, that my life has been nothing else (since I *came here*) *but* one continued round of *annoyance and fatigue;* in short, no pecuniary *recompense* could induce me to undergo what I *have, especially* as I expect, by shewing so little countenance to irregularities and public *abuses* to render myself very obnoxious to a greater part of the People."[14]

Shortly thereafter, he wrote in more diplomatic phrases to John Hancock: "It gives me great Pain to be obliged to sollicit the Attention of the Hon. Congress to the State of the Army in terms which imply the slightest Apprehension of being neglected: But my Situation is inexpressibly distressing to see the winter fast Approaching upon a naked Army, the Time of their Service within a few Weeks of expiring and no Provision yet made for such important Events." The army was ragged, unpaid, and on short rations. "I know not to whom to impute this Failure, but I am of opinion if the Evil is not immediately remedied . . . the Army must absolutely break up." His troops were "in a State not far from Mutiny."[15] This gloomy report produced immediate results in Philadelphia; Congress appointed a committee including Benjamin Franklin and Benjamin Harrison to proceed to Cambridge at once.

Washington had a most sympathetic and understanding relationship with Schuyler, then busy at Ticonderoga preparing for the campaign he expected soon to launch on Lake Champlain. On the last day of July, Schuyler wrote he was "assiduously employed in collecting materials for building boats"; that he had one on the stocks capable of carrying three hundred men and another of equal size "putting up." Washington replied by an express that he had just received a deputation of Abenaki Indians, whose chief, Swashan, had confirmed former accounts of "the good Disposition of the Indian Nations, and Canadians to the Interests of America."

For some time past, Arnold had been proposing an operation against Canada. When Washington next wrote Schuyler, he said he had been thinking of an expedition to "penetrate into Canada by Way of Kennebeck River, and so to Quebec. . . . I can very well spare a detachment for this Purpose of one Thousand or twelve Hundred men . . . it would make a Diversion that would distract Carleton and facilitate your Views." But "Not a Moment's Time is to be lost in the Preparations for this Enterprise if the Advices received from you favor it."[16] He did not wait for a response to this suggestion; he proceeded to get his detachment organized and selected Benedict Arnold to command it.

Arnold's exploits on Champlain, which he perhaps slightly exaggerated, had brought him reputation and a deserved fame. The colonel was daring, ingenious, and robust. If any senior officer could bring it off, Arnold might. And it would be no easy task. The route the colonel proposed to follow was difficult, but fairly well known. Celerity was the essence; Arnold immediately set himself to drawing up plans and making such arrangements as he could from headquarters at Cambridge.

In letters to the secretary during the summer, Gage repeatedly complained of his inability to act vigorously, and as consistently urged the desirability of changing the British base of operations to New York, a strategic position "preferable to all others," where, he assured Dartmouth, numbers of friends of government would "join the King's Standard." The troops would be better supplied and operations made easier "by having the convenience of a large Navigable river," possession of which "would render the Communication difficult between the Northern and Southern provinces." Such, he reported, was prevailing opinion among the general officers in Boston.[17] In none of his many reports did Gage mention the fact that British soldiers were deserting. They were not departing in streams, but the trickle was steady, and had a demoralizing effect on their comrades, who were doing demanding duty on monotonous rations.‡

He was sorry to inform Dartmouth that "Friends of Government" who sought refuge in Boston were beginning to feel distressed. Most had fled their country estates with no more than the clothes on their backs, a few cherished possessions, and very little money. This they had quickly spent; Gage found it necessary to advance small sums out of his pocket, which was not exactly bulging. No one in Boston or New York would honor his drafts; credit for his officers, formerly generously extended, had suddenly dried up. He had asked London for £50,000. Rigby, paymaster of the forces, sent him £10,000 and diverted the remaining £40,000 to his brokers to buy consols for his personal account. (Burgoyne "wondered" who was drawing interest on this sum.) The general could neither pay his troops nor could his officers discharge their personal debts.

Gage was not the only general in Boston who was writing letters in August. Burgoyne was busy with his quill, and on the twentieth informed Lord George Germain, a friend of the King's soon to move into the Cabinet, that Gage was passive and irresolute; that he could render no report on what Admiral Graves was doing, but could relate what he was *not* doing, i.e., supporting the beleaguered army. He thought John Adams "as great a conspirator as ever subverted a state"; he had "cajoled the opulent, drawn in the wary, deluded the vulgar till all parties in

‡ Washington did what he could to encourage Redcoats to desert. Handbills of various sorts were prepared and smuggled into Boston. One such read:

PROSPECT HILL	BUNKER'S HILL
I Seven dollars a month	I Three pence a day
II Fresh provisions in plenty	II Rotten salt pork
III Health	III The Scurvy
IV Freedom, ease, affluence and a good farm.	IV Slavery, beggary and want.

America and some in Great Britain are puppets in his string." He continued: "Be assured, my Lord, this man soars too high to be allured by any
offer Great Britain can make to himself or to his country. America, if his
counsels continue in force, must be subdued or relinquished. She will not
be reconciled."[18] On the same day he wrote the Earl of Rochford and observed that Adams wrote "with the conciseness of Tacitus; he opens matters for a volume in half a sentence." He added his hope that Adams's
political judgment was "not . . . as acute as his expression."

Burgoyne also wrote a discursive epistle to the adjutant general. This
depressing catalogue of assorted woes undoubtedly discomfited those in
London who read it: "Our situation here is exceedingly Disagreeable—
without an Army fitt to undertake any business of Consequence . . .
were they to be drove from this Camp, we could not Establish ourselves
Six miles from Boston . . . Nor could we cover the Least Extent of Country." An attack might be worthwhile provided victory "wou'd Give us
possession of the Enemies Cannon . . . Yett my private opinion is that it
will not happen." If the army could move to New York, the situation
would in all respects be improved, so "The Three Major Generals" had
lately "presumed" to advise Gage, who had "not yett determined anything upon it."

In the meantime, the army was suffering from want of fresh provisions: "We shall probably Lose a Great many Men in the Winter—our
Sickness increasing Daily in fluxes—the Wounded Recover Slowly and
many of them Dying . . . Change of Air and fresh provisions would
probably Save a Great many men." Unless "a *very large* Addition" were
provided, the ministry "need not flatter themselves" with any expectation
that the war would soon be terminated.

Possibly it would be a good idea to withdraw the Army from the rebellious colonies, leaving them "to Quarrel and Fight among themselves"; aid could then be given to loyal colonies on a selective basis. He
urged "a Viceroy with full powers" for "There is no possibility of carrying on a war So Complicated as this will be, att the Distance we are from
the Fountain Head without these full powers being att hand."[19] No one
in London was prepared to consider appointment of "a Viceroy with full
powers."

He also wrote Solicitor General Thurlow complaining of the "insignificant part" allotted him. He was already planning great things for
himself for 1776. He had received the King's permission to return to England at the end of the campaigning season, and would soon sail to take
his seat in Parliament and enjoy a winter in London. While he waited,
the junior major general in America laid the groundwork. He was a distinguished member of the House of Commons with many politically
powerful friends. And he was well aware that he was not likely to be favored if he hung on to the coattails of a discredited commander. Bur-

goyne had been a political warrior for some years; he knew where the sources of power were. Nothing could have persuaded him to waste his time in Boston if he could possibly get out of the "cursed place."

As the summer waned, criticism of Graves waxed; officers ashore deemed him culpably inefficient; his captains bombarded London with letters urging his recall. Lord Rochford wrote Sandwich the complaints could not be controverted: "Many of our vessels have been taken, officers killed, men made prisoners . . . swift boats called whale boats have been supplied to the enemy from well known towns on the coast, in which boats they have insulted and plundered islands immediately under the protection of our ships, and at noonday landed in force and burned the light-house in Boston harbor almost under the guns of two or three men of war . . . The King, who is apprised of all this has authorized me to tell you that he does not see how the command can be left in such improper hands."[20]

Graves's subordinates wondered why the admiral had not taken the punitive measures the situation obviously demanded: to bombard and lay in ashes the coastal towns that furnished boats, where swift-sailing privateers were fitting out, where prizes were carried in, and livestock and fresh provisions for His Majesty's forces refused. In justification of his inactivity, Graves could point out that he was short of shipping and undermanned and that his landing force—the marines—had been turned over to Gage. Further, he had received no specific directives from the Admiralty.**

By late August, Graves had concluded that punitive action against the sources of his afflictions was imperative. He appealed to Gage to give him two small transports which he could modify to carry cannon for bombardment. Gage thought this a good idea and gave the admiral two ships. Graves had these modified and by early October was ready to order out the first of the planned expeditions. He chose Lieutenant Henry Mowat to command.

The admiral had a long list of targets, including Marblehead, Newburyport, Portsmouth, and Falmouth (now Portland, Maine). He allowed Mowat discretion as to those he was to bombard. Mowat, with his four small ships, sailed from Boston harbor on October 8. Vagaries of weather precluded an attack on Newburyport, and in the afternoon of October 16, the small squadron found itself off Falmouth.

Mowat sent an officer ashore with an ultimatum. In this he dwelled on the unpardonable activities of the rebels, from whom His Majesty, actuated by forbearance and benevolence, had for too long withheld the "Rod of Chastisement." He had come, he said, "to Execute a just Punish-

** Not until September did the Admiralty direct him to seize and detain "Ships and Vessels belonging to the Twelve Colonies" and to impress the seamen aboard them.

ment" on Falmouth, and ordered the residents "to remove the Human Species" from the town. A committee of townsmen was hastily selected and waited on him aboard his flagship, eight-gun *Canceaux*. Mowat demanded that all arms be surrendered immediately, and with this message the committee returned. At Town Meeting, the inhabitants decided not to comply with the demand and began removing their personal property.

A second meeting aboard *Canceaux* resolved nothing, and early on the morning of October 18, 1775, the ships commenced a destructive bombardment. Shortly, a large part of the town was in flames. During the afternoon a landing force completed the work. All the waterfront warehouses and wharves, a church, the courthouse, and 130 dwellings were reduced to ashes. Mowat captured two ships in the harbor and burned thirteen others. As he had expended practically all his ammunition on Falmouth, he could not attack other targets, and returned to Boston.

Graves, reading the lieutenant's report with pleasure, attached a disproportionate importance to destruction of the little town and planned similar expeditions. American reaction was violent. Newspapers described the British as "savages"; their policy as "cruel and barbaric"; and Mowat entered the pages of American history as an "execrable monster." Winter intervened; no other coastal towns were bombarded.

The action did not resolve the question of whether or not such a policy, if carried to extremity, would ultimately have had a decisive political effect in New England. But if response of Americans to the destruction of Falmouth is a criterion, it is reasonable to suppose that such a policy would have served no purpose other than to further solidify their determination to resist.

June, July, and August were unhappy months for Administration. Walpole recorded that "Bad news poured in from America." The livery of London reacted dramatically; "Wilkes and his party threw off all moderation" and drew up a remonstrance which they insisted the King receive on the throne. His Majesty curtly refused, whereupon the lord mayor ordered it to be published, together with assorted "other violent resolutions," one of which demanded that ministers responsible for the government's American policies be impeached at the next session of Parliament.

The King was probably one of the few people in government not perturbed by the "bad news" from America. On July 26 he wrote Lord North: "I am clear as to one point, that we must persist and not be dismayed by any difficulties that may arise on either side of the Atlantick. I know I am doing my duty, and therefore can never wish to retreat."[21] He thought Gage "too mild," and agreed with his First Minister that Graves, too, should be relieved. General William Howe could assume command, but according to the King's explicit instruction, only of those troops stationed in Boston. He would be commissioned "General in America" when he relieved Gage, but he was not to be "Commander-in-Chief in America" as Amherst had been. This decision was not protested by the First Minister, who indeed would not have protested any decision made by the King. Pitt had earlier conceived America as a theater of war, and put Amherst in command of it, but George III would confer no such executive authority on Howe.

Gage had no important political "connexion"; his recall posed no problem. His naval colleague, however, had a powerful friend and protector in the First Lord of the Admiralty. But feeling was running against this "do nothing" Seaman, and Sandwich wrote him that further resistance to his recall would be "utterly ineffectual." The First Lord appointed another personal friend, Rear Admiral Molyneux Shuldham, to take command in North American waters.

These changes presaged a more vigorous prosecution of the war, a policy that met with general approval: "Nothing is more certain than at this time . . . by far the greater part of the British people most earnestly and zealously upheld the King in his determination, according with their own, to maintain, as he and they conceived, both the rights of the Crown and the Authority of Parliament."[22] This assertion is not exactly correct. "The greater part of the British people" lived and worked in villages and small towns in the countryside; they had no vote; a struggle with a remote colony did not touch their daily lives. Certainly the country vicars and fox-hunting squires "earnestly and zealously upheld the King." But stalwart farm boys did not flock to enlist in the Army, nor did seamen and fishermen hasten to accept the bounty offered by the Royal Navy's recruiting parties.

In late July, the King had directed Lord North to frame a royal proclamation declaring the conduct of the Americans "rebelious" and warning persons from corresponding with them. For three weeks, the First Minister took no action; finally, on August 18 the King wrote complaining of the delay: "From the time it was first suggested I have seen it as most necessary; first, as it puts people on their guard, and also as it shews the determination of prosecuting with vigour every measure that may tend to force those deluded people to submission."[23] The First Minister's delay in drawing up a proclamation "For Suppressing Rebellion and Sedition" should not be ascribed to his habitual procrastination. Rather, Lord North probably realized that the hostile and aggressive language the King desired would inevitably produce a violent reaction in America. Such a proclamation would, in effect, be a declaration of war against the colonies. But the King would have it no other way, and North bowed as usual to his master's obstinate determination.

The proclamation declared the Americans to be in a state of "open and avowed rebellion" instigated by "dangerous and ill-designing men" who were "traitorously" levying war against the crown. The duty of all officers, civil and military, was "to exert their utmost endeavours" to suppress the rebellion and bring the traitors to the bar of justice. The King called on his loyal subjects "to disclose . . . all treasons and traitorous conspiracies." There followed a distinct warning that "all persons" found to be in correspondence with the rebels, or who aided and abetted their designs, would suffer "condign punishment."[24] This was a signal not only to the too-vocal Opposition press, but to the London livery, the Reverend John Horne, and others who supported the Americans but did not enjoy parliamentary immunity, that the government would proceed against them. The proclamation, issued on August 23, was, with the exception of the City of London, generally approved. Loyal addresses poured in; from them the First Minister drew renewed confidence in his course of action. The King's confidence did not require bolstering; his devout belief in the rectitude of his measures was unwavering.

The proclamation clearly enunciated the "conspiracy" thesis which, in reverse, was popular on the other side of the Atlantic. His Majesty found it impossible to believe that any but a very small number of radical agitators, who should be incontinently hung up, would oppose acts of the supreme legislature to which he had given royal assent. This conviction, shared by most of his trusted advisers, was to have a decisive effect on formulation of British strategy and prosecution of the war.††

His Most Christian Majesty's ambassador to the Court of Saint James, M. le Comte de Guines, assessed Great Britain's intentions toward the rebellious colonies in a letter to Vergennes. The ambassador did not doubt that a decision had been made "to annihilate America if they cannot subdue her, to burn the cities, the ships, the forests, and to turn this country into a desert." He described the policy as barbaric, but one he thought would best serve Great Britain's interests, because "America will hardly be her slave, never her ally, and forever her enemy."[25] At Versailles, Vergennes had already arrived at similar conclusions.

In early August a British intelligence agent interviewed two French officers en route from the West Indies to Paris via America, who had stopped in London to enjoy the tag end of an exceptionally gay season. The meeting was convivial; the agent reported "What I have been able to collect from the two French officers by employing every art and all the

†† At this time the King was more interested in the question of a pension for the Earl of Chatham and his family than in the American rebellion, and was anxiously awaiting news that Chatham, "a trumpet of sedition," had passed to his reward. His Majesty, hopeful that the event would not be too long delayed, did not want to authorize payment of pensions of £3,000 per annum until he learned that Chatham was "totally unable to appear on the public stage."

address I am master of." The two officers, M. le Comte de Bonvouloir and M. le Chevalier d'Amboise, talked freely enough: ". . . that vin de Champagne produced the desired effect."

They agreed "the common people of America have been worked up to a pitch of enthusiastic frenzy that is beyond conception," but believed their leaders had "no settled, regular, well-digested plan, that there exists among their Chiefs more Jealousy than Unanimity, that all the Commercial people of substance" were beginning to tire of the situation, and that the British Government could no doubt "fall on methods to disunite them."

In Cambridge, where they spent several weeks before sailing from Newport, they had met Generals Israel Putnam and Artemas Ward. The former they described as "a good natured, civil, and brave old soldier, but a Head Strong, Ignorant and Stupid General. Ward they indeed hold very cheap." They thought "the rebel officers in general perfectly ignorant of their business . . . men of moderate, or rather mean, parts." They found the rank and file "well trained and remarkably well armed." The Americans lacked artillery and did not seem to know how to use what few pieces they had. However, a number of French officers had recently joined them and would soon teach them to employ artillery properly. This information was worth "that vin de Champagne" the agent provided.

Some powder and ball ammunition had been sent from the French West Indies to Newport. Lord Rochford directed H.M. chargé d'affaires in Paris to protest to Vergennes. The count coolly replied that the British Government was "certainly . . . misinformed." The chargé wrote the secretary: "I must do him the Justice to say that the whole tenor of his Language, which was frank and positive upon this occasion, convinces me that there is no Succour given to the American rebels with the countenance of Government." Neither Rochford nor his royal master was misled by Vergennes's beguiling double-talk. They knew "for certain the Particulars of several Cargoes loaded at Bayonne, St. Malo, and particularly Bordeaux, from whence a Ship was to sail [in early September] with 300 Casks of Gunpowder & 5000 Musquets with Bayonets complete." These supplies had been purchased with the proceeds of several cargoes of tobacco and rice.

In his summary of the state of affairs at the end of August 1775, the editor of the *Annual Register* wrote: "Thus the Boston Port Bill and its companions had even exceeded the prognostications of their most violent opponents. They had raised a flame from one end to the other of the continent of America and united all the old colonies in one common cause. A similar language was everywhere held; or if there was any difference in the language, the measures that were adopted were everywhere directed to the same object. They all agreed in the main points, of holding a Congress, of not submitting to the payment of any internal taxes, that were not, as usual, imposed by their own assemblies, and of suspending all commerce with the mother country, until the American grievances in general, and those of Massachusetts Bay in particular, were fully redressed."[26]

It was now obvious that many more troops would have to be raised, equipped, and sent to America. Both Major General Harvey and Viscount Barrington had for long expressed disapproval of major land operations, which they judged beyond the capability of Great Britain to sustain. They favored a strategy that would exploit the monopoly the Royal Navy might establish in American waters. Neither was a member of the Cabinet; their recommendations were not given serious consideration at that level. And for good reason: At the time, Britain did not have the means to impose an effective blockade on the Atlantic coastline of America. Such a strategy would have required four or five well-equipped and defended naval bases at such widely separated points as Halifax, Newport, New York, Norfolk, and Charleston. Nor were the types of ships needed available. A major building program which would take much time and have been extremely expensive would have been necessary. The Cabinet did not want to give the rebellion time to mature, but to nip it in the bud. Blockade, a protracted strategy, would not do.

The King realized this, and in his capacity of Elector of Hanover met the immediate emergency by ordering five battalions of electoral troops to be expeditiously embarked for Gibraltar and Minorca to free British garrisons there for service in America. He directed Lord North to advance £10,000 "To put them in motion. The officers are poor, and are not able to prepare their major equipage; many articles are wanting for the men. . . ."[27] His Majesty was delighted with the arrangement; it saved the Treasury a considerable amount of money as there would be no half pay for officers when they retired.

There was much gossip that the King was trying to hire 20,000 fully equipped Russian troops from the Empress Catherine. This was no idle rumor. Negotiations had been going on for some time in the Russian capital; on September 5 Dartmouth wrote Howe of the "confident hope he entertained of 'having a large Army in North America in the Spring." His Majesty's minister at St. Petersburg, having been "well instructed to sound the Empress," reported "Her Imperial Majesty has, in the fullness of her affection for the British Nation . . . made the most explicit declaration and given the most ample assurances, of letting us have any number of Infantry that may be wanted." The King had asked for 20,000 to be sent to America in the spring of 1776. Rochford wrote Eden he had been thinking "about those 20,000 Russians—They will be charming visitors at New York, and civilize that part of America wonderfully."

These rumors upset Walpole, who wrote Sir Horace Mann: "that miracle of gratitude, the Czarina, has consented to lend England 20,000 Russians to be transported to America. The Parliament is to meet on the 20th of next month, and vote 26,000 seamen—what a paragraph of blood is there! With what torrents must liberty be preserved in America! In England, who can save it? Oh! Mad, mad England! What frenzy to throw away its treasures, lay waste its empire of Wealth, and sacrifice its freedome that its Prince may be the Arbitrary Lord of boundless deserts in America and of an impoverished, depopulated and thence insignificant island in Europe."[28]

derly Book shows that he reduced but one sentence—that from six hundred to three hundred lashes.[1]

Rations were poor indeed. There were no fruits or vegetables; fresh meat was available only occasionally; scurvy and dysentery were endemic. The rank and file had nothing to do but get drunk, and this Howe's Redcoats did with consistency until the general closed the dramshops. Morale was steadily deteriorating and there is no evidence that Howe did anything to improve the situation. But he and his senior officers managed to live well. The general was putting on weight; he might have been a distant relative of the young, agile, audacious colonel who had scaled the cliffs at Quebec and gained Wolfe's accolade. He was an intellectual sluggard and physically indolent. He kept a good table over which his handsome young mistress, Mrs. Joshua Loring, "the Sultana," presided. He was a gambler, as were most of his contemporaries, and devoted many of his late night hours to faro. He passed most of his military responsibilities to Clinton, who was not exactly happy to have to occupy his time with routine administrative chores. Judge Thomas Jones of New York, the Tory historian, summed up Howe's activities in Boston during the winter of 1775–76 in a few words: "Nothing seemed to engross his attention but the faro table, the play house, the dancing assembly, and Mrs. Loring." Howe's infatuation with the luscious wife of a Boston Tory, whom the general commissioned "Commissary of Prisoners" as a reward for his complaisance, was widely celebrated by the Americans in dozens of ribald quatrains.

Howe did pay some attention to the recreational needs of his younger officers, and prepared a riding hall for them by gutting Old South Meeting House of its handsome carved pews and tearing out the aged oak floors, which provided him with a good supply of firewood during the approaching winter. So long as General Howe remained in command in Boston, Washington could devote himself to the problem of trying to create an army, a project in which the British general had no mind to interfere.

Benjamin Thompson of Woburn, Massachusetts, the ostensible patriot who later became Count Rumford, had spent considerable time at Cambridge when some of his friends were senior officers in the Massachusetts contingent. He thus had every opportunity to familiarize himself with conditions there. After he crossed the lines in October he prepared a report for Howe. Thompson had found Washington's army "badly *accoutered*" and "wretchedly *cloathed*"; in his opinion, "as dirty a set of mortals as ever disgraced the name of Soldier." As no women were permitted to live in camp, the men had to wash their own clothes. Most of them considered this chore demeaning, and rather than work over a washtub they let their linen "rot upon their backs." Sanitation was poor and "Putrid, malignant and infectious disorders . . . prevailed with unabating fury." As medical facilities were primitive at best, soldiers stricken with dysentery and hepatitis departed for their homes, where they could expect decent food and some attention. Thus, many "not only died themselves" but spread infection "among their Relations and Friends." The mortality in New England and particularly in Massachusetts was indeed appalling; worse than ever before known. The wasted men who staggered back to countless New England villages and farms during late summer and early autumn of 1775 were not particularly good advertisements for a life in Mr. Washington's army.

While Howe diverted himself with Mrs. Loring and at faro, and Washington gradually managed to impose a degree of discipline on officers and a militia reluctant to accept any, the political pot in London was coming to a boil. On the last day of August, the Duke of Grafton, Lord Privy Seal, had written the First Minister suggesting that Gage or his successor be immediately authorized to offer a cessation of hostilities and to invite the colonists to send a deputation to London "to state to Parliament their wishes and expectations." Grafton must have been aware that this suggestion would not possibly evoke a sympathetic response. In fact, seven weeks elapsed before he received any. Then, on October 20, Lord North replied, enclosing a cabinet draft of the speech the King would read from the throne when Parliament assembled a week later.

The minister wrote that he and his colleagues were determined to use "every species of force" to reduce the Americans to a becoming state of submission, after which his ministry would be pleased to discuss accommodation. The tenor was uncompromising; there was no suggestion of a moderating policy designed to promote the now remote prospects of reconciliation. This was too belligerent to suit the duke, who asked for an audience and was granted one on October 24. Here, he stated his unequivocal opposition to ministerial policy in America. The King assured him the rebellion would soon be put down, as he was arranging to hire great numbers of foreign mercenaries. Grafton replied that twice the number the King had mentioned "would only increase the disgrace, and never effect his purpose."

Two days later, Parliament assembled to hear the speech from the throne. His Majesty informed his loyal Lords and Commons that the Americans had openly avowed "their revolt, hostility and rebellion." Many of those "unhappy people" were no doubt still loyal, "yet the torrent of violence" had been "strong enough to compel their acquiesance till a sufficient force shall appear to support them." The King discounted the colonists' "vague expressions of attachment to the parent state" and their protestations of dutiful loyalty to his person, cunningly avowed only to distract the British whilst they raised an army and prepared a navy. He praised the "moderate" acts of Parliament: the Boston Port Bill, the Massachusetts Government Act, the Quartering Bill, all designed "to prevent . . . the effusion of blood." His Majesty admitted the rebellion had "become general" and was "manifestly carried on for the purpose of establishing an independent empire." Should this succeed, the results might well be fatal to Britain.

The King had no intention of supinely giving up colonies Englishmen had planted, nursed through many trials "with great tenderness, encouraged with many commercial advantages, and protected and defended at such expense of blood and treasure." He had therefore increased the naval establishment and augumented the land forces, but in the least burdensome way.[2] He had received "the most friendly offers of foreign assistance" and felt confident that the mighty forces he proposed soon to direct against "the deluded multitudes" would quickly impel them to recognize the errors of their ways and submit, at which time he was ready "to receive the misled with tenderness and mercy." Commissioners soon to be named would receive submissions and be authorized to grant "particular pardons." That the policy outlined in this speech and in the Royal Proclamation of August 23 was unhappily lacking in political sagacity may now appear too facile a judgment. But at the time, many thought it singularly inept.

Opposition took the speech to pieces and charged the ministry with having "brought the Sovereign into the most disgraceful and unhappy situation" of any monarch then reigning. The conduct of the King's ministers "had wrested the sceptre of America" from his hands, lost half the empire, reduced the remaining half to chaos, and spread corruption like a tidal wave over the land "until all public virtue was lost." Ministers had "inebriated the people with vice and profligacy" and in the "paroxysms of their infatuation and madness" taught them "to cry out for havoc and war." History could not show an instance of a great empire "ruined in such a Manner."[3]

In the Commons, the proposed address of thanks to His Majesty for his "gracious speech" touched off an acrimonious debate, as Lord John Cavendish moved a resolution that disorders in the colonies had been increased by policies ostensibly designed to allay them; that the measures taken were "injurious and inefficacious"; and that no good results could possibly have been expected from their application. Lord John called on Parliament to restore tranquillity by a prudent and temperate use of its powers, and vigorously condemned the alarming and dangerous expedient of hiring mercenaries to enforce British policy.

Lord North led his reliable phalanx of "King's Friends" and country gentlemen to the counterattack. Had not the illegal Congress usurped all the powers of government? Had they not fielded an army? Had they not

issued bills of credit? Were they not forming a navy? Had they not engaged in acts of war against duly constituted authority? Let the deeds of
these rebellious subjects speak rather than their hypocritical and deceit-
ful assertions of dutiful allegiance. They had construed Great Britain's
policy of indulgent leniency to be one actuated by fear and weakness.
They were contemptuous of Parliament and disobedient to its mandates.
The contest was for empire, and Great Britain could not recede from her
position without "shame, ruin and disgrace." The Americans must, and
would, be brought to heel. As dawn broke, Lord John's proposed amendments were put to the vote and defeated, 278 to 108.

But Opposition was by no means ready to call it a day, and after a
brief recess launched a concerted attack on the proposal to hire German
troops. This, one speaker after another asserted, was an illegal and unconstitutional procedure, repugnant to the Bill of Rights, and would set a
calamitous, alarming, and dangerous precedent. Lord North managed to
quell a revolt that might have brought down the government, but in
doing so finally lost any support he may have hoped for from General
Conway, who rose to condemn the war "in the most decisive terms."
Conway "declared it to be cruel, unnecessary and unnatural . . . a
butchery of his fellow subjects," and "reprobated every idea of conquer-
ing America upon all the grounds of justice, expediency and prac-
ticability."[4] The general was no longer on the active list, but he spoke
with undeniable authority and reflected the opinions of many senior serving officers in both the army and the navy that to subdue America by
force of arms was not a feasible project.

In the Lords, Grafton spoke for Opposition and added his voice to
those of Rockingham, Camden, Richmond, and Shelburne, who in view
of the duke's record were not inclined to receive him with acclamations
of unfeigned joy. Indeed, the defector "brought them nor sense, nor activity, nor harmony, nor six votes" (i.e., in the House of Commons).[5] He
resigned his office on November 9.

Grafton's resignation provided Lord North with an unexpected opportunity to make some changes in the Cabinet. Dartmouth, considered
by his colleagues to be lacking in determination and vigor, and known to
prefer a strategy of blockade to major commitment of land forces, was
with considerable difficulty persuaded to vacate the office of Secretary
for the Colonies and to accept the Privy Seal. This cleared the way for
Lord George Sackville Germain, who on November 11 was received by
the King, kissed hands, and took the oath as the third Principal Secretary
of State. His area of responsibility was America, and his appointment to
office was to prove possibly the most controversial in the history of the
British Cabinet.

Lord George was a man of strong convictions; in the House of Commons he was recognized as an effective speaker. He had earlier been a

supporter of the Marquis of Rockingham, but as he found himself in continuing disagreement with Rockingham's conciliatory American policy, had shifted his allegiance to Lord North. Even before reports of Bunker Hill reached Whitehall, he had urged the adoption of stern coercive measures, and had privately agitated for the recall of Gage and Graves. The general expectation was that he would add sorely needed backbone to a Cabinet over which the wobbly Lord North nominally presided.

Germain, who would be execrated in both England and America, was an enigma even to his friends and has proved a greater one to historians. He was the third son of the seventh Earl and fourth Duke of Dorset. Knole, the family seat in Kent where he spent a happy youth, is a great house, luxuriously furnished and appointed. When Lord George grew up there, platoons of butlers, footmen, cooks, chambermaids, grooms, and gardeners staffed the majestic establishment. This atmosphere, in which a child's whim had but to be expressed to be immediately satisfied by subservient retainers, was calculated to nurture the qualities of boundless egoism and arrogance both his friends and his enemies later observed to be his most marked characteristics.

Lord George was intelligent, handsome, active, and ambitious. Many of his forebears had served their kings in positions of authority and power. Naturally enough, Lord George was determined not just to equal their achievements, but to excel them. But his character was curiously flawed. He was far from being a friendly person—almost incapable, it would seem, of winning friends. Pride of birth and position, haughty dogmatism, a contemptuous disregard of social inferiors, were traits he shared with other Englishmen of his station in life. He was an accomplished political intriguer, as were most of his contemporaries, and never overlooked an opportunity to flatter those who by reason of position and influence could be persuaded to further his ambitions, nor to denigrate those of whom he was jealous. His more reprehensible qualities would surface only after the monumental disgrace that struck him down at Minden in August 1759. It is difficult to account for Lord George's later behavior unless we place it in the perspective of Minden, for what happened on that field was to hang around his neck like an albatross until his dying day, and to awaken dormant tendencies in his character that would make him detested by many and distrusted by most of his associates.

In the summer of 1758, Lord George Sackville (he had not yet come into the estate left him by his aunt Betty Germain, or assumed her name) was a senior major general in the British Army. He was generally regarded as a most able officer. He enjoyed the favor of King George II and the patronage of Pitt, at the time practically a dictator. In July he was promoted lieutenant general and sent to Germany, on Pitt's recommendation, to act as second-in-command to the Duke of Marlborough, then commanding the British contingent in the Allied Army serving under Prince Ferdinand, Duke of Brunswick.*

The day Lord George arrived in Germany he began writing letters criticizing both Marlborough and the allied commander in chief for their handling of operations. This was impolitic to say the least, as Ferdinand of Brunswick, esteemed the most accomplished general of his age, was much admired by George II. On October 28, 1758, the Duke of Marlborough died at Münster, and a few days later Lord George received his commission as "Commander in Chief of all His majesty's forces, horse and foot, serving on the lower Rhine or to be assigned there with the Allied Army under the command of Prince Ferdinand of Brunswick."[6]

On August 1, 1759, the allied foot, having stoically withstood four French thrusts, was ordered by Prince Ferdinand to go over to the attack. This the troops did, and with such élan and courage that total destruction of the French was within grasp. Urgently and repeatedly the prince sent couriers to Sackville with orders for him to lead the British cavalry forward to administer the *coup de grace* to the confused enemy. Lord George did absolutely nothing. When the cavalry did move, at the orders of his second-in-command, the Marquis of Granby, the moment had passed. The French Army, at the very instant of impending annihilation, escaped to safety behind the walls of Minden. The prince asked George II to recall his general immediately. Sackville was relieved of command and summoned to England forthwith. There, at his request, he faced a general court-martial.

Lord George was not tried for cowardice, though the imputation hung heavy. He had proved before Minden, and would later prove at pistol point when he faced one of the most dangerous duelists of the day who had publicly impugned his honor, that he was no physical coward. Deliberate disobedience? For what purpose? He could not possibly hope to advance himself by depriving Prince Ferdinand of a decisive victory, although this intent was alleged against him. For such a victory would have brought Lord George, as one of its architects, promotion and honor, possibly a Garter; from Frederick the Great of Prussia, royal recognition and grateful bounty. If he knew the reason for his inexplicable behavior, he never revealed it.

The sentence of the court, that he be immediately dismissed in disgrace from the British Army and deemed incompetent to hold any military post whatsoever, did not satisfy either King George II or Pitt, who were determined that he should suffer ineradicable disgrace. Lord George, however, was determined otherwise. He would rehabilitate himself by any means; he would gain that position in government to which he felt his birth and talents entitled him. He proceeded to do so by ingra-

* This Marlborough was a less than competent descendant of "the Great Duke."

tiating himself with the young Prince of Wales, soon to become George III. The ceremony held on November 11, 1775, when he kissed hands and received from his sovereign the seals as Principal Secretary of State for America, was the culminating act of a long, tortuous progress. Lord George Germain was finally at the top, where he had always known he belonged. And he knew the going there would not be smooth.

Indeed, it turned out to be even rougher than the noble lord had anticipated, for he immediately became Charles Fox's target in the House of Commons. At every opportunity Fox unloosed his vitriolic barrages at this "ill-omened and inauspicious character." When Fox, one of the toughest and most relentless infighters in the history of the House, was in "full feather," as he always was when he rose to attack Germain, his devastating polemic was not to be surpassed. He had a retentive memory, a blazing wit, and the well from which he drew his spontaneous flow of invective was apparently bottomless. Those who heard him in debate testified that his performances were coruscating. He had a thorough grasp of "that noble instrument" the English language; he could wield it either as a bludgeon or a rapier and with it he demolished his ministerial opponents.† All feared him, and even the King, who detested him, knew that when Fox was absent, ministers could shove bills through a reading with far less trouble and embarrassment than if he were there, waiting to tear them to shreds.

In his personal financial affairs, Fox was totally irresponsible. He borrowed from anyone he could touch for even a few guineas; his friends and acquaintances found it quite as difficult to resist his suggestions that they part with fifty or one hundred to ensure that Charles would be able to spend a pleasant day at Newmarket, or perhaps half an hour at a faro game. He borrowed from Peter to pay Paul and was heavily in debt at exorbitant interest to every moneylender in London. He called his reception room "the Jerusalem Room" because every midday it was crowded with Jewish usurers who hopefully came to collect anything they could. Sometimes, after a good day at the races (where he usually won) or a lucky run at cards (where he usually lost), his pockets would be heavy; his butler served the champagne and Charles paid off. On other days, he escaped his creditors by slipping out the back door and making his way to the House of Commons in a curtained chair.

Certainly Fox was (as his enemies never tired of asserting and his friends reluctantly admitted) a notorious womanizer, an incredible gambler, a wild plunger at Newmarket during the racing season, a gourmandizer, a heavy drinker, and a late sleeper. All these allegations were true but irrelevant, for his genius showed when he spoke in the House of Commons. But his brilliance, even when coupled with Burke's cold

† The description of the language is, I believe, Winston Churchill's.

analyses, did not suffice to wrench power from "the mangling hands of a blundering Ministry" seemingly intent not on the preservation, but on the destruction, of Britain's empire beyond the Atlantic.

In his speech from the throne, the King had stated his intent in unequivocal terms: to apply such force as necessary to suppress armed rebellion in America. The problem that now faced the ministry was how this aim was to be achieved in the shortest possible time and at the least possible expense. Here the Cabinet had to take into account a variety of factors. Principal among these was the question of French-Spanish policy. To what extent, short of a war for which Whitehall had reason to believe the Bourbon powers were not yet prepared, would Versailles aid the rebels? What would be the attitude of Spain? And what reliance could be placed on Loyalists in Virginia and the Carolinas? In New York? In New Jersey and Pennsylvania? How effective were the colonial troops likely to be when opposed by disciplined regulars in orthodox battle situations?

Obviously, many more trained troops and seamen were needed to settle this troublesome affair, and speedily, before the French and Spanish decided to take advantage of Britain's entanglement in a distant theater of war. Where were these to be found? How was the money to finance major overseas operations to be raised? And if primary emphasis were to be given to operations in the American colonies, what resources could be allocated to ensure the safety of the Sugar Islands, Canada, Gibraltar, Minorca? Newfoundland and India? How were the great merchant fleets to be protected? With access to American seamen, timber, and naval stores suddenly completely cut off, where was the Board of Admiralty to turn for men and assured supplies of materials indispensable to keep powerful fleets in American waters; to dominate the Channel; to provide frigates for convoys; and to keep watch on French and Spanish ports?

These questions would have challenged the imagination, determination, and planning and co-ordinating abilities of a First Minister more generously endowed with them than was Lord North. During the Seven Years' War, Pitt, blessed with a yokemate in Newcastle who had the thankless job of lining up votes in Lords and Commons, was free to plan and direct strategy. Lord North had no such help. He had not only to run the Treasury and Exchequer but to carry the burden in the House of Commons. There, he was principally assisted by Sir Gilbert Elliot, Thurlow, Wedderburn, and now Germain. This team could not possibly match the brilliant array mustered by the Opposition—led by Burke, Fox, Barré, Dunning, Conway. And Administration was but slightly better off in the Lords. Still, the First Minister could control the House of Commons; he had an assured working majority and he was a superb political manager. But he had no martial inclinations, and his feelings about the war in America were ambivalent. He intended to assume as little responsibility as possible for its prosecution.

The new Secretary of State was eager to do so. Germain was himself convinced, and had convinced others, including the King, that he had matured infallible plans to crush the rebellion, a task he did not believe would be onerous. From Dartmouth he had inherited an operation much to his liking; when he took office in mid-November, planning for this was in an advanced stage.

As there was no prospect that Howe could do anything more than hang on at Boston until ships could be provided to evacuate his army, the need for a stroke within the limited capabilities of the forces the ministry could muster was evident. Obviously, something had to be done quickly, or the cancer of rebellion would spread. Consensus in the Cabinet was that an opportunity existed in one or another of the southern colonies, whose deposed royal governors had for some time been insistently urging that an expedition be dispatched to those parts to re-establish the authority of the crown. In Virginia and North and South Carolina, so they vigorously asserted, thousands of Loyalists eagerly awaited the arrival of the King's troops to avow their allegiance. Ministers were naturally predisposed to accept these statements at face value, if for no other reason than that such a situation provided the basis for a relatively cheap, painless, and speedy way to re-establish royal authority in enclaves distant from the focus of rebellion. Lord Dunmore, Josiah Martin, and Lord William Campbell repeatedly assured anyone who would listen that once the Royal Standard was raised in the four southern provinces, recruits would pour in.‡ Such was the background for the cabinet decision taken in mid-September 1775 to mount an expedition against North Carolina.

On September 16 the King wrote Lord North approving the concept and authorizing the employment of four regiments (15th, 37th, 53rd, and 54th) then stationed in Ireland. These were to embark not later than December 12.[7] Apparently this approval was for planning purposes only, as it was not until October 16 that His Majesty finally gave explicit assent to the proposed operation. On the previous day he had written Lord North that "every means of distressing America" met with his concurrence; possibly the proposed expedition would bring the rebels "to feel the necessity of returning to their duty." He was "clear," too, that North Carolina was the proper target "as the Highland settlers are said to be well inclined."[8] A week later he approved an increase in the force to seven battalions. Howe had been directed to provide a general officer to command the landing force, which he was to augment by one battalion of foot. Howe did not approve of the project; not only did it diminish his

‡ Royal governors respectively of Virginia, North Carolina, and South Carolina. All three had taken refuge on British warships.

slender resources of infantry, but its objective was distant from any target area he considered strategically important. He named Clinton to command the expedition.

Charles, Earl Cornwallis, was in active command of his regiment in Ireland when he heard of the proposed expedition against the southern colonies. He immediately applied to Germain to be considered as second-in-command. His letter was laid before the Cabinet, and Lord North wrote the King recommending his appointment: ". . . it would be useful to permit Lord Cornwallis to go, as his example will give credit & spirit to our proceedings against America. The Ardor of the Nation in this cause has not hitherto arisen to the pitch one could wish, & [it] certainly should be encouraged wherever it appears." His Majesty concurred; the earl was to proceed with his regiment.

As a young officer, Cornwallis had distinguished himself on German battlefields and was promoted colonel at the age of twenty-six. He had later represented a family-controlled constituency in the House of Commons, and in 1762, on the death of his father, succeeded to the earldom and moved to the Lords. At the time he was selected as second-in-command to Clinton little more was known of his abilities than that as a junior officer he had been a vigorous and courageous combat commander, respected by his seniors and peers and admired by his subordinates. He was well educated, and through a Prussian tutor and attendance at a military school in Turin, had acquired something more than the smattering of theory common to most of his contemporaries. For a short time he had acted as a junior ADC to the King, who conceived for him a lasting affection which none of the earl's later mistakes and tribulations could extinguish. Germain, too, was an admirer, and when Clinton learned of the assignment he expressed his pleasure.

The earl's wife was unhappy at the prospect and did what she could do to have her husband's orders revoked. But he was determined to go across the Atlantic. For a relatively young, ambitious, and competent officer, the road to fame was in America, not in Westminster or in Irish backwaters. He was named "Major-General in America," given command of the contingent scheduled to sail from Cork, and ordered to join Clinton at Cape Fear, North Carolina.

At the same time, Sandwich informed Admiral Shuldham that shipping to lift five battalions, each of 477 officers and men, 60 women, and 12 servants, would be ready at Cork on December 1. There the troops were to embark immediately for North Carolina "in order to take possession of that province and to make a powerful diversion by that means to the attacks of the rebels in the North." Commodore Sir Peter Parker was "to have the conduct of this expedition."[9] Ten thousand stand of arms, brass cannon, shot, and a generous supply of ball ammunition and powder designed for Loyalist recruits to be assimilated into the royal establishment were loaded. After the successful operation in the South, the force would join Howe in New York for the campaign of 1776. It was not Clinton's mission to occupy permanently any area in North or South Carolina. He was to establish an enclave to which Loyalists could resort; re-establish royal government; embody, arm, and train provincials willing to serve the crown and then depart to join Howe.

Assuming (as Whitehall did with considerable reason) the validity of the premise that Loyalists would respond, the plan seemed sound. Even allowing for vagaries of winter weather on the Atlantic, which could be avoided by careful routing, the force should certainly reach its rendez-vous at Cape Fear with the contingent from Boston not later than mid-February, complete assigned operations by mid-May, and join Howe in New York in early June 1776. No major problem was apparent to Lord George, who, new to office, plunged at once into the bureaucratic jungle and devoted himself energetically to resolving the difficulties incessantly raised by the entrenched and inefficient boards responsible for various aspects of the expedition. His first action was to augument the Carolina force by ordering the 57th Regiment of Foot to prepare to embark at Cork on short notice. This augmentation brought the strength of Major General Earl Cornwallis' contingent to about 2,600.

Sir James Murray, a young captain who commanded the 57th's Light Infantry Company, wrote his sister that he considered the attempt to put down the rebellion a futile exercise: "To subdue by force of arms a coun-try of several thousands of miles in extent, almost entirely covered with wood, is not an easy operation, if there were no inhabitants at all: but when we consider that there are no less than 3,000,000 exasperated to the last degree and inflamed to the highest pitch of enthusiasm; we have too many instances of what that enthusiasm has been capable of producing not to be very doubtful of the event."[10] Murray was not convinced the Americans were in the wrong, for if they believed it better for them to cast off the yoke of dependency, and could succeed in doing so, "they are most indisputably in the right to make the attempt." But Britain had "an undeniable right" to attempt to preserve her American dominions. He thought this "matter of right" could not be decided "till toward the end of next summer."[11]

The 57th and other regiments now designated for the "Southern Ex-pedition" were destined to wait in Cork for a considerable period as one delay followed another. The first hitch was provided by the Admiralty. Although Sandwich had promptly allotted one fifty-gun ship and eight smaller shallow-draft ships for convoy and support, only one was at the moment ready. All others were in various states of refitting, loading stores, or taking on water and firewood. The early December em-barkation date projected could not be met. A thirty-day postponement was inevitably accepted. Both the King and Germain, who realized the necessity for dispatch, were disappointed.

For several weeks, the King had been expecting good news from Sir Robert Gunning, his ambassador in St. Petersburg. Gunning had previously reported that the Czarina would provide the troops His Majesty had requested to assist him in quelling the rebellion in America. Whether the Empress had actually promised the ambassador that she would rent 20,000 "well-disciplined" mercenaries is a question that cannot be resolved, but Gunning thought that she had and had been dissuaded from doing so by Frederick of Prussia. However that may be, Catherine sent the King a letter which he received on November 2. The epistle, so the King wrote Lord North on the following day, was a "clear-cut refusal, and not in so genteel a manner as I should have thought might have been expected from her. She has not had the civility to answer in her own hand, and has thrown out some expressions that may be civil to a Russian ear, but certainly not to more civilized ones."[12]

Unable to hire Russian peasants to fight his war in America, the King had to look elsewhere. For the American war was not popular in England. Had it been, there would have been no need to solicit troops from the Empress of Russia, and when these were refused to apply to assorted German princelings. A number of high-ranking officers in both the army and the navy refused to serve against the Americans. Prominent among these were Admiral Augustus Keppel and the Earl of Effingham. Chatham's son also resigned his commission. General Howe had expressed his distaste, but when ordered to go, went.

But where it mattered politically, the King was supported. The country gentlemen and practically all the well-to-do townspeople were solidly behind him. Loyal addresses poured into London. The enfeebled Opposition managed to procure a few critical of policy. These could be, and were, ignored. But loyal addresses by themselves solved no practical problem. The immediate need was for soldiers and sailors, and Britons were not interested in enlisting.

✄ 4

To Restore Liberty to Our Brethren in Canada

Governor Carleton was well aware of the activity at Ticonderoga, and of course deduced an invasion force was being mounted there. But there was not much he could do about it. He established his headquarters in Montreal and sent most of his available regulars to hold the forts at St. Johns and Chambly on the Richelieu. He had less than three hundred available to defend Montreal and Quebec.* And his confidence had been severely shaken by news that several hundred Canadians had joined Montgomery.

On September 25 Ethan Allen, ambitious to repeat his coup at Ticonderoga, suddenly appeared before Montreal with an ill-assorted troop and demanded the surrender of the city. Here, however, he encountered not another Captain de la Place, but Carleton and a tough Major Carden, whose small garrison sallied out, and in a short fire fight put the invaders to flight and captured their brash leader, who was immediately put in irons. Allen's reckless foray alerted the countryside; dozens of able-bodied men came in to help defend the city against another attempt.

* Some five hundred regulars were at Fort Niagara, Detroit, and Michilimackinac. He had earlier sent two battalions to Gage.

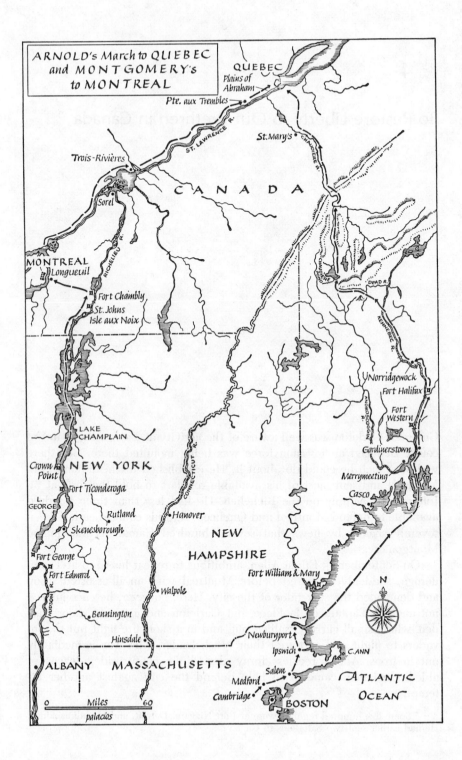

ARNOLD's March to QUEBEC
and MONTGOMERY's
to MONTREAL

QUEBEC
Plains of
Abraham
Pte. aux Trembles
St. Mary's
ST. LAWRENCE R.
CHAUDIERE R.
Trois-Rivières
C A N A D A
Sorel
RICHELIEU R.
MONTREAL
Longueuil
Fort Chambly
St. Johns
Isle aux Noix
DEAD R.
KENNEBEC R.
ANDROSCOGGIN R.
Norridgewock
Fort Halifax
Fort Western
LAKE
CHAMPLAIN
Crown
Point
NEW YORK
Gardinerstown
Fort Ticonderoga
Merrymeeting
L.
GEORGE
Rutland
Hanover
Casco
Skenesborough
CONNECTICUT R.
NEW
Fort George
HAMPSHIRE
Fort Edward
HUDSON R.
Walpole
Fort William & Mary
N
Bennington
Hinsdale
Newburyport
Ipswich
C. ANN
ALBANY
MASSACHUSETTS
Salem
Medford
ATLANTIC
OCEAN
Cambridge
BOSTON
0   Miles   60
palacios

When he heard Allen had been taken prisoner, Schuyler wrote the president of Congress he feared the "disagreeable consequences from Mr. Allen's imprudence. I always dreaded his impatience of subordination." So had his neighbors, who earlier had refused to give him command of the Green Mountain Boys and had elected Seth Warner as their colonel. The British sent Allen to England, where he spent the next two years in prison.

In late September, Schuyler informed Hancock he was ill and had passed field command of the expedition to Canada to Brigadier General Richard Montgomery. The president replied several weeks later to assure him that while Congress "most heartily lamented" his "Loss of Health . . . their Concern for the Public is greatly alleviated by the Abilities and Zeal of General Montgomery, in which they cannot but place the highest Confidence." Hancock then outlined the objective of the expedition: to induce the Canadians "to accede to an Union with these Colonies . . . and send Delegates to this Congress." Schuyler was to assure the Canadians that Congress would exert the "utmost Endeavours to obtain for them and their Posterity the Blessings of a free Government" and to guarantee them "the free enjoyment of their Religion." He directed Schuyler "to collect the Sentiments of the most discreet and sensible among the principal Canadians and English . . . and communicate *their* Opinion with *your* Remarks. . . ." The president was happy to report that Congress had "borrowed one Ton of Gun Powder" from Pennsylvania, and would send it forward without delay.[1]

Several days later, a most disconcerting letter from the commander in chief arrived in Philadelphia. In this missive, which demanded the immediate attention of Congress, Washington reported the alleged traitorous conduct of his director of hospitals and chief physician, Dr. Benjamin Church. With Joseph Warren, the two Adamses, and John Hancock, Church had been a member of the Provincial Congress and the Massachusetts Committee of Safety. He was a Boston aristocrat, a physician of excellent professional standing, and ostensibly an ardent Whig. His treachery, detailed in Washington's letter of October 5, shocked and dismayed the delegates. For if Benjamin Church could betray, who could not?

The records do not show when Church began to give, or perhaps to sell, information to the British, but he was active in March 1775, if not earlier. In mid-May he had informed Gage that the Americans proposed to fortify Bunker Hill, a piece of valuable intelligence to which Gage paid no attention. The doctor frequently visited Boston, ostensibly for professional reasons. A blunder by the doctor's mistress revealed his treason. Washington ordered the lady apprehended and interrogated her himself. She finally broke; her lover was arrested. He blustered in vain.

Church's betrayal of the cause gave Washington great anxiety, for Church was "privy to much information of a sensitive nature."

Samuel Ward's reaction was probably that of most delegates: "Dr. Church, Who could have thought or even suspected it, a man who seemed to be all animation in the cause of his Country, highly caressed, employed in several very honorable and lucrative departments, and in full possession of the confidence of his country, what a complication of madness and wickedness must a soul be filled with to be capable of such Perfidy! What punishment can equal such horrid crimes! I communicated the affair to the Massachusetts Delegates. They could hardly conceive it possible."†[2]

Montgomery now stood before St. Johns, which he expected to reduce in short order. No doubt he would have succeeded in doing so had it not been that a determined major named Preston, commanding most of the regular troops in Canada, had no intention of forsaking his duty. Preston defied Montgomery to take the fort. The general wisely decided not to attempt it; he had not sufficient weight of artillery to batter a breach in the stout walls.

Lack of cannon was not, however, his principal problem. This was provided by New England militia, many of whom were averse to serving under a New Yorker; thought the project a waste of time; and were determined to return to their homes the moment their obligated service expired. Had Montgomery's command been reliable rather than unruly and intransigent, he would probably have masked St. Johns and pushed on to Chambly and Montreal. But he did not dare take this chance; he felt sure many militiamen left to invest St. Johns would desert, Preston would sally out, cut the remainder to pieces, and be on his back. He urgently pled for reinforcement; Schuyler ordered Brigadier General David Wooster with his Connecticut militia, then in the Northern Department, to march to Ticonderoga at once. In mid-October, Wooster and his command arrived at the fort, where most of the men refused to be mustered into the Continental Army and announced their intention to depart for home forthwith. Schuyler, the aging Connecticut general, and the local chaplain did all possible to persuade them to proceed to St. Johns. On October 22, Wooster sailed down the lake with about 330 officers and men.

While he was waiting for Wooster, Montgomery decided he would move against Chambly. The officer in command there, Major Stopford, had no stomach for a fight and upon demand, ignominiously struck his colors (October 19). The Americans took some brass cannon, 140 barrels

† Congress permitted him to leave the country. The ship on which he took passage was lost at sea. His widow, who had gone to England, was granted a pension for her husband's services to the King.

of the King's good powder, and about one hundred muskets. Montgomery returned from that successful foray to St. Johns, where he found Wooster with his reluctant militiamen. The tough old Connecticut general was almost seventy, but without hesitation put himself under command of the younger man. Happily, Colonel Seth Warner and 150 Green Mountain Boys had unexpectedly arrived on the scene, a timely reinforcement.

Carleton, meanwhile, had collected a motley force at Montreal to move against Montgomery and ordered Colonel Allen MacLean and his Royal Scots Emigrants up from Quebec. Warner met Carleton's detachment near Sorel and drove the governor off. MacLean wisely decided his small group would be more useful at Quebec than as prisoners of war and returned to the capital. News that Chambly had fallen and Carleton's relief column had retired was conveyed to Preston, who only then decided that St. Johns was no longer tenable. On November 2 he capitulated, and on the following day led out his half-starved garrison. Montgomery accorded him deserved honors of war. One of the officer prisoners was a handsome and talented lieutenant named John André, of the 7th Regiment of Foot.

Montgomery was now free to advance on Montreal. Carleton decided he could not hold the city. He directed the few defenders to abandon it and to make the best of their way to Quebec. Montgomery arrived before Montreal on November 13 and entered without opposition. The campaign to drive the British from Canada, a project Washington, Schuyler, and the Congress deemed indispensable to the security of the northern borders, seemed finally to be progressing. But Preston's stubborn defense at St. Johns had delayed Montgomery for six vital weeks, and the Canadian winter was closing in.

After the capture of Montreal Montgomery's army started to evaporate. The men had not expected to campaign in an arctic wasteland, and began leaving by companies, claiming that Montgomery had promised to relieve them from service after he had taken the city.‡ One thing only—a commodity Montgomery lacked—might have persuaded them to extend enlistments and see it through: a generous bounty paid in "hard money."

These men were not totally devoid of patriotic sentiment. They had enlisted for one year, and they (and thousands of others) looked on their term of service as a "door-to-door" contract, which began to run the day they left home and terminated when they returned. And they timed their departure from the army accordingly. Even Colonel Seth Warner and his Green Mountain Boys set off for the New Hampshire Grants. As the men drifted through Ticonderoga, Schuyler, also penniless, exhorted and pled

‡ When told of the projected invasion of Canada, Montgomery is said to have exclaimed: "A winter campaign in Canada! Posterity won't believe it!"

in vain. He was a "Yorker"; New England men did not trust him. He wrote, desponding, to Washington.

Carleton was keeping the ministry well informed of American projects to acquire "a fourteenth province" by persuasion and subversion if possible, and by force of arms if these means failed. Reports of Montgomery's occupation of Isle aux Noix and the surrender of Chambly and St. Johns aroused much hostile feeling in Great Britain, where the invasion was seen as a wanton act of aggression. "To invade a province to which they could lay no claim, nor pretend no right, seemed such an outrage, as it not only overthrew every plea of justifiable resistance, but would militate with the established opinions, principles and feelings of mankind in general."[3]

British resentment and anger were not entirely justified. Congress had every reason to believe Carleton was rousing the Canadians and enlisting the services of the Indians. Whether the governor's capability to strike into New England and New York would support his desire to do so was beside the point; Congress decided to disarm him before he could stab the colonies in the back. Indeed, Congress had little choice; "there was no natural law nor convention among mankind, by which a person was bound to be a simple and inactive looker-on while an enemy was loading a gun for his destruction. . . . The sword was already drawn. . . . It was too late now to look back, and to waver would be certain destruction."[4]

From Whitehall's point of view, the situation in Canada was far from hopeful. Carleton had but few regulars and could not be reinforced until the ice broke in the St. Lawrence in late April. The French peasant farmers and woodsmen—the *habitants*—although nominally relieved from a state of vassalage to *les grands seigneurs* whose extensive estates they worked, were at best apathetically loyal to the British, and Congress had some reason to hope for their active co-operation. Most British residents in Canada were noncommittal. The majority opposed the Quebec Act, which Carleton had been instrumental in framing; in Quebec "great heartburnings prevailed among the English civil subjects."

Two weeks after Schuyler and Montgomery left Ticonderoga, Arnold marched out of Cambridge at the head of his confident "army" of 1,150 to meet with Schuyler's column on the Plains of Abraham. While Montgomery, unable to cow the Redcoat regulars who held St. Johns, invested the small fort, Arnold relentlessly pushed his overloaded bateaux up the Kennebec toward the heart of the wilderness.

Washington's purpose in sending Arnold's expedition to Canada by the wilderness route was to pose a sudden threat to Quebec from an unexpected direction, and so to face Carleton with a dilemma. The governor had limited resources. If he deployed his available troops to deal with Montgomery, Arnold should be able to take the capital. If he chose to defend Quebec, the column to move down Champlain and the Richelieu to the St. Lawrence could easily seize Montreal and then join Arnold. Or, if he divided his meager forces in an attempt to deal with both invading columns, the Americans should be able to defeat him in detail.

The strategic concept was sound, but only if co-ordination of the two widely separated movements could be assured. This was a big "if." For should either be delayed, Carleton, who enjoyed the benefit of interior lines, could turn the tables on the Americans by meeting and defeating one column and then marching with what force he could assemble to cope with the other. Washington was aware that he was taking a risk, but deemed the possible gain commensurate. And so, on the morning of September 11, 1775, Arnold had set off from Cambridge to march to Newburyport, there to embark in eleven assorted schooners and sloops for the Kennebec.

His force consisted entirely of volunteers. The Pennsylvania and Virginia "rifflers" would have volunteered for anything to escape the deadly monotony of routine guard duties and laborious working parties. They were, in fact, vastly unpopular in the camp at Cambridge, where for some time they had enjoyed a favored position. Almost every day, two or three went without permission to the forward pickets where they spent pleasant afternoons indulging in their favorite pastime: sniping. As most were expert marksmen, and from a prone or sitting position could hit a target eight or nine inches square at 150 yards, the pickings were good. These exercises usually evoked a response in the form of a furious cannonade brought down on the offending redoubt. The result was that riflemen were soon quite as unpopular with the Americans as with the Redcoats. They were tough men: Morgan had brought his company from Virginia to Cambridge, 650 miles, in twenty-one days. No man fell out during the march. The Pennsylvanians were equally well fitted for the difficult expedition on which they so readily embarked.

The riflemen were not as highly esteemed by some of their contemporaries as they have been by starry-eyed historians: "Of all useless sets of men that ever incumbered an Army, surely the boasted Rifle-men are certainly the most so. To be sure, there never was a more mutinous and undisciplined set of villains that bred disturbance in any camp." They would certainly be more valuable in Canada than they were in Cambridge.

Washington gave Arnold explicit instructions as to his behavior, and that of his men. The Canadians were friends and were to be treated as such. He directed Arnold to make every effort to encourage the neutrals to join him. He was to deal immediately and severely with any soldier found plundering: The soldier was to be shot. He closed the letter with this adjuration: "Upon the whole, Sir, I beg you to inculcate upon the Officers and Soldiers the necessity of preserving the Strictist Order during their March through Canada; to represent to them the Shame, Disgrace and Ruin to themselves and Country, if they should, by their Conduct, turn the Hearts of our Brethren in Canada against us."[5]

The commander in chief also entrusted Arnold with a proclamation in which he exhorted the Canadians to overthrow the tyrannous government the British had fastened on them, and promised them full enjoyment of all liberties, including that of their cherished religion. If Arnold found the Canadians unfavorable, he was "by no Means to prosecute the Attempt."

This arduous and challenging undertaking suited Arnold perfectly. As he had demonstrated in his foray to St. Johns, where he had seized *Betsy* and brought her up the lake to Ticonderoga, he was a courageous, imaginative, and energetic leader willing to take risks and to face difficulties which he appeared to believe existed only to be overcome. He would encounter many. The route he was to take involved passage through, or carriage around, a number of stretches of "white water" and tedious portages around falls. Then there were three long carries between ponds before he reached the "Height of Land," the watershed dividing waters flowing north into the St. Lawrence from those flowing south and east to the Atlantic. The route was fairly well known; some years earlier Captain John Montrésor, now General Howe's assistant engineer officer, had traveled, blazed, and mapped it. Missionaries, hunters, trappers, traders, and Indians had traveled it. Few of their reports and rough sketches were readily available, but Arnold prepared himself for the journey as best he could. All information was rudimentary; important details of terrain and watercourses were lacking.

Arnold's trip from Newburyport to Merrymeeting, where five rivers, including the Kennebec and the Androscoggin, pour into the bay near Bath, was uneventful; the run up the Kennebec to Gardinerstown (now Pittston, Maine), peaceful. By evening on September 22, practically the entire expedition bedded down in comfort at Major Reuben Colburn's, where Arnold was to pick up the bateaux Washington had directed the major to build. This had been a "crash" job; Colburn had exactly eighteen days' notice to construct two hundred light bateaux "Capable of Carrying Six or Seven Men each with their Provisions and Baggage." Each was to be provided with "four oars . . . Two Paddles and two Setting Poles." The commander in chief had further instructed Colburn to find "Artificers, Carpenters and Guides" and to "bespeak" all the "Pork and Flour" he could locate.[6] Arnold was not entirely pleased with the bateaux, which had been built of green timber. He ordered twenty more; these were built in three days.**

Arnold waited one day at Colburn's to receive a report from two scouts the major had sent upriver to investigate the proposed route to the headwaters of the Chaudière. There were several very rough portages on the Kennebec, and others between the Kennebec and Dead River. When they arrived at Dead River, the scouts encountered an Indian who informed them he was employed by Governor Carleton to watch the area. There was an outpost, so the Indian said, at the headwaters of the Chaudière where several hundred Mohawks in Carleton's employ were encamped. The scouts, who valued their scalp locks, did not linger to hear more, but hastily returned to the nearest settlement and sent a pessimistic message to Arnold. He wrote Washington that he placed no credence in the Indian's story, as he was a "noted villain."††

The next day the expedition proceeded to Fort Western (now Augusta, capital of Maine). Most marched by the east bank; the more hardy poled and rowed the bateaux. The broad river, tidal for this stretch of nine miles, is gently flowing and placid. But just above Fort Western it radically changes character. Here was half a mile of churning, swirling, white water. Arnold gave the troops little leisure to contemplate these difficulties; he employed them from sunrise to sunset portaging bateaux and carrying baggage and supplies to quiet water above the rapids.

From Fort Western, Arnold sent forward two scouting parties, one to proceed to Dead River, the other to the Chaudière, and on the following day dispatched Colonel Daniel Morgan and his riflemen upriver as an advance party. Morgan was to proceed to "the Great Carrying Place," the series of difficult portages between the Kennebec and Dead rivers, cut a trail, and await the main body, which Arnold sent forward in three divisions with instructions for all to assemble at the second portage. Before he left Fort Western, he sent a final report to Washington. Arnold was in high spirits; this was the sort of completely unorthodox undertaking that suited him. "There is at present the greatest harmony among the officers." He left Fort Western on Friday, September 29, "in a Bark Canoe," but as it proved "very leaky" he soon shifted to a dugout.

By this time, only six days after leaving Gardinerstown, all the bateaux were leaking. Flour and powder were mush; the men's tents, blankets, and spare shirts soaked; their shoes and stockings soggy. One officer expressed the general feeling: "Could we then have come in reach of the villains who constructed these crazy things, they would fully have experi-

** Colburn's handsome colonial house has been beautifully restored and is now headquarters of the Arnold Expedition Historical Society.
†† This "noted villain" later joined Arnold's column.

enced the effects of our Vengeance." Fortunately for him, Major Colburn
did not accompany the expedition.

The first of many arduous carries was at Taconic Falls (present Wa-
terville), a mile above Fort Halifax, where Arnold paused to dry powder,
clothing, and blankets. Here every four-hundred-pound bateau had to be
unloaded, and it and the contents manhandled on a forest trail for half a
mile. The labor was backbreaking, and this was but the initiation.
Twenty miles farther upriver (present Skowhegan) there was dangerous
white water and a twenty-five-foot falls. Again, the laborious process of
unloading, carrying cargo over rough trails, shouldering the heavy and
clumsy bateaux, and reloading. Here the column was "occasioned much
delay and great fatigue."[7] Between this point and Norridgewock Falls,
Arnold recorded "quick water," "Swift water," "Rips," "ripples."[8] For
those traveling the water route, the journey had been trying; those who
marched had an equally difficult time. But all were in good health and
spirits. They were to draw heavily on their reserves of both.

At Norridgewock Falls, Morgan's echelon faced a mile of capricious
white water; on this stretch, the river dropped almost a hundred feet.
The captain located two yoke of oxen and two sledges, and when Arnold
arrived on October 2 with his bateaux, Morgan was above the rapids.
The other three divisions spent a week portaging, repairing bateaux, and
drying out. All bateaux were waterlogged, many stove in. Practically all
barreled salt provisions were ruined; much was rotten and was dis-
carded. They were now on the verge of the wilderness, and a few days
later were deep in it.

On October 13 Arnold wrote from Dead River "about 160 miles from
Quebec" to friends there that he hoped to have the pleasure of seeing
them soon. His expedition, he explained, was co-operating with General
Schuyler "to frustrate the unjust and arbitrary measures of the ministry,
and restore liberty to our brethern in Canada." He asked his friends to
write at once "of the disposition of the Canadians, the number of troops
in Quebec, by whom commanded, and every advice you have received
from General Schuyler, and the situation of matters in general, what we
have to expect from the Canadians and merchants in the city."[9] Arnold
addressed his missive to "John Manir, Esq., or in his absence to Captain
Wm. Gregory, or Mr. John Maynard" and entrusted it to "one Eneas, a
faithful Indian," who would hasten back to him with the reply. He
enclosed a letter to be forwarded to General Schuyler, whom he hoped
to meet in Quebec "in a fortnight."

He wrote Washington on the same day. Since leaving Fort Western,
the column "had a very fatiguing time more than half way up the river."
He reported his "amphibious" boatmen "in high spirits"; he expected to
reach the Chaudière "in eight or ten days." He had "about nine hundred
and fifty effective men" with provisions sufficient for twenty-five days

and had ordered one hundred barrels of salt pork and flour to be sent up to the Great Carrying Place "to secure our retreat." He had heard nothing from General Schuyler, nor had he any reports from Canada. He assured the commander in chief that he had pushed on as rapidly as possible, and despite the onerous work in forcing their way "up against a very rapid stream" and "the great fatigue in portage . . . the officers, volunteers and privates, have in general acted with the greatest spirit and industry."[10]

Arnold's attention to detail, particularly his arrangements for care of the ill and disabled, was uncommon for the time, as was his prudence in securing a safe retreat "in case of accident." He expected intelligence at Chaudière Pond (Lake Megantic), and there he would decide whether to go down the river to the St. Lawrence and Quebec or return to the Kennebec. But before the army could reach Megantic, the weather turned. By October 24 rain had been falling steadily for a week. Rivers and streams were rising fast, camp sites were flooded out, and much food and powder lost and ruined. A Council of War decided to winnow the ranks, to return ailing and feeble men to the Kennebec, and to bring up the best men of Colonel Enos's division provisioned for fifteen days. All others were to be sent back. Arnold directed Enos to hasten forward "with all possible expedition" and wrote Colonel Green, whose division lay between his temporary headquarters and Enos's camp, to the same effect.

Arnold did not wait for these reinforcements, but pushed north, leading his starving and exhausted men through raging, freezing rains and intermittent snowstorms. But the volunteer force maintained cohesion, partly because every man realized he was in imminent peril; partly because Arnold and Morgan provided examples of dogged determination which each felt he must emulate. Marching through the wilderness in advance of his troops, Arnold reached Megantic with seventy men and again wrote Washington. A scout previously sent ahead had returned from the lower Chaudière; he reported the French *habitants* "very friendly, and by the best information he could get, will very gladly join us." The scout also brought news that "there were few or none of the King's troops at Quebec, and no advice of our coming." He proposed, he continued, to move as fast as he could, and if "there is any prospect of surprising the city, I shall attempt it as soon as I have a proper number of men up."[11]

Arnold reached Sartigan, the first French settlement on the Chaudière, on October 31.‡‡ Here bad news from Quebec awaited him. The "faithful Indian" to whom he had incautiously entrusted his indiscreet letter to friends in the city had either betrayed him or been taken by the British, who now knew he was on the way. Although Lieutenant Gover-

‡‡ On the site of the present Beauceville.

nor Hector Cramahé despaired of holding the capital, he pulled himself together sufficiently to order all canoes and bateaux immediately removed from the south bank of the St. Lawrence. Colonel MacLean had not yet returned from Sorel; Carleton was in Montreal. About that time, H.M.S. *Lizard* arrived, and Captain John Hamilton, senior naval officer present, ordered his forty-odd marines and every seaman who could possibly be spared into the city.

A week later, Arnold arrived at St. Mary's, some twelve miles below Quebec, where discouraging news from the rear caught up with him. Lieutenant Colonel Enos had received Arnold's order of October 24 late on the same day, and had at once called a council of his officers. Here, he and his subordinates took the ignominious decision to disobey their commander's orders and to abandon the expedition. Some few—a minority— were for going ahead. Enos provisioned them and they set off. He and most of the command turned back.*

Arnold had set out to take Quebec and could do without cowardly subordinates and their fainthearted men. He was angry when he learned of Enos's desertion, but generously ascribed the action to "a shortage of provisions" rather than the commander's want of courage and determination. If his spirits were low, they were soon raised when a courier brought in a letter from Montgomery, to whom he had previously dispatched several messages. He replied at once: His intent was to cross the river as soon as the remainder of his straggling column arrived.

Small groups, restored by milk, butter, bread, cheese, and beef provided by *habitants,* joined him every day. The ordeal of three days with practically nothing to eat before they reached the settlements on the Chaudière had almost finished them. They had killed and roasted two dogs, eaten roots, and chewed on boiled moccasins. Not surprisingly, they discovered they could not macerate moose hide. Nearly all had dysentery, several died of exposure, and the wretched survivors were nearly dead when on November 3, as they stumbled down the east bank of the Chaudière, they met French farmers driving half a dozen cattle sent back by Arnold. The beeves were at once butchered, cooked, and greedily devoured—too greedily indeed, for some ravenously ate more half-cooked meat than they should and were violently ill.

Along the south bank of the St. Lawrence, Arnold collected forty canoes which Cramahé had neglected to sweep up and on November 11 was ready to cross. But for three days the river was lashed by rain and driving winds. Finally, on the night of November 14/15, his "army" crossed, surmounted the precipitous cliffs without molestation, and at dawn stood on the Plains of Abraham. Arnold paraded his ragged command and summoned the city. The defenders fired on the young officer

---

* Enos was later tried by general court-martial and acquitted.

bearing his message under a flag of truce. He tried again the following day with the same result.

He was now dealing with an officer quite as determined as he. Colonel Allen MacLean, who had arrived from Sorel on November 10, had immediately summoned a Council of War to meet at Lieutenant Governor Cramahé's residence. Captain Hamilton of *Lizard* attended. Here the decision was taken "to defend the place to the last." Hamilton, too, was a determined man: "Their Lordships [of the Admiralty] may depend upon it no means in my power shall be neglected to destroy the King's ships, if the place should be destroyed." He was not too hopeful of success. "The King's forces are few, the Canadians in general in the interest of the rebels, many of the merchants indifferent so they can secure their property." The defenses were faulty, the garrison "in a wretched state and confusion, many things wanting," but Hamilton begged leave to inform their lordships "that everything in my power and ships under my command will be used for the protection of this garrison and province."[12]

A few minutes after Hamilton signed this letter to the First Lord, Governor Carleton, who had come downriver disguised as a peasant in a birch canoe, arrived safely in Quebec. Hamilton had ordered Lieutenant Pringle to proceed to England in H.M.S. *Polly*, recommended him to the attention of their lordships at the Admiralty, and assured them that the courier would give "a very clear and particular account of the whole." The governor hastily drafted a dispatch to Germain and sent it off with Pringle. The tenor was pessimistic.

Having learned that Montgomery possessed Montreal and would soon set out to meet him, Arnold withdrew from the environs of Quebec. Already the winter cold was closing down. Days were short, nights long, and the temperature falling. The men's clothes were little better than rags, their tow shirts tattered, their breeches ripped, their shoes and moccasins falling apart. All were thin, bearded, and as tough as they appeared to be. Of 1,050 who had set out, some 650 were present, among them Aaron Burr, Arnold's young aide-de-camp, a future Vice-president of the United States.

Arnold established a camp at Pointe aux Trembles, twenty miles west of Quebec, where he awaited Montgomery. He now devoted several days to a minute inspection of arms, ammunition, and clothing and discovered to his "surprise" (as he wrote Montgomery) that almost his entire stock of cartridges to be "unfit for service . . . we had no more than five rounds for each man, and near one hundred guns unfit . . . add to this, many of the men invalids, and almost naked, and wanting everything to make them comfortable." He had no cannon and very little "hard money," barely enough to "last ten days . . . and as the French have been such sufferers by paper, I don't think it prudent to offer it them at present."

He estimated the British force at 1,900, including 500 "obliged to bear arms against their inclinations, and who would join us if an opportunity presented." Arnold had not the slightest doubt that he and Montgomery would "knock up a dust with the garrison at Quebeck, who are already panic struck." Had he arrived ten days earlier, he could have taken the city: "My brave men were in want of everything but stout hearts, and would have gladly met the enemy . . . though we had not ten rounds of ammunition a man, and they double our numbers."[13] On December 3 Montgomery arrived at Pointe aux Trembles with 300 men; two days later the ragged Americans stood before the walls of Quebec. The entire command could not have exceeded 1,000 of all ranks fit for duty. Montgomery had brought with him some small cannon, muskets, powder, clothes, and shoes for Arnold's almost naked, shivering troops. He brought also an unquenchable spirit.

Arnold was overjoyed and wrote a brief report to Washington. With it, he forwarded a return of his detachment, now totaling 675. He had lost almost 400 men, most of whom had turned back with Enos. He and Montgomery were confident; they were busy "making all possible preparations to attack the city, which was a wretched, motley garrison of disaffected seamen, marines, and inhabitants, the walls in a ruinous situation, and cannot hold out long."[14]

The walls may have been in "a ruinous situation" but the spirits of Governor Carleton, Colonel MacLean, and Captain Hamilton were not. Carleton had more than the ordinary share of courage; MacLean's Highland Emigrants, chased away from Sorel by Seth Warner, were ready for a fight, and Hamilton's marines and sailors were totally reliable, as were the British inhabitants Carleton had summoned to bear arms. He had screened the male population and pushed the doubtful out of the gates.

On December 5 Montgomery summoned Carleton; the governor contemptuously rejected this demand and refused to accept Montgomery's letter. Within the walls, which, however "ruinous," could not be breached by Montgomery's puny cannon, the governor had adequate supplies of food and ammunition. Montgomery had no option; he must assault the fortress. Some enlistments expired on New Year's Day, and the men insisted they were going home. Several dozen were down with smallpox contracted in Montreal. Neither he nor Arnold would for a moment consider an ignominious retreat; the little army could not winter in the snows, and the British would reinforce as soon as the ice broke. It was now or never.

Scaling the massive walls was not practicable. Montgomery had no choice but to fight his way into the Lower Town, and from that as his base, move against the Upper. And no time could be lost. At a Council of War on December 16 the decision was taken to storm on the first dark night while falling snow obscured the attackers and deadened the sound of their approach. The plan was to distract the defenders of the Upper Town with two feints while two storming columns hit the Lower. Montgomery's column would attack the Lower Town from the west and force the barricades on what is now Champlain Street. Simultaneously, Arnold would carry the Sault-au-Matelot barricade on the east. The two columns would meet in the market place, where plans to assault the Upper Town would be concerted. A deserter carried this information to Carleton.

The days went by until lowering skies on the afternoon of December 30 presaged the conditions Montgomery sought. All preparations were made before dawn in the morning of the last day of the year. But both Montgomery and Arnold were moving slowly, and when Arnold stormed the first barricade he was brought down with a ball through his leg and carried to the rear. Morgan pushed on and forced his way through and over several barricades. Finally, his riflemen lost in the narrow twisting streets, he surrendered.

Montgomery, leading his advance party, impatiently awaited his straggling main body. He could wait no longer; he pushed on, and with his own hands helped rip apart two barricades. There remained but one obstacle—a blockhouse. The defenders saw the Americans approaching, shadowy figures fitfully obscured by falling snow. When the leading group was within ten yards of the blockhouse, a small cannon roared. Grapeshot wiped out the advance party. At that moment, the second-in-command should have rushed the blockhouse, whose defenders, believing that he would do just that, incontinently fled. But Colonel Donald Campbell was no Montgomery. He withdrew. Montgomery lay dead in the snow.†

† Richard Montgomery did not live to learn that on December 9 Congress had made him a major general in the Continental Army. His death cast a pall of gloom over the struggling Americans; even in England he was described as a hero, and in the colonies generally lamented. Elegiac poetry flowered:

Montgomery's dead! A Man by all rever'd!
By Patriots loved! By dastard tyrant fear'd!

The editor of the Annual Register (1776, p. 6) wrote: "In all transactions with our forces, Montgomery writ, spoke and behaved with that attention, regard and politeness to both private men and officers, which might be expected from a man of worth and honor. . . ." And Arnold said that had the general lived, "Quebec would have been ours."

5

Parole: *The Congress;* Countersign: *America*

After transit of the Atlantic from Boston in record time, Major General John Burgoyne arrived in London to enjoy the holiday season. He brought dispatches from Howe, and his own "Reflections Upon the War in America," a paper he had prepared during the voyage, which he proposed to submit to the Cabinet.

In this, Gentleman Johnny recommended that a special type of harassing and blockading force be created. His idea was that a dozen frigates, each with "a number of smaller armed vessels" attached, be dispatched to America. "Each of the great ships would . . . resemble a pimary planet with its satellites oscillating around it; the lesser cruisers or satellites being from their size adapted for peeking into every hole and inlet."[1] His suggestion failed to arouse the interest it deserved; no one—at least no one in Whitehall—was thinking in terms of a prolonged war; one decisive campaign would put an end to the rebellion. Besides, the sort of naval force Burgoyne urged would cost money, and a great deal of it.

Burgoyne drew a good picture of how the Americans operated: "Every private man will in action be his own general who will turn every tree and bush into a kind of temporary fortress from whence, when he hath fired his shot with all the deliberation, coolness and certainty which hidden safety inspires, he will skip, as it were, to the next." He urged doubling the number of light infantry companies, which, if the men were properly trained, could cope effectively with these tactics. This sensible recommendation died somewhere in Barrington's files. Finally, he suggested (as both Gage and Howe had done) that two co-operating armies operate from New York and Canada on the Hudson River–Champlain axis.[2]

Howe reported he expected to winter safely in Boston; he was "under no apprehension of Attack or Surprise by the Rebel Army," but as he had many men sick and an extensive front to defend, his force was not "adequate to any undertaking of Consequence." He also set forth in general terms tentative plans for the campaigns he proposed to conduct in 1776: He would seize Manhattan and Staten islands and Newport on Aquidneck Island in Narragansett Bay, but he required a very strong reinforcement, including artillery. For the train of the army, he would need wagons and horses. Shortly thereafter, he wrote that transports and storeships he had been expecting had not yet arrived. This gave rise to "very alarming apprehensions" that the vessels had been taken by "Rebel Privateers, which in great Numbers infested the Bay of Boston," and which Admiral Graves seemed either indisposed or unable to put down.[3]

Howe was indeed facing serious problems. The army suffered from a scarcity of firewood and fresh and salt provisions. He had sent ships to New York to gather up any food available there, to Georgia for rice, and to St. Eustatius for barreled pork and beef. Happily, one victualer came in with a consignment of porter, and another with "Oats Flour and Pease." And he had finally managed to get his troops into winter quarters. Fatigue parties were busy every day demolishing wharves, docks, buildings, and fencing for firewood. They did not confine their depredations to wharves and warehouses. They tore down old North Church and turned Faneuil Hall into a theater, where amateur dramatics were staged. A "smash-hit" was a play by Burgoyne: *The Blockade of Boston*. Old South, previously gutted, became a riding arena.

Howe's manifold difficulties and the threat to the British position in Canada, documented in dispatches Pringle brought from Quebec, raised at once a number of serious questions. Until these reports arrived in Whitehall, few in Administration seemed to realize that a transoceanic continental war would impose hitherto unheard-of demands on a creaking and inefficient executive and administrative machine. Rear Admiral Sir Hugh Palliser, an able officer recently assigned to the Admiralty, was an exception. On December 29 he wrote Sandwich: "It seems the demands of a small army now in America are so great as to be thought impossible to be furnished. The wagons and draft cattle is prodigious. If this is the case, what will it be when we have another army there of above 20,000 men, if they can't make good their quarters, and command carriages and cattle, and subsist and defend themselves without the aid and defence of the fleet, who whilst so employed can perform no other service?" Some people (of whom Palliser was one) were beginning "to be astonished and staggered at the unexpected difficulties we are in."[4]

Germain was displeased with Carleton's pessimistic report. But when the governor wrote, only a few minutes after he had arrived in Quebec following a hazardous trip down the St. Lawrence, he was in no mood to paint rosy pictures. He had found the situation in Quebec critical, and so reported it. After perusing Carleton's message, Germain wrote Sandwich that the governor had given little encouragement the city could be held: "I take the General to be one of those men who see affairs in the most unfavourable light, and yet he has the reputation of a resolute and persevering officer."[5] This was the opening shot in the campaign of innuendo Lord George was to wage against Guy Carleton.

In Versailles, M. le Comte de Vergennes, recently summoned to the Foreign Ministry, followed the Anglo-American situation with obsessive interest. From London, Louis XVI's chargé d'affaires, Charles Jean Garnier, sent reports of secret debates in both Houses of Parliament; in the Commons, the chargé's "man" was a member whose election campaign he had substantially financed. For the paltry sum of £500 a year, a well-placed informant with access to files in the American secretary's office kept Garnier *au courant* with British plans, troop movements, and developments in Boston as reported by Gage and Howe. Vergennes's agents in America forwarded regular reports on the temper of the rebellious colonists; the activities of the Continental Congress; the equipment and capabilities of Washington's army; and the operations—or, more precisely, the lack of them—of Gage and Graves.

French nobles, officers, and intellectuals made no secret that their sympathies lay wholly with the colonists; the first two groups, closely knit by blood, marriage, and social outlook, because they welcomed any action that would weaken the hereditary enemy; the last, primarily because *"les Bostonnais"* espoused republican principles. But Vergennes, a cautious and calculating minister, did not permit emotion to cloud his judgment. France was not yet prepared to confront Great Britain. Anne Robert Jacques Turgot, Minister of Finance, unequivocally opposed any policy that would bring bankrupt France close to war.

And in the background was the shadow of Chatham. The possibility that in a crisis George III might summon the earl had to be considered. This thought tormented Vergennes and was a powerful deterrent to ill-considered action, for he knew that if Chatham returned to power he would immediately throw out the North ministry and put in train a conciliatory policy toward the Americans. Chatham was a tiger; he would brook no provocation, however slight, from France or Spain, but in concert with the reconciled Americans would attack them fiercely and tear from them their remaining Caribbean possessions.

These influences, together with Madrid's less than enthusiastic responses to discreet inquiries as to the co-operation to be expected from that quarter, held the minister back. But others pushed him forward. Courtiers, notables, officers, and intellectuals deluged him and his royal master with *mémoires* urging at least clandestine aid to the Americans. By early December, Vergennes had been in office long enough to digest the flow of reports coming to him from European capitals and French agents in England and America, and to review the numerous plans his predecessor had drawn up.

Revenge on England had been the Duc de Choiseul's consuming passion; over the years his secretariat had prepared a variety of war plans, many of which took into account rebellion of England's American colonies, which Choiseul had anticipated. To these, Vergennes fell heir. His ultimate aim was the same as Choiseul's: to humble England. But first, France's position on the Continent must be made secure and her power enhanced. The keystone of policy was thus to be the Bourbon Family Pact with Charles III of Spain. "It is natural that the King should regard the Family Pact as the corner stone of his policy, and that, as long as Spain remains faithful to the spirit of their union, His Majesty's prime concern should be to strengthen it." The defensive alliance with Austria, in effect since 1756, would be maintained. England would not be provoked.

Stability in Europe permitted the minister to devote himself assiduously to study and analysis of the dynamic developments in America. The question that perturbed him was fundamental: Would the Americans fight; did they have the courage and stamina to make a durable effort? Or would they give up, retract their most extreme demands, and accept some sort of conciliatory proposals? As to the determination of the Americans to resist, the minister (although he received conflicting reports) believed they would, and toward the end of December he and his trusted assistant, Gérard de Reyneval, drew up an estimate of the situation which might serve as a guide to the policy to be pursued. This paper, entitled "*Réflexions: sur la situation actuelle des colonies anglaises, et sur la conduite qu'il convient à la France de tenir à leur égard,*" is one of the most important in the history of the American War of Independence.[6]

Only two others—the King and M. de Maurepas—saw the draft of this study. Vergennes's basic premise was that the Americans would persist in their insurgency, but if left to fight alone must inevitably succumb to the vastly superior forces Great Britain could deploy to crush them. Although at great effort and expense the British could probably suppress

the rebellion, they could not entirely subdue the ineluctable tendency toward independence. Still, if they were successful, they would preserve a
commercial monopoly that would augment their power. But should
America gain independence, her developing strength would swing the
balance in favor of other nations.

The minister proceeded: "England is the natural enemy of France—
and she is a rapacious, unjust and faithless enemy. The invariable object
of her policy is the destruction of France, or at least her abasement, humiliation and ruin." Self-preservation dictated that France "should seize
every possible opportunity to enfeeble the might and power of England
. . . it suffices to ascertain whether the present state of affairs and the actual situation of the Colonies are of a nature to conduce to this end: they
are now in open war with their mother country; their aim is to free themselves from British dominion; they have solicited succor and assistance
from us."

Thus, he went on, ". . . should we accede to the pleas of the
Colonies, and assuming the assistance we can render to be efficacious, it
appears that the following advantage would accrue:

1. England's power will be diminished, and ours correspondingly increased.
2. Her commerce will suffer an irreparable loss while ours will
   flourish.
3. It is probable [following such developments], that we shall be
   able to recover some of the possessions the English have taken
   from us in America. . . . One does not mention Canada."

What would be the disadvantages of the rise of an independent
power in North America, should that state be animated by a spirit of
conquest? Would it not then pose a danger to both French and Spanish
colonies? Vergennes thought two considerations militated against development of such a threat. First, the war would so exhaust the Americans
that for some time they would not be able to mount naval and land
forces in sufficient strength successfully to attack their neighbors; second, if they threw off Britain's yoke, they would probably establish a
decentralized republican form of government and would not be inclined
to be predatory. Further, the Americans were aware of the advantages of
peaceful commerce, and as they would need to develop their own indus-
tries they would require various commodities to help them do so. On the
whole, Vergennes judged fears of American aggression to be groundless.

If the conclusion was that the best interests of France required that
she assist the Americans, what should be the nature of such assistance; at
what time should it be rendered, and what effect might be anticipated?
In addressing himself to the first of these questions, the minister attempted to evaluate the strength of the opposing forces in America. He

estimated that by the summer of 1776 the British could deploy there 20,000 of their own troops plus an almost equal number of mercenaries. To oppose them, he believed the Americans could field armies aggregating 50,000 "regulars, well clothed, well armed, well disciplined and well commanded." These would be augmented by an equal number of volunteers who did not demand money, but only desired to fight. This optimistic estimate of American capabilities proved to be wildly incorrect.

Vergennes's appreciation of the strength of a navy the Americans could put into action by the next spring was somewhat more realistic, but still by far too generous. They lacked ships, weapons, and equipment to create an effective navy. These were, then, the items to be supplied. He mistakenly believed they had "treaties of neutrality, and in case of need, of alliance, with the Five Nations of Savages who detest the English."

There was no great problem in supplying arms. The Americans could ship various commodities to merchants in St. Domingue or elsewhere in the West Indies and exchange them there for weapons and ammunition. This commerce could be carried on without the government's hand appearing; "Intelligent, reliable and discreet" merchants or brokers in various ports could deal directly with ships' captains, and all such commerce would be "at the risk, peril and expense of the Americans." At the same time, this policy would encourage Congress and American traders to help dismantle Britain's monopolistic commercial system. Merchants in the French Islands were begging for wheat, flour, lumber, salt fish, horses, barrel staves, beef, and pork, and scores of merchants there would eagerly exchange sugar, molasses, and rum to get their hands on any or all of the products Americans could supply.

As to money: ". . . at first glance this would appear to be the great difficulty." But as the colonies were using paper money internally, they had no requirement for specie for domestic circulation. This was a rather facile treatment of the monetary problems that beset the colonies, where the financial situation was by no means as stable as Vergennes presumed.

Providing the Americans with vessels of war was considerably more complicated. France could not overtly transfer fighting ships to the colonists without danger of provoking war with Great Britain. Nor was clandestine transfer feasible. Armed merchant ships might be transferred at St. Domingue at American risk, but any other course would give the English a just reason to accuse Versailles of giving aid to the Americans. If Vergennes thought transfer of armed merchantmen would escape the notice of the British intelligence service, he grossly underestimated the capabilities of William Eden's French *apparat.**

---

* William Eden, an undersecretary in the Southern Department, had gradually taken over direction of intelligence operations in France from John Robinson, one of Lord North's undersecretaries at the Treasury.

The minister's second point, *Époque a laquelle la France devrait as-sister ouvertement les Colonies,* was indeed a most delicate one. In his discussion, Vergennes presumed that the arms, munitions, and other supplies France could furnish would enable the Americans to sustain an effective resistance for the short term. But these items had to be provided on a generous and regular basis, for shortages would affect their resolve to resist. It was essential that France "sustain their courage and per-severence"; "flatter them with the hope of effective aid when circum-stances permit"; make them understand that the precise moment of overt assistance would depend entirely on their own successes; and encourage them to believe that such assistance would be forthcoming "at latest, at the end of the next campaign" (i.e., by the end of 1776). Only in this manner could France hope to avoid compromising herself both with the colonists and with the court in London. But, Vergennes pointed out, one had to try to determine in advance *"le moment critique; le moment de la guerre."*

As to the minister's third point: *"Quels Effets Notre Assistance En-trainera-t-elle?"* First, as it was necessary to encourage the Americans, it was essential not later than the coming spring to correctly assess Whitehall's capabilities and probable intentions. England was now mak-ing "immense preparations" to suppress the rebellion in 1776. If at the beginning of the campaign she did not enjoy "successes which prognos-ticate the submission or collapse of the colonies," one might conclude that Great Britain did not have the means to attain her goal. At that point, France would not be risking too much to enter the war, and by so doing would ensure victory for the Americans.

He concluded *Réflexions* with a summary: "Affairs in America pre-sent one with two hypotheses; the first: England will triumph over the Americans and they will submit; the second: Great Britain will be re-pulsed by them, and obliged to admit their independence. In either case, it is possible that England will decide to attack our colonies; in the for-mer, to avenge herself for the aid which she will suspect we will have given her colonies (for she will take that view if she finds it exigent to do so, irrespective of our passivity); in the latter, to indemnify herself at our expense, or at the expense of Spain." This would be relatively simple, as England, whether she won or lost, would have powerful land and sea forces in America. If the war there were lost, the ministers would seize upon the opportunity to take the French Sugar Islands to re-establish their reputations, to acquire some glory, to avoid the inevitable censure of the nation, or "perhaps, even to save their heads."

Thus, Vergennes concluded, from whatever point of view one looked at the issue, and regardless of the conduct of France, prospects of an en-during peace were remote. France must base her policy on measures cal-culated to ensure her self-preservation, and since all circumstances tended toward war, prudence dictated that she prepare in advance the means to conduct it to her advantage, and with success.

Vergennes "dared think" the most essential of these means were "to assist the Colonies, and in case of need, to make common cause with them." All aid would have to be clandestine; an *apparat* that the French Government could disavow would be required. At the same time she surreptitiously assisted the colonies, she must ostensibly maintain a diplomatic position of undeviating neutrality until "*le moment critique.*"[7]

Horace Walpole opened his *Journal of the Reign of George III* for the year 1776 with a summary of the Administration's activities: "The year began with mighty preparations for carrying on the war in America with Vigour. Lord George Sackville Germain, who had been brought into power for that end, was indefatigable in laying plans for raising and hiring troops, in sending supplies and recruits and more naval force." Although response to recruiting campaigns was less than enthusiastic, those most anxious to chastise the Americans—Mansfield, Gower, Weymouth, Germain, Wedderburn, and Rigby—constantly advocated deployments sufficient to reduce the colonists to submission in one campaign. Others (as Walpole described them "the more sober sort") saw the "wildness and profusion of the expense" and were apprehensive that "if the business could not be effected in that time, the Administration would be blown up."[8]

This would have suited Walpole, who held the First Minister and his colleagues in contempt. "Lord North was a pliant tool, without system or principle; Lord George Germain of desperate ambition and character"; Wedderburn "a thorough knave"; Sandwich a "more profligate knave"; Lord Gower a villain "capable of any crime"; the pious Dartmouth, formerly a Secretary of State and now Lord Privy Seal, had bequeathed to his successor Germain "his hypocritic secretaries"; Barrington, apparently a fixture as Secretary at War, clung to office like a limpet to do the official lying for the ministry; Weymouth, totally "insensible to honour," connived with Thurlow, "who was fit to execute whatever was to be done." Lord Justice Mansfield, a "poltroon" and a "Machiavel," had the King's ear and "breathed nothing but war."

Opposition, disunited and lifeless, seemed powerless to call the ministry to account for "all the blunders, violent and absurd measures, and disgraces" of the recent past; Rockingham and his colleagues, "disheartened by repeated defeats," preferred the pleasures of their country estates, fox hunting, and racing to drafty town houses in London. While Walpole attempted with no success to fire the Duke of Richmond "with industry," Fox bustled about and "tried to animate both the Duke and Marquis [of Rockingham] but abandoned neither his gaming nor rakish life. He was seldom in bed before five in the morning, nor out of it before two at noon."[9] This regime allowed Fox scarcely more time than necessary to reanimate himself. Chatham, as usual, was ill and incommunicado; Shelburne, his *alter avis,* warbled unavailingly from his isolated perch. The King, in Walpole's eyes an obstinate and blind despot, had brought his colonies to revolt, laid them waste, and "impoverished and exhausted his subjects at home."

These characterizations, loaded with Walpole's prejudices, are not entirely unwarranted. Lord North was a man of unquestioned personal integrity, but had no "system," nor held to any steadfast political principles. He bent with the wind that daily blew from the direction of Kew or Queen's House, wafting messages of advice, admonition, or encouragement. Sandwich may have been a profligate rake, as he was generally described; he had betrayed John Wilkes, one of his closest friends, and took good care of his sycophantic favorites. The First Lord of the Admiralty was thoroughly disliked by most senior naval officers and deemed incompetent by many more. He had still to demonstrate how well or how badly he would perform as First Lord during a war. Despite the fact that Sandwich was a notorious gambler and openly kept a most attractive and expensive mistress, he stood high in the King's favor because he agreed with his master as to the proper policy to pursue toward the Americans, in a word: harsh. Gower, who was Lord President of the Council, Wedderburn, and Thurlow had been Bedford's followers, and were a bellicose lot; Dartmouth, feckless; Mansfield, an inflexible, tough, and reactionary justice, but far from a "poltroon."

It would seem axiomatic that a war Cabinet should be united and its counsels animated by one common imperative: to win the war quickly and at minimum cost in blood and treasure. But the British Cabinet, which functioned only sporadically as a corporate body at weekly dinners, usually at Lord North's, was not so united. Frequently no more than three or four members of the Cabinet attended these meetings. Lord Gower usually did, imbibed copiously of wine and port, and invariably fell asleep.

Walpole observed that the difference in the characters of the First Minister, an indolent, easygoing compromiser, and Germain, ambitious, active, bellicose, "kept up a sort of division or ambiguity in the conduct of government; Lord North still retaining an affected propensity to peace, Lord George pronouncing authoritatively for decision and exaction of full submission from the colonies."[10] Germain may have been an extremist, but at least he attempted to pump life into an apathetic First Minister, a task that almost continuously also occupied his royal master. Sandwich was not on good terms with Germain; Thurlow and Wedderburn quarreled constantly. All, with the possible exception of Lord George, feared Mansfield. Each jealously guarded his own domain and took care of his loyal henchmen.

Lord George had indeed been "indefatigible in laying plans for hiring troops"; negotiations for German mercenaries were progressing satisfactorily. After having been rudely rebuffed by the Czarina, the King had turned to the German principalities. Preliminary arrangements had been in train for several months. In late August the King wrote his First Minister complaining bitterly of the avidity of "contractors for raising recruits" eager "to finger English money." All they had to do was to "deliver them at Hamburg, Rotterdam, or any other port they may propose" in good condition. The King's representative would inspect them at ports of embarkation. "On the recruits being approved," the contractors would be paid ten pounds "per man ready money." This system did not work satisfactorily. Frederick of Prussia let it be known he would levy the same tax per head on mercenaries passing through his dominions as he did for cattle en route to the slaughterhouse. The King was not amused.

George III was now forced to deal with avaricious brokers, each well aware of his pressing need for cannon-fodder and each determined to get his hands on as many golden guineas as he could squeeze out of His Britannic Majesty's purse. This was no easy task, as the King was not precisely a spendthrift. The grasping princelings were not content with hard cash. They insisted on being treated as allies, and demanded as a *quid pro quo* guarantees that Britain would defend their domains. The principal members of this venal sextet were the Duke of Brunswick, the Landgrave of Hesse-Cassel, the Hereditary Prince of Hesse-Cassel, and the Prince of Waldeck. Each agreed to supply men at an average charge of about seven and a half pounds per poll. As the initial treaties stipulated that some 18,000 rank and file were to be provided, brokerage fees alone totaled £135,000. This was but the initial payment, for each was also to receive an annual subsidy.

The Duke of Brunswick would collect well over £15,000 a year; the landgrave, who was providing the majority of the mercenaries, £108,281; and the two princes about £6,000 each. Each would enjoy a number of fringe benefits: The British would pay, equip, feed, and transport the troops, and guaranteed payment for at least a year after they returned to their homelands. Additional articles provided for bounties to be paid for those killed in action—but not, of course, to their survivors. Naturally, none of this money found its way into the pockets of the officers and men sent across the Atlantic to kill or to be killed.†

It has been fashionable to make a moral issue of these transactions, but no moral issue was involved. For centuries employment of mercenaries had been standard procedure. Since the days of the Romans,

† Further treaties brought the total number of Germans for service in America to almost 29,000. Of this number, about 4,000 were taken prisoner and 5,000 deserted. Of the latter number, some had been prisoners of war.

rulers had rented soldiers. In the eighteenth century it was a commonly accepted practice, as, indeed, it has been since. But in the context of the American war, the use of mercenaries was a stupendous political blunder, not only because it enraged the colonists, but also because it bared British weakness. At Potsdam, Paris, Madrid, Vienna, and St. Petersburg rulers wondered what sort of a power this was that could not muster the resources to put down a colonial uprising, particularly if the American rebels were as pusillanimous as the King, his ministers, and His Majesty's friends in Parliament consistently averred they were.

Had generous bounties been offered to English, Scots, and Irish recruits, the ministry could have found many thousands of men willing to serve. But as such soldiers would someday return to the British Isles, those ill or disabled by wounds would be a continuing charge on the Exchequer. And there was the problem of desertion to consider. To the enticements of the Americans, Germans who could neither speak nor read English would be less vulnerable. Nor would the mercenaries be afflicted with humanitarian compunctions which might inhabit British troops confronting Americans. The Germans would be dealing with an alien soldiery and an alien population.

Howe was by no means pleased to spin out a dismally cold winter in Boston; as early as October 9 he had written Dartmouth setting forth his reasons "for not opening the campaign [in 1776] from Boston," and had urgently requested sufficient transport tonnage to move the army to New York "or to some other place to the southward." In one of his numerous letters to friends in London, Burgoyne echoed Howe's plea: "The Army shou'd Gett away from Hence." The secretary had anticipated these suggestions; on September 5 he had given the general authority to move at discretion, but had provided no shipping. When Dartmouth's letter reached Boston in mid-November, winter was closing in, and with insufficient shipping to move his army in one lift, Howe was stuck.

If Howe had little reason to feel festive during the holiday season, Washington had even less. On December 25 he sent Christmas greetings to John Hancock, and in a politely curt letter informed the president of Congress that the pay of his troops was two months in arrears and that he could not pay them because his paymaster general had no money. Thus, there was "a great murmuring" among the militia, whose terms were due to expire in six days. The general needed "near 275,000 Dollars."[11]

By New Year's Day his spirits had picked up: He issued a General Order (Parole: *The Congress;* Countersign: *America*) in which he marked the birth of "the new army, which, in every point of view, is entirely Continental." The commander in chief optimistically flattered himself that "a laudable Spirit of emulation" would soon animate both officers and men "and pervade the whole." He was lacking men, money, muskets, bayonets, powder, cannon, flints, tents, blankets, shoes, shirts, and stockings. But he had fathered a Continental Army.

In early January an anonymous pamphlet entitled *Common Sense* was published in Philadelphia. This, one of the most powerful pieces of revolutionary literature ever penned, was composed by Thomas Paine, a recent arrival in America. Shortly before crossing the Atlantic, Paine, who had been dismissed from his minor post in the Excise, called on Franklin in London and procured from him letters of introduction to friends in Philadelphia. When Paine reached Philadelphia, he at once threw in his lot with the radical Whigs; for about a year and a half he had been editing their Philadelphia mouthpiece, *The Pennsylvania Magazine*.

Paine was a master of spare, forceful, declarative prose. He was not a legalist. He wasted no words attempting in constitutional jargon to justify the stand the radicals had taken, but moved immediately to an attack on his primary target: hereditary monarchy. This institution, he avowed, was essentially ridiculous and oppressive, and the functions of a monarch absurd and useless, as were those of the hereditary peers who supported him and shared with him the plunder. These "remains of an aristocratical tyranny" had assisted the King of Great Britain in engrossing all power and in corrupting the House of Commons, packed with pensioners and placemen.

Lexington and Concord had shattered the dream of reconciliation: All plans and proposals made prior to April 19, 1775, had become as useless as an old almanac. The Americans had no need to remain in a state of dependency; the concept was utterly absurd: "To be always running three or four thousand miles with a tale or a petition, waiting four or five months for an answer, which when obtained requires five or six more to explain it in, will in a few years be looked upon as folly and childishness —there was a time when it was proper, and there is a proper time for it to cease." That time had arrived: "Everything that is right or natural pleads for separation. The blood of the slain, the weeping voice of nature cries, 'Tis TIME TO PART.'"

Copies of this pamphlet were snapped up as fast as printers could turn them out, and within two weeks Paine's thesis was common talk in every tavern in America. His argument seemed conclusive and irrefutable; the impact was immeasurable. Copies of *Common Sense* soon reached Cambridge, where the essay was avidly read by Washington, his officers, and the men in the lines.‡ Paine had hit hard and hit home.

At least one American in Cambridge did not need to draw on this

‡ About 90 per cent of the adult population of Massachusetts was literate. John Adams wrote that an illiterate man in Massachusetts was "as rare as a comet."

powerful polemic to strengthen his determination. Washington had no intention of allowing Howe to pass a quiet winter in Boston and on January 4 wrote Hancock he proposed to attack the city "the first moment I see a probability of success." Circumstances, "and not want of inclination," had delayed this. "It is not in the pages of history perhaps to furnish a case like ours. To maintain a post within musket shot of the enemy for six months together without powder, and at the same time to disband one army and recruit another within that distance of twenty odd British regiments is more than probably ever was attempted."[12]

A few days earlier, Rear Admiral Molyneux Shuldham had sailed into the harbor, accompanied by a fanfare of salutes, to relieve Graves. The prospect of the imminent departure of this incompetent and unco-operative admiral was enough to raise spirits in Boston, and the British greeted the new naval commander in chief in American waters with an exuberant expenditure of gunpowder, of which they had an ample supply. There was much activity in the harbor. Obviously the British were preparing an expedition. But what was the target?

Washington feared it was New York. (Actually, Howe was readying Clinton's small convoy for the Carolinas.) Charles Lee, too, thought the object was New York and suggested he be sent there forthwith to provide for the security of the city and to round up "that dangerous banditti" of Tories who infested Long Island. "Not to crush those serpents before their rattles are grown would be ruinous."[13] He proposed to pick up 1,500 short-term volunteers in Connecticut en route. Washington wrote Governor Jonathan Trumbull begging his assistance and issued orders to Lee on January 8. He also directed Colonel William Alexander, claimant to the Scots title of Lord Stirling, to bring his regiment of New Jersey militia across the Hudson and report to Lee in New York.** Lee's orders directed him ". . . to put that City into the best Posture of Defence which the Season and Circumstances will admit of." He was also to disarm all those whose conduct was inimical to America.

Two days after Lee left for New York, the commander in chief received first personnel reports on the strength of the new army. These were extremely disappointing. The general had hoped for a return of at least 10,000 rank and file. The reports he received showed but 8,212 recruits, of whom 2,500 either were not then present or were unfit for duty. "We are now without any money in our treasury, powder in our magazines, arms in our stores."[14] He found himself much weaker than he dreamed he could possibly be, and wrote the legislatures of Massachusetts and New Hampshire urging them (to no avail) to prevail upon their unpaid militia to stay with him until the end of January.

The patriots from New Hampshire let it be known that they had not

** Alexander was known in the Continental Army as "Lord Stirling," and he will so be known in this book.

the slightest intention to stay "any longer than they engaged for . . ." and departed forthwith. Many carried with them a new musket, dozens of scarce flints, and pounds of precious powder. The situation was "Truly Alarming." Enlistments were slow, and the general was "more and more Convinced that we shall never raise the Army to the New Establishment by Voluntary Inlistment."[15] Still, he was every day and every night thinking of ways to attack Howe, who with the co-operation of Mrs. Joshua Loring had become reconciled to long winter nights in Boston.

The Americans' determination not to be pushed around, his abiding antipathy to regimentation and imposed discipline, his inherent dislike and distrust of hierarchy and the accompanying status differentiation, all militated against the commander in chief's patient efforts to create an army. Washington knew that to cope successfully with the British he would need a disciplined "standing army," an army that many feared would constitute an ever-present threat to freedom and liberty. He was one of the few who understood that without such an army neither could be achieved. In his attempt to convince others of this imperative necessity, the commander in chief had used a phrase—"new-modelling the army"—which aroused dark suspicions, for the words conjured visions of a Cromwell and helmeted Roundheads usurping constituted civil authority: a host of evils too malign to comtemplate, as history clearly testified. Only with grudging reluctance would Congress eventually face the reality that the war could not be won by bands of militiamen, however momentarily inspired.

Washington's plan to "new-model" the Army raised a hot debate in the Continental Congress. Sam Adams was unalterably opposed. The Grand Incendiary usually agreed with his cousin John, but debate on the issue of a standing army found "the brace of Adams" divided. Sam, who was in constant touch with political sentiment in Massachusetts, championed (as he always did) the popular side: He would have none of it; he would permit "so dangerous a Body to exist only temporarily, in times of dire necessity." To his way of thinking this was not such a time, and in early January 1776 he wrote James Warren: "A standing Army, however necessary it may be at some times, is always dangerous to the Liberties of the People. Soldiers are apt to consider themselves as a Body distinct from the rest of the Citizens. . . . Men who have been long subject to military laws and inured to military Customs and Habits, may lose the Spirit and Feeling of Citizens." Young gentlemen who chose the military profession, and received instruction in the art of war, should at the same time be taught "the Principles of a free Government, and deeply impressed with the indispensable Obligation which every member is under to the whole Society." After they had learned their civil and military lessons, they would be qualified to command militia. Massachusetts farmers had driven the British Army from Concord to Boston; at Bunker

Hill they had shown they could stand and fight. All this talk of a professional army with an officer caste was dangerous nonsense.

Washington had to deal personally not only with a variety of policy problems, but also with a gallimaufry of administrative details that a competent staff—had he such—could have handled. Gates, an efficient adjutant general, took expeditious care of many routine matters, but still the burden carried by the commander in chief was relentless. To his dismay, Joseph Reed, his trusted confidential secretary, left the army to take a seat in the Provincial Congress of Pennsylvania.

One of the prickly policy matters that came to a head at this time was the enlistment of free Negroes, of whom there were several hundred serving at Cambridge. Congress had intimated that this was not a particularly good idea, but Washington prevailed upon delegates to change their minds and on January 16 they passed a resolution "That the free negroes who have served faithfully in the Army at Cambridge may be reinlisted therein, but no others."[16] He enlisted individual Indians, who were in the same status for pay and allowances as any other Continental soldier. He attempted also (without marked success) to enroll "companies" of Indians, who were to serve under their own chiefs.

Copies of the King's speech to Parliament had arrived in Boston and soon found their way across the lines. Washington, describing it as "full of rancour and resentment," forwarded a copy to Hancock. He presumed, he added, that Howe imagined the Continental Army would now lay down its arms and give up the struggle. If so, the British general was to be disillusioned; he was determined to kick the British out of Boston and, if he could, administer a stinging defeat in the process.

Until early February Washington lacked sufficient artillery to take decisive action, but as the cannon captured at Ticonderoga, which Colonel Knox had brought over the mountains with incredible toil, arrived in Cambridge and were emplaced, the general felt he would soon be able to mount an attack. Accordingly, on February 15 he called a conference of general officers and outlined an imaginative plan developed by Nathanael Greene. To this, Major General William Heath made a "most pointed opposition"; in his opinion the plan would "most assuredly produce only defeat and disgrace." The army was neither properly equipped nor sufficiently disciplined to execute an amphibious assault on the well-defended town of Boston. Howe, he said, may have been inactive, but he was not a blockhead. The assembled generals reluctantly voted to support the attack, but with the opinion of his counselors so divided, Washington sensibly decided to postpone the attempt.

Washington's correspondence during the late winter of 1776, and the position he took at the various councils of war he summoned at Cambridge, indicate quite clearly that he proposed to be an active and aggressive commander in chief, but one who would bow to the opinions of his colleagues. Indeed at this time his initiative was restricted, for Congress had instructed him that he must take the advice of his generals before he committed the army to a major enterprise. By nature he was inclined to be impetuous rather than cautious and was willing to take risks (as he would later do) when he calculated that prospective gains outweighed possible losses. On this occasion he outlined his battle plan, listened to the arguments of his generals, and abided by the decision of the majority.

In early March, Silas Deane, a delegate from Connecticut recently appointed by Congress to act as purchasing agent in France, received his instructions from the Committee of Secret Correspondence. These, drawn by Franklin, directed him to proceed immediately to Bordeaux in *Rachell,* a brigantine chartered by the committee expressly to convey him. He was to travel "in the character of a merchant"; his ostensible mission being to purchase and ship to America certain "goods for the Indian trade." If *Rachell* should be taken by a British frigate en route, Deane would no doubt find it embarrassing to explain why the Indians were in such pressing need of brass cannon, tentage, military uniforms, muskets, cannon balls, bayonets, flints, powder, and swivel guns. From Bordeaux, the agent was to hasten to the capital. "It is scarce necessary," the letter of instruction read, "to pretend any other business at Paris, than the gratifying of that curiosity, which draws numbers thither yearly, merely to see so famous a city." On arrival, he was to call on one M. Barbeu Dubourg, a friend of Franklin's, who would introduce him "to a set of acquaintance, all friends to the Americans." Conversation with these sympathizers would afford him "a good opportunity of acquiring Parisian French," he would find M. Dubourg "a man prudent, faithful, secret, intelligent in affairs," and capable of giving him "very safe advice."

Through M. Dubourg, Deane was to make application to wait on M. le Comte de Vergennes. The committee gave Deane specific and detailed instructions as to the subjects he was to open for discussion should the minister prove receptive. First, of course, was provision of arms, ammunition, and uniforms. Deane was given no money; he could offer the minister nothing more than vague promises to pay bills in such commodities as tobacco, rice, and indigo at some indeterminate future date. Next, he was discreetly to inquire as to the disposition of Versailles should the colonies "be forced to form themselves into an independent State." Would France recognize them, consent to exchange ambassadors, and enter into treaties of commerce and alliance? If so, on what conditions?

The committee also instructed its agent to arrange a meeting with Dr. Edward Bancroft, to whom he was to write "under cover to Mr. Griffiths, at Turnham Green, near London," and suggest that he come over to the

Continent for a meeting "on the score of old acquaintance." He also was to arrange to communicate with Arthur Lee, former colonial agent who was still living in London, and "obtain acquaintance with M. Garnier, late *Chargé des Affaires de France en Angleterre*," who was "extremely intelligent and friendly to our cause."[17]

Deane's friendship with Dr. Edward Bancroft had begun some seventeen years earlier, in Hartford, Connecticut, when for a short time after graduating from Yale, he had been a schoolmaster and young Bancroft, an intelligent lad, one of his scholars. He had later been involved with Bancroft, who was a friend in London of Dr. Franklin's, in promoting a trans-Allegheny land scheme called the Vandalia Company. Deane wrote Bancroft, care of Mr. Griffiths, from Philadelphia, informed him he was soon sailing for Bordeaux and would be in Paris in early July, and hoped Bancroft would meet him there. He also sent a letter to his wife in Wethersfield, Connecticut, informing her that he was about "to enter on the great stage of Europe," where he hoped, by his zeal and enterprise, to be "of the most extensive usefulness" to the cause.

Before Governor Josiah Martin of North Carolina fled the palace his predecessor had built at New Bern, he had managed to stir up emigrant Highland Scotch and loyal back country "Regulators" and had commissioned Donald MacDonald (brother of the famous Flora who had hidden the Pretender in 1745) a brigadier general in His Majesty's Army to command them. When Brigadier General James Moore heard Mac-Donald was collecting Tories, and designed to march on Wilmington, he directed Colonel Richard Caswell to block them at Moore's Creek Bridge.

There on February 27 the Loyalists ". . . made their attack . . . and in the most furious manner advanced within thirty paces of our breastwork and artillery, where they met a very proper reception . . . and in a very few minutes their whole army was put to the flight, and most shamefully abandoned their General who was next day taken prisoner." Caswell reported that his officers and men "behaved with the spirit and intrepidity becoming freemen contending for their dearest privileges."

This victory aroused "a noble ardour" in every part of the state: *Dunmore* to the North and *Martin* to the South have already made the whole Province soldiers." With almost 10,000 militia embodied and drilling daily, the North Carolinians did not fear Clinton (then encamped at Cape Fear, where he impatiently awaited Cornwallis): "Let General *Clinton* land where he pleases, we are ready for him at all points . . . the whole Province considers Regulars in the woods as an easy Conquest."[18]

Regulars in Boston, protected by the guns of Shuldham's fleet, would be no "easy Conquest." But despite the obvious reluctance of his generals, Washington was determined to bring on a major action. As a prelude, he ordered occupation and fortification of Dorchester Heights, an eminence overlooking the harbor. The British could have occupied this dominating feature at will at any time during the preceding eight months, but Howe had neglected to do so. Preparations to fortify the Heights were made secretly and in meticulous detail. Scores of oxcarts were assembled, fascines prepared, and hundreds of barrels to be filled with earth collected.

The Americans moved to the Heights after dark on March 4, excavated the frozen earth, cut down hundreds of trees and prepared them as abatis, filled barrels (which they planned to roll down the hill should the Redcoats attempt to ascend it), and built emplacements for cannon. Washington did not plan Dorchester Heights to be an inconclusive reprise of Bunker Hill, but part of a larger action designed to destroy Howe's army. On the Charles above Cambridge, he collected a large number of flat-bottomed boats. Whaleboat men, augmented by soldiers trained as oarsmen, were prepared to embark two divisions ordered to be in readiness on short notice to attack Boston from the rear when Howe was fully committed to an assault on the Heights.

Howe was now faced with two equally unpleasant alternatives: the first, to eject the Americans from the Heights before they blew him out of Boston; the second, to evacuate. The latter was a course too humiliating to contemplate. Howe rose to the bait: Instead of concentrating everything he had to burst through the thinly held line of circumvallation, and destroy Washington's army, he decided to attack the Heights precisely as Washington hoped he would do. Nature intervened to save Howe's army from the inevitable consequence of his questionable decision. On the night he planned his assault, a violent storm arose: ". . . the wind blew almost a hurricane from the south; many windows were forced in, sheds and fences blown down, and some vessels drove on shore; and no attempt was made on the works."[19]

Perhaps it is fortunate a storm did blow up, for there is some question whether the American contingents supposed to land in Boston while Howe was attacking Dorchester could have forced their way into the city. Barricades covered by cannon had been erected in every street. There was no factor of surprise built into this assault; defenders would have had ample time to prepare a bloody reception for the assailants as whaleboats approached selected landing sites and troops scrambled to find cover ashore. Indeed, Shuldham could have broken up this attempt with very little trouble and no loss to himself.

During the next few days, as the Americans continued to improve their fortifications, Colonel Henry Knox's cannon began dropping shot into Boston and harassing Admiral Shuldham's ships. On March 8 Howe took the decision to evacuate, and on the following day began to put his field artillery, ammunition carts, and stores aboard transports. Heavier guns and mortars were thrown off the wharves; other guns were spiked, their trunnions broken and their carriages destroyed, and contents of warehouses were consigned to the harbor waters. Many ships in the harbor were scuttled, and masts of others chopped down. Washington, fearful Howe would put the torch to the city, ceased his desultory cannonade and on March 13, now reasonably sure Howe was leaving, ordered Major General Heath to march with five battalions to New York.

Howe was under pressure, for in addition to embarking 7,000 rank and file fit for duty and almost 1,000 ill, wounded, and convalescent, he had the responsibility for 1,100 Tories. These men, women, and children and their servants boarded Shuldham's ships with the few pitiful possessions they were allowed. Most would never again see Boston. The embarkation was slipshod and disorganized. Howe had issued rigorous orders to prevent pilfering, but his officers took no measures to enforce them. Many usable stores were left in warehouses and were recovered by Washington's troops.

On March 17, led by fifes and drums, and with assorted flags and banners flying, the Americans marched into the almost empty city. "The town had been much injured in its buildings and some individuals had been plundered."[20] The inhabitants, who had endured much, greeted the troops with "joy inexpressible." Their fellow Americans were equally exuberant, and had reason to be, for not a single Redcoat now stood on American soil.

As a final salute to Boston, Howe blew up what was left of Castle William, which Gage had earlier demolished. But with the army aboard, Shuldham's fleet lingered in Nantasket Roads.

1. Lieutenant General Charles Cornwallis

2. Vice-admiral Sir George Brydges Rodney

23. Lieutenant Colonel Banastre Tarleton

24. Thomas Jefferson

25. John Adams

26. Samuel Adams

27. Martha Washington

28. Abigail Adams

29. Mercy Otis Warren

31. Thomas Paine

32. John Hancock

30. Benjamin Franklin

BOOK IV

America Is an Ugly Job, A Damned Affair Indeed

🎏 1

Really Gaming Deep

Although deserters reported Shuldham's fleet bound for Halifax, Washington was unable to confirm the information. He was uncertain "where they may go from hence. Long Island or New York is, in my Opinion, the Place of their Destination." He sent one rifle battalion and five battalions of the Continental Line to New York, and planned "to remove the Rest of the Army there" by detachments when reasonably certain Howe had "fairly left these Parts."[1] He wrote William Alexander, Lord Stirling, recently promoted brigadier general, and since Charles Lee's departure for Charleston, South Carolina, to take command of the Southern Department, senior officer in New York, to urge "most strenuous and Active Exertions in preparing to prevent any Designs or Attempts, they may have against it."[2]

The moment the governors of Rhode Island and Connecticut heard Howe had embarked his army they wrote Washington asking for troops to protect coastal towns against possible attacks. The commander in chief answered their pleas politely and firmly: His object now was to prevent the British from gaining command of the Hudson River; he considered it "absolutely and indispensably necessary, for the whole of this Army . . . to be marched from hence . . . with all possible expedition," for should New York be lost "the most fatal consequences" would inevitably follow.[3]

Shuldham's wind-bound men-of-war and transports still lay too near Boston for comfort. Washington was on his guard; he did not fear marauding parties, but possibility of a "capital stroke" existed so long as the "Ministerial Army" was in the vicinity.* "The continuance of the fleet in Nantasket Road . . . surpasses my comprehension and awakens all my suspicions." On March 24, a week after his troops had entered Boston, he wrote Hancock he was unable to account for the delay in sailing: ". . . to my surprize and disappointment the Fleet is still in Nantasket Road"; the British had "the best knack at puzzling people" he had ever known. "My opinion of the matter is, that they want to retrieve their disgrace before they go off." In five days he would lose ten regiments of militiamen whose terms expired on April 1. "From former experience, we have found it equally practicable to stop a torrent, as these people, when their time is up."[4] This might be the moment Howe would choose to strike.

Fortunately services of short-term militiamen would not be required. On March 27 the general, obviously relieved, wrote from Cambridge to report "the whole of the Ministerial Fleet" under way and standing out to sea. Howe had in mind either some "grand manoeuvre" or had made "an inglorious retreat." Washington immediately issued movement orders and directed General Israel Putnam to proceed to New York to assume command until he arrived.

In one of his frequent letters to the commander in chief, Joseph Reed passed on rumors that "Peace Commissioners" were soon to sail from England. Some in Congress and influential men outside were pressing for a declaration of independence. Others were alarmed at the prospect. Reed was "infinitely more afraid of these commissioners than of their generals and armies," for "If their propositions are plausible, and behavior artful, I am apprehensive they will divide us." Washington replied immediately; unless the commissioners were empowered to deal directly with Congress, it would be better "if they never put their feet on American ground." He, too, divined the ministry's "insidious" intentions: "to distract, divide, and create as much confusion as possible." He knew misguided Tories would humble themselves in the dust and "kiss the rod" held out for chastisement, but how could "any man . . . be so blinded and misled as to embrace a measure evidently designed for his destruction?" He was aware a strong feeling existed against declaring independence. "My countrymen I know, from their form of government, and steady attachment heretofore to royalty, will come reluctantly into the idea of independence, but time and persecution bring many wonderful things to pass . . . I find 'Common Sense' is working a powerful change . . . in the minds of many men."[5]

---

* No one was as yet ready to hold the King responsible for hostilities.

The general spent another week at his Cambridge headquarters and then set out for New York. En route, he was everywhere acclaimed. He assumed command in New York on April 14.

Lord North's propensity to delay decisions, forget appointments, and neglect his correspondence extended on occasion to a more serious dereliction: to fulfill his political promises. One such lapse created an administrative tempest that blew into St. James's Palace and contributed to the appointment of Vice-admiral of the White Richard Viscount ("Black Dick") Howe as commander in chief in American waters. North had promised Howe, a Rockinghamite, that on the demise of Sir Charles Saunders he would inherit the lucrative post of lieutenant general of marines. Unfortunately, when Sir Charles breathed his long-anticipated last breath, the viscount was at his country estate, and Lord North, pressured by Sandwich, forgot his prior commitment to Howe and agreed that Rear Admiral Hugh Palliser should be given the well-paid sinecure.†

When Howe heard that Palliser had kissed hands, he came to London determined to track down the perfidious Lord North and demand an explanation. Horace Walpole provides an amusing and instructive account of this unedifying confrontation, during which Howe threatened to resign all his appointments, and added, "I flatter myself my brother the General will resign, too, when he learns how I have been used."[6] The First Minister, "in a great fright," begged the admiral to delay any action while he untangled the situation. As usual, "the Noble Lord in the Blue Ribband" dumped the unsavory mess into the lap of his royal master.

Before Lord George Germain took office, ministers had informally discussed the question of sending a peace commission to America, an idea fathered by Dartmouth and approved not too enthusiastically by Lord North. Admiral Howe had been approached. The idea did not appeal to Germain, who disliked the prospect of treating with colonial rebels quite as much as he disliked the prospective nominee, which is to say considerably. Germain could not stop the effort, but he did effectively sabotage it by agreeing to go along only if Howe should be tied down by such instructions as he thought proper. North desperately needed Germain's support and co-operation and agreed to hobble Howe.

The admiral, who soon got wind of these activities, now stipulated he would not go to America unless his brother the general was named joint commissioner. The Cabinet accepted this demand with some reluctance. The admiral had another shot in his locker: He would accept only if given command of the fleet in American waters. The First Minister referred this demand to Sandwich, whose close friend Shuldham would

† The lieutenant general of marines exercised no command over the marines. The holder of the title received a generous annual emolument for doing nothing other than supporting administration policy.

thus be superseded. Sandwich replied that he did not "chuse to give him [Howe] command of the Fleet." The First Lord could control Shuldham; "Black Dick" Howe, who disliked and distrusted Sandwich, was not equally amenable.

The situation had reached an impasse which His Majesty resolved in Howe's favor, subject to such negotiating restrictions as the American Secretary deemed necessary. The King, not too happy with these appointments, soothed Shuldham with the twin emollients of an Irish peerage and a generous pension. He considered Howe "wrongheaded" and thought "it would be better for himself as well as the Service" if he voluntarily gave up the office of commissioner, a concession the King, who valued a golden guinea, must have known Howe would not consider. The remuneration of the peace commissioners had been set at £5,400 per annum.

One of those artful and engaging characters who all too rarely enliven the historical drama now made his entrance. This was Pierre Augustin Caron de Beaumarchais, son of a watchmaker, who had married considerably above his station.‡ His musical and artistic talents, his consummate effrontery (described by jealous courtiers at Versailles as "insolence"), and his native wit and flamboyance gave him a passport to high society. He had purchased a minor office at court; his political acumen had so impressed Vergennes that the count sent him on a confidential mission to the French embassy in London to recover compromising correspondence from Chevalier d'Éon, an extravagant and indiscreet diplomat who enjoyed wearing women's clothes when not engaged in state business. Beaumarchais wooed the transvestite with such success that he managed to steal the key to d'Éon's strongbox, recover the damaging letters, and earn Vergennes's gratitude and confidence.

He succeeded, too, in ingratiating himself with powerful political personalities, including the indiscreet Earl of Rochford, formerly Secretary of State for the Southern Department, who in course of a conversation told him the King and Cabinet were disturbed to learn that despite Lord Stormont's protests, Versailles had not moved to stop the clandestine traffic in munitions to the rebellious Americans. The earl intimated clearly enough that George III expected the French King and his ministers to take action. Beaumarchais replied in spirited fashion that French merchants would trade with whomever they wished. The interview waxed hot; Beaumarchais, flushed with anger at Rochford's arrogant presumption, informed the earl his expectations were "out of place." When tempers cooled, Beaumarchais announced he had come to London to buy Portuguese gold coins on behalf of his government, and produced

---

‡ Beaumarchais was also a master watchmaker. He invented a new and improved escapement for clocks and watches; he designed a fob watch for Louis XV and a ring watch for the King's mistress, Madame de Pompadour.

a letter signed by Comte de Sartine, Louis XVI's Minister of Marine, directing him to do so. This flimsy cover ostensibly satisfied British counterespionage agents, who allowed the coin buyer plenty of rope in anticipation that he would manage to hang himself. They seriously underestimated Caron de Beaumarchais, who had enough sense to be discreet, and who entrusted no correspondence to the mails.

In his next letter to Vergennes, Beaumarchais reported that he had dined with John Wilkes, where he had a conversation with an American, Arthur Lee (brother of Richard Henry and Francis Lightfoot), who had put in a plea for French engineers: "We want arms and powder, but above all, we want engineers. There is nobody but you who can help us. . . ." If the French would not lend engineers, they could lend money. "We will [then] get engineers from Germany, Sweden, Italy, etc., and you will not be compromised." Beaumarchais thought this a reasonable request and urged Vergennes to grant an immediate secret loan of one or two million livres. Engineers might talk. Money was mute.**

Beaumarchais kept his finger on the political pulse, and frequently attended debates in the House of Commons. He was not kind to Administration: Lord North, he reported, was floundering; the ministers knew not which way to turn. Barré, Burke, Conway, and Fox led the assault. Fox "in an inspired tone, invokes, interrogates the honour of the Ministers, and replying to himself, he says—'For a long time past the honour of the Ministers has been a chimera; it is null and has no voice in the public affairs of today.'" North, who had the votes, sat in silence.[7]

Beaumarchais insistently urged Vergennes to extend credit to the Americans. "Will you not try to convince his Majesty that this poor help which they ask and upon which we have been debating for a year past, must enable us to gather all the fruits of a great victory without having gone through the dangers of a battle; that this help may bring us, while we sleep, all that the shameful peace of 1762 [sic] made us lose; and that the success of the Americans, reducing our rivals to be nothing more than a second-rate power, replaces us in the first rank, and gives us, for a long time, preponderance over all Europe."[8]

Beaumarchais was impatient; Vergennes moved too slowly and circumspectly to suit him. Earlier, without the Foreign Minister's knowledge, he had submitted a lengthy memoir addressed "To the King Only." In this he proposed an ingenious plan for supporting the Americans without in the least compromising Louis XVI: "Your Majesty will begin by placing one million at the disposal of your agent, who will style himself Roderique Hortalez and Company, this being the signature and title of the firm under which I have agreed to conduct the entire business." Half the sum advanced would be invested in Portuguese gold coins to be sent to America to support rapidly depreciating Continental paper; the

** At the time, a million livres exchanged for approximately £ 45,000.

remaining half would be used for purchase of munitions and equipment, for which the Americans would pay in tobacco and other products.

Beaumarchais worked into his plan a rather complicated scheme which (he assured His Majesty) would triple the King's original investment in short order. He dwelt at considerable length on the financial aspects of this trade and referred to himself, to the King's amusement, as "the merchant, economist, and politician Hortalez de Beaumarchais."[9] The only problem, one easily overcome, was that Roderique Hortalez and Company needed royal permission to purchase muskets, bayonets, powder, tentage, cannon and cannon balls, gun carriages, entrenching tools, and assorted other items from royal arsenals. These would be loaded in French ports into vessels under charter to Hortalez and manifested for St. Domingue where cargoes would be exchanged for tobacco, salt fish, indigo, and hemp.

Vergennes, although anxious to take every advantage of the situation, did not allow himself to be influenced by Beaumarchais's bubbling enthusiasm. The minister moved toward a decision with analytical care, and in early March, after considerable cogitation, presented to His Most Christian Majesty an appreciation entitled: *Considerations on the Affairs of the English Colonies in America*. This, based on his earlier *Réflexions*, he sent, with a royal command for comment, to Count Maurepas, Louis XVI's *chef de conseil;* to Turgot (Comptroller General of Finance); to De Sartine (Minister of Colonies and Marine); and to Comte de Saint-Germain (Minister of War).

Not yet wholly convinced American independence would best serve the interests of France and Spain, Vergennes examined various possibilities. He reasoned first that England, "feeling the insufficiency of means" to put down the rebellion, might attempt reconciliation with the colonies. Or, should she succeed in suppressing the rebels, George III might seize the opportunity to subjugate his own people and then attack France or Spain. Or, should the English be beaten in America, the ministers, in an effort to save their own heads, might seek an indemnity at the expense of the Bourbon powers by seizing their transatlantic colonies. And, finally, if the Americans won, they might embark on a career of conquest in the Caribbean or Louisiana. This the count considered an unlikely possibility. The situation thus demanded the most thoughtful appraisal and "the most measured steps."

Were the two monarchs not wholly "dedicated to peace," and were their "military and financial means appropriate," they might seize the moment "Providence has marked . . . for the humiliation of England . . . struck with the blindness which is the most certain precursor of destruction." Decisive blows at this time would "cause England to return to the ranks of secondary powers; would take from her the Empire which she claims to exercise in the four quarters of the world with so much

pride and injustice, and would deliver the universe from a rapacious tyrant who wishes to swallow up at the same time all power and all
riches."

But if Their Most Christian and Most Catholic Majesties found this
course of action unacceptable, measures of a noncompromising nature
could be put in hand. The best interests of France and Spain dictated
that the war be kept going for at least another year: "A year gained for
measures of vigour and foresight may, in many respects, change the aspect of affairs." The most certain means of attaining this end would be
on the one hand "to keep the English ministry persuaded that the intentions of France and Spain are pacific, in order that it may not fear to embark in the operation of a brisk and expensive campaign; whilst, on the
other hand, we should sustain the courage of the Americans by some secret favours," by vague hopes of future massive assistance, and by encouraging the idea of independence, now only in the bud, "to burst
forth."[10]

This low-risk policy was a compromise. Turgot, worried by the precarious state of finances, advocated a policy of retrenchment and
vehemently opposed spending more than absolutely necessary on arms.
Certainly, if much were to be spent, it should not be devoted to equip-
ping the Americans. He favored them because they weakened the hereditary enemy, but he did not propose to encourage their resistance by
draining an already nearly exhausted treasury and bankrupting the country. De Sartine knew his fleet was not yet ready for a major showdown
with Britain and could not approve a policy that would probably precipitate hostilities. His colleague Saint-Germain depreciated the possibility
of a continental war and was ready to go along with Vergennes.
Maurepas was not too happy with the Foreign Minister's plans; Spain's
attitude was ambivalent; Louis's conservative *chef de conseil* felt a firm
commitment from Madrid essential before France embarked on an ad-
venturous policy that would put at risk her precious Sugar Islands and
valuable fishing rights.

But Vergennes's influence was paramount. He had friends among the
King's intimates; perhaps most important of all, his proposals were enthusiastically supported by Queen Marie Antoinette, who adored *"les
Bostonnais"* as fervently as she detested the British. She persuaded her
young and impressionable husband to rid himself of Turgot, who stood
as the only obstacle to adoption of the policy advocated by M. le Comte
de Vergennes.

As Clinton awaited the expedition from Cork at the Cape Fear rendezvous, he learned that impatient North Carolina Scots Loyalists, who
had responded to the summons of Donald MacDonald, the aged brother
of the famous Flora, had donned their kilts, sharpened their claymores,

summoned their pipers, marched on Wilmington, North Carolina, and had been intercepted, defeated, and dispersed at Moore's Creek, some eight miles from the town, on February 27. This thoughtless impetuosity wrote a definite finis to any hope for successful collaboration of Loyalists and restitution of His Majesty's government in North Carolina. Clinton now could do nothing but fret until Major General Earl Cornwallis joined him, at which time a new plan could be formulated. He was to have a considerable wait; the Southern Expeditionary Force did not depart Cork until mid-February and was still somewhere in the middle of the Atlantic, laboriously beating its way westward against contrary seasonal winds. The embarkation, a model of confused inefficiency, had been conducted (so Murray wrote) "in such a harum scarum humble jumble manner" that he was ashamed to admit he had previously approved Administration's measures.

What little news arrived from America was not calculated to confirm His Majesty's hopes that the rebellion would subside, or could soon be put down. The last word from Howe was that he was penned in the Boston cul-de-sac, and with the St. Lawrence frozen solid no accounts of recent events in Canada could be sent out; no one in London knew the fate of Quebec, when last heard from invested by Montgomery and Arnold. Walpole's current report to Mann was even gloomier than usual: "Indeed I do not think the general language is so prophetic of certain success as it was some months ago and people seem to grow much more clear of the unpromising aspect of affairs than they were." He thought America a gamble; Britain was "really gaming deep—we have set 12 provinces on the cast of a die."[11]

His Majesty's expensive treaties with German princelings raised a storm of protest in London; on March 23 the lord mayor, aldermen, and Council presented "a humble Address and Petition" protesting the disgrace of the arrangements. They looked forward with horror to the impending "Dismemberment of the Empire . . . increase of the National Debt and of Burthensome Taxes . . . distresses of Merchants and Manufacturers; those deficiencies of the Revenue; that effusion of the blood of our Countrymen and Brethren, that failure of public Credit," and other unspecified dreadful "Calamaties and Convulsions." They implored the King to extend his justice and mercy to America and to grant her just and honorable terms before his powerful armaments commenced "their dreadful operations." Should the Americans reject such terms, then, assuredly, they would be in a state of rebellion which "the zealous hearts of a determined, loyal and united people" would rally to suppress. His Majesty replied, deploring the miseries his subjects in America had "brought upon themselves by an unjustifiable Resistance to the constitutional Authority of the Kingdom" and promised to extend "Mercy and

Clemency" when "the Rebellion is at an end" and the authority of Great Britain re-established.

One division of Hessians arrived in England in April and embarked at Portsmouth for New York in early May. Assorted contretemps prevented sailing as scheduled; Admiral Palliser hastened to Portsmouth to speed embarkation. The Germans refused to sail until supplies of beer had been put aboard; they had been promised a generous daily ration and intended to have it. Palliser took care of that. Major General Philip de Heister preferred to await the arrival of his second division; Palliser persuaded him to proceed. Just as all seemed ready, half the crews of a dozen transports jumped ship. Commodore William Hotham raged; he twice missed fair winds; Palliser described the whole business as "mortifying beyond expression." Patrols rounded up most missing sailors and returned them to their ships, where they received routine floggings.

Palliser was far from satisfied with the state of the Hessian embarkation. "The ships are so full of baggage, artillery, stores, wagons, coaches, and other carriages that I fear the men are too much crowded . . . they must not be so crowded as to endanger the men's health and thereby endanger the success of the expedition."[12] He laid hands on two extra transports, did some last-minute rearranging, and finally saw the convoy off.

The British contingent destined for Canada had sailed in April. Several weeks later a convoy bearing Major General Baron Friedrich von Riedesel and some 4,000 Brunswickers overhauled them in mid-Atlantic, and Burgoyne, gazetted second-in-command to Carleton, paid a mid-ocean call on the German who was to be his colleague in the invasion of New York from the north.

In early May the fleet bearing the British troops entered the Gulf of St. Lawrence. Some leagues below Quebec a packet boat met them with news that Montgomery's attempt to storm the city had been beaten back; that he had been killed, and Arnold grievously wounded. Shortly after, Burgoyne learned that on May 6 Carleton had marched out of the city to attack. The rebels, ill clad, short of ammunition and provisions, decimated by desertion, and riddled with dysentery and scurvy, had fled in confusion, abandoning their few light cannon and all their camp equipment. Some six hundred, ill with pneumonia and infected with smallpox, were captured. The thoroughly demoralized remnants scarcely stopped to draw breath until they reached Sorel at the mouth of the Richelieu, where hastily collected reinforcements commanded by Brigadier General William Thompson awaited them.

On the last day of May, to the delight of Captain William Digby of the Grenadier Company, 53rd Regiment of Foot, the ships cast anchor twelve leagues above Quebec. The scene entranced him: lovely weather, a majestic river, towering forest trees "in all appearance as old as the world itself." On the following day the troops began to disembark. Digby's company marched to Trois-Rivières, "a neat village . . . half way from Quebec to Montreal." More troops under command of Lieutenant Colonel Simon Fraser came ashore every day.

The reinforcement was timely, for at dawn on June 8 three American columns commanded by Thompson approached the town. Fraser met them, put them to flight after a brief skirmish, and took nearly three hundred prisoners including Thompson. On the following day, Burgoyne assigned the grenadier and light infantry companies of ten regiments plus the 24th Foot to Fraser, appointed by Governor Carleton "Brigadier General in America" and named him to command the advance corps of the army. Fraser, then forty-seven years old, an introspective and reserved Scot, a competent professional who had fought at Louisburg and Quebec, was respected by his superiors, much admired by his associates, and esteemed by his men. Under him, Major Alexander Lindsay, Sixth Earl of Balcarres, a young, tough, fighting Scot, commanded the light infantry battalion, and John Acland, a hard-drinking, violently anti-American M.P., whose courageous and attractive wife, Lady Harriet, accompanied him, commanded the grenadiers.

The strength of the new army in Canada (including Riedesel's Brunswickers) was now almost 10,000. The troops were well equipped, in good health, and eager to move against the Americans gathered at Sorel under Major General John Sullivan, who had recently taken command. Sullivan was quite unable to meet the overwhelming force Carleton had to throw against him. The governor, burning to repay the rebels for the humiliations they had inflicted on him, arrived before Sorel on June 14 and immediately ordered the advance corps to take the place. This turned out to be no problem; Sullivan had withdrawn in disorder at dawn. On the following day, Burgoyne landed, assumed tactical command, and immediately started for Chambly. On June 18 his advance corps arrived hard on the heels of the Americans, who barely escaped in the greatest confusion. The general moved at once on St. Johns; en route, trails littered with abandoned equipment indicated the routed Americans were flying. Burgoyne, smelling annihilation, ordered three companies of light infantry forward "on a trot." They arrived at St. Johns to find the fort abandoned and blazing. "Thus was Canada saved with much less trouble than was expected on our embarking from Great Britain."[13]

Carleton had driven the Americans from Canada. His next objective was to move up Lake Champlain and take Ticonderoga. To the successful British, now immobilized at St. Johns for lack of water transport, "the tediousness" of preparations necessary "for so great an expedition was far from pleasing. We had everything to build, battows to convey the troops over, and armed schooners and sloops to oppose theirs. . . . It was thought that everything would be ready in 7 or 8 weeks, but the undertaking was a great one."[14] Carleton immediately ordered forward naval carpenters and artificers and summoned hundreds of Canadians to fell trees, set up lumber mills, cut trails, and build roads and bridges.

The remnant of the beaten American Army—an army wrecked by battle losses, smallpox, and desertions; hungry, exhausted, ragged, unpaid, and totally disorganized—huddled fearfully at Crown Point awaiting bateaux from Ticonderoga to extricate them from the imminent dangers of torture and scalping by Indians, a slow death by starvation, or, perhaps, a more immediate one by bayonets of Carleton's Redcoats.

Hancock forwarded Washington a "melancholy" report from Samuel Chase and Charles Carroll, congressional commissioners who had earlier been ordered to inquire into the condition of the army. They had found the situation "truly alarming. Our Army in that Quarter is almost ruined for Want of Discipline and every Thing else necessary to constitute an Army, or to keep Troops together." In this crisis, Congress resolved to relieve Major General Wooster, then commanding at Ticonderoga, and to replace him with Major General John Thomas. Obviously, much more than a change in top command was needed. Congress, however, persisted in the belief that a new general was a panacea for all ills, including a raging epidemic of smallpox, which took Thomas off.

When Washington learned the army had retreated in disorder, he knew the game in Canada was about played out. He had small hope the situation could be retrieved: "This unfortunate affair has given a sad shock to our Schemes in that Quarter, and blasted the Hope we entertained of reducing that Fortress [Quebec], and the whole of Canada to our Possession."[15] But he wanted to hold a position as far forward as possible, and under any circumstances to hold Lake Champlain. From New York, he attempted to satisfy Schuyler's urgent requests and sent him carpenters and sailmakers, anchors, cordage, nails, and other items necessary to construct a fleet sufficiently powerful to maintain naval supremacy on Champlain.

The conquest of Canada was not a project gentlemen in Philadelphia were yet ready to abandon. The New Englanders, obstinately determined to inject new life into an irretrievable situation, urged that Horatio Gates be appointed to proceed to Canada and assume command. John Adams, ever jealous of the commander in chief, made it a point not to consult him, and on June 18 wrote Gates: "We have ordered you to the Post of Honour, and made you Dictator in Canada for Six Months, or at least until the first of October. . . . We don't Choose to trust you Generals, with too much Power for too long Time."[16] At that point Gates and Adams were on the best of terms. Although Gates had served Washington well as adjutant general at Cambridge, he had no qualifications to recommend him for an important independent command. He was a fierce radical; he wanted to exterminate the verminous Tories, an attitude that found favor with Adams, who engineered his appointment to major general and assignment to command the army in Canada.

En route to Ticonderoga, Gates stopped in Albany to pay his respects to the ailing Schuyler, who informed him there was no longer an army in Canada. This automatically placed him under Schuyler's command—to Gates, not a particularly pleasing prospect. However, amenities were observed, and after enjoying his host's celebrated hospitality, he hastened to Ticonderoga. Here, he discovered affairs to be in a mess that beggars description. Hundreds of militiamen were convalescing from wounds or were down with smallpox, dysentery, and scurvy. Medical services were utterly inadequate; graft and corruption rampant. The situation at Crown Point was even worse. A young Connecticut officer described the dismal scene. He found "not an army, but a mob, the shattered remains of twelve or fifteen very fine battalions, ruined by sickness, fatigue and desertions and void of every idea of discipline or subordination."[17] The "shattered remains" wanted only to get home.

The invasion of Canada was indeed "a new and perilous undertaking. It seemed totally to change the nature of the ground on which [the Americans] stood in the present dispute. Opposition to government had hitherto been conducted on the apparent design and avowed principle only of defending certain rights or immunities of the people." A resistance so based could be considered by many "to be entirely consistent with the principles of the British constitution. . . . But to render themselves the aggressors, and not content with vindicating their own real or pretended rights, to fly wantonly in the face of the sovereign, carry war into his dominions, and invade a province to which they could lay no claim, or pretend no right, seemed such an outrage as not only overthrew every plea of justifiable resistance, but would militate with the established opinions, principles, and feelings of mankind in general."[18] Such were the sentiments of Edmund Burke, who wrote the articles on American and European affairs published in The Annual Register. If Burke considered the attempt to conquer Canada an unwarrantable outrage, it must have appeared to His Majesty not less than criminal; certainly, it confirmed his determination to crush the rebellion.

Thus ended the attempt launched with such sanguine hopes in the preceding autumn. Had the effort been under way six weeks earlier, with troops adequately equipped and their commanders supplied with specie to buy fresh food and pay Canadian volunteers in cash, it would probably have been successful. But Congress had very little "hard money" and few Canadians had volunteered. Although Arnold emerged with an enhanced reputation, the "Canada Army" was shattered.

Ships of the convoy bringing Cornwallis and his troops to America began arriving at the Cape Fear rendezvous in mid-April, but the last few did not straggle in for another four weeks, some ninety-odd days after departing Cork. As neither Commodore Sir Peter Parker nor General Clinton had a directive as to what to do should the projected operation in North Carolina blow up, they at once fell into an altercation as to a proper target. Clinton wanted to go to the Chesapeake; Parker— "tempted in an evil hour"—to seize Charleston. The commodore won this round; in late May troops broke camp at Cape Fear and the fleet set sail for Charleston.

A diligent search of the annals of amphibious warfare would not discover an expedition conducted with an equal measure of the ineptitude which characterized the attempt to take Charleston, in Captain Murray's opinion "one of the most singular events that has yet conspired to degrade the name of the British nation."[19] Everything that could go wrong went wrong. Tides, winds, depth of water, and fog co-operated in favor of the Americans and against Parker's ships.

Parker persuaded Clinton that the first step was to reduce the fort at Sullivans Island which commanded the approaches to Charleston harbor and was defended by a small but determined garrison under Colonel William Moultrie. Again, army-navy co-operation left much to be desired. Clinton landed his troops on Long Island with the idea they could wade across a relatively narrow channel at low tide to storm the fort. While Parker bombarded Moultrie's palmetto-log stronghold with no effect—the spongy logs simply absorbed British cannon balls—Clinton discovered an unpleasant fact a reconnaissance would have revealed: At the lowest of low tides the water in the channel was seven feet deep. While the general puttered about seeking a nonexistent ford, Moultrie's guns did frightful execution, repeatedly hulling Parker's ships. An explosion on the quarter-deck of His Majesty's flagship *Bristol* removed the commodore's britches. After three weeks of futile flailing, three hundred casualties, loss of a frigate and severe damage to two others, the fleet set sail for New York.

En route, Captain Murray wrote his sister an account of the bungled operation. He, at least, had learned a few things: "The gentlemen who have undertaken to conquer America with single regiments might have likewise had an opportunity of making some few observations in this camp: that the artillery of the *Yankies* was admirably well served, their works admirably constructed." But the captain optimistically wrote that notwithstanding all misfortunes and mistakes, "I'm persuaded that we shall beat them this autumn if we know how to set about it."[20]

When the King read the reports, he dispatched a laconic memorandum to Sandwich: "Though the attack upon Charles Town has not been crowned with success, it has by no means proved dishonourable; perhaps

I should have been as well pleased if it had not been attempted."[21] The King's memory was unusually good; that he had encouraged the expedition seems conveniently to have slipped his mind. The fiasco provided material for a popular Yankee war ballad, "The Commodore Reports to the Lords of the Admiralty." Two verses convey the flavor:

> With much labor and toil
> Unto Sullivan's Isle
> I came fierce as Falstaff or Pistol
> But the Yankees ('od rod 'em)
> I could not get at 'em
> Most terribly mauled my poor *Bristol*

> Bold Clinton by land
> Did quietly stand
> While I made a thundering clatter
> But the channel was deep
> So he could only peep
> And not venture over the water[22]

Lord George Germain had drawn plans to end the rebellion in 1776. Essentially these provided that Carleton gain control of Champlain, seize Ticonderoga, and take Albany. Howe was to take New York, and then, presumably, push up the valley of the Hudson. These orders arrived in Halifax just before Howe sailed. He wrote Germain on June 7; his army was embarked, Shuldham awaited a favorable wind. He assured Lord George he would not "hazard any disadvantageous attacks" but would await arrival of reinforcements before undertaking operations against Manhattan Island. Howe fully expected to put himself under Carleton's command: "No difficulties could possibly arise respecting his [Carleton's] command on the junction of the two armies."

On the following day he wrote a personal letter to Lord George: "I cannot take my leave of your Lordship without expressing my utter Amazement at the decisive and Masterly Strokes for carrying such extensive Plans into immediate execution as have been effected since your Lordship has assumed the conducting of this war." He was certain Lord George would "finally receive the acknowledgements of a grateful country and the lasting Glory which such Services Merit."

The wind now blew fair; the packet sailed for England, and Shuldham's fleet set course for New York. On the same day, the secretary wrote Howe: "If our news with respect to Quebec is true, and we have the strongest reasons to think it is, much may be done from that side to facilitate the Success of your Operations, and if ever your two armies can join the Rebels must submit. . . ."

2

An Impudent and Atrocious Proclamation

During the last days of May 1776, independence men both in and out of Congress pressed the policy with unrelenting vigor; Adams wrote: "Every Post and every Day, rolls in upon us Independence like a Torrent." This conveys the idea that support for independence was massive; that letters favoring it were pouring into Philadelphia in floods; that the public demanded action, and that, soon. Pressures on the men in whose hands the decision lay were indeed constant and mounting, but "Independence" was not a slogan that was sweeping the colonies. Still, Adams was not alone in feeling that he and his colleagues would soon be called on to deal with "the most decisive Measures and the most critical events."[1]

In Philadelphia all political talk—and at this time there was little else —resolved around "Three Capital Measures": a declaration of independence, confederation, and foreign treaties. All felt the storm would soon break: "Our affairs are hastening fast to a Crisis; and the approaching Campaign will in all Probability, determine the fate of America." The words are John Hancock's in a circular letter calling on governors, conventions, and assemblies to summon the militia and warning them the abominated ministry had hired foreign mercenaries to carry on their business "without Remorse or Compunction." He exhorted them to "Exert every Nerve" to hasten their preparations, for only if they did so would they be able to lead their people "to Victory, to Liberty and to Happiness."[2]

News that George III had negotiated "infamous treaties" with the Prince of Brunswick, the Landgrave of Hesse-Cassel, the Count of Hanau, and lesser assorted avaricious princelings, to most of whom he was related, and had agreed to pay the staggering sum of almost £1 million a year for six, seven, or eight years aroused indignation in the colonies. Americans were not wholly ignorant of history; they had a good idea of the treatment they might expect at the hands of alien mercenaries: "The tidings were everywhere received with surprise, indignation, and cruel anxiety. Those feelings were strongest in the quiet, well-ordered homesteads of the settled districts which, ever since the red man had retreated westward, had been exempt from the terror of rapine, and conflagration, and outrage. It was indeed grievous for farmers who lived along the Hudson River or to the east of the Delaware. The German officers, and a great majority of their men, might be respectable and law abiding . . . but the rank and file in some of the regiments was composed of refuse from all the barrackrooms in Europe."[3] Americans had previously heard of the King's abortive efforts to hire "Tartars"; German mercenaries were equally detestable.

The decision to employ foreigners changed the character of the American war. Had hostilities been confined to Americans versus English, a chance, however slight, for accommodation still existed. With the injection of thousands of mercenaries no such opportunity remained. The King and his ministers regarded these contracts as a supreme coup. Surely the sweepings of every jail in Brunswick and Hesse would shortly bring the rebels to the suppliant attitude His Majesty stubbornly demanded.

Although the question of declaring independence had been the principal topic of conversation "out of doors" during April and May, proponents of the measure did not directly attempt to force the issue. New Englanders and their allies from Virginia were discreet; they realized New York, New Jersey, and South Carolina were not ready to commit themselves to severance from Great Britain. Delaware sat on the fence; Pennsylvania and Maryland, the two great proprietaries, were less than lukewarm. As R. H. Lee wrote his brother, "The Proprietary Colonies do certainly obstruct and perplex the American Machine."[4] Quakers in Pennsylvania and Tories in Maryland and Delaware were sufficiently influential to make their opinions felt; they were "exerting themselves, but these exertions are no more than the last struggles of expiring faction."

Everyone in Philadelphia knew Richard Henry Lee had in hand a resolution declaring the colonies to be free and independent states. He offered this on June 7. Jefferson's *Notes of Proceedings in the Continental Congress* for Friday and Saturday, June 7 and 8, give the outline of the drama. On Friday "The Delegates from Virginia moved in obedience to instructions from their constituents that the Congress should declare that these United Colonies are & of right ought to be free & independent states, that they are absolved of all allegiance to the British crown, and that all political connection between them and the state of Great Britain is & ought to be totally dissolved; that measures should be immediately taken for procuring the assistance of foreign powers, and a Confederation be formed to bind the colonies more closely together."[5] Debate on the propositions was deferred until the following morning, when members were ordered to attend punctually at ten o'clock.

On Saturday at ten o'clock, delegates took their places. The roll was called; the resolution for independence offered. Rutledge of South Carolina took the floor. He described the attempt to push through the measure at this time as foolish and inappropriate, and labeled the effort a typical example of New England "impudence." The people, he argued, were not ready to unite; the colonies were in "a disjointed state." There was as yet no reason for "pressing the measure." But others, including Jefferson, were convinced that sentiment for independence was fast rising, and that in a short time those who appeared hesitant "would join in the general voice of America."

Obviously, Congress had no authority to take the momentous step of declaring independence until delegates from all colonies were specifically so instructed by their constituents, and a number were not yet so instructed. If the delegates from certain colonies had no power to declare for independence, delegates from others surely had no power to declare it for them; should they presume to do so, their uninstructed colleagues would probably disavow the action and walk out. Such a step would at once raise the possibility that "certain" colonies (Pennsylvania, Delaware, New York, and New Jersey) might then not accede to the proposed declaration and confederation. In the event of such a division, "foreign powers would either refuse to join themselves to our fortunes, or having us so much in their power as that desperate declaration would place us, they would insist on terms proportionably more hard & prejudicial."

John Adams never stood in the ranks of the uncertain. This determined man had a clear-cut program and proposed to push it with all the energy and influence he could summon. "The lives and liberties of millions yet unborn" depended on the events of the next few weeks in Philadelphia. He could not return to his family "in the very midst of a revolution, the most complete, unexpected and remarkable, of any in the history of nations." Each colony, he wrote Cushing, must institute "a perfect government"; they must then confederate; Congress must declare the colonies "free and independent" and send ambassadors abroad empowered to solicit recognition and negotiate treaties." When these things are once completed, I shall think that I have answered the end of my creation, and sing my *nunc dimitus* [*sic*], return to my farm, family, ride circuit, plead law, or judge causes, just as you please."[6] On June 11, the question of the declaration was again postponed, this time until July 1. However, a committee consisting of Jefferson, John Adams, Franklin, Roger Sherman, and Robert Livingston was appointed to draft a document. All agreed Jefferson should draw it. He did so, and submitted his draft separately to Franklin and Adams for comments and corrections. They had but few, none particularly material.

While this committee, or to be more precise, its chosen instrument, Mr. Jefferson, labored, Congress attended to the long-neglected business of establishing a "Board of War and Ordinance." Hancock too optimistically assured Washington that this "great event" would be "attended with essential advantages." The infant Navy, established in October 1775, was not distinguishing itself; Hancock laid its "shameful Inactivity" to "neglect or disobediance of Orders in Commodore Hopkins" and to unspecified derelictions of duty on the part of Captains Dudley Saltonstall and Abraham Whipple. He ordered all three to repair at once to Philadelphia by most rapid conveyance "to answer for their Conduct."[7]

As the month of June drew to a close, excitement in Philadelphia rose. The first day of July had been set aside "for the greatest debate of all." Before he left his lodgings that historic morning to walk to Carpenters' Hall, John Adams wrote a friend: "A declaration that these colonies are free and independent States, has been reported by a committee appointed some weeks ago for that purpose, and this day or tomorrow is to determine its fate. May Heaven prosper the new-born republic, and make it more glorious than any former republics have been!"[8]

That evening, after eight hours of debate, he was impatient and less ebullient. The day had been "an idle mispence of time for nothing was said but what had been repeated and hackneyed in that room before, a hundred times, for six months past."[9] John Dickinson, first to speak, announced his opposition to the Virginia resolves. Adams, no longer an admirer of "the Farmer" as he once had been, conceded that his opponent had prepared himself "with great labor and ardent zeal." When Dickinson finished, Adams rose in response to Rutledge's earnest plea to speak in rebuttal. He was reluctant "to speak again to this subject"; he had repeatedly expressed his views and his reasons for holding them. To him the question seemed one "of plain common sense." Delegates from New

Jersey who had just arrived pressed him urgently. He then "summed up the reasons, objections and answers, in as concise a manner as I could, till at length the Jersey gentlemen said they were fully satisfied, and ready for the question, which was then put and determined in the affirmative."*

On the following day the resolution was carried in Committee of the Whole without a dissent. (The New York delegates had not yet received instructions and hence did not vote.) On July 3, Adams wrote his "Dearest Friend": "Yesterday the greatest question was decided which ever was debated in America, and a greater, perhaps, never was nor will be decided among men."[10] Later that night, still under the spell of the drama in which he had played the leading role, he again took his quill in hand to Abigail:

> The second day of July, 1776, will be the most memorable epoch in the history of America. I am apt to believe that it will be cele- brated by succeeding generations as the great anniversary Festi- val. It ought to be commemorated, as the day of deliverance, by solemn acts of devotion to God Almighty. It ought to be solem- nized with pomp and parade, with shows, games, sports, guns, bells, bonfires, and illuminations, from one end of this continent to the other, from this time forward, forevermore.[11]

On July 4 the Declaration of Independence was adopted, authenticated, and ordered to be printed.†

Jefferson had spent many hours drafting and revising the preamble, which had it been the only paragraph he ever composed, would have as- sured him deserved position as one of the most powerful political writers in history. Jefferson never asserted that the philosophy he so succinctly and forcefully expressed was original. Indeed, he specifically disavowed any such claim; it was his purpose, he later wrote,

> Not to find out new principles, or new arguments, never before thought of, not merely to say things which had never been said before; but to place before mankind the common sense of the sub- ject, in terms so plain and firm as to command their assent, and to justify ourselves in the independent stand we are compelled to take. Neither aiming at originality of principle or sentiment, nor yet copied from any particular and previous writing, it was in- tended to be an expression of the American mind, and to give to that expression the proper tone and spirit called for by the occa- sion.[12]

* On July 2 Congress resolved itself into a Committee of the Whole. Debates on Jefferson's draft of the declaration were secret and not recorded.

† The engrossed declaration was signed on August 2, 1776.

The preamble reads:

THE UNANIMOUS DECLARATION OF THE THIRTEEN UNITED STATES OF AMERICA

When in the Course of human events, it becomes necessary for one people to dissolve the political bands, which have connected them with another, and to assume among the powers of the earth, the separate and equal station to which the Laws of Nature and of Nature's God entitle them, a decent respect to the opinions of mankind requires that they should declare the causes which impel them to the separation.—We hold these truths to be self-evident, that all men are created equal, that they are endowed by their Creator with certain unalienable Rights, that among these are Life, Liberty and the pursuit of Happiness.—That to secure these rights, Governments are instituted among Men, deriving their just powers from the consent of the governed,—That whenever any Form of Government becomes destructive of these ends, it is the Right of the People to alter or to abolish it, and to institute new Government, laying its foundation on such principles and organizing its powers in such form, as to them shall seem most likely to effect their Safety and Happiness. Prudence, indeed, will dictate that Governments long established should not be changed for light and transient causes; and accordingly all experience hath shewn, that mankind are more disposed to suffer, while evils are sufferable, than to right themselves by abolishing the forms to which they are accustomed. But when a long train of abuses and usurpations, pursuing invariably the same Object evinces a design to reduce them under absolute Despotism, it is their right, it is their duty, to throw off such Government, and to provide new Guards for their future security.—Such has been the patient sufferance of these Colonies; and such is now the necessity which constrains them, to alter their former Systems of Government.

Jefferson next submitted "to a candid world" a catalogue of twenty-seven charges drawn against King George III, whose intent, he wrote, was to establish "an absolute Tyranny over these States." He was careful not to use the world "Parliament"; he focused on a single identifiable target. However valid the charges, they were sufficiently grave, in his mind, to justify "the independent stand" the Americans, who had repeatedly appealed in vain for redress of grievances, had finally been "compelled" to take. Whether the King had personally planned the "abuses" alleged against him or directed the "usurpations" stipulated was not relevant to Jefferson's purpose, which was to hammer home the charges that

George III was unfit to rule a free people. This section of the declaration is a masterful example of persuasive political propaganda.

Congress had tactfully deleted Jefferson's philippic charging the King with responsibility for the slave trade and had considerably improved his last paragraph. As amended on the floor, this reads:

> We, therefore, the Representatives of the united States of America, in General Congress, Assembled, appealing to the Supreme Judge of the world for the rectitude of our intentions, do, in the Name, and by Authority of the good People of these Colonies, solemnly publish and declare, That these United Colonies are, and of Right ought to be Free and Independent States; that they are Absolved from all Allegiance to the British Crown, and that all political connection between them and the State of Great Britain, is and ought to be totally dissolved; and that as Free and Independent States, they have full Power to levy War, conclude Peace, contract Alliances, establish Commerce, and to do all other Acts and Things which Independent States may of right do.—And for the support of this Declaration, with a firm reliance on the protection of divine Providence, we mutually pledge to each other our Lives, our Fortunes and our sacred Honor.

Hancock wrote William Cooper: "I hope we shall be a free and happy people, totally unfetter'd, and Releas'd from the Bonds of Slavery. That we may be thus free, Congress have done, and will still do, more, to promote it."[13] These were brave words. On the same day he wrote Washington: "Altho it is not possible to foresee the Consequences of Human Actions, yet is it nevertheless a Duty we owe ourselves and Posterity, in all our public Counsels, to decide in the best Manner we are able, and to leave the event to that Being who controls both Cause and Events to bring about his own determinations." He forwarded an attested copy of the declaration which he requested Washington to have "proclaimed at the Head of the Army in the way you shall think most proper."[14]

The appeal to "Posterity" was a constant theme in letters delegates wrote their wives and friends before and after the declaration. "Generations yet unborn" would hopefully enjoy a new quality of life in a new world. And members of Congress optimistically presumed "Divine Providence" must necessarily favor any struggle against a despot. The King, in his nightly prayers, presumably importuned the same God to withdraw His support from a cause instigated by rebels and supported by seditious traitors.

On Tuesday, July 9, John Adams wrote Samuel Chase, ". . . the river is passed and the bridge cut away," and gave him a brief description of events of the preceding day in Philadelphia. A great crowd assembled in the State House yard where the declaration was proclaimed by the Committee of Safety. "Three cheers rended the welkin. The battalions paraded on the Common, and gave us the *feu de joie,* notwithstanding the scarcity of powder. The bells rang all day and almost all night. Even the chimers chimed away."[15] Men deliberating in Philadelphia knew they had taken the irrevocable step: "a few weeks will probably determine our fate—perfect freedom or Absolute Slavery—to some of us, freedom or a halter."[16]

While delegates debated in humid Philadelphia, British warships and transports came into the waters off Long Island. On June 29 "a fleet of more than one hundred square rigged vessels" arrived at Sandy Hook. The British, so dispatches said, had sailed from Halifax and had come to New York "with a view of putting their cursed plans into execution. But Heaven, *we hope and trust,* will frustrate their cruel designs." H.M.S. *Greyhound,* with General William Howe aboard, anchored off Staten Island, where the general proposed to establish his headquarters. Howe was aware that behavior of his troops ashore might well be the critical factor that would influence American attitudes. He believed that most of the citizens were "well-affected to Government," and in his first General Order made it clear that any person found guilty of plundering would be executed "on the Spot."

His Majesty's general in America had scarcely settled himself and his official family in new surroundings before he and Admiral Shuldham began to quarrel. The general wanted Shuldham to send ships to patrol the North River above New York with a view to distressing Washington's army "upon the island of New York by obstructing their supplies." Shuldham at first agreed. Several days later, he had second thoughts; the river was too narrow; the channel was covered by numerous well-served rebel batteries; he did not think it either "prudent or advisable to risk two of His Majesty's ships." They would be much safer riding comfortably at anchor.

The British general expected soon to be heavily reinforced. He knew, too, that arrival of the fleet had been a beacon that would summon the militia—possibly more effectively than would urgent pleas from either Hancock or Washington. But he had high hopes of substantial help from well-disposed Americans, and on July 7 wrote Germain: "I have the satisfaction to inform your Lordship that there is great reason to expect a numerous body of the inhabitants to join the army from the provinces of New York, the Jerseys, and Connecticut, Who, in this time of universal apprehension only wait for opportunities to give proof of their loyalty and zeal for government." The general had been on Staten Island for a week when he wrote these words.‡ His letter served to confirm Lord

‡ Possibly he had been drinking too often and too long with Governor Tryon.

George in his opinion that a Redcoat presence would suffice to bring thousands to the royal standard.

The general, impatiently awaiting the arrival of his elder brother, now due any day, felt "the powers with which he is furnished will have the best effect on this critical time." But he still believed there could be no King's peace in America "until the rebel army is defeated." A few days later, H.M.S. *Eagle*, a newly commissioned 64 wearing the flag of Vice-admiral of the White Richard Viscount Howe, dropped the hook off Staten Island. For the first time a reasonably harmonious relationship between army and navy commanders in America seemed assured.

Viscount Howe had succeeded to the peerage when his elder brother, George, serving under the feckless and timid Abercrombie, had fallen at Ticonderoga during the War for Empire. George was highly esteemed in America. He had commanded Massachusetts troops, and the Bay Colony had raised a popular subscription for a monument to him which stands today in Westminster Abbey. Richard thus fell heir to American good will. He was a dour man, little given to words. In the Navy he was known as a fighting admiral: "Black Dick" always sailed toward the sound of the guns. He detested Lord George Germain and had little use for Sandwich. He enjoyed the confidence, if not the favor, of the King. He was a poor speaker who had trouble stringing his ideas together sequentially and developing them logically, and was liked, rather than respected as a debater, by parliamentary colleagues. But the admiral had not come to America to make speeches. He had come to make peace if he could, and if not, to make war. Both he and his younger brother thought the Americans misguided, but neither was personally hostile.**

The brothers had some appreciation of the potential strength of the colonies, and realized that putting down the rebellion would require a tremendous effort. The admiral, indeed, was secretly skeptical that the revolt *could* be put down by force of arms. Their enemies and detractors would later allege that their conduct was ambivalent, that they were too lenient, that they showed undue sympathy for traitors and rebels. None of these allegations can be sustained. The Howes were professional officers with distinguished records; there is no reason to believe either was disloyal to his King. But it is difficult to carry an olive branch in the left hand and in the right an unsheathed sword.

Viscount Howe brought with him a royal commission which granted him and his brother authority to pardon those who would lay down their arms, take an oath of allegiance, and submit. The brothers were specifically prohibited from negotiating with any rebel body, nor could they make any commitments respecting the rights and privileges Americans might expect to enjoy after they had cast themselves on their knees

---

** When standing for Parliament in the most recent election, the general had assured his constituents he would not fight against his transatlantic brethren.

before the throne. The admiral had battled long in London to gain more substantial bargaining authority. He had failed. Finally, he had accepted the best he could extract from an administration reluctant to concede anything to rebels, and set sail for America. He could not have been too sanguine.

He may well have become even less so when he read dispatches his brother and Admiral Shuldham brought him when they boarded *Eagle* to pay their respects, for he now learned that a few days earlier the Congress had declared American independence. A copy of the declaration that Ambrose Serle, the admiral's secretary, read with mounting anger, reduced him to an apoplectic state: ". . . the Villainy & the Madness of these deluded People . . . A more Impudent, false and Atrocious Proclamation was never fabricated by the Hands of Man." Serle's anger changed to "Horror at the daring Hypocrisy of these Men" who had called "upon GOD to witness the uprightness of their Proceedings." Worse, the signers had the "Audacity to calumniate the King and People of Great Britain."[17]

Serle's rage abated when Admiral Howe informed him an army commanded by Generals Carleton and Burgoyne was en route to Albany with 1,000 Indians; that the British had overtaken the fleeing rebels, "driven them into a Swamp and put about 500 of them to the Sword. The Troops hold them very cheap and long for an opportunity of revenging the Cause of their Countrymen, who fell at Bunker's Hill."[18]

On the following day, Viscount Howe sent a tactful letter to his old friend Franklin notifying the doctor that his flagship was lying off New York and informing him that he and his brother hoped their joint efforts as royal commissioners would promote the establishment of lasting peace and union with the colonies. At the same time, the general dispatched a letter to "George Washington, etc. etc., etc.," which the American commander in chief refused to accept. The young aide-de-camp who delivered this missive blandly informed Washington that the string of etceteras was meant to include "everything." "And anything," Washington is said to have remarked. Washington's insufferable behavior raised Serle's blood pressure; "So high is the Vanity and Insolence of these Men!" who were not in the least disposed to recognize "the Duties of Humanity, Law and Allegiance."

General Howe had testily announced he would recognize only titles and ranks conferred by the King; he soon realized that if he were to have any communication with Washington, he would have to address the American commander as "General." Thereafter, he reluctantly did so. The admiral's secretary continued to rage; the Americans "had blocked up every Answer to Peace"; there remained "No Alternative but War and Bloodshed."[19] Serle, a well-educated, observant young aristocrat, dined daily with Admiral Howe and high-ranking officers aboard *Eagle;* the sentiments he confided to his journal reflect his personal opinions, but no doubt mirror those expressed by senior admirals and generals after the cloth was drawn and bottles of madeira moved from hand to hand around the candlelit table in the admiral's cabin.

Washington knew the day of decision could not be long delayed. He feared a major landing momentarily and addressed the army in the following General Order:

> The time is now near at hand which must probably determine whether Americans are to be Freemen or Slaves. . . . The fate of unborn Millions will depend, under God, on the Courage and Conduct of this army—our cruel and unrelenting Enemy leaves us no choice but a brave resistance or the most abject submission. . . . We have therefore to conquer or die . . . and if we now shamefully fail, we shall become infamous to the whole world.

Some time in late June, Dr. Edward Bancroft, F.R.S., received the letter Silas Deane had sent from Philadelphia, and at once deduced that public rather than private business called this eminent Connecticut delegate to the Continental Congress to Paris. Secret Service agents in the London Post Office, who read all foreign mail, had no doubt arrived at a similar conclusion.

Before he left his native New England, Bancroft had apprenticed himself to a doctor, had picked up a rudimentary knowledge of medicine, and had learned how to compound pills and potions. He decided to practice his art in the Caribbean and eventually landed in Guiana, where on the Demerara River he encountered a British planter of substantial means named Paul Wentworth, who was related to the wealthy and aristocratic New Hampshire family of that name and distantly to the Marquis of Rockingham. Wentworth, a gentleman of obliging disposition, engaged the young man as plantation doctor and took him into the "big house" as a member of the family. Feeding pills to ailing Negroes did not occupy too much of Bancroft's time, most of which he devoted to serious study of tropical plants and experiments with medicinal herbs used by the natives to cure maladies peculiar to the region. The doctor, observant and analytical, became interested in arcane hallucinatory compounds of various sorts. He was ambitious, and determined not to waste his talents on a remote river plantation in the tropics. In 1767 he forsook Guiana and set out for London.

Bancroft was suave, and in no time talked himself into a staff position at St. Bartholomew's Hospital, where he made a good impression on his colleagues. He also found time to write several learned and instructive monographs that brought him to the notice of Benjamin Franklin, who encouraged him, as he did all those who devoted themselves to scientific endeavors. The doctor sponsored Bancroft for election to the Royal Society and interested him in the Vandalia Company, a speculative Ohio land scheme that was going to make the shareholders very rich indeed. But in the wake of colonial disturbances the Vandalia Company had collapsed; Franklin had left London, and the Americans, in this summer of 1776, were at war with the mother country. When he received Deane's letter, Bancroft made haste to put his personal and professional affairs in order, and set out for the rendezvous with his respected schoolmaster and business associate.

Deane arrived at Bordeaux in late June. Here he tarried until near the end of the month. He kept busy; he made connection with many leading merchants and bankers and reported to his partner Robert Morris that those he talked with seemed favorably inclined to his proposals for trade. He discovered prospects for grain cargoes to be good, and left for Paris in an optimistic mood.†† In the capital, he proceeded at once to call on Dr. Franklin's friend, M. Barbeu Dubourg, who would introduce him to Vergennes. At his banker's, Deane found a letter from one Monsieur de Beaumarchais, who wrote that for some time past he had "cherished a desire to aid the brave Americans to shake off the British yoke" and had attempted in various ways "to begin secret and reliable business relations between the general Congress and a firm that I have formed for this purpose." He had discussed the matter with "a person in England" (Arthur Lee), but as nothing concrete had developed, he was now hoping to conduct negotiations "in a surer and more connected manner." Beaumarchais's decision to deal with Deane rather than with Arthur Lee, whom he did not trust, was the genesis of the undercover campaign Lee waged to ruin his compatriot.‡‡

Dr. Bancroft arrived in Paris several days later. Over a bottle of bordeaux, one of the three or four dozen Deane had brought along from the port without the formality of paying French excise taxes, the onetime Hartford schoolmaster and his star pupil renewed an old friendship. After several convivial suppers, a contract was drawn. By its terms the doctor agreed to act as Deane's confidential agent in London and to forward regular reports on political and military matters. Deane provided Bancroft with instructions, a code, and made a down payment for services to be rendered.

Bancroft was well equipped by character, temperament, and intelligence for the assignment. In London he was in a position to pick up a great deal of valuable information and had the wit to put together the bits and pieces. And he was above suspicion. Deane took Bancroft com-

†† A certain proportion, perhaps as much as 30 per cent of the grain or tobacco shipped to France, was to be shipped on private account. Morris and Deane then stood to make fortunes.

‡‡ Arthur Lee's subsequent behavior proved him to be an irresponsible and meretricious intriguer. Fortunately for the American cause, Beaumarchais chose to deal exclusively with Silas Deane.

pletely into his confidence, revealed to him details of his instructions from the Secret Committee, and outlined several projects to which he proposed the eminent doctor devote his attention when he returned to London.

Shortly after his sessions with Silas Deane, Dr. Bancroft met another old friend—Paul Wentworth, who years earlier had put the young man on his payroll in Surinam, and who, since his return to London from the tropics in 1772, had been agent for his native colony of New Hampshire. Since 1772, Wentworth had also been working for William Eden, Lord Suffolk's undersecretary, and in the absence of John Robinson, responsible for British intelligence in France. Eden, a guileful and ambitious schemer, had recently sent Wentworth to Paris wth a good expense account, encouraged him to find a mistress and rent a carriage, and entrusted him with the task of organizing and controlling an espionage network targeted on the increasing French aid to the colonies and the developing informal relationship between them and Versailles. Wentworth already knew who Silas Deane was, and suspected why he was in Paris.

In the course of several pleasant conversations with Bancroft, it became clear to Wentworth that the doctor was the answer to his prayers. Apparently, no discreet recruiting procedure was necessary. Bancroft was in a position to supply what Wentworth needed: current reliable reports of political and supply transactions between France and the rebellious Americans. Wentworth had what Bancroft wanted: money, and plenty of it. In a few days the contract was drawn up and duly signed, and Edward Bancroft, M.D., F.R.S., cover name "Mr. Edwards," went to work for the British.

Bancroft's initial report to Wentworth was comprehensive. He gave full details of Deane's first interview with Vergennes, during which the Foreign Minister discreetly refused to commit himself other than to promise his ministry would "favor the United Colonies in every reasonable way." He did, however, express his private opinion that were the colonies "finally determined to reject the Sovereignty of His Brittanick Majesty, it would not be the Interest of France to see them reduced by Force." Finally, he assured Deane that the Americans enjoyed "the unanimous good Wishes of the Government and People of France." As a result of this meeting, Vergennes ordered French arsenals to release 13,000 muskets, which Deane immediately arranged to have shipped from Nantes.

During the next week, Deane met frequently with Conrad Alexandre Gérard, senior secretary in the Bureau of Foreign Affairs, and on July 20 was again received by the minister. At this audience, Deane revealed the full extent of his instructions from the Secret Committee: 25,000 stand of small arms, an equal number of complete uniforms, and 200 brass cannon. Vergennes promised the weapons, and M. le Rey de Chaumont, "a gentleman of great Property who lives at Passy," undertook to supply the uniforms on a generous basis. He personally advanced Deane a credit of one million livres.

Vergennes had previously written Deane recommending "a Mr. Beaumarchais . . . as one who would with great Secrecy, & on the best Terms supply the Congress with such other Goods and Commodities as they might want, and Mr. Beaumarchais offered to credit them with Merchandise, etc., to the Amount of Three Millions of Livres." Deane had been wary of dealings with Beaumarchais, but shortly after receiving assurance from Vergennes, opened negotiations.

In mid-August, Dr. Bancroft set out for London. For the moment, at least, he had learned almost everything his British employers wanted to know. Rarely has any secret intelligence service been so well served as was William Eden's by Dr. Edward Bancroft in the summer and autumn of 1776.

3

A Glorious Achievement

New York was seen by both Americans and British as a pivotal position of great strategic value. Once in firm possession of Manhattan Island, with its surrounding waters dominated by his brother's men-of-war, Howe could swing quickly into either New Jersey or Connecticut, or punch up the Hudson to seize the Highlands and co-operate with an invading force from Canada. Protected waters gave ample space for a great fleet and the train of transports and victualers required to move and support his army. Residents of lower New York, Long Island, and adjacent New Jersey and Connecticut were reported favorably inclined to the King's cause; Howe's optimistic expectation was that he would have no trouble recruiting a number of Provincial battalions.

Manhattan offered useful conveniences for docking, billeting, and warehousing. The island could be held with ease by a fairly small force supported by the navy. Here ships could be hauled out, careened, cleaned, and refitted, and amphibious expeditions secretly and securely mounted. There was reasonable hope that a variety of fresh food and forage could readily be had in exchange for the King's golden guineas. Obviously, domination of the waters around Manhattan and the Hudson to the Highlands opened a wide variety of tactical combinations to the brothers Howe, who could land troops and artillery anywhere they chose.

This was quite as apparent to Washington as it was to the British. With control of the surrounding waters held by Viscount Howe's fleet, he could not hope to hold New York for long. Why then, despite the advice of several of his generals, did he decide to try to do so? On May 5 he wrote Congress he was unable to form an "accurate opinion" of Howe's plans, as "the designs of the Enemy are too much behind the Curtain." But it appeared to him a practical certainty the British objective would be New York, as no place ". . . seemed of more Importance in the execution of their grand Plan than possessing themselves of Hudson's River."[1]

Surely he must have considered factors since overlooked. First, during April, May, and June, the question of a declaration of independence hung in balance. As of late June, New York and New Jersey, two populous and wealthy colonies, had not taken the irrevocable decision. Not until June 25 did New Jersey elect five delegates instructed to support the Virginia resolution offered by R. H. Lee. New York, where Tory sentiment ran strong, made no move. The situation in Canada had deteriorated rapidly; by early June it was disastrous. A decision to abandon the city, the most important on the Atlantic seaboard, would profoundly influence opinion in the two wavering colonies, as well as in adjacent Connecticut. Following on the Canadian debacle, it would almost certainly put an emphatic period to negotiations Silas Deane was bidden to undertake in France. At home, it would undermine the prestige of Congress and the army, and otherwise cause irreparable psychological damage. Patriots would be disheartened, Tories vastly encouraged, and neutrals, still by far the majority, strongly influenced to cast their lot with the crown. Too, it would have serious repercussions in England, strengthening the position of the ministers and weakening that of Opposition. If Washington would not fight for New York, what *would* he fight for?

Washington was reasonably confident that on ground of his own choosing he had a chance to defeat the British, or at least to inflict unacceptably high casualties. He had talked to many who had seen Howe in action at Bunker Hill. Obstinate indeed the British general was. But what tactical imagination did he have? Washington's opinion that he was not an aggressive commander had been formed during the long winter in Cambridge when Howe had quietly allowed him to pay off one dissatisfied army and create an almost wholly new one.

To defend the city Washington had fewer than 18,000 troops. Of these, 3,600 were sick and unfit for duty. His miscellaneous manhandled ordnance was inadequate as to both number of pieces and weight of metal. He had no cavalry; a single troop of fifty horsemen for patrol and picket duties would have been invaluable. Only eight soldiers in ten had muskets; two in ten, bayonets. A considerable number were armed with homemade pikes and old sabers. The army was perennially short of flints, powder, shoes, tentage, and blankets. Most of the troops, short-term militiamen who would not face cold steel, were ill disciplined and thought of nothing but going home. Any realistic assessment must have indicated that Washington could not hope to hold Manhattan with the force available.

But unorthodox tactics could exact a heavy toll of British and German regulars. He should have learned this lesson from "the affair" of April 19. Instead he spread his army from King's Bridge on the northern tip of Manhattan Island to Bedford on Long Island, a front of almost sixteen miles. Apparently anticipating that Howe would again perform as he had at Bunker Hill, he put 5,500 in the Brooklyn lines. He underestimated the force Howe had to throw against him, and what impelled him ultimately to hazard more than half his effectives in a forward position was a mystery to some of his generals. He had not yet developed that full appreciation of the flexibility of sea power which would later distinguish him. Nor had he assessed William Howe accurately; the British general *had* learned something at Bunker Hill.

Daily, frigates and transports came in and anchored. On August 1 Clinton and Parker, no longer on speaking terms, returned from their wasteful enterprise in South Carolina, and soon thereafter Commodore Hotham arrived from England with a string of transports crammed with sick and sweating Hessians. General officer and staff conferences were now the order of the day. From dawn to dusk boats flitted from ship to ship. As they came alongside, crews tossed oars, and belaced young staff officers, tightly hugging dispatch boxes, climbed swaying rope ladders. On deck, side boys were prepared to hoist aboard corpulent captains. A covy of barges lay off Staten Island waiting to return Lord Howe's commodores and his brother's British and German generals and colonels to their ships.

"A fleet majestical" rode the waters off Long Island. Here Viscount Howe had assembled four hundred sail. Victualing ships and transports were packed with regiments of foot, Highlanders, dragoons, Hessians, light infantry, grenadiers. This army, by far the largest Britain had ever yet sent beyond the seas, numbered 32,000.* Howe commanded a superb fighting force, well equipped, well disciplined, and anxious to be turned loose on the rebels. Officers and men who the year before had endured the galling humiliation of two bloody encounters, nine months of close confinement in Boston enforced by rebellious warders, and a long and bitter winter in Halifax, were anxious to wet their swords and bayonets in Yankee blood.

General Howe decided to make an initial landing on the west end of

* Rank and file.

Long Island. He organized his landing force into seven tactical brigades: five battalions of light infantry and dismounted dragoons, and a formidable reserve consisting chiefly of four battalions of grenadiers. He selected Gravesend Bay as the landing area and set the assault for Thursday, August 22. He proposed to move next against the American battle positions on Brooklyn Heights, from which his artillery could command lower Manhattan.

During Wednesday night, a torrential rain deluged the area: "A most terrible Evening of Thunder, Lightning, Wind & Rain; the most vehement I ever saw, or that has been known here by the Inhabitants for many Years." The heavenly electrical display terrified American militiamen huddling under soaked blankets; half a dozen were electrocuted by bolts of lightning or crushed by crashing trees. Was this an ominous portent? Many untutored men huddling in trenches on Long Island and waiting sleepless in shredded tents on Staten Island or in crowded quarters aboard His Majesty's transports no doubt believed it was.

At dawn, British and Germans with sharpened bayonets and three days' supply of cooked food and ammunition began embarking in flat-hulled landing craft that soon after would beach on the sands of Gravesend Bay. The landing, precise and methodical, met no opposition; assault troops advanced to a previously selected beachhead line and immediately posted strong pickets. Inland, farmers set fire to their haystacks and standing grain and drove livestock toward the east. Viscount Howe's secretary described the scene:

> The Soldiers and Sailors seemed as merry as in a Holiday, and regaled themselves with the fine apples which hung everywhere upon the Trees in great abundance. . . . the Disembarkation of about 15,000 Troops upon a fine Beach, their forming upon the adjacent Plain, a fleet of above 300 Ships & Vessels with their Sails spread open to day, the Sun shining clear upon them, the green Hills and Meadows after the Rain, and the calm Surface of the Water upon the contiguous Sea and up the Sound, exhibited one of the finest & most picturesque Scenes that the Imagination can fancy or the Eye behold.

Still, all this might did not guarantee victory, for "there is no assurance but in Him . . . who giveth the victory when and where and how He pleaseth."[2]

On the three days following, British and Germans sent out reconnaissance patrols. American riflemen harassed them, and on the nights of August 25 and 26 Colonel Edward Hand's Pennsylvania rifle battalion tried without much success to beat up the Hessian cantonment. The Germans were not accustomed to this grossly unethical way of conducting a war and complained bitterly. Howe had taken his time, but by the eve-

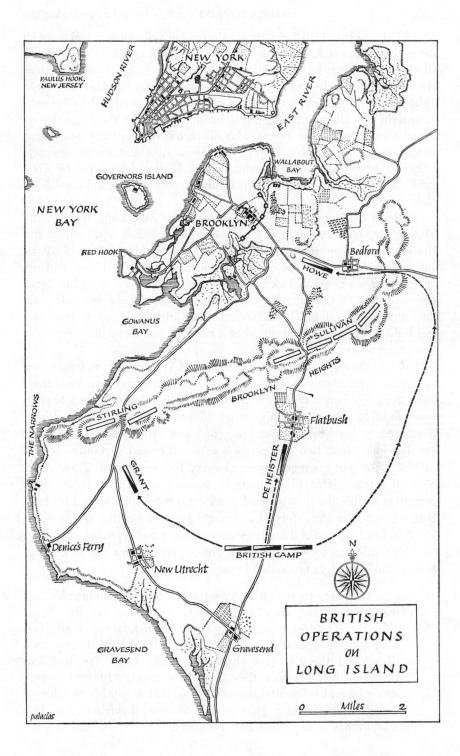

PAULUS HOOK,
NEW JERSEY

HUDSON RIVER

NEW YORK

EAST RIVER

WALLABOUT
BAY

GOVERNORS ISLAND

NEW YORK
BAY

BROOKLYN

RED HOOK

Bedford

HOWE

GOWANUS
BAY

SULLIVAN

HEIGHTS

STIRLING

BROOKLYN

Flatbush

THE NARROWS

GRANT

DE HEISTER

N

Denice's Ferry

BRITISH CAMP

New Utrecht

GRAVESEND
BAY

Gravesend

BRITISH
OPERATIONS
on
LONG ISLAND

0   Miles   2

palacios

ning of the twenty-fifth his patrols, after some skirmishing, had marked the outline and left flank of the forward American position. The general studied the reports; he planned a fixing operation in the front (Lieutenant General Philip de Heister), a secondary attack on the American right (Major General James Grant), and a main blow, commanded by himself, to turn the American left, hanging in the air, and get to their rear. Howe hoped thus to crush the rebels who distracted on the front and right, would be smashed by his deep envelopment. At 2 A.M. on the twenty-seventh a powerful column commanded by Clinton set off led by Tory guides well acquainted with the roads and bypaths. Howe enjoined complete silence.

At dawn De Heister's artillery opened on the Americans; on the British left, Major General Grant, who not too long before had assured the House of Commons that with 5,000 troops he could march easily from one end of America to the other, advanced skirmishers. Howe had ordered these two generals to keep the Americans "in play" until his signal guns indicated that the striking force was well into the enemy's rear. This they did to perfection. The defenders, their attention fixed to the front and right flank, had no warning that a cataract was about to overwhelm them from the rear.

Only on the right, commanded by General William Alexander, known in the American Army as Lord Stirling, was there sustained resistance. Here a bloody battle raged for hours; Brigadier General Lord Stirling was a fighting general, and his troops, who admired and respected him, responded to his lead. It was said (and generally believed) that his lordship loved best two things—wine and battle—and certainly on that August 27 he and his men contested every foot of ground. Their stand held off Grant (later to be unjustly accused of lack of vigor) long enough to enable the disorganized American center commanded by John Sullivan to flee to the safety of a strongly fortified position on Brooklyn Heights. Lord Stirling and Sullivan were among 1,100 captured.

This battle was serious, but not a critical, setback for the Americans. It was bloody enough, no doubt of that:

> . . . the Scots regiments behaved with the greatest bravery and carried the day after an obstinate resistance on the Rebel side. . . . The *Hessians* and our brave *Highlanders* gave no quarters; and it was a fine sight to see with what alacrity they dispatched the Rebels with their bayonets after we had surrounded them so that they could not resist. Multitudes were drowned and suffocated in morasses—a proper punishment for all Rebels. . . . It was a glorious achievement, my friend, and will immortalize us and crush Rebel Colonies.

The British command had propagated a rumor that the Americans would give the Hessians no quarter "which made them fight desperately, and put all to death that fell into their hands." The writer, a Highland officer, concluded this cheerful epistle by assuring his friend that "the affair will be over this campaign, and we shall all return covered with *American* laurels and have the cream of *American* land allotted us for our services."[3] The night of August 27, 1776, these expectations seemed reasonable.

But now Howe, with everything going for him, his enemy bloodied, despondent, and in almost total disarray, did not follow up. Instead, he sat down in front of the entrenchments on Brooklyn Heights and prepared to run orthodox approaches to Washington's lines. The Americans were at a loss to understand just what he was up to. They thought the engineering effort was some sort of elaborate ruse: "Our intrenchment was so weak that it is most wonderful the British general did not attempt to storm it after the battle in which his troops had been victorious."[4]

Washington crossed to Long Island on the morning of the twenty-eighth, inspected the Brooklyn Heights position, and proceeded to compound his initial near-fatal mistake by ordering two more battalions to cross the East River. During the twenty-ninth the commander in chief was under constant pressure from his subordinates to withdraw from Brooklyn. That afternoon he decided to do so, and after darkness fell the troops began to thin out and file quietly from the works they were no doubt delighted to leave.

This evacuation in the face of a vastly superior enemy, meticulously planned, perfectly co-ordinated, and executed in silence, was eloquent testimony to good staff work. During the night of August 29, Colonel John Glover's Marblehead fishermen, hands blistered, arms numb, and backs aching, made repeated trips across the East River, and brought 9,000 men to safety on Manhattan Island. The commander in chief crossed in the last boat in a dismal dawn. When the fog lifted, Howe's cautious patrols found the Brooklyn positions abandoned. The admiral could and should have stationed rowing boats in the channel to observe American actions. Had the withdrawal been detected, as under such circumstances it must have been, his brother's army could have broken it up, or at least impeded it. The oversight was quite unlike Lord Howe, ordinarily a most thorough officer.

One immediate result of the battle on Long Island was to increase British contempt of the Americans. Serle thought they behaved "very ill . . . a hopeful Rabble and worthy of their Cause." He conversed at length with Sullivan and Lord Stirling who dined with the admiral the night of their capture. Sullivan was too loquacious; he must have expressed himself unreservedly, for Serle wrote that Washington's army was "rent with Distractions, about 3000 sick of a contagious Disorder [dysentery?] distressed in their Circumstances, and all in a Panic." The admiral's secretary was sure "the Hand of GOD" was upon the Americans, who had "little to hope & every thing to fear."[5] Major General Sullivan would have served the cause better had he imbibed less of the admiral's madeira.

Although he rejoiced in the victory gained, Serle was worried over reports of depredations committed by Hessians on Staten Island: "I fear our Employment of these upon this Service will tend to irritate and inflame the Americans infinitely more than two or three British Armies upon such an Occasion." "Some Deference," he wrote, "should be paid to the Goodwill of Mankind." When he visisted Long Island a few days later he was appalled at "the Devastations which the Hessians have made upon the Houses and Country Seats of some of the Rebels. All their Furniture, Glasses, Windows and the very Hangings of the Rooms are demolished or defaced."[6] Howe had issued strict orders against ravaging and plundering, but as their future behavior amply testified, something more than a piece of paper was required to control the rapacity of the Germans.

So ended the Long Island campaign, from which Howe emerged as an able tactician. But a good army commander is supposed to know what to do with victory. On August 27 Howe threw away opportunity. He later attempted to justify his failure to push home an attack with the plea that it would have been too costly. Possibly. But strengths and weaknesses of the defense could have been determined by a series of probing attacks. His enemy was demoralized; the odds were all in his favor. One can scarcely imagine Wolfe allowing Washington to escape this trap. After animadverting on Howe's lack of drive, Fortescue, in his *History of the British Army,* wrote of Washington: "It is less easy to defend the American general who, for no possible advantage, deliberately exposed an advanced detachment to the certainty of destruction by a superior force."[7]

Two days later, Nathanael Greene wrote Washington, urging him to pull the army off Manhattan. He concluded:

> I give it as my opinion, that a general and speedy retreat is absolutely necessary, and that the honour and interest of *America* require it. I would burn the city and suburbs and that for the following reasons: If the enemy gets possession of the city we can never recover the possession without a superior naval force to theirs; it will deprive the enemy of an opportunity to barracking their whole army together which, if they could do, would be a very great security. . . . It will deprive them of a general market. . . .

> All these advantages would result from the destruction of the city, and not one benefit can arise to us from its preservation, that I can conceive of.[8]

Charles Lee, just returned from South Carolina, concurred. Washington, however, possibly conceived a benefit that could arise, namely, that if he spared the city the war might be kept within bounds. Putting the torch to New York might indeed temporarily deprive Howe of barracking facilities, but it would invite devastation of every coastal city and town Black Dick's fleet could bring under its guns.

The morale of Howe's army was now at a peak. British and Germans had tasted easy victory on Long Island and were enjoying the deserved fruits. Farmers drove in herds of well-fattened hogs, sheep, and beeves. Their wives peddled Indian corn, beans, peas, apples, and pears; fishermen brought their varied catches. Long Islanders sensibly (if unpatriotically) preferred solid money that weighted their pockets to Continental paper. Officers appointed for the purpose of administering oaths of allegiance to the crown and granting the King's pardon worked endlessly to serve long queues of Americans only too eager to get their hands into Howe's inexhaustible golden treasury.

But despite the glorious achievement of August 27, few joined the army. Lieutenant Frederick Mackenzie, who had marched with Colonel Francis Smith to Concord, was with his regiment, the Royal Welch Fusiliers, on Long Island. He had expected many Americans to come over: "When the Army was on Staten Island, we were made to expect that as soon as we should land on this Island, many thousand of the Inhabitants would show their loyalty and join the Army. But we have seen very little to induce us to believe that the Inhabitants of this Island are more loyal than the others."[9]

While the army was fighting the British on Long Island, Congress, safely cloistered in Philadelphia, pushed ahead with unwonted alacrity to complete long-deferred projects. A Committee of the Whole approved a working draft of Articles of Confederation and of significant amendments to Articles of War for the governance of the armed forces. Most important of all, "a plan of a treaty of foreign alliance" received committee approval. And great news had come from William Bingham, the able agent in Martinique: "France will soon take an active part in our favor. She has opened all her ports to our Merchandize, privateers and prizes, and has offered us Warlike Stores in the Islands, and every other Article which may tend to induce an intercourse with her."[10]

On the first day of September, Major General Sullivan appeared in Philadelphia on parole. He brought a message to Congress from Viscount Howe, the purport of which was that the admiral wished to meet with several delegates "in their private capacities" to discuss reconciliation. Many members considered the invitation delusive and insulting, and were not interested in listening to Sullivan. After debate, he was received on September 3, when he informed Congress that the British naval commander in chief, in his capacity of peace commissioner, desired to explore the possibilities of an accommodation: "he was very willing to meet at almost any place, a number of the members of Congress" (as private gentlemen, for he could not recognize any such body as Congress) "to try if they could make any proposals. . . ."

John Adams wrote Warren on the following day: "Lord Howe is surrounded with disaffected American Machiavellians, Exiles from Boston and elsewhere, who are instigating him to mingle Art with Force. He has sent Sullivan here, upon Parol, with the most insidious, 'tho ridiculous message which you can conceive. It has put Us rather in a delicate Situation, and gives Us much Trouble."[11] Congress was indeed in a delicate situation; should the delegates accede to Howe's request, radicals would assail them for grasping at straws; if they rejected it, moderates would accuse them with equal vigor of seeking needlessly to prolong strife and bloodshed. As Adams later wrote, times were critical: "The attention of Congress, the army, the States, and the people, ought to have been wholly directed to the defence of the country. To have it diverted and relaxed, by such a poor artifice and confused tales, appeared very reprehensible" (i.e., of Sullivan, to have accepted such a mission).[12] Even as Sullivan was speaking, Adams whispered to a colleague that he wished the first musket ball fired on Long Island had gone through the general's head.

Although most members of Congress were convinced the Howe brothers had nothing substantial to offer and feared acceptance of the admiral's invitation would strengthen the Tories and dishearten the army, they reluctantly decided to accept, and elected Dr. Franklin, John Rutledge, and John Adams members of an informal embassy to Howe "to ask a few questions and take his answers." Adams did not wish to accept the charge. He had been "against the idea from first to last." Nevertheless, on September 9 the three emissaries set off for Staten Island via New Brunswick, Franklin and Rutledge in horse-drawn chaises and Adams, perhaps desirous of maintaining the character of a staunch New England farmer, on horseback.

The trip across New Jersey was instructive and for the observant Adams a disheartening experience: "On the road, and at all the public houses, we saw such numbers of officers and soldiers, straggling and loitering, as gave me, at least, but a poor opinion of the discipline of our forces, and excited as much indignation as anxiety. Such thoughtless dissipation, at a time so critical, was not calculated to inspire very sanguine hopes, or give great courage to ambassadors."† The following morning the three proceeded to Perth Amboy, embarked in the admiral's barge, and were rowed to Staten Island.

Viscount Howe met them at the landing and made apologies for his absent brother, unfortunately detained by press of business. "We walked up to the house between guards of grenadiers, looking fierce as ten Furies, and making all the grimaces, and gestures, and motions of their muskets, with bayonets fixed, which, I suppose, military etiquette requires, but which we neither understood nor regarded." Howe had prepared "a large handsome room" in the house, "otherwise dirty as a stable," to receive his guests. A carpet of moss covered the floor; the walls were decorated with green sprigs, shrubs, and flowers. Adams found it "not only Wholesome, but romantically elegant; and he entertained us with good claret, good bread, cold ham, tongue and mutton."

After the collation, Howe stated his power was limited to conferring, advising, and consulting. He was not a plenipotentiary, but a commissioner, empowered to grant the King's pardon to those who would lay down their arms and return to allegiance. He did not mention the fact that certain Americans, among them two of the three present (Franklin and Adams), had been specifically excluded from royal clemency.

Having perused a copy of his lordship's commission, Franklin replied that as it contained no other offer than "pardon upon submission" he was distressed the admiral "had been sent so far on so hopeless a business. . . . It is impossible we should think of submission to a government that has with the most wanton barbarity and cruelty burnt our defenceless towns in the midst of winter, excited the savages to massacre our farmers, and our slaves to murder their masters, and is even now buying foreign mercenaries to deluge our settlements with blood. These atrocious injuries have extinguished every remaining spark of affection for that parent country we once held so dear. . . ." He reminded Howe of his own unremitting endeavors "to preserve from breaking, that fine and noble China vase, the British empire," and closed with the assertion that the war was both "unjust and unwise. . . . I am persuaded that cool dispassionate posterity will condemn to infamy those who advised it; and that even success will not save from some degree of dishonor, those who voluntarily engaged to conduct it."[13]

The ambassadors made it clear that America "would not again come under the domination of Great Britain" and would "never treat in any

---

† Adams's observations on the distressing state of the army in New Jersey were confirmed by an English traveler who happened to be in Newark at the same time the three reluctant emissaries from Philadelphia were en route to Staten Island. In his journal, Nicholas Cresswell wrote that "the Yankeemen" he saw were "the nastiest devils in creation . . . ragged, dirty, sickly and ill disciplined. If my countrymen are beaten by these ragamuffins I shall be much surprized."

other character" than as a sovereign, independent state. The discussion apparently ended on this note. Adams had predicted that nothing would come of the meeting, and nothing had. Had the admiral arrived in late May armed with plenary powers, or even with power to declare a cessation of hostilities pending future negotiations, the course of history might conceivably have been changed.

During early September Howe began moving his brigades to Hell Gate. There he lingered for several weeks. This delay allowed Washington ample time to have withdrawn all but outposting and harassing detachments from Manhattan and to have moved the main body of the army inland, away from the water to an area where he could be approached only from landward, where he could find stronger defensive terrain and unrestricted maneuver room with escape routes into Connecticut or across the Hudson if dangerously pressed. But he was reluctant to abandon "the Key to the Northern Country." He compromised: He left a sizable force in lower Manhattan and some 3,000 others to man the Kip's Bay position on the East River.

He was, however, groping for a strategy to guide him in future campaigns, and wrote Hancock on September 7: ". . . the War should be defensive . . . we should on all Occasions avoid a general Action or put anything to Risque unless compelled by a necessity, into which we ought never to be drawn."[14] He saw clearly that the best "System" was to prolong the war. In London, Horace Walpole, whose opinions so often reflected the private views of his admired cousin, General Henry Seymour Conway, had written: "The best chance of the Americans was by protracting the war."[15]

Although Clinton had developed the scheme of maneuver which won Howe a signal tactical success on Long Island, the commander in chief was not sympathetic to his deputy's suggestions for future operations. Howe wanted to land at Kip's Bay (East 34th Street); cross Manhattan to the North River; realign; move on Harlem Heights and King's Bridge and literally push the Americans off the island. This cautious, regulated, step-by-step operation involved little risk, but ceded the advantage of time to Washington. Clinton's purpose was more imaginative: He urged Howe to move to Hell Gate, cross into Westchester, and march north to block Washington's escape routes eastward toward Connecticut. He would then be forced either to give battle at grave disadvantage or attempt to flee across the Hudson, a move Admiral Howe's men-of-war could readily block. The difference in tactical concept is striking. Howe's objective was Manhattan Island; Clinton's, to trap and destroy Washington's army.‡

For some days tidal conditions prevented Viscount Howe's landing

‡ Because of the tidal currents, crossing at Hell Gate would indeed have been difficult; possibly Admiral Howe vetoed Clinton's plan.

craft from getting up the East River under a cover of darkness, but on Sunday, September 15, after a furious cannonading of the American works, Clinton's assault troops landed at Kip's Bay. "The Rebels . . . apparently frightened by the horrid din—deserted all their works in the utmost precipitation." According to Admiral Howe's flag secretary, the populace received the British with open arms. Possibly these "manifestations of Joy" delayed Clinton, for he did not push rapidly across the island to the Hudson. Several thousand Continentals thus managed to escape from the southern tip of Manhattan to Washington's lines on Harlem Heights. Howe now realigned and turned north, but at Harlem ran into a strong position in considerable depth, with both flanks anchored on water—the right on the Hudson, the left on the Harlem. The position could not be turned except by an amphibious operation. Clinton had earlier suggested a landing north of King's Bridge, but his proposal was rejected by Admiral Howe, who feared his fleet could not safely run upriver past the batteries at Fort Lee on the Jersey shore and Fort Washington on Manhattan.

On the early morning of September 21 a fire broke out in the city. The Americans had made off with every church bell in town for melting down and casting into cannon, so there was no way to give the alarm. The fire engines were broken and the few leather buckets available leaked. Wind favored the flames, and soon about one fourth of the city was caught in a roaring conflagration, eventually brought under control only thanks to a shift in the wind. The British, naturally enough, blamed the Americans for this "excess of villainy." Actually, Washington had received explicit instructions from Congress to take "special care" that his troops did no damage to New York, as "Congress had no doubt of being able to recover same."

The morning after the fire a young Yale graduate, a captain in the Continental Army who had been picked up in New York dressed in civilian clothes, his pockets stuffed with sketches and notes, was hanged as a spy. A British captain who witnessed Nathan Hale's execution recorded that he behaved "with great composure and resolution."**

The fire gave the British general a few days to make up his mind about what to do next. He had apparently landed on Long Island with no plan that embraced the contingency of a successful American withdrawal; now he was stopped before the Heights of Harlem. Obviously, instead of trying to batter down the barred front door, he should go around to the side and kick in the garden gate. But he wasted three weeks before he arrived at this conclusion.

Possibly at this time Howe was simply waiting for the Continental Army to disintegrate, for it was indeed on the verge of doing so. Washington was frustrated and as close to despair as he ever allowed himself

** Legend has it that the Yale Club stands upon the site.

to be. At Kip's Bay, when he and other officers made vain efforts to rally the fleeing troops, the general was "so exasperated that he struck several officers in their flight, three times dashed his hatt on the ground, and at last exclaimed, 'Good God, have I got such troops as those.'"[16] In his report to Congress he said the defenders ran off in disorder; troops ordered to support them flew "in every direction in the greatest confusion." Conduct on this occasion was "disgraceful and dastardly."[17]

There is ample evidence that many senior officers were losing confidence in the commander in chief, who himself admitted that he was then in "a divided state of mind." Apparently, he was in the trough of a profound depression: what Boswell (and much later Winston Churchill) described as "the Black Dog." He certainly had every reason to be. Even Henry Knox, the optimistic and redoubtable chief of artillery, was deeply worried: ". . . the bulk of the officers of the army are a parcel of ignorant, stupid men. . . . I am chagrinned . . . many late affairs, of which I've been an eye-witness, have so totally sickened me that unless some very different mode of conduct is observed in the formation of the new army, I shall not think obliged by either the laws of God or nature to risk my reputation on so cobweb a foundation."

At this time Washington sent John Hancock a long letter, surely one of the most important he ever dispatched to a president of Congress. In this analysis of the current situation and the temper of his troops the general wrote: "We are now, as it were, upon the eve of another dissolution of our army." Prospects for the future were "gloomy"; Washington foresaw "beyond the possibility of doubt" that the cause would be lost "unless some speedy, and effectual measures are adopted by Congress." The essential business was to establish the army "upon a permanent footing," that is, enlistments for a period of at least three years or the duration. One-year enlistments had been tried; they had been found to be far more trouble than worth. Men must be offered substantial inducement to join the army: a suit of clothes, a generous bounty, regular pay, an allotment of a hundred acres at honorable separation from the service, pensions for themselves and their widows.

Equally imperative was a system to induce "Gentlemen and Men of Character" to take up commissions. As things stood, the men had no respect for their officers, whom they regarded as little better than "broomstocks." There was far too much egalitarianism in the army; this induced a spirit of insubordination. Officers were finding it increasingly difficult to control their men, and the more depraved among them had actually participated in plundering expeditions. General courts-martial were reluctant to convict, and many who should have been ignominiously cashiered were suffered to remain in service.

Congress had placed its hopes in the militia, but "To place any dependence upon Militia is, assuredly, resting upon a broken staff." The

principal ailment afflicting them was homesickness; "such an inconquera-
ble desire of returning to their respective homes" that there were wholesale "shameful and scandalous Desertions." Nor would the militia brook
necessary restraints "without which licentiousness, and every kind of disorder triumphantly reign."[18]

The commander in chief chose a good moment to dispatch this particular letter; events of the next few weeks brought home to Congress the
necessity for speedy and radical remedial action if the Continental Army,
and the cause it served, were to be saved. The series of almost desperate
letters Washington wrote John Hancock from Harlem Heights and White
Plains produced the desired effect. He had help from his corpulent chief
of artillery who for some time had been urging "a permanent standing
army . . . to exist during the war." On September 16 Congress resolved
that eighty-eight battalions of infantry should be enlisted for the duration. Bounties were authorized, as were grants of land ranging from five
hundred acres to be given a colonel to a hundred for a private.

Debate on creation of a standing army had been lengthy and acerbic.
John Adams was a persuasive proponent of the measure; even before the
battle on Long Island he had written Henry Knox: "I am a constant Advocate for a regular Army and the most masterly Discipline, because I
know, that without these We cannot reasonably hope to be a powerful, a
prosperous, or a free People, and therefore, I have been constantly
labouring to obtain an handsome Encouragement for inlisting a permanent body of Troops."[19] Something more than Adams's constant labors,
both indoors and out, had been needed to allay the apprehensions of
those who rested their hopes upon the "broken staff" of a militia. The
British victory on Long Island, and Washington's urgent pleas, provided
the necessary impetus.

Belated recognition of need for an army enlisted for three years or
the duration was one thing; raising it, quite another. Hancock appealed
to the states "to bend all attention" to enlisting the quotas assigned:
"When the bloody Standard of Tyranny" was raised "in a land of Liberty, no good man, no friend of his country, can possibly remain an inactive Spectator of her Fall." Despite Hancock's exhortations, many who
should have joined would remain "inactive Spectators."[20]

Next on Adams's agenda was to gain congressional assent to proposed
revisions of the Articles of War. He and Jefferson were members of the
committee that had worked on this project, but as Jefferson rarely spoke,
Adams had to fight the amended articles through, paragraph by
paragraph, on the floor. He argued with zealous conviction and considerable emotion. "Discipline, discipline" had been his constant theme, for
he "saw very clearly that the ruin of our cause and country must be the
consequence, if a thorough reformation and strict discipline, could not be
introduced."[21] The commander in chief had written that the Mosaic

thirty-nine lashes, the limit he was authorized to inflict, were not enough to deter men from deserting, plundering, and gross insubordination.

Washington was still not at all happy with officer's pay scales, or bounty offered men to enlist. Congress was on the whole opposed to increasing pay for officers. To many radicals, the differentials the commander in chief urged seemed a renunciation of the democratic principles to which they professed to be dedicated. The proposition would have been "irreversibly negatived" had not Washington, in terms "moving, pathetic, rational and nervous," presented it as "an absolute necessity." Congress reluctantly yielded to his pleas and raised officers' pay 50 per cent across the board. This generated new fears. William Hooper of North Carolina reported that although inducements to pursue a military career were "enormous," some officers were not yet satisfied. In his opinion, Congress had given way "to the extortion of the Army"; if more were yielded, everyone would become "Slaves" to the soldiers' "Avarice and Caprice."

The behavior of Howe's army in New York was not such as to win friends for the King; the general's orders designed to prevent plundering were simply not obeyed. Tory Judge Thomas Jones commented acidly that when the British entered New York "the soldiers broke open the City Hall, and plundered it of the College Library, its Mathematical and Philosophical apparatus and a number of valuable pictures." Troops looted the Subscription Library and the Corporation Library, "the whole consisting of not less than 50,000 volumes. This was done with impunity and the books publicly hawked about the town for sale by private soldiers, their trulls and doxeys."[22] Judge Jones and other Tories who had expected the conduct of the Royal Army and the mercenaries to be exemplary were sadly disappointed: ". . . plunder, robberies, peculation, whoring, gameing, and all kinds of dissipation were cherished, nursed, encouraged and openly countenanced."[23]

The situation outside the city was worse than that within it. Militiamen marching to join Washington's army were never properly supplied with foodstuffs, blankets, shoes, and stockings and took what they needed from townspeople, villagers, and farmers. Those returning to their homes were equally lawless. Armed bands of Tories and plunderers who called themselves Patriots roamed the countryside, robbing, stealing livestock and poultry, burning barns, and terrorizing the inhabitants. Although the lower Hudson Valley was the focus of these depredations, marauders operated with impunity on Long Island, in the southwestern counties of Connecticut, and in the eastern Jerseys. All brought discredit on the cause they professed to serve.

℀ 4

The Dissolution of Our Army Is Approaching

In late September reports arrived in London that the New Yorkers had pulled down the gilded equestrian statue of George III, beheaded it, and sent the headless corpse and its mount to a smithy to be melted down for bullets. This obscene news, diplomatically withheld from His Majesty, struck his supporters with horror: "The Ministers were quite in despair at the unprosperous state of their affairs. The King could not disguise his concern, which increased his indisposition; and at the reviews every body remarked his weariness, and how much he had fallen away. It was thought that Lord North had a mind to resign."[1] The last statement was certainly true. For some time the First Minister had been of this mind; the King visited him at Bushy Park and held him rigidly to his duty. Major General Harvey, adjutant general of the army, and the King's confidential adviser on military matters, was pessimistic; he thought America "an ugly job; a damned affair indeed."

Travelers arriving shortly thereafter from Nantes brought rumors that Howe had won a decisive victory at Long Island; others reported he had barely escaped a disastrous defeat. No one knew what to believe until, on October 10, one of Howe's aides-de-camp arrived with official reports of the battle. These "filled the Court with an extravagance of joy, which they displayed with the utmost ostentation . . . though the Court endeavoured to stifle it, it was soon known that the Hessians had committed great butchery, and refused to give any quarter."[2] The "King's Friends" gave out that the rebels were now to be even more vigorously chastised and terrified into abject submission. Walpole did not view the prospect with particular pleasure; to support an army of occupation in America would require a vast amount of money. Members of the bellicose "Bloomsbury Gang," whose principal spokesman in the House of Commons was Richard Rigby, a past master in the arts of corruption, "vapoured that it might be right to destroy their towns, and that America was so powerful it ought to be set back fifty years."[3]

Sandwich wrote Admiral Howe a fulsome letter of congratulation "upon the very great and successful outset" of the campaign; ministers had formed "the most pleasing ideas" of what was to follow. Germain wrote the general in similar tenor. He had received reports that Washington's army would soon disperse, and thought Rhode Island should also become "the first object" of Howe's attention. He also suggested a descent on Philadelphia: "The punishing that seat of the Congress would be a proper example to the rest of the Coloneys." He hoped Howe would be able to find time to attack Boston, so the rebels there would feel the distress of a war "their detestable principles have occasioned, encouraged and supported."[*] This letter makes one wonder if Germain had ever looked at a map of North America, or if he had, whether he was capable of reading it. He apparently believed Howe could move from New York against three such widely separated points as Philadelphia, Newport, and Boston quite as easily as one could travel in a coach from London to Brighton, Bath, or Cambridge.

Fox was soon writing Rockingham from Newmarket, where he spent much time during race meetings, that the news from Long Island was "terrible." He was worried about defections and expressed the hope that Rockingham's followers would "support the Americans in adversity as much as we did in their prosperity." It is impossible to assess his motives at this time. Many of his colleagues were convinced they were self-serving; that Fox was using the war with America as a means to promote his own career. Others thought him a traitor, and in private conversation did not hesitate to say so.

Admiral Howe took advantage of the opportunity afforded by his brother's victory to ask for more ships of the line. Precisely why he needed ships of this type he did not bother to explain. The First Lord promised to support him to the extent possible, but was careful to pro-

---

[*] A personal letter from Earl Percy no doubt contributed to the secretary's euphoria. His lordship had written that the battle "was ably planned and nobly executed." The Americans had felt the blow: "I may venture to foretell that this Business is pretty near over" (Sackville German Papers, Vol. V). Percy was feuding with Howe and would soon return to England.

vide himself with a parenthetical escape hatch: Great preparations were going forward "both in the French and Spanish ports, where they are putting a very large number of capital ships into readiness to receive men." What Howe required was not ships of the line but frigates and sloops. Sandwich sent him twelve, and promised him two forty-gun two-deckers. This was the type Howe needed to cruise off the principal American ports—to close them down and keep them closed. By mid-September 1776 the admiral had seventy fighting ships under his command in North American waters. The force represented some 40 per cent of the Royal Navy's strength in ships and men, and included practically all seaworthy frigates available.

The navy at this time faced a severe manning crisis. Recruiting was slow; bounties did not attract the men needed. And small wonder. Life belowdecks was vastly uncomfortable; once aboard, there was no shore leave; rations provided by cheating contractors were frequently inedible; scurvy, endemic; pay, ridiculously incommensurate with the hard service; promotion, slow; discipline, savage. With great secrecy, the Admiralty laid on a "hot press." Press gangs gathered in every man who could not give a meticulous account of his employment. Thames rivermen and merchant seamen were kidnaped. Wastrels, pensioners, derelicts, vagabonds—all were swept up. After this human debris had been winnowed and the totally unfit released, His Majesty's ships were still short of hands.

Man power was by no means the only shortage Sandwich had to reckon with, for both shipwrights and critical materials were in short supply. For many years mast and spar timbers, particularly those suitable for fitting out line-of-battle ships, had come from New England—New Hampshire and the virgin forests of the area now the state of Maine. Suddenly those supplies were cut off, as were many essential naval stores such as turpentine, tar, and hemp, formerly supplied by the southern colonies.

Privateers had already become something more than a nuisance, particularly off the New England and Canadian coasts. Off Newfoundland, they were invading the cod fisheries and reaping a rich harvest of "Bankers." The British commanders there needed small, fast flush-deck ships of twelve to twenty guns to protect the fishing fleet from Yankee ravaging. Enough vessels of this type were not available. Several of those on station had run aground, been caught in the ice, or dismasted in violent North Atlantic storms. Replacement was frustratingly slow.

During 1776, American privateers took 229 British merchant ships, victualers, and transports, of which 50 were retaken. But net captures totaled 179 for a loss of 6 privateers. Booty included three companies of Highlanders, 10,000 muskets, tons of cannon balls, many barrels of powder, salt pork, flour, dried peas, tentage, ball ammunition, sugar, hogsheads of rum and wine, and uniforms. One prize cargo brought £25,000 at auction—a fortune for the officers and crew of the ship that took her. A record must have been set by *Revenge* and *Montgomery*, which between them took nine ships in six days (May 28–June 2) cruising off Matanzas.

Still, as far as the lords of the Admiralty were concerned, these were side issues. The Baltic would supply mast and spar timber and some proportion of naval stores, and the building program would in time provide the ships necessary to put down the privateers. At the Admiralty the focus of attention was not America but France, where great efforts were under way to ready fleets capable of challenging British supremacy on the high seas. The First Lord, however much maligned, never allowed his attention to be distracted from his principal objective: to have in being a Channel fleet that could defeat the French should they attempt to assault the home islands. Practically all his energies were devoted to this end. He did the best he could for Lord Howe, but the admiral's alleged requirements were not the primary object of Sandwich's concern, either in 1776 or later.

Nor was army recruitment progressing satisfactorily. Vagrants, pickpockets, thieves, debtors—even felons who formerly would have been transported to the colonies to work out their sentences—were turned out of jail and handed over to the army. An increasing number of those who attempted to keep themselves well informed were reluctantly arriving at the conclusion that Britain faced a long, expensive, and possibly indecisive war in America.

Recruiting was indeed a major problem, but provisioning His Majesty's land and naval forces in America a more difficult and complex one never resolved to the satisfaction of frequently hungry and disgruntled consumers. Muddling inefficiency of a complicated bureaucracy totally unsuited in organizational terms to handle a war of this scope at such great distance from the supply source increased expenses and contributed to peculation, confusion, and delays. A handful of able and dedicated men struggled with little success to cope with conniving and criminal contractors, unavoidable irregularities in freighting and sailing schedules, unpredictable vagaries of Atlantic weather, and ever-increasing demands of forces in Canada and the rebellious colonies.

Commissioners of the Treasury, responsible for victualing the army, had initially complacently assumed that a large proportion of meats, vegetables, and grains required could be had in America. Both Gage and Howe, who had been quite unable to live off the country when in Boston, attempted to dissuade them of this conception. Howe had fared reasonably well while on Staten Island, and better after his victory on Long Island, but he still could not derive from the countryside even half of what he needed. He reported with some asperity that he could not depend on local supplies of food and forage; he would have to be provisioned from home.

The situation dictated a drastic shake-up in the logistics organization, centralized control of all aspects of supplying the forces overseas, and an executive endowed with the authority necessary. At the time, and under the circumstances, any such innovation would have been next to impossible. The traditional bureaucracy, parochial and strongly entrenched, was jealous of its prerogatives and would have fought to defend them. Lord George Germain recognized the need for changes and managed to effect some, but obstacles were too many.

The principal port and major depot for shipment of provisions was Cork. Here, as at other depots, the first problem arose: condition of food at time of delivery. As a rule it was not better than fair, and sometimes indescribably bad: meat, rotten; flour, bread, and biscuit, weevily; peas, alive with maggots; butter, rancid; cheese, spoiled. Packaging was slipshod, barrels and casks flimsily made, bagging cheap. In a long voyage bags often disintegrated, or, if they had held together, fell apart during unloading. Rats infested warehouses and the holds of victualing ships.

When victualers left Cork they faced an Atlantic voyage which, with considerable luck, might take only six weeks. But frequently an east-to-west crossing took ten to fourteen. Yankee privateers captured many victualers; others, perhaps destined for Quebec or New York, wound up dismasted in Bermuda or the Barbados. Some were blown all over the Atlantic and eventually limped into port in the British Isles with shattered bowsprits, tattered sails, minus half their rigging, and foodstuffs in their holds ruined.

When ships arrived at destination, fresh hazards awaited their cargo. Thievery on the docks was a thriving business. Many officers of the commissary department of the British Army in New York were not as honest as they should have been. Inspectors there frequently declared a considerable proportion of barreled meats contaminated or otherwise unfit for human consumption and (theoretically) destroyed the contents. But somehow quantities of food, beer, molasses, and rum purchased for the Redcoats found its way to markets and taverns.

Despite the graft, waste, delays, and bureaucratic inefficiency, the troops overseas were supplied. Howe complained, as all generals do, of sporadic shortages and of Government's failure to support him properly, but with rare exceptions the British Army in hostile America never suffered, as Washington's did, from chronic lack of provisions and continued shortages of arms, ammunition, clothing, and equipment.

While General Howe was attempting to come to grips with Washington's army, a momentous struggle was being waged for control of Lake

Champlain. As in all naval armaments races, Act I was played out in rival shipyards: the British, at St. Johns on the Richelieu, where Captain Thomas Pringle, R.N., was superintending the construction of a flotilla he would command; the Americans at Skenesborough on South Bay, where Benedict Arnold drove his workmen around the clock.

Captain Charles Douglas, R.N., who had pushed his little flotilla through the ice of the St. Lawrence to help break the American investment of Quebec, wrote the First Lord in mid-August from his flagship *Isis* that Pringle's yard was booming. Shipwrights had put together three gunboats sent from England in sections. *Royal George, Maria* (named for Carleton's wife), and *Inflexible* had been beached near Sorel, taken apart, sent by oxcart to St. Johns in bits and pieces, and were there being reassembled. "A great deal of business has been done, my Lord, since the 6th of May."[4] Douglas prophesied the fleet would "very shortly cut a noble figure." He had sent Pringle every available artificer and detachments of qualified seamen, marines, and gunners to man His Majesty's ships soon to sail.

Major General William Phillips, Carleton's artillery commander, was irritated at the delays. The season for campaigning was nearly over. He wrote Fraser on September 7 his opinion that the naval force then ready was adequate to drive the Americans off the lake. "We must risk and depend on [this force] . . . it will be vain, nay madness, to wait for more." He had no doubt of success "as the General is cool and sensible, a deliberate judgement and not heated like some I know, and I include myself, I have great confidence that things will go well."

Some 150 miles to the south, American artificers were short of almost everything they needed—forges, files, saws, iron, oakum, spikes, rope, anchors, cable, sailcloth, nails. There were no sailors to man the ships being built, a want that did not seem to bother Arnold. He sent off the three vessels he had (schooners *Royal Savage* and *Liberty* and sloop *Enterprise*), manned by hastily trained militiamen, to patrol the lake. As needed supplies trickled in, shipwrights who had recently arrived from Rhode Island constructed "gundelos" and row galleys.† The commander in chief fully appreciated the strategic importance of Lake Champlain; as early as June 28 he had written Schuyler he deemed it "a Matter of infinite Importance to have a considerable number of Gondolas on the Lakes to prevent the Enemy from passing."[5] He was, therefore, sending forward items requested by the general including "Anchors and Cables, Mill Saws and Files." He also sent sailmakers and other artisans.

By mid-September workmen at the Skenesborough yard had built a

---

† "Row galleys" were sixty to seventy feet in length, were propelled by thirty-six oarsmen, and carried forty-four equipped soldiers.

respectable fleet. In addition to the three ships already commissioned, they were finishing a schooner, eight "gundelos," and three galleys. These mounted a total of 94 guns and 176 small-bore "swivels." Captain Pringle's fleet, in which Carleton and Burgoyne were to be embarked as passengers, could discharge twice the weight of metal. If Arnold knew this, it did not deter him—apparently nothing did. In early October, after some days spent teaching farm-bred militiamen how to make sail, handle lines, load and fire cannon and row, Arnold proceeded to a position he had selected in the channel west of Valcour Island, where he anchored and awaited the British.

They were not long in coming. One of Arnold's patrol boats descried the bellying sails of Pringle's miniature armada on October 10 and immediately ducked for cover. Pringle, sailing before a fair wind, passed Valcour; the British then laboriously came into the wind and tacked to get within range. When they did, about noon, weight of metal and experienced gunners told the tale. As darkness fell, the American fleet appeared to be trapped.

Arnold, however, was determined to salvage what he could, and summoned his captains to a Council of War. All agreed that discretion was the better part of valor, and the "admiral" slipped away during the night, towing his damaged ships. When the mist lifted on the morning of October 12 Valcour Bay was empty. Carleton was enraged, but Pringle was equal to the occasion. He at once set off in hot pursuit and on the following day (October 13) caught the fleeing Americans. Arnold ordered several badly damaged ships to be sunk, and beached and set fire to the others. The Americans reached the safety of Ticonderoga.

Both Carleton and Pringle wrote Sandwich shortly after the second fight. As usual with him, the governor was laconic; Pringle gave the details. Douglas, anxious to garner as much credit as possible, got off a letter to the First Lord from Quebec. He hoped, he said, that the many "eccentric acts done throughout the whole course of this novel and eccentric scene" would meet with his lordship's approbation.[6]

What most decidedly did not meet with their lordship's approbation was Carleton's failure to push on to Ticonderoga. For this he was to be severely criticized in Whitehall, particularly by Lord George Germain. The King wrote Sandwich: "Yesterday it was pretended (you can guess by whom) that too much time has been lost in building more ships of force than necessary. . . ."[7] The "whom" was Lord George, who never lost an opportunity to denigrate any officer of whom he was jealous. But the King respected Carleton and was immune to the minister's vindictive insinuations. Possibly Carleton had built more ships of force than the secretary thought necessary, but Germain was neither on the spot nor responsible, and the governor was. The Americans had forced on him a shipbuilding program which delayed his planned operation by several months, until the season was too far gone.‡

Actually, Carleton had not the means to pass a force of any significant size up the lake to Ticonderoga much earlier. After he defeated Arnold at Valcour, he might, indeed, have proceeded to Ticonderoga and seized the fort, but he was familiar with the deadly ferocity of the winters. He could not possibly have supported a garrison there from mid-December until ice broke in early April. Ministers in London who would criticize the governor had no comprehension of the insuperable supply problems that would have faced him had he pushed on.

The war was certainly going to be long and expensive if General Howe's lack of activity during the three weeks following the fire in New York was any criterion. Finally on October 12, when control of Champlain was in balance, he began landing in force on Throgs—or, as Washington called it, Frog's—Neck. This was a most unhappy choice, for the Neck was connected to the mainland by a narrow causeway, frequently covered by water at high tide. A maze of intersecting stone walls provided ample cover for defenders. The general could readily have ascertained the situation had he ordered a reconnaissance, which he neglected to do. He spent the following week deciding what to do next, and on the afternoon of the eighteenth put assault troops ashore at Pell's Point about a mile to the eastward. Three days later he was in order of battle at New Rochelle, in position to threaten Washington at White Plains. He had squandered twenty precious days. Now the nights were cold; in the chilly dawns frost glistened on the fields. If he hoped to accomplish anything, he would have to start moving.

At the time, the British in New York expected Carleton and Burgoyne to press on toward Albany; when they did so American resistance would almost certainly collapse. "From the discontent which prevails in the Rebel army, and among the people in general, and the dangerous situation in which they will find themselves as soon as General Burgoyne makes any progress through the Country toward Albany, it is highly probable that, if the intended plan is Crowned with moderate success, we shall have very little more trouble with the Rebel army, and that they will never make another stand of any consequence."[8]

‡ Admiral Alfred Thayer Mahan wrote later that Arnold's appreciation of the fact that Carleton must at any cost be impeded bought the Americans in the Northern Department a full year of grace to prepare for the inevitable drive south from Canada. The precious time gained by Arnold's perspicacity and activity, Mahan averred, was the key factor in the defeat of Burgoyne the following year. Mahan praised Arnold: "In conduct and courage, Arnold's behavior was excellent throughout." He had with boundless energy created an efficient flotilla, he had "handled his inferior force to great advantage," and "His personal gallantry was conspicuous there as at all times of his life." A. T. Mahan, Captain, U.S.N., *The Major Operations of the Navies in the War of American Independence*. p. 27.

Although some of Howe's junior officers were not entirely satisfied with his strategy, Lieutenant Mackenzie confided to his diary:

> The cautious conduct of Genl Howe in all the operations of this Campaign is generally approved of; and altho many are of opinion that he should have followed up the advantage he gained on the 27th August, and either on that day, or the following, attacked the Rebels in their lines at Brooklyn, yet it must be allowed that it was extremely proper in him to consider what fatal consequences might have [been] received in the first action of the campaign. He has therefore conducted every enterprize in that cautious, circumspect manner, which, altho not so brilliant and striking, is productive of certain and real advantages, at the same time that very little is set at stake. Great Britain has at an immense expense, and by great exertions, assembled an Army from which the Nation expects an entire suppression of the Rebellion, it would therefore be the heighth of imprudence in the Commander in Chief, by any incautious or precipitate conduct, to give the Rebels any chance of an advantage over it.[9]

Had Howe known more than he did of the conditions prevailing in the American camp, he might have been less dilatory than he was, for since early September, Washington had been faced with snowballing problems. Shortly after the reverse on Long Island the militia began drifting away. They were leaving the army not by ones or twos but "by whole Regiments, by half ones, and by Companies at a Time." This he found "sufficiently disagreeable." But there was more: The vagrant and undisciplined behavior of the militia had infected the Continentals. Alarmed, and deeply concerned for the future, the commander in chief confessed his "want of confidence in the generality of the troops." He had every reason to express a want of confidence. Desertions, increasing since Howe took New York, had reached alarming proportions. Mackenzie wrote: "Great numbers of the Rebels desert to us daily, and among them are some officers. Near 80 deserters came in one day lately, by which we may judge of the very great desertion in their Rebel army, as there can be no doubt that much greater numbers leave them to return to their own homes, and to other places in the Country." A week later he recorded: "Scarce a day passes that several deserters do not come in from the Rebels. They all agree that the Rebels are discontented, and tired of continuing so long in Arms, especially since the misfortune they have suffered since we landed on Long Island. They are ill-clothed, and must suffer exceedingly for want of good warm clothing when the severe weather sets in."[10]

Of 8,000 militia from Connecticut present in August, more than 6,000 had by late September quit the army; contingents sent to replace them arrived without tentage, blankets, pots, pans, or kettles. Washington directed his brigade commanders "to stuff the men thicker in their tents" and to take immediate inventory of cooking equipment so what little there was could be shared equally. To Governor Trumbull, he complained bitterly of the militiamen: "Their want of discipline, the Indulgences they claim, and have been allowed, their unwillingness, I may add, refusal, to submit to that regularity and order essential in every Army" had the pernicious effect of poisoning the entire force. This understanding man did not condone their behavior, but appreciated that it must be expected; he closed his letter with these words: "For men who have been free and never subject to restraint or any kind of control cannot be taught the necessity, or brought to see the expediency, of strict discipline in a day."[11]

Plundering, which he abhorred and which never failed to evoke his wrath, continued endemic. The men were stealing everything they could lay their hands on. He enjoined his officers to exert themselves to curb this "diabolical practice." If officers did not restrain their men, "e'er long, Death will be the portion of some of the offenders. . . . No plundering army ever was a successful one." A copy of Howe's order relating to plundering had fallen into Washington's hands, and on September 19 he issued a General Order pointing out that while the British were "exceeding careful" to restrain this abuse, "The abandoned and profligate part of our own Army, countenanced by a few Officers who are lost to every sense of Honour and Virtue, as well as their Country's Good, are by Rapine and Plunder, spreading Ruin and Terror wherever they go. . . ." He promised to inflict immediate and severe punishment on those found guilty of this "most abominable practice."**

These were a few of the many difficulties that had kept his mind "constantly upon a stretch"; his feelings had been deeply hurt by "a thousand things that have happened contrary to my expectations and Wishes. . . ." For the first time, and happily the last, he seriously questioned his ability to see it through. Certainly, he was convinced he could not unless there was "a thorough change in our Military System."[12] Three days later he wrote his brother ". . . if I were to wish the bitterest curse to an enemy on this side of the grave, I should put him in my stead. . . . In confidence I tell you I was never in such an unhappy divided State since I was born." He was "bereft" of every peaceful moment, and profoundly distressed.[13]

Fighting for three days around White Plains was inconclusive as Washington fended off the British general and fell back toward the Croton River. Howe considered an attack at White Plains; American ac-

---

** The British were not "exceeding careful" to restrain plundering. Howe, of course, did not condone it, but did little to put a stop to it.

counts relate the Hessians several times probed their right wing and were thrown back in disarray, "scattered like leaves in a whirlwind." The defenders suffered one hundred killed and wounded, the attackers three times that number. Some Germans deserted; a number were taken prisoner. These expensive and tactically unsatisfactory forays may have decided Howe not to entrust a major attack on this particular position to his German allies. He would later testify he did not attack "for political reasons." To have reshuffled the army in the face of an enemy strongly posted would have been a precarious undertaking and one the Hessians would have regarded as an insult.†† As Washington withdrew, Howe advanced cautiously to Dobbs Ferry.

Washington was now in a dilemma and he did not handle the situation as well as he might have done. He had "spun the Campaign without letting Genl Howe obtain any advantage" and had limited him "to the conquest of a few pitiful islands." Although he was convinced Howe had nowhere to go but to New Jersey, he wanted to sound his generals. At the Council of War he expressed his opinion that Howe could not "close the Campaign and sit down without attempting something more. I think it highly probable and almost certain that he will make a descent with part of his troops into Jersey. He must attempt something on Acct of his Reputation, for what has he done yet, with his great Army?"[14]

Charles Lee expected Howe to attempt something; certainly the British were "not going to remain kicking their heels in New York." Lee thought Howe would cross the North River and march on Philadelphia, and wrote Congress to rouse themselves: ". . . for Heaven's sake, let ten thousand men be immediately assembled and stationed somewhere about Trenton." Two days later he wrote Gates from Fort Constitution, ". . . inter nos the Congress seem to stumble every step. I do not mean one or two of the Cattle, but the whole Stable. I have been very free in delivering my opinion to 'em." He urged Washington to threaten resignation unless Congress stopped its "absurd interference" in operations.

Washington's generals sustained his opinion: Howe had to go to New Jersey, cross the Delaware, and drive the Congress from Philadelphia. There the British general could "sit down" for the winter at the close of a successful campaign and contemplate his conquests. Lee urged Washington to move into New Jersey before the British did. He decided to do so and sent Stirling's corps over on November 10 and 11; on the night of the thirteenth he crossed to join Greene.

But he left valuable hostages on the east bank. He directed Lee to hold at Croton with almost 4,000 men until further orders; he sent 3,000 more to Peekskill to report to Major General William Heath for defense

†† The rigid demands of existing military protocol and the necessity of maintaining good relations with his allies would land more than one British general in hot water.

of the Highlands.‡‡ He decided also to hold Fort Lee on the Jersey side of the river. He had urged Congress to permit him to abandon Fort Washington on the east shore; the delegates, indisposed to give up another fortress without a fight, reluctantly allowed him to exercise his discretion. He delegated this authority to Major General Nathanael Greene, who believed Fort Washington could be held. Such dispersion of the small army was inexcusable. Both forts should have been evacuated.

For several days common gossip in British officers' messes was that the army would move on Fort Washington. Mackenzie thought Howe's next step would be "to land a body of troops as soon as possible on the Jersey side . . . from the general appearance of matters it is probable that the moment Fort Washington is taken General Howe will land a body of troops in Jersey from the right of his Army [i.e., British formations] and after taking Fort Constitution [Fort Lee], penetrate into that Province toward Philadelphia. If, at the same time, a force was landed at Amboy, and a fleet with troops sent into the Delaware, Pennsylvania would be attacked by Three Columns, which must infallibly penetrate to Philadelphia, route the Congress, and establish the left of our line [i.e., German formations] in that City." Mackenzie believed "Numberless advantages would arise from the execution of this plan," as indeed they would have. Nor would this be "difficult to effect. . . . The Rebels have very few troops that way." Mackenzie thought "the appearance of a formidable force in Pennsylvania, where the measures of Congress are now much condemned, would induce numbers of the deluded inhabitants to seize the favorable opportunity of returning to their Allegiance, and the enjoyment of their ease, peace, and happiness. Many of the leading men in Congress might also take the opportunity to make their peace by an early submission. If anything of this nature should happen, the strength of the Rebellion is at an end and Washington's army would disperse."[15] Clinton, whose unwelcome suggestions Howe habitually disregarded, gave his commanding general substantially this advice.

Despite Charles Lee's urgent appeal to "draw off the garrison" of Fort Washington, Greene ordered Colonel Robert Magaw "to defend it to the last extremity." Magaw held out for two assaults; when he surrendered, 2,818 officers and men, who should have been evacuated to the Jersey side, one hundred guns, and much other valuable equipment was lost. Only General Howe's presence prevented the Hessians from repeating their Long Island massacre and turning Fort Washington into an abattoir. Howe had given explicit orders that the troops were to drive the Americans from their outer works into the fort, at which point they would again be summoned to surrender. Had he not held his troops, "there is no doubt that they (especially the Hessians, who were ex-

‡‡ Many left on the east side of the Hudson were New Englanders who had no desire to cross the river.

tremely irritated at having lost a good many men in the attack) would have gone on and taken it by assault. The Carnage then would have been dreadful, for the Rebels were so numerous they had not room to defend themselves with effect, and so frightened they had not the power. Indeed, after having rejected the offer made them on the 15th, they had no right to expect the mild treatment they met with. . . ."[16]

The men taken at Fort Washington were a fairly representative cross section of the American Army. Washington had frequently complained that far too great a proportion of militiamen sent him were either too young or too old to endure the rigors of a campaign. From White Plains, he had sent one group of "grandfathers" back to Connecticut with the laconic observation that their aggregate age exceeded one thousand years. Many "grandfathers" taken at Fort Washington would not outlive their captivity.

Although Howe treated the American officers in his hands with decency, the fate of enlisted men was a miserable one; while officers were "suffered to walk about in every part of this town [New York] on their parole and in their Uniforms," soldiers were confined aboard leaky transports and storeships unfit to hazard the return trip to Britain. Rations were barely sufficient to maintain life; the holds of the ships, cold, damp, and insanitary.

When Lee heard that Fort Washington had fallen (as he had predicted it would), he wrote Benjamin Rush a most indiscreet letter: ". . . Heaven alone can save you." Although his troops were ill clad, on short rations, and had no blankets, they did not "want courage." What was needed, he asserted, was vigorous direction, which he could supply if allowed to dictate "but one week." Rush kept this letter to himself; although he was not one of Washington's admirers, he had enough common sense to realize that Lee's intemperate expressions bordered on treason.

Two days after Magaw surrendered Fort Washington, Cornwallis surprised General Greene at Fort Lee. The Americans left breakfast in cooking kettles and ran off with no more than their muskets and the tattered shirts on their backs. The loss of Forts Washington and Lee cost the Americans dear: The British took several thousand stand of arms, cannon, powder, tentage, and large stocks of dry and salt provisions.

Cornwallis drove the Americans hard. Howe sent the earl nine fresh battalions, but ordered him to wait at Brunswick, where Howe joined him on December 6. The delay was critical, and even though Howe pushed on to Princeton on December 7, he had dallied too long. Even so, he entered Princeton on the heels of Lord Stirling's retiring rear guard. Here he stopped for eighteen hours to refresh the troops, there again squandering irretrievable time. Washington had ordered boats to be on the east bank of the Delaware to transport what was left of his army to safety on the Pennsylvania shore. Cannon and stores went over on December 7; the army crossed during the night with the rear guard getting over early on Sunday, the eighth. Cornwallis arrived at river's edge at noon that day. No boats were to be found.

The bedraggled collection of miscellaneous understrength regiments and battalions that was the American Army, with its several dozen assorted pieces of manhandled artillery, had finally reached a haven on the west bank of the Delaware. There in a position of comparative safety Washington had an opportunity to refresh, re-equip, and rehabilitate his exhausted troops, to reanimate them, and with his most competent and trusted generals—Greene, Sullivan, Stirling, and Knox—to plan the riposte he knew to be necessary.

Before Howe had become involved in the New Jersey campaign, he had mounted an expedition against Rhode Island; on the morning of Saturday, December 7, Sir Peter Parker (of the Charleston fiasco) appeared in Narragansett Bay with seventy sail and anchored off Newport. The militia, awed by this display of British might, sensibly spiked their few brass cannon, collected their belongings, and took off in the general direction of Bristol, whence they proceeded at a more dignified pace to Providence. The townsfolk were quite pleased to see Clinton's Redcoats, whose pockets were well lined with hard money. According to the American press, the British were greeted "by a set of well-known infamous Tories who have long infested that town, and who may yet possibly meet with the fate justly due to their atrocious villainies."[17]

Clinton and Parker had patched up their relationship since the affair at Charleston, and both the general and Lord Percy, his second-in-command, sailed with the commodore in H.M.S. *Chatham*. They talked of seizing Providence, and thus getting astride the principal line of communication from New York and Connecticut to Boston, but nothing was done. The presence of Parker's ships did, however, put a stop to privateering based on Narragansett Bay. And the British were now in full possession of the harbor Admiral Rodney later described as "the best and noblest in America." Howe committed a force of about 6,000 to Rhode Island. He had done so for two reasons: first, to take the pressure off New York during the coming winter, where billeting and supply of food and forage would be most severe problems, and second, to form a base from which to mount a drive toward Boston, or possibly through Connecticut, in the spring of 1777. Frederick Mackenzie's regiment, the Royal Welch Fusiliers, formed a part of Clinton's force. Mackenzie found Newport "delightful," even in mid-December, and thought that "In the beginning of summer" the view across the bay, its "adjacent waters,

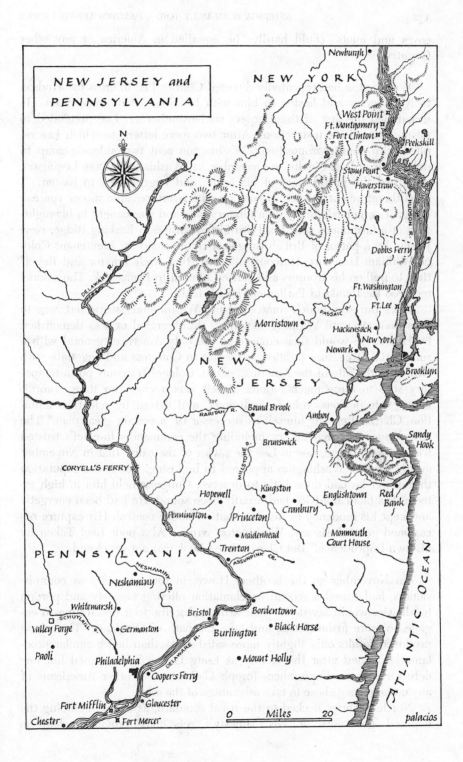

NEW JERSEY and PENNSYLVANIA

N

NEW YORK

Newburgh
West Point
Ft. Montgomery
Fort Clinton
Peekskill
Stony Point
Haverstraw
Dobbs Ferry
Ft. Washington
Ft. Lee
Hackensack
New York
Newark
Brooklyn
Sandy Hook
Morristown

NEW JERSEY

DELAWARE R.
PASSAIC R.
RARITAN R.
Bound Brook
Amboy
Brunswick
MILLSTONE R.

CORYELL'S FERRY
Hopewell
Kingston
Pennington
Princeton
Cranbury
Englishtown
Red Bank
Maidenhead
Monmouth Court House
Trenton
ASSUNPINK CR.

PENNSYLVANIA

NESHAMINY
Neshaminy
Whitemarsh
Bristol
Bordentown
SCHUYLKILL R.
Valley Forge
Germanton
Burlington
Black Horse
Paoli
Philadelphia
Mount Holly
DELAWARE R.
Cooper's Ferry
Fort Mifflin
Gloucester
Chester
Fort Mercer

ATLANTIC OCEAN

HUDSON R.

0   Miles   20

palacios

coves and inlets" could hardly "be equalled in America or any other Country."[18]

Washington had repeatedly directed Charles Lee to cross the Hudson to New Jersey and hasten to him with his brigades of some 3,000. He dispatched the first of these orders on November 21. Lee pretended to misunderstand the instructions. After two more letters, to which Lee replied with counterpropositions, Washington sent two aides-de-camp to deliver his orders. Finally on December 11, Washington wrote Lee again, described the pitiful state of his army, and begged Lee to hasten: "I must therefore entreat you to push on with every possible succor you can bring." Lee moved, finally, in a dilatory way and was caught in his nightshirt at a farmhouse near Lord Stirling's mansion in Basking Ridge, New Jersey, by a patrol of British dragoons commanded by Lieutenant Colonel William Harcourt. Harcourt allowed "that Arch Traytor and Rebel" time to pull on his trousers and carried him off to Brunswick. The colonel received the thanks of Parliament for his feat.

Lee's purpose, which some (but not Washington) suspected, was to bide his time until Washington's army disintegrated or was demolished by Howe. He would then emerge as the only American general with a substantial force, in a position to dictate to Congress and negotiate with Howe for the fate of the American cause. Colonel Harcourt put a temporary stop to these machinations. But it was a close-run thing. Inordinately vain, jealous, volatile, indiscreet, and driven by relentless ambition, Charles Lee saw himself as successor to "a certain great man." The real danger was that others, including the commander-in-chief's trusted friend Joseph Reed, saw in Lee the savior of the cause that in November and December Washington appeared to be losing. Lee had a reputation that as yet he had done little to deserve. Congress held him in high esteem. His tactical advice had usually been sound. He had been energetic and kept his tendency to insubordination under control. His capture occasioned general dismay. Washington wrote, "Alas poor Lee! Taken by his own Imprudence!" But Charles Lee's book was not yet closed.

On November 30 the brothers Howe, in their capacity as commissioners, had issued a second proclamation offering amnesty and pardon to all who would lay down their arms, subscribe to a declaration to engage no more in hostilities, and take the oath of allegiance. This ukase produced results only slightly more satisfactory than had a similar proclamation issued after the victory at Long Island. They gained but one defector of some importance—Joseph Galloway. No other Americans of any consequence chose to take advantage of the offer.

Nor had Tories flocked to the royal standard, as many, including the deposed governors of His Majesty's rebellious provinces, had so confidently predicted. In New York, Oliver De Lancey, an immensely wealthy landed proprietor and formerly a politically potent figure, had assured Howe he could enlist a brigade of fifteen hundred with no trouble. Howe commissioned him a brigadier. Despite generous bounties paid in specie, he managed to round up fewer than six hundred, practically all tenants on his various estates. In New Jersey the tale was much the same. There, Howe commissioned Courtland Skinner a brigadier, but Skinner never produced the brigade he promised. Washington wrote Hancock he would do all he could "to prevent these parricides from accomplishing their design."

On Washington's urgent advice, conveyed by General Thomas Mifflin, Congress had resolved on December 9 to adjourn to Baltimore, "as it was judged that the Council of America ought not to Sit in a Place liable to be interrupted by the rude Disorder of Arms." And Congress was worried, too, that the British, in connivance with suspected Loyalists in Philadelphia, might, in a *coup de main,* capture many members. Samuel Adams apprehended that "the people of Pennsylvania, influenced by Fear Folly or Treachery," would give up "their Capital to appease the anger of the two brothers." These fears were not entirely fanciful—the Pennsylvania militia had been most reluctant to join Washington in New Jersey, and the Committee of Safety, "a bunch of water-gruel Sons of B——es," dithered.[19]

Congress had left Robert Morris behind to regulate business. This was not exactly easy: "There is the greatest scene of confusion in the management of the Continental Horses, Wagons and Expresses that ever was exhibited . . . it was bad enough before Congress departed, but it is ten times worse now. . . ." However, he promised to "bestir" himself until Congress could appoint an executive committee to act. Morris was more or less on his own and took advantage of his position to push his sensible and necessary arrangement. On December 16 he wrote the Committee of Secret Correspondence blasting Congress for failure to delegate authority: ". . . if the Congress mean to succeed in this contest, they must pay good executive men to do their business as it ought to be and not lavish millions away by their own mismanagement."[20] A week later, Congress appointed an executive committee of three (Robert Morris, George Clymer, and George Walton) and directed them to remain in Philadelphia to deal with routine matters.

The congressmen detested Baltimore—"too dirty and too dear." One delegate who had thought Philadelphia the dirtiest place he knew changed his mind when he saw Baltimore—"the Damndest Hole in the World." All yearned to return to the city of the Quakers where streets were cobbled, society cultured, meals well cooked and reasonably priced, and wine cheap. In this "worst of all terrestial places" streets were quagmires and prices extravagant: "the poorest of board without any Liquor a dollar a day"; wine, twelve shillings the bottle; rum, thirty shillings the gallon. "Infamous!"

But delegates resolved several critical problems. Here the question of establishing the Continental Army on a regular basis was finally decided. Congress set strength at 110 infantry battalions plus artillery and a regiment of light dragoons, provided for bounties on enlistment for three years, promised land grants to honorably separated veterans, and agreed that invalids and widows would receive pensions.

Despite the unwelcome presence of Arthur Lee, Silas Deane managed to transact a great deal of business in Paris. He enjoyed the confidence and friendship of the Foreign Minister, of his secretary, Gérard de Reyneval, and of the director of Roderique Hortalez and Company.* But in Arthur Lee, Deane had a jealous and vindictive enemy. Lee felt he should have been given the mission entrusted to Deane and devoted considerable time and energy to composing letters designed to ruin Deane's reputation, to his brother Richard Henry and assorted other delegates to the Congress.

One of Deane's missions in Paris was to contract for services of French artillerists and engineers; to this activity he devoted considerable attention. No doubt he greatly exceeded his authority; his misguided zeal would eventually land him in deep trouble with Congress. In September he signed an agreement with Sieur Phillipus-Charles Jean Baptiste Tronson du Coudray, a major in His Most Christian Majesty's artillery. Deane was so anxious to acquire the services of this officer that he promised Du Coudray a commission as major general and "direction of whatever relates to the Artillery and Corps of Engineers"; agreed that Congress would pay passage and incidental expenses for him, his suite and servants; and guaranteed that he and all who accompanied him to America would receive half pay for life when they quit the American service. Details of this unfortunate contract could not be kept secret. Du Coudray was an ambitious and indiscreet braggart, and in no time adventurers of every description and nationality besieged Deane's offices, begging appointments. Some were competent, some were not, but all were fluent and with few exceptions guileful, and for a price, unreservedly dedicated to assisting America to free herself from the yoke of Great Britain.

By mid-October, Deane had been in Paris for three months. During that time he had received no communications from the Secret Committee. On October 17 he "once more put pen to paper, not to attempt what is absolutely beyond the power of language to paint, my distressed situation here, totally destitute of intelligence or instructions," but to beg for more ample negotiating authority. Although his representations had been

* Gérard de Reyneval was the younger brother of Conrad Alexandre Gérard.

favorably received at Versailles "the *sine qua non* is wanting—a power to treat from the United Independent States of America."[21]

He urged the committee to forward without delay 20,000 hogsheads of tobacco and large quantities of rice which he could readily dispose of at a good profit. Two weeks later he again wrote, pleading for shipments of tobacco, indigo, wheat, and rice, all in great demand in France and Holland. "I must say your silence . . . discourages me at times. Indeed, it well neigh distracts me . . . it has greatly prejudiced the affairs of the United Colonies of America . . . it has occasioned the greatest hazard and danger (to success of the American cause) and thrown me into a state of anxiety and perplexity which no words can express. . . . I have made one excuse after another until my invention is exhausted . . . hope itself has almost deserted me."[22]

At Wentworth's behest Dr. Bancroft commuted between London and Paris. From the British capital he gave his American employer inconsequential information probably fed him by Eden, but took care to include enough significant detail to ensure Deane's continuing gratitude, gratuities, and confidence. Deane first learned of the Declaration of Independence from Bancroft, who read of it in the London press. Finally, on November 16 he received an authenticated copy, with instructions to deliver it to the French Foreign Minister. He immediately wrote Vergennes asking to be received.†[23]

Dr. Benjamin Franklin was seventy-one when he sailed from Marcus Hook in late October to join Deane in Paris. He had enjoyed a variety of careers. He now was to embark on the service that crowned his life, one that would assure his country's existence as a sovereign state, and his place in history as one of the very few men instrumental in laying the foundations of a new nation. As an augury of his mission, sloop *Reprisal* (Captain Lambert Wickes) on which he sailed picked up two prizes on the way.

The doctor landed at a fishing village in Brittany on December 3, traveled by coach to Nantes, where he rested ten days, and then went on to Paris, where he arrived shortly before Christmas. News that he was en route preceded him. Walpole wrote "there could be no doubt but he came with the fullest powers from the Congress to announce the fullest independence of the Colonies, and to offer the most advantageous terms of alliance and commerce to France . . . ," and thought it "difficult to suppose that France can resist such tempting offers of ruining us for ever."[24]

The French were vastly excited by the presence in their country of

---

† The Secret Committee had sent instructions, but the ships bearing them had been intercepted. Normal procedure was to send instructions in duplicate or triplicate by different vessels.

the respected philosopher and scientist, who wore spectacles, a fur hat, and homespun. Within forty-eight hours after he arrived in Paris he was the toast of the city. He hastened to present his credentials and respects to Maurepas and M. le Comte de Vergennes, who received him cordially. The doctor must have made an agreeable impression, for Louis's Foreign Minister promised him an immediate loan of two million francs. Vergennes was not inspired to offer such generous assistance because of a fondness for Americans, of whom he had not met more than half a dozen, or because he was sympathetic to the republican philosophy they embraced. His ambition was to humble proud and insolent Britain.

A free and independent America would throw open her ports to French trade. England's commercial monopoly on the North American continent had to be broken; a sovereign United States would break it. What the minister sought, and what Franklin was empowered to give him, was an unqualified assurance that America proposed to fight until she secured her independence. Franklin gave it at once. With that, Vergennes opened the purse strings. Equally important, he assured Franklin that ports would continue to be open secretly to American ships of war, privateers, and their prizes. He also gave permission for Americans to sell prizes and cargoes to French bidders. This, it would turn out, was a qualified commitment which the minister could and did suspend and disavow when British pressure proved too great. France was not yet ready for open war.

Though Franklin's presence delighted the French, it naturally troubled Lord Stormont, who was well aware that the doctor was up to no good in Paris. He immediately set spies on him, and wrote Weymouth that the doctor was a "subtle, artful man" who would "use every means to deceive" his hosts.[25] But Franklin would have had to be considerably more artful than he was to deceive William Eden or Paul Wentworth, who ran Eden's espionage network in France.

Franklin had not been in Paris a week when Wentworth signed a new contract with Dr. Bancroft, who had complete access to the commissioners' office and their most private papers. Wentworth wanted details of discussions relating to the Franco-American treaty he (and everyone in Paris) knew Franklin had come to negotiate. He wanted the names of Congress's agents in "ye foreign Islands of America" and the names of those in Versailles and Madrid responsible for arranging credits. Most important, Wentworth wanted copies of "Franklin's and Deane's correspondence with the Congress and their Agents of the Secret as well as the ostensible letters of the Congress to them." The contract stipulated that all reports were to be written in invisible ink. Bancroft's "drop" was a hole in a root of a certain tree in the Terrace of the Tuilleries, where he was to deposit reports every Tuesday evening at half past nine.[26]

Several days after the doctor called on Vergennes, Madame du

Deffand invited him to attend her weekly salon, a small, intimate gathering. Franklin arrived as bidden *"avec un bonnet de fourrure sur la tête et des lunettes sur son nez, et puis, tout de suite, Mme de Luxembourg, M. Silas Dean . . . Monsieur le Duc du Choiseul. . . ."* Charles Fox, in Paris to attend the holiday racing, arrived a few moments after the Americans had left.[27] Shortly after Madame du Deffand's doors closed on the last departing guests, Wentworth knew what the topics of conversation had been.

Meanwhile, Beaumarchais, who did nothing in niggardly fashion, had established Roderique Hortalez and Company in a mansion on Rue Vieille du Temple, and had moved in his current mistress, sisters, brothers, nieces, nephews, accountants, secretaries, and kitchen and household staff. In mid-December he was supervising the loading of three ships Roderique Hortalez had purchased. Aboard *Amphitrite* he put 52 cannon, 20,000 cannon balls, 6,000 muskets, twelve tons of musket balls, 9,000 grenades, six tons of powder, and hundreds of shovels, axes, picks, billhooks, and mattocks. On *Amélie* he loaded nineteen brass cannon, thousands of cannon balls, and assorted tools. Practically everything—certainly all the weapons, ammunition, and tentage—came directly to Roderique Hortalez from French government arsenals. *Amélie* and *Amphitrite* sailed in January and would arrive safely. A third ship, loaded at the same time, was taken by a British frigate.[28] Beaumarchais, a busy man, somehow found time during these months to amuse himself with (among others) mesdames, the King's four sisters, who found him a diverting companion.

Thanks to "Mr. Edwards," who dropped the mail regularly at the Tuilleries, Paul Wentworth was well informed of the precise nature of Beaumarchais's private transactions with the Americans, with government officials, and with contractors. Wentworth's agents trailed Franklin and Deane. Nor did they overlook the director of Roderique Hortalez, his assorted relatives, his assistants and his menials from the moment they left Beaumarchais's *hôtel* in the morning until they returned. Wentworth had infiltrated Franklin's offices at Passy, the Paris post office, and had spies in every French port and building yard.

But neither the King nor his First Minister gave Wentworth's reports the attention they deserved. Both were inclined to give more credence to those sent to Whitehall by Viscount Stormont, who had little information other than that provided by Vergennes. Stormont did not believe the Foreign Minister's duplicitous assertions, but neither did he put much faith in Wentworth's reports. Whitehall was receiving conflicting reports from Paris.

⚡ 5

To Strike Some Stroke

On December 14 Howe issued a General Order to the army:

> The Campaign being Closed with the Pursuit of the Enemies
> Army near 90 miles by Lt. General Lord Cornwallis Corps much
> to the Honour of his Lordship & to the Officers and Soldiers under
> his Command. The Approach of the Winter putting a stop to any
> Further Progress the Troops will Immediately march into Quar-
> ters and hold themselves in readiness to assemble on the Shortest
> Notice![1]

At Cornwallis' urging, Howe outposted Trenton, Bordentown, and
Burlington with strong contingents of Hessians. He backed these with
the light infantry of the army, a brigade of foot, and a troop of dragoons
at Princeton. This deployment, dictated primarily by supply difficulties
in New York, was sensible in the political context as Howe saw it and
was militarily sound. All detachments were within mutually supporting
distance. He deemed the disposition desirable "because a considerable
number of the inhabitants had come in with their arms," and more, he
was certain, would do so if they had protection. He posted Hessians in
advanced positions because the left was the post of the Hessians: "Had I

changed it upon this occasion it must have been considered as a disgrace
. . . and it probably would have created jealousies between the Hessians
and British troops, which it was my duty carefully to prevent."[2]

Howe apparently believed that Washington had no offensive capability, but had he been slightly more imaginative, he might had deduced
that Washington could scarcely afford to sit on the west bank of the Delaware during the long winter and might consider an aggressive action politically essential. But Howe and all his generals held Washington and
his ragged army in complete contempt. He had not developed that respect for an opponent which is one mark of a superior general.

Washington did not concede that the approach of winter put a stop
to further operations. He had been considering various possibilities, and
on the day Howe ordered his army into winter quarters, he summoned
Greene, Knox, Sullivan, and Lord Stirling to a conference at his headquarters at New Town. Hopes and spirits of even the most ardent patriots were fast ebbing. The preceding four months had witnessed a dismal catalogue of retreats, surrenders, and staggering losses of men and
material. Many officers now talked seriously of resigning their commissions. Congress had sought refuge in Baltimore; the loyalty of Philadelphians was at best questionable. Enlistments of most Continentals
would expire on the last day of the year, but two short weeks away.
Washington realized that the cause to which he and many others had
committed their lives, their fortunes, and their honor was at stake. He
had to strike somewhere, and strike successfully, for if he did not, the
bone and muscle of the army—his Continentals—would soon be gone.
Then nature would step in on the side of the British. The Delaware
would freeze, Howe would move in force from Brunswick, Amboy, and
Princeton, cross the river, and take Philadelphia. As someone said at the
time, Howe had a mortgage on the American Army and was only waiting
for an appropriate moment to foreclose.

Washington's information on Colonel Johann Gottlieb Rhall's dispositions at Trenton and those of Colonel Emil Kurt von Donop at Bordentown indicated that neither had yet prepared proper redoubts; that
security (particularly at Trenton) was lax; and that both posts were
vulnerable to carefully planned suprise attacks. To assure secrecy, he
limited final planning conferences to a select group—the generals named
plus Brigadier General James Ewing and Colonel John Cadwalader. His
friend Joseph Reed, unaware of Washington's intentions, sent the commander in chief an almost hysterical letter on December 22: "Some Enterprise must be undertaken in our present Circumstances or we must
give up the Game. . . . Will it not be possible My dear Genl. for your
Troops or such Part of them as can Act with Advantage to make a Diversion or something more at or about Trenton. . . . If we could possess
ourselves again of New Jersey or any considerable Part of it, the Effect

would be greater than if we had never left it. . . . I will not disguise my own Sentiments that our Cause is desperate and hopeless if we do not take the Oppy. of the Collection of Troops at present to strike some Stroke. Our Affairs are hastening fast to Ruin if we do not retrieve them by some happy Event. Delay with us is now equal to a total Defeat."[*3] Washington did not reply to this indiscreet letter. The commander in chief was as well aware as his volatile and pessimistic correspondent that he had "to strike some Stroke," even more for political and psychological reasons than for any immediate and possibly transitory military advantage he might hope to achieve.

His plan was to cross the Delaware in three columns and to hit Trenton and Bordentown simultaneously at first light the day after Christmas. His column (some 2,400 Continentals under Sullivan and Greene, with Knox's artillery) would cross at McKonkey's Ferry (now Washington Crossing) and move on Trenton from the north. Ewing, with 1,000 militia, was to cross south of the town and set up a blocking position. Cadwalader was to create a diversion at Bordentown, and so discourage Von Donop from sending help to his beleaguered colleague. This scheme of maneuver might fail ingloriously unless Washington achieved surprise. The river was running high, the passage made precarious by floating islands of ice. The eight-mile march from the selected landing site must be made in freezing darkness over icy, rutted roads. The risks were great. Washington accepted them.

Of the three columns his alone succeeded in crossing the river on this bitter Christmas night. Sleet, snow, and hail delayed the march; he was not able to launch the attack before 8 A.M. Surprise was complete. Dozing sentries were disarmed or shot down. Rhall and his officers and men, sleeping off the effects of a twenty-four-hour German Christmas party, staggered out of their billets in a state of stupor. Knox got his guns into position and swept the streets with grapeshot. The half-clad Hessians panicked; some ran away; most lay down their arms. Rhall, mortally hit, surrendered his sword to Lord Stirling. The attackers suffered four casualties—two officers and two enlisted men wounded. Two soldiers were frozen to death. Happily, the Americans discovered several hogsheads of rum, "large draughts of which preserved the lives of many." Rum was not the only booty. Had Ewing and Cadwalader struck as planned, the bag of prisoners would probably have been 3,000 German officers and men rather than the 30 officers and 861 enlisted, including "a band of musicians" the general scooped up. He managed to drag off "Six Pieces of Brass Artillery," but could not take captured supplies other than one thousand muskets, ammunition, and fifteen standards back across the Delaware.

The conduct of his troops fulfilled the general's highest hopes: "In

---

* When Reed mentioned "Collection of Troops" he was referring to contingents of the Pennsylvania Militia, then reporting to New Town.

justice to the Officers and Men, I must add, that their Behaviour upon this Occasion, reflects the highest honor upon them. The difficulty of passing the River in the very severe Night and their March thro' a violent Storm of Snow and Hail did not in the least abate their Ardour. But when they came to the Charge, each seemed to vie with the other in pressing forward."[4] So he reported to Hancock from headquarters at Newton the day following his victory.

Colonel von Donop evacuated Bordentown, Burlington, and Mount Holly "in the greatest hurry and confusion." By December 28 the weather had relented, and Cadwalader and Mifflin crossed to New Jersey with about 3,000. Clearance of the Germans from the east bank relieved the incipient threat to Philadelphia. The victory at Trenton was particularly pleasing because it was gained at the expense of Howe's detested Hessians.

The army was now ready to undertake anything. Many Continentals and some militiamen extended their terms of service. A rest of three weeks in a safe haven, fresh supplies of ammunition, and a respectable diet had restored the soldiers' spirits and their bodies to physical vigor; the smashing success at Trenton convinced junior officers and rank and file that under Washington's inspiring leadership they could go on to further victories. The general shortly gave them opportunity to do so. On December 29 he again crossed the river and occupied Trenton. Cadwalader with 1,800 moved into abandoned Bordentown and swept out Mount Holly, Black Horse, and Burlington. On New Year's Day, Washington assembled three corps totaling 6,500 at Trenton.

This effrontery could scarcely be borne. Howe immediately canceled Cornwallis' home leave, ordered him to resume tactical command, and to restore the situation along the Delaware. The earl, a marching general, arrived at Princeton with a corps of almost 8,800 on the evening of New Year's Day, and early the following morning set out for Trenton with some 5,500. He left the Fourth Brigade of three regiments, several batteries, and a troop of light dragoons at Princeton under command of Colonel Charles Mawhood with orders to follow him the next morning.

This unexpectedly rapid reaction, which Washington had not anticipated, put him in an extremely critical position. He had no time to get back across the river. Cornwallis had been trying "to run the Fox to ground" for months; now he sensed the kill. Washington had taken position south of Trenton along Assunpink Creek, where his Continentals and militiamen were making the dirt fly. He had outposted the road from Princeton in strength with Hand's Pennsylvania riflemen, several other battalions, and four cannon. The earl's advance guard hit them about 11 A.M., and there was hot skirmishing as the Americans fell slowly back. At dark, they slipped through Trenton, crossed the creek, and occupied prepared positions.

Cornwallis decided to lie in Trenton overnight and attack the Americans shortly after dawn the following morning. His men were tired. Most had marched almost fifty miles in two days, and several regiments had been fighting for six hours. One of his generals did not concur in this decision and is reported to have said, "My Lord, if you trust these people tonight, you will see nothing of them in the morning." But Cornwallis, too, was tired. He went to bed.

Washington called a Council of War shortly after dark. He knew the situation in Princeton; a spy had arrived with full details of Mawhood's dispositions. He took the decision to march on Princeton, surprise and overwhelm Mawhood's brigade, and press on to capture Howe's great magazine and military chest at Brunswick. He ordered campfires to be built up, and as working parties continued to wield picks and shovels, the army filed off. The British slept as the Americans "March'd by a round about road to Princeton . . . we found Princèton about Sunrise 3 January with only three Regiments of Infantry and three Troops of Light Horse in it." Mawhood's regiments "made a gallant resistance," but in killed, wounded, and prisoners "must have lost near 500 men." The figure seems reasonable as Washington had "near 300 prisoners, 14 of wch. are Officers, all British." He reluctantly gave up the idea of pushing on to Brunswick for ". . . the harassed state of our troops (many of them having had no rest for two nights and a day) and the danger of losing the advantage we had gained by Aiming at too much, Induced me, by the advice of my Officers, to relinquish the attempt." He informed Congress he was moving on to Morristown, there to establish winter quarters and put the troops under cover: ". . . hitherto we have lain without any, many of our poor soldiers quite bearfoot and ill clad in other respects."[5] His decision provides one of the best examples of his calculated prudence.

On January 6 Washington established headquarters at Morristown. In two bold strokes he had possessed himself "again of New Jersey," or certainly "a considerable Part of it," cleared the province of the British and their plundering allies, regained the initiative, thrown Howe with his vastly superior force on the defensive, instilled new life into the army, and given heart to the patriots in New Jersey, who now in considerable numbers offered their services. In a brilliant campaign, he had completely outgeneraled Howe and made Cornwallis, his best corps commander, look an amateur. Clinton, who had little respect for Cornwallis' professional ability, later wrote that the earl, "deceived by Washington's fires . . . neglected to patroll to Allen's Town, over which Bridge Washington's whole Army and the last hopes of America escaped. I am sure no Hussar corporal would have been so imposed upon."

The impact of the operations Washington conducted between December 26 and January 3 can scarcely be exaggerated. Howe described

Trenton as "an unfortunate and untimely defeat" and admitted that the American victory there had given new life to an expiring cause. He saw no prospect of terminating the war "but by a general action," and this he had learned from experiences Washington could avoid, for his troops moved "with so much more alacrity than we possibly can."† Major General William Tryon assessed recent events correctly when he wrote that American leaders were conscious of the need to strike a stroke "to give life to their sinking cause." And until Washington reversed the situation in New Jersey during that critical week, the cause was sinking, and sinking fast. Washington's imaginative and audacious plans, his energy and his personal qualities of leadership, had combined not only to reanimate the spirit of his countrymen and to depress those of their enemies but to re-establish his own reputation, sadly impaired on Long Island, on Manhattan, by the needless loss of the garrison at Fort Washington, the surprise at Fort Lee, the precipitate retreat across New Jersey, and the abandonment of that state.

The commander in chief modestly ascribed his recent successes to favorable circumstances. Although he described Trenton as "our late lucky blow" and wrote Putnam that fortune had favored him at Princeton, the press wallowed in praise so lavish as to be embarrassing. He was hailed as America's "deliverer and guardian genius." The editor of the *Pennsylvania Journal* was completely carried away: "Had he lived in the days of idolatry, he had been worshipped as a god. One age can not do justice to his merit, but the united voice of a grateful posterity shall pay a cheering tribute of undissembled praise to the great asserter of their country's freedom."

Jubilant Americans were unsparing in criticism and ridicule of their enemies. As for 1777: "His Majesty intends to open this year's campaign with ninety thousand Hessians, Tories, Negroes, Japanese, Moors, Esquimaux, Persian archers, Laplanders, Feejee Islanders and light horse. With this terrific and horrendous armament . . . he is resolved to terminate this unnatural war the next summer."[6]

Although Howe, his staff, Governor Tryon, and the Tory community in New York were privately extremely critical of the Germans surprised at Trenton, the line taken in public was to depreciate the American victories there and at Princeton as of no particular import. Ambrose Serle, close to the small group of senior commanders, was "exceedingly concerned on the public Account, as it [Trenton] will tend to revive the drooping Spirits of the Rebels and increase their Force." He disconsolately resigned himself to a long winter in New York.

† Howe failed to draw the logical conclusion that British and Germans could move more rapidly if combat loads of the individual soldier and the excessive amount of officers' baggage and other impedimenta in the trains were drastically reduced.

Serle felt sympathy for "the poor ignorant Souls" who came daily to his office to pledge allegiance to the King and to receive His Majesty's pardon. The lines were long, but men stood for hours in bitter weather, anxious to receive their pardons before the January 29 deadline set by the Howes. Serle was sympathetic to these plain folk, "deluded to their own Destruction by the Artifices of the Congress and other Demagogues." He met daily with Galloway for a dish of tea or a glass of wine, which he imbibed with a considerable amount of misinformation. According to Galloway, there was "every Reason to expect a speedy Famine." Even in Connecticut, "one of the most plentiful Colonies," the inhabitants were "distressed for Salt, and many other Necessaries of Life. All this is the diabolical Work of a few wicked men, called *the Congress.*"

When Serle was not busy making out pardons to be given all—and there were hundreds—who voluntarily took the oath of allegiance, he spent considerable time discussing political affairs with William Allen, a prominent Philadelphia Tory to whose advice both Serle and his seniors gave a great deal more weight than it merited. Over a cup of tea, Allen told Serle that "three fourths of the People are against Independency"; that they were suffering "under the Dominion of a desperate Faction, formed by the worst Characters," and that "opinion among all sensible People in Philadelphia" held "the Force of opposition was breaking, and that it wd. be impossible to establish the Point of Independency."

Allen's two brothers confirmed this view, as did Joseph Galloway, who declared the "Power of the Rebellion to be pretty well broken." Galloway thought that while "the Colonies may make some further Efforts" they could "only be feeble and ineffectual." This opinion was commonly held in New York. When Serle suggested that Loyalists in Philadelphia might seize leaders of Congress, Allen replied the measure had been secretly discussed by "some of the first people" and rejected as too "perilous," as there were "no Arms in the Hands of any but the violent Faction." Serle dryly replied that it rested with loyal Philadelphians to determine whether "the Object was not worth the Peril."

Andrew Allen, one of William's brothers, who knew Samuel Adams, paid the Bostonian the merited compliment of being the one man of all he had ever known "most capable of leading or inflaming a Mob. He has vast Insinuation and infinite Art, by wch. he has been able to impose upon most Men." The thesis that Adams and a small group of desperate and conniving men had deluded the unhappy Americans fit neatly with unconfirmed assertions of refugees from Philadelphia that "the three lower counties upon Delaware . . . and Maryland" awaited an opportunity to rise against the Congress: There was no doubt of their making "a formal Renunciation" when the British Army would "advance to support them."[7] Charles Lee, then a prisoner, told the Howe brothers the same story. Galloway reported a deplorable state of affairs in Philadelphia, where the unhappy inhabitants suffered under "the iron Dominion of the Rebels." These reports and others corroborating them confirmed the convictions of the King and his ministers, who apparently made no attempt to evaluate information derived from self-serving sources, that tens of thousands of Loyalists would respond to a Redcoat presence.

Queen Charlotte's birthday was celebrated in New York with public and private ceremonies. Guns of forts and ships fired numberless salutes; such bells as the Americans had not removed for casting into cannon rang joyously. General Howe and the admiral were cohosts at "a grand Entertainment to the officers and others." At this affair Lord Howe invested his younger brother with the Order of the Bath. Sir William, as he now became, was not particularly anxious to receive the red ribbon, which was not especially prestigious; Knights of the Bath were a shilling a dozen. Serle rejoiced: "Everybody agreed that the Ribbon was never more honorably conferred, nor more honorably invested." Drinking, eating, gaming, and dancing were succeeded by "A very fine Piece of Firework." The ignorant locals gaped, enchanted: "To most of them it seemed a most wonderful Phoenomenon."[8]

"Everybody," including Judge Thomas Jones, did not agree that the investiture was an honorable one. The judge had nothing to say of the ceremony or the brilliant rout that followed, but he dealt harshly with the new knight: "This month was remarkable for the investiture of General Howe with the order of the Bath; a reward for *evacuating* Boston, for *lying indolent* upon Staten Island for near two months, for *suffering* the whole rebel army to escape him upon Long Island, and again at the White Plains; for *not putting an end to rebellion* in 1776 when so often in his power; for making such *injudicious cantonments* of his troops in Jersey as he did, and for *suffering* 10,000 veterans, under experienced generals, to be cooped up in Brunswick and Amboy." The judge, disillusioned and embittered, loathed Howe, who, he wrote, spent his time "Lolling in the arms of his mistress, and sporting his cash at the faro bank," when he should have been attending to his duties in the field.

Historians have repeatedly raised questions relating to Howe's conduct of the campaign of 1776, which optimists in London had good reason to believe would crush the rebellion in America. To some of these there are satisfactory answers; to others there are not. In his professional relationships the British commander in chief was a taciturn man. He kept a great deal of his thinking to himself. He frequently consulted Cornwallis and was usually attentive to his suggestions. He listened reluctantly to Generals Clinton and Grant. He never took more than cursory notice of recommendations made by his Hessian subordinates, General de Heister or, later, Major General Baron Wilhelm von Knyphausen.

Why did not Howe attack Washington on Long Island before he did —shortly after he arrived from Halifax? He considered doing so and rejected the idea because he had not the means to mount an assault with any realistic hope of success. He had but meager intelligence of Washington's strength, and of his dispositions, none. He had no information on the Long Island beaches nor the terrain inland. He was short of landing craft, tents, other camp equipment, horses, spare parts for muskets, and engineering tools. He was awaiting promised reinforcements. Most important, when he arrived off Staten Island his troops had been crammed on transports, living on salt provisions and bread for three weeks. They had endured a cold winter of privation and frustration in Boston and had fared little better in Halifax. They needed, and deserved, a full month for refreshment; for hundreds of sick to convalesce on an adequate diet and in reasonably pleasant surroundings, and for officers and sergeants to re-establish the control inevitably eroded during protracted periods of incarceration on troopships.

The next question—and this was by no means satisfactorily explored during the later (1779) parliamentary inquiry—is why Howe did not press the victory he gained on August 27 to its conclusion. His failure to do so was incomprehensible to at least one senior American commander. Apparently, the British general had not forgotten Bunker Hill. He knew what execution Yankees protected by entrenchments could do on troops advancing in ordered ranks. He perforce weighed prospective gain against possible loss. To put this in brutal terms—as he did—how many casualties could he accept in a storming operation? 1,000? 1,500? 2,000? Whatever the number, he juggled figures of dead and wounded in his mind, and concluded the price he would have to pay would be more than an army 3,000 miles and three to four months from the source of replacements and resupply could afford.

In his later exculpatory statement before the House of Commons, the general cited his report of September 3, 1776, to Germain: "Had the troops been permitted to go on, it is my opinion they would have carried the redoubts, but as it was apparent the line must have been ours at a cheap rate by regular approaches, I would not risk the loss that might have been sustained in the assault and ordered them back to a hollow way in the front of the works, out of reach of the musketry." He would not "wantonly . . . commit his Majesty's troops when the object was inadequate."[9] But was it? A general more bold than Howe would have been willing to pay the price—and it would have been heavy, but perhaps in political terms not exorbitant. Annihilation of the major part of Washington's army might well have been worth the sacrifice. At the time both Clinton and Cornwallis acquiesced in Howe's decision.

Next, what explanation is there for Howe's inactivity between August 29 and September 15? Two factors must have influenced him. First, it would have been impolitic to undertake offensive action before Viscount Howe talked with the gentlemen from Congress; second, he had to adjust his movements to conditions of moon, tides, sunset, and sunrise. He desired to put in his attack on the Kip's Bay position as a surprise. As in any amphibious operation—and he and his brother were experts in this form of assault—plans must be adjusted to suit the prescriptions of nature. The admiral had to get his landing craft up the East River secretly, and he could only do this on certain nights when all conditions were right.

As we look at Howe's movements during the six weeks following Harlem Heights, we must remember his purpose was always to maneuver Washington into a position where he would be forced to fight on unfavorable terms—in open ground, where British infantry, unequaled in orthodox tactics and supported by an excellent artillery, could easily dispose of the American "ragamuffins."

The general wrote Lord George Germain on September 23, 24, and 25 to report successful action at Kip's Bay, the fire, and conclusion of the second phase of his planned operation to seize New York. He ascribed his delay, for which he was well aware he would be severely criticized, to the nature of the country "so covered with wood, swamps and creeks, that it is not open in the least degree to be known but from post to post." There is but one certain way of discovering terrain details, and that is by sending out reconnaissance parties. Howe's problem here was similar to that Gage had encountered: Junior officers who should have led these patrols were unable to map or sketch. He added he found Americans "not so well disposed" to join him as he "had been taught to expect" and thought "further progress for the present precarious." In the last of these letters he stated bluntly that he saw "no prospect of finishing the war that campaign."[10] With a commanding general so easily discouraged there was indeed no prospect of reaching a decision in that or any other campaign.

Howe's complaint that the terrain imposed severe restrictions on his operations was indeed true. The more open terrain of Europe, uncluttered with natural obstacles—gullies, streams, underbrush—was perfect for maneuvering of close formations advancing in dressed ranks at uniform pace. In many engagements in America the British were unable to utilize their excellent artillery with maximum effect. As a young surveyor and Indian fighter, Washington had developed a keen eye for the lie of the land; he knew that ground is the handmaid of victory and took great pains in selecting and organizing his positions at both Harlem Heights and White Plains to derive full advantage from its accidents. He had to depend on this and on indefatigable work with pick, shovel, and ax to nullify the effect of British and German cannon fire and to break up orderly formations of assaulting infantrymen advancing in rhythmical cadence to close quarters.

Various theses have been suggested as to why Howe attacked Fort Washington instead of simply masking the place and moving quickly into New Jersey with a striking force. One answer is that he needed a victory, any sort of victory. The opportunity to achieve one at Fort Washington was given him by an American officer who deserted and brought with him full details of the strength of the garrison and the defenses. Howe had accomplished little since mid-September, and the ministry wanted, and had reason to expect, some good news. They had provided the general with a magnificent army, which for two months had done little more than march and countermarch and eat its total weight. But he did not reduce Fort Washington until November 16. The operation may have advanced Howe's reputation in Whitehall, but it gave the Americans a start of five full days. And Washington's "ragamuffins" could march. The final scene of the campaign was laid in New Jersey. There, Howe not only let slip the opportunity to destroy Washington, but allowed both British and Hessians to deal mortal blows to the cause of the crown.

Howe should have ordered and led a relentless pursuit of the demoralized and disintegrating American Army. True, Cornwallis' troops were tired, but when Washington's retreating army arrived at Princeton on the morning of December 2, his men were exhausted and their morale at the nadir. "We are in a terrible situation, with the enemy close upon us, and whole regiments of Marylanders and Jerseymen leaving us."[11] His strength was less than 4,000, and had Cornwallis' light infantry and grenadiers clung close to his rear guard, they might well have brought his tattered army to bay. There was chance for a great victory. But Howe had not pushed.

Worse, Howe's troops plundered their way across New Jersey, carrying off cattle, chickens, pigs, sheep, horses, farm carts, and grain. Burning, looting, raping, and intimidating, they indiscriminately terrorized the rebels, the apathetic, and the Loyalists. Howe was to state later that in New Jersey he had "endeavoured to conciliate his Majesty's rebellious subjects, by taking every means to prevent the destruction of the country."[12] He certainly did not actively encourage devastation of the countryside or terrorization of its inhabitants, but neither did he take steps to control the rapacity of his troops.

Judge Jones, who undoubtedly acquired some of his information of the New Jersey campaign from good sources, was unsparing in his criticism: ". . . a victorious army, in full pursuit of a flying inconsiderable enemy, were stopped upon the banks of the Delaware, and instead of taking the necessary steps for the security of New Jersey, a licentious army was suffered to plunder, and to commit every kind of rapine, injustice and violence indiscriminately upon the inhabitants, the consequence of which became dismal. It ended in the loss of the province, the ruin of hundreds, and the lives of thousands."

Although considerable evidence was available that most Americans were not in the slightest degree interested in again subjecting themselves to Great Britain, or in submitting to the questionable clemency of a now detested King, this intelligence did not find its way to London through official channels. Indeed, in Whitehall, such a conclusion would have been most unwelcome. Biased reports from across the Atlantic invariably confirmed ministers' preconceived notions of American loyalty, which objective reporting and analysis might have dissipated.

Howe was frustrated and his British and Hessians exasperated by Washington's consistent refusal to be sucked into a position where he would have to accept battle on Howe's terms. At New Rochelle and White Plains, Howe had maneuvered in approved European style, but Washington would not rise to the bait. As he had written Hancock, he was determined to take no "Risque." He would fight not when victory seemed possible, or even probable, but only when he deemed it practically certain. Just as it was to Washington's advantage to prolong the war, it was to Great Britain's to end it as quickly as possible. To do this, General Howe had to move rapidly, push his enemy relentlessly, and take calculated risks. But he was not temperamentally so inclined.

The net result of the operations Howe conducted between August 1776 and mid-January 1777 was slightly better than zero. He held New York and its environs. His New Jersey holdings had been reduced to tenuous garrisons at Amboy and New Brunswick. His army had suffered considerable casualties, and British arms had lost immeasurable prestige. His troops had alienated many citizens in New Jersey; the four weeks the British spent in Princeton were long remembered as the "twenty-six days of tyranny."

When one examines the record, it seems apparent that Howe should have been relieved, and another "General in America" appointed. Possibly the most competent British general then in North America was Guy Carleton, but he had no chance of a change of scene so long as Germain held office. The Howe brothers were politically powerful, and thanks to the adultery of a grandmother, related to the King. Nothing short of a cabinet revolt could have forced George III to relieve Sir William Howe. But with Lord North as First Minister, this was inconceivable. Had someone of Pitt's caliber been in office, things might have been different. There is no record that the question of Howe's recall was seriously discussed.

Some two weeks prior to the time Washington took up winter quarters at Morristown, Congress passed a resolution unique in American history, one that stands as singular testimony to the trust and confidence the delegates reposed in the commander in chief. On December 27, Congress conferred "full, ample and complete Power" on Washington to raise six-teen Continental battalions; to appoint their officers; "to raise, officer, and equip three thousand Light Horse, three Regiments of Artillery and a Corps of Engineers, and to establish their pay." The resolve was due in part to the desperate situation, and in some measure to a personal letter General Nathanael Greene, bypassing established channels, had written Hancock on December 21, in which he urged that Congress delegate to Washington "full Power to take such Measures as he may find Necessary to promote the Establishment of the New Army." Greene averred he was "no advocate for the Extension of Military Power," but was fully con-vinced the measure was "absolutely necessary." Congress need not be ap-prehensive: "There never was a Man that might be more safely trusted, nor a Time when there was a louder Call."[13]

Congress granted these extensive, indeed almost dictatorial powers over the army none too soon. And as Greene had affirmed, there would be no cause for fear that the general would abuse the trust. On New Year's Day, 1777, he assured Congress he would employ all his faculties "to direct properly the powers they have been pleased to Vest me with, and to advance those Objects, and only those, which give rise to this honourable mark of distinction."[14]

The first weeks at Morristown were busy ones for the general, partic-ularly as Adjutant General Reed had again resigned.‡ During the last three weeks of January, letters and reports streamed out of his head-quarters. His small team of overworked secretaries must have spent eighteen hours a day taking dictation, drafting and redrafting "roughs," and producing smooth copies of letters for the general's signature.

Much of this correspondence concerned prisoners of war. Congress had sent Washington many reports alleging mistreatment of American prisoners confined aboard prison ships in New York harbor. Men taken from privateers were particular objects of Viscount Howe's animosity. From Morristown, the commander in chief wrote the admiral a strong but tactful letter of protest. He could not suppose Howe was "privy to proceedings of so cruel and unjustifiable a nature" and hoped his lordship would so regulate matters "that the unhappy Creatures, whose Lot in Captivity may not in future have the Miseries of Cold, disease and Famine, added to their other Misfortunes."[15] Howe's neglect of the pris-oners on the hulks in New York was in marked contrast to the humane and almost benevolent treatment prisoners in Carleton's hands had re-ceived. The governor's leniency had been reprobated by Germain, a fact that did not escape the attention of the admiral and his brother.

‡ It appears likely that Washington tactfully suggested this. He had by mistake opened and read a letter Charles Lee had written Reed in which Lee had most disloyally and indiscreetly asserted that "a certain great man" was by no means fit to hold such high position. Washington's confidence in Reed's fidelity and discretion was inevitably destroyed.

Inhumane treatment of prisoners was a question frequently raised by both sides, and with reason. The British commissary of prisoners, Joshua Loring, husband of General Howe's mistress "the Sultana," was a Boston Tory who had been deprived of his property and vindictively took every opportunity to square accounts. That the general had deprived him of his wife did not seem to bother him. She was at least seeing his bread was buttered.

Washington's general plan for the winter was to restrict the British to Brunswick and Amboy, to distress them as much as possible, to ambush their foraging parties, and to compel inhabitants of New Jersey to sell livestock and grain to the Americans. The British were short of feed for their horses; Washington's idea was that if he could cut off supplies of hay and grain the animals would starve, and so immobilize Howe in the spring. He reported to Congress that these operations promised to be highly successful; his patrols skirmished with British parties daily; Howe was beginning to feel the pinch: "I think do what they will, they must be distressed greatly before the Winter is over."

The army was now in another recurrent state of dissolution. As of mid-January, one Pennsylvania battalion had departed; two more daily threatened to leave; five Virginia regiments had been reduced to "a handful," and most of Hand's riflemen had taken off for home. Of the New England Continental Troops, fewer than 800 of 1,400 remained in camp. Several Pennsylvania brigades stayed "from day to day, by dint of Solicitations." Happily, General Warner had just arrived with 700 Massachusetts militia, engaged for ninety days. The commander in chief sent out every officer he could spare "to collect the scattered Men of the different Regiments, who are dispersed almost over the Continent."[16] He was, however, successfully maintaining a front; constant patrol activity completely deceived Howe as to his effective strength. As usual, the army wanted shoes, shirts, stockings, blankets, and tentage; the military chest was in its normal condition: empty. No bounty money was available to entice recruits.

Washington felt if he could survive the winter, he could field a respectably effective army in late spring. By that time, he hoped to have the establishment on a regular footing. He optimistically presumed state authorities were busy engaging men to serve for the duration in the battalions Congress had authorized. Some were making the attempt, albeit halfheartedly; others, such as Governor Nicholas Cooke of Rhode Island, were sabotaging the program by enlisting men for duties only within the boundaries of the state.** Washington wrote Cooke a strong but discreet remonstrance, and begged him to set matters right, for "If

** Allotments of these battalions, by states, was as follows: New Hampshire three, Massachusetts fifteen, Rhode Island two, Connecticut eight, New York four, New Jersey four, Pennsylvania twelve, Delaware one, Maryland eight, Virginia fifteen, North Carolina nine, South Carolina six, Georgia one.

I am properly supported, I hope to close the Campaign Gloriously for America."[17]

This hope was not soon to be realized. Guerrilla-type detachments had many minor local successes, but so long as he had "a full Army one day and scarce any the next" he could not possibly project any major operations. Strategically, he was on the defensive, but he held the tactical initiative and made the most effective use of this advantage. He was eager to "stab" Howe hard during the winter in ambushes and forays and to "strike a decisive Blow before Spring." Howe, living in comfort in New York, had no intention of exchanging Mrs. Loring's warm bed for a cold tent in New Jersey.

While Washington's army made the best of short rations and leaky hutments, a rump Congress sat in Baltimore. On the first day of February 1777, only twenty-two delegates answered roll call. All others had departed for their own more cheerful firesides: "New York, Delaware and Maryland may almost as well desert the Cause as so lamely support it by their appearance in its publick Councils." The southern colonies were equally remiss. The "crime" carried its own punishment: ". . . if there are two Interests . . . that must necessarily prevail which always has its advocates on the spot. . . ."[18]

Among other matters, Congress was considering wage and price controls. As the value of Continental paper steadily dropped, inflation reached even higher levels. John Adams found prices in Baltimore "intolerable," his expenses "infinite." He was in favor of controls, but as he wrote Abigail, he expected "only a partial and temporary relief," and feared that "after a time, the evils will break out with greater violence. The water will flow with greater rapidity for having been dammed up." There was only one cure—"to stop the emission of more paper and draw in some that is already out."[19] He continued to advocate taxes.

Most members were anxious to return to Philadelphia. Benjamin Rush was indefatigable in urging his colleagues to remove to the more civilized banks of the Delaware: "We live here in a Convent. . . . We are precluded from all opportunities of feeling the pulse of the public upon our measures. Our return will have the same effect upon our politicks that General Washington's late successes have had upon our Arms. Its operation perhaps may not be confined to the Continent. It may serve our cause even in the Court of France."[20]

But not for three long weeks were delegates to pack their trunks and boxes and with considerable difficulty hire coaches, "chariots," wagons, chaises, and horses to transport them and their baggage to "Jerusalem," where all hoped they could settle in cultivated surroundings, with reasonably priced claret and madeira, and return to a productive schedule. Hancock detested Baltimore; the sojourn there had been a total loss: "the Stagnation of all Business for a Season."

But Congress had found time to debate selection of general officers; these sessions were stormy, "perplexed, inconclusive and irksome." Benjamin Rush, who fancied himself a classical scholar, harked back to Rome, which he described as "a powerful and happy commonwealth." According to him, "Rome called her general officers from the plough and paid no regard to rank, service or seniority." He advocated total control over appointment and recall of generals. Unless Congress preserved supreme power, he argued, all "civil power" might as well be turned over to the army. The army had to be restrained and kept subservient to the Congress. John Adams respected Washington, but "in this house I feel myself his Superior."[21]

Although Washington never contested the thesis that the army must be subservient to the will of Congress, he had no particular desire to have any more general officers "called from the plough." He had repeatedly emphasized that merit should be the sole criterion in their selection. But demands of section were powerful; delegates could not neglect them. The number of battalions provided by each state automatically dictated the number of native sons who would enjoy general officer rank. Parochial loyalties were unavoidably decisive.

In Philadelphia, Morris, Clymer, and Walton acted as an executive committee for Congress; on February 27 Morris wrote the commander in chief confidentially lamenting the loss to that body of so many good men: Jay, two Livingstons, Duane, Deane, Nelson, Rutledge. Some were temporarily absent; others had given up their seats and had not yet been replaced. Morris was worried for what would happen to America and the cause "if a constant fluctuation is to take place among its Councillors. . . ." Several men of superior abilities had recently been replaced. Morris viewed these changes with regret. He also sent Washington his estimate of Howe's capabilities; citing the many difficulties the British general had to contend with, he concluded that Howe could not make a serious offensive move for some time.

Washington replied with a long analysis of Howe's situation as he saw it. He believed Morris was too sanguine and was viewing but "one side of the Picture, against which let me enumerate the advantages of the other." Then, he went on, one might "determine how we would act in his situation." Howe had 10,000 men in the Jerseys (Brunswick and Amboy) and barracked aboard transports. Washington had but 4,000 fit to fight. Howe's troops "are well disciplined, well Officered and well appointed: Ours raw Militia, badly Officered and under no Government." Washington could hope for fresh troops, but they would have to be such as he could rely on (an unlikely prospect), "or the Game is at an End."

In respect to fit horses and supplies of forage, Howe's situation was "bad, very bad." He proposed to take measures to make it considerably worse.

Constant pressure might induce Howe to try a movement by land to Philadelphia. Howe had an efficient network of informers; he could not be ignorant of the condition of Washington's army, hutted in primitive shelters at Morristown. Taking Philadelphia would give great "Eclat to his Arms" and "strike a damp upon ours." Howe could send all heavy baggage and stores by sea, so that he would not be encumbered and delayed by a train. If Howe was not contemplating such a move, why had he recently come to Brunswick? Here was no contemptuous underrating of the British commander in chief and his forces, but an objective appraisal of relative strengths and weaknesses and a rational attempt to assess Howe's capabilities.

What actually held Howe in New York was not, as so frequently and ribaldly alleged, the indubitable charms of Mrs. Loring, but an acute shortage of provisions for the army and of hay and grain for his horses. He did not have enough horses to mount his chasseurs, to transport officers' baggage, and to pull his guns, ammunition carts, and wagons loaded with rations, beer, rum, and camp equipment. Washington's tactic of sweeping up all animals and fodder had effectively immobilized him for the winter.††

Actually, neither army was clothed or equipped for sustained winter operations. And for the British general there was the problem of crossing the Delaware, where ice would break during four or five days of reasonably mild weather. Altogether, Washington accorded Howe a capability he did not at the time possess.[22] But it is more prudent slightly to overrate the enemy than to underrate him.

On February 19 Congress made five new major generals. Brigadier General Benedict Arnold was not on the list; all those promoted—Lord Stirling, Thomas Mifflin, Arthur St. Clair, Adam Stephan, and Benjamin Lincoln—were junior to him. The real reason Arnold was passed over at this time has never been discovered. (True, his accounts were in arrears, and his letters had antagonized several powerful members who felt his attitude to Congress was not sufficiently respectful.) Washington was

†† To put the problem of provisioning and otherwise supplying His Majesty's forces overseas in proper perspective, it must be recalled that the army was literally spread from Minorca to Michilimackinac; from Halifax to the Sugar Islands; from Jamaica to the west coast of Africa. In the winter of 1776–77 Howe's army in New York and the Jerseys stood at a strength of some 30,000 effectives; Carleton's in Canada numbered 10,000. Possibly 5,000 were in or en route to the West Indies and Florida. Gibraltar was defended by 4,000, Minorca by 2,000, Halifax by 1,000. To this total (52,000) there must be added the Provincial troops, friendly Indians, and thousands of Loyalists in New York who had fled there for safety. When the requirements of the Royal Navy on station in American and West Indian waters is added, the staggering scope of the logistics problem becomes readily apparent.

dismayed. As soon as the list was published he wrote Arnold begging him not to take "any hasty step." Probably some error had been made which would soon be rectified. At least, his own "endeavours to that end shall not be wanting."[23] New brigadiers were also appointed; Washington wrote to each congratulating him, exhorting him to renew his zeal, and issuing miscellaneous instructions

The question of how to effect the speedy release of Major General Lee agitated the delegates during their last days in Baltimore. Howe had threatened to send Lee to England to stand trial for treason. Washington reminded him that he had thirty Hessian mercenary officers in his hands and knew precisely what to do with them should Howe carry out his threat. The British general stopped his blustering; he and his brother decided they might use Lee to advantage by persuading him to write Congress suggesting a "conference."

Congress received the letter and promptly rejected the idea as "degrading." "It was the General Sense of Congress that no Conference ought to be held with any but Embassadors properly authorized by the Court of Britain to treat of Peace." And peace could be discussed with such emissaries only after a solemn declaration that the United States was an independent and sovereign nation. John Adams thought the proposal "an artful strategm" designed by the conniving brothers "to hold up to the public view the phantom of a negotiation in order to give spirits and courage to the Tories, to distract and divide the Whigs at a critical moment when the uttermost exertions are necessary to draw together an army." He considered the proposition a political ploy and gave his opinion that Lee had allowed himself to be duped "so far as to become the instrument" of the brothers' machinations. The Staten Island meeting had done "great and essential injury" to the American cause at the court of Versailles and also pulled the rug from under the Opposition in Parliament. "Lord Howe knows it, and wishes to repeat it."[24] So Adams wrote General Nathanael Greene, who had interceded in his brother officer's behalf. Charles Lee would have to languish yet awhile in New York.

Finally, after much acrimonious argument, a majority of delegates voted immediate adjournment to Philadelphia. Some gentlemen were apprehensive; one less timid than his colleagues observed that it made not the slightest difference if they were "all killed or Captivated" as "public Business would suffer no other Injury except the delay until other members could be chozen; he knew his country [State] had men much better than himself."[25] The motion was carried, but not "without some Difficulty and some warmth." James Wilson believed the move essential and would "give a Spring to the Sinews of War."

The delegates assembled in Philadelphia on March 3, and on the following evening attended a dinner at the City Tavern in honor of Thomas Wharton, president of the Supreme Executive Council of the Commonwealth of Pennsylvania. A delectable meal was followed by seventeen toasts, among them "The Congress," "General Washington and the Army," "The Navy," "Agriculture," "Dr. Franklin," and "General Charles Lee." Cannon roared, church bells pealed. Indeed, "the whole was conducted with the utmost decency, and no accident happened of any kind."[26]

News of Washington's successes at Trenton and Princeton, and Howe's subsequent abandonment of New Jersey, was received in London with consternation. Howe's dispatches to this point had been complacently optimistic; now the Administration was struck by a totally unexpected bombshell. Walpole, generally pessimistic, wrote Mann on April 3: "Washington, the dictator, has shown himself both a Fabius and a Camillus. His march through our lines is allowed a prodigy of generalship. In one word, I look upon [the] great part of America as lost to this country."[27]

At Versailles, the persuasive Dr. Franklin was doing what he could to see to it that America *would* be lost to Great Britain. In a memoir to Vergennes, the doctor questioned the minister's policy of avoiding open interference, based, he said, on the fallacious assumption that England "would so far exhaust herself as to give France an opportunity of more advantageously beginning a war at a later period." This was *"too dangerous to be any longer pursued by a wise and provident administration."*

He predicted Britain would exert herself to bring the war to an end in 1777. There was even a distinct possibility she would grant independence and promptly engage with her former colonies in alliance against France. One could scarcely doubt that when peace was concluded, "whatever may be the Conditions of it, the whole force on the Continent of America will be suddenly transported to the W. Indies and imployed in subduing the French Sugar Islands there to recompence her Losses and Expenses in this War and to avenge the secret encouragement and assistance which France is supposed to have given the Colonys against Great Britain." The ministry would thus be enabled to palliate a disgraceful failure in America and divert the anger of the people from themselves to France.[28] Bancroft passed a copy of Franklin's memoir to Wentworth, who commented at length and sent it on to Eden.

Eden had another reliable agent in Paris, code name "George Lupton," who reported directly to him. "Lupton" was an American from Philadelphia, ostensibly a merchant, and one of Silas Deane's intimates. Deane, who had no conception of the meaning of the word "discretion," talked freely; all his convivial guest need do was listen. In a humorous passage which sheds light on Deane's doings, "Lupton" reported that the commissioner had moved into a new *hôtel* on fashionable Place Louis XV "where he struts about like a Cock on his Dunghill, and is as well pleased as a Child with a new plaything, but I perfectly join with you in the opinion that his pride must have a downfall."[29] Deane was in fact bemused by the brilliant society in which he was able to move. He was spending a great deal of money and devoting a considerable portion of his time and energies to fitting out a privateer at Marseilles in which he had a financial stake. This ship was to prey on the British silk trade; fabulous profits were projected.

The third American emissary, Arthur Lee, was even less help to Franklin than Deane. Lee, an extremely difficult person, was a trouble-maker; he and Deane were constantly at sword's points. He was jealous of Franklin's influence and popularity and contributed little to help the doctor in his delicate negotiations. He, too, talked too much. His confidential secretary was a Wentworth agent—indeed, the offices of the commissioners were so many sieves. Everything Franklin or his colleagues said or did was shortly known in Whitehall. Copies of what they wrote were usually available to William Eden within seventy-two hours.

The interminable winter in New York was not conducive to improving morale and discipline in Sir William Howe's idle army. No fresh provisions were available, and those of the salted variety, as well as beer, rum, and firewood, were strictly rationed. The shivering soldiers mounted guard, chopped wood, fetched water, turned out reluctantly for occasional ceremonies, grumbled, cursed their luck, the weather, their sergeants, played cards, got drunk as often as possible, consorted with prostitutes when they could afford this indulgence, and wished they were almost anywhere but in New York. Many deserted.

When Sir William read the most recent epistle from the Secretary of State, he, too, probably wished he was not in New York. Germain found "the disagreeable occurrence at Trenton . . . extremely mortifying" and warned Howe that the Americans "should not be held too cheap." He reminded the general that commanders should "never think so meanly of their Enemies as to permit themselves to be off their Guard," and wound up his homily by expressing his hope that the brothers would soon adopt "such modes of carrying on the War that the Rebels may be effectually distressed and brought as soon as possible to a proper sense of their Duty." The message was clear: The mood in Whitehall was no longer one of unqualified approbation of Howe's activities, but of irritation at his negligence and dissatisfaction with his conduct of operations in New Jersey.

The secretary's rude letter arrived at Howe's headquarters at about the time he received confirmation of reports that a principal American magazine at Danbury in western Connecticut held large stocks of provisions, ordnance stores, and camp equipment of all descriptions. This information provided Major General Tryon opportunity to revive his earlier suggestion that he be given command of a small force to sail down Long Island Sound, land near Norwalk, make a quick march to Danbury, conduct a raid on the depot, collect what foodstuffs and tentage he could to alleviate shortages in New York, and destroy what he could not carry off in requisitioned wagons. Tryon observed that the operation would certainly "distress" the rebels. Howe agreed. He approved Tryon's plan, assigned him a landing force of some 1,900 (including a battalion of Provincials known as the Prince of Wales Royal American Volunteers), and promised a diversion up the Hudson to prevent American troops at Peekskill from marching to the relief of Danbury or interfering with the subsequent withdrawal.

During late afternoon on April 25, the British landed at the mouth of the Saugatuck River, which flows into Long Island Sound a few miles east of Norwalk, marched inland ten miles, and bivouacked. Several hours before dawn the following day they took the road to Danbury, where the advance guard arrived at 4 P.M. They had met no resistance. This valuable depot was protected by some fifty Continentals and fifty militia who had no choice but to withdraw. Notice that Redcoats were marching inland had reached Danbury at dawn, ten hours before the advance guard set foot in the place, but as no plans had been made to move valuable stores, nothing more than several wagonloads of medicines had been taken from the town. The patriotic citizens, unwilling to turn over their horses and wagons for this purpose, hurriedly crammed them with wives, children, chickens, pigs, bedding, pots, pans, and pewter, hitched up their teams, and took off in all directions.

As soon as Tryon realized he could not find transport to move the captured food, tents, and other supplies, he ordered them destroyed. This proceeded in a methodical fashion. The British made no attempt to burn the town and evidence does not support later lurid accounts of drunken depredation and indiscriminate plundering.‡‡ In any event, circumstances did not permit such soldierly indulgences as these. There was too much work to be done in the short time Tryon had allowed.

Before noon on the twenty-seventh the British took the road south through Ridgefield. Here they encountered a small force under command of Brigadier General Benedict Arnold, who happened to be in the vicinity drumming up militia, then commanded by Major General David Wooster. Several short, hot fights ensued. In the first of these Wooster was wounded mortally. In the second Arnold had a horse shot from under him and barely escaped with his life as he shot a Redcoat who attempted to bayonet him. He rallied the militia and led two attacks. In

‡‡ Only twenty dwellings of some four hundred were destroyed by fire. The reasonable supposition is that these were adjacent to structures that contained stores, or caught sparks from the several huge bonfires in the streets. Tryon had issued explicit orders forbidding plundering.

these the British suffered heavily, but Arnold, despite his heroic example and his best efforts, could not persuade the militia to follow him for a third time. He later reported that they had behaved "*as usual*—I wish never to see another of them in action." Tryon embarked without suffering further serious opposition. He had lost 170 in killed, wounded, and prisoners. For months he had been telling Howe that western Connecticut teemed with Tories. He had expected hundreds to flock to his column. None had.

The cost to the Americans of Tryon's raid was tremendous. At Danbury the British destroyed 4,000 barrels of salt beef, 1,000 barrels of flour, and several hundred hogsheads of rum, sugar, wine, coffee, and molasses. Upwards of 1,000 precious tents were fed to the flames, as were chests of medicines, thousands of pairs of shoes and stockings, and tons of wheat, corn, and oats. Months would be required to replace destroyed stocks. The tents, lately arrived from France, could not be replaced in America.

Although Governor Trumbull of Connecticut appeared cast as the logical scapegoat, he was by no means to blame for the failure to protect Danbury or to grievously damage the raiding column. For several weeks Washington had been urging him to send forward all the militia he could muster, and the governor had done so. Actually, no single individual could justly be held accountable. Howe's diversion up the Hudson had completely fooled Washington, as it had Brigadier General Alexander McDougall, commanding at Peekskill. The only senior officers to emerge with credit were Wooster and Arnold, who was promoted to major general and given a horse "properly caparisoned" by Congress "as a token of their admiration of his gallant conduct." Wooster was buried several days later.

For several weeks prior to Tryon's appearance, the Americans had received information pointing almost unmistakably to Howe's intent. None had paid it proper attention. While in no sense decisive, the raid once again demonstrated the ability of the British, who enjoyed uncontested naval control in American coastal waters, to hit at will almost any seaport they chose or even any town within thirty or forty miles of water. The operation, imaginatively conceived, meticulously planned, and vigorously executed, testified as well to superior British staff work, to excellent army-navy co-operation, and to the marching and fighting ability of well-led Redcoats. On the other hand, the affair provided a dismal commentary on American intelligence and on their ability to counter such operations.

BOOK V

Organized Disaster

1

Thoughts for Conducting the War
from the Side of Canada

In early December 1776, Major General the Honourable John Burgoyne
returned to England from Canada. He arrived in London on the ninth.
The general had comported himself well as second-in-command to Carleton during the inconclusive campaign up Lake Champlain. Although he
professed to admire Carleton, he let it be known that he was not entirely
pleased with the governor's conduct of the campaign of 1776. Before he
left Quebec, he and Carleton had discussed a plan for similar operations
in 1777, in which two British columns, one driving south from Canada,
one north from New York, would meet at Albany. He was sufficiently
discreet to do no more than hint at his ambition to command the northern force.

Although Albany was not a flourishing commercial entrepôt, as New
York, Boston, Philadelphia, Charleston, and Newport were, it was one of
the few large inland towns in America; it lay astride the New York–Montreal axis; from it, post roads led eastward through the New Hampshire
Grants to Springfield and Boston and westward through the rich farming
country of the Mohawk Valley to Lake Ontario.* Many in the region

* Population of Albany at this time was about 4,500.

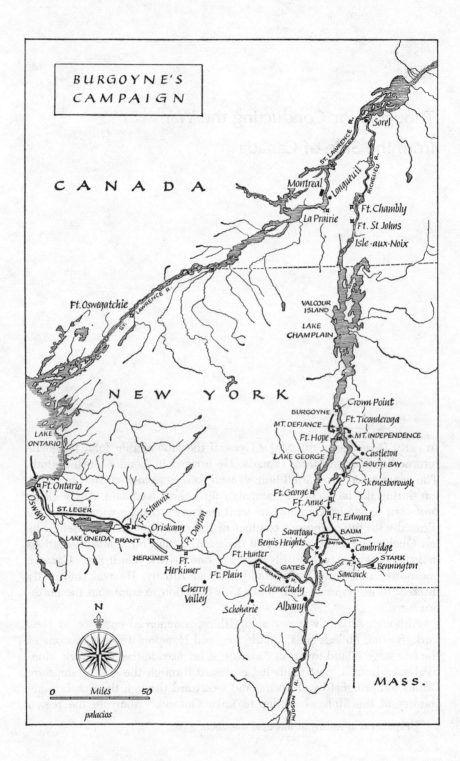

BURGOYNE'S
CAMPAIGN

CANADA

St. Lawrence R.

Sorel

Richelieu R.

Montreal
Longueuil

La Prairie
Ft. Chambly
Ft. St. Johns
Isle-aux-Noix

Ft. Oswegatchie

St. Lawrence R.

VALCOUR
ISLAND
LAKE
CHAMPLAIN

NEW YORK

Crown Point
BURGOYNE   Ft. Ticonderoga
MT. DEFIANCE
Ft. Hope   MT. INDEPENDENCE
Castleton
LAKE GEORGE   SOUTH BAY
Skenesborough

LAKE
ONTARIO

Ft. George
Ft. Anne

Ft. Ontario
ST. LEGER
Oswego
Ft. Stanwix
Ft. Dayton
LAKE ONEIDA   BRANT
Oriskany
HERKIMER
Ft.
Herkimer
Ft. Plain
Ft. Hunter
MOHAWK   R.
GATES
Cherry
Valley
Schoharie
Schenectady
Albany

Ft. Edward
Saratoga   BAUM
Bemis Heights   BATTEN KILL
Cambridge
STARK
HOOSIC R.   Bennington
Sancoick

HUDSON   R.

N

0   Miles   50

palacios

MASS.

were confirmed Loyalists; others, noncommittal, would cast their lots with the winning side. Some prominent Albanians were believed to be discreetly awaiting a Redcoat presence to declare openly for the King. An administration located in Albany could deal effectively with the powerful Indian tribes, and a garrison based there could control the "Northern Country" and live off a countryside rich in cattle, corn, fruits, and vegetables. Albany was thus a strategic center well worth possessing.

The concept of isolating New England, "the focus of rebellion," from the other colonies by control of the Hudson from Albany to New York had been much discussed. Shortly after Bunker Hill, Burgoyne had outlined such a plan in a private letter. Gage had urged a third force to move west across Massachusetts, and Howe, during his sojourn in Halifax, had recommended operations similar to those now proposed by Burgoyne. Indeed, the plans for 1776 had contemplated a junction of Northern and Southern armies. This strategy had collapsed because Arnold had delayed Carleton on Lake Champlain, and because Howe's operations around New York had started late in the season and been unduly protracted. The assumptions in London were that such impediments would not exist in 1777, and that as the Americans could not field a force strong enough to do more than harass Burgoyne, he should not have too much trouble reaching Albany.

The feature common to the various plans proposed was that of driving a wedge deep into the heart of the rebellious colonies by establishing control of the Hudson River–Champlain line. This concept exerted an almost hypnotic influence alike on generals in America—Gage, Carleton, Howe, Clinton, Burgoyne—and ministers in London. The generals favored it because they believed the King's land and naval forces would then be able to stop significant flow of men, arms, grain, livestock, and other supplies in both directions. It appealed to Germain because he was convinced it would enable the British to capitalize on Loyalist sentiment he believed to be preponderant in western Connecticut, the Hudson and Mohawk valleys, northern New York, and eastern New Jersey.

Shortly after Burgoyne reached London he met with Germain to discuss the plan he and Carleton had developed. That it was speedily approved at cabinet level and referred to the King is evident from His Majesty's letter of December 12 to Lord North:

> That there is a great prejudice, perhaps not unaccompanied with rancour, in a certain breast [Germain's] against Governor Carleton is so manifest to whoever has heard the subject mentioned, that it would be idle to say more than that it is a fact. Perhaps Carleton may be too cold and not so active as might be wished, which may make it advisable to have the part of the Canadian army which must attempt to join General Howe, led by a more enterprising commander.[1]

The Cabinet was to meet the following day on the subject of strategy for 1777. The King cautioned his First Minister to pay no attention to Germain's "invections" against Carleton, but to send the governor notice that plans for the next year were being "maturely" considered. Further, "in the present posture of affairs 3000 Men at least must be left in Canada; part of the Army must proceed on the lakes to Ticonderoga, and another by the Mohawk River." Army recruiting was proceeding slowly, and for the campaign from Canada foreigners would have to be used, as they "are the only forces we can raise, and at a reasonable charge, for they do not cause an additional Half pay when the business shall be completed." He closed this letter with the sentence: "Burgoyne may command the Corps to be sent from Canada to Albany. . . ."[2]

Germain apparently did not consider this explicit statement of the royal wish a command. Burgoyne's previous close association with Carleton, the object of Lord George's unremitting enmity, predisposed the secretary to favor Henry Clinton. Burgoyne got wind of this challenge and before leaving London for Bath to take the waters and do a bit of gambling wrote Germain he would be available to report on the situation in Canada "upon one days" notice. He added that in a private audience with the King he had "humbly laid" himself at His Majesty's feet "for such active employment as he might think me worthy of." He closed this epistle with assurances of his "solid respect and sincere personal attachment" and solicited the secretary's valued patronage. Germain was noncommittal. But the King, the final arbiter in such matters, had expressed his preference for Burgoyne.

The "Northern Army," commanded by Carleton during the previous campaign, would comprise essentially the same elements and would strike due south from St. Johns up Lake Champlain to Ticonderoga. These British and German troops, who were wintering in Canada after the campaign of 1776, had adjusted well to the climate, and were in excellent health and high spirits. A much smaller force, a highly mobile mixed group of regulars, Canadians, Indians, and Tory sympathizers totaling some 1,700, would proceed from Lake Ontario eastward along the Mohawk Valley to the Hudson. Indians under Sir John Johnson and Chief Joseph Brant were to make up half the force to be commanded by Brigadier General Barry St. Leger, whose mission was to take the undermanned forts in the Mohawk Valley and effect a junction with Burgoyne's column where the Mohawk flows into the Hudson a few miles north of Albany. Burgoyne conceived St. Leger's operation as essentially a military diversion, but one with political content. Allegiance of the Six Nations was fragile. Two tribes had declared themselves neutral; a third, the Oneida, was collaborating with the Americans. A successful operation down the Mohawk would, so it was hoped, inspire the neutrals to commit themselves, win over the Oneida, and gain active support of the many Loyalists in the area.

While the prospective commander of the Northern Army was enjoying the holidays at Bath, a letter from Howe dated November 20, 1776, reached London and was logged in at Germain's office on December 30. In this, Howe set forth his proposals for the next campaign, with the force he would require "in order if possible to finish the war in one year." His propositions were "that we should have 10,000 men to act on the side of Rhode Island, and penetrate eastward into the country toward Boston, leaving 2000 for the defence of Rhode Island, 10,000 in the province of New York, to move up the North River to Albany, 5000 for the defence of New York Island and its dependencies, 8000 to cover Jersey and to keep General Washington's army in check by giving a jealousy to Philadelphia," which he proposed to attack in autumn.[3] To execute these operations, he deemed a reinforcement of 15,000 rank and file "absolutely necessary, besides an additional battalion of artillery."

Howe was shortly to modify this plan, but it may be noted that a principal feature was a drive north up the Hudson to Albany, presumably to meet there an army driving south from Canada. The concept is otherwise interesting because it reveals Howe's limitations as a strategic planner. It was, in fact, a hodgepodge, for he was proposing to field three columns to operate divergently. There was no strategic axis. No one of these scattered columns could render support to another nor was any sufficiently powerful to assure victory over Washington's army. Finally, it should have been obvious that the projected operations imposed monumental—if not indeed insuperable—logistical problems. Germain answered Howe's proposals on January 14. He could not provide the reinforcements required; he promised 7,800. In the meantime, Howe had concluded there was little prospect of his getting 15,000 additional troops. He therefore drew up a second plan and sent it off to Whitehall in December.

Burgoyne was not privy to this correspondence. During January and February he worked happily on his plan, elaborating it in considerable detail, setting forth the assumptions on which it was based, and listing his operating force requirements in terms of regulars (not fewer than 8,000 rank and file), artillerymen, "a corps of watermen, two thousand Canadians, including hatchet men and other workmen, and one thousand or more savages."[4] Apparently Carleton was to be responsible for the horses, oxen, and carts required, and for preparation of the naval forces to be used on the lakes. He was also to raise Canadian provincial formations, enlist a corps of woodsmen, and make necessary arrangements to line up the Indians to be employed by both Burgoyne and St. Leger. Burgoyne anticipated he would be able to embody a considerable number of Loyalist sympathizers during his progress to Albany.

In "Reflections upon the War in America," a paper he probably prepared at Germain's request before sailing to join Carleton for the Champlain campaign of the previous year, Burgoyne gave an interesting and accurate description of American fighting men and their conduct in combat in difficult terrain:

> Accustomed to felling of timber and to grubbing up trees, they are very ready at earthworks and palisading, and they will cover and entrench themselves wherever they are for a short time left unmolested with surprising alacrity. . . . Composed as the American army is, together with the strength of the country, full of woods, swamps, stone walls, and other enclosures and hiding-places, it may be said of it that every private man will in action be his own general, who will turn every tree and bush into a kind of temporary fortress, from whence, when he hath fired his shot with all the deliberation, coolness, and certainty which hidden safety inspires, he will skip as it were to the next, and so on for a long time till dislodged either by cannon or by a resolute attack of light infantry. In this view of the American militia, rebels as they are, they will be found to be respectable even in flight. Light infantry, therefore, in greater numbers than one company per regiment, ought to be an essential part of the general system of our army.

Burgoyne was aware of the variety of other difficulties he would en-counter. He had some idea of the nature of the terrain to be passed, and specifically requested "hatchet men and other workmen" to help his army traverse it. He anticipated a lengthy and possibly expensive operation to reduce Ticonderoga. He had discussed this with Carleton and Phillips and they had agreed on the number and size of cannon and mortars re-quired. After taking Ticonderoga he did not expect to meet any resist-ance his own strong force could not overcome. His operations after tak-ing Ticonderoga would necessarily depend to a great extent on enemy reaction as well as upon the general plan of campaign finally decided.

Burgoyne expressed his concept in these words: ". . . that it be the *sole purpose of the Canada army to effect a junction with General Howe, or after co-operating so far as to get possession of Albany and open the communication to New York, to remain upon the Hudson's River and thereby enable that general to act with his whole force to the south-wards*" (italics mine).[5] He offered two alternative plans; the first, to swing south and east from Ticonderoga and move down the valley of the Connecticut River, where he could be within a week's march from Howe in New York; the second, to join Howe by sea, if enlistment of Canadians and Indians and procurement of an adequate number of horses, carts, drovers, and teamsters proved impossible. This last, Burgoyne wrote, was a measure "not to be thought of but upon positive conviction of its necessity." He was thus reasonably trying to ensure for himself some strategic flexibility, given the existing state of communications, the uncertain situation in Canada, and his exposed position in difficult country whose inhabitants might prove actively hostile.

The first point to be noticed is that the mission of the army moving south from Canada was expressed imprecisely and ambiguously. Was the Northern Army to effect a physical junction with Howe's force at or near Albany, or was Howe to act on the Hudson line in a co-operative endeavor which would assist Burgoyne's army to take Albany, and, by so doing, open communication from the St. Lawrence to New York? Once the British were in secure possession of the line of the Hudson, "that general" (Howe) could *then* "act to the southward." Despite the ambiguity, Burgoyne clearly conceived Howe would "act to the southward" only *after* the British controlled the line of the Hudson from Albany to New York. Revisionist historians have made much of the fact that Burgoyne knew Howe proposed to act to the southward in 1777. Of course he did, but he expected co-operation, too. The two forces were to be mutually assisting participants in a shared mission, which, when successfully accomplished, would "enable" Howe to go south.

The general completed work on his plan on February 28 and submitted it to Germain several days later. The Cabinet approved it (apparently without dissent) and sent it on for royal assent. The King went over it carefully, reduced the contingent of regulars to 7,000—he was apprehensive about the defense of Canada—and observed laconically, "Burgoyne certainly undervalues the German recruits." His Majesty also directed that Indians be employed and that the force from Canada must "join Sir William Howe in Albany." He greatly disliked the idea of shipping any part of the army from Canada by sea to join Howe, and, as it later developed, Germain was not in favor of Burgoyne's proposal to swing left through the New Hampshire Grants into Connecticut, although at the time the secretary did not inform the selected commander of the Northern Army of this.

Thus, as of early March 1777, Burgoyne's plan was approved strategy for co-operative operations to be undertaken the following summer on the Champlain-Hudson axis. This fact must be borne in mind, for if it is not, the searcher for the ultimate truth respecting Burgoyne's campaign will be led wildly astray by the charges and countercharges that later fogged the air in London and by Administration's efforts to confuse the picture by a whitewash of ministerial incompetence.

Gentleman Johnny's concept was attractive, but in the strategic context was not a solution, and this for several reasons. The first was that the proper objective was Washington's army, not real estate along the Hudson Valley and south of Champlain. For as long as that army remained in being as a combat instrument, the rebellion could not be broken. And both Burgoyne and Germain had overlooked the possibility that another American Army, or armies, might contain or conceivably defeat either or both British forces in detail. Actually, too, the British could not possibly support forces of sufficient strength effectively to isolate New England by the concerted operations Burgoyne projected.

That Carleton, Burgoyne, and ministers in London all believed the strategy could be decisive indicates their ignorance of the obstacles terrain would impose on rapid movement and continuous effective supply; their too sanguine expectations of Loyalist support, and their underestimate of the zeal, ingenuity, and capabilities of their American adversaries. Here it is only fair to Germain to point out that his generals had put him in the same position many other ministers, in other wars, have found themselves in. A strategy recommended by three senior professional soldiers, all presumably familiar with the terrain in America, the rebels' capabilities, and the character of the people, could be overruled by a minister only at the peril of his reputation and his place. Germain did not have much of the former to preserve—that had been lost years before at Minden—but he had a cabinet post, the ear of the King, the confidence of the First Minister, and a profound conviction of his own strategic sagacity. The secretary indeed had no reason to overrule Burgoyne's plan. He approved of it—at least so long as Carleton would not reap any honors as its executant. He therefore took care to have the activities of that capable officer restricted to his Canadian domain, and professed to be delighted he had been able to help Burgoyne get the independent field command many thought Carleton deserved.†

While Burgoyne was putting final touches to his "Thoughts," Howe's letter of December 20 arrived in Germain's office. In this, Howe informed the secretary that the government's inability to provide the reinforcements he had requested for early 1777 made it necessary for him to revise his plans. Basing these on the forces he realistically expected to be available, he now envisaged a principal operation against Philadelphia for the summer. He could not operate against New England. That would have to be deferred until reinforcements arrived. The corps he proposed to leave at New York under Clinton would be strong enough "to act defensively upon the lower part of Hudson's River, to cover Jersey on that side, as well as to facilitate in some degree the approach of the army from Canada."

Clearly, Howe had chosen Philadelphia as the target of first priority, and to its possession he proposed to subordinate other operations. He based this determination on the conviction that sentiment there and in Delaware was swinging toward a return to allegiance, and was therefore "fully persuaded the Principal Army should act offensively on that side."

† As early as August of the preceding year Germain had written Carleton that he was to confine himself to Canada. Carleton received this directive ten months later.

Precisely what part Major General Charles Lee played in persuading the British commander in chief to adopt this view is not entirely clear, but Lee certainly assured him that Loyalist sentiment in the area was running strong.

Germain received this letter on February 23. It should have been immediately apparent to him that Howe did not propose to act with vigor along the line of the Hudson and that a strategic muddle was incipient. Burgoyne was still in London, and, as Howe later testified, "the Minister had full opportunity of communicating the contents [of his plan] to that general and of making such changes as he might judge expedient to coincide with the northern operations."[6] But Germain did not summon Burgoyne.

On January 20 Howe sent a revision of this second plan to Germain. He again asked for more troops and categorically confirmed that his "principal object" for 1777 would be Philadelphia. Now he wanted to send a "detached corps" by sea "whilst the main body might penetrate by way of Jersey." This letter also arrived in England prior to General Burgoyne's departure.[7] Germain answered Howe's letters on March 3, 1777, and approved Philadelphia as his target.

Apparently the secretary, the Cabinet, and the King then conceived Howe would march the main body of his army across New Jersey, possibly in late May or early June when green forage could be had and roads were sufficiently dry for his supporting artillery and train to move speedily. If Howe could take Philadelphia by the end of June, or even by mid-July, he could then release a powerful column to move north and east toward Albany. But nowhere in his letter had Sir William stated he had any intention of moving in force toward Albany or that he expected Clinton to do so. He had written only that when Burgoyne arrived there, the "subsequent operations" of the Northern Army would "depend upon the state of things at the time."

A fundamental question—one now impossible to resolve—is to assess to what extent personal ambitions for rank, honors, and more tangible rewards influenced strategy for 1777. The American historian Bancroft believed this factor decisive: "The scheme originated with Carleton, the Governor of Quebec, who, as he outranked Howe, nursed the ambition of leading ten thousand men victoriously into the United States, and on his arrival assuming the supreme direction of the war."‡[8] Howe, jealously nursing his own ambition to end the war and so to gain sole acclaim, was not willing to share honors.

It was Germain's responsibility to straighten out this muddle. The remedy was simple. He could have summoned Burgoyne and discussed the question of 1777 strategy with him before laying Howe's new plan before the Cabinet. There is no evidence this idea crossed Lord George's

‡ Actually, "the scheme" did not "originate" with Carleton.

mind. Yet he was not stupid. It is possible he hesitated to balk the politically powerful Howe brothers. Or did he simply fail to comprehend the basic incompatibility of the operations proposed? In late March he wrote Carleton: "With a view of quelling the rebellion as soon as possible, it is become highly necessary that the most speedy junction of the two armies should be effected."[9] Yet not until too late would the secretary inform Howe the Cabinet expected his force, or part of it, to move north and so facilitate Burgoyne's drive on Albany.

"Thus, as of early March, Howe was left with directions to attack Philadelphia and Burgoyne with positive and unconditional commands to advance to Albany and there to place himself under Howe's orders. . . . Never was there a finer example of the art of organizing disaster."[10]

2

Messengers of Justice and Wrath

Burgoyne has received a bad press for almost two centuries. This much-maligned general was born in 1723. In later years he was said to have been illegitimate, fathered by Lord Bingley upon an adulterous mother. Horace Walpole, ever ready to retail scandalous gossip, gave wings to this malicious rumor, accepted subsequently by several historians. It is not necessary to delve into Burgoyne's early years other than to remark that he eloped with Lady Charlotte Stanley, an attractive daughter of the Earl of Derby, resigned from the army, and fled to France with his bride to escape his creditors.

The Burgoynes traveled extensively on the Continent; the ex-officer, ambitious for a military career, perfected his French and learned all he could of contemporary continental military thought. In 1756 the earl forgave his daughter, paid Burgoyne's debts, and purchased for him a commission in the 11th Dragoons. During that assignment he wrote a guide for young officers which was considered quite radical, as he encouraged them to read widely and study the military art assiduously, occupations that at the time few officers had the inclination to undertake. British soldiers, he reminded them, "are thinking beings" and should be treated as such. In Burgoyne's command, no one was allowed to curse or strike a soldier.

When Spain threatened England's ally Portugal during the War for Empire, Pitt replied with an expeditionary force: "I do not mean that we should carry the King of Portugal on our shoulders, but we should set him on his legs and put a sword into his hand." Burgoyne was a member of this force and distinguished himself as a cavalry commander. The King of Portugal gave him a diamond ring, and the allied commander wrote Lord Bute that Burgoyne had conducted himself "with great presence of mind and all possible valor." One of his subordinates, Lieutenant Colonel Charles Lee (later to become George Washington's second-in-command), led the imaginative cavalry attack on Villa Velha, which Burgoyne planned.

Burgoyne returned to England and enjoyed a hero's welcome. He was received at court and made colonel commandant of the 16th Light Dragoons, a regiment he had raised in 1759. He resumed his seat in the House of Commons where he soon made his mark as a debater. At about this time his wife inherited a considerable sum of money and the colonel was able to indulge his expensive tastes. He was a gambler accustomed to risking heavily on the turn of a card, a handsome man of great charm and ready wit, a favorite with the ladies, a poet of some ability, and a successful dramatic writer. His *Maid of the Oaks,* produced by David Garrick, was a "smash hit" at Drury Lane. He wrote in a "cultivated but ornate style," which Horace Walpole dubbed "pompous." He spent a great deal of time at Newmarket during the racing season. Sir Joshua Reynolds did a portrait of him.

In the general election of 1768 the colonel stood for Preston. He was threatened, should he dare appear at the hustings on election day. He did so, with a loaded pistol in each hand. Charged with inciting to riot, he was found guilty and fined a thousand pounds. He paid the fine and again took a seat in the Commons. In 1774 he sailed for Boston to serve briefly under Gage. In 1776 he was second-in-command to Carleton. Now in the spring of 1777 he was returning to America as a lieutenant general to assume an independent command.

This was to be the year of decision. London was optimistic; Germain wrote Sir William Howe he was inspired "with no small degree of hope that this campaign will put an end to the unhappy contest." As Burgoyne left England, he cherished the conviction that he was destined to effect this happy consummation—a view shared by a large number of his associates. Many were muttering over Howe's poor performance in New Jersey—his stock was no longer at the buoyant high it had hit a few months previously; these critics were sure Gentleman Johnny would inject new life into a stagnant situation.

The Americans anticipated another offensive up Champlain in the spring and summer of 1777, but during the winter were powerless to strengthen Ticonderoga or significantly to improve the extensive works already begun on a bluff directly across the narrow channel connecting Lake Champlain with South Bay. Schuyler deemed the positions complementary, and in a letter to Washington in July 1776 had pointed out the great value of fortifications on the hill he had christened Mount Independence. A week later, after a thorough reconnaissance, he wrote: "Can they drive us out of the strong camp on the east side? I think not. I think it impossible for twenty thousand men to do it. . . ."[1]

The troops left to garrison the twin forts during the winter were ill clad, half-starved, freezing, and riddled with a variety of diseases. As early as December 4, 1776, Thomas Wharton of Philadelphia wrote the Pennsylvania Council of Safety: "One third at least of the poor wretches is now barefooted and in this condition obliged to do duty. This is shocking to humanity. It can not be viewed in any milder light than black murder." Many were sleeping on the frozen ground "in poor thin tents." Some had not even this flimsy protection against the biting wind which swept, often with hurricane force, from Canada up the lake across one hundred miles of ice and snow. Temperatures held consistently below zero; barracks were totally inadequate; "if you was here, your heart would melt." Wharton had just returned from visiting a primitive shelter "called a hospital." There "The first object presented my eyes, one man laying dead at the door, the inside, two more laying dead, two living lying between them." There were no blankets; medicines were in short supply. Wharton, sickened at what he had seen, cried in despair: "This was too much to see and too much to feel for a heart with the least tincture of humanity."

Joseph Wood's and Anthony Wayne's Pennsylvania regiments were "lying out in poor worn out tents, we have from ten to fifteen every week that Bids fare well to this world, its Shoking to Humanity, our distress." If these regiments were not relieved, he wrote, "and moved from this D——d Sink of a Place," they would shortly be unable to turn out as many as a hundred men. Indeed, there were "not one thousand men that fits to turn out if the Enemy Should attack."[2] Not until April did Congress move to alleviate the horrors at Ticonderoga.

The physicians, surgeons, their staffs, and four wagonloads of medicines and equipment they brought to Ticonderoga in early spring were welcome, but during that appalling winter almost 1,000 men had "Bid fare well to this world," many literally frozen to death. The survivors, emaciated, weak, their morale shattered, wanted nothing more ardently than to leave Ticonderoga behind them forever.

The general chosen to command the Northern Army arrived at Quebec in H.M.S. *Apollo* on May 6 and had not been ashore twenty-four hours when he discovered to his horror that details of his plans were common gossip and had even been published in the press! The portentous leak was ascribed to various sources, including Lord George Germain, who was "utterly unable to keep his own counsel." Burgoyne, a club man, may have talked indiscreetly over cards in London or at a race meeting at Newmarket. But he and Carleton set to work, and although the force ultimately available was considerably less than the strength he had requested, Burgoyne did not cavil. He professed to be satisfied with the allotment of 7,200 rank and file regulars. He never had more than 200 Canadians; he would later pick up some 400 Indians. The Canadians he got were not the sort of men he wanted. He needed woodsmen expert with the ax "who know the nature of the woods and paths and can see and trace the footsteps in the woods." There were hundreds of such men in Canada, but they were not anxious to join the British Army and Carleton could not conscript them. The political situation in Canada was delicate, and the governor knew the limits of practical authority.

There were other problems. One was horses to mount Major General Baron von Riedesel's dragoons; another, draft animals to pull the rickety two-wheeled carts being hastily put together with unseasoned lumber. Carleton could not confiscate horses and oxen the French farmers needed for spring ploughing and planting, and it was politically impossible to order a mass levee of carriers. But he did his best to help Burgoyne prepare the expedition, as the general attested both at the time and later.

Before sailing from Plymouth, Burgoyne had written a personal letter to Howe on the subject of his operation and the nature of his orders, and shortly after arriving at Quebec he again wrote Howe in the same tenor. He also wrote Germain to express his chagrin at failure of Canadians to come forward in the numbers he had hoped for. Carleton, he said, had been of inestimable help. The governor's zeal was "manifest, exemplary and satisfactory."[3]

Burgoyne and his staff left Montreal on June 9 and arrived at St. Johns two days later. On the sixteenth the general boarded flagship *Royal George* which would lead the Northern Army in its passage up the lake. Soon thereafter, Lieutenant Colonel Robert Kingston, deputy adjutant general, issued an order entitled "General Disposition of the Army." This prescribed an advance corps, commanded by Brigadier General Simon Fraser, consisting of the 24th Foot; the British light infantry under Major the Earl of Balcarres; the grenadiers, commanded by Major John Acland; Captain Fraser's rangers; a detachment of inept Loyalists; the reluctant Canadians; and a "body of Savages"—Iroquois, Algonquins, Abnaki, Ottowas, Sauk, and Fox—led by a fearless and thoroughly ferocious Canadian woodsman, St. Luc de la Corne. St. Luc, sixty-seven, had fought the British and had previously attempted to sell his services to Montgomery; now he and his son-in-law were to devote their benevolent talents and those of their Indians to terrorizing the Americans.

Following the precedent established by Carleton, Burgoyne grouped his British and German contingents into two wings, one of two British, the other of two German, brigades. The British line regiments (Major General William Phillips, who also commanded the artillery and engineers) were posted on the right; the Germans (Major General Baron Friedrich von Riedesel) on the left. From the right (west) flank the Order of Battle was:

Brigadier General Henry W. Powell—47th, 53rd, and 9th Foot
Brigadier General James I. Hamilton—21st, 62nd, and 20th Foot
Brigadier General W. R. von Gall—Frederick and Hanau regiments
Brigadier General Johann F. Specht—Retz, Specht, and Riedesel regiments

This was the order in which the regiments were to encamp and fight throughout the campaign.

The Corps of Reserve commanded by Lieutenant Colonel Heinrich Breymann, a dogmatic martinet, embodied the German grenadiers, the chasseurs (or Jägers) armed with short-barreled rifles, and the light infantry. Riedesel's horseless dragoons would provide security for the headquarters; two companies of freshly enrolled Provincials, as yet untrained, were also held "out of the line." The Northern Army at St. Johns mustered 7,213 rank and file regulars, of whom 3,724 were British and the balance German.*

By any definition, Burgoyne commanded a combat-effective army. Phillips, irascible and choleric, and Fraser, reserved and laconic, were battle-experienced and competent general officers, and there were many superior officers in field and company grades. Among these Majors the Earl of Balcarres and John Acland were outstanding. Artillery officers were professionally able. Riedesel was courageous and thorough; his competence as a general officer under the pressures of campaign and battle remained to be proved. His senior subordinates on the whole were too mechanistic and not up to the standard of their British colleagues. A pro-

---

* Strength and casualty reports of both British and American armies abound with discrepancies. In 1951 Charles W. Snell, a staff member at Saratoga National Historical Park, did a painstaking statistical study, which resolved most of the problems. His figures for Burgoyne's army as of July 1, 1777, are these:

	OFFICERS	SERGEANTS	DRUMMERS	PRIVATES	TOTAL
British	257	216	170	3,509	4,152
German	178	371	116	3,278	3,943
	435	587	286	6,787	8,095

Charles W. Snell, *A Report on the Strength of the British Army under Lieutenant General John Burgoyne July 1 to October 17, and on the Organization of the British Army on September 19 and October 7, 1777* (February 28, 1951, Saratoga National Historical Park, File 834). On July 1 there were 426 fewer rank and file present than had mustered at St. Johns. Some of these were probably returned to Canada sick. Others were presumably left at Crown Point to assist in forwarding supplies.

portion of the enlisted men, both German and British, were farm-bred and tough. They would show they could cope with the hardships of the trail—the backbreaking labors of clearing roads, building bridges, and getting supplies up—and still, in a fire fight, give a good account of themselves.

About the Germans, Phillips had reservations. Many were too old to endure the hardships of campaigning under primitive conditions. They were "raw," and while the general was sure they would "behave nobly being brought early to a premeditated action," he was "fearful for anything unprepared." He had organized the artillery train, which consisted of a large number of weapons. Both he and Carleton deemed heavy cannon and mortars essential to batter down the ramparts at Ticonderoga and Independence, which the Yankees were reported to be daily strengthening. Burgoyne had "the finest brass train" ever assigned to a British Army. Thomas Anburey, a young subaltern, observed that the troops were vigorous, in good health and spirits, and ready in all respects: "As to our army, all I can say is that if good discipline joined to health" and the general confidence the men reposed in their commander "who is universally esteemed and respected, can ensure success, it may certainly be expected."[4]

Gentleman Johnny certainly expected it. He had no doubt he could deal with any force the disorganized Yankees could field. He did not anticipate encountering more than sporadic guerrilla activity after he had taken Ticonderoga, and before setting forth drew up in considerable detail a set of "Standing Regulations," corresponding to "Standing Operating Procedure" (SOP) of the present day. These had to do with all aspects of camp security, clearance of fields of fire, hasty fortifications, posting of sentries, camp hygiene, foraging, flank and rear "Piquets" and "Alarm Posts." He added teeth to his orders on straggling and plundering: "the Savages as well as the Provost will have Orders to punish Offenders in these respects, instantly, and with the utmost vigour."

The Americans, he said, could not hope to stand up to the King's troops in open spaces or "hardy combat"—indeed, they were "infinitely inferior." But the rebels were "well fitted by disposition and practice for the Strategms and enterprizes of little Wars."† During his tour in Boston he had learned that Yankee marksmen were effective and warned his troops to be ever watchful. Neither forests nor rivers could be counted on to afford security.

In attack, men were to place ultimate reliance on cold steel: "The officers will take all proper opportunities, and especially at the beginning of the campaign, to inculcate in the mens' minds a Reliance upon the Bayonet. Men of half their bodily strength and even cowards may be their match in firing; but the Onset of Bayonets in the hands of the Val-

---

† Burgoyne probably picked up the word *guerrilla*, diminutive of *guerra*, during his service against the Spanish.

iant is irresistible." The enemy relied wholly on fortifications and "riffle Pieces." It would be to the glory of the army to "storm where possible."

In one critical area, preparations were woefully haphazard and totally unrealistic. This was in respect to assured supplies of food and forage. After the army left Canada, and until it arrived in the vicinity of Albany, it could not hope to draw on the adjacent countryside for adequate sustenance for man or beast. Arrived at Albany, a large share of the food and forage required could be purchased or taken from the inhabitants and nearby farmers—but Albany was a long way from Ticonderoga.

Europe, to which British and German veterans were accustomed, was a totally different terrain. There the country had been farmed for hundreds of years. Market towns and villages lay three or four miles from each other and were connected by networks of roads. Streams and rivers were generally bridged. These waterways and canals facilitated transport of artillery and heavy equipment. Magazines could be built up with relative ease. The terrain afforded an imaginative commander a wide range of movement options. And, further, this terrain was familiar to many senior British officers who had fought over it and to their juniors who had done the "Grand Tour." The cities and fields of western Europe were close to home. In an emergency, replacement troops and needed supplies could be provided in ten days or two weeks to the Low Countries, France, or Germany west of the Rhine.

In the forested wilderness there were no cathedral spires to help guide the march; no towns or villages whose terrified inhabitants could be made to provide information or disgorge their scanty stores of meal and flour; no fields or farmyards with fat stock waiting to be taken; no duck ponds or chicken houses to be raided; no shuttered wineshops, taverns, or cellars to be plundered of their casks of beer and bins loaded with dark dusty bottles; no rich burghers' houses to sack. Here were only forbidding and well-nigh impenetrable forests, frightened rabbits, rattlesnakes, flighty deer, rocky trackless hills and streams, gulleys, bogs, and swamps swarming with billions of mosquitoes and vicious deer flies. Nature was an ever-present enemy.

In British experience on the Continent, supply had never been so critical a factor as to be decisive. But to feed his men and animals in the hostile country he planned to move through, where he could expect no help from the inhabitants, Burgoyne required a reasonably sustained minimum flow of not less than 25,000 pounds of food and grain per day plus ammunition, clothing, medical supplies, and assorted camp and transport replacement and maintenance items.‡ Scores of smiths, wheelwrights,

‡ One can argue that the daily tonnage requirement was slightly more (or slightly less) than the figure given, which is based on a total personnel strength of 9,000, and included women with the army, Canadians, Provincials, and Indians. If we allow two pounds per person per day (including beer, rum, porter, and wine), the total for personnel rations is nine tons. The balance would be grain for horses and oxen.

and harness makers, with their sundry equipment, were needed to keep several hundred rickety carts on the move. The immensity and complexity of the problem was simply not comprehended. Even had it been, logistic organizations in London and Canada were incapable of giving Burgoyne the continuous effective support he would so urgently need. The existing bureauracy was understaffed and unimaginative, but had it functioned at maximum efficiency, it would have been unable to meet the heavy demands laid upon it.

Another problem, muted during the campaign of the previous summer when Carleton commanded, was the relationship between British and German officers. Even during the final planning phase in Montreal, Burgoyne did not take Riedesel, Specht, and Von Gall as fully into his confidence as he did Phillips, Fraser, Powell, and Hamilton. The language barrier had something to do with exclusion of the Germans, but there was more to it than that.

The British officer caste was a very select club. Outsiders—and particularly Germans who had been *hired*—were not acceptable. British army officers of the time were probably, as a group, the most arrogant and parochial snobs who ever lived. Later, in her *Letters and Journals* Baroness von Riedesel wrote that from the beginning of the campaign of 1777 her husband was "neither admitted into the war councils of the English generals . . . nor were the instructions, which General Burgoyne had received from the British Ministry upon the manner in which the campaign should be conducted, ever imparted."**[5] Burgoyne's attitude toward his German allies was condescending.

Junior British officers took their cue from the comportment of their seniors; sergeants and enlisted men, from that of their company officers. Thus, a breach that time and the rigors of a difficult campaign would only widen was created before the expedition left Canada. One of Burgoyne's most important responsibilities was to create harmony and fellowship between British and Germans under his command and embarked on a common mission. He failed to establish this essential rapport. Gentleman Johnny could be charming and usually was—but only in the company of those he considered his equals.

The restrictions the government had laid upon Carleton foreclosed any significant assistance from that quarter. Carleton's only responsibility

---

** It is difficult to believe this statement. Both Burgoyne and Riedesel spoke French, and the baron some English. John Luzader, formerly historian at the Saratoga National Park, who has inspected Riedesel's papers, suggests that the translation of Riedesel's *Memoir* may be faulty: "His journals and personal papers in the archives at Wolfenbüttel contain too many evidences of frequent written and oral communication with Burgoyne. . . . Riedesel certainly knew the instructions Burgoyne had received in detail, and there are copies of significant portions of the British instructions in his papers. Unless Burgoyne received orders or instructions that are not reflected in his State of the Expedition and the Germain Papers, the German commander was aware of everything that was committed to paper."

after the campaign began was to forward supplies. He was specifically prohibited from leaving Canada or from depleting his own relatively weak forces to assist Burgoyne. It apparently had not occurred to either the King or Germain that a powerful thrust up Champlain, reduction of Ticonderoga, and a drive into the heart of New York was the best possible insurance against a renewed American attempt to conquer Canada.

The Americans had no resources to mount another expedition against Canada. British control of the great lake could not be challenged in 1777. The burned, half-submerged hulks of the fleet Arnold led at Valcour lay rotting along the east shore of Champlain. Another fleet could not possibly be built. The Americans could not stop Burgoyne from parading his fleet just out of range of Ticonderoga's cannon and landing his troops, supporting artillery, and supplies at any points he chose.

On May 22 Congress relieved Horatio Gates from the Northern Department and replaced him with Schuyler who, delegates felt, would be better able to command support in his native state than would the former British officer from Virginia. Schuyler established his headquarters in Albany. Three weeks later another former British officer, Major General Arthur St. Clair, assumed command at Ticonderoga. He came to an undermanned fortress. Food was scarce and there was small prospect the situation could be improved. Less than a week after he arrived, St. Clair wrote despairingly to Schuyler asking what anyone could expect "from troops ill-armed, naked and unaccoutred."

Neither Schuyler nor any member of the Congress would have been disposed to answer this embarrassing question honestly, for in the American mind Ticonderoga, an impregnable bastion, a symbol of strength and determination, stood guard over the northern wilderness. But how could Ticonderoga hold for long against an enemy with the means to take it? The question plagued St. Clair. And there was an equally important corollary: How could he get his troops out if Ticonderoga were no longer tenable? Suppose, despite his previous assertions to the contrary, the British *could* take Mount Independence? St. Clair had every reason to be apprehensive, and the few reports his scouts brought in were not calculated to dispel his anxiety. At a Council of War called by Schuyler, the decision was taken to hold Ticonderoga as long as possible, and then to defend Mount Independence.

On June 19 and 20 elements of Burgoyne's advance corps embarked at Cumberland Point. Lieutenant James M. Hadden, Royal Artillery, a conscientious diarist who sailed up the lake with the first echelon, noted: "This day was very fine and the passage pleasant, the *Lake* affording many beautiful prospects."[6] In late afternoon the fleet arrived at the mouth of the Bouquet River, where Fraser's corps and some of St. Luc's painted Indians were establishing a camp. The general arrived on June 21. At breakfast the next morning he and his staff were introduced to pancakes. Burgoyne was so pleased with this woodsmen's breakfast dish, which he may have enjoyed with molasses or maple syrup, that he recommended it to the army as easy to prepare and most tasty.

On the following day, reveille sounded before dawn at Cumberland Point. Schooners and brigs lay offshore; scores of canoes and hundreds of large, thirty-man bateaux were drawn up on the beach. At the boom of a morning gun, the army struck and rolled tents, and units formed in columns, leading ranks at the water's edge. When Major General Phillips, second-in-command, saw that all was in readiness, a gun was fired, and the fore-topsail on *Maria* loosed. The troops then began to embark; as bateaux loaded, they moved into assigned positions and oarsmen lay on their oars. When bateaux cleared the beach, flat-bottomed boats and radeau *Thunderer* moved in to take aboard mortars, siege guns, and ammunition.††

Some four hundred women, many with young children, who accompanied the army, officers' mounts and bât (baggage), and draft horses and oxen, pulling two hundred cumbersome Canadian carts loaded with barrels of salt pork, beef, biscuit, sugar, and rum for the troops and cases of smoked hams and tongues, madeira, Rhine wine, and champagne for the generals and officers, moved by road with the sutlers down the west side of the lake. Finally, two signal guns boomed dully. The white smoke drifted slowly southward before a gentle breeze from Canada as Indians bent to their paddles and soldiers to their oars. The campaign to break the back of the rebellion was under way.

Burgoyne was a dramatist, and he planned the movement by water to make the most of the great lake dominated by mountains clad in majestic oaks, towering pines, maple, spruce, and hemlock. The *mis en scène* provided for an impressive and colorful formation as the Northern Army moved toward Ticonderoga, a fortress already wrapped in legend, the Gibraltar of North America. Ahead and on the flanks in a great crescent, fourteen war canoes, each with twenty greased and painted Indian paddlers; then *Maria* followed by two schooners and a brig, sails bellying and pennons snapping. The lieutenant general commanding the Northern Army, colonel of the Queen's Regiment of Light Dragoons, governor of Fort William in Northern Britain, one of the representatives of the Commons of Great Britain in Parliament, and commanding an army and fleet employed on an expedition from Canada, etc., etc., etc., had planned to lead his armada in person, but had changed his mind and gone up the lake in brig *Royal George* to meet Fraser where the Bouquet flows into Champlain. Phillips would thus be in the van, followed by columns of bateaux loaded with Redcoats and colorfully uniformed Brunswickers.

†† *Radeau:* a large, unwieldy, bargelike vessel.

Flat-bottomed boats and *Thunderer,* with heavy artillery and mortars to batter down Ticonderoga's walls, would bring up the rear. If ever stage was set for triumphant drama, it was on Lake Champlain on this June day in 1777. Unfortunately, a storm blew up; the departure was delayed.

At the camp on the Bouquet, Burgoyne feasted and addressed St. Luc's savages. He was sure his Indian allies were burning "to vindicate the violated rights of their benevolent parent" King George III, and exhorted them to go forth in all their valor to support the cause of law and justice by striking down the American rebels, "the disturbers of public order, peace, and happiness." The general cautioned his auditors against scalping the living, but allowed that scalps could be taken from the dead. Many commanders have made hortatory addresses to their troops before battle was joined, but history affords few equally fatuous.‡‡

Burgoyne then proceeded to pass out the rum, and his painted allies staged a war dance for his edification and amusement. Hadden had previously seen one such spectacle at Quebec. The men were tall, active, and well made: "a small Tuft of Hair is left on the back part of their heads, To which they fasten and wear a *feather* for every Scalp taken in War. . . . Their ears are slit and they wear a number of small Rings round their separated Gristle . . . the Gristle of the nose being bored serves to support a small kind of *Silver Bob and Ring.*" When they prepared to take the warpath, they daubed themselves with paint, "Vermillion and other colours. Their dress is a Blanket and Arse Clout, or covering for the Privities." At the great war dances such as that staged at the mouth of the Bouquet, the Indians were "totally Naked, at the end of the *Penis* the head and neck of some handsome bird is fastened." As war drums throbbed and rum flowed freely, the braves whooped and gyrated.[7]

The general was to be severely criticized for using Indians, but as a matter of historic fact the Americans were the first to persuade the savages to take up the hatchet. Indians had been used by both sides in the Seven Years' War, and in 1775 the Bostonians had not hesitated to appeal to the Stockbridge Indians for their help. (They alleged these were "tame" Indians.) Nevertheless, the Americans seized on this as a good propaganda ploy and circumstances were to permit them to exploit it to the limit.

On the night of the twenty-fifth, the Northern Army moved south to Crown Point, where the deputy adjutant general directed troops "to make up cartridges according to the standing orders of 100 rounds p. man . . . the greatest care to be taken of the musket cartridges" because

‡‡ When copies of Burgoyne's address reached London, it was ridiculed in the press and made the subject of a famous speech by Burke in the House of Commons which convulsed Lord North and elicited roars of laughter alike from members of the ministerial majority and Opposition.

of "the difficulty of fresh supplies across the lake." So soon had supply realities become apparent to the general and his staff.[8] There, on the last day of June, Burgoyne issued the customary pre-battle exhortation:

> The army embarks tomorrow to approach the Enemy. We are to contend for the King and the Constitution of Great Britain to vindicate Law and to relieve the Oppressed. A Cause in which His Majesty's Troops and those of the Princes His Allies will feel equal excitement.
>
> The services required of this particular expedition are critical and conspicuous. During our progress, occasions may occur, in which, nor difficulty, nor labour nor life, are to be regarded. This army must not Retreat.

Here he also found time to compose a bombastic proclamation to the disobedient and recalcitrant Americans. He declared the "present unnatural rebellion" a foundation "for the completest system of tyranny that ever God, in his displeasure" suffered "to be exercised over a forward and stubborn generation." The assorted enormities inflicted on the Americans by those governing them, including arbitrary imprisonment, torture, and execution, had never been equaled, even by the "inquisitions of the Romish Church." He concluded this remarkable document with the threat that if the rebels did not come meekly to heel, he would "give stretch" to his thousands of Indians to overtake the King's enemies, and warned them that his disciplined and valorous troops, "messengers of justice and wrath," would execute the vengeance of the state upon all those who persisted in a deluded resistance.*

"The high-sounding terms and impolitic menaces of this manifesto had no other effect than that of exciting the indignation of the revolted colonists, and impelling them to the most obstinate resistance."[9] It also aroused a storm of derision. Gentleman Johnny was lampooned in the press and in pamphlets, and amateur poets produced a crop of parodies in which he was made to appear ridiculous. But the Americans did not find his threat to unleash St. Luc's savages quite so amusing. With good reason St. Luc's name was feared in upper New York and the New Hampshire Grants, where the frightful barbarities of his Indians after the surrender of Fort William Henry on Lake George in 1757 were not likely to be forgotten. Burgoyne's announced intention to "give stretch" to this monster and his ferocious bands no doubt terrified the timorous, but in most of the frontier farmers it provoked a spirit of savage determination.

General Riedesel described the American positions as he surveyed them from Burgoyne's flagship *Royal George* on the morning of the first

---

* Digby (*Journal*, pp. 188–92) states Burgoyne issued his "Proclamation" at St. Johns.

day of July: "The Americans were estimated at from four to five thousand men, consisting of twelve regiments divided into four brigades commanded by General St. Clair. The enemy's position was covered on the right flank by Fort Independence, built on a considerable eminence, and fortified by three successive lines. . . . It was separated by water from Fort Carillon [Ticonderoga] which lay on the opposite side and consisted of nothing but the old French works. Between the forts were four armed vessels, in front of which was a bridge. . . . In front of this bridge there was a very strong iron chain hanging across the water. To the left of Fort Carillon there was another fortification upon a hill."†[10]

As the German general was peering through his telescope, Fraser's scouting parties pushed through the forest bordering the west shore of Champlain to within sight of Ticonderoga and satellite Forts Independence and Mount Hope. Early the next day, Indians "bold with rum pushed on with the greatest rashness"; the small garrison at Mount Hope set fire to the blockhouse, spiked two guns, and withdrew hastily to the shelter of Ticonderoga. Fraser established several outposts along the creek and the portage road to Lake George.

Phillips arrived on the scene shortly thereafter. As an experienced artilleryman, he had a keen appreciation of terrain, and the minute he laid eyes on Sugar Loaf Hill (Mount Defiance) which overlooks Ticonderoga, he dispatched Lieutenant Twiss, his young Swiss-born engineer, on a reconnaissance. Twiss returned to report the height undefended and accessible. A few goats were grazing on the hillsides. This was all Phillips needed to know: "Where a goat can go, a man can go, and where a man can go, he can drag a gun." He directed Twiss to cut a trail to the top. Twiss immediately called for a fatigue party of seven hundred men and put them to work.

While Redcoats toiled on the northwest slopes of Sugar Loaf, Riedesel's Brunswickers, who had landed on the east shore, attempted to surround Mount Independence and so cut off an American retreat through the Grants or via South Bay. The baron's heavily laden troops spent the better part of two days trying to work their way through a swamp to assigned positions.

General St. Clair was awakened on the morning of July 5 to hear the news that British cannon on Sugar Loaf overlooked him and could interdict the bridge of boats leading to Fort Independence. The general snatched his telescope. In a minute he could see more than he cared to see. Ticonderoga was no longer tenable and the safety of the army was imperiled. The commandant of the supposedly impregnable fort gave orders to evacuate when darkness fell. During the night, amid scenes of indescribable confusion, the garrison pulled out, some via the footbridge over the narrow channel to Mount Independence, others in bateaux up South Bay to Skenesborough (now Whitehall, New York). Total disorder

† Shortly to be christened Mount Hope by General Phillips.

reigned as the troops abandoned a hundred unspiked guns, barrels of powder, cannon balls, salted provisions, tentage, and other camp equipment. The detachment left to guard the footbridge proceeded to get drunk as speedily as possible; grenadiers racing across the bridge found the defenders prostrate.

At dawn on July 6, as ships battered their way through the boom, the exulting British broke the royal standard over Ticonderoga.

The Fickle Goddess Fortune

Most of the Americans fled east over a forest road that shortly bent toward the south to Hubbardton and thence to Castleton. Here the trail intersected a slightly better but still primitive one leading from Skenesborough to Manchester. The Americans moved fast, but the light infantry moved faster and came up with them at Hubbardton at dawn on July 7. The Redcoats of Balcarres's advance corps pressed the Americans hard. Balcarres later said "they certainly behaved with great gallantry." Gallantry was not enough. The British were better trained, better armed, and better led, but the Americans did not break until Riedesel reached the scene with a battalion of Brunswickers.

Burgoyne made much of this victory, but Hadden felt differently: ". . . whatever footing the General might wish to put the Action near Hubbardton upon, that Corps [Fraser's] certainly discovered that neither they were invincible nor the Rebels all Poltroons; On the contrary many of them acknowledged the Enemy behaved well, and looked upon General Riedesels fortunate arrival as a matter absolutely necessary. . . ."[1] The British had gained the field, where the Americans left nearly 200 dead, including their colonel, Ebenezer Francis. Many were wounded and 18 officers and 210 men made prisoners. British casualties were about 200.

As Balcarres set off toward Hubbardton on the morning of July 6, Burgoyne ordered Lieutenant Colonel John Hill with the 9th, 20th, and 21st Foot to embark at once, move rapidly up South Bay, disembark on the eastern shore, push overland, block Wood Creek south of Skenesborough, and cut the road leading to Fort Anne. Hill found the terrain between the bay and the creek too rough to negotiate, re-embarked his men, and proceeded by water to Skenesborough. On the following day he sent a detachment to seize Fort Anne. Some of St. Clair's Yankees were still there and disposed to fight. The battle, short and vicious, ended when the Americans set fire to the stockade and withdrew. The British left their wounded in care of Sergeant R. Lamb of the Royal Welch Fusiliers and returned to Skenesborough.

The maneuvers Burgoyne ordered were sound enough, but had a result Gentleman Johnny had probably not clearly anticipated: They pulled the remainder of the army toward Skenesborough, where on July 10 he assembled his British regulars, St. Luc's vagrant and ferocious Indians, the spiritless Canadians, and a motley collection of Tories, most of whom needed arms and ammunition. Riedesel's Brunswickers lay on the left flank in the direction of Castleton. The wings of the Northern Army were within mutually supporting distance. Morale was high. The Yankees, chased out of Ticonderoga and Independence, and beaten at Hubbardton and Fort Anne, had disappeared east into the Green Mountains or fled south to refuge at Fort Edward, where St. Clair had established his headquarters.

Burgoyne had reason to be pleased with the success of his operation to this point. He issued a congratulatory General Order designating the following Sunday as "a day for rejoicing"; directed that divine service be held to give thanks to the God who had so manifestly favored British arms; remitted all fatigue parties; ordered a *feu de joie* to be fired by all ships in South Bay, the cannon, and the infantry of the army; and sent off a courier to England bearing tidings of his victories. He empowered Major Phillip Skene, his political adviser, to receive Loyalists and penitents who had seen the error of their ways and had come to profess allegiance. Many did appear at Skenesborough.

The general now found himself in a dilemma, for he had originally intended to go south from Ticonderoga by Lake George. His desire to annihilate St. Clair's fleeing troops had brought him almost twenty-five miles south of Ticonderoga. He did not want to turn his victorious army around. He considered, too, the question of relative distances: At Skenesborough, he was but twenty-two miles from Fort Edward on the upper Hudson. And there is reason to believe Skene's advice to push on by the overland route influenced the decision to go ahead.

Burgoyne's decision did not meet with unqualified approval. Lieutenant William Digby, who served with the advance corps, wrote that many "were of opinion the general had not the least business in bringing the army to Skenesborough, after the precipitate flight of the enemy from Ticonderoga, and tho we had gained a complete victory over them, both at Fort Anne and Hubberton, yet no visible advantage was likely to flow from either except proving the goodness of our troops at the expense of some brave men." Only in his diary did Digby question the wisdom of the decision; other officers, "discontented," asserted the army should not delay at Skenesborough but should take advantage of the enemy's panic and confusion and push on as rapidly as possible. Digby, however, did not entertain "the least doubt" that the general "had his proper reasons for so acting though contrary to the opinion of many."[2]

At Skenesborough, comfortably ensconced in Skene's stone mansion with his recently acquired mistress, "the wife of a Commissary," Burgoyne found time to write to Major General Harvey a letter denigrating the Americans: "The manner of taking up the ground at Ticonderoga convinces me that they have no men of military science . . . they seem to have expended great treasure and the un-wearied labor of more than a year to fortify, upon the supposition that we should attack them upon the point where they were best prepared to resist." Obviously Burgoyne had as yet little reason to believe that he would encounter any obstacles he could not overcome. He had quickly cracked the supposedly impregnable bastion at Ticonderoga; at the moment he foresaw no other challenge.

On the same day, he drew up an official report to the American Secretary. He again complained, as he had from Quebec, of the restrictive nature of his orders; had he been given liberty "to march in force immediately by my left [i.e., toward Rutland, Windsor, and the Connecticut River] instead of by my right," he could easily have subdued New England, that cradle of treason and sedition, "the provinces where the rebellion originated," before winter set in. However, he would proceed as directed "to force a junction at Albany." He had ordered Riedesel with six battalions to Castleton in order to influence the Americans to believe his ultimate object was to operate on the Connecticut River and to mask his true intentions.

By this time, any confidence the general may have reposed in his Indian allies was rapidly evaporating. He found them "little more than a name. If under the management of their conductors they are indulged . . . in all the caprices and humours of spoiled children, like them they grow more unreasonable and importunate upon every new favour. Were they left to themselves, enormities too horrid to think of would ensue;

---

* The King had studied his maps while Burgoyne's plan rested on his desk in late February, and had written in his "Remarks":

> If possible, possession must be taken of Lake George, and nothing but an absolute impossibility of succeeding in this, can be an excuse for proceeding by South Bay and Skenesborough.

guilty and innocent, women and infants, would be the common prey."[3] Burgoyne marked this bit "confidential"; he was aware the King had commanded that savages be employed and that the American secretary was an ardent advocate of their use. He and his officers found the Indians unreliable, capricious, superstitious, rapacious, cowardly, incompetent, ill humored, drunken, and mutinous. No tribe was better or worse than any other—all were "of equal depravity . . . their only pre-eminence consisted in ferocity."

Burgoyne also wrote Carleton an account of his progress and requested him to provide a garrison for Ticonderoga. To this plea the governor promptly replied that Germain had restricted him to the boundaries of Canada, as he thought Burgoyne must have known. He could, and would, immediately send forward rear echelons of Burgoyne's regiments; that was all. As to Germain: "I am very ready to acknowledge that I think the whole of our Minister's measures, civil and military, very strange; indeed, to me, they appear incomprehensible, unless they turn upon private enmity and resentment. I was so convinced of this that I lost no time in entreating the King's permission to resign and return home, in hopes that wiser measures might be pursued by his Lordship after my departure; I will only add on this head that part of the Troops his Lordship stations so ably are mere paper."[4]

The British now had to remain at Skenesborough to await supplies. Transport of ammunition, provisions, and stores sufficient to build up a level of thirty days was attended with many delays. Not nearly enough bateaux were available, and Canadian contractors had failed to supply the agreed number of horses, oxen, and carts. Sergeant Lamb wrote later: "The British were now obliged to suspend all operations and to wait at Skenesborough for the arrival of provisions and tents."[5] No foodstuffs were available locally; the army subsisted on a few stray cows, weevily flour, hard biscuit, and salted beef and pork from England, transhipped at Montreal. Burgoyne was at the far end of a 4,000-mile supply line.

Groups of Indians from the distant country bordering Lake Huron arrived daily at Skenesborough; on July 19 "His Excellency the Lt. General held a congress with the Indian nations"; after rum was served out, His Excellency, who loved making speeches, delivered an oration to which the various chiefs responded. The tribes then "each separately danced their several war dances, very much to the entertainment of the spectators. They were highly dressed with feathers and painted with great taste, which added greatly to the appearance of their natural ferocity."[6] At first light the next day Indian scouting parties left camp to range the country.

As the British worked slowly and laboriously to clear Wood Creek and improve a road to Fort Anne, the Americans were active. No small working party was safe from harassing snipers. Time was working against Burgoyne; the Americans realized this and made the most of the general's inactivity. In the Grants, Committees of Safety sent urgent pleas to the towns and villages of New Hampshire and Massachusetts for powder, bullets, and militia.

When they were not working on the roads to Fort Anne, or the back-breaking task of clearing Wood Creek for bateaux, soldiers at Skenes-borough managed to find and consume considerable amounts of liquor. Women camp followers procured rum from sutlers, which they promptly sold to the men. One of Burgoyne's brigade commanders found it "very mortifying . . . to perceive so much licentiousness" and threatened any woman caught purveying spirits with immediate expulsion from the camp.

During June, Howe had conducted a series of moves designed to pull Washington out of the strong defensible ground he occupied some ten miles north and west of New Brunswick. Sir William's two corps, commanded by Cornwallis and De Heister, marched and countermarched in vain; Washington was not to be tempted. He correctly diagnosed the maneuvering as an attempt to entice him to accept a general action on ground of Howe's choosing. This interlude, punctuated with small patrol actions, afforded the Hessians opportunity to indulge in their favorite occupation: "Great symptoms of a disposition to plunder being perceived in the Troops, the commander in chief sent a message to General de Heister desiring him to warn the Hessians not to persist in such outrages, as they would be most severely punished."[7] Howe could have stopped the rampant pillaging had he held commanding officers strictly responsible. This he never did.

The Americans harassed the enemy around the clock. Roads between Brunswick and Amboy "were infested by ambuscades which fired on our patrols and out sentries"; "Rebel Light Horse were frequently seen hovering about Lord Cornwallis' Camp."[8] Howe now dropped back on Amboy preparatory to crossing to Staten Island. Lord Stirling deployed his division to watch the British and press them when they began to embark. Howe still hoped to draw Washington out of the broken country south of Morristown, but the American general would not take the bait. On June 28 Sir William gave up, and three days later his rear guard left Jersey soil for Staten Island. He had thrown away two precious months.

The British in New York were dejected at the failure of Sir William's maneuverings to bring on a decisive battle; they were "full of Regret that the Cause of our King and Country does not proceed so quick as our Desires." On July 3 Serle took "a long, pensive walk" with Galloway, now General Howe's trusted political adviser. They "discoursed upon the dejection of our Army, the state of the Rebels and the present Posture of

Affairs." Galloway let slip the interesting fact that "a Person" with whom he had lately conferred had given up "every Hope of obtaining America by Arms." There was, however, one cheerful item: Major General Robert Prescott, who commanded British troops in Rhode Island (Newport),† had been taken from his bed in the middle of the night by a Yankee raiding party and hustled off into captivity for a second time: "He is not much regretted."[9]

Two days later Sir Henry Clinton arrived from England and reported to Sir William as second-in-command. This was a mismated pair. Neither cared for the other personally; Howe was not impressed with Clinton's professional abilities, and Sir Henry had little confidence in his superior's military judgment. This small confidence was destroyed when he learned, as he did shortly after reporting, that Howe proposed to embark the army and sail off to the south.

Clinton spent the better part of the next week in a futile attempt to dissuade Howe from undertaking his seaborne expedition to Philadelphia. Sir William was adamant. His plan had been approved by King and Cabinet; he would go to Philadelphia. Burgoyne could get to Albany without help from him. Sir Henry's persistence got him nowhere; he gave up in disgust. He could not believe that Howe was really going to sail off to the southward.

While Burgoyne's armada lay before Ticonderoga and his troops prepared to invest the fort, Americans in Boston, Philadelphia, and elsewhere were noisily and somewhat tipsily celebrating the first anniversary of their Declaration of Independence. Brass cannon fired numberless salutes, church bells pealed, and troops paraded "to the approbation of the spectators." Philadelphia pulled out all the stops and provided "an elegant dinner" for Congress enlivened by "the Hessian band of music taken in Trenton the twenty-sixth of December last. . . . After dinner a number of toasts were drank, all breathing Independence. Each toast was followed by a discharge of artillery and small arms and a suitable piece of music by the Hessian band."[10] Festivities in Boston commenced with "an excellent discourse" delivered by the Reverend Mr. Gordon. Later, many salutes were fired, and gallons of rum punch, claret, and madeira consumed. After sunset, the citizens enjoyed a display of fireworks. The young ladies of Amelia County in Virginia pledged themselves "not to permit the addresses of any person . . . unless he has served in the American armies long enough to prove by his Valor that he is deserving of their love."[11] But the festive mood of this day was soon to be replaced by an equivalent despondency.

News that St. Clair had evacuated Ticonderoga without firing a shot and had abandoned one hundred irreplaceable cannon and great quanti-

---

† Prescott was colonel of the 72nd Foot but held the rank of "Major General in America."

ties of stores of all descriptions reached Washington, then at Morristown, during the night of July 10/11. The general wrote Congress immediately, recommending that a "brave and judicious officer" be ordered north at once to salvage the deteriorating situation. He urged the appointment of Major General Benedict Arnold. Congress approved; John Hancock wrote Arnold to proceed north at once "to collect the militia to check the progress of Gen. Burgoyne, as very disagreeable consequences may be apprehended if the most vigorous measures are not taken to oppose him." Major General Benjamin Lincoln was also ordered north to take command in the New Hampshire Grants.[12] All anticipated that Howe would move up the Hudson; Washington placed his army in position to interpose.

The loss of Ticonderoga, believed by most members of Congress and the public to be impregnable and the consequent baring of upper New York and the western flank of New England was a grievous blow. To many it seemed inconceivable the fortress could have been so casually abandoned. In taverns and coffee shops there was much talk of treachery; poisonous rumors of bribery circulated. New England delegates mounted a campaign to relieve Schuyler forthwith and replace him with Gates. This proposal touched off a furious row. Each general had his adherents. Gates was popular in the New England colonies where Schuyler, a patrician landowner from upper New York state, was distrusted. As the altercation boiled, the Board of War, instead of devoting its energies to coping with the situation in the north, spent days in fruitless argument about the desirability of sending an expedition from Georgia to conquer West Florida, and another overland through trackless forests and malarial swamps to the lower Mississippi. Thomas Burke of North Carolina finally put a stop to this nonsense with the laconic observation, "We had best send our whole force against the enemy's army."

At Washington's instigation, Congress ordered Schuyler and St. Clair to report at once to his headquarters to face an inquiry for dereliction of duty. John Adams, busy in committees from morning till night, found time to write his "Best Friend" that Burgoyne was overextended and would have to retreat. As for St. Clair: "I think we shall never defend a post until we shoot a general. After that, we shall defend posts. . . . we must trifle no more." Adams had learned nothing from the disasters at Forts Washington and Lee. A defense of Ticonderoga against the overwhelming force Burgoyne had at hand to throw against it would have delayed the British for no more than several days at most and would have cost the garrison. Presumed cowardice of generals was not the only problem that worried Adams; finances lay heavily on his mind: "Taxation as deep as possible is the only radical cure. I hope you will pay every tax that is brought you, if you sell my books, or clothes or oxen, or your own, to pay it."

As Congress debated the debacle at Ticonderoga and Adams fulminated on the incompetence—or worse—of trifling generals, Viscount Howe quietly embarked his brother's expeditionary force at Staten Island. At Quibbletown, Washington received continuous reports of the progress of embarkation, mulled over Sir William's options, and warily held his swing position, prepared to move north and east to the Hudson, or south and west toward Philadelphia.

Admiral Howe's fleet of 260 sail dropped down from Staten Island to Sandy Hook on Sunday, July 20. Serle described the scene as "very good and picturesque." These sentiments were not shared by Sir Henry Clinton, K.B., who sometime later wrote: "Notwithstanding that my instructions and many other unequivocal demonstrations tended to show that Sir William Howe's army was destined for an expedition to the southward, I own I could not to the very last bring myself to believe it. For I was satisfied in my own mind that it was all a feint." Even as Howe was about to sail, Clinton told the commander in chief he "was persuaded *he intended to deceive us all, and, though he was pleased to say he was going to sea with the present northerly wind, I should expect to see him return with the first southerly blast and run up the North River.*"[13] Howe, who had no intention of returning with the first "southerly blast," ordered Clinton to defend Manhattan Island and its environs with a force Sir Henry deemed altogether inadequate for the purpose.

Two hundred miles to the north, Burgoyne was struggling with the obstacles of a rugged terrain, its natural difficulties vastly aggravated by Yankee woodsmen, who with their steel-bladed felling axes could drop a forest oak two feet in diameter precisely where they wanted the giant tree to fall to block a narrow trail. His next objective, Fort Edward on the upper Hudson, lay some twenty-two miles south of Skenesborough. The Americans had not only blocked narrow, tortuous forest trails but had turned clear-flowing streams into clotted swamps by felling hundreds of trees. Clearing "was attended with incredible toil." The army built forty bridges and laid two miles of corduroy road across a morass.

While sweating Redcoats labored in the forest, Indian war parties actively sought scalps and loot. On July 25 the savages massacred ten people, including a young lady named Jenny Macrae, three other women, two children, and a babe in arms. The bodies were mutilated and the victims scalped. Burgoyne learned of Miss Macrae's murder the next night and immediately wrote Fraser: "The news I have just received of the savages having scalped a young lady, their prisoner, fills me with horror. I shall visit their camp tomorrow morning." He directed that all Indians be present.

Burgoyne intended to hang the leader of the marauding band, but St. Luc de la Corne prevailed upon him not to do so, for if he did, his Indian allies would certainly desert en masse and so deprive the army of its scouts. He informed St. Luc that he would "rather lose every Indian in his army than connive at their enormities," and made it emphatically clear he would tolerate no more murderous forays.[14] That night, his Indians started leaving. If they could not loot and scalp without fear of retribution, there was no point in staying around.

On August 5 their chiefs informed Burgoyne the Indians were going home. The general immediately called a congress "and with the promise of a little rum attended with the usual ceremonies, they agreed to stay till we approached Albany." Burgoyne's address to his savage allies must have been a persuasive masterpiece. The chiefs replied with war speeches; "one in particular who was called *Le Bouf de la Prairie* was particularly conspicuous on the occasion. He spoke with energy, drew his knife like a Garrick, and declared, that knife should not be sheathed, till he had revenged his Father's injuries (by Father they mean the King) and that if the warriors of his nation would not attend, he alone would move on with the army."[15]

The wholesale massacre at Allen's farm and the wanton murder of Jenny Macrae produced an explosive reaction in upper New York and the New Hampshire Grants. In this vast area, where many men might conceivably have been won over, hatred of British Redcoats, German mercenaries, and their savage allies rose to white heat. Overnight Gentleman Johnny became "Butcher Burgoyne," and his King, who had directed that Indians be employed, the personification of evil.

The immediate result was that farmers set the torch to their standing grain, left the area with their families, their livestock, and their possessions, and joined the nearest militia unit. Foragers found a desert: deserted cabins, blackened, smoking sheds, and charred stubble. A German officer wrote that the Americans had taken great pains to clear the countryside, ". . . to sweep its few cultivated spots of all articles likely to benefit the invaders. . . . All the fields of standing corn were laid waste, the cattle were driven away, and every particle of grain, as well as morsel of grass, carefully removed, so that we could depend for subsistence, both for men and horses, only upon the magazines which we might ourselves establish."[16] This was, in truth, a most uncivilized way to run a war! As the army moved toward Albany its very life would depend on the tenuous and vulnerable arteries running south from Skenesborough and Lake George.

Since taking Ticonderoga, Burgoyne had been trying frantically to establish communication with General Howe. On July 29 he sent Carleton an account of his recent activities. For the first time, the general realized he was in deep trouble: "I have no news of Sir William Howe." He again begged Carleton to garrison Ticonderoga. The following day he wrote Germain a long letter. His couriers could not get through to New York; some were caught and summarily hanged; others probably destroyed their compromising messages and joined the Americans. Thus Burgoyne was "in total ignorance of the situation or intentions of that General." He was in a serious predicament. If he advanced, and Howe did not, he was putting his army at grave risk; if Howe advanced, and he did not, "that General" might well lose his. "Every cause conspired to increase the General's anxiety for nothing was more certain than that the enemy's numbers were augmenting in his front and flanks. The New Englanders had been roused to madness by the outrage of the Indians, and every day's delay meant accession of strength to the Americans."[17] But on August 3 a messenger from New York got through to him.

Just before he sailed, Howe had written laconically. He first congratulated Burgoyne on the capture of Ticonderoga, and then informed him that he, with his army, was about to embark in Admiral Viscount Howe's mighty fleet to seize Philadelphia: "My intention is for Pennsylvania, where I expect to meet Washington, but if he goes to the northward contrary to my expectations, and you can keep him at bay, be assured I shall soon be after him to relieve you. After your arrival at Albany, the movements of the enemy will guide yours; but my wishes are that the enemy be drove out of this province [New York] before any operation takes place in Connecticut. Sir Henry Clinton remains in command here and will act as occurrences may direct. Putnam is in the Highlands with about 4000 men. Success be with you."[18]

We may only imagine Burgoyne's consternation when he read this nonchalant letter in which His Majesty's general in America washed his hands of responsibility to co-operate with the Northern Army. He must have been utterly dismayed. If so, he kept his own counsel. Unquestionably he wondered what had been going on in Whitehall; when he sailed from Plymouth, he had understood that his plan was the approved strategy to win the war in 1777.

Now he was on his own.

At least the ordeal in the forest was behind him; the army was encamped on cleared farm land in sight of the Hudson. "As yet, the fickle Goddess Fortune had smiled upon our arms, and crowned our wishes with every kind of success, which might easily be seen from the great spirits the army in general were in; and the most sanguine hopes of conquest, victory, etc. etc. were formed of crowning the campaign with, from the general down to the private soldier. . . ."[19] The smile of "the fickle Goddess" may have been sardonic, for "it was soon found that in the situation of the transport service at that time, the army could barely be victualled from day to day, and that there was no prospect of establishing a magazine in due time for pursueing present advantages. . . ."

The news from Skenesborough was received with joy in London. The King rushed into the Queen's apartments waving a paper and exulting:

"I have beat them; I have beat all the Americans." The fact that his general had taken a vacated fort and that St. Clair had preserved the nucleus of his army seems to have escaped him. Germain immediately proposed Burgoyne for a red ribbon (Knight of the Bath) and announced a great victory in the House of Commons. The general had anticipated that his victory would be rewarded with a signal mark of royal favor, but for reasons he never made clear had written his father-in-law, the Earl of Derby, not to accept the red ribbon if it were tendered. We may be confident modesty had not impelled the general to ask the earl to reject the proffered red ribbon. This honor might have satisfied a man of less ambition than Burgoyne, as indeed it had satisfied Clinton, but Gentleman Johnny must have had his eye on bigger things. A marquisate? the Garter? Earl of Champlain?

Reports of success in America were exhilarating, but the Admiralty was concerned with serious problems close to home. American privateers operated boldly off the coasts; there was "certain intelligence of many rebel cruisers in the Chops of the Channel"; two Dover packet boats had recently been seized by Yankee privateers and taken into Dunkirk; Newfoundland traders "in great anxiety" bombarded the Admiralty for convoys, as did merchants in the Irish linen trade. Liverpool shippers were "very pressing for a frigate to be constantly employed to attend their trade to a certain distance into the sea," and the Scots demanded frigates to protect Ayr, Irvine, Rothesay, Greenock, and Port Glasgow from Yankee depredations.[20]

"American privateers swarmed on all our coasts, kept Ireland and Scotland under alarms, and interrupted all their trade. Several pieces of cannon were mounted in the harbor of Dublin."[21] Ships destined to be sold to the Americans were fitting out in French ports: St.-Malo, Nantes, Rochefort, Morlaix. The lords of the Admiralty were familiar with the names of already famous privateer captains: Wickes, Conyngham, Johnson. They had not yet heard of Captain John Paul Jones, U.S.N., then superintending the fitting-out of United States sloop of war *Ranger* at Portsmouth, New Hampshire.

During the summer of 1777, French aid to America built up rapidly. William Eden's watchful agents in France gave him regular reports of activities of Roderique Hortalez and Company and other contractors supplying arms and equipment. A private letter from Eden to the First Lord dated July 20, 1777, testifies to the scope of the aid operation: Two frigates, *Subtile* and *Pour-Voyeuse*, were loading sails, rigging, and other warlike stores for America; a large privateer was fitting out at Le Havre; two merchantmen were loading at Marseilles; at Nantes the *Anomine* was scheduled to take on "1000,000 lbs virgin copper and some 30,000 stand of arms." She was also to take as passengers Chevalier Bretigny and thirteen other volunteer officers. Two ships were ready to sail from

Le Havre "with linen and other clothing, lead, steel, etc.," and the American commissioners were "in treaty" for several frigates, plus "sailcloth, cordage and anchors" to equip three ships building at yards in America.

As French merchantmen cleared with cargo manifested for Martinique, captains of British frigates who hailed them on the high seas could do no more than board and examine papers. Later, the French ships altered course for the American ports which were their true destinations. These experiences were frustrating; British captains frequently had a good idea of what cargos were in the holds, and of their ultimate disposition, but short of provoking hostilities they could do nothing.

Great Britain was not ready to take on another enemy, particularly one thirsting for revenge, and still the most powerful nation on the Continent. Her immediate strategic aim was to placate France and liquidate the rebellion in America. When the colonists had been sufficiently chastised to persuade them to make due submission, she could deal with the incipient threat from the Bourbon powers.

Viscount Howe's formidable armada entered Delaware Bay on July 29. Here Captain Andrew Hamond, H.M.S. *Roebuck*, boarded *Eagle*. *Roebuck* had patrolled the lower river and bay for some time and Hamond was presumably familiar with terrain on the west bank of the river, as well as with American activity. No one knows precisely what Hamond told the Howes, but Serle's *Journal* entry reflects his distress when he learned of the decision taken: "The ships lay on and off all the day; and at length it was determined by the General not to land here— the Hearts of all Men were struck with this Business, everyone apprehending the worst. *O Quanta de Spe!* is the universal Cry; and without the Loss or Risque of a Battel—What will my dear Country think and say too, when this News is carried Home? *Horreo.*" In the evening "it was given out that the fleet would sail to the Chesapeake." Serle could bear no more. "May GOD defend us from the Fatality of the worst Climate in America at this worst Season of the Year . . . I can write no more; my Heart is full."‡²²

‡ General Howe would adduce testimony at the later House of Commons inquiry into his conduct of operations in America which tended to support his assertion that a landing on the west bank of the Delaware in the New Castle–Wilmington area was impossible. Actually the river as far as Chester, some twelve miles upstream, was navigable for any vessels of Viscount Howe's fleet, or of his convoy. Indeed, in early October, flagship *Eagle* and other ships of force would ascend the river, with no trouble, to Chester. There were no obstructions in the river or fortifications on its banks south of that point. This the Howes could have determined by ordering a reconnaissance before they took the decision to go to the Chesapeake. Such a reconnaissance would have located suitable landing areas on the west bank of the Delaware. Washington could not possibly have managed to defend fifteen miles of riverbank between Port Penn, where the river was two miles in width, and Wilmington. Howe's change in plan cost three valuable weeks and would put him as far from Philadelphia as he had been before he left Staten Island.

As soon as Howe's fleet was sighted, couriers set off for Philadelphia with news that the British had "arrived at the offing in the capes of Delaware" and were "standing in for the bay with a fair wind. . . . No doubt therefore [could] remain that the city of Philadelphia is the object of their destination and attack."[23] Then, suddenly, Howe had disappeared. The great bay was empty. Was the general now on his way to the North River? Or to Rhode Island? Or, possibly, to South Carolina? Washington thought the move a feint designed to pull him south, and that Howe would return to New York, sail up the Hudson, and meet Burgoyne.

Actually the fleet was slowly beating to the south, with the object of sailing up Chesapeake Bay. Howe's plan was now to land at Head of Elk, march north, seize the rebel capital, and thus end the revolt. When a European capital was taken, the government usually sued for peace. Obviously the way to put an end to the rebellion in America was to take Philadelphia, capture as many delegates to the illegal Congress as he could lay hands on, hang up the lot, and embody thousands of Loyalists in Pennsylvania and the "Lower Counties" (Delaware) who, he had been assured, were only waiting his arrival to affirm their allegiance to the crown. Germain's recent letter was optimistic. The secretary wrote that accounts "from all quarters which arrive relative to the good inclinations of the inhabitants" indicated that Sir William should be able to raise sufficient provincial forces to defend the province and thus free the army for offensive operations.

Washington had to take a critical decision. Should he remain within easy striking distance of the Hudson, or should he start to move the army south and west across New Jersey toward the Delaware? Could Gates's army, stiffened by the presence of the audacious Benedict Arnold and the portly and determined Benjamin Lincoln, stop Burgoyne on ground of their choosing, harass him, cut his tenuous supply line, and starve him out? Would John Stark stop sulking and grumbling because Congress had again passed him over for promotion to a Continental brigadier and march out of the New Hampshire hills?

Washington considered these imponderables during many candlelit conferences as he canvassed his staff and senior commanders. Finally, he took the decision: to fight for Philadelphia. Essentially, the decision was based on political and psychological factors; he simply could not afford to give up the city and with it all of eastern Pennsylvania and western New Jersey without a fight. Before he took up the march to the south, he wrote: "Howe's in a manner abandoning Burgoyne is so unaccountable a matter that till I am fully assured of it, I cannot help casting my eyes continually behind me."[24]

As the army plodded toward the Delaware, Congress continued to boil with the Schuyler-Gates controversy and finally, on August, 5, over the strenuous objections of New York delegates, appointed Gates to relieve Schuyler in command of the Northern Department. William Williams wrote the governor of Connecticut on the following day: "I hope N. England will take their own measures to drive Burgoyne into the Lakes . . . can it be that N.E. will be long driven and distressed by 6000 men. Surely we can eat them up at a Meal."[25] Samuel Adams, leader of the New England faction, determined to discredit and displace Schuyler, thought the patrician New Yorker "excellently well qualified for a Commissary or a Quarter-Master," but certainly not for field command. Indeed, he intimated that Schuyler and St. Clair must have done a deal with the British: "The whole Conduct [at Ticonderoga] seems to carry the evident marks of Deliberation and Design."[26]

This was vicious slander. Adams was not in the slightest degree qualified to condemn the two generals until he had heard their stories. But feeling of the New England delegates ran strongly against the arrogant patrician from upper New York. Schuyler had made enemies in New Hampshire and Massachusetts by his stubborn support of New York's claim to the New Hampshire Grants. His dilatory conduct during the campaign of 1776, in which hundreds of Massachusetts and Connecticut men were needlessly sacrificed, had increased smoldering antagonisms; New Englanders simply refused to serve under Schuyler. They distrusted him and no longer reposed confidence in him as a commander. They would serve under Gates. However, in mid-August Washington suspended his orders to Schuyler to proceed to his headquarters, and directed him to stay near Albany without a specific command, to influence the New York militia who were loyal to him and not at all anxious to serve under his rival. Inquiries into Schuyler's conduct were suspended until a decision was reached in upper New York.

Congress was also attempting to deal with another perplexing and embarrassing question: how to handle the shoals of French officers who were presenting themselves with commissions granted by Silas Deane. Many who had made their way to Philadelphia were impudent charlatans, unable to speak English, who optimistically believed Congress was duty-bound to honor Deane's frequently absurd commitments. In late July "a fresh quantity" arrived in Philadelphia. Their commissions were "2 Majors General, two Brigadiers, 2 Lt Cols. 2 Majors, 3 Captains and two Lts." Of this particular group, six men, including Baron de Kalb, had come with the Marquis de La Fayette. These gentlemen at once proceeded to present themselves to the President of Congress, who consigned them to the not so tender mercies of James Lovell, chairman of the Committee for Foreign Affairs.

Lovell, completely exasperated with Deane, a "weak or roguish man" who should be recalled, reminded La Fayette and his comrades that as they had come uninvited Congress did not propose to do anything. The young marquis would not accept this. He had crossed the Atlantic at his own expense after fleeing from a *lettre de cachet* which peremptorily forbade him to go to America. He at once offered to serve as a volunteer without compensation and without command. On the last day of July, Congress formally repudiated Deane's commission, but resolved that in consideration of the marquis's "illustrious family, his zeal and his connections," he should "have the rank of Major general in the army of the United States, but without pay and without command." La Fayette, who asked only to serve "near General Washington," was sent to the commander in chief's headquarters at Neshaminy, in Bucks County. In five weeks he would celebrate his twentieth birthday.

At this time, the plot known in American history as "the Conway Cabal" was in the bud. The object of these designs was to displace the commander in chief. Two ambitious adventurers, Thomas Conway, an Irish soldier of fortune, and Tronson du Coudray, who had recently arrived in America bearing the contract made with Silas Deane, impertinently injected themselves into the Schuyler-Gates wrangle. Modesty was not one of Du Coudray's attributes; en route from Boston, where he landed, he talked freely of his expectations to command the artillery and engineers. Washington met him and thought him probably able; he was certainly suave, and sweet-talked Congress into the major general's commission Deane had promised him. Shortly thereafter, Du Coudray, who was apparently slightly inebriated, rode his horse onto one end of a Schuylkill River ferry and off at the other. He drowned. The horse swam ashore, a distinct gain to the American cause. Conway was cut from another cloth—the Irish one. He was a big talker, flashy, and debonair, but he had courage and some command experience. Congress made him a brigadier general. He lost no time ingratiating himself with Gates, about to move north to replace Schuyler.

There were, indeed, grounds for dissatisfaction with the commander in chief's recent performances. His determination to defend New York had resulted in the nearly disastrous battle on Long Island; he had evacuated the city without burning it to the ground as both Charles Lee and Nathanael Greene urged him to do and had then fought two inconclusive battles before extricating his army. He had lost Forts Washington and Lee with their irreplaceable guns and stores of all descriptions. His reputation as a field commander had fallen to a low point. The ultimate test of a general's ability is success in the field; Washington had not failed it, but despite his successes at Trenton and Princeton, many—and not all of them his inveterate detractors—believed he had passed it.

John Adams inadvertently assisted these machinations. Indeed, he had written a year earlier he was "much distressed to see some members of this house disposed to idolise an image which their own hands have molten. I speak here of the superstitious veneration that is sometimes paid to General Washington." His opinion was perhaps motivated in some degree by personal jealousy. He had an abiding distrust of generals, the commander in chief not excepted. He had written Gates, when that general had been sent to the Northern Department to pick up the pieces after the Canadian debacle: "We don't trust you Generals with too much Power, for too long a Time."[27] What Adams feared was a military dictatorship. He did not want an American Cromwell. But he did not know his Washington, who never harbored such designs.**

Despite their preoccupation with this wrangle, delegates to Congress managed somehow to find time to debate a fantastic scheme to embark 1,000 men in "Battoes" at Fort Pitt, from whence they were to float down the Ohio to the Mississippi and on to New Orleans, where, it was assumed, the Spanish governor would provide them with money, cannon, and stores sufficient to enable them to march overland to attack Pensacola. Henry Laurens of South Carolina, who had only recently taken his seat, made a reasoned speech against "so mad an enterprise" and prevailed upon his colleagues to abandon it. Laurens was vastly annoyed to find Congress wasting valuable time on a variety of matters he considered either absurd or inconsequential, and wrote his friend John Rutledge, the president of South Carolina, that he could hardly "forbear concluding that a great Assembly is in its dotage and that happily for us, our Enemy is at the Same time very infirm."[28]

** British agents in America kept Whitehall well informed of the progress of the plots against Washington. The King thought these "discontents" would not "only greatly facilitate the bringing that deluded country to some reasonable ideas, but will make France reconsider whether she ought to enter into a war when America may leave her in the lurch."

✄ 4

A Gathering Storm

The day before Admiral Howe's fleet entered Chesapeake Bay, Burgoyne moved his headquarters from Fort Edward south some ten miles to Fort Miller. The flanks of his main body were well protected. Fraser's advance corps was preparing to cross the Hudson south of Fort Miller and take up a strong position near Saratoga (now Schuylerville, N.Y.); General von Riedesel's Germans covered the left. All elements were within mutually supporting distance, the Yankees were nowhere to be seen, and the general was confident he could force his way to Albany without major assistance from the south—if he could build up magazines. He realized that his supply problem was serious. A general less optimistic than the Honourable John Burgoyne would have assessed it as critical.

Some time previously Riedesel had suggested a foray into the Grants to procure mounts for his dragoons, collect draft animals, and pick up livestock to augment the salted meat diet on which the army had been subsisting. Burgoyne had disapproved this request, but now, just before leaving for Fort Miller, he reconsidered and decided to send a strong detachment on a swing to the east and south. He directed Riedesel to draw up the orders. The baron was reluctant. He pointed out that the situation in the Grants had changed drastically during the last weeks, that militiamen had responded to calls from Seth Warner and the General Court of New Hampshire, and that the prospective returns would no longer justify the risk. "But the English Commander was not a man to be dissuaded by anyone from any project he had determined upon."[1]

Had it not been for Skene, the baron's well-founded arguments might have prevailed. But Burgoyne listened rather to his political adviser, who informed him the area around Bennington was teeming with Loyalists and that there was in the town "a great deposit of corn, flour and cattle." Bennington sounded like the Promised Land; Burgoyne changed the plan Riedesel had submitted and set Bennington as the objective. Lieutenant Colonel Frederick Baum was named to command the expedition to march from the Batten Kill.

The purpose of the operation was "to try the affection of the Country; to disconcert the councils of the Enemy," to enlist provincial Tories, and "to obtain large supplies of Cattle, Horses and Carriages." Almost 350 horses would be needed to mount the dragoons; the army stood in need of an additional 1,300, plus draft oxen to haul the large numbers of carts and "other convenient carriages" Baum was directed to requisition and load with saddles, bridles, harness, and whatever else he could collect. All cattle (milch cows excepted) were to be rounded up; to ensure delivery, "the most respectable People" were to be taken as hostages. Baum did not need any cash. He was to confiscate property of rebels and to tender receipts to Loyalists. Burgoyne gave him explicit instructions as to how stock was to be guarded "when graizing" and how he was to arrange his bivouacs to ensure security. He directed Baum not to hazard his force.[2] Burgoyne gave this assignment to a German contingent under a German commander because military etiquette demanded that he do so. The Germans were on the left (east) flank and the operation was to be toward the left (east). Both Phillips and Fraser went over the orders. Phillips approved them; the Scot did not like the look of things: "The Germans are not very active people. Still, it may do."

Baum's composite command totaled nearly 600: 170 dragoons, about the same number of light infantry and Jägers, 40 or 50 Indians, 50 rangers, nearly 100 Canadians, and several dozen Tories. At dawn on August 13 Baum mustered the troops, and his column, complete with band, took the dusty road to Cambridge, fifteen miles to the southeast and halfway to Bennington.* Skene, who was to advise him as to how "to distinguish the good subjects from the bad," rode at his side.

Fraser was not alone in taking a dim view of this project. That a column was to be sent on an extended operation to conciliate the inhabitants and encourage Loyalists to enlist might have suggested that it would be a good idea to have sent several fairly senior English-speaking

---

* Several miles of the road Baum took to Cambridge exist today as a narrow, graveled, rural road.

officers with it. Skene, described by Hadden as "a famous marplot," was well known in the area and was detested and distrusted. The Riedesel dragoons, with their ridiculous pomaded pigtails, overburdened with equipment and long sabers that weighed ten pounds, were entirely unprepared for the sort of opposition they might meet, and were probably the one unit in the Northern Army least qualified for the mission. Hadden wrote they were sent on a task "the British Light Infantry of this Army are not fully equal to."[3] Here, regard for military protocol (which had previously got Howe into serious difficulties) prevailed.

During the afternoon Baum moved cautiously. His scouts captured a few rebels, who informed him that 1,800 militia were at Bennington. The colonel reported this to Burgoyne and added that he would be particularly careful in his approach. "Your Excellency may depend on hearing how I proceed at Bennington, and of my success there."[4]

A rebel colonel whose name the German had never heard commanded the militia encamped near Bennington. This was John Stark, a fearless officer who had campaigned during the War for Empire as a lieutenant under Robert Rogers. Stark, a veteran forest fighter who knew all the tricks of the trade, had fought at Trenton and Princeton, and when he heard Baum had marched from Cambridge at first light on August 14, he dispatched small groups of armed militia, instructed to wear Loyalist cockades on their hats, to meet the advancing column.

Baum made good time in the cool of the morning and at about eight o'clock arrived at Owl Kill, a small stream that empties into the Hoosic River. Here, at Sancoick, a demolished bridge had to be rebuilt. Baum encountered scattered resistance but by nine was across the stream and had taken a mill the Americans had neglected to destroy. He sat down, and using a barrel head for a table, composed another report to Burgoyne. "By five prisoners taken here, they agree that from 1500 to 1800 are in Bennington, but are supposed to leave it on our approach, I will proceed so far today, as to fall on the enemy tomorrow early . . . people are flocking in hourly, but want to be armed; the savages cannot be controlled; they ruin and take everything they please."[5]

Burgoyne received this letter in the afternoon; he replied immediately. A note of apprehension was apparent: "Should you find the enemy too strongly posted at Bennington, and maintaining such a countenance as may make an attack imprudent, I wish you to take a post where you can maintain yourself till you receive an answer from me, and I will either support you in force, or withdraw you."[6]

By midafternoon, Baum's column had put in a wearying twelve-hour day, and when his scouts reported a large body of Americans marching out of Bennington, he sensibly concluded that he might be in serious trouble. He selected a strong defensive position atop a steep hill overlooking the valley of the Walloomsac, set his men to trenching and throwing up parapets, got off a message to Burgoyne asking for immediate assistance, and settled down to await the morrow.

When dawn came, rain was falling; vaporing mists rose from the valleys of the Walloomsac and the Hoosic. Toward nine o'clock on the morning of the sixteenth, small bodies of armed men, most of them in shirt sleeves, appeared from different directions. "They did not act as if they intended to make an attack; and Baum, being told by the provincial [Skene] . . . that they were all Loyalists, and would make common cause with him, suffered them to encamp on his side and rear." Shortly thereafter, a strong body appeared and launched an attack on the rear of Baum's position. "This was the signal for the seeming royalists to attack the Germans."[7] The Americans hit Baum's position simultaneously on the front, rear, and both flanks. His Indians, who well knew the fate awaiting them if they were taken, fled to the woods. Soon it was over. Baum lay mortally wounded; many of his men had been killed and others captured. A few escaped and headed west, abandoning cannon, packs, headgear, standards, muskets, sabers, and other equipment to Stark's Yankees.

Help was on the way in the form of a column led by Baum's colleague, Colonel Breymann. But help was coming to Stark, too; Colonel Seth Warner's regiment was marching toward the field. Stark collected his men, who were busy going through the pockets of the dead, and the combined force "put a stop to their [the Germans] Career." The action, "very warm and desperate," lasted until sunset, when the Germans broke. Stark reported, ". . . we took two Pieces more of their Cannon, together with all their Baggage, a number of Horses, Carriages, etc." He reported twenty-seven German officers captured, including "1 Lieut Coll since dead, and 1 Baron."[8]

The lesson of Bennington was clear, unequivocal, and menacing, but Burgoyne, nurtured in the tradition of orthodox continental warfare, could not read it. There, Stark had brought together an efficient force of temporary soldiers, untrained in the complicated evolutions of European battlegrounds, but ready to hazard their lives to protect their families and homes and defend their cherished liberties. Their fathers and grandfathers—and some of them, too—had fought red Indians, and they were equally willing to fight red-coated soldiers and their detested allies. Stark's tactics had been imaginative and his assaulting columns, which struck Baum's position simultaneously at four points, skillfully planned and commanded. "The English, as usual, endeavored to lay the entire blame of the ill-success of this expedition upon the Germans."[9]

Though the Americans fought well, Burgoyne would not have been wise to report this to Lord George Germain, who held the general's future in his keeping and had frequently and vigorously expressed himself on the inherent inferiority and cowardice of the colonists. Still, Burgoyne could not sweep the Bennington affair under the rug, and on August 20 wrote the secretary a pessimistic letter: "The great bulk of the country is undoubtedly with the Congress in principle and in zeal; and their measures are executed with a secrecy and dispatch that are not to be equalled. Wherever the King's forces point, militia, to the amount of two or three thousand, assemble in twenty-four hours. . . . The Hampshire Grants in particular, a country unpeopled and almost unknown in the last war, now abounds in the most active and most rebellious race of the continent, and hangs like a gathering storm upon my left. In all parts the industry and management in driving cattle, and removing corn are indefatigable and certain."†[10]

A few days later, in a General Order to the army, he explained the disaster as owing to the "Credulity of the Department of Intelligence— the ill-founded confidence of Colonel Baum . . . the slow movement of Lieutenant Colonel Breymann's Corps." The enemy, he asserted, "had surely felt their little Success, and there is no circumstance to affect the Army with further regret or melancholy."[11]

But inevitably the morale of the army *was* affected. The troops saw stragglers coming in dejected, soaked with sweat, exhausted, hungry, weaponless, defeated. They soon learned that St. Luc's son-in-law had made off to Canada, that many Canadians had followed him, and that most of the Indians had departed. The troops "felt unusual mortification from this unexpected check. Though it did not diminish their courage, it abated their confidence." Further, "it deranged every plan for pursuing the advantages which had been previously obtained. Among other embarrassments it reduced them to the alternative of halting till the supplies were brought forward from Fort George, or of advancing without them at the risque of being starved."[12]

Equally distressing news now arrived from the west. On August 3 St. Leger had arrived at Fort Stanwix (now Rome, New York) and summoned Colonel Peter Gansevoort, who commanded the isolated fort, to lay down his arms. The usual promises were made that if he did so, his troops would be protected from the savagery of the Indians. Gansevoort declined the invitation and St. Leger set about investing the fort. Two days later, he learned that a relief column commanded by Nicholas Herkimer, chairman of the Tryon County Committee of Correspondence and Safety, was on the way to raise the siege. He immediately sent Brant and his Indians off to lay an ambush, and on August 6 the militia walked into it near Oriskany. Although the militiamen were surprised and momentarily panicked, they pulled themselves together, and after a hot fire fight, in which Herkimer was mortally wounded, broke up the ambuscade and scattered the howling Indians, who took off through the forest for their camp near Fort Stanwix.

† When Alexander Wedderburn heard of the march to Bennington, he observed that because one general had been "a blockhead" (Howe garrisoning Trenton with Germans) was not sufficient reason for a second general to emulate him.

While this was going on Gansevoort sent a column commanded by Colonel Marinus Willett to assist Herkimer. En route, Willett's scouts discovered the camp of Brant's Indians; the few sentinels fled to the surrounding forest and the Americans proceeded to sack the camp. What they could not carry back to the fort, they destroyed. The Indians returned to a scene of desolation. Willett's men had carried off all their cooking pots, kettles, robes, and blankets and burned everything else.

News of Herkimer's fight reached Schuyler at Stillwater the following day, and on the eleventh he dispatched Brigadier General Ebenezer Learned with a column eight hundred strong to deal with St. Leger. Two days later he directed Benedict Arnold with a brigade of six hundred "to repair thither with all convenient speed" and assume over-all command. Arnold, who knew something about psychological warfare, sent ahead a half-witted Dutchman who told the Indians he was on the way with a host as numberless as the leaves on the trees. They did not wait to hear more. St. Leger at once raised the siege, abandoned his few small cannon and his camp equipment, and retreated with indecorous haste to Oswego. On the way, his savage allies stole all the officers' liquor. Burgoyne could no longer expect help from that quarter.

In the fights at Bennington, Riedesel's corps had been seriously hurt. Burgoyne sent the walking wounded off to Ticonderoga, where after a tedious and dangerous trek, they would embark for the journey down the lake, the first step on a long trail back to the German villages and farms most had come from. Shortly after the engagement, Lieutenant Colonel Robert Kingston, Burgoyne's adjutant general, submitted a personnel return showing a total of 4,646 rank and file present and fit for duty. This figure reflected a two months' rank and file attrition of 1,649. The return did not include officers, sergeants, gunners (some 400), drummers, Indians, Canadians, and Provincials. Of the Indians, fewer than 100 remained, and they, sensing calamity, continued to drift off. Canadians in all scarcely exceeded 100. Provincial Tories, many of whom joined at Fort Edward, mustered about 600. Burgoyne had found the Loyalist recruits not readily amenable to British discipline and fit only for "searching for cattle . . . clearing roads, and guiding detachments on the march." They were, he later said, "an even heavier tax on time and patience" than the Canadians. He had to count on his regulars, British and German, to see him through.

Had Bennington been a success, Burgoyne would have reinforced Fraser; now he sensibly decided to consolidate and ordered the Scot to abandon his position at Saratoga. This maneuver was executed with considerable difficulty; the Hudson, swollen by days of rain, had carried away the bridge of bateaux, but the enterprising young naval officer on Burgoyne's staff collected enough "scoules" and skiffs to get Fraser's command to the safety of the east bank at Batten Kill.

Burgoyne no longer had the slightest doubt the "great bulk of the country" supported Congress. Before leaving London he had been told quite the opposite by Germain, whose prejudices precluded any objective estimate of American sentiment. There, he had also discussed the American temper with Hutchinson, and in Quebec, Carleton had assured him he would be joined by hundreds of Loyalists eager to support the King. The general discovered, and reported, that this support, ephemeral at best, derived not from any attachment to the crown, but was motivated in most cases by selfish personal reasons. His estimate was accorded no weight by the ministry, whose self-appointed expert on the subject would continue for the next four years obstinately to assert the opposite.

French Canadians, Provincials, and Indians were one personnel problem; another, common to all European armies, was women. More than four hundred camp followers, many with children, trudged with the soldiers or rode in the army's carts. The general's mistress, wife of a complaisant commissary officer, tenaciously followed along; Baroness von Riedesel, with three children and two servants, trailed loyally after her husband in her calash. Other officers had wives or mistresses who had followed them across the Atlantic or had been acquired en route. Altogether, this female corps and accompanying baggage required a great number of carts, horses, and men that could ill be spared. A European army was on the march. But this was America, and a different war.

No one paid much attention to Burgoyne's orders to strip down. Why should they? He and Riedesel had not. One had his compliant mistress, his candlelit table, his champagne, and his card games, the other his doting wife and his Rhenish wine. Burgoyne's baggage and that of his small official "family" required thirty carts. The adjutant general, when later questioned as to the number of women attending the army, replied that he was so occupied that he had no leisure "to pay attention to the ladies" and knew very little "either of their beauty or their numbers." He maintained the women were more of a comfort than an impediment to the King's army.

The reverses at Bennington and Stanwix destroyed the last vestiges of Gentleman Johnny's optimism: "Had I latitude in my orders I should think it is my duty to wait in this position near Saratoga, or perhaps as far back as Ft. Edward, where my communication with Lake George could be perfectly secure until some event happened to assist my movement forward."[13] The event he anxiously awaited was a move north from New York. "When I wrote more confidently, I little foresaw that I was to be left to pursue my way through such a tract of country, and hosts of foes, without any cooperation from New York. . . . I yet do not despond."[14] He knew Americans were flocking to join Gates at Stillwater where "he can get as many militia as he pleases"; that Major General Israel Putnam, who held the Highlands, had sent two brigades to Gates, and that these troops were "strongly posted at the mouth of the Mohawk River." Still, he was determined to carry out the orders he had received "to force a junction at Albany." This irrational decision strongly suggests ambition had impaired Burgoyne's judgment to the extent that he was no longer able to assess the situation objectively. As an independent commander he was responsible to take decisions that would assist him to attain his objective, or if a reasoned appreciation indicated that to be impossible, to preserve his army.

The bulk of the Northern Army, on short rations and plagued by dysentery, was encamped at Batten Kill on the east bank of the Hudson. Officers and men suffered "with fevers and agues so common to the climate . . . the heats there were very severe and violent. All sorts of meats were tainted in a very short time and the stench was very prejudicial."[15] But the army had recovered its spirit. One of Burgoyne's aides, in his circuit of the camps, found morale high. He thought it impossible "for any army to have been in higher spirits . . . or more desirous of coming to an engagement with the enemy."[16]

Major General Horatio Gates, who had relieved Phillip Schuyler as commander of the Northern Department on August 19, 1777, was preparing for the inevitable engagement, which he designed to take place on ground of his own choosing. He and his Polish engineer, Colonel Thaddeus Kosciusko, reconnoitered the terrain, and Gates decided to stand on Bemis Heights, strong defensible ground about nine miles south of Saratoga. Gates immediately ordered the army to march north from Stillwater.

Although Arnold and Learned had joined him, he anxiously awaited the arrival of John Stark. At Stark's headquarters, Benjamin Lincoln was having no success in his attempts to persuade the victor of Bennington to join Gates or to move against Burgoyne's vulnerable communications. Stark, independent as always, refused to come out of his hills. He was angry at Congress because for a second time he had been passed over for promotion to brigadier. Gates would have to do without him. That was that.

John Hancock now intervened and in late August wrote the New Hampshire Assembly a rather severe letter:

> It is with the utmost Regret the Congress hear, that Genl. Stark has Instructions to act independent of the Army of the United States, if he should be so inclined, as Nothing can be so destructive of military Subordination, or produce greater Confusion in the Service, than the Existence of any Corps or Body of men free from the Control of the Commander-in-Chief and the Rules of Dis-

cipline that bind the Rest of the Army. It is the earnest Desire of Congress that General Stark may be subjected to the same Regulations by which all other General Officers of the Militia have been hitherto governed when called out at the Expense of the United States. I am therefore to request you will give Genl. Stark Instructions to govern himself accordingly.[17]

Congress could do nothing to enforce its "earnest Desires." The General Court of New Hampshire had appointed Stark a brigadier; he was under no obligation to Congress, and he did not propose to march—at least, not yet. Still, Gates had under command more than 12,000 troops. Approximately half were Continentals. And he knew that Morgan's riflemen would soon be on the way.

Burgoyne waited at the Kill until September 13, when a pontoon bridge of bateaux and planking was ready. On that afternoon and the day following, the Northern Army crossed the Hudson. Gates did not move to contest the crossing; he was well pleased with his position commanding the river and the road to Albany; with his right anchored on the Hudson, his front protected by ravines, his left in the forest, and his army behind log-reinforced earthworks, Gates was confident.

He had other reasons to feel fully competent to cope with the British general. He had known Burgoyne when they both served His Majesty. Not intimately, for Gates was never accepted in the same social circles. But that he well knew Burgoyne's character is attested by letters he wrote at the time. He was aware his opponent was a gambler who would chance all "on the turn of a card." Gates was taking no risks. He would sit. His strength increased daily; Burgoyne's decreased. Gates had plentiful supplies of food; Burgoyne but little, and that little would soon be eaten. Gates expected six or seven hundred Pennsylvania and Virginia riflemen to arrive at any moment; he could stay behind his entrenchments until the Northern Army starved, and he was prepared to do so. He would fight, but on his own terms.

On September 15, with his army standing on the west bank of the Hudson, Burgoyne ordered "the Bridge to be Broke."

Washington had found Viscount Howe's movements perplexing. When the British fleet left Delaware Bay and disappeared over the eastern horizon, he wrote Sullivan, then marching toward the Delaware: "From this event it appears Genl. Howe has been practising a deep feint merely to draw our attention and whole force [toward Philadelphia]. I am to request that you will countermarch the Division under your command and proceed with it, with all possible expedition, to Peeks Kill, as there is the strongest reason to believe, that the North River is their object. . . ."[18] Two days later he directed Sullivan to halt and encamp upon "convenient and healthy Ground" until further orders. He regretted that necessity required so much marching and countermarching and urged Sullivan to "use every means to refresh the Troops and to get their Arms in good order."

The governor of New York, Major General George Clinton, had requested more Continental troops to help check Burgoyne; Washington replied he could not spare them. He wrote Governor Trumbull urging him to supply the Connecticut quota to the Northern Department without delay. The situation was indeed "gloomy," but "a steady perseverance, and our spirited exertions will put things right again." Surely the militia were not disposed to be "supine spectators of their own and their country's ruin."[19] But it was difficult to persuade militiamen to move outside the boundaries of their native states.

Howe's peculiar behavior kept Washington in a constant state of suspense. "The advantages they receive from having command of the water are immense." His imagination was "constantly in the field of conjecture"; his troops fatiguing themselves in marching. "I wish we could but fix on their object. Their conduct is really so mysterious that you cannot reason upon it."[20]

Washington knew that when he moved, he would have to do so unexpectedly and march rapidly, and from his headquarters at Germantown issued orders designed to ensure "the utmost Celerity." Officers were to take only the indispensable minimum of clothing; men's packs would be carried in wagons provided by the quartermaster general; "But these packs are not to be stuffed with loads of useless trumpery . . . and the officers are to see that they are not."[21] As Howe's intentions were still unclear, Washington held the bulk of the army on the east side of the Delaware, prepared to march toward the Highlands of the Hudson or south toward Philadelphia.

On the first day of August, Howe's fleet left Cape May and dropped over the horizon. The armada was next sighted a week and a half later, when the ships were seen beating to the south. "This is the first information we have had of them since they left Cape May, and I am now as much puzzled about their designs, as I was before; being unable to account, upon any plausible Plan, for General Howe's conduct in this instance or why he should go to the Southward, rather than cooperate with Mr. Burgoyne."[22]

Pleas for assistance from the Northern Department poured in every day. Washington directed Colonel Daniel Morgan to march his five-hundred-man rifle corps from Trenton to Peekskill, where General Israel Putnam would have vessels waiting to take them to Albany. He wrote Putnam to prepare for Morgan's arrival and to "give out" that he was marching with one thousand riflemen. Although Washington was in no position to influence developments in the north decisively, he exerted himself to keep informed. He had heard that it was "in contemplation to unite all the Militia and Continental Troops in one body and make an opposition wholly in front." He wrote Governor Clinton he thought this a "very ineligible plan." The general had his eye on Burgoyne's fragile and vulnerable communications: "a tolerable Body of Men" in the Grants would give him considerable anxiety," oblige him to advance circumspectly, and "leave such Strong Points behind as must make his Main body very weak and extremely capable of being repulsed by the force we shall have in front." As he was not fully acquainted with the situation, he could not give specific advice; "Let those on the Spot determine and act as appears to them most prudent."[23]

As late as August 20 Washington was still in a quandary. Where were the Howe brothers? He was uncertain whether he would have to move to the north or south. The general was now convinced the British meditated an attack on Charleston, or possibly a move against New England. "The danger of the Sea, the injury his Troops and Horses must sustain from being so long confined, the loss of time so late in the Campaign, will scarcely admit the supposition, that he is merely making a feint and still intends to return either to Delaware or North River." If his objective was indeed Charleston, Washington could not arrive there in time; his only course of action was to wait in place, north of Philadelphia, alert to move either toward Philadelphia or the Hudson at the moment Howe conclusively revealed his intent.

All doubts were resolved on the following day. Viscount Howe's fleet had arrived in Chesapeake Bay. Washington immediately ordered the army to cross the Delaware and take up the march toward Wilmington. He wrote Putnam: "As there is not now the least danger of General Howes going to New England, I hope the whole Force of that Country will turn out, and by following the great stroke struck by General Stark near Bennington, intirely crush Genl. Burgoyne, who by his letter to Colo. Baum seems to be in want of almost everything."[24] He ordered Sullivan to join the army at once.

Howe's passage from the Delaware to Cape Charles was laborious and unpleasant. The heat was "immense"; many horses died; their carcasses were hauled out of the fetid holds and thrown over the side. Water was strictly rationed; soldiers and sailors sickened and died of "putrid and bilious Fever common in this Region of the World." Serle recorded temperatures in the shade of 84° to 86°. During this leisurely but vastly uncomfortable sail, a packet brought General Howe mail from England. The bag contained a rather curious letter from Germain dated May 15 in which the secretary expressed his hope that the general would conclude operations against Philadelphia in time to assist Burgoyne. In justice to Howe, it may again be observed that he never had any intention of personally leading an army north to meet Burgoyne at Albany, or, indeed, to employ any sizable force for that purpose.

Had the American Secretary belatedly come to appreciate the full implications of the strategy for which he bore ultimate responsibility? He had not conceived Burgoyne's operation, nor that of Sir William against Philadelphia, but as the executive responsible for conduct of land operations he had approved them. He had carried both, presumably with cabinet approval, to the King. Apparently not until May did he fully appreciate that the plans he had approved for strategy in 1777 were dispersive rather than co-operative. One deduces the secretary suddenly realized he must cover himself.

As Viscount Howe's majestic armada sailed north before a fair wind, Washington, at last certain of Sir William's ultimate intention, left his headquarters in Bucks County and led his Continentals, spruced up for the occasion, through Philadelphia. La Fayette, who witnessed this parade, wrote that many of the soldiers were half naked; that thousands wore soiled and greasy buckskin and tow hunting shirts, but that all marched proudly to the music of fifes, drums, and tambourines.

Fortunately for Howe's troops, the landing at Head of Elk on August 25 was not opposed. For thirty-four days they had been aboard transports, jammed together like cattle, subsisting on salted meat, weevily biscuit, rancid cheese, wormy peas, stale water, and curtailed rations of beer and grog. Five weeks on a modern troopship with a reasonably wholesome and balanced diet, sufficient fresh water, and some facilities for exercise and recreation is an episode no soldier is anxious to repeat; one who has endured it can imagine the inexpressible relief British and Hessian troopers must have felt as they staggered and splashed wearily through the tepid tidal muck to the beach on that muggy day in 1777.

Washington could not seriously have opposed this landing, backed as it was by the guns of the fleet, but a few score riflemen could have created tremendous confusion by picking off officers and sergeants as the tired troops clambered out of flat-bottomed assault boats and waded ashore. The opportunity was neglected, however, and the landing went off smoothly. Admiral Howe had planned the operation in meticulous detail; troops and stores flowed ashore in good order. By nightfall of the twenty-sixth the British general had his beach head and was ready to move. But now, when he should have pushed hard, he dallied.

His troops began to plunder before their gaiters were dry. Howe had determined to take stern measures, and by sunset of that "D day" his provost marshal had hanged two and ordered five more severely whipped. "If this had been done a year ago, we sh'd have found its Advantages."[25] But these seven men and dozens of others who escaped the noose and the "Catt" had done the damage: A proclamation Howe issued the following day assuring "the peaceable Inhabitants of the Province of

PENNSYLVANIA, the lower counties on DELAWARE and the counties of Maryland on the Eastern Shore of CHESAPEAK BAY" that he proposed to inflict exemplary punishment on looters evoked no response but curses. Nor did his promise of clemency to those who would take an oath of allegiance have any effect. Inhabitants of the area around Cecil Court House ran away and drove off their livestock.

British and German troops alike considered abandoned cottages and farmsteads fair game; Serle spent three days ashore and was "mortified with the Accounts of Plunder, etc. committed on the poor Inhabitants by the Army and Navy." He stopped "several Depredations" and was not too unhappy to record that forty-seven "Grenadiers and several other Parties straggling for Plunder were surprized by the Rebels." But no severities of punishment could check the Hessians, "more infamous and cruel than any. It is a misfortune, we ever had such a dirty, cowardly Set of contemptible Miscreants."[26] Most British officers shared Serle's sentiments, which would not have found favor with Lord George Germain, who was convinced the Howe brothers had treated the Americans far too leniently.

As Sir William edged cautiously toward the capital, the admiral's warships, empty transports, and victualing ships fell down the Elk to the bay. Here the fleet awaited results of the battle soon to be fought for Philadelphia. Serle made a few notes on the nature of the country and its inhabitants: "Scarce a white Person was to be seen; but negroes appeared in great abundance. They live in Huts or Hovels near the Houses of their Owners, and are treated as a better kind of cattle. . . . Such is the Practice or Sentiment of Americans, while they are bawling about the rights of Human Nature."[27]

Delegates to the Congress, responsible for a considerable volume of this bawling, now became apprehensive. In Philadelphia there was a great deal of underground Loyalist sentiment, particularly among the Quakers, and Richard Henry Lee wrote his friend Patrick Henry, governor of Virginia, that some had been arrested "to prevent their mischievous interposition in favor of the enemy." The most outspoken were being sent under guard "forthwith" to Staunton, where he hoped the governor would see they were "well secured, for they are a mischievous people."

The British commander in chief, undoubtedly one of the most dilatory generals in the history of the British Army, did not reach Brandywine Creek, where Washington had laid out his defenses, until September 11, seventeen days after his first waves had hit the beach. His advance skirmishers on the southwest bank of the Brandywine reported the Americans in force and entrenched on the opposite side. Howe determined to turn the American right and selected the man to do it: Cornwallis. This general, remembered in American history only for the surrender at Yorktown, was a vigorous corps commander, and at Brandywine demonstrated that he could move fast and strike hard. Washington was here the victim of conflicting information, and before he was aware of the rapidly developing threat to his right, Cornwallis, after marching nearly eighteen miles, was in position to turn it and rampage into the rear of the Continental Army. Washington hurried Sullivan to that flank, and fearing the worst, hastily dispatched Greene to the rear to cover the road to Chester.

Actually, Cornwallis could not get his corps into position to launch an attack on "Rebels very strongly posted" until 5 P.M. The British, fatigued from the long march, still managed a bayonet charge; the Americans scrambled from the steel. Lieutenant Henry Stirke of the Light Infantry Battalion wrote: "Had there been but one more hour of daylight, all their Waggons, and baggage would have fallen into our hands."[28]

Meanwhile, Lieutenant General Knyphausen, whose artillery had been playing on the Americans, hit their front at Chadd's Ford. The American position was now crumbling into disaster, which only darkness averted. Howe had planned to destroy Washington's army; his commanders and troops had moved energetically and fought bravely. Sullivan's division had been demolished. To this point, Howe had handled the battle well; the Americans retreated toward Chester in great confusion. La Fayette, a musket ball through his leg, was taken to the rear in a carriage with other wounded officers. He described the retreat as "pell-mell; the route was complete." Howe's horses, starved during the tedious voyage from New York, were in no condition for his dragoons to follow and saber the fleeing Americans. La Fayette thought Howe had "lost a precious night." A more vigorous commander would have put his light infantry and grenadiers on the road to Chester before dawn on the following morning.

Shortly after midnight, Washington got off an express to John Hancock. The president of Congress received the courier at 1 A.M., summoned Congress to an emergency meeting two hours later, and sent an urgent call for 4,000 New Jersey militia. This was really whistling up the wind. Thomas Burke (North Carolina) had arrived in the city several hours earlier direct from the battlefield burning with anger at General Sullivan, the "marplot of our army," whose "total want of military genius" had, he asserted, led to Washington's defeat.

On September 18 Washington sent Colonel Alexander Hamilton riding to the capital with a plea to the delegates to leave the city, and by the following morning most had departed. "You may depend upon it," one wrote, "we were soon on the wing." Destination: Lancaster. "We thought it not best at this time to remove out of this State lest in this Critical Situation of Affairs there whould be a total defection of this State." John Adams, not in the least perturbed, wrote his "Dearest

Friend": "Don't be anxious about me, nor about our great and sacred cause. It is the cause of truth and will prevail. If Howe gets the city, it will cost him all his force to keep it, and so he can get nothing else."[29] Thus amid scenes of undignified confusion, Congress left Philadelphia, "that mass of cowardice and Toryism."

The opposing generals, each designing to bring the enemy to battle on terms favorable to himself, indulged in a series of inconclusive maneuvers. Washington's principal problem was not Howe, but preservation of the army. Brandywine had not enhanced his reputation; Major General Baron de Kalb assessed him as "the most amiable, kind hearted and upright of men; but as a General he is too slow, too indolent and far too weak; besides, he has a tinge of vanity in his composition and overestimates himself." Kalb felt that whatever success Washington might enjoy would be "owing to good luck and the blunders of his adversaries, rather than to his ability. I may even say that he does not know how to improve upon the grossest blunders of the enemy."[30]

Now resigned to the loss of Philadelphia, Washington hoped to harry and distress Howe by attacking his communications, and entrusted this mission to Brigadier General "Mad Anthony" Wayne, who posted his division in a wood near Paoli. Through deserters, Howe had learned of Wayne's location, and directed Major General Charles Grey to deal with him. Grey planned a midnight bayonet assault on the sleeping Americans. He ordered all flints removed from muskets and bayonets fixed. The British approached silently. Surprise was complete. "The sentries fired and ran off." Grey's light infantry rushed into Wayne's camp, "putting to the bayonet all they came up with, and overtaking the main herd of the fugitives, stabbed great numbers."[31] American casualties were between two and three hundred; British less than a dozen.‡

Several days after the "Paoli Massacre," Cornwallis marched into Philadelphia, where Tories accorded him a handsome welcome. Howe arrived a few days later. The British commander in chief had taken the rebel capital. But he had not destroyed Washington's army. And his position was insecure, for as he could not get supplies safely across New Jersey, he relied on his brother to bring all supplies by sea. Ships with reinforcements, replacements, provisions, and all supplies required to maintain the combat effectiveness of his army must proceed by the route he had followed. The shorter route up the Delaware could not be used until Yankee forts at Red Bank and Fort Mifflin below the city were taken and the river cleared of obstructions.

In London general belief was that Howe would sail and march north from New York to meet Burgoyne, or at least send a respectable force to-

‡ The general was thereafter to be known in the British Army as "No Flint" Grey.

ward Albany. When news arrived that he had embarked his army and set off for the south, "the Ministers were so confounded . . . when they wished he should have gone to the North and endeavour to get Washington between him and Burgoyne, that they sent orders to Burgoyne not to advance beyond the Albany till he could hear from and concert with Howe."[32] Walpole's statement that the ministers were "confounded" is interesting; he had very good high-level sources of information, and his remark raises the question of precisely how much Germain's colleagues knew of his plans. Apparently very little; there is no record that any of His Majesty's confidential servants voiced objection to the harebrained strategic concept that in 1777 dispersed the efforts of the only two British striking forces in America.

🎙 5

Not More than Mortal

During the afternoon of September 17 the Northern Army encamped on "advantageous ground" some three miles north of Gates's position on Bemis Heights.* Redcoats immediately began to scavenge nearby potato fields for supplementary fare. One such group was ambushed; twelve were killed and twenty taken prisoner. Burgoyne, properly incensed, "solemnly" informed the army he did not propose to lose men whose lives belonged to the King "for the pitiful consideration of a few potatoes. . . . The first Soldier caught beyond the Advanced Centrys of the Army will be instantly hanged."

Gates's scouts, operating in small groups in Burgoyne's rear, kept the American general informed. From them, he received "certain Intelligence" that Burgoyne had ordered forward his detachments at Skenesborough, Fort Anne, Fort George, and Fort Edward with their artillery, stores, and provisions. He at once wrote Governor Clinton: "From this it is evident, the General's Design is, to risque all upon one rash Stroke, it is therefore the indispensable Duty of all Concerned, to exert themselves in reinforcing this Army, without one Moments Delay—the Militia from

* The site of Burgoyne's headquarters has been clearly identified. There, a spring provided the general with clear, cold water then, as it does today to any visitor.

every Part, should be ordered here, with all possible Expedition."[1] John Stark and his New Hampshire militia arrived on the following morning, but to Gates's consternation, Stark lingered for but a few hours; he explained that as the men's term of service expired that very day, they were determined to go home. And go home they did, although they knew from sounds of occasional musket fire that battle was impending.

Having committed the army to the west bank, and marched to a confrontation, the British general had two tactical options—he must either drive Gates from the position on Bemis Heights or pry him out of it—and he had no time to lose. Broken ground and boggy ravines choked with heavy brush and tangled thickets limited the scope of maneuver. On high ground west of the river, around Freeman's Farm and John Nielson's cabin, the land was partially cleared, but patches of woodland limited visibility and easy movement. Terrain dictated the pattern of attack. Here, the Heights press closely on the river and command the road. An advance down this natural bottleneck was not feasible. The general decided to maintain simultaneous pressure on both the river road and the center, and to turn Gates's left (west) flank, anchored in the woods. His problem was that scouts had been unable to determine where this flank lay.

Burgoyne conceived that a wide sweep to the west and south would force the Americans to uncover their position; appropriately, he entrusted this difficult and decisive task to Fraser's advance corps. Fraser's column included as usual the light infantry, grenadiers, Canadians, Loyalists, and a few Indians, with twelve guns attached. The center column consisted of the 9th, 20th, 21st, and 62nd regiments. Burgoyne would accompany this column, commanded by Brigadier General James Hamilton. Riedesel's Germans were to press down the river road.

Tactically, this battle plan could have been much improved. No more than a remote possibility existed that Riedesel could force the river road. A relatively small force with adequate artillery support could, however, create a threat and keep the Americans there fully occupied. Obviously, a decision had to be sought in the west or at the center. This should have suggested a strong infantry reserve posted behind the interval between Hamilton and Fraser, alert to reinforce an advantage gained by either. Burgoyne did not allocate preponderant weight to the area where he sought a decision, but rather to the river road. To compound this error, he assigned nineteen guns to Riedesel and directed Phillips to remain with the baron. None of the general officers took exception to this plan.

September 19 dawned warm. The Heights were clear, but fog hung heavily over the river as Fraser set off on his wide swing to the west to seek the American left. Hamilton followed for about a mile, then turned south, and sent forward scouts and skirmishers. Shortly after noon, American scouts picked up Fraser's columns; Gates immediately ordered out

Daniel Morgan's riflemen and sent Enoch Poore's brigade of Arnold's division after them. Morgan's men did not, however, run into Fraser, but into Hamilton. The riflemen, unaccustomed to regulars pressing on them with glistening steel, fled into the woods. Here, during a brief respite, Morgan rallied them with repeated "turkey calls."

Gates now began feeding Continental troops into the contested area around Freeman's Farm. Morgan ordered his riflemen to "take off" the officers, which they did with great effect and to the outrage of the British, who conceived that while "private men" might be mown down and laid out in windrows, officers were sacrosanct. American sharpshooters took a more democratic view, and when a Redcoat in lace and braid exposed himself they zeroed in on him. Gunners were other prime targets. Fire of riflemen posted in treetops and hidden in underbrush was so effective that in one four-gun battery of forty-eight, the battery commander and thirty-six gunners were killed or wounded.

The center was held only because of quick reaction by Riedesel, who, hearing heavy firing from that direction, hastily gathered together his regiment, two odd companies of another, Captain Georg Pausch's gunners with two brass cannon, and set off at quick step toward the scene of battle. The British regiments in the center had withstood six attacks by "steady relays" of Americans. When Riedesel arrived they were "thinned down to one half." He found "a small band surrounded by heaps of dead and wounded." He attacked at once; Pausch's gunners manhandled their brass cannon into a front-line position and opened fire with grapeshot.[2]

The baron had again saved the day, as he had earlier at Hubbardton. At dusk, the Americans retired to their fortifications, ceding the bloody field. That night Burgoyne's spent regulars rested uneasily on their arms on the ground they had held. The general called the day "a victory." Baroness von Riedesel, a loyal wife who was convinced her husband never received the credit due him, later wrote: "General Burgoyne and a few other English commanders, regarded the German general with secret envy. Indeed, they would gladly have passed over his merits, had such a thing been possible. British pride did not desire the acknowledgment of bravery other than their own."[3]

Sergeant Lamb, who was present, recorded his opinion that General Burgoyne "behaved with great personal bravery, he shunned no danger; his presence and conduct animated the troops (for they greatly loved the general); he delivered his orders with precision and coolness; and in the heat, fury and danger of the fight maintained the true characteristics of the soldier—serenity, fortitude, and undaunted intrepidity."[4] That night many Canadians, Loyalists, and Indians left camp. But the candles on the general's table burned into the early hours as he went over the casualty lists submitted by Colonel Kingston. Freeman's Farm had cost him over 500 killed, wounded, and missing in action. More than 350 of these were in British regiments of the line.

During the later House of Commons inquiry, the Earl of Balcarres, who had driven the Americans before him at Hubbardton, was asked why, at Freeman's Farm, the Yankees had not stayed in their entrenchments. He replied: "The reason they did not defend their entrenchments was that they always marched out of them and attacked us." They fought, he testified, "with courage and obstinacy . . . we were taught by experience that neither their attacks nor resistance was to be despised."

The precise part Benedict Arnold played in the first battle of Freeman's Farm is obscure. Many years later James Wilkinson, aide-de-camp to Gates at Saratoga, wrote:

> It is worthy of remark, *that not a single general officer was on the field of battle the 19th Sept.* until the evening when General Learned was ordered out; about the same time General Gates and Arnold were in front of the center of the camp, listening to the peal of small arms, when Colonel Mr. Lewis, deputy quartermaster general returned from the field, and being questioned by the General, he reported the undecisive progress of the action; at which Arnold exclaimed *"By God, I will soon put a stop to it,"* and putting spurs to his horse gallopped off at full speed; Colonel Lewis immediately observed to General Gates "You had better order him back, the action is going well, he may by some rash act do mischief." I was instantly despatched, overtook, and remanded Arnold to Camp.[5]

Others said they saw Arnold on the field.

For some time, the two generals had been at odds over the question of the most effective tactics to use against Burgoyne. Gates, cautious and methodical, planned a careful and controlled defensive battle. Arnold, always impetuous, audacious, and aggressive, wanted to carry the fight to the British. In this tactic there was an element of risk Gates was not prepared to accept. He could not afford to hazard the army, and his was the ultimate responsibility. Over a bottle of wine, Arnold had contemptuously referred to Gates as an "old woman," an indiscretion scarcely calculated to restore mutual cordiality.

A General Order Gates issued several days later did not help matters. In this, the general directed Colonel Daniel Morgan "to make returns and reports to headquarters only; from whence alone he is to receive orders." Arnold no sooner read this order than "he repaired to headquarters in great warmth, asserted his pretensions to the command of the élite, and was ridiculed by General Gates: high words and gross language ensued and Arnold retired in a rage."[6] While the riflemen had not been technically attached to Arnold's division, Morgan, who had served under

Arnold on the march to Quebec and admired him, had camped in Arnold's area when he arrived and obviously considered himself to be under Arnold's command. When Arnold returned to his tent, he immediately wrote Gates requesting a pass to proceed to Philadelphia "where I propose to join General Washington, and may possibly have it in my power to serve my country, although I am thought of no consequence in this department."[7] This intemperate blast inaugurated a paper war that raged for a week.

Freeman's Farm was a drawn battle. Only half Burgoyne's available force engaged less than one third of Gates's command. The British regiments in the center, particularly the 20th, 21st, and 62nd, bore the weight of battle. All took very heavy casualties. The 62nd, which had marched out of Canada at its full strength of five hundred rank and file, emerged from this day with a strength of four officers and sixty enlisted. The general issued the usual congratulatory order, but added, ". . . the Impetuosity and Uncertain Aim of the British Troops in giving their Fire, and the Mistake they are still under in preferring it to the Bayonnet is much to be lamented. The Lt. General is persuaded this Error will be corrected in the next engagement."[8]

As Burgoyne discussed with his generals and staff the various lines of action he could adopt, a courier from Clinton was announced. Sir Henry was anticipating a draft from England; when these troops arrived, he would immediately move up the Hudson. Burgoyne replied at once—he would consolidate and await Gates's reaction to the developing threat from the south. Should the American commander detach a sizable force to deal with Clinton, Burgoyne could strike with good prospect of breaking through the American lines on Bemis Heights.

Disquieting rumors drifting in from Lake George soon dispelled optimism induced by news from New York, for on September 20 Colonel John Brown, operating under orders from Benjamin Lincoln, had surprised British outposts, moved on Ticonderoga, taken possession of Mount Hope and Mount Defiance, captured almost three hundred British and Canadians, released one hundred American prisoners, burned two hundred bateaux, and summoned Brigadier General Henry Powell, who commanded Forts Ticonderoga and Independence. Powell's response was terse; "The garrison intrusted to my charge I shall defend to the last." Brown, short of provisions, fell back to Lake George. Ticonderoga was now completely cut off from the land side.

On September 29 a courier from Burgoyne arrived safely in New York with ominous news and a request for immediate assistance. Burgoyne had but three weeks salt provisions; his communications with Canada were cut. Any move Clinton could make would help. Sir Henry, who had been meditating relieving the pressure on the Northern Army by a surprise attack on Forts Montgomery and Clinton, conferred immediately with Commodore Hotham. The commodore was skeptical, but after considerable persuasion reluctantly agreed to co-operate, and on October 3 Clinton began his move up the North River with a force of 3,000. To give the Americans "jealousy for every object but the true one," Hotham's flotilla anchored off Verplanck's Point on the east bank on October 5.

Here Sir Henry received a despairing missive from Burgoyne. The bearer, Captain Campbell, described in detail the deteriorating situation of the Northern Army and conveyed Burgoyne's urgent plea that Clinton send him "as soon as possible . . . most explicit orders, either to attack the enemy in his front or to retreat across the lakes while they were clear of ice . . . hinting at the same time that *he would not have relinquished his communication with them had he not expected a cooperating army at Albany.*" Clinton was not going to take any share of the onus for the disaster he apprehended, nor could he comprehend why "the General should seem to entertain hopes of my being able to force my way to Albany." Although responsibility for the safety of New York lay heavily upon him, he determined at once to do what he could to assist the Northern Army. At dawn the following morning he landed at Stony Point, on the west bank of the Hudson.

After a circuitous march of upwards of seventeen miles over very rough terrain the two British columns were in position to assault Forts Montgomery and Clinton, and before dusk carried both positions at the point of the bayonet. Sir Henry had taken the two forts with celerity and efficiency; he now considered it possible to push a column up the river toward Albany. He detached Major General John Vaughan with 2,000 men and ordered him to "feel his way to General Burgoyne, and do his utmost to assist his operations, or even join him if required." The small flotilla commanded by Captain Sir James Wallace reached Kingston on October 15; Vaughan burned the town and Wallace sailed up the river to Livingston's Manor, some forty-five miles south of Albany. Here, pilots refused to take Wallace's squadron any farther.

At this juncture Clinton, obedient to peremptory orders from General Howe, recalled Vaughan to New York and dismantled Fort Clinton, which he had strengthened and garrisoned. "I was under the mortifying necessity of relinquishing the Highlands and all the other passes over the Hudson, to be re-occupied by the rebels whenever they saw proper." This episode did nothing to ameliorate Sir Henry's growing animus toward Howe and confirmed his opinion of his commanding general's poor judgment.

On October 3 Burgoyne put the army on half rations. On that day he also issued a General Order in which he assured his troops that "powerful armies" were "acting in co-operation" and that help from New York was on the way. But the army sensed something had gone awry: Rumors that Sir William Howe had embarked the major part of his force and sailed off to the south had circulated for some time. That under these circumstances morale did not collapse reflects great credit on the army commander and his officers and men. Burgoyne knew, too, that General Lincoln and John Stark and their Yankee militia, well armed, now lay in strength across the road to Fort Edward and Lake George.

The general's situation was no longer critical—it was desperate. Men and animals were hungry and there was no possibility of getting more food.

> The situation of General Burgoyne already began to grow dangerous. The outposts were more and more molested; the army was weakened by sick, wounded and the sending off of detachments; the enemy swarmed in its rear, threatening the strongest positions; the army was as good as cut off from its outposts; while in addition to all this, in consequence of the close proximity of the enemy's camp, the soldiers had but little rest.

The army was further weakened by desertion. "The want, moreover, of everything to which the English soldier especially, was accustomed, and the hard service, made matters worse yet. There were already, besides the sick who were with the regiments, eight hundred men in the hospital."[9] The Northern Army was slowly, inexorably, disintegrating.

Burgoyne realized he had not much time left. He must either attack, and attack very soon, or retreat; at a conference of his general officers, he presented a bold plan designed to envelop the American left. He proposed now to leave a relatively small force to hold his position and protect the hospital, baggage, supplies, and bateaux. He would lead the bulk of the army, marching light, in a wide swing to the west and then deep into Gates's rear. The idea did not appeal to Phillips, Riedesel, or Fraser, who recommended reconnaissance in force as an essential preliminary. This did not suit Burgoyne, who summoned a second conference on the following evening. At this meeting, Riedesel emphasized the critical nature of the situation; there was no time to be lost. The army must attack at once or withdraw across the Hudson to the Batten Kill, re-establish lines of communication to the north, and await help anticipated from the south. Fraser agreed. Phillips said nothing. "General Burgoyne with whom it went hard to make a thoroughly backward movement declared, that on the 7th he would make a reconnaissance as near as possible to the enemy's left wing in order to ascertain whether it could be attacked."[10]

This was a desperate gamble. Terrain favored the Americans. Between the two camps the ground was heavily wooded and crazily intersected by ravines and streams that ran in every direction. Visibility in the tangled underbrush was limited to a few yards. British and German formations could not fight effectively in terrain of this sort. But Burgoyne determined to chance it, and in early afternoon on the seventh sent out a column under command of Fraser.

With some 1,500 regulars and ten guns, Fraser advanced from the British right and seized a piece of commanding ground half a mile from the American camp. This immediately stirred up a hornet's nest. The Americans "advanced in great numbers, pouring in a superiority of fire from Detachments ordered to hang upon our flanks, which they tried if possible to turn." Burgoyne was unable to support his reconnaissance in force and ordered the detachment to retreat, "but not before we had lost many brave men. Brigadier General Fraser was mortally wounded, which helped to turn the fate of the day." Burgoyne arrived on the scene shortly before Fraser was hit; he "seemed then to feel in the highest degree our disagreeable situation." For a few minutes the British held the Americans off, but the Yankees "rushed on with loud shouts" and forced them to abandon their cannon. The fight seesawed until the British reached the security of their works, where they held off the assailants with grapeshot.

Toward sunset, Arnold, who "needed but his own irritated pride and the smell of gunpowder to rouse him to acts of madness," rushed from his tent, threw himself into the saddle, and galloped toward the sound of the guns to animate the troops and encourage them to a final assault on the British right. "It was remarked that in the progress of the engagement he rode about the camp betraying great agitation & wrath, and it was said that he was observed to drink freely; at length he was found on the field of battle exercising command, and not by order or permission of General Gates. His conduct was exceedingly rash and intemperate and he exposed himself with great folly and temerity."[11]

With Arnold in the lead, the Americans closed on the Balcarres redoubt, which, with another held by Colonel Breymann, secured the deep right flank of Burgoyne's army. The light infantry held fast; Arnold spurred his mount toward the left and led the way into Breymann's redoubt. His horse, hit by a musket ball, reared and fell. Arnold could not get clear. The leg broken at Quebec was broken for the second time.† Within a minute the redoubt was a shambles. The Americans, wildly wielding clubbed muskets, battered the desperate Germans who held them off with bloodied bayonets. Tomahawks flashed. A man who took time to load his musket was brained as he bent his head to ram a charge home. The slaughter was brutal and primitive. No quarter was asked and none given. Breymann was shot. He died on the blood-soaked ground he and his men had bravely defended. The surviving Germans staggered off,

† The musket ball that killed the horse apparently also broke Arnold's leg bone between knee and ankle.

dragging their wounded comrades. The Americans, too exhausted to pursue, collapsed. They had demolished the right flank of the British Army. Burgoyne's position was no longer tenable. As Arnold was being carried to the rear on a litter, Colonel Wilkinson, General Gates's aide, reined up beside him, reminded him politely that he had broken arrest, and suggested that he return at once to his tent.

On this bloody day, Fraser had been "taken off" by an American "riffler." The quiet, soft-spoken general had been highly respected by his superiors, associates, and subordinates. Burgoyne praised him for his "activity and bravery," his intelligence, his "extensive merits." Balcarres thought him "warm, open and communicative, but reserved in matters of confidence." He was certainly one of the finest general officers to serve in America during the war, and in his death the British Army suffered a very real loss. As he died, he whispered: "Poor General Burgoyne. My poor, dear wife."

Burgoyne was now confronted with the options of again attempting to break through the Americans or retreating. He, his senior commanders and staff thoroughly canvassed both. The omens were bad, but the general put a brave face on the situation and sent General Phillips to invite the Riedesels to supper. The baroness had planned a supper party herself, but her board dining table was put to another use that night. On it, General Fraser lay dying.

The decision was to retreat, and on the night of October 8 the Northern Army fell back toward Saratoga. "It rained incessantly . . . the roads were bad; the cattle were nearly starved for want of forage and the bridge over the Fish Kill had been destroyed by the enemy." All night rain fell in torrents; half-starved horses and oxen could not pull bogged-down guns and ammunition wagons through calf-deep muck, and they were abandoned. Exhausted and dispirited infantrymen staggered along, hungry, soaked, half asleep. "The state of our army was certainly as bad as possible. Their numbers were few, their provisions short, and their position not a good one." The army, mortally wounded, dragged itself to Saratoga.

During the next few days and nights Burgoyne had many other things to think about than his mistress and their cozy suppers. Should the army abandon what heavy equipment remained, strip down, attempt to break the American encirclement, and try to fight its way to the north? Baroness von Riedesel was certainly not one in favor of surrender: "the greatest misery and utmost disorder prevailed in the army. . . . The whole army clamored for a retreat and my husband promised to make it possible, provided only that no time was lost. But General Burgoyne, to whom an order had been promised if he brought about a junction with the army of General Howe, could not determine upon this course, and lost everything by his loitering."[12] Possibly the attractive little baroness was too harsh. She had no particular respect for the British general.

Neither the baroness' courageous husband nor anyone else could have led the dying army north to safety. Gates mustered over 16,000 men under arms present with almost 4,000 more dug in on the east bank of the Hudson, ready and able to resist a crossing should one be attempted. The forest trails to Fort George and Ticonderoga were blocked by John Stark and Morgan's "rifflers"; the woods swarmed with militiamen. A last desperate and despairing attempt to break out would have been repulsed with slaughter. Nor could the army for long maintain a defense against the full-scale assault Gates would inevitably mount.

On the night of October 13 Burgoyne called a council of all senior officers and on the following day asked for terms. Those proposed by Gates were found generally acceptable but for Article VI, which read:

> These terms being agreed to and signed, the troops under his Excellency General Burgoyne's command, may be drawn up in their encampments, where they will be ordered to ground their arms and may thereupon be marched to the river side on their way to Bennington.

The council summoned to consider the terms rejected this indignantly; Burgoyne replied in uncompromising language:

> This article is inadmissible in any extremity. Sooner than this army will consent to ground their arms in their encampments, they will rush on the enemy determined to take no quarter.[13]

The terms, amended by Gates to allow the British to march out under arms, with drums beating, to the banks of the river and there to pile arms, were accepted. Burgoyne requested authority to send off three couriers, one to Carleton, one to Howe, and one to carry his account of the surrender and the events leading up to it to Whitehall. Gates acquiesced. The articles prescribed that all standards be delivered to the Americans. Both British and Germans blatantly evaded this—Burgoyne told Gates all colors had been left in Canada. Baroness von Riedesel later boasted that colors of the German regiments were sewn up in her mattress and were taken back to Brunswick.

The formal ceremony was held at Gates's headquarters tent on the morning of October 17. After signing the "Convention," as the instrument of surrender was euphemistically described, Burgoyne tendered his sword. Gates immediately returned it. The American Army then passed in review. Balcarres, who was present, estimated that 13,000 or 14,000 participated: "They marched in good order and were silent." There was no vulgar rejoicing. Gates served an excellent luncheon. Amenities were preserved.

Americans lining the road from the British camp to the Hudson, where the troops were to pile arms, watched silently as British and Germans marched to beating drums. Lord Francis Napier wrote: ". . . they behaved with the greatest decency and propriety, not even a smile appearing in any of their countenances, which circumstance I really believe would not have happened had the case been reversed." One of Riedesel's officers described the men as tall, tanned, and lean, physical types he wished he could have recruited. Baroness Riedesel, whose calash (carrying the mattress) passed between the victor's ranks, was complimentary.

Lord Francis concluded his *Journal* entry: "Thus ended a campaign which at the beginning was attended with every Appearance of Success. The facility with which we obtained Ticonderoga contributed in a great measure to bring us into our disagreeable Situation. From their quitting that post before our attack began, We had conceived the idea of being irresistable. What afterwards followed plainly evinced We were not more than Mortal."[14]

On this memorable day, Horatio Gates had every reason to be a happy man. He was. That night he wrote his wife: "The voice of fame, ere this reaches you, will tell how greatly fortunate we have been in this department. Burgoyne and his whole army have laid down their arms and surrendered themselves to me and my Yankees. . . . If Old England is not by this lesson taught humility, then she is an obstinate old Slut, bent upon her ruin."[15] Colonel Wilkinson carried the general's report to Congress in York. Gates did not have the elementary courtesy to send a copy to his commander in chief, who learned indirectly of the victory which was to prove of critical—indeed of decisive—importance.

Americans, British, and Germans had endured much and fought bravely. Burgoyne was a courageous officer. The records attest that he was esteemed by his officers and admired by his men. He maintained his composure despite continuous difficulties and repeated disappointments and setbacks. Many years later a distinguished British historian wrote an epitaph for this fighting army: "What men can do, Burgoyne and his army did."

Burgoyne and some members of his staff spent the first days of their captivity in General Schuyler's spacious Albany home, where they and Baroness von Riedesel, with her three girls, were treated as distinguished guests. Burgoyne took advantage of this opportunity to write a number of letters, including one to Lieutenant Colonel Richard Phillipson, an aide-de-camp to the King, exculpating his conduct. He sent his father-in-law, Lord Derby, a copy of this letter, together with copies of all his dispatches to Germain, "in order that it may be published by him in case the Ministry should mangle or curtail any part of it in their Gazette."[16] The general correctly anticipated he would be the target for ministers' accusations, and in a private letter to Germain, who would be the first to seek a scapegoat, tried to forestall them by claiming he had saved, rather than lost, an army. For when his troops arrived in England, which he assumed would be quite soon, an equal number could be sent to America to reinforce Sir William Howe.

Burgoyne most unfairly blamed Riedesel's Germans for his failure and asserted that if his command had been wholly British, he could have fought his way through. He did not then, nor would he ever, admit any faulty judgments. Humility was a virtue unknown to Lieutenant General the Honourable John Burgoyne.

On November 5 Eliphalet Dyer, one of Gates's supporters in Congress, wrote congratulating him on his victory. "The Almighty," said Dyer, had crowned the general's "Indeavours" and made him "the Happy Instrument in bringing down the lofty pride and haughty Insolence of a vain glorious *Burgoyne*, who had spread terror and Consternation through our Northern Country, Untill Providence over ruled (against a Violent Opposition) to replace you in the chief Command."[17] This epistle probably irritated the general, who was not one to give credit either to the Lord God of Hosts or to Benedict Arnold.

While Dyer's letter was being borne by courier to the "Northern Country," Burgoyne's defeated army trudged across the New Hampshire Grants toward Massachusetts and a prisoner-of-war camp in Cambridge, destined to be the first stopping place on a long and weary trail. There, Burgoyne received a letter from Carleton: "This unfortunate event, it is to be hoped, will in future prevent Ministers from pretending to direct operations of war in a country at three thousand miles distance, of which they have so little knowledge as not to be able to distinguish between good, bad, or interested advices, or to give positive orders upon matters which from their nature, are ever on the change." The hopes of Carleton and many others, who with reason expected Germain to be dismissed and a more effective American Secretary installed, were frustrated. Lord George remained in office.

Riedesel was the only senior officer who criticized the conduct of the campaign, and the baron was most discreet. From Schuyler's house in Albany he wrote Prince Ferdinand expressing his disappointment. Years later, when he wrote his memoirs, he was less reserved. His baroness was more caustic. Burgoyne, she wrote, indulged too frequently in supper parties and often "spent half the night in singing and drinking and amusing himself with the wife of a commissary who was his mistress and who, as well as he, loved champagne."

Before his wings were clipped at Bennington and Stanwix, Burgoyne made an error of judgment that would prove of critical importance. This was to pursue the demoralized and disorganized Americans who fled from Ticonderoga. He had taken the fort at no expense; his troops were in high spirits and full vigor. At this moment, calculations affecting immediate future employment of the army were in order. Cool deliberation should then have suggested the obvious advantages of the Lake George route. But in the moment of victory very few generals can be expected readily to refrain from delivering the *coup de grâce* to a routed enemy.

Having assembled the British component of the army at Skenesborough, and holding momentarily an overwhelming psychological advantage, Burgoyne should have ordered the advance corps forward with all speed, left his park artillery to join later, marched the mass of the army to Lake George, and pushed for the Hudson. Such a move would have shaken St. Clair and his affrighted troops out of Fort Edward.

Burgoyne issued repeated orders to the army to "strip down"—for officers to rid themselves of nonessentials. But he himself never did so. His thirty carts loaded with furniture, champagne, china, linen, crystal, and silver, his mistress and her maids and their trunks, bedding, and boxes, creaked ponderously along in the army's train. A resolute general, determined to reach Albany (as Burgoyne insisted he was), would have jettisoned all this paraphernalia and seen to it that the army followed his example. But Gentleman Johnny would not give up his sensual indulgences. He wanted his woman, his drink, and his cards, and he had them.

Phillips, who was not accompanied by a lady, gave similar orders. His artillery carriages and Canadian carts were breaking down due to overloading. The artillery commander directed that all carts be examined and everything "not a part of the Artillery preparation to be taken out; a fire to be made and such Baggage and Luggage to be immediately burned."[18] When Phillips learned thirty carts had been sent forward from Fort George "loaden with Baggage said to be the Lieutenant General's," he blew up. He was sure his commanding general would "on no account suffer his private conveniency to interfere with the public Transport of Provisions."[19]

Both Howe and Clinton were in part responsible for Saratoga. Perhaps the King's general in America cannot technically be charged with culpable negligence; he can, however, be charged with an astonishing indifference to the fate of the Northern Army. Clinton, who was well aware Burgoyne's situation was desperate, later went to great lengths to justify his excess of caution.

But ultimate responsibility must be placed squarely on Lord George Germain, who although not the architect of the disastrous strategy of 1777 was endowed by virtue of his office with executive authority to alter proposed plans so as to ensure co-ordination of effort. Full effects of the secretary's failure to exercise this authority were soon to be manifest: "So uncommon an event as the capture of a whole army animated [the Americans] with fresh ardor, invigorated the exertions of the Congress,

lessened in the mind of the American soldier the high opinion which he
entertained of British valour and discipline, and inspired him with a
juster confidence in himself."[20] The "uncommon event" was also to
inspire His Most Christian Majesty's Minister for Foreign Affairs, M. le
Comte de Vergennes, to move vigorously to the policy so urgently advocated by Dr. Franklin.

But many French officers who had served with distinction in America
were not equally impressed with the victory at Saratoga. Among those
who had a poor opinion of Louis XVI's transatlantic allies was Colonel
Louis le Bèque du Portail, Washington's chief of engineers. Shortly after
Burgoyne's surrender, Du Portail wrote to Comte Claude Louis de Saint-
Germain:

> It is not due to the good conduct of the Americans that the
> campaign in general has been terminated so happily, but by the
> faults of the English. It was a capital fault of the British govern-
> ment in wishing General Burgoyne to traverse more than 200
> leagues of country almost a desert to join forces with Generals
> Howe and Clinton. This plan might have seemed to be a great one
> in the cabinet in London, but appears miserable in the eyes of
> those who had an exact knowledge of the nature of the country.

This was not written in hindsight; two months before Saratoga, Du Portail had written Saint-Germain that the greater part of the Northern
Army would be destroyed by hunger, fatigue, and desertion; by constant
alerts and by militia ambushes. "Had the English, instead of amusing
themselves in this manner, directed their attack against General Washington . . . I do not know what might have become of us." In Du Portail's opinion, Sir William Howe had failed to do all he could have done.
Throughout his operations in 1777 the British general had demonstrated
a slowness and timidity Du Portail thought "astonishing."

His estimate of the Americans was equally unflattering. He deemed
them to be indolent and self-indulgent: "They move without spring or
energy, without vigor and without passion for the cause in which they
are engaged. . . . There is an hundred times more enthusiasm for this
revolution in any one coffee house at Paris than in all the Thirteen Provinces united."

BOOK VI

Obstinate Rebels

1

You Cannot Conquer America

Congress tarried but one day in Lancaster and then moved to York. There three problems central to the continued existence of the new nation absorbed delegates. First was currency; second, reorganization of the army; and third, confederation. American finances were in a frightful state. Emissions of unbacked paper had precipitated a relentless and uncontrollable inflation. The viability of the United States and their ability to wage war depended on reasonable financial stability, but no one would accept Continental paper. Debates on the question were constantly interrupted by heated partisan disputes. Before Congress left for York, Henry Laurens wrote that since he had been sitting (about seven weeks) he had discovered "parties within parties, divisions and Subdivisions to as great a possible extent as the number 35 (for we are never more together) will admit of."[1] Congress had decided to borrow from France. Laurens opposed this vigorously: "If we have not virtue enough to Save our Selves, easy access to the Treasury of France will only hasten our ruin." He favored issues of loan certificates at 6 per cent redeemable after a year, and compared the attempt to borrow abroad to "the folly of a Young Man borrowing money from a designing Sharper upon the credit of an expected Heirship. We are unwary and love ease and pleasure, we will borrow because we will save trouble." Many delegates still refused to recognize the obvious necessity to tax, a policy for long advocated by John Adams. Congress, powerless to levy general taxes, could do no more than recommend that they be levied by state governments, but the states were reluctant.

Congress now also bent itself seriously to formulation of articles of confederation. York was quiet. As James Duane wrote: ". . . we are sufficiently retired and can deliberate without interruption." In Philadelphia there had been far too many legislative and social demands. In the safe backwater of a small farm community delegates could get some work done. But to succeed in confederating thirteen states, each jealously determined to guard its prerogatives, demanded a sense of nationalism that did not yet exist. No state would surrender controlling legislative, executive, or judicial powers to a central government. They would grant Congress authority to send ambassadors abroad to negotiate treaties and solicit foreign aid, but not the power to impose uniform tariffs. States refused to accept Continental currency; all insisted on the right to emit bills. Nor would they permit Congress to name any but general officers in the army. They would not concede authority to settle boundary questions or delegate to Congress control of lands they claimed by virtue of royal charter. Small states, adamant on the question of voting, insisted that substantive matters be determined on the basis of one vote per state. Thus, a handful of delegates representing three or four states with an aggregate population of several hundred thousand were able to stop, and did stop, proposals favored by delegates from states with an aggregate population of nearly two million.

Washington had taken up a position along Shippack Creek, northwest of Philadelphia and some fifteen miles from Germantown, where Howe had established his headquarters and a garrison of about 9,000. In hope of repeating his victory at Trenton, Washington decided to make a surprise attack on Germantown at dawn on October 4. For the purpose he formed four columns, two of regulars under Sullivan and Greene, and two of militia, one on each flank. The approach march would be made under cover of darkness. Sullivan's brigades were to attack the British center, Greene's the right. The militia column on the right was to "amuse" the British left while that on the left got into Howe's rear. Such a complicated scheme of maneuver would have taxed capabilities of a well-trained staff, experienced unit commanders, and disciplined troops.

A few minutes after dawn, British pickets fired on Sullivan's column as it marched east down the Shippack Road toward Germantown. Sullivan deployed astride the road, one brigade (Wayne) on the north side, another on the south side, with his third (William Maxwell) bringing up the rear. At this moment, a dense fog enveloped the field and reduced visibility to thirty or forty yards. Under this cover several depleted companies of the British 40th Foot, commanded by Lieutenant Colonel Thomas Musgrove, occupied a stone house belonging to Judge Chew, barricaded the doors and windows, and poured concentrated volleys on Maxwell's men, who attempted valiantly and with considerable loss to drive them out. Such was the situation when one of Greene's brigades (Adam Stephan), groping its way south toward the British right, took position behind Wayne, and opened fire. This produced an immediate panic. Men of Sullivan's and Wayne's brigades streamed to the rear, utterly demoralized.

During this time, Musgrove defended against repeated attacks "with great Bravery and Slaughter to the Rebels, 'till they were drove entirely out of the Town by the arrival of more Troops." The attack had been "made with some degree of Spirit, and the battle lasted four hours before the Rebels began to retreat; when We pursued them above Eight miles: Their loss was pretty considerable, as they left numbers dead on ye field."[2] Parliament ordered a silver medal struck to commemorate Musgrove's gallant stand.

Major John André, "No Flint" Grey's aide-de-camp, was present during the battle; he thought Washington's plan "too complicated; nor do their troops appear to have been sufficiently animated . . . altho' the power of strong liquor had been employed. Several, not only of their Soldiers, but Officers, were intoxicated when they fell into our hands."[*]

Germantown was a battle lost that might have been a battle won. Washington wanted to bypass the Chew house. Knox and others persuaded him from doing so. Here again he accepted bad advice. He lost six hundred killed and wounded and four hundred prisoners. Howe's battle casualties were about four hundred. Washington got the army safely to Whitemarsh, where he entrenched and awaited a riposte which did not materialize.

The Pennsylvania campaign of 1777 was nearly finished, and so was the Continental Army.

September brought its usual invigorating weather to London. Although news from the other side of the Atlantic was encouraging, that from across the Channel was not. His Majesty found French behavior "very irksome . . . very changeable; whether from duplicity or timidity it is equally distressing." The King advised his First Minister to move cautiously, to take "no hasty step . . . which may hasten on a war."[3] He put little faith in intelligence reports from Paris. ". . . as *Edwards* is a stock jobber as well as a double spy, no other faith can be placed in his intelli-

---

[*] When rum was available—and it usually was—the common practice was to serve a rum ration during an arduous march. No doubt some had partaken too liberally. Obviously, André had not been in the neighborhood of the Chew house, when neither attackers nor defenders showed any lack of "animation."

gence but that it suits his private views to make us expect the French Court means war."[4] He deemed Paul Wentworth, also a dabbler in stocks, equally unreliable.

In fact, reports coming to Eden from his two "stock jobbers" were on the whole reliable. Very little that went on in the offices of the American commissioners escaped Bancroft. According to him, Silas Deane's loyalty was wavering; he was disgusted with "the Vilany of Congress" and "the deceit of the French Court," which he described as "insufferable," and confided his opinion that "nothing but the power of G.B. re-established can save us from the worst of evils." Franklin, "with his usual apathy," seemed not yet too perturbed by French delay to declare a position. He was "averse to the necessity of incuring obligations from France which may bind America beyond its true Interests." William Carmichael, one of Franklin's able young assistants, said the doctor thought America would "derive Resources" from her own distress, "like the earth-bound Giant Anteus, who derived new strength from his Falls . . . he wishes no European connection—He despises France and He hates England."

Franklin did not "despise" the French people. He was an avowed admirer of French culture; his friends were intellectuals, and he met them on common ground. He did not have to seek them out; they sought him. He certainly did not approve of arbitrary and despotic government, but he was discreet. Everyone with whom he associated in Passy and Paris knew he had dedicated his life and his talents to help create a free and independent nation, and respected his unfaltering republican convictions. They also respected his scientific achievements, and when his friend Turgot introduced him to the French Academy, he did so in five words:

Eripuit coelo fulmen
Sceptrumque tyrannis.

For the members of this erudite body, who spoke Latin as fluently as they did their native tongue, no translation was necessary.†

Eden passed everything he considered important to Viscount Weymouth; some reports he sent directly to the King with his perceptive comments. One, enclosing a copy of a letter the commissioners had written the Committee for Foreign Affairs, should have been sufficiently convincing to remove any lingering doubts as to French policy. The commissioners wrote that Vergennes and his colleagues continued to act "with their former duplicity—on one hand promising to England a strict Neutrality and a Faithful observance of Treaties, and giving her assurance of the most pacific intentions," while on the other they assured the commissioners of their "most friendly wishes and intentions, and verified

---

† "He wrenched the thunderbolt from the Heavens, and the sceptre from the tyrant."

33. Major General Nathanael Greene

34. Major General Philip Schuyler

35. Major General Horatio Gates

36. Captain John Paul Jones

38. Brigadier General Francis Marion

37. Major General John Sullivan

39. Major General the Marquis de La Fayette

40. Major General Henry Knox

41. General Anthony Wayne

42. Brigadier General Daniel Morgan

43. Captain George Rogers Clark

44. Major General Baron von Steuben

YOU CANNOT CONQUER AMERICA

these assurances by substantial Proofs and favors, directly affording many essential aids . . . shewing every kind of indulgence and favour to the American Commerce." If this policy continued, Franklin anticipated "an Open Rupture at an early date."[5]

Wentworth informed Eden frequently and precisely of the extent of these indulgences and favors. One agreement with Sieur de Montieu, in the amount of one million livres, provided that he procure and ship 10,000 uniforms, 100,000 pounds of red copper "of the best quality suitable for casting cannon," 20,000 pounds of sheathing for coppering hulls, 4,255 "soldier's superior guns fitted with bayonets," and 8,000 ordinary muskets. While De Montieu supervised lading these cargoes at Nantes, Beaumarchais was similarly engaged at Marseilles, where he was packing for immediate shipment 13,000 bombs; 27 "Brass Mortars with their Beds"; 60 "Brass Field Pieces with Carriages"; 25,000 axes, saws, picks, spades, mattocks, and other engineer tools; 6 "large Hogsheads of Soldier's Knives"; 18 tons of powder; 25 tons of sulfur; and "a large quantity of cannon balls." He had recently shipped on *Heureux* 44 brass field guns with carriages; 20 brass mortars; 5,000 cannon balls, and 2,000 bombs.[6] These "essential aids" were indeed "substantial Proofs" of French intentions.

Bancroft picked up a considerable amount of interesting gossip from privateer captains and other Americans who were constantly in and out of Paris. Toward the end of October Wentworth passed some of these tidbits to his employers in London. There were interesting rumors of a quarrel between Richard Henry Lee and Washington. Lee, so the story went, was not too popular with his colleagues in either Virginia or Philadelphia, who found "His Violence, Rapacity and Insincerity" unbearable. "This Lee, with Saml and John Adams, with Morris, rule the Congress; the first and His party are inimical to Washington; the latter are his friends." The Lee faction (which now included Richard's brother Francis Lightfoot Lee) was insinuating that Washington was bidding "for the Imperial Station." Reflecting Bancroft's gossipy reports, Wentworth opined that "Political profligacy" was rampant; perhaps a "well-timed offer of indemnity and impunity to these Cromwells and Barebones may serve, like a strong ALKILI, to reduce the Effervescence of the Mass of the People, or turn their frenzy on their Mis-Leaders."[7]

The King now addressed himself to the delicate problem of Lord North's personal finances. The First Minister was not a gambler nor did he keep expensive mistresses. But he could not maintain his family, spend the sums on entertainment expected of one in his position, and for long stay solvent. Indeed, he was deeply in debt. He owed considerable sums on loans, on mortgages, and to tradespeople; financial worry was a source of constant distraction. In a private interview with John Robinson, North's undersecretary at the Treasury, His Majesty did some discreet

probing and directed Robinson to present him with a summary of the
First Minister's personal financial situation.

With obvious reluctance Robinson did so, and the King determined
to alleviate Lord North's burden: "I must insist you will now state to me
whether 12 or 15,000 *l* will not set your affairs in order; if it will, nay if
20,000 *l* is necessary, I am resolved you shall have no other person concerned in freeing you [from debt] but myself. . . . You know me very ill
if you do not think that of all the letters I have ever wrote to you this one
gives me the most pleasure, and I want no other return but you being
convinced that I love you as well as a man of worth as I esteem you as a
minister."[8] Lord North accepted the bounty, and with it further obligation to serve his master.

Long-awaited reports from Viscount Howe and his brother reached
Whitehall in the last days of October. In these the general described his
laborious passage from New York to Head of Elk; his army was ashore;
he expected to encounter Washington near Wilmington. The King, not
entirely pleased with this dalliance, thought a stiff letter to his general in
America might impel Howe to "turn his thoughts to the mode of war
best calculated to end this contest as most distressing to the Americans,
and which he seems as yet carefully to have avoided." He had always
believed, so he informed Lord North, that there was more cruelty in protracting the war "than in taking such acts of vigour which must bring the
crisis to the shortest decision."[9]

Walpole wrote Sir Horace Mann in a pessimistic vein: "If Burgoyne's
army is destroyed, little force left in Canada, only seven thousand men in
New York and Howe's army not increased . . . where are we . . . to conjure up new armies? And what will less armies achieve, which such large
ones have not compassed in three campaigns?" He was sure the Americans would continue to fight. "And can you conquer them without beating them? Can you maintain the country when you have conquered it?
Will a destroyed country maintain your army? . . . We are like Lord
Holland paying the debt of his sons; he ruined himself and left them
beggars."‡ He anticipated war with France, a prospect he viewed with
dismay.[10]

On Thursday, November 20, Parliament reconvened to hear the customary speech from the throne. The King informed assembled lords and
gentlemen that the revolt in America unhappily continued, but assured
them of his firm intention, with God's blessing, to re-establish "constitutional subordination" in his rebellious colonies. He still hoped that "the
deluded and unhappy multitude of America," suffering under an "arbitrary tyranny," would return to allegiance and that an attitude of dutiful
submission to their sovereign would be "rekindled in their hearts." How-

‡ Lord Holland was the father of Charles James Fox, who before his twenty-first
birthday had run up gambling debts of £140,000.

ever, it would be necessary to prepare for such other operations as "the obstinacy of the rebels might render expedient." Both France and Spain seemed to be preparing for war; these activities required an augmentation of the navy. His Majesty asserted his pacific intentions and vowed to maintain the honor of the British crown. The usual addresses of thanks, "full of the most lavish panegyric," praised the "profound wisdom of ministers" and the demonstrable "rectitude of their measures."[11]

During the parliamentary recess, the ministry had busily disseminated propaganda through its subsidized press accusing those who spoke against Administration's American policy as a set of "unprincipled, clamorous and seditious men."[12] These threats did not deter members of Opposition from launching full-scale attacks on Lord North and his government. In the Lords, the Earl of Coventry prophesied Britain's ineluctable doom should she in monumental folly persevere in a contest she was incapable of winning. Chatham followed. The King's speech, he asserted, was based on "an ill-founded confidence . . . supported hitherto only by a succession of disappointments, disgraces, and defeats." The ministers in whom the King reposed confidence had misled him and permitted England to be humiliated in the eyes of the world:

> No man thinks more highly than I of the virtue and valour of British troops; I know they can achieve anything except impossibilities; and the conquest of English America is an impossibility. You cannot, I venture to say it, *you cannot conquer America.* . . . What is your present situation there? We do not know the worst, but we know that in three campaigns we have done nothing, and suffered much. . . . Conquest is impossible: you may swell every expense and every effort still more extravagantly; pile and accumulate every assistance you can buy or borrow; traffic and barter with every little pitiful German prince that sells his subjects to the shambles of a foreign power; your efforts are forever vain and impotent; doubly so from this mercenary aid on which you rely; for it irritates to an incurable resentment the minds of your enemies. To overrun them with the mercenary sons of rapine and plunder; devoting them and their possessions to the rapacity of hireling cruelty! If I were an American, as I am an Englishman, while a foreign troop was landed in my country, I never would lay down my arms, never—never—never![13]

Chatham then assailed the ministry for allying to British arms "the tomahawk and scalping knife of the savage." Who, he asked, had dared authorize this desperate alliance, which would "leave an indelible stain on the national honour" and, he continued, "Besides these murderers and plunderers, let me ask our ministers what other allies have they acquired? . . . Nothing is too low or too ludicrous to be consistent with their Counsels."[14]

He then launched into a peroration:

> You cannot conciliate America by your present measures. What then can you do? . . . the time demands the language of truth; we must not now apply the flattering unction of servile compliance or blind complaisance. To support a just and necessary war, to maintain the rights or honour of my country, I would strip the shirt from my back: but in such a war as this, unjust in its principle, impracticable in its means, and ruinous in its consequences, I would not contribute a single effort nor a single shilling. I do not call for vengeance on the heads of those who have been guilty; I only recommend retreat; let them walk off and let them make haste or speedy and condign punishment will overtake them. . . .[15]

On the first day of December a courier from General Howe (who for some time had been agreeably bedded in Philadelphia with "the Sultana") arrived in London. His news—that the rebel Congress had fled the city and that Washington's decimated and debilitated army was encamped near Whitemarsh—confirmed ministerial optimism. But occupation of Philadelphia, whose Quaker inhabitants had displayed a "uniform, fixed enmity to American measures," meant little. Members of the Congress had made good their escape to resume seditious deliberations in York; the Continental Army, although in a sad state of disarray, short of everything, and with desertion endemic, was still in being. Happily for the American cause, Howe had not (as Dr. Franklin would remark later) captured Philadelphia—Philadelphia had captured Howe.

Exhilaration in Whitehall was destined to be short-lived. Near midnight on the following day Captain Moutray, a courier bearing urgent dispatches from Sir Guy Carleton, brought unconfirmed reports of Burgoyne's surrender. The news, Walpole wrote Sir Horace, "occasions some consternation, but none at all I assure you in the temple of Concord."** Walpole was wrong. There had been considerable discord in "the temple" on the preceding day when Fox again moved for papers relative to Burgoyne's expedition, as well as for instructions given Sir William Howe for his "intended cooperation" with the Northern Army. The demand occasioned acrimonious debate and was rejected.

Before an expectant House, Germain rose to detail troop deployment in America; he coolly neglected to mention Burgoyne. This startling omission brought Barré to his feet to ask what had "become of General Burgoyne and his brave troops." Lord George replied he had no "authen-

** The House of Commons. Walpole also refers sarcastically to the Lords and Commons as the "Temples of Honour and Virtue."

tic information" respecting the reported surrender, and imputed the failure of the campaign—if it had failed—to the ineptitude of the general. This was more than Opposition could swallow. Burke and his cohorts violently assailed the minister, and "roaring like bulldogs" ascribed blame for the loss of an army to Lord North and his arrogant Secretary for America.

Charles Fox, to whom his friend Burgoyne had thoughtfully sent a copy of his final report to Germain, attacked the American Secretary furiously; asserted that an army of 10,000 officers and men had been destroyed through "the obstinate willful ignorance and incapacity of the Noble Lord" and expressed the hope that Lord George would be brought to a well-deserved trial for a second time. The imperturbable First Minister, dozing on the treasury bench, roused himself to defend his colleague; he spoke coolly and wittily as usual. When the House rose, he walked over to Fox and said, "I am glad you did not attack me today, Charles, for you was in full feather." On the following day Lord North's royal master congratulated him on "the manly, firm, and dignified part" he had taken to bring the House "to see the present misfortune in true light as very serious, but not without remedy."[16]

While the storm over Burgoyne's surrender continued to rage in the lower House, Chatham moved for relevant papers in the Lords. As Fox had done two days previously, Chatham defended Burgoyne. He ascribed the general's "misfortune" to a "want of wisdom in our councils, want of ability in our ministers," described the strategy Germain had approved as a "most wild, uncombined and mad project," and denounced employment of Indians as "bloody, barbarous and ferocious."

The King, who rarely lost his composure, thought "the Wisest step" would be "to act only on the defensive with the army, and with great activity as to the troops. Canada, Nova Scotia, the Floridas, New York and Rhode Island must probably be the stations." Amherst, who had great experience "in those parts . . . must be consulted, and will be able to point out what is best."[17]

Captain John Paul Jones, United States Navy, whose activities in the seas around their long-inviolate islands would soon exceedingly perturb the British, arrived at the mouth of the Loire on December 2 in sloop of war *Ranger*, which he had put in commission at Portsmouth, New Hampshire. *Ranger* was a well-found sloop, but in the thirty-two-day passage, during which she picked up two prizes, Jones decided her masts should be restepped and her rigging altered. He brought a duplicate set of dispatches from Congress to the commissioners informing them of Burgoyne's surrender. He sent these immediately to Passy. Rumors that Jonathan Austin, a courier from Boston, had landed at Nantes two days previously and was on route to Passy were already circulating. On De-

cember 3 the American commissioners awaited him in Franklin's
graveled courtyard.

> When Mr. Austin's chaise was heard in the court they all went out
> to meet him, and before he had time to alight Dr. Franklin cried
> out, "Sir, is Philadelphia taken?" "Yes, sir," replied Austin. Upon
> hearing this Dr. Franklin clasped his hands and turned as if to go
> back into the house. "But sir," said Austin, "I have greater news
> than that. General Burgoyne and his whole Army are prisoners of
> war."[18]

This news, Deane said later, was "like a sovereign cordial to the dying."
Franklin at once notified Vergennes, and Caron de Beaumarchais set off
in a chaise for Paris to spread the word. He drove with reckless speed—
his chaise broke down, he was thrown from it and dislocated an arm.
Within forty-eight hours reports of Burgoyne's surrender had reached
The Hague, where general opinion was that America was irretrievably
lost. On international exchanges, British bonds dived to new lows.

A week later, Jones found time during refit to write a friend in Portsmouth whose young son was a member of his crew. Captain Jones was
obviously a poet manqué: "The Ranger was wafted by the Pinions of the
gentlest and most friendly Gales, along the Surface of the Blue profound
or Neptune; and not the swelling bosom of a Friends, nor even an
Enimi's Sail, appeared within our placid Horizon, untill after we had
passed the Everlasting Mountains in the Sea (called Azores) whose Tops
are in the Clouds and whoes Foundations are in the Center. When lo!
This Halcyon Season was interrupted! the gathring Fleets o'er-spread the
Sea! and Wars alarms began! Nor ceased day or night untill aided by the
mighty Boreus, we cast Anchor in this Asylum the 2nd curr^t. But since I
am not certain that my Poetry will be understood, it may not be amiss to
add . . . a marginal note."[19] In the "marginal note" the captain gave a
factual account of his crossing. Capture of prizes had given him "the
most agreeable Proof of the Active Spirit of my Officers and Men." He
was disappointed to learn that a French offer of a fine frigate had been
withdrawn because of "some difficulties" the commissioners had met
with, but he could still write: "My Heart glows with the most fervent
Gratitude for every unsolicited and unexpected instance of the favo'r and
Approbation of Congress."[20] He sent his compliments to the "agreeable
Ladies" he had met in Portsmouth. On December 15 the commissioners
summoned him to Paris.

Captain Jones enjoyed his holiday. He and Franklin became fast
friends; the handsome young sailor could not have found a better spon-
sor. The ladies lionized the doctor, and thanks to his introduction, Jones
soon became something more than a friend to Madame le Rey de
Chaumont, whose husband's business as a naval contractor frequently

called him from Paris. The captain did not allow his amorous entanglement to interfere with his campaign to get the frigate he had been promised, but Stormont, who had learned of the pending transaction, had made vigorous protests. Vergennes replied with suave falsehoods, but the frigate was not forthcoming. However, Franklin managed to find Jones enough "hard money" to refit *Ranger*, and on January 28, after embracing Madame de Chaumont, he set off to assume active command of his ship. Before leaving Paris, he persuaded Franklin to sign a set of orders he had drawn up for himself. These gave him considerable leeway; they authorized him to distress "the Enemies of the United States, by sea or otherwise." The captain had plans—"several Enterprizes of some importance," he wrote Congress. "When an Enemy thinks a design against them is improbable, they can always be surprised and attacked with advantage." He had concocted several such "improbable designs."[21]

Confirmation of Burgoyne's surrender produced a flurry of ministerial activity in London. Shortly after the first unofficial reports arrived, Sandwich had done some serious thinking, and on December 8 sent Lord North, via Germain, a detailed analysis of the strategy he believed should henceforth be pursued in America. This was to be essentially naval, based on "possession of several places along the coast which are tenable . . . against any force the Americans can bring against them. These places must be such as the King's ships can resort to at all times and seasons, and which will give them shelter and refreshments for their men." From such strongly garrisoned enclaves, which the First Lord proposed to supply with naval artificers and all equipment and tools necessary for careening and refitting ships, the fleet could operate continuously against American ports and shipping. This was precisely the strategy Viscount Barrington had proposed early in 1775.

Sandwich realized he could not allocate sufficient ships to American waters to block up all the rebels' ports or put a total stop to privateering. "However, we may certainly distress them infinitely more than has hitherto been done, and throw such burdens upon their trade and privateering as to make it difficult to carry on either without considerable loss, which it is to be hoped, together with their want of necessaries from Europe, would soon make them tired of the war."[22] The First Lord reminded Lord North that although he had specifically directed Viscount Howe to select several suitable harbors on the American coast for development as fleet bases, the admiral had paid no attention whatever to this imperative instruction. A new directive should be sent, ordering him "to block up the American ports [and also to cooperate with the army in any attempts that may be thought advisable and practicable for making ourselves masters of those ports, destroying their shipping and alarming and attacking their coast upon every proper occasion.]"[23]

The part of the foregoing in brackets was added to Sandwich's memorandum by Lord George Germain and altered the character of the First Lord's concept. Sandwich was urging that primary emphasis be placed on blockade and destruction of coastal shipping and privateers; Germain, additionally, that dispersive amphibious raiding operations be undertaken. Experience of the preceding year should have made it evident (particularly in view of the increasing likelihood of war with the Bourbon powers) that the Royal Navy did not have the capability simultaneously to deploy sufficient ships of appropriate classes to distant American waters to carry out both these missions, maintain a Channel Fleet adequate to protect the Home Islands, support the West Indies, Gibraltar, and Minorca, keep open the Mediterranean lines to the Levant, cover British coastal holdings in India, and convoy outgoing and returning East and West Indiamen.

Here the question of strategic priorities was unequivocally posed. Could the English temporarily forgo objectives "C" and "D" in order to be sure of "A" and "B"? Certainly, protection of the Home Islands against seaborne assault must be accorded priority "A." What then was "B"? What "C" and "D"? America? The Sugar Islands? The Mediterranean? In the King's mind, conquest of the French West Indies Islands had replaced subjection of his former colonies as a priority task.

Again rumors that Chatham was to be returned to power ran through drawing rooms and coffeehouses and inspired Horace Walpole to write to the Countess of Upper Ossory: "Send for Lord Chatham! they had better send for General Washington, Madame." He went on to inveigh against "the abject, impudent poltroonery of the Ministers" and the "blockish stupidity of Parliament." Saratoga confirmed his belief the French would come in and the American war would last "forever"; "till the end of the century"; "for a millenium." He described Burgoyne sarcastically as "Julius Caesar Burgonius"; the general's proclamation to the Americans was so much "rhodomontade," surpassed only by his "supernatural" exhortation to his savage allies.

Walpole was convinced nothing could be expected of the Rockinghams, "the most timid set of time-serving triflers that ever existed." The elegant marquis, leader of these "triflers," His Grace the Duke of Richmond, and Edmund Burke were at the moment attempting to put together a patchwork reconciliation with Chatham. Messengers hurried to and from Hayes but the planning and the scurrying resulted in nothing. Both Chathamites and Rockinghams agreed the war with America must be stopped. The stumbling block was the earl's refusal to concede independence. Nor would the marquis give ground. He wished to recognize American independence and attempt to forge an alliance with the new nation against the Bourbon enemies. The fractured Opposition was impotent.

While Walpole and his circle desponded, the "King's Friends" did not. Spontaneous offers to raise battalions arrived from every quarter. The King, delighted, wrote Lord North he was "glad to find the spirit of many parts . . . rising on the late catastrophe; indeed, the country would have greatly fallen in my opinion if that event had not roused the lion."[24] The lion may have been roused but so was Opposition, particularly when the ministry's plan for a holiday recess of six weeks commencing December 11 became known. In the Commons, Burke and Fox lashed out, as did Chatham in the upper House: "At so tremendous a season it does not become your Lordships, the great hereditary council of the nation, to neglect your duty: to retire to your country seats for six weeks in quest of joy and merriment, while the real state of public affairs calls for grief, mourning and lamentation, at least, for the fullest exertion of your wisdom."

On the same day, Chatham delivered another scathing attack on Administration. The earl ascribed the unhappy fate that had overtaken "that spirited officer, Mr. Burgoyne, and the gallant troops under his command" to "the wanton temerity and ignorance of Ministers," and applauded the "generous, magnanimous conduct, the noble friendship, brotherly affection, and humanity of the victors."†† He concluded: "The nation has been betrayed into the ruinous measure of an American war by the arts of imposition, by its own credulity, through the means of false hope, false pride and promised advantages of the most romantic and improbable nature."

Members of Opposition were by no means the only ones dismayed. A few days after Christmas William Eden wrote Sandwich: "The disgraces of this year have followed each other to the end of it without a single episode of any event honourable or fortunate: our land officers surrender with fourscore barrels of dry gunpowder in their possession, and yield the colours of their regiments without drawing a single trigger or spilling one drop of blood in defence of them; our admirals prefer the destruction of defenceless towns to the defence of our most valuable provinces; and if the extent of our naval power compared with that of the rebels is to be determined by the balance of the captures in number and value, the decision is certainly much in favour of the latter."[25]

General Sir William Howe's British and Hessians, received by the inhabitants of Philadelphia on September 26 with "acclamations of joy," behaved themselves for two or three days. Young Robert Morton, son of

†† Chatham spoke too soon. The treatment accorded Burgoyne's surrendered army by the Congress, which refused to honor the Convention signed at Saratoga, was precisely the opposite of generous, magnanimous, and humane. The conduct of Generals Burgoyne and Phillips in Cambridge, where the "Convention Army" was to winter, was not calculated to placate Congress.

a pacific Quaker who had been banished to the wilds of Winchester, Virginia, as a suspected Tory, was delighted to see the Redcoats. He and others who had "too long suffered the yoke of arbitrary Power" hoped now to enjoy the King's peace. Omens were good. Howe had issued a proclamation guaranteeing security and protection to all peaceable citizens; Galloway and the Allen brothers, who had returned with the British Army, assured old friends still in town they need have no apprehensions. Morton went to Howe's headquarters, where he chatted with a number of officers; all "appeared well disposed toward the peaceable inhabitants, but most bitter against, and determined to pursue to the last extremity the army of the U.S."[26]

This disposition did not, however, extend to British and Hessian soldiers habituated to plundering and looting; officers commanding patrols and foraging parties either would not or could not control the men. Morton's father's house in the country was broken into, and desks, bookcases, and closets ransacked. On the following day a neighbor's house was vandalized and looted. Morton protested to an officer who told him that if looters were discovered they would be punished. One was caught and summarily hanged; another, severely whipped. Unfortunately most were not discovered. "The ravages and wanton destruction of the soldiery will, I think, soon become irksome to the inhabitants, as many who depended upon their vegetables, etc., for their maintenance are now entirely and effectually ruined by these soldiers being permitted, under the command of their officers, to ravage and destroy their property."[27]

Foraging parties took livestock, potatoes, grain, and hay and gave fortunate farmers promises of reimbursement. Those who had fled their farms returned to find their livestock missing, their homes plundered, and their rail fences removed for firewood. British troops who had frozen in Boston, Halifax, and New York did not propose to freeze in Philadelphia. Most citizens had relied on Howe's proclamation, "but, Alas! Melancholy experience has convinced them of the contrary, and the ruin of numbers has stamped it with infallible certainty."[28] The British were losing friends, and losing them fast.

Indiscriminate foraging in the adjacent countryside was no more than a partial solution to Sir William's formidable supply problem. The army could not for long be supported over the tortuous and vulnerable road from Head of Elk. The Delaware must be cleared, and without delay, so that transports and victualers could sail upriver unmolested and lay alongside Philadelphia quays. Immediate reduction of Fort Mercer (Red Bank, New Jersey) and Fort Mifflin on the Pennsylvania side some seven miles below the city was imperative. Colonel von Donop, who had withdrawn from Bordentown after Washington took Trenton, was anxious to restore his blemished reputation and appealed to Howe to give him command of the operation against Fort Mercer. Howe acquiesced, and on October 21, 1777, Von Donop crossed the Delaware with 2,000 Hessians.

In the early afternoon of the next day Von Donop invested the fort and summoned Colonel Christopher Greene to surrender, with the threat that if Greene rejected his demand, the Hessians would storm and give no quarter. Greene's position was strong, and he and his four hundred Rhode Islanders were plentifully supplied with courage, cannon, grapeshot, powder, and ball ammunition. He rejected the summons. Three attacks failed. Von Donop fell, mortally wounded. The Hessian Jägers, grenadiers, and the Regiment von Mirbach, which composed Von Donop's assaulting force, lost almost four hundred. American losses were fewer than forty.

On the day after Von Donop's defeat, defenders of Fort Mifflin had the pleasure of watching H.M.S. *Augusta,* a 64, and *Merlin,* a sloop, run aground within range of their cannon. Both were set afire and burned to the water's edge. Severe cannonading from the land side finally forced the defenders of Fort Mifflin to flee to Fort Mercer, which Greene, threatened by a strong column under Cornwallis, evacuated on the night of November 20. Viscount Howe's ships could finally ascend the river safely.

As flagship *Eagle* anchored off Fort Mifflin, Ambrose Serle went ashore to view "this celebrated place. Nothing, surely, was ever so torn and riven by Cannon-Balls. A more dismal Picture of Ruin can scarcely be conceived." Serle thought the Americans had "certainly defended with a Spirit they have shown no where else to an equal Degree during the War."[29] Serle was not impressed with Philadelphia: "There are some handsome Public Buildings, and some houses not inelegant, but the Generalty of the last are rather mean Edifices." He found the market poor—no meat, no fowl, very few vegetables. After inspecting the market, Serle breakfasted with Galloway. Both gentlemen bewailed "the misery of the Times" and "the loss of that Happiness (perhaps the greatest ever enjoyed by human Society in this depraved State of things), wch had been wantonly thrown away in Gratification of the dishonest & ambitious views of smuggling merchants and turbulent Demagogues."[30]

During the last days of November and the first week of December, Admiral Howe's ships tied up at wharves and anchored in the river "in great numbers." With the navy came merchants who with their wares moved into deserted and boarded-up stores. "But the English merchants that came in the fleet will not dispose of their goods without hard money"; citizens who had no specie were soon "reduced to beggary and want." Morton observed, as Serle had, a growing scarcity of provisions: "Hard to pass the paper money"; with Continental paper useless, "our ruin must be certain and inevitable."[31]

In early December, Howe had marched his army out of the city, presumably to seek battle. Three days later, "to the great astonishment of the citizens, the army returned." The Hessians, as usual, "committed great outrages on the inhabitants . . . as if the sole purpose of the expedition was to destroy and to spread desolation and ruin, to dispose the inhabitants to rebellion. . . ."[32]

Robert Morton was eighteen; he had seen his father secretly arrested and carried away by the Pennsylvania Committee of Safety and sent with scores of other Quakers to the concentration camp in Virginia, where they would be none too mildly treated. He was one of hundreds in Philadelphia who had witnessed arbitrary power arbitrarily exercised. He was bitter. A week before Cornwallis marched in, he had written "the day must come when the Avenger's hand shall make thee [the Supreme Executive Council of Pennsylvania] suffer for thy guilt."[33] He was delighted to see the oppressors of honest, God-fearing people, who had held steadfastly to their pacific convictions, chased out of town. He had expected better of the British. After three months, he was a totally disillusioned young man.

Ambrose Serle, who no longer cherished hope that His Majesty's forces would soon bring the Americans to acknowledge loyal and dutiful subordination, left Philadelphia two days before Christmas bound for New York en route (he hoped) to his family in England. His despondency may well have been induced by the pessimistic mood prevailing at British headquarters.

In late October, when news of Saratoga reached him, Howe had written Germain a letter exculpating himself from any blame for the loss of Burgoyne's army. He closed with the following paragraph:

> From the little attention, my Lord, given to my recommendations since the commencement of my command, I am led to hope that I may be relieved from this very painful service wherein I have not the good fortune to enjoy the necessary confidence and support of my superiors.

The allegation was a gross distortion of the record, for Germain had approved practically every one of Howe's recommendations, and on the whole had given him effective support.

Howe had squandered a precious year. At Philadelphia he had reached a dead end. His professional reputation was shattered. He was under attack at home, and he could not rehabilitate himself by lingering in America. He saw no prospect of ending the war without another full-scale campaign, and not even then "unless ample succors are sent from Europe" and Washington somehow brought to a decisive action. He added that unless a "respectable reinforcement" was sent at an early date the eventual outcome was "doubtful." General Sir William Howe, K.B., was a frustrated, angry, embittered, and defeated man.

As Louis XVI sought a definite commitment from Madrid, Franklin kept the pressure on Vergennes. The count was ready to arrive at an arrangement, but Louis would permit him to sign nothing until the courier returned from Spain with assurances from his royal uncle. George III and his First Minister were kept *au courant* of proceedings at Versailles and Passy by Paul Wentworth, who received detailed reports from Bancroft, from Arthur Lee's secretary, who was also a British agent, and from assorted other spies. Although members of Opposition were aware that negotiations at Passy had reached a critical stage, Administration, misled by Stormont's reports, publicly professed belief in His Most Christian Majesty's pacific intentions.

Informal peace feelers from members of Opposition reached Franklin from time to time. Several months earlier, he had replied to a long letter from David Hartley, an Opposition M.P. and an old friend from the doctor's London days:

> Happy should I have been, if the honest warnings I gave of the fatal separation of interests as well as of affections, that must attend the measures commenced while I was in England, had been attended to, and the horrid mischief of this abominable war had been thereby prevented. I should still be happy in any successful endeavours for restoring peace, consistent with the liberties, the safety and the honor of America. As to our submitting to the government of Great Britain, 'tis vain to think of it.

Franklin then summarized the "numberless barbarities" England had inflicted on the Americans; these, he said, had created so deep an impression of British "depravity" that he and his countrymen "would never again trust her in the management of our affairs and interests." Afraid that perhaps his letter was "too warm," Franklin thought to "strike out some parts," but on further reflection decided to send it as it stood. In closing, he suggested that Hartley ask his fellow countrymen why they stubbornly persisted in making inveterate enemies, not only of the "present inhabitants of a great country, but of their infinitely more numerous posterity; who will in all future ages detest the name of *Englishman*."[34]

Madrid was exceedingly cautious. Charles III, willing to extend limited clandestine assistance to the revolting Americans, was not yet ready to acquiesce openly in a war policy that would imperil Spain's dominions beyond the seas. The Spanish King's calculated dilatoriness, Franklin's exhortation that "there was not a moment to be lost" if Louis XVI "wished to secure the friendship of America, and detach her entirely from the mother-country," and Vergennes's suspicion that Lord North was seriously contemplating some sort of conciliatory measures, decided the minister to press the King for a decision.

King Louis acted immediately. On December 6 he dispatched Gérard to Franklin's residence to inform the doctor verbally that "His Majesty had resolved to recognize the independence of, and to enter into a treaty of commerce and alliance with the United States of America, and that he would not only acknowledge their independence, but actually support it with all the means in his power."[35] Several days later Vergennes formally confirmed his master's decision.

There is a pleasant myth that La Fayette was influential in persuading Vergennes to this decision. The young nobleman, a knight errant ambitious for personal glory, fired by a consuming hatred of Great Britain and inspired by American aspirations to achieve liberty, was not another eighteenth-century soldier of fortune. He had not braved the wrath of his King and the anger of his family to line his pockets. The marquis, charming, persuasive, and obviously dedicated, had not thought to create a legend. His secret departure from France, his harrowing voyage to America, the toilsome trip from Charleston to Philadelphia, his acceptance by the Congress and later by the commander in chief, who became to him a father figure, are the texture of the romantic story which has endeared his name to generations of Americans. But La Fayette's adventure had nothing to do with Vergennes's decision to enter the war. That a young and inexperienced nobleman had fled a *lettre de cachet* to join the rebellious colonists made not the slightest difference in the objective calculations of Louis XVI's Foreign Minister.

Both Vergennes and his predecessor had repeatedly and thoroughly canvassed all conceivable contingencies that might arise should the Americans resort to arms to seek redress of their grievances. Given the circumstances, a French decision to assist the revolting colonies in some way was inevitable. The question was not whether France would join forces with America to bring England down, but how, with respect to her own security and best interests, she could do so, and when. These were the questions Vergennes had pondered in *Réflexions* in December 1775. He, not the British enemy, would choose *le moment de la guerre*.

2

To Starve, Dissolve, or Disperse

The joy that the news of Saratoga excited at Passy, where Franklin and his colleagues were comfortably housed, well fed, and lionized alike by courtiers, courtesans, intellectuals, and the public, affords a grim contrast to the clouds of despondency settling over the new nation on the other side of the Atlantic.

For this was to be a winter of severe trial; of further machinations of the clique supporting Horatio Gates, the ambitious general soon to be made president of the Board of War, whose secret hope was to supplant Washington; of unrelenting financial crunch; of almost total lack of blankets, shoes, stockings, shirts, soap, vinegar, or candles for the shivering, hungry, and unpaid army encamped at Valley Forge. Washington had selected this site some twenty miles west of Philadelphia because provision contractors asserted they could conveniently supply him there, and because, if he hung close to Howe, he could prevent the British from ravaging the countryside and deprive them of beef, flour, and forage. And there was a most important political consideration: Eastern Pennsylvania was predominantly neutral or Tory. The presence of the Continental Army would intimidate those whose sympathies lay with the British.

On December 19 the army marched into "this wooded wilderness, certainly one of the poorest districts of Pennsylvania; the soil thin, uncultivated and almost uninhabited, without forage and without provisions! Here we are . . . to lie in shanties, generals and privates, to enable the army, it is said, to recover from its privations, to recruit, to re-equip, and to prepare for the coming campaign, while protecting the country against hostile inroads." Obviously displeased with the choice, Baron de Kalb continued: "The idea of wintering in this desert can only have been put into the head of the commanding general by an interested speculator, or a disaffected man." He thought Washington too susceptible to influence: "He is the bravest and truest of men, has the best intentions and a sound judgement," but was convinced that those who enjoyed his confidence were "the worst of advisers. . . . If they are not traitors, they are certainly gross ignoramuses."[1]

The baron may have been a respectable brigade commander, but he was no judge of terrain. Washington was, and when he rode over the ground tentatively selected by Colonel Louis le Bèque du Portail, chief of engineers of the Continental Army, he must have realized at once that this was the place. To the north, the Schuylkill, with few fords and those easily guarded; to the west, the deep ravine formed by Valley Creek. The only approaches to the wooded convoluted hills on which Du Portail proposed to establish the first and second lines and the final battle position, which outposting units could speedily occupy, were across furrowed fields. Sentries posted in observation towers erected on the heights of land could readily detect any major movement from Philadelphia and give ample warning of an impending attack. Troops could then be moved to any threatened area. Washington had not selected Valley Forge because he thought it would be a pleasant place to spend the winter.

De Kalb, probably the most experienced soldier in the American Army, was extremely critical: "Now we have only been here six days, and are already suffering from want of everything . . . the generals never think of sparing their men," and turned them out on ceremonial parades and guard mounts when they should have been building shelters. The baron found his recommendations unwelcome and had "abandoned the practice of suggesting improvements." He deplored the lack of professional competence: "I have had the greatest trouble in making them understand the necessity of strong patrols for visiting the posts. They have no idea of a system of pickets and outposts." De Kalb's French colleagues thought of nothing but "incessant intrigues and backbitings. They hate each other like the bitterest enemies, and endeavor to injure each other wherever an opportunity offers. . . . Lafayette is the sole exception." He thought it fortunate "we have an enemy to deal with as clumsy as ourselves."[2]

Several days before Christmas, Washington received positive information that a large British party had marched from Philadelphia to forage near Darby. He ordered the troops to be in readiness to move out "When, behold! to my great mortification" the men "were unable to stir on Acct. Provisions." The troops were no longer on reduced rations; they were slowly starving. "A Dangerous Mutiny" the previous night "with difficulty was suppressed by the spirited exertions of some officers." The commissary "had not a single hoof of any kind to slaughter and not more than 25 Barls. of Flour."[3] The general informed Congress he was "convinced beyond a doubt that unless some great and capital change" suddenly took place in the administration of the Commissary Department, "this Army must inevitably be reduced to one or other of these three things. Starve, dissolve, or disperse. . . . Rest assured Sir this is not an exaggerated picture."

Foraging was not the answer. "No Sir: three or four days bad weather could prove our destruction." The situation was approaching the catastrophic. Washington was being blamed for the condition of the army; his failure to act offensively was being severely criticized "not only by the common vulgar, but those in power." He therefore determined "to speak plain," and did: "No Man, in my opinion ever had his measures more impeded, by every department of the army." The general did not complain about the lack of soap; there was very little occasion for it; very few men "had more than one shirt; many only the Moity of one, and Some none at all." There seemed to be no point in having a quartermaster general, a commissary general, or a clothier general. Thousands were shoeless; indeed, 2,898 rank and file were unfit for duty because they were "barefoot and otherwise naked."[4] Muster rolls of December 23 showed but 8,200 fit for duty; over 25 per cent of the army was immobilized.

Every night now the ground froze. In the pale cold morning sunlight the frost melted, and after several hours potholed roads and rutted paths were ankle-deep in clinging icy mush. Men without blankets (and nearly 4,000 were) "set up all night by fires instead of taking comfortable rest in a natural way."

The Pennsylvania Legislature, rather than bending every effort to assist this emaciated and exhausted army, had the supreme effrontery to attack Washington for going into winter quarters. Did they think his "Men (the Soldiers) were made of Stocks or Stones," insensible to driving, freezing rain, frost, and snow? The "Gentlemen" of Pennsylvania and New Jersey had promised clothing and blankets; none had arrived. "I can assure those Gentlemen that it is a much easier and less distressing thing to draw remonstrances in a comfortable room by a good fire side than to occupy a cold, bleak hill and sleep under frost and Snow without Cloathes or Blankets; however although they seem to have little feeling for the naked and Distressed Soldiers, I feel superabundantly for them, and from my Soul pity those miseries wch. it is neither in my power to relieve or prevent."[5] He wrote Governor Patrick Henry of Virginia asking for clothing and told him it was impossible to give "a just and accurate Idea of the sufferings of the Troops."

But he did not resign himself to despair, as lesser men did. In fact, he was planning the spring campaign; many abuses must be rectified before April: "We have not more than 3 months to prepare a great deal of business in." He urged Congress to appoint a committee immediately to visit the camp and confer with him and his divisional and brigade commanders. Washington's humanity, his sense of justice, his devotion to the army, his profound faith in the cause it served, are nowhere shown more clearly than in this letter. Nothing daunted him—he spent most of Christmas Day drawing up secret plans for a surprise attack on Philadelphia.

Only dire necessity would persuade him to allow even the most carefully regulated foraging; when he learned that parties of soldiers had been intimidating the inhabitants and taking food from them, he issued a stern and angry General Order. He had heard of these "cruel outrages and robberies" with "inexpressible grief and indignation." The base and wicked crimes committed by such villains injured the army and the common cause; they deserved and would receive "the severest punishment."

New Year's Day, 1778, brought good tidings. The Americans at Wilmington under command of Brigadier General William Smallwood had captured a brig and a sloop bound to Philadelphia from New York loaded with butter, flour, pork, poultry, 1,000 stand of arms, powder, officers' baggage, and 2,000 new uniforms. All this treasure had been en route to General Howe.

Washington and his small staff spent that day planning army reorganization. Each of two wings—right and left—was to consist of triangular divisions each of three brigades, under Major Generals La Fayette, Baron de Kalb, St. Clair, Lincoln, McDougall, and Lord Stirling. Arnold, whose leg had not yet properly healed, commanded the Corps de Réserve: two brigades of infantry and the light horse under Count Casimir Pulaski, wintering in Trenton. Although current muster rolls showed a total strength of slightly more than 18,000, probably not more than 10,000 to 11,000 were present and fit for duty.* Some less sanguine than Washington doubtless conceived the reorganization as no more than a paper exercise.

Although before Christmas the commander in chief had warned Henry Laurens, now president of Congress, that the army would proba-

---

* The muster rolls of the American Army are far from being models of accuracy. Muster rolls of December 23 showed 11,098 rank and file present. The balance, about 6,000, included officers, sergeants, drummers, fifers, surgeons, surgeon's mates, deserters, all those on detached duty, on furlough, and in hospitals elsewhere than Valley Forge.

bly dissolve unless Congress took immediate steps to provide essential supplies of food and clothing, little was being done. He was using "every exertion that may be expedient and practicable for sustaining the Army and keeping it together."[6] But something more than expedients was needed. Morale at Valley Forge continued to slide: "The discontent prevailing in the army from various causes, has become but too prevalent, and I fear, unless some measures can be adopted to render the situation of the Officers more comfortable than what it has been for some time past that it will increase." Continuing depreciation of Continental paper was the root of all evils: ". . . the difficulty of procuring necessaries and the exhorbitant prices officers are required to pay for them" created mounting dissatisfaction.[7] The malaise was not confined to junior officers —disillusioned brigadiers and colonels tendered their resignations.

Officers in a position to steal who thought they could get away with it did so. All were not successful. On January 5, one Dunham Ford, commissary officer in General Greene's division, was tried by general court-martial and found guilty of theft. The court sentenced him "to be brought from the Provost guard mounted on a horse back foremost without a saddle, his coat turned rong side outward his hands tied behind him & to be Drum'd out of the Army, never more to return, by all the Drums of the Division to which he belongs."

Although troops were neither decently clothed nor adequately fed, the army had on hand a supply of rum, and each officer and man received a small daily ration. Individuals supplemented this by purchase from sutlers and women camp followers who engaged in the forbidden but lucrative business.† General Knox thought the rum ration should be increased; a generous quantity "would support the men through every difficulty."[8] Drunkenness, a common offense, was by no means confined to the rank and file.

Sanitation was execrable—indeed, nonexistent. Knox's artillery horses were dying of starvation and exposure; their carcasses lay where they fell; in several days of relatively mild weather they bloated and putrified. Only the fact that temperatures held generally below freezing prevented an epidemic of dysentery. Bathing was next to impossible: "Our men are also infected with the itch, a matter which attracts very little attention either at the hospital or in camp." De Kalb had seen many "poor fellows covered over and over with scab."[9] In his division, he isolated the afflicted and made some effort to get them and their clothes clean.

Perhaps the problem that distressed Washington most was failure of states to replenish their battalions. The obligated time of thousands of militiamen would soon expire; Continental units were progressively re-

† In a General Order issued January 26, Washington authorized sutlers to sell liquor, and set prices: Peach Brandy at 7/6 the quart; Whiskey and Apple Brandy, 6/; Cider, 1/3; and Strong Beer, 2/6.

duced by sickness and desertion. The Pennsylvania Legislature had passed a draft law; Washington thought it vain to hope quotas could be filled any other way and suggested other states enact similar legislation. Baron de Kalb gloomily wrote M. le Comte de Broglie, "All things seem to contribute to the ruin of our cause. If it is sustained, it can only be by a special interposition of Providence."[10]

Congress assembled briefly on New Year's Day and met to work on the day following. One of the first resolutions, passed unanimously, was to dismiss Commodore Esek Hopkins. Hopkins had been suspended from his naval duties in the preceding March; with him out of the way, there was at least a possibility that the navy would be able to function to better effect.

But a far more serious matter than the dismissal of the once-respected commodore troubled many members. The clique plotting to replace Washington had crystallized. Henry Laurens wrote his son, an aide-decamp to Washington, on January 8: ". . . our whole frame is shattered; we are tottering, and without the exertion of wisdom and fortitude, we must fall flat down."[11] He went on to say that General Mifflin, a member of the Board of War, was a "pivot" in these machinations. A man of "fawning mild address and obsequiousness," Mifflin had gained favor with many—not, however, with Laurens, who judged him duplicitous. The president found it difficult otherwise to identify participants in this junta, for "in all such there are prompters and Actors, accomodators, Candle Snuffers, Shifters of scenes and Mutes."[12]

La Fayette had earlier written Laurens his suspicions of a cabal against Washington.‡ The president was aware of the maneuverings, "but I think the friends of our brave and virtuous General, may rest assured that he is out of the reach of his Enimies. . . ." To assuage La Fayette's obvious alarm, Laurens dismissed the whole affair as "little more than tittle-tattle." He was dismayed at the extent of scheming and maneuvering: "Very early after my arrival at the State House Philadelphia I discovered the spirit of party triumphant." He ascribed discord in large measure to provincialism, which he assured the marquis would be overcome by realization of danger from the common enemy. "We are in a State of Infancy, yet thank God, we are not quite so foolish nor so wicked as our Parent."[13]

Washington's reports of the shocking conditions at Valley Forge moved Congress to appoint a committee of three, plus Gates, Mifflin, and Timothy Pickering, to proceed to the camp. Naturally none of the three

‡ Dr. James Craik, Washington's friend and physician, who had recently left Valley Forge, wrote him on January 6 from Port Tobacco, Maryland: "It was said, that some of the eastern and southern members were at the bottom of it, particularly one, who has been said to be your enemy before but denied it, Richard Henry Lee; and that General Mifflin, in the new Board of War, was a very active person."

members of the Board of War, among the most active of the commander in chief's detractors, wished to go. All were excused. Charles Carroll of Carrollton and Gouverneur Morris were appointed in their stead. Detachment of delegates to Valley Forge critically reduced members available to perform "the ordinary drudgery of Committees" and to forward essential business. Laurens described the situation succinctly in a letter to John Rutledge: ". . . consider, Sir, the Circumstances of Congress, left to reap the fruits of former shameful Idleness and dissipation of time." Sometimes twenty-one members appeared, more often thirteen or fourteen, "sometimes barely 9 States on the floor, represented by as many persons."

Financial matters absorbed a major proportion of time and attention. As managers of the lottery (previously authorized by Congress) reported to the Committee on the Treasury that Howe's invasion of Pennsylvania had considerably obstructed sale of tickets, the drawing was again postponed, but Congress, "being desirous . . . to fulfill the expectations of the adventurers," directed the managers to proceed with it on "the 1st day of May next." Still reluctant to urge taxation, Congress emitted paper—$3 million in January—and authorized the Treasury Board to float a $10 million loan at 6 per cent. Given the existing rate of inflation, this proposition was not likely to attract too many investors.

Much time was devoted to debates concerning Burgoyne and the "Convention Army" wintering unhappily in Cambridge, where Gentleman Johnny, displeased with the quarters assigned, engaged in a paper war with his warder, Major General William Heath, and Horatio Gates. Heath, no match for Burgoyne in a duel of words, answered the general's missives politely and forwarded them, with his replies, to Congress, where Burgoyne was not particularly popular. The result was a resolution "That the embarkation of Lieutenant General Burgoyne and the troops under his command, be suspended till a distinct and explicit ratification of the convention of Saratoga shall be properly notified by the court of Great Britain to Congress." Congress was of course aware that the court of Great Britain would not ratify the Convention, for to do so would amount to recognition of American independence.

The activities of the Board of War might well have been designed to hasten the ruin of the cause. In late January, and without planning consultation with Washington, these master strategists decided to mount a winter expedition to seize Montreal, and named Major General La Fayette to command it, with Conway and De Kalb as his deputies. The young marquis was not exactly delighted with the appointment of Conway, an officer he thoroughly detested. Still, fame, honor, glory, beckoned. When the gentlemen at York belatedly wrote the commander in chief of their plan, he was decidedly cool: "In the present instance, as I neither know the extent of the Objects in view, nor the means to be employed to effect them, it is not in my power to pass any judgment upon the subject." He expressed hope the expedition would be "advancive of the public good" and would bring honor to the "Marquis de la Fayette, for whom I have a very particular esteem and regard."[14] The records do not indicate precisely the origin of the absurd idea; it may have been in Congress. At least that body approved it. Apparently, the design was to get La Fayette out of the way, and in the process to dishonor this devoted and able defender of Washington. Possibly Conway was sent along to win over the marquis if he could, or, if he could not, to neutralize his influence, which was considerable.

The three officers named by the board proceeded as ordered to Albany, where they met with Major Generals Schuyler, Lincoln, and Arnold, none of whom had been consulted, and all of whom vigorously opposed the scheme, as did John Stark. The Board of War had provided the generals, but had neglected to arrange for troops. Washington had reluctantly sent forward Colonel Hazen's battalion of Continentals, but less than 1,500 men were found available in the Northern Department. This abortive affair was enlivened by a ridiculous dispute between Conway and De Kalb respecting relative rank. The disappointed marquis and his quarreling deputies soon turned their backs on Albany and set off for Valley Forge.

There, Washington and his general officers were engaged with the committee of Congress which had recently arrived. The gentlemen from York chose not to stay at Valley Forge, where they might have witnessed and endured the hardships suffered by the army. Rather, they moved into a commodious mansion several miles distant from the general's headquarters, thus establishing a precedent invariably followed by similar committees.

Washington had prepared a commendable staff study in which he frankly and at length presented the existing situation in the army and made specific recommendations designed to correct defects. He hoped the visitors were fully impressed with the "necessity of speedy and decisive measures" required to put the army "upon a satisfactory footing." The general admitted that although his picture of "the wants and sufferings of the army" was disagreeable, it was "a just representation of evils equally melancholy and important; and unless effectual remedies be applied without loss of time, the most alarming and ruinous consequences are to be apprehended."[15]

Several days after the delegates (presumably informed and suitably entertained) departed for York, Henry Laurens sent Washington a copy of an anonymous handbill, surreptitiously circulated, which contained a vicious attack on him. The allegations wounded Washington deeply. He at once wrote a moving letter to Laurens. He knew "a malignant faction" had formed and was working against him. But, as he had "no other view than to promote the public good," and was ambitious for no honors except those "founded in the approbation" of the nation, he did not "desire in the least degree to suppress a free spirit of enquiry" into any part of his conduct "that even faction itself may deem reprehensible." He requested Laurens to lay the paper before Congress.[16] He hoped to dismiss the matter from his mind and enjoy for a time some domestic felicity: Martha—"Lady Washington," as the army knew her—was expected soon at Valley Forge.

Gates, Conway, and their friends in Congress, including the two Lees, intensified their covert campaign of denigration and innuendo. The general was now well aware of the details; he had received reports confirming information earlier provided him by Stirling and La Fayette and had written a lengthy letter to Gates. He considered Conway "capable of all the malignity of detraction, and all the measures of intrigue, to gratify the absurd resentment of disappointed vanity, or to answer the purpose of personal aggrandizement, and promote the interests of faction."[17] He did not need to add that this pungent description fit the president of the Board of War as aptly as it did his scheming Irish protégé.

Washington spared no efforts to assure the army an adequate supply of provisions. Although the approved daily ration was one and a half pounds of fresh meat and one pound of bread, plus salt, sugar, tea, milk, and rum, the troops rarely saw meat and were getting but half the bread ration. The army was living from day to day on a bare subsistence level. Mifflin, the quartermaster general, was simply not functioning. Whether he was indolent and incompetent or whether he was motivated in part by some sinister design will never be known, but Washington could no longer tolerate him at this critical time. He wrote Israel Putnam in the Highlands and Governor Trumbull of Connecticut begging them to collect cattle. Without supplies of beef, the army would disband. He faced "a Melancholy and Alarming Catastrophe."

Finally, he resigned himself to the absolute necessity of wholesale foraging, appointed Major General Nathanael Greene quartermaster general, and ordered him to sweep the countryside for cattle, horses, sheep, oxen, and "every kind of forage that may be found." He directed Greene to give certificates of valuation for the stock and "Provender" taken. Greene, a tough and uncompromising officer, wasted no time carrying out his unpleasant mission. Had Washington not taken this harsh but essential decision, the army probably would have ceased to exist. General Greene produced, as he had promised he would. The lingering food crisis was at last almost over.

The state of discipline in camp demanded severe measures. Theft was endemic. General courts-martial sat daily; dozens of officers were cashiered, and others, such as Lieutenant Grey, found guilty of absence without leave, robbing, and "infamously stealing," were sentenced to public humiliation. Grey was "unanimously sentenced to have his sword broke over his head on the grand parade," to be ignominiously dismissed and "rendered incapable" of ever again serving in the Army of the United States. Sentences of one hundred lashes "on the bare back well laid on" were becoming everyday occurrences. After review of the evidence, Washington often reduced or remitted severe corporal punishment adjudged on enlisted men; in egregious cases, he approved.

Washington's forty-sixth birthday, celebrated quietly on February 22 at Valley Forge, could not have been a particularly festive occasion. The next afternoon, a middle-aged Prussian soldier, Friedrich Wilhelm Ludolf Gerhard Augustin, Baron von Steuben, presented himself at headquarters.

In the summer of 1777 the baron had found himself in Baden, and out of work. He had served as a junior aide-de-camp to Frederick the Great and was an accomplished professional soldier. When he learned that American commissioners in Paris were hiring officers to serve in the Continental Army, he hastened to the French capital. There he encountered Beaumarchais, who introduced him to Deane and Franklin. The commissioners reluctantly informed the baron that Congress, irritated by the flood of adventurers who at American expense had crossed the Atlantic seeking rank and emoluments, had put a peremptory stop to recruiting. Von Steuben was a persistent man. He continued to call on Franklin and Deane and offered to pay all his expenses provided they would write a suitable letter of recommendation to Washington. During these negotiations the baron quietly promoted himself from captain to lieutenant general, and the letter he carried to America so identified him.

Von Steuben, with a young French nobleman he had acquired as "military secretary," and a valet, sailed on one of Beaumarchais's ships from Marseilles. After a tempestuous passage which included two shipboard fires and a mutiny, *Le Flamande* had anchored at Portsmouth, New Hampshire, on the first day of December, where her passengers no doubt considered themselves fortunate to be able to disembark. From Boston, where he was received with ceremony, the baron sent off letters to Congress and to Washington. In due time he was bidden to York. He and his entourage arrived in mid-February and were handsomely accommodated and suitably entertained. Von Steuben discreetly stated his desire to assist the cause as a volunteer; Congress accepted him as such. He was perhaps the most valuable volunteer acquired by the American Army.

At Valley Forge he went to work immediately. With General Washington's enthusiastic approval, he established a corps of inspectors. He was a stern disciplinarian and an excellent drillmaster. He formed an exhibition drill company and in two months his system had greatly improved the discipline and professional standard of the army. Washington was not slow to appreciate that in this volunteer he had a gem, and recommended that Congress commission the baron a major general.

When Franklin remarked that Philadelphia had "taken" Sir William Howe, he knew whereof he spoke, for he was familiar with both the general and his own city. Howe, his staff, and his officers were received in the best society with more than toleration and soon discovered that at least some attractive young ladies in the Quaker City were not as impregnable as they had been led to believe. Philadelphia Tories, happy to have the British with them, displayed their hospitality in more ways than with food and drink. Masques, gambling, balls, banquets, concerts, flirtation, and more serious love-making were the order of the day.

Sir William consoled himself in the arms of the available beauty who had followed him from Boston to Halifax to New York and finally to Philadelphia. His infatuation with Mrs. Loring was generally known, as the following stanza, no doubt read with glee wherever a patriot printer could function, suggests:

> Sir William he, snug as a flea,
> Lay all this time a snoring
> Nor dreamed of harm as he lay warm
> In bed with Mrs. Loring.

Both the general and "the Sultana" were avid gamblers. Faro, played for high stakes, was the popular game. (In one unfortunate evening Mrs. Loring dropped three hundred guineas.) Howe's subordinates were not slow to follow the general's example.

Taking the field was the last thing Sir Billy contemplated. He knew the strength of Washington's Valley Forge position; he felt that with forces available he could not risk an attack. Based on information he had, this was a reasonable decision. But he apparently had neither the imagination nor the energy to exploit the political situation in eastern Pennsylvania, where many had Tory leanings, and many more, for want of encouragement and protection, were apathetic neutrals. The British dispensed solid specie; the Americans, depreciating Continental paper; farmers who would not grind corn and wheat for Washington's starving army ground it readily for Howe's Redcoats. The British ate beef, pork, and chicken; Americans at Valley Forge rarely saw a side of beef.

The British general could have organized, armed, and generously rewarded Tory guerrillas to lie in wait for American foraging parties and to continually harass Washington's outposts. He could have deprived Washington of very considerable amounts of food by establishing three or four mutually supporting enclaves, and from them, sent out strong columns to sweep the countryside. Many Americans deserted; the British had good sources of information, and Howe must have known of Washington's condition. Was he waiting for the American Army to disintegrate: "to starve, dissolve, or disperse"? The apathy of this general was incomprehensible to many of his junior officers.

The King affected to pay little attention to the approaching crisis in Anglo-French relations; his holiday correspondence with Lord North, who had sought "joy and merriment" at Bushy, was almost entirely concerned with details of commissions he proposed to award to deserving applicants—or to withhold from the undeserving—in the new corps being raised by subscription in Manchester, Liverpool, Middlesex, Yorkshire, and the Highlands. These details should have been left to Lord Barrington's office, but it was precisely such minutiae that too often engrossed the Sovereign's attention, to the detriment of great affairs of state. The King was a dedicated bureaucratic quill-driver. It would perhaps be unjust to describe him at this juncture as complacent. He was already mentally and emotionally prepared for war with the allied Bourbon powers. He wrote Lord North he could meet "the very unhappy event" with equanimity, for he had "scrupulously attempted" to avoid hostilities. He had. In any event, his conscience (as always) was clear: ". . . without one single grievance, France chuses to be the aggressor."[18]

The King wrote an important letter to his First Minister on January 13. The course France would finally adopt appeared to him to be uncertain. He opined that the Americans at Passy were gradually drawing a rather reluctant Louis XVI and his ministers into a war they really did not want. Contingent planning for a war with the two great continental powers was certainly necessary; he had discussed the subject at length with Lord Amherst, who had confirmed his opinion that continuation of an offensive land war in America was impracticable, that it would be wise to abandon all North America save Canada, Nova Scotia, and the Floridas, and to base strategy on operations vigorously conducted by the Royal Navy, designed to prevent any supplies of whatever description reaching the rebels. This strategy, the King believed, would "make them come into what Britain may decently consent to," for "to treat with Independence can never be possible."[19]

Rockingham, still wooing Chatham, wrote the earl his concept of proper Opposition policy: ". . . the best service which now can be done for the public is to point out, and if possible, fully convince them, of the impossibility of going on with the war: to show them how much blood and treasure have already been wasted; the present state of the army and navy, and most particularly, the miserable state of the funds; to point out the weakness and inability with which the military operations had been planned, and indeed the folly of every measure which the Ministers have taken in this horrid war."[20]

But the marquis was not inclined to exert himself to pull his followers together or to give them guidance. He was not exactly a dilettante but he did prefer his country seat to London; only with great difficulty could Burke persuade him to forsake the pleasures of life outside the metropolis to come up to the capital. "The Manifico of his day" spoke infrequently in the House of Lords. Indeed, he rarely graced the chamber with his presence. He owned and trained thoroughbreds, and during racing season was usually to be found at the course. He was immensely wealthy and enjoyed the respect of the Yorkshire gentry. He had controlled the county for years and nominated those who would stand for its seats in Parliament. But he was not equipped either intellectually or temperamentally for the role history had assigned him in this most critical period.

After the prolonged holiday recess, Parliament assembled on January 22. Fox immediately moved again for ministerial instructions to Howe and Burgoyne, and Sir Phillip Clerk asked for a precise account of the number of troops recently raised by subscription, a procedure Opposition described as dangerous, infamous, disgraceful, and unconstitutional. Nothing came of this particular uproar, the principal purpose of which was to further embarrass Administration.

Lord North reluctantly agreed to provide the papers requested, and did so a week later. Germain, however, did not appear; Opposition deemed the papers supplied by the First Minister wholly unsatisfactory, and the absence of the American Secretary unconscionable. The ministry, embarrassed by continual attacks, was obviously stalling.

Certainly the King's First Minister was despondent. On January 30, he resumed his campaign to gain permission to retire from office. His royal master wrote him the following evening:

> You must feel how very entirely I have confided in you since you have presided at the Treasury, how fairly you have been supported by your colleagues in the administration, how sincerely you are loved and admired by the House of Commons, and how universally esteemed by the public; indeed, these reflections must rouse your mind, and enable you to withstand situations still more embarrassing than the present.[21]

"The Noble Lord in the Blue Ribband" would indeed have to withstand many more embarrassing situations; they were to become routine.

Several days later, both Houses went into committee to consider the State of the Nation. Fox opened in the Commons with a long speech in which he reviewed Britain's relations with her colonies since 1774, dwelt at length on the misconduct of the American war and the probability of embroilment with France and Spain. He then moved that no more troops be sent out of Britain. The motion was lost, 259 to 165. For the first time,

Opposition had mustered a respectable following on an important division, and Fox exulted.

This showing, combined with the ill-concealed desire of Lord North to retire, again sparked the always latent rumor that Chatham would be called back on a rescue operation. Walpole thought it most unlikely; he saw no point at this critical juncture in sending for "an old commander without Soldiers," particularly one "so fractious, so unsettled, and so impracticable" as the Earl of Chatham.[22] Indeed, "No man at this period could feel a stronger wish to see the Prime Minister displaced" than did the unwilling incumbent of that office, who, totally frustrated and overwhelmed by responsibilities he was unable to handle, was now privately and discreetly agitating conciliatory measures.

🎍 3

Our Situation Is Alarming

Great Britain stood alone, and this time there was no Pitt to guide her. In his place was Lord North, the pliable tool of an obstinate King. His cabinet colleagues, arrogant, calculating, and slippery politicians, looked not to him for future perquisites and preferments, but to their common master in St. James's Palace. Among themselves, they quarreled and bickered. Germain held himself aloof from these petty squabblings. He was a man of strong will, not afraid to speak his mind, and he meant what he said. He held courageously to his convictions and stood firmly with his King. But Germain had become something of an embarrassment to Lord North's riven administration, now under constant attack in both Houses of Parliament, in the City, and in the opposition press. Rumors were that Lord George would go. But Lord George had no intention of leaving; he was dedicated to suppression of the rebellion in America. This, he must have felt, was his personal cause, and he was determined to see it through. Germain was a stubborn man.

Not a single European nation wished England well. All hopefully anticipated her downfall and disintegration of the empire constructed by Chatham. France was about to make her choice; Spain would probably join her. At Potsdam, Frederick watched events with unconcealed pleasure. He had previously informed avaricious German princelings anxious to provide more mercenaries to fight for the English King in America that he intended to impose the usual "cattle tax" on all Hessian troops marching through his dominions "because though human beings they had been sold as beasts."

Many able to assess the dimensions of the crisis felt only one man could pull the state through. That man, so they believed, was Chatham, who, mentally despondent and in great pain from gout, sat silently in a darkened room at Hayes and allowed no one save Lady Chatham to approach him. Lord North now again wrote the King begging to be allowed to retire and urging his royal master to send for the earl. The King replied immediately with an attack on Chatham "and his crew" and agreed to accept the "perfidious" earl only if he would support "the fundamentals" of administration policy and guarantee if he took office to retain most of "the present efficient Ministers," i.e., North, Suffolk, Gower, Mansfield, Weymouth, Sandwich, Thurlow, and Wedderburn.* His Majesty was prepared, if necessary, to sacrifice Germain. Otherwise, the road would be "opened to a set of men who certainly would make me a slave for the remainder of my days."[1] The King was not interested in ministers who might advocate a pacific resolution of the American rebellion; all those he named had for years violently attacked the Americans and were execrated by them.

Tentative and informal advances were, however, made to Chatham by an emissary dispatched by Lord Shelburne. As might have been anticipated, the earl rejected the overtures and made it abundantly clear (apparently by verbal message, as no written records of these transactions are known to exist) that he was not interested in taking office under the terms proposed. He would serve if the King summoned him, but he would control appointments and policy. The King refused to accept this ultimatum and wrote Lord North he would rather risk his crown than do what he thought "personally disgraceful." If the nation would not stand by him, they should "have another king." The threat to abdicate temporarily silenced the importunate pleading of the First Minister, but only temporarily; four days later he resumed his entreaties to be allowed to give up office.

At this time Lord Barrington, one of the "King's Friends" who had access to the Closet, requested to be received. He spoke to His Majesty briefly and to the point; described "the general dismay, which prevailed among all ranks and conditions" arising from a "universal" opinion that "Administration was not equal to the times," and assured the King he was not purveying coffeehouse gossip but reflecting a conviction prevail-

---

* "Efficient" in the context means "active," or "serving." These ministers were otherwise known as the King's "Confidential Servants."

ing among those "most dependent on and attached to his Ministers, and even among the Ministers themselves." The warning had little more effect on his obdurate master than had the series of events that had motivated it.

However, and probably as a direct result of this interview, the King agreed that Amherst should command the army in Great Britain, have some responsibility for overseas strategy, and be given a voice in the Cabinet. To the knowing, this appointment clearly signaled a major change in strategic emphasis. Amherst had long advocated an essentially naval strategy in America; redoubled efforts to prepare the fleet to defend the home islands; attacks on the French at sea wherever they were to be found; and conquest of their Caribbean islands.

Sandwich was aware of the danger posed by the combined Bourbon fleets, and in an urgent letter to Lord North gave his opinion that war with France was "inevitable at a very little distance." He provided a detailed assessment of the naval situation, and closed: "I own I think our situation so alarming that I cannot avoid unburdening my mind and begging of your Lordship most seriously to resolve this business in your thoughts, and to consider how fatal it may be to this kingdom if another hour be lost in our naval equipments."[2]

Great Britain's only logical strategy was to seek a speedy accommodation with the United States. The First Minister therefore proposed appointment of peace commissioners armed with power to grant all American demands short of recognition of independence, and privately directed William Eden, Thurlow, and Wedderburn to prepare bills to be introduced in the House of Commons. The King was not yet persuaded of the necessity for conciliatory measures, "not from any absurd idea of unconditional submission my mind never harboured, but perceiving that whatever can be proposed will be liable not to bring America back to a sense of attachment to the mother-country."† George III wanted instead to transfer most of the troops to the West Indies and use the remainder in an amphibious raiding role to destroy "the trade and ports of the rebellious colonies."[3] His Majesty was determined to avenge the humiliations the colonists had inflicted; he conceived the American revolt as an affront to the dignity of the crown and to himself.

Despite the attitude of his royal master, Lord North thought it essential to proceed as rapidly as possible with the legislation. A draft study, probably prepared by Eden, indicates that Administration was reconciled to accepting the best terms the commissioners could get: "Under the apparent Difficulties that must attend the Prosecution of the war, the Conditions Cannot be equal to the Rights of Great Britain and to the Expectations on which the War was commenced." Some concessions would

† This was a falsehood. The King had for years insisted on unconditional submission.

have to be made; what it was decided to yield "had better be given up in the Outset, because the object at present can only be to gain an opening for Treaty."[4]

Eden had some idea of concessions that might be made, and sent a paper for consideration to Lord Chief Justice Mansfield, a gentleman not disposed to grant anything to rebels. Several days later, he visited Mansfield; the lord chief justice informed his guest that during the preceding forty-eight hours he had thought of nothing but the Peace Commission: ". . . it had spoiled his Digestion and broke his Sleep"; he did not see how commissioners could be endowed with powers that would inevitably diminish those of Parliament. He promised, however, to do what he could to help Eden frame the legislation.[5]

Uncertainty over taxation and finances, the decided possibility that many country gentlemen were inclined to desert the ministry and throw their votes to Opposition, and the increasing probability of war with France impelled the King to change his mind. On February 9 he wrote Lord North that intelligence from Wentworth "shews the veil will soon be drawn off by the Court of France, which makes me wish you would not delay bringing your American proposition . . . into the House of Commons." For "Should a French war be our fate, I trust you will concurr with me in the only means of making it successful, the withdrawing the greatest part of them [the troops stationed in America] from America, and employing them against the French and Spanish settlements; but if we are to be carrying on a land war against the rebels, and against those two powers, it must be feeble in all parts and consequently unsuccessful."[6]

A week later the First Minister presented his Conciliatory Bills to the House. The first was entitled "For Removing All Doubts and Apprehensions concerning Taxation by the Parliament of Great Britain in any of the Colonies"; the second empowered the King to appoint commissioners to treat with the rebellious colonials. Lord North admitted the war had gone contrary to his expectations and stated bluntly the nation could not much longer carry it on. Burke later wrote that when the First Minister sat down "a dull melancholy silence for some time succeeded . . . [he] had been heard with profound attention, but without a single mark of approbation to any part, from any description of men, or from any man in the House. Astonishment, dejection, and fear overclouded the whole assembly."[7] Opposition gloated, but could not strenuously object to an administration policy designed to implement a program its members had for long been noisily and ineffectually advocating. Both bills passed easily.

Walpole wrote Mann that Administration's attempt at accommodation "had one defect—it came too late. . . . Nobody knows what to think. To leap at once from an obstinacy of four years, to a total concession of everything; to stoop so low without hopes of being forgiven . . . all that remains certain is that America is not only lost, but given up."[8] Several days later he opined Great Britain had "leaped from outrageous War to a most humiliating supplication for peace," and compared Administration to a patient suffering from the ague "who moves from a shivering fit to a burning one." Possibly Lord North's government was "in its dotage." While he did not believe war with France imminent, he dared not look into the future; his wisdom consisted only "in abstaining from conjectures."

Although lack of progress in America and the First Minister's Conciliatory Bills had agitated Lords and Commons to some extent, the consuming question was the state of Franco-American negotiations. On this subject Richmond, Grafton, Temple, and Shelburne "handled Administration very roughly" in the Lords; they were rewarded with the usual evasive replies—indeed, Lord Weymouth dodged the question by stating he had received no "authentic" information that a Franco-American treaty was "in existence or contemplation."

Actually, translators and clerks in Versailles were busy putting into final form a Treaty of Amity and Commerce between His Most Christian Majesty Louis XVI and the Independent States of North America. This, as well as a secret treaty of alliance, was signed on February 6, for France by Conrad Alexandre Gérard (soon to become the first envoy to the new nation) and for the United States by Franklin, Deane, and Arthur Lee.

The secret treaty, which provided for a defensive alliance between the two countries, would become effective should hostilities break out between France and Great Britain. At this juncture, "the good and faithful allies," embarked in a common cause, would aid one another to maintain the sovereignty and independence of the United States. Each signatory staked its territorial claims: the United States to Canada and Bermuda; France to all other British islands in the western Atlantic, including Newfoundland and Cape Breton. Article VIII provided that neither party would make a truce or sign a treaty of peace with Great Britain without first obtaining formal consent of her ally. Further, neither party would lay down arms until the independence of the United States had been explicitly assured.

On the face of it, this treaty seemed disproportionately favorable to the United States. But the treaty also satisfied Vergennes's imperial ambitions: to humble England, to take Great Britain's Sugar Islands, and by giving birth to another maritime power, to break Britain's commercial monopoly in the north Atlantic and so open the vast continent of North America to unrestricted trade. American agreement to give the French a free hand in Newfoundland and Cape Breton Island, with their valuable fisheries, contributed decisively to the success of the negotiations, which history has correctly viewed as Benjamin Franklin's most important contribution to the cause of American independence.

Happily, Bancroft did not then see the secret treaty, but he probably had a good idea of what was in the wind, as no doubt did Arthur Lee's secretary. The two traitors must have spent a busy night preparing detailed reports. Bancroft delivered a copy of the Treaty of Amity and Commerce to Lord Stormont the following morning; the ambassador immediately sent it to Weymouth. Franklin gave copies of both treaties to trusted couriers to carry to America and confided the originals in French and English to Simeon Deane, brother of Silas, who would soon sail from Brest in a French frigate.

Some accused Vergennes of having acted precipitately. Perhaps he had. But his sense of historical timing cannot be faulted; he felt that Charles III was not yet ready to commit Spain to a maritime war which might well result in loss of her slave empire in Latin America. Although Count Pedro d'Aranda, His Most Catholic Majesty's ambassador to the Court of Versailles, urged Madrid to accede to the secret treaty, José Moñino Floridablanca, his superior, a prudent and calculating minister, saw no prospective gains for Spain but rather the possibility of inestimable losses. If France would absolutely and unconditionally guarantee her Gibraltar, she would accede. Otherwise, the answer was an unqualified no.

Reports from "Mr. Edwards" were laid before His Majesty on March 3. These convinced the King "that France will inevitably go to War." As to Spain: If Madrid were not "very explicit, a fleet must be stationed to seize the flotta coming from Havana, and a corps of 2000 men to be sent by Sir Henry Clinton to conquer New Orleans."[9] The situation in the rebellious colonies was most disturbing. Howe's letter exculpating himself from the Saratoga disaster and blaming the ministry for lack of success in America had arrived in Whitehall. This impolitic missive was a "matter of equal astonishment and indignation to the parties against whom that charge was made; while it inevitably led the unprejudiced and impartial spectator to contrast the langour and reluctance so visibly apparent in the conduct of Sir William Howe with that alacrity and zeal with which the ministry, and particularly the Minister for American affairs, provided and furnished the measures for carrying on the war. . . ."

Sir William's second-in-command was a very unhappy man. Howe's latest requisition had reduced Sir Henry Clinton's rank and file strength fit for duty to about 6,000. Clinton thought this left him "too low to admit of more than the strictest defensive," and renewed his "solicitations for leave to return home, as I plainly saw that my continuance in America was not likely to contribute to the service of my country or the advancement of my own honor. But the Commander-in-Chief being of the opinion that my services could not be dispensed with for the present —especially as General Burgoyne's late misfortune had left the enemy at liberty to employ the whole army which had been opposed to him, either against General Pigot [then occupying Newport] or me—I was obliged to submit to the mortification of enduring my situation somewhat longer."[10] At this point he dispatched an ADC, Major Duncan Drummond, to England to submit his request to come home.

Carleton had also written the minister a rude letter, and Germain considered retiring, alleging that the King, by conferring a sinecure on his inveterate enemy Carleton, had insulted him. By this time both George III and his First Minister were quite ready to see the Secretary for America, whose continued presence in the Cabinet was an increasing embarrassment, retire to his country estate. The King described Lord George as "malevolent" and remarked that his resignation "would save us all trouble."

Ten days after the Versailles treaties had been signed, Marquis de Noailles, Louis XVI's ambassador to the Court of Saint James's, delivered a note to Lord Weymouth which announced that the Most Christian King had lately concluded a Treaty of Friendship and Commerce with the United States of North America, now "in full possession of independence" and asserted his "constant and sincere devotion" to peace. The note did not mention the secret Treaty of Alliance signed at the same time, nor the mutual pledge given by both parties not to make peace with Britain until independence had been conceded and confirmed by a treaty of peace. The secretary listened in stony silence and dismissed the ambassador, who hurried off to the embassy to burn his papers and pack his belongings. Weymouth informed Lord North and ordered Stormont to quit Paris at once without taking leave.

That night the King wrote his First Minister:

> The paper delivered this day by the French Ambassador is certainly equivalent to a declaration, and therefore must entirely overturn every plan for strengthening the army under the command of Lieut-Gen Clinton with an intent of carrying on an active war in North America: what occurs now is to fix what numbers are necessary to defend New York, Rhode Island, Nova Scotia, and the Floridas: it is a joke to think of keeping Pennsylvania for we must from the army now in America form a corps sufficient to attack the French islands, and two or three thousand men ought to be employed with the fleet to destroy the ports and warfs of the rebels.[11]

His Majesty had reluctantly concluded that orthodox operations could not subdue the rebellious Americans. His plan now was to harass and distress them to the greatest extent possible without further major commitment of forces. He directed that secret orders be sent Clinton, shortly to supersede Sir William Howe as "General in America," to evacuate Philadelphia and return at once to New York. Clinton was to cooperate with the King's ships to attack "the ports on the coast from New York to Nova Scotia, and to seize or destroy all wharfs, stores, and materials for shipbuilding, in every harbor or creek which it should be found practicable to penetrate." When these operations were concluded, presumably about the end of September, he was to mount attacks "upon the southern provinces, with a view to the conquest of Georgia and South Carolina."[12] The mirage of gaining decisive Loyalist support in the southern colonies was to control future strategy.

Three peace commissioners were named. They were the young and inexperienced Earl of Carlisle; William Eden, director of British intelligence and ostensibly a deputy secretary of state; and George Johnstone, M.P., a half-pay captain in the Royal Navy and onetime governor of West Florida, who earlier had been extremely critical of Administration's American policies.‡ The commissioners were not told of the orders already dispatched to General Clinton and Admiral Howe and when they sailed were unaware that strategy had been reoriented and that, in Lord Amherst's words, the war in America had become "a secondary consideration."

The King's eye was fixed on the French Sugar Islands. Santa Lucia, a superb base for fleet operations against Martinique, was the chosen target. On March 21 Sandwich dispatched orders to Rear Admiral the Honourable Samuel Barrington, commander in chief, Leeward Islands, to rendezvous at Barbados with an expeditionary force to be organized by Admiral Howe and General Clinton; his mission: to seize Santa Lucia.

One of the principal purposes of the French alliance was to neutralize the British fleet, for although Congress had authorized a navy, the Americans were well aware they could not challenge His Majesty's battle fleets. They could and did build a handful of small frigates, but their reliance was necessarily on privateering. For a *guerre de course*, they could build fast sailing flush-decked ships or could get them in France; they had daring and experienced masters to command them, and thousands of experienced sailors to man them. Privateering was a lucrative business, especially in the Caribbean, in the narrow seas off Holland and Denmark, in the Irish Sea and the Channel where prizes could be disposed of in French ports, in the Bay of Biscay, and off Gibraltar. From 1775 to the end of 1777 American privateers took 457 British merchantmen without the loss of a single ship.[13]

The Americans could not prevent the British from sending convoys

‡ Johnstone had no command.

with troops and supplies to any place they wished from Portsmouth, New Hampshire, to Savannah, Georgia. They could not seriously challenge a major, or indeed a minor, amphibious operation, or a raid directed against any target the British selected. They could not prevent British movement along their shores into the bays and estuaries and up the rivers. Against line-of-battle ships and frigates they were impotent.

But France had fleets-in-being. France could challenge British sea power ship to ship and gun to gun. Her navy could convey French troops, cannon, and supplies of all descriptions safely to America, could hopefully deprive the British of naval supremacy in American waters and seize the maritime initiative in the Western Hemisphere. This was the great object of the alliance Dr. Franklin had successfully consummated.

The only questions in Whitehall were where and when the guns would begin firing. The Cabinet gathered for dinner at Lord Weymouth's on March 14 to assess and discuss the situation. Fleet dispositions were given first priority. Howe's command in American waters totaled seventy fighting ships, including five 64's, five 50's, three 44's, and fourteen 32's. Some of these, under Commodore William Hotham, were to proceed on order to the West Indies for the operation against Santa Lucia; others were to come home for refit before sailing to the Mediterranean. Despite his earlier refusal to serve against the Americans, and his known antipathy to the First Lord of the Admiralty, Vice-admiral the Honourable Augustus Keppel, a staunch Rockinghamite, was named to take command of the Channel fleet.

Three days later the King informed his loyal lords spiritual and temporal and members of the House of Commons of the "just indignation" excited in his breast by the late "most offensive proceedings of the Court of France." Germain, in a *"Most Secret"* letter of March 21 to Clinton, wrote: ". . . his Majesty, in consequence of the advice of his most confidential servants, has taken the resolution to avenge the insulted honour of his Crown and vindicate the injured rights of his people by an immediate attack upon the French possessions in the West Indies."

British agents reported increased activity in French ports, particularly Brest, where eighteen sail of the line were making ready for sea. "Four large ships . . . laden with arms, warlike stores and various goods for the use of the rebels, and some thousand uniforms for the rebel army" lay at St.-Malo. Rear Admiral de la Motte-Picquet, with seven of the line and half a dozen frigates, was under orders to convoy these ships across the Atlantic. At Toulon, Vice-admiral Comte Jean Baptiste d'Estaing assumed command of a powerful squadron fitting out.

The ultimate destination of this squadron could not be ascertained. Was D'Estaing going to America? Or would he join a squadron at Brest commanded by Comte Louis d'Orvilliers? If he set course for America after passing Gibraltar, help must be immediately sent Howe. If he came north to join D'Orvilliers, the Channel fleet must be reinforced. The Admiralty dealt with the dilemma by holding in hand thirteen of the line, commanded by Vice-admiral the Honourable John Byron, until D'Estaing's destination could be confirmed.

That the French would attempt to land an expeditionary force in southern England or somewhere on the Irish coast was a very real and every day increasing possibility. To meet the threat, Keppel would have available, as of mid-April, twenty of the line and fewer than half a dozen frigates. The French alone would significantly outgun him, and should Spain enter, as Sandwich apprehended she might, the enemy line of battle would hold considerably more than a two-to-one advantage in ships and broadside weight of metal.

The King took a keen interest in the developing naval situation. He received Admiral Keppel, who had temporarily called off his feud with Sandwich and ceased (for the time, at least) making political noises. Indeed, Keppel was entirely aware of his responsibility and was busy from morning to night doing all he could to ready the "Great Fleet" to meet the anticipated challenge. He could not, however, resist the temptation to observe that if so many ships had not been sent Viscount Howe, his own command would have been in better condition to meet the combined fleets of Louis XVI and His Most Catholic Majesty.

Lord North chose this time of crisis to renew his campaign to retire from office and to plead yet once more for leading members of Opposition to be given places in the Cabinet. His Majesty, excessively "grieved," wrote the First Minister that "no consideration in life" would make him "stoop to Opposition." He was prepared to abdicate "rather than be shackled by those desperate men." Surely "in this hour of danger" Lord North could not desert him. The royal epistle apparently shamed "the Noble Lord in the Blue Ribband"; he did not revert to the subject for some time.

A new ambassador from the Court of Madrid was expected soon to arrive at St. James's; it was generally anticipated he would deliver a note similar in tenor to that Marquis de Noailles had recently handed Weymouth. Rumors flooded London: Spain had concluded a treaty with the independent United States of North America and would back France. This was no sooner circulated than contradicted. Walpole was morose: "We, the herd . . . must take the beverage our rulers brew for us." He was thankful he had not contributed to the baneful potion: "I believe it will be a bitter one."

Despite Washington's continued efforts, conditions at Valley Forge had only marginally improved. Men deserted and officers tendered their resignations daily. Contingents from every state had fallen far below established quotas. Washington appealed by Circular Letter to the executive of each begging him to adopt at once "the most early and vigorous measures" to bring regiments to authorized strengths. With a "respectable force" available in the spring, he would find "Opportunity of Striking a favorable and happy Stroke." He believed Britain would reinforce Admiral Howe and General Clinton: "Her views and schemes for subjugating these states and bringing them under her despotic Rule will be unceasing and unremitted." There was much speculation that France would soon publicly declare her position: ". . . be this as it may, our reliance should be Wholly on our own strength and exertions."[14]

On several occasions Washington had urged Congress to authorize raising "a body of horse" to augment the several cavalry squadrons under command of Count Pulaski; in early March, delegates "earnestly recommended" to "young gentlemen of property and spirit" in the several states "forthwith to constitute . . . a troop or troops of light cavalry, to serve at their own expense" except for rations and forage, presumably to be provided. Apparently, very few young gentlemen who enjoyed "in a peculiar degree the gifts of fortune and of a cultivated understanding" had any desire "to stand forth in a disinterested manner in defence of their country, and by a laudable example to rouse and animate their countrymen to deeds worthy of their brave ancestors, and of the sacred cause of freedom," and this despite the provision that "all booty taken from the enemy shall belong to the troop by whom it shall be taken."[15]

While the commander in chief's first consideration was naturally the combat capability of his army, he was forced daily to cope with dozens of lesser problems. Some time earlier, the anti-Washington clique in Congress had managed with the help of Gates to arrange for the appointment of Conway, a vain, ambitious, mendacious, vindictive, and impertinent adventurer, as inspector general. He had spoken indiscreetly to both La Fayette and Lord Stirling, who warned the commander in chief that Gates was working to supersede him, and that Conway was an instrument. Washington replied to La Fayette, and, after unmistakably identifying Gates (but not by name), wrote: "His ambition and great desire of being puffed off as one of the first Officers of the Age could only be equalled by the means which he used to obtain them." As Washington would not indulge this ambition, Gates had become "an inveterate Enemy, and has, I am persuaded, practised every Act to do me an injury." The general intended to continue his "uniform code of conduct . . . regardless of the Tongue of Slander or the powers of detraction." But, he continued, "we must not in so great a contest expect to meet with nothing but Sun shine. I have no doubt that everything happens so for the best; that we should triumph over all our misfortunes, and shall, in the end, be ultimately happy, when, My Dear Marquis, if you will give me your company in Virginia, we will laugh at our past difficulties and the follies of others."[16]

Some in Congress were considerably less optimistic than the commander in chief. William Ellery wrote a friend that "Shoals of Officers" were "rioting on the Spoils of the Publick," and that avarice and peculation raged: "The Love of country and public virtue are annihilated. If Diogenes were alive and were to search America with candles, would he find an honest man?"[17] Obviously Ellery thought the philosopher would be wasting his time.

Congress had taken steps to curb misappropriation of public money by requiring every officer who handled government funds to subscribe to an oath that he would render an honest accounting of all monies entrusted to him. Those who refused to take such an oath were to be cashiered and rendered forever incapable of executing any office under Congress. Auditors attached to the army were to inspect accounts periodically. These measures checked wholesale graft, but with accelerating inflation could not stop it. Congress continued to emit paper; during February and March, $4,000,000 in new bills went into circulation.

Many people were making fortunes. Anyone who could raise the money bought as many shares as he could in privateers. This was practically a gilt-edged investment; even should one ship of three be taken by British cruisers, returns from the other two would give a speculator a profit of 100 per cent. And when captured ships and cargoes were sold in French and Spanish ports, or the West Indian Islands, returns were in "hard money"—not in Continental paper.

Contracting for the army was a lucrative proposition riddled with graft. "Pay-offs" and "kickbacks" were so common as to be complacently overlooked. Here again, if one had money he could make a great deal more. Clever men connived with crooked contractors to sell the Board of War shoddy blankets, poor flints—French flints were the best, as was French powder—underweight cannon balls, and diluted rum. Barrels of flour were too often liberally sanded, and salt provisions of poor quality. Edmund Burke earlier remarked that British contractors were savoring the *haut gout* of wartime profits; their American cousins were not lagging far behind. Although Congress corrected many evident evils, it was powerless to enforce its resolutions except over the armed forces and those in its immediate employ.

In General Orders, Washington appealed to the army to accept inevitable shortages: "Thank Heaven! our Country abounds with provision and with prudent management we need not apprehend want for any length of time. Defects in the Commissaries department, Contingencies of weather, and other temporary impediments have subjected and may again subject us to a deficiency for a few days, but soldiers! American soldiers! will despise the meanness of repining at such trifling strokes of Adversity. . . ."[18]

In private correspondence he admitted "strokes of Adversity" had not been exactly "trifling." He confided a true picture of the state of affairs to Brigadier General Cadwalader: "By death and desertion we have lost a good many Men since we came to this ground, and have encountered every species of hardship, that cold, wet, and hunger, and want of Cloathes were capable of producg." Contrary to his expectations, the soldiers had not mutinied "although, in the single article of Provisns, they have encountered enough to have occasioned one . . . as they have been (two or three times) days together, without Provisions, and once Six days without any of the Meat kind." Could "the poor Horses tell their tale, it would be in a strain still more lamentable."[19]

Dr. Benjamin Rush, until recently surgeon and physician general of the Middle District, Continental Army, visited Valley Forge in March. He found conditions appalling: "The encampment dirty and stinking, no forage for 7 days—1500 horses died from ye want of it. 3 Ounces of meal and 3 pounds of flour in 7 days. The Commander-in-Chief and all ye Major Generals live in houses out of ye camp." Rush was ambivalent about Washington, but certainly not about some of the major generals. A few months earlier he had written in his *Historical Notes*, under the heading "State and Disorder in the American army," that although Washington was *"the idol of America"* he was under the baneful influence of Generals Greene and Knox and "Col. Hamilton, one of his aids, a young man of 21 years of age." As to Major Generals Greene, Sullivan, Stirling, and Adam Stephan: "The 1st a sycophant to the general, timid, speculative, without enterprise; the 2nd, weak, vain, without dignity, fond of scribbling, in the field, a madman. The 3rd, a proud, vain, lazy, ignorant, drunkard. The 4th a sordid, boasting, cowardly sot." (His judgment was corrected in the case of Adam Stephan, court-martialed and cashiered in disgrace for drunkenness.) The state of the army was not impressive: "The troops dirty, undisciplined and ragged; guns fired 100 a day; pickets left 5 days and sentries 24 hours, without relief; bad bread; no order; universal disgust."

At about this time, Washington drew up "Thoughts Upon a Plan of Operation for Campaign 1778." He saw three options: first, to recapture Philadelphia; second, to attack New York; and third, "to lay quiet in a secure Camp and endeavour by every possible means to train and discipline our Army, thereby making our numbers (tho' small) as formidable as possible." The first two, which would require the help of militia, would "be attended with considerable expense; great waste of Military Stores, and Arms, and will call for great supplies of Provisions." The third would give the enemy time to receive reinforcements, to "spread

their baneful influence more extensively, and be a means of disgusting
our own People."

None of the three particularly appealed to him. If Philadelphia were
invested, Howe could withdraw by water; nothing was to be gained except the empty honor of driving the enemy from the city. An attack on
New York would be tremendously expensive, complicated, require a
complex cover plan, and rapid, secret convergence of forces. The army
was not ready to take the field; levies from the various states had not yet
come forward as he had hoped. Both his first and second plans depended
essentially on co-operation of militia, which if it failed him, as he thought
it probably would, would turn into total disaster. As of the end of March,
he had taken no decision. Many factors would bear: the state of Continental currency, the credit situation, the temper and expectations of the
people. This last he considered of decisive importance, for "in such a
contest as the one we are engaged in," everything depended "on the
Spirit and willingness of the People."[20] He leaned cautiously to the third
option.

He circulated his "Thoughts" to general officers and asked for comments. The replies were not particularly helpful, as some favored the first
course, some the second, and several the third. He would have to wait to
see how the situation developed.

Howe's officers were vastly enjoying the winter in Philadelphia. Amateur playwrights produced several farces; London favorites were resur-
rected. These theatricals, in which local belles took part, relieved the monotony of garrison duty. Balls mitigated boredom and afforded young
officers opportunity to appear to advantage. Taverns did a flourishing
business, there was no lack of good wine, madeira, cognac, and champagne. Certainly, life in the City of the Quakers had never been as gay as
it was in the winter of 1777–78.

America Takes Her Rank Among the Nations

The King's First Minister, afflicted with another seizure of despairing inadequacy, again implored his master to permit him to retire; he had just learned that Opposition had closed ranks and was sending the Marquis of Granby to Hayes with yet another plea to Chatham to assume active leadership. Lord North thought it essential "in this very alarming crisis . . . to employ the greatest man of business and the most consummate statesman that ever existed"; the increasing responsibilities were "infinitely more than Lord North can undertake"; if the King insisted that he continue to bear the burden, "National disgrace will be the consequence." Accordingly, he advised his royal master to send for Chatham, the only man of eminence who had enough credit with the Americans to end the war. Having dispatched this plea to Queen's House, the noble lord fled London for a day of solace in the country.

His Majesty received this epistle late Saturday evening and was at his desk before eight o'clock the following morning. He was willing, he wrote, to strengthen North's administration, but was "extremely indifferent whether Lord Granby goes or does not go with the abject message of the Rockingham party this day to Hayes; I will certainly send none to that place." And he concluded, ". . . if I will not by your advice take the step I look on as disgraceful to myself, and destruction to my country and family, are you resolved agreable to the example of the D. of Grafton at the hour of danger to desert me."

Lord North was in no mood to be flattered, cajoled, or threatened; he wanted to get out. "In much quieter times" he had "repeatedly requested His Majesty's permission to withdraw." Now "the times are become more arduous and difficult, and Lord North consequently more unequal to his situation." If the King was resolved to retain him as First Minister, the "almost certain consequence" would be "the absolute ruin of His Majesty's affairs." He therefore supplicated the King to choose "a Leader for the Administration out of some other quarter, if not out of the Opposition."

Lord North was surely unique among men of his class—rather than seeking power he wanted above all to divest himself of it. He did, however, undertake to stay until his royal master should find a suitable replacement.[1] The King, who had no intention of looking for a replacement for a satisfactorily subservient First Minister who could manage the House of Commons, replied curtly, expressing his pleasure at Lord North's "determination not to desert at this hour."[2] The appropriate word was not "determination," a quality the noble lord notably lacked.

The King was now pressing Lord North to get the peace commissioners on the way. He conceived it desirable to end the war with America as soon as possible in order "to be enabled with redoubled ardor to avenge the faithless and insolent conduct of France." Although he gagged on the word "independence," he thought it might be helpful to keep open a channel of communication to the scheming and "insidious" Dr. Franklin.[3] One such channel, and a most unlikely one, was James Hutton, a venerable Moravian remarkable for piety, who had been a close friend of Franklin's when the doctor was in London. Hutton, almost totally deaf (he carried a huge ear trumpet), was in high favor at St. James's, and very probably at the direct instigation of the King went to Paris to renew his friendship with the senior commissioner and sound him out. Hutton had several long conversations with Franklin and Deane, but nothing came of them. Subsequently, the doctor wrote him, addressing him as "My Dear Old Friend," and said that although he had no proposition to make, he had some advice:

> You have lost by this mad war, and the barbarity with which it has been carried on, not only the government and commerce of America, and the public revenues and private wealth arising from that commerce, but what is more, you have lost the esteem, respect, friendship and affection of all those great and growing people, who consider you at present, and whose posterity will consider you, as the worst and wickedest nation on earth.

Franklin then threw out a few casual suggestions as to terms America might consider: "In proposing terms, you should not only grant such as the necessity of your affairs may evidently oblige you to grant, but such additional over as may shew your generosity." He suggested the British "throw in" Canada, Nova Scotia, and the Floridas.[4]

Shortly after Hutton received this letter, an enfeebled Chatham rose to speak in the House of Lords. He mumbled in a voice scarcely audible, gasped, and collapsed. The King, pleased to be rid of "this trumpet of sedition," observed only that his "political exit" would no doubt persuade Lord North to remain in office.

With the American war relegated to a position of secondary importance, the focus of activity shifted from Germain's office to the Admiralty. Sandwich and Keppel were in complete agreement that defense of England and Ireland was "the first object." Keppel was worried; on April 16 he wrote the First Lord "upon the critical situation of this country regarding its fleet. One mistake or accident ruins all." He urged no further detachments than absolutely essential. Gibraltar must be supplied—the "Rock" could not withstand a protracted siege—otherwise, the fleet must be kept in hand.[5] The King was impatient; both he and Germain wanted to send a squadron to intercept D'Estaing at the Strait of Gibraltar. Keppel scotched this idea in a memorandum to His Majesty: the "Great Fleet," the "Bulwark and real safety of these dominions, I cannot but think that in every view of it, It should be *preserved in Force* superior to the Enemies If Possible, and depend on good Intelligence for Adopting any *separation* . . . of it . . . detachment & separation is dangerous & risks too much."[6] Sandwich agreed.

On April 13 D'Estaing's squadron cleared Toulon. Silas Deane and Conrad Alexandre Gérard were passengers; the former, recalled by Congress to be replaced by John Adams; the latter, to present his credentials as Louis XVI's minister to the United States. British intelligence operatives had been diligent. From their knowledge that Deane and Gérard were sailing and of cargo taken aboard they correctly deduced the destination to be America. Actually, the Admiralty learned from an agent in De Sartine's Ministry of Maine that the count's destination was America, but considering the source it was essential to confirm this information. Fast sailers were disposed to track D'Estaing after he passed Gibraltar. If he set a westerly course, conjecture would become certainty. Tracking ships were then to bend on all the canvas they could carry and head for home.

Continental ship *Ranger*, Captain John Paul Jones, the first ship of war to display the American flag and to receive a salute in European waters, finished her refit at L'Orient in February; Jones brought her to Brest, where for two months she lay alongside quays. Her crew was unhappy and rebellious; their friends on privateers were making small fortunes. Captain Jones, anxious to begin distressing "the Enemies of the United States by sea, or otherwise," may have felt equally frustrated but was sufficiently discreet to disguise such sentiments. During some of this time he was in Holland on a secret mission for Dr. Franklin.

While Jones was so engaged, a furious debate between Franklin and Arthur Lee concerning *Ranger*'s employment raged at Passy—Franklin, a peerless psychological warrior, planned to use this aggressive young captain, who had confided to him some of his "improbable designs," on operations off the coasts of the British Isles. Lee, a jealous and vindictive schemer, under the influence of his confidential secretary, an American he trusted but who was a British agent, wanted to order *Ranger* back to America. Franklin listened courteously, and blandly replied that Jones would carry out the instructions he, the doctor, had some time previously issued.

Franklin, a gentleman of normally equable temper, had taken about all he proposed to take from Lee, who was now writing his brothers that the doctor and Silas Deane were a pair of embezzlers who had mishandled public accounts. On April 1 Franklin wrote him: "Sir, There is a Stile in some of your Letters, I observe it particularly in the last, whereby superior Merit is assumed to yourself in point of Care and Attention to Business and Blame is insinuated on your Colleagues without making yourself accountable by a direct Charge, of Negligence or Unfaithfulness, which has the Appearance of being as artful as it is unkind." Lee replied with an abusive letter, and on April 3 Franklin wrote him that he had too much to do to waste precious time in angry altercation. He had borne Lee's "Magisterial snubbings and Rebukes" without reply; his concern was "for the Honour & Success of our Mission, which would be hurt by our Quarrelling." The doctor pitied Lee's "Sick Mind, which is forever tormenting itself, with its Jealousies, Suspicions and Fancies. . . . If you do not cure yourself of this temper it will end in Insanity of which it is the Syptomatic Forerunner . . . God preserve you from so terrible an evil; and for his sake pray suffer me to live in quiet."[7]

Ranger sailed from Brest on April 10; Jones set course for the Irish Sea. En route, he sank a brigantine bound for Ostend; two days later he captured a ship laden with porter and merchandise, put a prize crew aboard, and ordered her to Brest. Jones had not, however, ventured into the Irish Sea with the primary object of taking a few prizes. In Paris he and Franklin had agreed that one way to distress the British was by raiding unsuspecting coastal towns. Jones had tentatively selected Whitehaven, on the southern (English) shore of Solway Firth, as a likely target. He had been born near Dumfries on the Scottish shore; he knew the local waters and coasts, and when he learned that scores of small merchantmen and fishing boats were lying in Whitehaven, he decided to make a surprise descent to burn the shipping. An imaginative and audacious foray would be the last thing unwary seamen and townsfolk and the indolent militiamen stationed in two small forts guarding the harbor would anticipate. If things went well at Whitehaven, other raids would follow; the psychological effect on the inhabitants of inadequately protected coastal towns would be out of all proportion to any material damage Jones might inflict.

He planned to land just before dawn on April 18, but contrary winds thwarted him. Two days later he learned that His Majesty's sloop of war *Drake* was at Carrickfergus in Belfast Lough. He determined to lure her out and engage her. Again, winds rising to gale force foiled him. At dawn on April 22 wind and sea subsided; the sky was clear. Captain Jones wrote: "The weather was once more fair, though the three kingdoms, as far as the eye could reach, were covered with snow."[8]

To this time, the British had no idea an American ship of war was in their home waters; Jones felt perfectly safe and decided to return to Whitehaven. With some difficulty he persuaded thirty-one members of *Ranger's* crew to accompany him as a landing party. The party proceeded in two boats to the pier, which they reached at dawn. Leaving some of the men under the master and the first lieutenant to fire the shipping, the captain led the rest to one of the small forts, which they entered through the embrasures. As Jones had anticipated, the sentinels were sound asleep in the guardhouse. He locked them up, spiked the guns, and proceeded to the second fort, where he repeated the process.

In the meantime, the parties supposed to set fires had not done so; Jones managed to get a fire going on only one ship. By this time the sun was up—and so were the affrighted citizens of Whitehaven. "The inhabitants now began to appear in thousands, and individuals ran hastily toward me. I stood between them and the ship on fire, with a pistol in my hand, and ordered them to retire, which they did with precipitation. The flames had already caught the rigging, and begun to ascend the mainmast; the sun was a full hour's march above the horizon, and as sleep no longer ruled the world, it was time to retire."[9]

A second adventure later the same day did not enhance Jones's reputation. This was his attempt to kidnap the Earl of Selkirk from his home on St. Mary's Isle, and to use him as hostage to secure better treatment and the possible release of American seamen held as prisoners. Fortunately for himself, the earl was absent; members of the party sent to take him contented themselves with a sheetful of his lordship's silver plate. Lady Selkirk testified that Jones's sailors were decent and polite.*

Two days later, *Ranger* was again off Carrickfergus. *Drake's* captain

---

* Jones later bought and returned the silver.

decided to investigate. Jones wrote: "The tide was unfavorable so that the *Drake* worked out but slowly . . . at length the *Drake* weathered the point, and having led her out to about mid-channel, I suffered her to come within hail. The *Drake* hoisted English colors, and at the same instant the American stars were displayed on board the *Ranger*." *Drake* hailed, "demanding what ship it was. I directed the Master to answer 'the American Continental ship *Ranger*; that we waited for them, and desired that they would come on'; the sun was now a little more than an hour from setting, and it was therefore time to begin."[10]

Jones crossed *Drake*'s bow, raked her deck from stem to stern, and maneuvered to fire a crucial broadside; "the action was warm, close and obstinate. It lasted an hour and four minutes, when the enemy called for quarters." *Drake*'s hull was "very much galled"; topside, she was a wreck: ". . . the sails and rigging cut to pieces, her masts and yards all wounded."[11] Jones put a prize crew aboard her and directed the prize master to follow *Ranger* to Brest. Jones had two killed and six wounded; *Drake*, forty-two, including both captain and first lieutenant. Captain Jones had won his first sea fight in clear view of hundreds of spectators and had imposed his will on an unco-operative and rebellious crew. Indeed, when he announced he planned to engage *Drake*, his sailors were on the verge of open mutiny: "I ran every chance of being killed or thrown overboard."[12] But he faced them down.

Jones's exploit at Whitehaven threw the citizens into a panic; they hastily drew up an appeal to Sandwich to station cruisers in the Irish Sea to protect their town and to track and sink the insolent Yankee pirate. Panic was by no means confined to Whitehaven. Stocks tumbled, insurance rates rose, the militia was hastily called out. Walpole wrote Mann: "We shall be in no want of sights this summer every county will have a camp of its own: the coasts will be amused with seiges. An American privateer has attempted Whitehaven and plundered Lord Selkirk's house."[13]

The captain was not going to venture a return to Brest through the Irish Sea with his valuable prize, for *Drake* was the first British ship of war to be taken in battle. Jones appreciated to the full the psychological impact his victory would produce in England and was aware of the excitement it would generate in France and Holland. He therefore set his course to the north, sailed down the west coast of Ireland, and when he thought himself clear of English cruisers, steered for Brest. On the night of May 8 he entered the harbor. Hailed by a French frigate and asked to identify himself, he replied: "The American Continental ship *Ranger*, of eighteen guns, Captain Paul Jones, and the man-of-war prize is His Brittanic Majesty's late ship the *Drake*, of twenty guns."[14] Captain Paul Jones, United States Navy, had brought the war to Great Britain's door and fractured the myth of inherent British naval superiority. Ship to ship, gun to gun, man to man, American sailors could hold their own on the seas.

His Majesty's captains and seamen would soon have to deal with a more menacing maritime threat than that posed by Captain Jones and Continental ship *Ranger*. News of D'Estaing's departure reached London almost two weeks after the admiral sailed from Toulon. Germain was apprehensive the French fleet would be joined "by all the Marine force of the Rebellious provinces, and in that case will be able to attack and destroy our fleet in those seas. . . ." The secretary, lamenting that his cabinet colleagues had not accepted his earlier advice to send a fleet to intercept D'Estaing at the Straits, now entreated Lord North "maturely to consider of the very alarming situation of this country"; a strong squadron should be sent to reinforce Howe. This action, he hoped, would "probably prevent the disgrace of this Kingdom."[15] North consulted Sandwich; the tentative decision was to send a squadron under command of Rear Admiral Hyde Parker to Halifax at once. Germain vigorously opposed sending Parker, who upon arrival at Halifax would automatically come under command of Rear Admiral James Gambier, an incompetent in whose abilities no one save Sandwich reposed the slightest confidence. The outcome of this ministerial wrangle was that Vice-admiral the Honourable John Byron, known to sailors as "Foul-weather Jack," who some time previously had been alerted to sail, and was senior to Gambier, was assigned to command.

The King, well informed in naval matters, was concerned as to the condition of the "Great Fleet." He had visited H.M.S. *Victory* and was pleased; he planned to travel with his Queen to Portsmouth to inspect the dockyards and Keppel's ships preparing there for sea. Sandwich wrote the admiral suggesting he arrange "whatever may be necessary for their proper reception and amusement." Should Keppel be ready to sail when Their Majesties were on the spot, "it would naturally be the highest entertainment they could receive; but serious business must always have the preference even over the amusement of crowned heads."[16]

Although the King insisted on informality, the royal visit caused no end of trouble, as all such do. But His Majesty *was* informal; he enjoyed every minute of his stay. He felt his visit had improved morale, and it no doubt had. He chatted with seamen, marines, and dockyard workers. He was indefatigable; he tired his aides and the assorted admirals who dined with him daily. The whole business bored the Earl of Sandwich excessively; the First Lord was losing a full week of gambling nights. The King had planned to leave Portsmouth on a Thursday; he was so entranced he decided to stay over a few days and wrote Lord North he would remain at Portsmouth until several ships ordered to join Byron's squadron sailed: ". . . this has put great allacrity into all of them. . . . I have no object but to be of use if that is answered I am compleatly happy." George III would have made a far better admiral than most he had.

Since receiving recommendations from the committee appointed to visit Valley Forge, Congress had devoted many hours to debate on the subject of the army. Washington had urged upon the gentlemen who conferred with him the vital necessity of offering some inducement to officers to stay for the duration. Far too many had resigned and others were seriously considering doing so. Pay, perquisites, and retirement benefits offered were not sufficient to persuade men of education and ambition to continue in service or for younger men to seek commissions.

Thomas Burke summarized the problem to Governor Richard Caswell of North Carolina: The present situation afforded officers "no prospects but of pain, danger and ruin to their private fortunes." At the same time, many men who were protected by officers' valor and exertions were "emassing princely fortunes." Unless half pay for life could be promised officers who would agree to serve for the duration, and generous pensions established "for Widows of officers who may be slain, . . . we cannot long expect to have an Army." Delegates who had visited Valley Forge agreed that unless something of this kind were done the army would soon disintegrate "because the Officers, being unable even to subsist on their pay, have already expended much of their private property, and would be entirely ruined were they to continue."

Many members strongly opposed the general's recommendations and held that officers "ought to be actuated by the principles of patriotism and public spirit, and ought to disdain motives of private interest." They should deem the opportunity to serve their country and to earn its gratitude ample compensation for the hardships and dangers they suffered. Gentlemen who indulged in this flag-waving argument—which Thomas Burke described as "specious"—were as well aware as anyone that neither officers nor their widows and fatherless children could subsist on gratitude. What they really feared, Burke thought, was the specter of a standing army in time of peace "to be at the disposal of the Congress," and that "the rights of the States of appointing the regimental officers will be reduced to nothing." In times of crisis, Congress could call for the militia; at other times—so opponents of the measure argued—this horde of idle pensioners would be battening on public funds.

There was, of course, a constitutional issue involved, for the Continental Congress had no authority but that freely granted by states. Congress could not legally provide for any peace establishment. Fears of a standing army carried no great weight with Burke: "The few in each State whom the fatigues and consequent infirmities of a long and painful War will induce to indulge an indolent ease" were not, in his opinion, "an object of any consequence."[17]

Francis Lewis (New York) reported Congress had met for a week *de die in diem,* debating in secret the subject of half pay. Nothing had been determined; "The half-pay scheme meets with great opposition." Lewis's description of the argument as "warm" was obviously an understatement, for sixteen members declared they would "not speak more than Ten minutes, seldom more than once, never more than twice," and would "unite in supporting order and pursuing decency and politeness in debate."[18]

While Congress dithered over the question of half pay, scores of officers had given up hope of relief and had submitted resignations. Washington, pained that this important matter could continue to meet with difficulties and delays, wrote a Virginia delegate emphasizing the necessity for speedy action: Officers "will not be persuaded to sacrifice all views of present interest, and encounter the numerous vicissitudes of War, in the defence of their Country, unless she will be generous on her part, to make a decent provision for their future support." Although he would not "pronounce absolutely, that we shall have no Army if the establishment fails," he was convinced "the Army we have will be without discipline, without energy, incapable of acting with vigor, and destitute of those Elements necessary to promise success, on the one hand, or to withstand the shocks of adversity, on the other."[19] The commander in chief did not exclude "the Idea of Patriotism." He recognized it as a powerful motivating force, but did not believe it alone could support a long and bloody war. Those who relied on it entirely would find themselves "deceived in the end. . . . We must take the passions of Men as Nature has given them." This letter was sent from Valley Forge in April—the army had last been paid in January.[20]

What held that army together? Certainly, Washington's obvious dedication to the cause, his devotion to the soldiers, his complete integrity, were decisive factors. Although outwardly invariably calm and dispassionate, passages in his personal correspondence clearly suggest that inwardly he was raging at the manifest injustices his army suffered at the hands of a dilatory, suspicious, and unsympathetic Congress. He of course knew which men were devoting their energies to blocking essential reform—the New Englanders, whose radical republicanism found no particular favor with him. But he was diplomatic, prudent, and a superb politician who understood the temper of Congress and knew precisely when and how to advocate his policies and to apply the discreet pressure necessary for their acceptance.

In personal letters he was often distinctly outspoken. The indecision of Congress galled him exceedingly and was "productive of a variety of inconveniences." A second point was "the *jealousy* which Congress unhappily entertains of the Army, and which, if reports are right, some members labour to establish." Washington felt such sentiments were based in prejudice, and the activities of delegates who fostered them, injurious. He could not comprehend fear of some "that standing Armies are dangerous to a State." In other countries, this distrust was founded in the fact that officers and soldiers were "hirelings"; in America they were citizens: "We should all be considered, Congress, Army, &ts. as one people, embarked in one Cause, in one interest, acting on the same principle and to the same End."

He thought the drawing of distinctions, as some delegates were doing, encouraged jealousies and served no good purpose. This attitude was unjust, he wrote,

> because, No Order of Men in the thirteen States have paid a more sanctimonious regard to their proceedings than the Army, and, indeed it may be questioned whether there has been that scrupulous adherence had to them by any other for without arrogance, or the smallest deviation from truth, it may be said, that no history, now extant, can furnish an instance of an Army's suffering such uncommon hardships as ours have done, and bearing them with the same patience and Fortitude.

He and his officers had seen "Men without cloathes to cover their Nakedness, without Blankets to lay on, without Shoes, by which their Marches might be traced by the Blood from their feet, and almost as often without Provisions as with; Marching through frost and Snow, and at Christmas taking up their Winter Quarters within a day's March of the enemy, without a House or Hutt to cover them till they would be built and submitting to it without a Murmur, is a mark of patience and obedience which in my opinion can scarce be parallel'd."[21]

Washington's indictment of Congress was entirely deserved. The caliber of delegates had sadly deteriorated. Many who had signed the declaration had left to assume important posts: John Adams and Benjamin Franklin were in Paris; Hancock had returned to Massachusetts; others had taken up commissions in the army, were serving their states, or had retired to a less hectic life. Of those present, some were callous and others indifferent. Some who quailed before responsibility were anxious to pass sticky questions to committees or to the Board of War.

Individual delegates could (and did) write their governors imploring co-operation, as did Washington and his senior generals, who had developed the arts of exhortation and persuasion to a remarkable degree. But even when governors and assemblies accepted supply responsibilities, they had no way effectually to enforce their desires. They had to retain good will and naturally hesitated to confiscate livestock, blankets, clothing, shoes, and other necessaries urgently required by the army. And purchasing was not easy. No farmer was anxious to trade half a dozen hogs for even a barrow-load of Continental paper. Commissary officers, who normally had to deal in promises, tried to alleviate food shortages, but state governors feared to allow too much livestock to be driven across their boundaries to disappear forever with prospects of eventual remuneration dim at best. Truly, as Thomas Paine had written, these were the times that tried men's souls. The winter of 1777–78 proved that too many Americans were "Sunshine Patriots."

Copies of Lord North's Conciliatory Bill arrived in America in mid-April; Howe immediately had a large number printed for circulation. Washington wondered whether this "insidious proceeding" was genuine or had been "contrived in Philadelphia." Provenance of the document was immaterial, but the bill was "certainly founded on principles of the most wicked, diabolical baseness, meant to poison the minds of the people, and detach the wavering, at least, from our cause." He thought it expedient for Congress to investigate the bill and expose its "injustice, delusion and fraud."[22] Laurens agreed and wrote Governor George Clinton of New York that the bill was spurious, concocted by Howe in Philadelphia.

Laurens referred Washington's letter, with copies of the bill, to a subcommittee, which reported its findings on April 22. Members of the committee were inclined to believe the "paper being industriously circulated" was probably not a propaganda trick, but reflected a variety of British misconceptions, among them that Americans were weary of war and would accede to Lord North's terms for the sake of peace. The ministry probably hoped, too, that the measure would "detach some weak men in America from the cause of freedom and virtue." King George would need his fleets and armies at home; every day made it "more manifest" that since the British could not possibly subjugate America, their interest was "to extricate themselves from the war upon any terms."[23]

The subcommittee had then proceeded to rip the Conciliatory Bill to pieces. Not only was it a clear indication of Great Britain's weakness, but also a manifestation of her wickedness and guileful insincerity. It appeared evident to the committee

> that the said bills are intended to operate upon the hopes and fears of the good people of these states, so as to create divisions among them, and a defection from the common cause, now by the blessing of Divine Providence, drawing near to a favorable issue; that they are the sequel of the insidious plan, which from the days of the stamp act down to the present time, hath involved this country in contention and bloodshed; and that, as in other cases, so in this, although circumstances may force them, at times to recede from their unjustifiable claims, there can be no doubt but they will, as heretofore, upon the first favorable occasion, again display that lust of domination which hath rent in twain the mighty Empire of Britain.[24]

The committee stated its opinion that any persons or group of men who presumed to deal with the commissioners "ought to be considered and treated as open and avowed enemies of these United States." Further, members of the committee believed "the United States cannot, with propriety, hold any conference or treaty with any commissioners" until Great Britain withdrew her "armies and fleets," or else, "in positive and express terms, acknowledge the independence of the said states." The report was read and debated; Congress unanimously approved and confirmed it, and ordered it to be published. Delegates considered this a good day's work and adjourned until the morrow.[25]

The commander in chief learned in late April that his constant efforts to effect the exchange of Major General Charles Lee had finally met with success. He wrote Lee a cordial letter, congratulating him on his "restoration" to the country and to the army. He asked Lee to come to Valley Forge as soon as he conveniently could "to take an active part with us."[26] Possibly he had been attracted to Charles Lee because Lee's character—flamboyant, extrovert, expansive—was almost precisely the opposite of his own. He respected him because Lee was truly a professional; he admired him because Lee, once a dashing lieutenant colonel in a famous British cavalry regiment, had chosen to become an American and had drawn his sword in her fight for independence. Washington had many attributes; one he unfortunately lacked was the ability correctly to assess the motives that drove many lesser men, men not inspired with his dedicated idealism.

On the last day of April more dramatic news reached Valley Forge. Simeon Deane had arrived in Casco Bay (now in the state of Maine) aboard French frigate La Sensible with copies of the treaties negotiated by the American commissioners, and was hastening to York, where he arrived on May 2. The commander in chief was not surprised; he had long anticipated this news: "France appears to have acted with politic generosity towards us, and to have time her declaration in our favor most admirably for her own interests and the abasing of her ancient rival."[27]

The Continental Army celebrated May Day "with mirth and jollity." Maypoles were erected in every regimental area; the soldiers, "their hats adorned with white blossoms," paraded and paid due honors to King Tamany.† The various parades circled the camp to music provided by fifes and drums, "Huzzaing as they passed the poles." Later, whiskey was given out, and "each man retired to his own hut without any accident hapening throughout the whole day."[28] Obviously, the commander in chief no longer suffered morale problems.

Nor in the future would he have to endure Conway, who had submit-

† "King Tamany" was a seventeenth-century Delaware Indian chief, sometimes facetiously canonized as a patron saint of the independent United States of North America.

ted his resignation in the confident expectation that Congress would not accept it. To his mortification, Congress did. This cleared the way for appointment of Baron von Steuben as major general inspector of the Continental Army.

Washington had received a note form Simeon Deane "with the outlines of the good tidings" and communicated the news unofficially to his officers: "No event was ever received with a more heart-felt joy." Laurens summoned Congress to meet in unscheduled session on the night of Saturday, May 2. The treaties, including secret codicils, were read, and President Laurens hurried off an express with a note to Washington.[29] The Virginia delegates wrote Governor Patrick Henry they found His Most Christian Majesty had "been governed by principles of Magnanimity and true generosity, taking no advantage of our circumstances, but acting as if we were in the plenitude of power." York rejoiced: Samuel Chase declared the French alliance "a singular unmerited mark of God's favor and protection: America has now taken her rank among the nations." He exhorted Governor Thomas Johnson, Jr., of Maryland to "exert every means" to support the war. This called for "speedy and liberal loans of money" and "a respectable Army."[30]

The question of half pay for officers at retirement continued to agitate delegates, who had spent days and weeks in debate, much of it heated. Laurens viewed the scheme as "Altogether unjust and unconstitutional in its nature and full of dangerous consequences." He did not want to be obstinate; he would go along if the majority wished it. He felt with others that Washington had faced Congress with an unhappy dilemma: either provide for the officers "in terms dictated . . . or lose all the valuable Soldiers among them." He believed the measures proposed would go "against the grain of the People . . . Republicans will at a proper time withdraw a Grant which shall appear to have been extorted."[31]

As Laurens penned his letter, the commander in chief was engaged in planning festivities to celebrate the French alliance. Due credit was accorded Divine Providence: "It having pleased the Almighty Ruler of the Universe propitiously to defend the Cause of the United American States and finally by raising us up a powerful Friend among the Princes of the Earth to establish our liberty and Independence up[on] lasting foundations, it becomes us to set apart a day for greatfully acknowledging the Divine goodness and celebrating the important Event which we owe to his benign Interposition."[32] The celebration would commence at "half after eleven" when troops were to take position: Major General Lord Stirling commanding the right wing, La Fayette the left, and Baron de Kalb the brigades arrayed in rear. First, "discourses" by brigade chaplains, then a thirteen-gun salute, then a *feu de joie* fired by the entire army; then, upon signal, "the whole Army will Huzza! Long Live the

King of France." A second salute, a second *feu de joie,* then "Huzza! And long live the friendly European Powers." Finally, a "last discharge of thirteen Pieces of Artillery," followed by a third *feu de joie* and a "Huzza! To the American States."[33] Rum would then be served to the troops.

All went according to plan. Spectators were duly impressed. The troops moved with "animation," their uniforms clean, their arms in good order. "During the whole of the review, the utmost military decorum was preserved." When troops marched off the Grand Parade, officers marched to "elegant marquees" where an abundant collation awaited. "The officers approached the place of entertainment in different columns, thirteen abreast, and closely linked together in each other's arms. The appearance was pretty enough. The number of officers composing each line signified the thirteen American States; and the interweaving of arms a complete union and most perfect confederation."[34]

An excellent band of music provided entertainment. Washington was animated, mingling with the officers and their ladies, among whom were "Mrs. Washington, the Countess of Stirling, Lady Kitty her daughter, Mrs. Greene." There was no lack of wine; countless toasts were proposed "descriptive of the spirit of free men." The commander in chief "wore a countenance of uncommon delight and complacence"; the French officers seemed "peculiarly pleased." At six o'clock "the company broke up, and his Excellency returned to headquarters." A happy, triumphant day in Washington's career, and one he would long remember. "What may be reckoned somewhat remarkable, not one accident happened to lessen or disturb the joy of the day."[35] The commander in chief marked the day by pardoning two soldiers "misled by designing Trayters" who lay under sentence of death. Lesser malefactors were likewise pardoned. On this "truly joyful day" Washington emptied prison cells at Valley Forge.

In a long letter to his wife, Baron de Kalb described the ceremonies and festivities. Louis XVI's action had won the hearts of the Americans: "No means could have been better adapted to bruise the colossal power of England, and to snatch this great country forever from its allegiance." At the "grand banquet . . . wine, meats, and liquors abounded, and happiness and contentment were expressed on every countenance." French officers and their King were repeatedly huzzaed and toasted: "It was a fine day for us, and a great one for General Washington. Let me say that no one could be more worthy of this good fortune. His integrity, humanity and love for the just cause of his country, as well as his other virtues, receive and merit the veneration of all men."[36]

Congress was fidgety. Delegates wanted to know what plans were being formulated for the campaign of 1778. On May 8 Washington summoned a full-scale Council of War. Present: Gates, Greene, Stirling, Arnold, Mifflin, La Fayette, De Kalb, John Armstrong, Von Steuben, Knox, and Du Portail. After summarizing both his own and enemy situations, he dwelt on deficiencies that would affect operations. He was not optimistic. He estimated Howe's strength in Philadelphia at 10,000 (it was actually almost double this—19,300, including 1,500 Provincials) and anticipated Continental strength would not exceed 20,000 rank and file able and fit. He could not depend on substantial assistance from militia. Ordnance and stocks of ammunition would not support siege operations. For some time, the commissary department had been "in such a defective and disordered state" he could form no accurate estimate of prospects for provisioning. He closed his pessimistic summary with a request that participants deliver their opinions to him in writing. His generals decided unanimously that forces were insufficient to besiege either New York or Philadelphia, and recommended the army "remain on the defensive and await events; without attempting any offensive operation of consequence, unless the future circumstances of the enemy should afford a farther opportunity than at present exists."[37]

On May 20 Major General Charles Lee, who had been received at Valley Forge three weeks earlier with military panoply, returned from a visit to Congress in York. Washington rode out to greet him personally and gave him command of the right wing of the army. Elias Boudinot, commissary general of prisoners, the man responsible for Lee's exchange, had little use for him. "He immediately began to cabal against Gen[l] Washington and to quarrel with Marquis Lafayette"; Lee had assured Boudinot "that Gen[l] Washington was ruining the whole Cause." Boudinot had spent a night with Lee in New York—where Admiral Viscount Howe had assigned his captive a commodious house, fully staffed —to arrange for his exchange and Lee had then talked as he habitually did: indiscreetly. This man Washington so admired and trusted had treated Boudinot to a diatribe and asserted "the Improbability of our Troops under such an ignorant Commander-in-Chief—not fit to command a Sergeant's guard—ever withstanding British Grenadiers and Light Infantry." The commissary general was deeply shocked and therefore "could not but entertain the greatest Jealousy of the integrity of Gen[l] Lee." Boudinot thought him mentally unbalanced.[38] Why he never reported the substance of these conversations to Washington is a mystery.

Washington's agents in Philadelphia kept him up to date on activities in the city: "Every piece of intelligence from Philadelphia makes me think it more and more probable, that the enemy are preparing to evacuate it . . . there are some reasons that induce a suspicion they may intend for New York." He wished to be in instant readiness to respond to any move the British made; he directed Quartermaster General Nathanael Greene to "strain every nerve to prepare without delay the necessary provisions"; ordered Knox to alert his artillery to move "on the

first notice"; and arranged for stocks of food to be collected at depots between Coryell's Ferry on the Delaware and the North River. "No time is
to be lost."[39]

Two days before Lee returned to the army, British officers in Philadelphia staged a gala for Admiral Viscount Howe and General Sir
William, who was to be relieved on the morrow as His Majesty's "General in America." This was the famous *MISCHIANZA,* an afternoon of
lavish pageantry followed by a night of dining, dancing, drinking, gambling, and no little love-making. It is difficult to understand how the general and his more modest brother could have sanctioned this expensive,
vulgar, and garish display.‡

While some of Howe's sycophantic juniors undoubtedly regretted his
departure, most citizens of Philadelphia certainly did not. An officer who
served there under Cornwallis later wrote: "During the winter a very unfortunate inattention was shown to the feelings of the inhabitants, whose
satisfaction should have been vigilantly consulted, both from gratitude
and from interest." Here, where the British had many supporters and
could have won over many more, Howe took no effective steps to curb
the depredations of Redcoats and Hessians: "The soldiers insulted and
plundered [the citizens]; and their houses were occupied as barracks
without any compensation." The immorality their commanding general's
personal behavior encouraged in the younger officers shocked staid Philadelphians: ". . . individual officers were even indecent enough to introduce their mistresses into the mansions of their hospitable entertainers."

For the royal cause, the winter of 1777–78 was a calendar of lost opportunities. The King's general in America, anxiously waiting to go
home, indulged his habitual indolence and his penchant for pleasure. Although he openly expressed contempt for the ragged Americans at Valley Forge, he hesitated to attack them or even seriously to harry them.

Sir Henry Clinton, K.B., assumed command of His Majesty's Army in
the former colonies on May 24. He was not too happy with the assignment, and later wrote: "The great change which public Affairs had un-
dergone, in Europe as well as America . . . had so clouded every prospect of a successful issue to the unfortunate contest we were engaged in
that no officer who had the least anxious regard for his professional fame
would court a charge so hopeless as this now appeared likely to be. For
neither honor nor credit could be expected from it, but on the contrary a
considerable portion of blame, however unmerited, seemed to be almost
inevitable."[40]

The day before he relieved Howe, Clinton received Germain's instructions to detach several units to the West Indies and Florida: "When

‡ "This entertainment was probably the most magnificent exhibition of extravagance and folly ever witnessed in America."

these detachments have been made, or while they are making, Philadelphia is to be evacuated; all the troops to be embarked, with everything belonging to the army, and to proceed thence to New York, where they will await the issue of the negotiation, which the commissioners have been authorized to propose to the Congress." Obviously, Germain had made not the slightest attempt to examine the situation or he would have known at once there was no possibility of lifting Clinton's army, with its ordnance, ammunition, horses, provisions, and assorted impedimenta by sea to New York. Clinton immediately wrote Germain he "found it impracticable to embark the forces in order to proceed to New York by water, as there are not transports enough to receive the whole at once and therefore a great part of the cavalry, all our provision train and the persons whose attachment to the Government has rendered them objects of vengeance to the enemy must have been left behind. . . . These reasons have induced me to resolve on marching through Jersey."

℀ 5

Will Mr. Washington Attack?

William Pitt, Earl of Chatham, died on May 11, 1778. The House of Commons moved a state funeral and ordered a monument to be erected at public expense. The earl's debts, amounting to £20,000, would be liquidated by the Treasury; his widow was granted £4,000 a year, with reversion to her eldest son. "With all his defects," Walpole wrote, Chatham would be "a capital historic figure. France dreaded his crutch to this very moment." In the Lords, Shelburne moved that the earl's colleagues walk in his funeral procession. The motion failed; the King was pleased.

"Lord Chatham was a meteor, and a glorious one . . . A minister that inspires great actions, must be a great minister and Lord Chatham will always appear so by comparison with his predecessors and successors. He retrieved our affairs, when ruined by a most incapable administration; and we are fallen into a worse state since he was removed." Walpole thought posterity would "allow more to his merit, than it is the present fashion to accord to it." The specter of Chatham in power would no longer haunt the dreams of M. le Comte de Vergennes.

Lieutenant General Burgoyne, a prisoner on parole, landed at Portsmouth on May 13, posted to London, requested an audience of the King and was firmly denied one.* His Majesty had no time for a general who had surrendered an army to rebels. Burgoyne asked that a Board of Enquiry be convened to hear his story; while he waited to exonerate himself, he talked with Rockingham, Fox, and other members of Opposition, and on May 26 appeared in the House of Commons, "which was so exceedingly crowded that they were forced to turn out the strangers, though Burgoyne begged they might stay and hear his defence."[1] The general asked for a committee of the House to hear him; he said "nothing hard on General Howe, did great justice to the Americans . . . he made great encomiums on General Schuyler."

Germain protested vigorously. As a prisoner on parole, Burgoyne had no right to state his case in the Commons. Fox and Temple Luttrell, always ready for a go at the American Secretary, castigated him severely. Luttrell "compared the conduct of Burgoyne with that of Lord George Germaine who, he said, had been promoted for disobedience and timidity."[2] "Lord George started up in the most violent rage, and clapping his hand on his sword, said, tho he was an old man, he would not hear such an insult from a young man, who was an assassin, and of the most wretched character."[3] This threw the House into a two-hour turmoil. Luttrell, who despised Germain, stalked out, inviting a duel. The speaker called him back. Germain apologized for laying his hand on his sword, and Luttrell "was forced to disclaim any farther resentment."

The motion for appointment of a select committee to hear Burgoyne was lost, and the Board of Enquiry he had requested ruled out. Gentleman Johnny, who promptly cast his future fortune with Opposition, was to be left to justify his conduct as best he could. Administration was not anxious to afford Opposition an opportunity to attack ministers responsible for the muddled planning that wrecked the expedition from Canada and lost an army.†

Lord North was yet again talking retirement; the King forestalled this plea by naming him warden of the Cinque Ports during pleasure. The First Lord humbly objected; he had expected to enjoy the sinecure for life. His Majesty would have none of it: "I daily find the evil of having put so many employments out of the power of the Crown, and for the rest of my life I will not conferr any in that mode but where constant

---

* Burgoyne had written Congress and Washington in February requesting permission to return to England as a prisoner on parole to defend himself against those determined to disgrace him. Washington replied he could sympathize with Burgoyne's feelings "as a man whose lot combines the calamity of ill health, the anxieties of Captivity, and the painful sensibility for a reputation, exposed where he most values it to the assaults of malice and detraction." He was happy Congress had acquiesced in the general's request, and wished him "a safe and agreeable passage, with a perfect restoration of . . . health."

† Burgoyne was later afforded an opportunity to justify his conduct before a committee of the House. The inquiry into his campaign and that of General Sir William Howe embarrassed Administration and was abruptly terminated when the King prorogued Parliament. The inquiry was not resumed.

practice has made it matter of course."[4] But the King was worried; perhaps Lord North would take it into his head to retire "at an hour still more inconvenient if possible than the present." His Majesty trusted a "Summer's repose will enable you to rouse your mind with Vigour to take the lead again in the House of Commons, and not let every absurd idea be adopted as too recently appeared."[5]

The First Minister replied immediately and at length. He found his present situation "most arduous, most irksome and most embarrassing." He had not the slightest desire to continue to bear the debilitating burdens of public life; he would stay on until the King had made satisfactory arrangements, but could promise nothing more. During the previous session of Parliament, he had carried on "the business of Government unsupported and alone"; he anticipated "no more cordiality in the next session"; his "personal defects" would probably increase and render him "every day less and less fit" for employment. Again, he reiterated his desire to retire. Otherwise, he would certainly "sink under the burthen of public business, at the most critical moment." He assured his royal master he was not actuated by "hope of pecuniary emoluments" but was "prompted solely" by obedience to the King's commands, attachment to His Majesty's person and government, and by the gratitude he felt for countless instances of royal kindness. He thought £4,000 per year, due the lord warden of the Cinque Ports, excessive, begged the King to reduce it, and stated that he would take the office without any salary. Several days later the King quieted him with a draft for £4,000.[6]

"Major" Thornton, Arthur Lee's secretary in Paris, was earning his money as a British spy. He had traveled to London, ostensibly as an American agent authorized to discuss exchange of prisoners, where he had three private conversations with Lord North. Mr. Thornton was more interested in fattening his pocketbook than in alleviating the pitiful condition of Americans rotting in British prison ships and jails. "Mr. Thornton is a friend to D[r] Franklin and speaks of him probably better than he deserves. . . . He says of Deane that he is a selfish man, who has made an immense fortune by the present troubles & wishes to see them continue."‡ Thornton told Lord North he believed the first French attack would be against British posts in the Mediterranean, "& points out Gibraltar as the most probable object."[7] Thornton's sources probably deliberately misled him.

On June 2 frigate *Proserpine* arrived in Falmouth; her captain sent an express to Whitehall: D'Estaing had passed Gibraltar and was in the Atlantic with thirteen of the line and eight frigates. Captain Sutton tracked until he felt certain of the admiral's destination: "From the regu-

‡ Deane had lost money rather than made any. Thornton had been listening to Arthur Lee's vicious diatribes.

lar course the fleet steered and the great press of sail they carried I cannot help supposing it is for the West Indies." Keppel ordered Sutton to proceed to the Admiralty and dispatched a hasty note to the First Lord: "Captain Sutton's information will require the order for Admiral Byron's proceedings to be speedily determined by the King's ministers." *Enterprise*, also a tracking ship, arrived twenty-four hours after *Proserpine*. Her captain confirmed Sutton's report.

The King was undecided. He did not think the course set was "certain proof of the West Indies being his destination. I should rather reason that it was to get in a certain track, to make the passage more secure to North America."** He suggested the Cabinet immediately direct Byron to sail at the earliest possible moment to reinforce Lord Howe. Admiral Palliser, a junior lord, and third in command of Keppel's Channel fleet, basing his estimate on "accounts of particular persons and things," embarked at Toulon, concluded D'Estaing would go either to the Chesapeake or the Delaware.[8] The lords of the Admiralty ordered Byron to sail at once for Sandy Hook with thirteen of the line and one frigate. "Foul-weather Jack" sailed on June 9.

Keppel sailed from Portsmouth with twenty of the line three days later. His immediate mission was to escort the Gibraltar convoy for several days and then take station to meet the Brest fleet. "As soon as he was fairly at sea he was surrounded by French frigates—or so it seemed, since he had so few of his own." Whether their mission was to shadow or harass the British was unclear; Keppel's orders were "to oblige them to desist" and should they refuse, to seize them. His attempt to capture several shadowers brought on a running fight during which British cruisers engaged French frigates *Licorne* and *Pallas*. Both struck, were boarded, searched, and sent in to Portsmouth. Neither French captain had the forethought to dispose of his papers; from them Keppel learned the Brest fleet was greatly superior to his own, both in ships of the line and in frigates. He accordingly decided to seek a temporary haven in St. Helen's until he had received the additional ships promised by Sandwich.[9]

Officially, France and England were not yet at war. The fleet under D'Orvilliers—twenty-seven of the line, plus some frigates—still lay in Brest. Keppel's force was considerably inferior, but his few coppered frigates had demonstrated they could outsail and outmaneuver any D'Orvilliers had.†† Lack of frigates perturbed Palliser, who wrote Sandwich that American privateers "may do a deal of mischief to the northward." He expected "so soon as hostilities commence the enemy will send many strong frigates and privateers to intercept our Baltic trade; if they are

** The King, who had studied winds and currents in Caribbean and Atlantic waters, was correct.

†† The Admiralty was making tremendous efforts to have all hulls sheathed in copper. "Coppering" was a significant technological break-through, as the sheathing kept hulls clean and preserved ships' timbers from rot.

successful it would very much distress us to support a fleet at sea with naval stores and masts." Keppel foresaw trade would be "much interrupted if you are not able to cover the sea with frigates."[10] A few days later, Palliser again wrote the First Lord: "I can't help adding my testimony to Admiral Keppel's of the excellent qualities of our coppered frigates and the superiority they have in sailing over all the French frigates we have seen."[11]

Keppel considered a *possible* defeat would "be attended with fatal consequences" and dared not put himself "in the scale against so much danger to my country."[12] This epistle irritated the King, who immediately wrote Sandwich: "I cannot conceal that I am much hurt at the resolution taken by Admiral Keppel of instantly returning to St. Helen's on hearing that the Brest fleet amounts to 27 sail of the line . . . I fear this step will greatly discourage the ardour of the country." His Majesty hoped that at the cabinet meeting scheduled for June 25 "it may be settled to represent unto me the propriety of ordering the Admiral to return to his station." He added he believed Keppel's retirement to St. Helen's roadstead would probably enable the French to intercept the convoy proceeding to Gibraltar with supplies and reinforcements.[13]

Tension increased daily, but neither side seemed anxious to make a formal declaration. Walpole was disposed to hope that both England and France were becoming rational: ". . . that is, humane enough to dislike carnage. Both kings are pacific by nature, and the voice of Europe now prefers legislators to *heroes,* which is but a name for destroyers of their species."[14] Mann was distressed: ". . . all Europe is against us!" He reported Arthur Lee in Vienna in the guise of "a simple traveller." Baron de Breteuil, the French ambassador, had presented him to the Chancellor, Prince von Kaunitz, but Empress Maria Theresa categorically refused to receive him, and Kaunitz gave him no encouragement.‡‡

Some days later Walpole wrote that the last news from America had "little spirit in it." The "Grand Fleet" had gone to sea; the country was "spread with camps." Sir William Howe was momentarily expected, but as Parliament had been prorogued for the summer months, "that topic may be suspended." Voltaire, "the meteor of the reading world," died on May 30: ". . . that throne is now vacant." Walpole believed that genius would revive from beyond the Atlantic: "they seem to set out with a politeness with which few empires have commenced. We have not shown ourselves quite so civilized."[15]

Clinton was pushing preparations to evacuate Philadelphia. He was not yet aware D'Estaing had sailed for the Delaware Capes, but "every circumstance of the moment"—and the possibility of French naval intervention was one such circumstance—directed a speedy redeployment,

‡‡ Lee also attempted to see Frederick the Great, who refused to receive him.

for, should he and Viscount Howe procrastinate, the army and its base at New York would be placed in jeopardy. He therefore hastened to get the sick, a number of Philadelphia Tories, two battalions of Hessians, army women and children, and heavy cannon and equipment aboard the admiral's ships and clear them for New York at the earliest possible moment. He sent two brigades to Point Gloucester on the Jersey shore south of Camden to establish bridgeheads to cover the army's crossing; ordered wagons to be loaded with food and ammunition for twenty days; and directed last-minute inspections of individual arms and equipment. The army would march light across New Jersey, and, he hoped, fast. Men were issued four days' salt and cooked provisions.

His Majesty's three peace commissioners arrived in the city to discover that the general was abandoning it. Cornwallis, returning from home leave, accompanied them. The earl carried in his pocket a dormant commission to succeed to command should anything befall Sir Henry. The commissioners, considerably disgruntled that ministers had not chosen to inform them of the decision to evacuate Philadelphia, applied to Washington to grant a pass to their secretary, Dr. Adam Ferguson, to proceed to York bearing their credentials and proposals. Washington refused the *laisser-passer*, but forwarded a packet of letters. Delegates, not in a conciliatory mood, read the mail, but firmly refused to receive Dr. Ferguson.

Samuel Adams wrote Warren: ". . . the Scene begins to open. You may depend upon it that Congress will not attend to any Propositions until Independence is acknowledged. . . . The contents of the Letter . . . showed plainly that their Design was to draw us back to a subjection to their King. Some expressions in the Letter gave particular Disgust to all the Members."[16] Laurens drew up a letter to former Governor Johnstone, a man much respected in America, in which he asserted that "the good people" of America would never recede from their stated position even if they were forced to retire "westward of yonder Mountains."[17]

All in York agreed the terms proposed were entirely inadmissible. Some described the letter as an insult. Robert Morris thought the trio should not be given one moment's hearing, but be sent packing. Richard Henry Lee wrote Jefferson the communication laid before Congress was "a combination of fraud, falsehood, insidious offers and abuse of France, concluding with a denial of Independence."* Lee wanted to return the letter "with contempt," but cooler counsels prevailed, and "31 members, the whole number in York Town" agreed unanimously to reject the terms proposed. "Acknowledge our Independence, or withdraw your fleets and armies and we will treat with you for peace and commerce."[18]

Delegates realized the thirteen American states were now in a posi-

* Reflections on his King and country enraged La Fayette, who challenged the Earl of Carlisle, the senior peace commissioner, to a duel. Carlisle sensibly paid no attention to the marquis's letter.

tion to dictate minimum conditions for retreating. France had joined; a powerful fleet was on the way; the Army had rebounded from the winter low point; the commander in chief and his generals were optimistic; Clinton was retreating. Pennsylvania and New Jersey would soon be cleared of Redcoat soldiers and Knyphausen's plundering Hessians. The King's commissioners had subjected themselves to the rigors of an uncomfortable voyage to no purpose. That they had been sent was generally interpreted as a certain sign of Great Britain's weakness. Terms Americans would probably have accepted early in 1776 were in this summer of 1778 deemed insulting and beneath contempt.

During his brief sojourn in Philadelphia, William Eden had heard enough to persuade him that negotiations would be futile, and wrote a friend his forebodings: "Our young Americanus will some Day succeed in Arms. . . . This is a noble Country, & if my Wishes and Cares wd. do the Business it wd. soon belong once more to Great Britain." On June 15, in a letter to his brother, he wrote that although he knew little more of America than he had seen coming up the Delaware, he had seen enough to regret "most heartily that our Rulers instead of making the Tour of Europe did not finish their Education round the Coast and Rivers of the Western Side of the Atlantic."[19] Several days later: ". . . the ignominious desertion of Pennsylvania took place this morning and the Army (16,000 of the finest troops in the World) is now marching with 5000 horses to New York."[20]

He unburdened himself in a private letter to Alexander Wedderburn; he had sacrificed his domestic happiness, his career, and his character "to a Commission obviously meant to make a mixture of ridicule, nullity and embarrassments." He was prepared to accept personal disappointment, but "in a public Light it is impossible to see what I can see of this magnificent Country and not to go nearly mad at the long Train of Misconducts and Mistakes by which we have lost it."[21]

By the evening of June 17, Clinton's main body had crossed the Delaware. Washington made no attempt to intervene. He considered attacking the bridgeheads and lamented "that the number of our sick (under inoculation, etc.), the situation of our stores and other matters, will not allow me to make a large detachment from this army till the enemy have actually crossed the Delaware, and began their march for South Amboy, then it will be too late."[22]

He planned to move the army, less 3,000 sick at Valley Forge, to a position on the Hudson to pose a threat to New York. He directed Brigadier General William Maxwell to observe Clinton's march, to harass and impede the British, "And when you find that it is needless to pursue any further, you are to file off and gain the North River as quick as possible."[23] Clearly, British politics were "aground"; what Clinton would do when he finally got the army safely to New York was problematical.

What Great Britain *ought* to do, Washington wrote Gouverneur Morris, was to relinquish "all pretensions to conquest in America . . . but how far obstinacy, revenge, and villainy may enduce them to persevere, I shall not undertake to determine."[24]

He ordered Major General Benedict Arnold, whose leg broken at Saratoga eight months before still caused him considerable pain and denied him the active command he desired, to move into Philadelphia and put the city under martial law. Arnold assumed command in Philadelphia on June 19 and immediately exercised the dictatorial powers conferred by the commander in chief. He boarded up stores and warehouses and ordered merchants to prepare detailed inventories of their stocks "in order that the quartermaster, commissary and clothing generals may contract for such goods as are wanted for the use of the Army." These orders, strictly in accordance with instructions Washington had given him, angered merchants who had entertained visions of fat profits.

As was his custom at moments when critical decisions were to be taken, Washington had summoned general officers to a Council of War to discuss his options. He was perplexed; he could not decide upon the most appropriate course of action. Should he move at once on New York? Should he reinforce Maxwell in New Jersey? Could the main body of the Continental Army occasion Clinton "any material interruptions"? If so, would it be prudent "to make an attack upon them"? Should such an attack be a partial or a general one? Or would it be more eligible to proceed to the North River "in order to protect communications between New England and the South"?[25]

As so often happened at such meetings, differing views prevented agreement. Greene, Wayne, and Cadwalader, his most aggressive generals, recommended immediate pursuit and forcing of a general action. Du Portail, Knox, and Von Steuben opposed. La Fayette was ambivalent. Charles Lee thought nothing serious should be done to obstruct Clinton's march. Henry Knox agreed: "It would be the most criminal madness to hazard a general action at this time." Colonel Alexander Hamilton, who was present in his capacity as Washington's ADC and secretary, expressed his opinion that the council "would have done honor to the most honorable society of mid-wives, and to them only, as the purport was that we should keep at a comfortable distance from the enemy."[26]

Washington resolved the question the following morning and at noon directed Lee to cross his First Division to Jersey by Coryell's Ferry (New Hope, Pennsylvania, to Lambertville, New Jersey). The Third (La Fayette) and the Fifth (Lord Stirling) would follow. The Second and Fourth would cross at Sherrard's Ferry. He directed Knox to assign appropriate artillery to each division. The Continental Army could not

stand on the Jersey side of the river, ready to move, until the morning of
June 22 at the earliest.

Clinton had a four-day start. But he also had a cumbersome train, including field artillery, fifteen hundred wagons, a thousand bât horses
with officers' personal belongings, their bedding and camp equipment,
sutlers with another thousand horses, many loaded with loot, and army
women, some with children. The British Army, strung out for almost
fifteen miles, would march by Haddonfield, Mount Holly, and Allentown
to Amboy or Sandy Hook, and then be ferried to New York.

On the afternoon of June 24 the Continental Army reached Hopewell,
about eleven miles east of the Delaware, and on the following night
camped at Kingston and Rocky Hill on the banks of the Millstone River,
some five miles north and east of Princeton. Washington detached Morgan's corps "to gain the enemy's right flank; Maxwell's brigade to hang
on their left," and gave Brigadier General Charles Scott instructions to
move fast and gall Clinton's rear.[27]

At Allentown, Clinton sensibly elected to take the road leading by
Monmouth Court House to Sandy Hook. The last thing Sir Henry
wanted was to be forced into accepting a general engagement. He
mistakenly believed Gates was hastening to Washington's assistance and
thought the Americans would not hazard an attack until the two forces
merged. By that time, he hoped to be safely in Sandy Hook.†

The weather was stifling. Temperatures climbed into the mid-nine-
ties. The Hessians were as usual overburdened with individual equipment and portable plunder. Throats were parched; drinking water a
scarce commodity. Most infantrymen staggered along; some, with
tongues swollen and woolen uniforms soaked with sweat, dropped by the
roadside. Others deserted. Tories whom Knyphausen was shepherding to
safety had left Philadelphia with wagonloads of furniture, blankets,
clothing, and household wares, which Sir Henry wrote "was a great in-
cumbrance during the march."‡[28]

Again June 24 Washington summoned a Council of War. Again the
vote was against a general action. The Americans were not immune to
the heat prostrating British and Hessians. They too were thirsty. But they
were more lightly clad and carried little equipment. Still, the consensus
was the retreating British would fight desperately under the circumstances; the risk seemed unacceptable. The generals recommended assignment of additional harassing forces; Washington directed La Fayette to
proceed south and east with a brigade and take over-all command.[29] He
ordered the marquis to attack "by detachment," but "if a proper opening

---

† Clinton would later write that he hoped "Mr. Washington" would attack him
on the march. At the time, he feared an attack.

‡ Sir Henry Clinton's words in a note written in the margin of one of his copies
of Stedman's *History*.

shd. be given," to move against the British with the whole force under his command, which would total some 6,000.[30]

On occasion it appeared that supreme command of the American Army was a co-operative enterprise, but Washington was to some degree bound by a resolution of Congress which directed him to confer frequently with his general officers as to operations to be undertaken. At this time there was no need to have summoned such a conference. In the tactical context, the American Army lay in an advantageous position and Clinton in an extremely vulnerable one. Washington could initiate the action and he could terminate it. He had it in his power to have captured or destroyed the train moving ponderously toward safety at Sandy Hook, and Clinton feared he would attempt to do precisely that. The train would be a great prize, but as Washington considered his options he correctly concluded that Clinton's army was the primary objective. The commander in chief had a keen political judgment; he was also blessed with an ability to assess the psychological benefits that would accrue from a victory—or even from a drawn battle—with British and German regulars. He was indeed playing for high stakes, for if he could destroy Clinton's army, or even wound it deeply, the war would probably wind down, and American independence be assured. But should he suffer a decisive defeat, the cause might well be ruined.

Washington's orders to La Fayette irritated Charles Lee, who wrote petulantly that he considered assignment of such a powerful force to a "Young Volunteering General" was not appropriate; he felt either he or Lord Stirling should command, otherwise "both myself and Lord Sterling will be disgrac'd."[31] Washington acquiesced; in a tactful letter to La Fayette he informed the marquis he felt "for Genl Lee's distress of mind" and had directed him to take command. Washington, with the main body, lay in Cranbury; La Fayette, short of provisions, was moving toward Englishtown, some eight or nine miles to the east and close to the north flank of Clinton's retreating column. The commander in chief had a healthy respect for his adversary. He adjured La Fayette "to observe the greatest circumspection."[32]

Supersession of La Fayette was a serious blunder, for Lee had unequivocally asserted his objection to operations that might bring on a battle with British troops he conceived to be immeasurably superior to the Continentals. Although La Fayette had not voted to seek a general engagement, he was anxious to inflict all the damage he could on Clinton's columns and believed the troops would comport themselves with spirit. Americans, he said, had stood up to British regulars before, and could again.

To assign a combat mission to a man who believes he cannot succeed is to ask for failure. Nor should an agreed plan, already in operation, and with contact imminent, be compromised by misguided regard for wounded sensibilities. On both counts, Washington was guilty.

Torrential rains on June 26 broke the heat wave and mired the roads. Washington could not get rations forward. Hamilton reported Anthony Wayne's division in extreme distress and almost starving. The troops "seem both unwilling and unable to march further till they are supplied."[33] On this day Clinton, apprehending a major blow, directed Knyphausen to press on with the train to Sandy Hook, and brigaded the elite formations of the army—grenadiers, light infantry, and chausseurs—into a "Rear Division" under command of Cornwallis. The earl assigned eight hundred light infantry as a rear guard. Hamilton reported the British march "very judiciously conducted. . . . To attack them in this situation, without being supported by the whole army would be folly in the extreme."

Stupefying heat, rain, unrelenting harassment, and the threat posed by Washington's army were not the only difficulties Clinton faced; each day he was losing scores of men by desertion. Washington thought "five or Six hundred is the least number that have come in . . . they are chiefly Foreigners."[34] On June 27 Clinton rested the army at Monmouth Court House. The day had been blistering and night brought little relief until toward morning the heavens again opened.

Lee spent this day at Englishtown, five miles from Monmouth Court House, waiting for explicit orders and for Washington, with the mass of the army, to close to supporting distance. Clinton had but twelve miles to march to reach defensible ground near Sandy Hook. His intelligence was poor, but he thought Washington "little desirous . . . of risking a general action."**[35] Actually, Washington had decided—without summoning a Council of War—to force a general engagement by an attack on Clinton's rear division as soon as the British Army broke camp on the following morning and was in motion. He directed Lee to initiate the action, at which time he would move forward in support.

"The sky was cloudless over the plains of Monmouth when the morning dawned, and the sun came up with all the fervor of the summer solstice. It was the sultriest day of the year; not a zephyr moved the leaves; nature smiled in her beautiful garments of flowers and foliage, and the birds carolled with delight. Man alone was the discordant note in the universal melody."[36] The British broke camp before dawn and marched shortly after sunup. The move was immediately reported to Lee, as it was shortly thereafter to Washington. The commander in chief at once sent an aide with a verbal order to Lee that he desired him "to bring on an engagement, or attack the enemy as soon as possible, unless some very powerful circumstances forbid it," and added that he would soon be up. This order should have been peremptory and in writing.

** Clinton Marginalia in one of his copies of Stedman's *Histories*.

Lee had not kept scouts in close touch with the enemy, as Washington had instructed him to do. He had little information of Cornwallis' dispositions and knew even less of the terrain. Indeed, he had not yet had time to make the acquaintance of senior officers serving under him. His instructions to them were confused and inconclusive; his attack was not timely and when he finally launched it, totally unco-ordinated. La Fayette, who sensed things were going badly, sent word to Washington to hasten to the field. Lieutenant Colonel John Laurens of Washington's staff, who had been assigned to Lee as liaison officer, twice sent similar messages to the commander in chief.

Washington arrived on the scene to find the army in disorderly retreat. He questioned Lee (and some say cursed him roundly), sent him to the rear, assumed personal command, and ordered the troops to hold in delaying positions until he could organize a battle position on strong ground behind a ravine (West Ravine). While this was taking place, Knox and Greene maneuvered guns into position to deliver enfilade fire.

Clinton had received favorable reports of the action and now determined to press his advantage. He first attacked the American left wing (Lord Stirling). The Americans checked the British and counterattacked. Sir Henry then switched his effort, first to the right (Greene), where the Americans defended desperately, then to the center (Wayne). Here the British charged three times and were three times driven back. The main battle position had been held. Clinton called off the attack.††

Both armies were physically spent as night settled on the Monmouth plains. Fifty-nine British soldiers died of heat prostration; 299 others were killed, wounded, or missing. American casualties were roughly the same. Neither army had any stomach for further fighting, and Clinton slipped away while the Americans slept.

Washington's first report to Congress was terse: He had engaged Clinton's army; the British had retired. In General Orders he congratulated the army and the New Jersey militia on their courage, coolness, and spirit. The discipline instilled by Von Steuben during long hours at Valley Forge had paid dividends on the field of battle. Washington's "ragamuffins" had stood up to Britain's elite corps; Henry Knox's artillerymen had distinguished themselves.

Americans celebrated Monmouth as a victory. In a sense it was, for the army had there proved itself to be an effective combat instrument. Washington's speedy and decisive reaction and his personal leadership in a critical situation renewed the army's confidence in him, convinced skeptics of his ability and determination to lead the cause to ultimate victory, and at least temporarily silenced his detractors.

†† The sequence of events at the Battle of Monmouth has been much disputed. Washington's temper was volcanic; there is every reason to believe he lost it at his encounter with Lee.

A not unimportant dividend of the day was that it wrote an abrupt
finis to the career of Charles Lee, who in Washington's words was "guilty
of a breach of orders and of misbehaviour before the enemy on the 28th.
Inst in not attacking them as you had been directed and in making an
unnecessary, disorderly, and shameful retreat."[37] Lee was brought to trial
before a general court-martial and sentenced to be suspended from duty.

Clinton garnered what laurels there were for the British. He accomplished his mission: He brought his army, its train, and its baggage
safely to New York.

During 1777 and 1778, while war in the seaboard colonies engrossed
the attention of Lord George Germain, Count de Vergennes, Congress,
and military commanders on both sides, another war was being fought
west of the Allegheny Mountains in a vast area stretching to the Mississippi. In this 150,000 square miles of virgin wilderness there were few
settlements and these lay at the mercy of Shawnee war parties supplied
by Lieutenant Governor Henry Hamilton at Detroit. Hamilton, known as
"the Hair Buyer" (he offered bounties for American scalps), provided his
Indian allies with muskets, powder, ball ammunition, blankets, rum, and
tomahawks and scalping knives made of the best British steel. Settlers in
isolated hamlets north of the Ohio—"the Beautiful River"—lived in constant fear of the sudden war whoop in the night and the fate it portended. Nor were those who lived in Kentucky—"the Dark and Bloody
Ground"—immune to savage depredations.

For some time it had been apparent to these frontiersmen that the
only solution was to take Detroit and so deprive the Indians of their base
of support. Two expeditions organized for this purpose had started from
Fort Pitt and had foundered. Congress had no resources in men, money,
or equipment to divert to further operations in those remote parts; the
settlers there would have to fend for themselves. This arrangement did
not please gentlemen in Virginia who held shares in Ohio Valley land
companies. Nor did it suit George Rogers Clark, an imaginative and
audacious young Virginia militia officer who had settled in Kentucky.

Clark and several colleagues worked up a plan to break the power of
the Shawnee. The ultimate objective was to be Detroit, but certain preliminary operations were projected. These involved taking over the predominantly French settlements at Kaskaskia and Cahokia on the east
bank of the Mississippi and at Vincennes on the Wabash. Clark thought
the threat to Vincennes would draw Hamilton out of Detroit; if it did
not, he proposed to march to Detroit and take the fort and "the Hair
Buyer" with it. In late 1777 he had crossed the mountains into Virginia,
ridden to Williamsburg, and laid his scheme before Governor Patrick
Henry, who proved to be a sympathetic listener. Henry conferred with
half a dozen leading men, including Thomas Jefferson and George

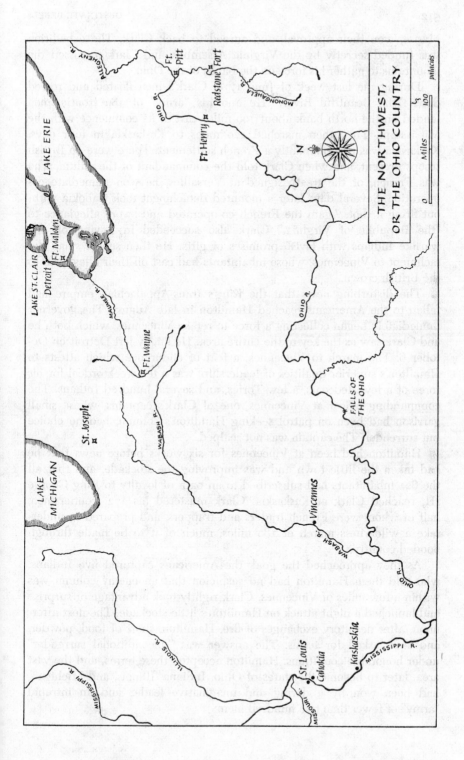

THE NORTHWEST,
OR THE OHIO COUNTRY

LAKE ERIE

ALLEGHENY R.

Ft. Pitt

Ft. Henry

Redstone Fort

MONONGAHELA R.

OHIO R.

LAKE ST. CLAIR

Detroit

Ft. Malden

MAUMEE R.

Ft. Wayne

LAKE MICHIGAN

St. Joseph

WABASH R.

FALLS OF
THE OHIO

Vincennes

WABASH R.

OHIO R.

ILLINOIS R.

St. Louis

Cahokia

Kaskaskia

MISSISSIPPI R.

MISSOURI R.

MISSISSIPPI R.

N

0   50   100
Miles

0   50   100
palacios

Mason, won their approval, and agreed to back Clark. The expedition was funded secretly by the Virginia Assembly, and Clark recrossed the mountains to gather his force on the banks of the Ohio.

During the last week of June 1778, Clark's men floated and rowed down "the Beautiful River." He and his "army" of 180 frontiersmen landed on the north bank about 100 miles east of its confluence with the Mississippi. They then marched 120 miles to Kaskaskia in four days. Kaskaskia was predominantly a French settlement. There were no British troops present, and when Clark told the commandant of the militia, who was French, of the treaty signed at Versailles, he won immediate co-operation. Several days later a mounted detachment took Cahokia without firing a shot. Again the French co-operated and swore allegiance to "the Republic of Virginia." Clark also succeeded in buying off the warlike Indians with lavish promises of gifts. He then sent a small detachment to Vincennes, whose inhabitants had cast off their allegiance to the British crown.

The disturbing news that the King's trans-Appalachian empire had fallen to the Americans reached Hamilton in late August. The governor immediately began collecting a force to retake Vincennes, which both he and Clark saw as the key to the entire area. He finally left Detroit on October 6. The march to Vincennes, a feat of endurance which attests to Hamilton's superior qualities of leadership, was a ten-week ordeal for his force of a few Redcoats, a few Tories, and several hundred Indians. The commanding officer at Vincennes, one of Clark's captains, whose small garrison had been on patrol seeking Hamilton's column, had no choice but surrender. The captain was not scalped.

Hamilton had been at Vincennes for six weeks before news that he had taken the little town and was improving the stockade, and that all the 621 inhabitants had subscribed to an oath of loyalty to King George III, reached Clark at Kaskaskia. Clark mustered his 172 frontiersmen, half of whom were French traders and trappers, and prepared to undertake a wilderness march of 180 miles, much of it to be made through flooded country.

As they approached the goal, the Americans captured five Indians, who told them Hamilton had no suspicion that an enemy column was within a few miles of Vincennes. Clark rightly took advantage of surprise and launched a night attack on Hamilton's little stockade. The next afternoon, after desultory exchanges of fire, Hamilton, short of food, powder, and shot, asked for terms. The answer was "unconditional surrender" under honorable conditions. Hamilton accepted these terms, and the vast area, later to become the states of Ohio, Indiana, Illinois, and Michigan, had been won by a daring and imaginative leader and an intrepid "army" of fewer than two hundred men.

BOOK VII

The Common Cause

☙ 1

Spirit Equal to the Risk

While Clinton's army and his ponderous baggage train wound across New Jersey toward the heights of Navesink from where he would march to Sandy Hook to embark for the passage to Manhattan Island, Viscount Howe's transports and storeships, impeded by head winds, dropped slowly down the Delaware with the tides to the capes where the admiral and his small fleet awaited them. By June 28 the last straggler had arrived and Howe immediately set course for New York. That afternoon a British packet joined with information that she had sighted D'Estaing's superior fleet steering for the coast of Virginia. The French admiral, in ninety-gun flagship *Languedoc,* with eleven other ships of the line and four frigates, arrived at the mouth of Delaware Bay on July 8. He had missed Howe by ten days.

D'Estaing detached a frigate to convey Louis XVI's emissary, Conrad Alexandre Gérard, and former Commissioner Silas Deane to Philadelphia, and sent two messengers to Washington "to offer to combine my movements with his own." In a letter to the president of Congress, D'Estaing announced his arrival and expressed the hope that he and Washington would be able "immediately and without any delay, to act in concert for the benefit of the common cause."[1] With his quarry gone, the

French admiral sailed for New York and on July 11, 1778, anchored four miles east of Sandy Hook.

Vice-admiral Howe, who realized he could not commit his inferior fleet to a running fight in the open sea, had designed a judicious defensive disposition. To repel D'Estaing, he anchored his men-of-war in an indented formation inside the Hook and directed his captains to put out spring cables so as to hold the ships in a position to rake the French as they crossed the bar in line ahead before an easterly wind. Should the French survive these devastating broadsides, the British ships could veer so as to enable each to deliver a full broadside at short range as D'Estaing's ships came abeam.*

On the day the French fleet anchored off the Hook, Congress informed Washington, whose headquarters were at Paramus, New Jersey, of D'Estaing's arrival in American waters and suggested that he cooperate with the French admiral "in the execution of such offensive operations against the enemy as they shall mutually approve." Washington sent an aide, Lieutenant Colonel John Laurens, son of the president of Congress and one of the few officers on his staff fluent in French, to greet D'Estaing. Several days later he ordered the army to move its camps in New Jersey to a position east of the Hudson to threaten New York.

But no decision had yet been reached as to the first objective of combined Franco-American operations, and on July 15 Washington wrote Major General Sullivan, then in Providence, to prepare to attack the British force at Newport on Aquidneck Island, should that be selected as the alternate target. He dispatched several regiments to Providence to reinforce Sullivan; directed him to collect the boats necessary for an amphibious assault; authorized him to call up 5,000 militia from Massachusetts, Connecticut, and Rhode Island, and ordered him to find competent pilots for D'Estaing should the decision be for an operation against Major General Sir Robert Pigot's force defending Newport.

While Washington waited at his White Plains headquarters, D'Estaing conferred with New York harbor pilots previously sent him. Their unanimous opinion was that they could not take the larger French ships over the bar. But on July 22 "a fresh northeast wind concurred with a spring tide to give the highest possible water over the bar." Still, D'Estaing hesitated, and by midafternoon reached the decision not to attempt to cross the bar. Clinton took advantage of D'Estaing's "state of suspense" to dispatch five battalions via Long Island Sound to reinforce Pigot's Newport garrison, and alerted an additional 4,000 troops to embark on a moment's notice.

---

* In nautical terms, this means that each ship of Howe's formation was anchored abaft the beam of the ships lying to its right (starboard). Thus each could deliver a full raking broadside against each ship in the approaching French column. When Howe's ships were veered 90°, each could deliver a full broadside as the French came abeam.

The British had naturally anticipated that their enemies, thus favored by fortune, would attack. One officer wrote: "We . . . expected the hottest day that had ever been fought between two nations. On our side, all was at stake. Had the men-of-war been defeated, the fleet of transports and victuallers must have been destroyed, and the army of course, have fallen with us. D'Estaing, however, had not spirit equal to the risk; at three o'clock we saw him bear off to the southward, and in a few hours, he was out of sight."[2]

"Spirit equal to the risk." If Washington had similar thoughts about his ally he kept them to himself and ordered La Fayette with two brigades to march "with all convenient expedition" to Providence and there place himself under Sullivan's command for an attack on Newport. He then wrote D'Estaing tactfully expressing his regret that "the brilliant enterprise" the French admiral had meditated "was frustrated by physical impossibilities."

A week later, D'Estaing arrived off Point Judith. He ordered two ships of the line to move into Narragansett Bay and anchor off Conanicut Island and sent two frigates to operate in Sakonnet Passage, to the east of Aquidneck Island. Major General Pigot, who unexpectedly found his garrison in an extremely critical situation, hurriedly concentrated all his forces to defend Newport. The French commanded the waters around the island; the British position was grim; the Americans optimistically anticipated another Saratoga. But in their tactical equation they had failed to take into account a most important factor: the will and courage of Vice-admiral of the White Richard Viscount Howe, R.N.

While D'Estaing was making ready for the combined operation against Rhode Island, sorely needed reinforcements arrived in New York and reported to Howe. Four ships came in during the space of ten days: two of fifty guns, a 74, and a 64. These were the first of "Foul-weather Jack" Byron's squadron (which sailed from England on June 9) to arrive in American waters. During his passage, Byron had encountered winds of gale force that scattered his ships from Nova Scotia to the West Indies.† Howe had no intention of waiting for Byron or any other of his ships. He deemed his available force sufficient to deal with D'Estaing, and as soon as the late arrivals had been watered and provisioned, he weighed and set course for Point Judith, where he anchored on August 9. D'Estaing had stood into the harbor on the previous day. As soon as the French fleet appeared, Sullivan crossed from Tiverton to the north end of Aquidneck Island, occupied Butts Hill, and entrenched. Now the fate of Pigot's army, of his American opponents, of both French and British fleets, and possibly of the British position in North America were to be put at stake.

On July 17 Keppel was ready to sail with the Channel fleet and ordered several ships not yet fully manned and provisioned to hasten final

† One was refitted in Lisbon.

arrangements and rendezvous with him off the island of Ushant, west of Brest. Before sailing he wrote Sandwich: "A battle with the French fleet must depend upon them: if they are eager, I shall endeavour to get them a little from their own coast, but I am apprehensive they will not allow me to lead them from their land."[3] The admiral, confident of his ability to defeat the French, was ready to begin the shooting war, but the First Minister was not. He wrote Sandwich he wished Keppel "to continue as if nothing had happened" at least until the richly laden merchant fleets from the East and West Indies had arrived safely.[4] Keppel could scarcely continue to behave as if "nothing had happened," for D'Orvilliers was at sea, and on July 24, the admiral wrote the First Lord that contact was imminent.

Three days later the equally matched fleets met off the French coast and engaged in the indecisive action known as the Battle of Ushant. The French, at least, did not wish to push the affair to a decisive conclusion; Keppel, claiming a victory, considered their withdrawal during the night following the action "shameful and disgraceful."[5] The battle was, as then described, "a misbegotten affair." The French retired to Brest, but their *langrage,* so Keppel admitted, had damaged British masts, torn sails, and sheared rigging "beyond any degree" he had ever seen.‡ Many British ships thus rendered unseaworthy would require extensive refit before they could again sail. Although D'Orvilliers's fleet had suffered considerable hull damage, his ships were in better condition than were Keppel's to renew the fight.

This engagement illustrates the difference in concepts of gunnery as between the English and French. English doctrine taught that the hull of an opposing ship should be the target of a broadside; the French, on the contrary, taught that fire should be directed at the upper decks, masts, and rigging for the purpose of disabling enemy ships and inflicting gundeck casualties and so forcing them to drop out of the line of battle. Keppel's testimony on this occasion indicates that French gunners had mastered the technique.

Both admirals had difficulty with subordinates, Keppel with Vice-admiral Sir Hugh Palliser, D'Orvilliers with the royal Duc du Chartres. Signals misunderstood or perhaps deliberately misconstrued prevented both commanders from executing desired fleet evolutions. The French scapegoat was the Duc du Chartres, who was immediately relieved. In England, Keppel's failure to crush the French was popularly ascribed to Palliser's negligence, or as his most vocal critics professed to believe, to his calculated treachery. Walpole gives some credence to these rumors: "As Palliser was Lord Sandwich's creature he was suspected of having acted by the Earl's orders, who hated Keppel for having complained to the King of the bad condition of the fleet." The rancorous feud in the

‡ *Langrage:* case shot loaded with pieces of iron of irregular shape.

Royal Navy engendered by the Keppel-Palliser controversy was to split the officer corps wide open.

But Keppel's "victory" (as the official *Gazette* and London newspapers described the action off Ushant) did much to raise public morale in Great Britain. For a full seven months news from America had been depressing. Now British arms had enjoyed at least a qualified success. Fears of imminent invasion subsided, and as neither side had yet declared war, a twilight peace prevailed. Walpole wrote Sir Horace Mann that communication with France was still open: "The packet boats pass as usual and French and English are allowed to go to Paris and to come to London as if to compare notes on all that happens."[6]

D'Estaing, confident of his superiority, had not expected Howe to follow him so closely, and when his frigates descried the British ships off Point Judith, he hurriedly called a Council of War to discuss available options. These the admiral saw as two: to retire further within the harbor or to take position near the entrance, and if the wind turned favorable, to sail out and engage Howe. The latter was his choice, and on August 10, with a following wind, the French fleet weighed and put to sea.

When viewed objectively, this decision is simply incomprehensible. The French admiral had a clear mission: to co-operate with the Americans in attacking the British garrison on Aquidneck Island. He had all the advantages of position. Howe would have had to enter the bay in line ahead. Each British ship in succession would inescapably have come under devastating broadsides. The French admiral had it in his power to destroy Howe's fleet if the British chose to enter the bay. If Howe did not so choose, the French and Americans could have destroyed or captured Pigot's army. The French admiral was a brave man. He was also excessively stupid.

On August 11, as the fleets maneuvered for advantageous position, a violent gale arose, dispersed the ships of both, and during the next several days drove some of them far to the southward. D'Estaing's flagship lost all her masts, her rigging, and her rudder; eighty-gun *Tonnant* lost all her masts save one. Howe's ships did not escape; many were severely damaged, and the British admiral put back to New York.

On August 20 D'Estaing with his crippled ships was again off the entrance to the bay.** Before sailing, he had promised Sullivan he would return, and he had. But he did not intend to stay. He summoned his officers to a conference; they were unanimous in the opinion that he should abandon the Rhode Island enterprise and sail immediately to Boston for repairs. In his report to the Minister of Marine, D'Estaing wrote: "All the opinions, very many arguments and the dictates of reason itself urged me to steer to that port [Boston]. . . . But my duty before all else

---

** *Languedoc* and *Tonnant* both jury-rigged.

was, to prove to the new allies of His Majesty that we are ready to sacrifice everything in order to keep a promise that we had once made. Our need of water, and the uncertainty as to what might happen, could not release us from a fixed engagement, and I felt that I must inform General Sullivan and assist him, by the presence of the fleet, either to conquer or to retreat."[7]

The assistance the French admiral gave Sullivan was nugatory, for on the following day he announced his intention to proceed to Boston for refit. Sullivan, Greene, and La Fayette immediately appealed the admiral's decision. Sullivan argued that the fleet could refit at Providence as well as at Boston, and promised to provide mast and spar timbers, cables, cordage, and all other items required.†† But D'Estaing was not to be moved; he sailed for Boston, designated in his orders as his base in North America. He thus left Sullivan to carry on the operation unsupported or to extricate his army as best he could from its embarrassing situation.

A Newport Tory wrote the New York *Royal Gazette* "the monsieurs and the rebels are likely to come to blows on account of the late movements in Rhode Island." D'Estaing had returned to Newport "dismantled and dismayed, having in his excursion not only had the British fleet against him but the wrath of Heaven, and soon after against the urgent solicitations of the rebel commander (Mr. Sullivan) he again set sail for Boston, to refit his scows and recover his equanimity."[8] It is difficult to take exception to D'Estaing's decision to proceed to Boston. He was aware that Vice-admiral Byron had sailed in early June with thirteen of the line to join Howe. Byron was long overdue; as far as D'Estaing could know, this powerful reinforcement might arrive any day. To preserve his fleet, it was essential that he refit speedily and clear North American waters at the earliest possible moment.

Sullivan made no attempt to conceal his resentment, and as Greene informed the commander in chief, had "very imprudently issued something like a censure in General Orders. Indeed it was an absolute censure." He added that D'Estaing's departure had "struck such a panic among the Militia and Volunteers that they began to desert by shoals."[9] He was not exaggerating. Sullivan's army of 9,000 rank and file had been reduced by nearly half.

Departure of half his force did not temper Sullivan's determination to assail Pigot's positions and drive the British and Hessians into the sea. He pushed his outposts well to the south of Butts Hill and advanced his batteries to within one thousand yards of Pigot's forward positions. This was mere bravado, for the range was too great to permit effective fire. Nor did he now have under command a force strong enough to storm the British redoubts with any hope of success. At a conference of general

†† At least three of the largest ships that had been dismasted could not have been refitted elsewhere than in Boston.

officers Green urged withdrawal and observed that while this maneuver might be calamitous, to remain longer on the island was to invite certain ruin. The decision was to withdraw to the mainland and during the night of the twenty-eighth the army struck tents.

Pigot was not one to miss such an opportunity, and the next morning marched north in three columns hard on the heels of Sullivan's retiring rear guard. Battle was joined in midmorning. On the American right, Lieutenant Colonel Christopher Greene's First Rhode Island Regiment, largely composed of Negroes, distinguished itself by repelling three successive attacks mounted by Major General Losberg's Hessians. In the center and on the left the Americans were equally stubborn. In late afternoon, with his casualties mounting and nothing accomplished, Pigot retired. During the night of August 30, Sullivan executed an orderly withdrawal to Tiverton and Bristol. He and La Fayette were the last two to leave. Two days later Sir Henry Clinton arrived at Newport with transports carrying 5,000 reinforcements.

American reaction to the news from Rhode Island was one of mixed disappointment and resentment. An intemperate protest signed by Sullivan and all his generals save La Fayette, and delivered to D'Estaing as he arrived in Boston, was not calculated to salve French feelings or to heal the incipient breach between already mutually suspicious allies. Washington wrote Major General Heath, commanding in Boston, that he was apprehensive "the unfortunate circumstance" would if not "prudently managed . . . have many injurious consequences." He feared the affair would discourage the people and "possibly produce prejudice and resentments" and urged upon Heath the necessity of providing D'Estaing with "Zealous and effectual assistance."[10] Several days later he wrote Governor George Clinton of New York that while differing opinions would be entertained on the propriety of D'Estaing's action "we ought all to concur in giving it the most favourable colouring to the people. It should be ascribed to necessity resulting from the injury sustained by the storm."[11]

Washington closed a letter of instruction he wrote Sullivan with these words:

> I will just add a hint, which, made use of in time, may prove important and answer a very salutary purpose. Should the expedition fail, thro' the abandonment of the French fleet, the Officers will be apt to complain loudly. But prudence dictates that we should put the best face upon the matter and, to the World, attribute the movement to Boston, to necessity. The Reasons are too obvious to need explaining. The principal one is, that our British and internal enemies would be glad to improve the least manner of complaint and disgust against and between us and our new Allies into a serious rupture.[12]

The tone of Washington's letters at this time indicates that if he was not as disgusted as many clearly were, he was certainly greatly disappointed. He realized that a victory shared by Franco-American forces in their first joint operation would produce incalculable political and psychological effects, not only in America, at Versailles, and in other European countries, but as well in England. For although the surrender of Pigot's army of some 7,000 would not have substantially imperiled the British position in New York, it might well have brought down Lord North's administration and induced the British Government to try more realistically to end an unpromising and unprofitable continental war.

Before he returned to New York, Clinton directed Major General Charles ("No Flint") Grey to attack and lay waste towns on the Connecticut shore of the Sound, and this Grey proceeded to do with thoroughness and dispatch. He put the torch to several towns including New Bedford and Fairhaven; destroyed about one hundred vessels, including several privateers and their prizes; and burned storehouses, docks, and shipbuilding facilities. He then proceeded to Martha's Vineyard where he levied a substantial cash contribution on the inhabitants, burned every ship and boat afloat, and collected three hundred oxen and ten thousand sheep, which Clinton observed "afforded a very seasonable refreshment to the garrison of Rhode Island and the King's ships and troops in New York."

Sullivan had saved his army and D'Estaing his fleet, but the first cooperative endeavor had been a disappointing failure. And it also generated considerable rancor in the breasts of French officers serving with the Americans. La Fayette thought it necessary to return temporarily to France to urge that more effective aid be given America and to attempt to counter the indignant letters some of his colleagues were sending home. One of his friends and admirers, Major General de Kalb, had recently written his patron Marshal de Broglie that French officers with Washington's army were complaining about their allies: "A man accustomed to order and subordination has continually to suffer. . . . With the greatest ignorance of the art of war, they all have the highest opinions of themselves, and as they are of English origin it will be very difficult to root out that old hatred for France."[13]

The botched affair at Rhode Island produced repercussions elsewhere than in the already strained relationships between French and American officers. Many in high position believed D'Estaing had squandered fair opportunities. One immediate result was reflected in an immediate drop in the value of Continental paper and as it depreciated, recruiting was seriously affected. Washington thought the bounty of twenty dollars designed to encourage re-enlistment in the Continental Army insufficient and urged Congress to increase it to thirty. Here he was in direct competition with states offering double and triple this sum to those who enlisted in the militia.

He had recently written La Fayette, soon to embark for France, that the designs of the British were "wrapped in impervious darkness" and that he could form no precise idea of their intentions. He thought it possible they might be planning to move by sea against Boston in the hope of trapping and destroying D'Estaing's fleet. Or perhaps Clinton was contemplating a move against the Hudson Highlands. Stray items reported by spies in New York suggested the British were about to embark a large force for operations against the southern states. Possibly they were preparing to evacuate New York.

Howe returned from an excursion‡‡ to Boston to find that Admiral Byron had finally arrived. Not reluctant to turn over command of His Majesty's fleet in American waters, Howe prepared to sail for home. He did not depart under a cloud as his brother had done. But he had made it sufficiently clear that he desired no further employment so long as the Earl of Sandwich presided at the Admiralty. Clinton did not wish to see Howe go; his departure "caused very great regret and concern to the army who as well as myself had the most unbounded confidence in His Lordship's abilities and cooperation."[14]

Although Byron and his second-in-command, Rear Admiral Hyde Parker, inherited several able commodores, notably William Hotham and John Elliot, they had the misfortune also to inherit Rear Admiral James Gambier, an irresolute, avaricious, and carping incompetent who bombarded his patron the Earl of Sandwich with tediously complaining letters which exasperated both the First Lord and the King. Howe had sensibly not trusted Gambier with a sea command, nor would Byron.

With the Franco-American effort against Rhode Island frustrated, Clinton was in a position to ready the expeditionary force destined for the capture of Santa Lucia. This, under the command of Major General James Grant, would consist of 5,000 "choice troops, most amply equipped with a complete battering train and every other suitable appointment."[15] Escort and support and supply during the amphibious phase would be provided by Commodore Hotham.

The peace commissioners still lingered in New York, whence William Eden wrote his friend Wedderburn: "The Rebels will be much Disgusted by the Desertion of the French Fleet from the Attack of Rhode Island." He thought D'Estaing might have destroyed Howe's fleet at New York "if he had pushed into the Hook on the first night of his arrival when our

‡‡ Howe had gone to Boston after refit in New York to look into the possibility of sailing into the harbor and attacking D'Estaing. After surveying the harbor defenses he changed his mind.

Force was desperately small and not collected." He believed the French admiral might have succeeded at Newport "had he shown the smallest degree of audacity." He closed with the despondent observation that Admiral Viscount Howe seemed "decided in his opinion that America must be abandoned."[16]

Unbeknownst to his colleagues on the commission, Governor George Johnstone, M.P., had for some time been engaged in conducting a covert operation of his own devising. With the connivance of a Tory lady in Philadelphia who was acting as his intermediary, Johnstone had tried to bribe Joseph Reed, president of the Supreme Executive Council of Pennsylvania and a delegate to Congress, with an offer of £10,000 and "any office in the colonies in his Majesty's gift" if he would attempt to bring the Americans dutifully to accept the terms offered by the peace commissioners. Reed reported the conversation to Congress and stated that his reply to the lady had been that he "was not worth purchasing, but such as he was the King of Great Britain was not rich enough to do it." Johnstone had earlier attempted to bribe Robert Morris, also from Pennsylvania, and through him Henry Laurens and George Washington.

Letters and other material relating to Johnstone's activities had been presented to Congress in mid-August. Delegates promptly expressed their "most pointed indignation" and resolved that Congress would neither have intercourse with Johnstone nor negotiate further with the other peace commissioners, tainted as they were by his corrupting influence. Although the resolves were not approved by a majority of delegates, they were published in the press, and a copy, signed by President Henry Laurens, was sent to the Earl of Carlisle.

Johnstone's crass stupidity thus blasted what frail hope for accommodation the other commissioners may still have entertained. He resigned his position and sailed for England breathing hate against Americans in general and Congress in particular. When he resumed his seat in the House of Commons, he took advantage of every opportunity to assail with bitter invective those who had exposed him. In time of war bribery of enemy leaders is a legitimate weapon. But when bungling efforts are disclosed and are given full publicity, they are likely to do considerable damage to the cause the briber is attempting to promote. And so it was with Governor Johnstone's ill-conceived schemes, which succeeded only in hardening American animosity toward Great Britain and increasing, if possible, detestation of the administration of which the governor provided a corrupt example.

On September 29 the Earl of Carlisle drew up a minute for a "Manifesto and Proclamation" which he, Eden, and General Clinton, acting in their capacity as joint peace commissioners, issued in New York five days later. The "interference" of France, said the earl, had given "a new colour to everything that relates to the American contest." As

America, with "equal malice and perfidy," had chosen to league herself with France, it had become necessary to pursue a strategy that would prevent the rebellious colonies from becoming "an accession of strength" to Great Britain's "natural enemies." America, the earl wrote, must be reduced "to the extremity of distress . . . by a scheme of universal devastation." Unless the rebellious Americans humbly and dutifully accepted their dependent position, His Majesty's armies and fleets had no recourse other than to invoke this "dreadful system."[17] The Manifesto and Proclamation provoked anger, contempt, and derision in America, and when copies arrived in London, a storm of hostile criticism in the press and in Parliament.

After an unhappy exile in York, Congress had once again gathered in Philadelphia and had received M. Gérard in an impressive ceremony "at once elevating . . . joyous, easy, graceful, Endearing and Noble." Henry Marchant (Rhode Island) thought the reception presaged "a happy Issue to the American Struggle and a growing and undecaying Glory that shall diffuse its grateful Influence thro' the World."[18] Indeed, he and his colleagues had reason to be optimistic. Clinton's Redcoats were confined to a few square miles on Manhattan and Rhode Island, and although D'Estaing's fleet had won no laurels, its presence in American waters provided visible proof of the good will of His Most Christian Majesty and of his intent to fulfill his obligations under the Franco-American treaty.

And there was a good prospect that proposed Articles of Confederation, dispatched to the thirteen state assemblies in November 1777, would shortly be ratified by all. Virginia had taken the lead. Less than a month after receiving the articles, her General Assembly unanimously resolved that speedy ratification would "confound the devices" of foreign enemies of the United States; "frustrate the wavering; contribute much to the support of their public credit and the restoration of the value of their paper money; produce unanimity in their councils and add weight to their negotiations abroad, and completing the independence of their country, establish the best foundation for its prosperity."[19]

Virginia's call to action had little immediate effect. Most assemblies, fearful of too much power centralized in the Congress, debated the articles interminably. John Mathews of South Carolina wrote Governor Rutledge, ". . . if we are to have no Confederation until the Legislatures of the Thirteen States agree to one . . . we shall never have one, and if we have not one, we shall be literally a rope of sand, and I shall tremble for the Consequences that will follow at the end of this war." As of early November 1778, all states save New Jersey, Delaware, and Maryland had ratified. These three had proposed changes which Congress had debated and rejected. There the matter rested, for until the three laggards ratified, there would be no Confederation.°

Although Congress devoted much of its attention to the perennial problem of finance, it had finally managed to find time to receive Silas Deane, who since mid-July had been waiting on the doorstep for an opportunity to justify his transactions, financial and otherwise, during his career in Paris. Many members believed Deane had wantonly abused his authority in giving commissions and granting passage money to French mercenary officers who wished to serve in America; others were persuaded he had diverted public funds to his private profit.† Richard Henry Lee and Samuel Adams were the leading spirits in the attempt to discredit the former commissioner. William Stevenson, who had earlier been at Nantes, and William Carmichael, who had been employed by Deane, were in Philadelphia prepared to appear.‡ R. H. Lee suspected Franklin had written friends in Congress denigrating Arthur and wrote his brother: ". . . virtue will prevail over vice in the end—the Doctor is old and must soon be called to account for his misdeeds; therefore bear with him if possible.°°20 He warned Arthur to be circumspect in his behavior and cautious in his correspondence.

The question in Passy was who was having to bear with whom, for Dr. Franklin, John Adams (who had replaced Deane), and Arthur Lee were not congenial. The doctor made no secret of his conviction that one resident commissioner would serve the interests of America more effectively than could three, for although some benefits might derive from joint counsels "all the advantages in negotiating that result from secrecy of sentiment and uniformity in expressing it and in common business from dispatch are lost."21 And there was the further item of expense, which the doctor thought "enormously great." This unhappy situation was further complicated by the presence in Paris of William Lee, another of the Virginia family, accredited by Congress to the courts of Frederick the Great and Emperor Joseph II, but as yet received by neither monarch, and of Ralph Izard, a friend of the Lee dynasty accredited to the court of the Grand Duke of Tuscany. Izard was as unwelcome in Florence as was William Lee in Potsdam and Vienna, and as both were to Franklin.

The principal mission of the ill-assorted commissioners was to raise money. Between January 1 and the end of September 1778, Congress had emitted $28.5 million in paper, $20 million in bills of credit, $6.5 million

---

° Confederation was doomed to languish until February 1781, when Maryland finally authorized her delegates to sign. They signed a month later.

† Deane's commission had authorized him to enlist engineer officers. He was indeed engaging in assorted speculative ventures, but there is no evidence that he misappropriated public funds.

‡ Carmichael's testimony before Congress turned out to be little better than a curious farrago of innuendo and hearsay, but on the whole supported Deane.

°° Parts of the letter, including the sentence relating to Franklin, were in cipher.

in bills of exchange, and $10 million in loan office certificates bearing 6 per cent interest. The total for this nine-month period was $65 million, a colossal amount secured only by the pledge of Congress and "the faith of the United States." The commissioners well realized the urgent necessity to secure commitments in "hard money," but very soon discovered they had considerable competition.

Great Britain was trying to float a loan in Amsterdam; Maria Theresa, on the verge of war with Frederick of Prussia over Bohemia, needed cash as did her son Joseph II; they and Jacques Necker, the Swiss financier who had taken Turgot's place as Louis XVI's Minister of Finance, were trying to find it in Amsterdam, Milan, and Genoa. Despite persistent efforts, Arthur Lee had been unable to tap private sources in Madrid. His correspondent there, James Gardoqui, thought a negotiation possible if the Americans could conquer Florida and would agree to cede it to Spain. Izard received no encouragement from Florence, where lenders were demanding solid security and asking high rates of interest, but Abbé Niccoli, with whom he corresponded, informed him the situation would be different if France would agree to act as America's guarantor. This role did not appeal either to M. Necker or to Vergennes.

John Adams viewed with distaste these frenzied efforts to negotiate loans. He had never believed in borrowing money, and wrote his cousin Samuel that there was but one way to give credit to American currency, "Taxes, my dear sir, Taxes!" In a letter to R. H. Lee he summarized financial prospects: "Loans in Europe will be very difficult to obtain. The powers at war, or at the eve of war, have such vast demands, and offer terms so much better than ours, that nothing but sheer benevolence can induce any person to lend to us."[22]

The commissioners seem to have had no agreed mode of conducting business. Dr. Franklin should have been given authority to oversee all operations, but although recognized (reluctantly) by the two Lees and Izard as *primus inter pares,* he apparently exercised little control over the political behavior of his colleagues. As each of the five gentlemen in Paris wrote the president of Congress, members of the Committee of Foreign Affairs, and any other person when the spirit moved him, it is no wonder that there was too often "little secrecy in sentiment and no uniformity in expressing it."

Personal animosities played their part. Adams wrote R. H. Lee: "It has given me much grief since my arrival here to find so little harmony among many respectable characters, so many mutual jealousies, and so much distrust of one another."[23] Unfortunately, several of the "characters" were not entirely respectable. Arthur Lee, almost insanely jealous of Franklin, had not hidden his animus. His brother William, a former alderman of the City of London, was devoting considerable time to speculative commercial transactions. Izard devoted his to denigrating Franklin and meddling in affairs which were none of his concern. When to these problems is added the fact that Dr. Bancroft and "Major" Thornton, confidential secretaries to Franklin and Arthur Lee, were British spies, one can only be amazed that the commissioners accomplished anything.†† That they had done so is the best possible testimony to the early efforts of Silas Deane and to the tact and discreet diplomacy of Dr. Franklin, recently elected by Congress to be minister plenipotentiary of the United States at the court of France.

Although the autumn of 1778 passed without Spain joining France, King George believed she would certainly do so by the following spring and in mid-October wrote Lord North he trusted the Royal Navy would then be in fit condition to cope with the combined Bourbon fleets. His Majesty had no doubt it would please the Almighty to ensure a favorable issue: "It must Now be decided whether Britain or France must yield; I trust in the justness of my cause and the bravery of the Nation."[24] The King urged his First Minister to exhibit "activity, decision and zeal" and pressed upon him the necessity for taking measures to ensure a good attendance in both Lords and Commons when Parliament assembled. Lord North was not sanguine; he was depressed and thought attendance would be "slack." Apparently, he intended to do very little to rectify this situation: "The strong measures that must be taken, the want of confidence & attachment to the present ministry, grounded in the bad success of their measures . . . will, Lord North fears, render the Members of Parliament very indifferent to the cause of Government."

The sorry state of the Royal Navy attested to the bad success of ministerial measures, and although the King was not perturbed at the prospect of Spain entering the war, the Earl of Sandwich was, and wrote Lord North that he found the state of affairs so "critical and alarming" that his mind could find no rest. What exertions, he wondered, could be used "to guard against the storm that is hanging over us"? Spain would go to war, and soon, unless she could be "bought off at a very high rate." The objectives of the Spanish crown were certainly Gibraltar and Minorca, and perhaps Jamaica. Madrid would impose harsh and disgraceful conditions which if accepted would not only "occasion the utmost confusion at home" but might also "be attended with very disagreeable consequences" to those responsible for conducting the King's affairs. Should Spain enter the war in the immediate future, she could easily take both Minorca and Jamaica. And unless reinforced and resupplied, Gibraltar too might fall.

The best, indeed the only present, policy, Sandwich wrote, was to temporize. Spain must not be offended, but she would not for long "be

†† Lee, finally convinced that Thornton was making use of his knowledge of secret transactions to speculate on European exchanges, dismissed him.

amused with fair words and professions of friendship only." Still, "This language will gain at least two months." But two months were not sufficient. He needed more time. The Bourbon powers were feverishly increasing their naval strength; Sandwich thought they would soon be able to deploy eighty ships of the line. By the end of the year he could count on no more than forty-nine in home waters ready for sea.‡‡ Not enough ships. And not nearly enough men; some method would have to be devised "to get the seamen from their lurking holes." Byron should be ordered to return to England; his marine battalion sent home at once, and "more troops should be raised by every possible means, for everything is now at stake." Possibly an emissary should be dispatched to St. Petersburg to urge the Russians to send a fleet to assist England: ". . . surely it is a great object to them not to suffer France and Spain to be superior to us on the sea."[25]

The First Minister again begged the King to allow him to quit office; he was "in a situation for which he was never fit & for which he is now less fit than ever." He thought his continuance in government "highly prejudicial to His Majesty's affairs" and entreated the King "to continue his search for a better arrangement." He hoped his royal master would consider that some men in high office were indifferent to their duties, and added: "In critical times, it is necessary that there should be one directing Minister, who should plan the whole of the operations of government & controul all the other departments of administration so far as to make them co-operate zealously & actively with his designs even tho' contrary to their own. . . . Lord North is certainly not capable of being such a minister as he has described. . . ."[26]

George III did not want the sort of First Minister Lord North had described, for such a man would have asserted his authority, insisted on dismissal of dilettantes, incompetents, and sycophants, brought order to a disorganized and feckless administration, and taken direction of a war being fought in America, in the Atlantic and Caribbean, and soon to be fought in the Mediterranean and the East Indies. The rebellion that broke out on the village green in Lexington, Massachusetts, on an early morning in April 1775, had become a war spread over vast oceanic expanses to remote islands and distant continents.* In this most critical period, George III had no choice but to assert his influence over all aspects of war policy. He was able and anxious to do so.

Walpole had little news to impart to Sir Horace Mann. He had found great difficulty in separating truth from falsehood: "Ten thousand lies are propagated every week. . . . Newspapers, that ought to facilitate intelligence, are the vehicles of lies and blunders and scandal, and truth cannot

---

‡‡ An optimistic estimate!

* The complicated situation in India was also absorbing British resources, but on a relatively small scale. In terms of the American war, the action there was peripheral and had no decisive effect on the American-Caribbean theater.

now get along the road for the crowds of counterfeits. An historian that
shall consult the gazettes of the times, will write as fabulous a romance
as Gargantua."[27]

In addition to his requisition of 5,000 men for the West Indies, Germain had ordered Clinton to reinforce Pensacola with three battalions
and to send a strong force south by sea to assist Brigadier General
Augustine Prevost, commanding in East Florida, in an attack on Savannah and the reduction of Georgia. Clinton assigned 3,000 officers and
men to Lieutenant Colonel Archibald Campbell and directed him to report to Prevost. The secretary had also ordered Clinton to provide Major
General Frederick Haldimand (who had relieved Carleton in command
of Canada) with several battalions, and to reinforce Halifax, Bermuda,
and the Bahamas. These deductions left Clinton with 13,661 effective
rank and file and in his opinion deprived him of any ability to do more
than hold New York.† His Majesty's commander in chief in America
viewed the prospect of a long and dismal winter on Manhattan Island
with no particular pleasure, and as soon as he had made the arrangements described dispatched an ADC by packet to London with a request
to Germain "to lay at His Majesty's feet" his "most humble and earnest
solicitations" that he might have permission to resign and return home.
Earlier, in a despondent mood, Clinton had urged that he be allowed to
abandon New York and withdraw to Halifax. This suggestion had produced consternation in Whitehall. But the ministry, instead of relieving
him immediately, decided to bribe him with promises of reinforcements
and more adequate support. That no general could be found to go to
America to relieve Clinton is a revealing commentary not only on the
paucity of able senior officers, but as well on the destructive influence of
factional politics.

The deployments Germain had directed would seem to provide yet
another example of the dispersive strategy to which the secretary was addicted. But any assessment of Germain's judgment must take into account that Whitehall accepted, as did all British generals and admirals,
that rigors of climate in the northern part of America restricted the campaigning season there to a period from late April to early December. The
army expected to spend December, January, February, March, and a
good part of April in reasonably comfortable winter quarters, a routine
procedure in the cold climes of Europe where major land operations
were habitually suspended in late November and were not resumed until
spring weather had dried out roads and green forage was available. Nor
could navies operate in American waters north of the Chesapeake during

---

† This was Clinton's figure. Other reports indicate that he had available nearly
16,000 effective rank and file. This total did not include approximately 6,000–7,000
at Rhode Island.

the season of violent dismasting and sail-shredding gales in the north Atlantic. Ships seeking haven in New York, the St. Lawrence, or Halifax might suddenly find themselves icebound for months on end. It was thus sensible to close down winter operations in America north of the Chesapeake and to move to the southern area, which ships and expeditionary troops could leave in April or May before the hurricane season arrived in the Caribbean. And in any analysis of British strategy during this time, it is important to bear in mind the great strategic and economic value assigned to possession of the Sugar Islands, which lay athwart Spain's routes to her Central American colonies, and from which fast sailing British frigates could attack and take her bullion *flottas* sailing out of Panama.

It is more difficult to make sense of the decision to reinforce Prevost and to order an expedition to Savannah, for nothing of strategic value was to be gained by reducing Georgia to submission. Nor, while the Royal Navy held command of the sea, was reinforcement of Halifax, Bermuda, and the Barbados necessary. Had Clinton been authorized to retain the seasoned battalions thus scattered about and to withdraw the useless garrison on Rhode Island, he would have had sufficient battle-tested troops under command to move rapidly against the Highlands and so force Washington either to give battle or to cede the strategic terrain. Thus another opportunity to bring Washington's ragged army to decisive battle was cast away by the strategist at the head of the American Department.

The various contingents sailed as scheduled. Commodore Hotham with five of the line escorting the transports carrying Grant's troops cleared New York harbor on November 4, 1778. On the same day D'Estaing sailed from Boston and set course for Martinique.

During early November 1778, Washington was occupied with the perennial problem of securing supplies of money, blankets, coats, shoes, stockings, jackets, breeches, medicines, and forage for the army he would soon put into winter quarters. His supplies of powder and ball ammunition and (happily for morale) of provisions and rum were adequate to meet immediate needs. Congress, dilatory and bumbling, again proved itself to be a weak reed. Other matters of moment demanded his attention. Among these was movement of Burgoyne's "Convention Army" from its prisoner-of-war camps outside of Boston to Charlottesville, Virginia. Washington's particular charge was to ensure that the prisoners, marching in four divisions, passed rapidly and safely through eastern New York state, crossed the Hudson without interruption, and continued their march toward the Delaware. The movement of so large a body required detailed planning and generated a mass of correspondence. As he thought it possible Clinton would attempt to rescue the prisoners as they were ferried across the Hudson, he retained direction and control, and ordered strong detachments posted to protect the crossing places.‡

He had lately received from Congress a set of resolutions and a plan drawn by La Fayette for an invasion of Canada in 1779 in conjunction with a French fleet and army. The commander in chief studied the proposed scheme and replied that although he viewed the emancipation of Canada "as an Object very interesting to the future prosperity and tranquillity" of America, he did not deem the plan "to be eligible." He then proceeded with customary tact to give Congress an elementary lesson in the principles that he believed should govern combined operations undertaken by allied powers:

> It seems to me impolitic to enter into engagements with the Court of France for carrying on a combined operation of any kind, without a moral certainty of being able to fulfill our part, particularly if the first proposal came from us. If we should not be able to perform them, it would argue either a want of consideration, a defective knowledge of our resources, or something worse than either; which could not fail to produce a degree of distrust and discontent that might be very injurious to the union . . . should the Scheme proposed be adopted, a failure on our part would certainly occasion in them, a misapplication of a considerable land and naval force, which might be usefully employed elsewhere; and probably their total loss.[28]

Should the operation fail, as because of an evident shortage of manpower and lack of other essential resources he was convinced it would, the inevitable result would be "to give a very unfavourable impression of our foresight and providence, and would serve to weaken the confidence of that Court in our public councils."[29]

In sum, he thought the invasion of Canada "as delicate and precarious an enterprise, as can be imagined." England would not complacently allow her Canadian empire to be wrested from her. The loss of Canada and the naval base at Halifax "would be a deadly blow to her trade and empire." A hope to find Halifax in a defenseless state must be founded, he wrote, in a supposition of the total incapacity of Britain, both by land and sea, to afford protection to this important base. "I should apprehend, we may run into a dangerous error by estimating her power so low."[30]

He then returned to the logistics aspects of the proposed invasion. These were staggering, and Washington discussed them in detail. Clearly, he foresaw a catastrophe should the plan be adopted. And such a disaster could not be confined to the military sphere. It might well

‡ Clinton did attempt to intercept, but the British arrived too late.

wreck the alliance and thus ensure the ruin of the cause. He wished to attempt "everything our circumstances will permit," but in his opinion, circumstances did not permit the project Congress had proposed. He elaborated his views in a private letter to Henry Laurens: "I have one objection to it, untouched in my public letter, which is in my estimation, insurmountable, and alarms all my feelings for the true and permanent interests of my country. This is the introduction of a large body of French troops into Canada. . . . I am heartily disposed to entertain the most favorable sentiments of our new ally . . . but it is a maxim founded on the universal experience of mankind, that no nation is to be trusted farther than it is bound by interest; and no prudent statesman or politician will venture to depart from it."[31] These letters produced the desired effect; he would hear no more of this project.

While the commander in chief was thus engaged, savage warfare blazed in the Mohawk Valley in western New York. On November 11, 1778, a force of Tories and Rangers under Major William Butler and Indians under Chief Joseph Brant surprised the small settlement at Cherry Valley, killed Colonel Ichabod Alden and some of his officers and men who were billeted in farmhouses outside the stockade, and brutally murdered thirty men, women, and children. Brant finally managed to stop the massacre.

Report of the attack on Cherry Valley roused Washington's anger; he immediately directed Pulaski's mounted legion to report to Governor George Clinton, and ordered other strong detachments to Albany for such operations into Indian territory in western New York state as the governor might direct. Washington was essentially humane, but he had had sufficient experience with Indians to realize that the only way to put an end to their sanguinary depredations was to move a force deep into their territory, destroy crops, kill or take their livestock, chop down their orchards, burn their villages, and drive them from the borderlands deep into the inhospitable wilderness. At the moment, he was unable to plan other operations; the force available to him was not adequate for a major offensive.

Sir Henry Clinton, left with what he described as "the debris" of an army, was equally unable to do more than order desultory raids into the adjacent countryside, and although Washington constantly complained of his lack of intelligence, he knew that detachments being made, presumably for the south, were sufficient to immobilize the British general and confine him to Manhattan. Rear Admiral Gambier, commanding the small and heterogeneous fleet based on New York, found himself in a situation even less pleasant than was Clinton's. The admiral had nothing for the lords of the Admiralty but a catalogue of complaints. His ships were unseaworthy, their hulls rotten, hundreds of his seamen ill, hospital facilities inadequate, desertions increasing. He saw no possibility that Clinton could conduct any offensive operations. Admiral Howe, he wrote, had left him with too few ships to carry out the tasks imposed; first Hotham, then Byron, had denuded him of officers and rated men. He had not been named a peace commissioner and no one in New York paid any attention to him; he had been reduced to the ignominy of breaking his flag on a troop transport; his impoverished family lived in anguish as they awaited his return to England, and so on, and so on.[32] Gambier laced his rambling letters to Sandwich with such fawning flattery that they must have disgusted even the First Lord, himself an accomplished sycophant.

Commander Hotham, escorting fifty-nine transports carrying Grant's expeditionary troops, arrived at Barbados on December 10, 1778, and reported to Rear Admiral the Honourable Samuel Barrington, commanding the Leeward Islands Station. Barrington had earlier learned that D'Estaing had arrived in Caribbean waters, and determined to move at once against St. Lucia, which lies about thirty miles south of the larger French island of Martinique. Troops were held aboard transports, and after a commanders' conference preparations were made to sail at dawn on December 12. The amphibious force arrived at Santa Lucia during early afternoon the following day, and troops immediately began landing on beaches north of the Grand Cul de Sac, a deep inlet on the northwest coast. The British moved rapidly against ineffectual resistance, seized key terrain and the small fort, and in late afternoon of December 14 broke the Royal Standard over the French governor's mansion, where General Grant established his headquarters. At this moment, D'Estaing's fleet appeared and closed rapidly. D'Estaing, it seemed, had Barrington at his mercy.

The British admiral's situation was even more precarious than Admiral Howe's had been some months earlier at Sandy Hook. For as at Sandy Hook, D'Estaing was greatly superior in ships and weight of broadside. Barrington could not fight him in the open sea. His first responsibility was at all hazards to protect the transports and supply ships, and to the best of his ability support Grant's landing force. Here, defeat meant not just the loss of a few fighting ships, but as well of a great train and of a British army.

During the night of December 14, troops ashore prepared to resist a French landing on the morrow and Barrington moved transports and supply ships deep into the Grand Cul de Sac. He disposed his seven of the line and three frigates to block the entrance. Shortly before noon on the following day, D'Estaing's fleet, in column formation, passed the mouth of the Grand Cul de Sac. His broadsides fell harmlessly short of or over Barrington's anchored ships. In the afternoon the French admiral repeated his maneuver with equal lack of success. Unable either to force his way into the Cul de Sac or to get Barrington out of it, he decided to land at the head of his troops and storm the British positions. Accordingly, on December 18 he landed and attacked. The defenders held their ground; in three frontal assaults 400 French officers and men were killed and 1,200 wounded. The admiral called off the assault and re-embarked his landing force. Barrington meanwhile had greatly improved his position in the Grand Cul de Sac, and when D'Estaing next appeared he looked in once and departed for Martinique.

Again, time had been a deciding factor, for had Barrington delayed at Barbados for one more day, or not commenced landing operations at the earliest possible moment, or not promptly arranged his defensive formation to protect the supply ships after arriving at the Cul de Sac, D'Estaing's fleet would in all probability have destroyed his inferior squadron.

One might speculate on the course of events in America during 1776, 1777, and 1778 had His Majesty's commanding generals there been endowed with the same degree of professional competence, vigor, and determination as were Admirals Viscount Howe and the Honourable Samuel Barrington.**

Several days before D'Estaing departed for Martinique, Lieutenant Colonel Campbell's motley force—two battalions of Highlanders, two of Hessians, and four of Loyalist Americans—arrived at the mouth of the Savannah River. Campbell had no idea as to the whereabouts of Brigadier General Augustine Prevost, to whom he was to report, nor did he have any information whatever as to the strength of the Americans under Major General Robert Howe who were defending Savannah and were said to be encamped near the river half a mile east of the town. Lack of precise information did not deter Campbell. He landed two miles below Howe's reported position, made a personal reconnaissance, decided to envelop the American right, and launched his attack. In less than an hour the defenders were fleeing in disorder. That night Campbell slept comfortably in Savannah. General Prevost, forced to make his way north by inland waterways, arrived on the scene of action ten days later. His small force had subsisted for days on a diet of fish and oysters.

After taking Augusta, Prevost proclaimed the "King's Peace" in Georgia. Royal government was once again established. The Georgians reacted immediately. Hundreds came to Savannah, Sunbury, and

** Mahan would later write: "This achievement of Barrington and of Major General James Grant . . . was greeted at the time with an applause which will be echoed by the military judgement of a later age. . . . The celerity, forethought, wariness and daring of Admiral Barrington have inscribed upon the records of the British Navy a success the distinction of which should be measured, not by the largeness of the scale, but by the perfection of the workmanship, and by the energy of the execution in face of great odds." (*The Major Operations of the Navies in the War of American Independence*, p. 104.)

Augusta with horses and arms, subscribed to the oath of allegiance, and
enlisted in battalions of foot and troops of cavalry. A state had been lost,
but the loss was of no particular importance. The issue would be decided
elsewhere than in Georgia.

℀ 2

Hourly Change of Circumstance

Henry Laurens, "sated with honor and worn out with fatigue," had recently resigned as president of Congress for what he tersely and tactfully described as "good and sufficient reasons."* John Jay of New York succeeded to the chair. Laurens had been a respected president, but of late not a particularly popular one, for he had allowed himself to become embroiled in the acrimonious controversy between Silas Deane and the Lees. Deane had powerful enemies in Congress, including Laurens. But he also had powerful friends there, as he did "out of doors," and he enlisted their services to bring this "ridiculous squabble" (as James Duane described the feud) to the attention of the public by anonymous letters in the press. Thomas Paine, now secretary to the Committee of Foreign Affairs, in turn assailed him over the signature *Common Sense*.† Thus were the energies of the disputing factions in Congress dissipated as the year 1778 drew to a close.

Washington, summoned from his headquarters at Middlebrook, New Jersey, to Philadelphia to discuss the condition of the army and his plans

* The "good and sufficient reasons" were that he was disgusted with the time wasted in the Deane-Lee controversy.

† Paine was shortly thereafter dismissed from his position.

for the next campaign, rode into the city on December 22. If the four young secretaries who accompanied him thought they would enjoy a vacation from their daily quill-driving, they were to be vastly disappointed.‡ During his first week in Philadelphia, the commander in chief met with Congress and dined with delegates, and on December 30 wrote Benjamin Harrison his impressions. He had seen nothing to give him cause for hope, but had "abundant reason to be convinced, that our Affairs are in a more distressed, ruinous, and deplorable condition than they have been in Since the commencement of the War." He was greatly worried as he assessed the caliber of the men sitting in Congress and the measures they had taken, or perhaps more exactly those they had failed to take. He beseeched Harrison to exert himself to see that the most able Virginians were sent to Congress. Where, he asked, were George Mason, George Wythe, Thomas Jefferson, Edmund Pendleton, and Thomas Nelson, Jr.? They "must not slumber or sleep at home in such times of pressing danger . . . while the common interests of America are mouldering . . . and sinking into irretrievable ruin."

He drew a frightening picture of the times and of the men who were determining America's fate: ". . . idleness, dissipation and extravagance seemed to have laid fast hold of most of them. . . . Speculation, peculation, and an insatiable thirst for riches seem to have got the better of every other consideration and almost of every order of Men." Factional disputes and personal quarrels were "the great business of the day whilst the momentous concerns of an empire, a great and accumulated debt; ruined finances, depreciated money and want of credit . . . are but secondary considerations . . . postponed from day to day, from week to week, as if our affairs wore the most promising aspect." Officers were daily leaving the army, and the "more virtuous few" who were staying were "sinking by degrees into beggary and want."[1]

It is a curious irony that this letter was written on the day Congress had set aside for a general Thanksgiving.

During the first weeks of January, Washington met daily with a Committee of Conference appointed by Congress. The commander in chief, relieved to learn that the proposed Canadian expedition had been abandoned, had little hope he could mount a major operation before the opening of the campaigning season. He thought it "advisable for the main body of the Army to lye quiet in some favorable position" and confine the British to Manhattan and Staten islands. As security of frontier settlements could be assured only by offensive action, he planned several expeditions "to scourge the Indians and prevent their depredations" and had ordered one such expedition to move into Indian country when the weather moderated. This, commanded by Brigadier General Lachlan

‡ The secretaries were Alexander Hamilton, Tench Tilghman, James McHenry, and Robert Hanson Harrison.

McIntosh, was to ravage Indian communities in northern Pennsylvania and western New York and attack Detroit, then held by a small British garrison.

Although "Minutes of Sundry Matters" which he prepared for the committee did not explicitly state that the army could do nothing more than "lye quiet," such was the fact, for the army could not march. Shoes, warm clothing, and blankets were, as usual, lacking.

Washington observed that as paper money was nearly worthless, flour and forage were difficult to obtain. In addition, the army needed muskets, powder, and ordnance stores; if these were not soon supplied in adequate quantities, the situation would be "ruinous." The clothier general's department was confused and inefficient and the maladministration of the Board of War and Ordnance a constant source of embarrassment to Brigadier General Knox. The medical department needed to be reorganized from top to bottom as did the engineer branch. The office of the inspector general, administered by Major General Baron von Steuben, required more officers.

At the request of the committee, Washington prepared specific recommendations. Congress, always jealous of its prerogatives and determined to assert control of the military, took immediate exception to establishment of "departments" within the army, particularly to that proposed for the inspector general. Such agencies implies "an independence of the Commander-in-Chief" and would be productive of "Inconvenience and Expence."[2] This was a paltry evasion of the constructive recommendations Washington had made; the reorganization he had proposed would have promoted efficiency and saved money.

On January 31, 1779, Congress informed the commander in chief he could return to his headquarters at Middlebrook. The general, delighted to depart from Philadelphia, returned to his army. Only time would tell whether his recommendations would eventually be accepted and implemented.

For three years Congress had sought some solution to the "alarming and embarrassed" subject of finances. But efforts had been sporadic and ineffective. As delegates groped to find paths of escape from the financial swamp, paper continued to depreciate. Washington wrote that Monday's paper dollar was worth but ninety-five cents on Tuesday.** The cancer of inflation was growing and ramifying. Most delegates were afraid to face the fact that the country was on the verge of bankruptcy, but Henry Laurens and some of his colleagues knew that drastic action could no longer be delayed. Fine-spun theorems and endless debate could not cure the disease; unless Congress struck at the root causes—"immense emissions, the peculation of great public Officers, the practice of monopolizers, etc., etc., we may drudge on, the Evil will remain and our Coun-

** Exactly, he wrote that paper was falling 5 per cent a day.

try will be reduced systematically to destruction." Patriotism was out of fashion, and unless speedily revived "we shall experience a violent convulsion which will go near to ruin us, and which will at least bring us into universal disgrace. I lament the prospect."[3]

Heavy taxation, which delegates had considered too delicate a matter to urge upon the states, had finally been accepted as unavoidable. By methods of their own devising, states were to collect a total sum of $60 million prior to the first day of January 1780. Emissions of 1777 and 1778 totaling $41 million would be called in and old paper replaced with new notes or interest-bearing loan certificates. These particular emissions had been counterfeited by the British to such an appalling extent that bills bearing those days were no longer negotiable. Congress was by no means sure these schemes would be acceptable or even that taxes in the sum specified could be collected, but at least the disease of inflation had been faced and a treatment prescribed.

Although finances absorbed a great deal of time, Congress had to wrestle with many other pressing problems. For weeks Henry Laurens had been urging the imperative necessity to reinforce Georgia and South Carolina. Congress ordered Benjamin Lincoln, a reliable but otherwise undistinguished major general, to proceed to Charleston, South Carolina, relieve Major General Robert Howe, who was not particularly popular in those parts, and assume command of the Southern Department. Militia from Virginia and North Carolina were ordered to march, but as usual there were delays in providing arms, powder, and other essential supplies.

Congress appealed to Gérard to request D'Estaing to come north with an amphibious force to recover Georgia and help defend South Carolina; the governor of South Carolina dispatched a similar message to the French admiral. Gérard created an obstacle by demanding financial compensation for the proposed expedition; Congress debated the subject for days on end, but in Philadelphia "we move no faster than we would do if the Southern States were in perfect peace and safety."[4] Washington had ordered Major General Count Casimir Pulaski's legion to Charleston, but the legion could not move until the commander's public accounts were settled. Laurens and other southern delegates had every reason to be exasperated, and were.

Washington's presence in Philadelphia had of course provided occasion for entertainments in his honor; one such, a lavish banquet, took place in the well-appointed mansion occupied by Major General Benedict Arnold, commandant of the city. Arnold was having some problems, but it is unlikely that he spoiled the gaiety of the evening by mentioning them to the commander in chief.

During January, he had been engaged in a running battle with the Supreme Executive Council of Pennsylvania over a variety of charges the

Council was investigating. And he was arguing with a committee of Congress over his accounts, for long unsettled. He was living in a style well beyond his means and was deeply in debt. His ostentation and arrogance and his obvious preference for the society of Philadelphians suspected of Tory leanings outraged radical Whigs, notably Joseph Reed, president of the Council, and Timothy Matlack, the secretary. That members of the Council disliked the general and that radical Whigs reprobated his flamboyant behavior was true enough, but scarcely constituted substantial grounds for charges to be brought against this distinguished soldier.

Arnold's constant need for money had led him to engage in assorted transactions, none criminal but all imprudent and unbecoming in an officer in his position. Solid evidence of his complicity in these shady deals was almost totally lacking, but by the end of January 1779, Reed and his colleagues had assembled enough to enable them to charge him publicly with "such illegal and offensive conduct as is cognizable in the Courts of Law." In a broadside published in Philadelphia on February 3 the Council announced that its members had "maturely considered the general tenor and course of the military Command exercised by Major General Arnold" and had unanimously resolved "That the same hath been in many respects offensive to the faithful subjects of this State, unworthy of his rank and station, highly discouraging to those who had manifested their attachment to the liberties and interests of America and disrespectful to the Supreme Executive Authority of the State." There followed a list of eight charges.

Arnold had not previously devoted much attention to squabbling with the Executive Council. His energies had been otherwise employed: He had fallen in love with Miss Margaret Shippen and had little time to spare for such indulgences as engaging in a paper war with self-important and misguided politicians who apparently could find nothing better to do than to harass him. But publication of the charges and Reed's insistence that they were a proper subject for investigation by Congress changed the complexion of the affair. Arnold had few friends in Congress and no political leverage. These facts did not dismay him, and when called before a committee chaired by William Paca of Delaware, he defended himself ably. The committee dismissed the allegations and cleared him.

Reed and Matlack howled in frustrated rage and raised such a clamor that Congress rejected the findings of the Paca committee and appointed another whose members were more amenable to the wishes of the Supreme Executive Council. This committee determined that four of the eight charges were of sufficient gravity to warrant trial by general court-martial. After some debate, and despite strenuous objections by Arnold's supporters, the recommendations were approved on the floor and the charges forwarded to Washington. Arnold immediately resigned his position as commandant of Philadelphia. He was now a general without a job.

Although his professional career was not prospering, his suit for the hand of Miss Margaret Shippen was. Peggy's family was no longer rich but was aristocratic. She was nineteen; the general, almost twice her age. This homely girl, endowed with a beautiful figure, who would later play such a decisive and dramatic role in Arnold's career, had a local reputation for gaiety and frivolity. But the gay Peggy Shippen, whose presence ensured the success of an intimate supper party, was a young lady of sensitive and perceptive intelligence. She was also an accomplished amateur actress. During the British occupation she had enchanted Lord Rawdon, Howe's deputy adjutant general, and Captain John André, who was soon to hold that position under Sir Henry Clinton. American officers, notably their general, had found her no less appealing. She and Major General Benedict Arnold were married in a quiet ceremony on April 8, 1779.

In his *Last Journals During the Reign of George III*, Horace Walpole wrote: "The new year [1779] was ushered in by a violent tempest of wind, which began in the night precisely as the old year ended." Although ancient historians might have regarded this as an omen of political storms to follow, he believed better-founded "prognostics" were "the folly of the Court and the wretched condition to which it had brought this country."[5] If proceedings in Parliament during the short meeting prior to adjournment for the holiday season provided a reliable forecast, storms which might wreck Lord North's administration were making up. Admiral Howe, his brother General Sir William, and Gentleman Johnny Burgoyne, all members of the House of Commons and all anxious to redeem their reputations at the expense of Lord George Germain's, could seriously embarrass Administration. His Majesty expected Lord Howe "to lay the foundation for much altercation for the rest of the Session." The admiral had his price: If the King would confer on Sir William "some military preferment," he could guarantee the Howe brothers would keep their mouths shut. The King, ordinarily not averse to discreet bribery if it could buy him support in the House of Commons, balked at awarding any accolade to a discredited general but offered Viscount Howe a place at the Admiralty. The admiral, who loathed Sandwich, promptly refused it. Another member of the Commons who could cause trouble was Governor Johnstone, the former peace commissioner who had returned from America seething with rage at the Howes, whose incompetent blundering, so he alleged, had unnecessarily prolonged suppression of the rebellion. Johnstone, a half-pay navy captain, was silenced by promotion to commodore and given command of a small squadron based on Lisbon. But the degree of embarrassment Administration might suffer from the charges of these gentlemen could not possibly equal the public odium it was preparing to bring upon itself.

Before Christmas Vice-admiral Sir Hugh Palliser, encouraged by his patron the Earl of Sandwich, brought serious charges against Admiral Keppel for unbecoming behavior during the engagement off Ushant. The First Lord was an astute politician; he must have been aware that calling this popular "High Whig" aristocrat before a general court-martial would induce Opposition factions to bury their differences and rally to Keppel's support, create serious morale problems in the officer corps of the Royal Navy, and provoke heated debates in both Houses of Parliament during which he himself would inevitably become a prime target. Nevertheless, the charges were preferred. Had tradition been followed, the court would have sat in the flagship. This procedure, favored by the Admiralty, would have deprived Keppel and his friends of the accessible and commodious forum they desired, for they had every intention of turning the proceedings into a political trial which they hoped would thoroughly discredit the First Lord of the Admiralty. The popular admiral, pleading ill health, requested that the trial be held ashore. Under the circumstances, Sandwich could not refuse, and on January 8, 1779, the court convened at Portsmouth dockyard.

The trial was the event of the season. The Rockingham squadron turned out in full force as did many other great Whig aristocrats and their ladies. Charles James Fox and Edmund Burke were among those present in the courtroom. Public opinion favored Keppel, and as the trial wore on it became apparent that not the accused but the accuser was in trouble: "Every day's trial heaped new glory on the prisoner."[6] Sandwich received daily reports of the proceedings which the King also read attentively. Although neither would admit that bringing the respected and popular Admiral of the Blue to trial had been a political blunder, there was no doubt in minds less prejudiced that it had been.

Keppel, honorably acquitted on February 10, arrived in London a few days later and was noisily acclaimed by great crowds who forced their way into Palliser's house, gutted it, and then broke all the windows at Lord North's and Lord George Germain's. General expectation was that Lord North's government would be forced to resign, or at least that Sandwich would have to go. But the earl had the best friend it is possible to have at court: the King. He stayed in office, and although there was much talk that changes would be made, none were.

The result of Keppel's trial dictated that Palliser must have his turn before a court-martial. Sir Hugh requested Sandwich to order one and resigned his post of lieutenant general of marines and his sinecure as governor of Scarborough Castle. In the Commons, Charles Fox argued that Palliser should be expelled from the House. The admiral, a ruined man, had reason to blame his predicament on political prejudice and partisan rancor.

All those in government anticipated that Sandwich, too, would soon be called to account, and on March 3, 1779, Lord North in a speech in the House of Commons made it clear that he would consider a vote of censure on the First Lord of the Admiralty a censure of his administration. The First Minister based his argument on a minute apparently prepared by Sandwich. This minute is of singular historical interest because it stated unequivocally and for the first time the principle of corporate cabinet responsibility:

> Every expedition, in regard to its destination, object, force and number of ships, is planned by the Cabinet, and is the result of the collective wisdom of all his Majesty's confidential ministers.†† The First Lord of the Admiralty is only the executive servant of these measures; and if he is not personally a Cabinet Minister he is not responsible for the wisdom, the policy and the propriety of any naval expedition. But if he is in the Cabinet [as Sandwich was] then he must share in common with the other ministers that proportional division of censure which is attached to him as an individual. In no situation is he more or less responsible to his country than his colleagues from any misconduct that flows from a Cabinet measure.[7]

This speech did not fend off attacks in either Lords or Commons, but votes of censure were defeated.

Sandwich had more important matters to consider than the disgrace of Sir Hugh Palliser or even his own political fate. Although the First Lord had not been reading the enciphered dispatches from Madrid to Marquis Almodóvar, His Most Catholic Majesty's ambassador to the Court of St. James's, he had been correct in his earlier estimate that Spain would demand a very high price to stay out of the war. Floridablanca, the Spanish Foreign Minister, had instructed Almodóvar to inform Lord Weymouth, Secretary of State for the Southern Department, that the price was Gibraltar: "that pile of stones which is only a matter of expense and care to them, disturbing to us, and an impediment to permanent friendship."[8] Weymouth made it clear that the price was too high. If the Spaniards wanted Gibraltar, they would have to take it. Spain was not anxious to enter the war but she wanted "that pile of

†† The "confidential ministers" or "efficient ministers" were those who had seats in the Cabinet. At this time, they numbered nine or ten and were: the First Lord of the Treasury, the three Principal Secretaries of State, the First Lord of the Admiralty, the Lord Chancellor, the Lord President of the Council, the Lord Keeper of the Privy Seal, and the Lord Chamberlain. Lord Amherst, the Commander in Chief, was a member, but the Secretary at War was not, nor (usually) was the Chancellor of the Exchequer. (Lord North was both First Lord of the Treasury and Chancellor of the Exchequer.)

stones," and if she could not get it by diplomatic pressure, she proposed to get it by force. She had only to cook up a pretext for joining France in active hostilities.

On April 3, Charles III, "wishing to give one more proof of his love of humanity," sent notes to Paris and London expressing his willingness to act as mediator between the two warring powers. As necessary preliminaries to any such arrangement His Most Catholic Majesty demanded that Great Britain agree to a cessation of hostilities in the American colonies pending negotiations to be held in Madrid, and, additionally, that the colonies be treated "as independent in fact."‡‡ Charles III and his advisers knew that the Court of St. James's would not accede to such an ultimatum.

Planning for joint operations of the Bourbon armies and navies had commenced in Versailles and Madrid three months prior to the ultimatum of April 3, 1779, and a variety of plans had been considered. From these emerged an agreed allocation of responsibilities to become effective when Spain declared war. Invasion of England with landings in force on the Isle of Wight and near Portsmouth was to be a joint endeavor conducted by Admiral d'Orvilliers. Reduction of Gibraltar and seizure of Minorca were to be Spanish operations. The allies agreed to conduct joint operations in the Caribbean and western Atlantic; Spain to seize Jamaica and Florida, France to fall upon the Sugar Islands. France would continue to extend assistance to the Americans. A secret treaty confirming these arrangements was signed at Aranjuez on April 12, 1779. Shortly thereafter, Charles III issued a flamboyant "Manifesto" consisting of a catalogue of fabricated charges against Great Britain. No possible doubt now remained that Spain would enter the war. The only question to be resolved was the timing.

Since he had been appointed comptroller of the navy in 1778, Captain Charles Middleton had devoted all his time to naval matters. In his opinion, the Royal Navy was in a perilous state, and not because of any shortage of ships. The navy list showed some 260 ships of war "from 40 guns downwards" in commission. Of these, 130 were coppered. Why, then, Middleton asked Sandwich, was it that so few enemy privateers were taken; that British trade was not safe even in the Channel, and the convoy system so irregular and inefficient? Why were there no plans for judicious employment of Great Britain's fleets, cruisers, and convoys? Measures never planned but always expedient had invariably produced only "confusion and misfortunes." He continued, ". . . I may venture to assert that, unless a new plan is adopted, and your lordship gives your

‡‡ But Charles would not give *de jure* recognition. He had an agent in Philadelphia, Don Juan de Mirelles, but Don Juan was not accredited.

whole time to the business of the admiralty, the misapplication of the fleet will bring ruin upon this country."

Middleton had had ample opportunity to observe Sandwich, who devoted most of his time to "amusements and private concerns."* He finally wrote the First Lord:

> The office you are in, my lord, is one of the first magnitude at this time, and the safety of your sovereign and his dominions depends on its operations. If I, my lord, who am a professional man, find myself unequal to the duties of the office I am in, with an application of twelve hours six days in the week, how is it possible that your lordship can manage yours, which is equally extensive, in three or four? Indeed, my lord, it cannot be.

The Admiralty, he said, was such "a mass of confusion" that he saw "no prospect of reducing it to order." He concluded this courageous letter with the statement that if he were to be questioned in Parliament he could say nothing favorable to the Admiralty as then administered by the Earl of Sandwich. "The whole system of the admiralty is rotten, and must tumble about your lordship's [ears] if it is not soon altered."[9]

On May 7, 1779, one of Middleton's close friends, Captain Richard Kempenfelt, R.N., reported aboard H.M.S. *Victory*, flagship of the Channel fleet, as first captain to Vice-admiral Sir Charles Hardy, who was given the command after Keppel struck his flag.† Hardy, an impatient, bumbling sexagenarian, had not been at sea for eight years and had enjoyed the comforts of a placid haven as governor of the Naval Hospital at Greenwich where he anticipated he would spend the few years remaining to him. He was not qualified to command the Channel fleet in this moment of national crisis, but he was the only senior admiral who would agree to accept. The King had urged Keppel to return to active duty; Keppel had refused. Nor would Vice-admiral Viscount Howe take this or any other command so long as Sandwich presided at the Admiralty. The choice was Sir Charles Hardy. Those who knew the old admiral were aware that he needed an intelligent and active officer to assist him to ready the fleet for action and to be at his right hand in the crucial battle for control of the Channel which all believed imminent. Richard Kempenfelt, perhaps the most able captain in the British Navy, had been selected by the King, who seemed to be well aware of Hardy's failings for this high command.

Kempenfelt had not been long aboard H.M.S. *Victory* when he wrote an almost desperate letter to Middleton. He described Hardy as a mar-

---

* On one recorded occasion "trouting" for a long weekend with two gentleman friends and three handsome ladies of questionable virtue.

† Kempenfelt's position as first captain would equate to the modern position of chief of staff.

tinet who had "not one grain of the commander-in-chief. I hear it often said the salvation of Britain depends upon this fleet. I never hear the expression but I turn pale and sink. My God, what have your great people done by such an appointment!" Kempenfelt's first object was to rid the fleet of this incompetent admiral always "in a hurry" who could not gain either the esteem or the confidence of his officers and men and who devoted his time to petty harassment of his subordinates: ". . . in this great national charge, the command of the fleet, the person you have chose is not in any degree equal to it . . . for the commander of a fleet he is totally unfit."[10] But it was with this admiral in command that Great Britain was to face the most critical threat to her existence since those remote days when the "Invincible Armada" sailed up the English Channel.

The omens were not auspicious. Should Spain enter the war, as the King and his ministers felt sure she soon would, the combined Bourbon fleets would outnumber Hardy's command by more than two to one in ships of the line and would hold a similar advantage in weight of metal thrown by broadsides. Although the competence of French and Spanish admirals, the courage of their fighting men, and the ability of their fleets to maneuver together were unknown quantities, they could not be discounted. Nor could the well-equipped French invasion force of 30,000 infantry, artillery, and dragoons standing ready to embark at St.-Malo and Dunkirk to cross the Channel under cover of the great fleet and to land somewhere on the southern coast of England or perhaps on Irish beaches near Cork.

Other problems afflicted those responsible for readying the fleet for defense of the homeland. The officer corps had been riven by the Keppel-Palliser feud and a strange and "dreadful distemper" raged aboard several ships. Most of the men pressed to fill Hardy's crews were scum of the London docks, totally untrained in gunnery and with little conception of demanding duties aloft. One captain reported his crew to be "the poorest dirty vermin that ever came on board a man of war."[11] And despite a secret "hot press" from which merchant seamen were not exempt, Hardy's fleet still lacked 25 per cent of authorized complement of sailors and marines.

The admiral's sailing orders dated May 29, 1779, directed him to block Brest, cruise off Ushant, and should D'Orvilliers manage to slip out and elude him, to give chase and bring the French fleet to a decisive action. Should the Bourbon fleets combine and be discovered in preponderant force, he was to retire to Portsmouth or Torbay. Admiral Baron Mulgrave objected to these orders. He believed thirty of the line could cut the unwieldy enemy armada to pieces. From Portsmouth, where he was expediting preparations to sail, he wrote Sandwich he had found Admiral Hardy diligent; the Channel fleet in good order; its officers and men zealous and their morale high. These official reports did much to revive drooping spirits in Whitehall and on Downing Street.‡

On the evening of the following day the King wrote his First Lord of the Admiralty: "I am much pleased at the hearing this morning that Sir Charles Hardy sailed yesterday and that his fleet was in such perfect order. I own I expect great efforts from this force, and shall not be satisfied if persons count what number of ships are brought against us. It was the vigour of mind shown by Queen Elizabeth and her subjects, added to the assistance of Divine Providence, that saved this island when attacked by the Spaniards. It is necessary to be active on the present occasion, and to bring the enemy as soon as possible to decisive action."[12]

Similar exhortations had no visible effect on the First Minister, who was trying desperately to fashion an "Arrangement"—any arrangement—that would allow him to retire. His behavior served only to encourage dissidence in a cabinet which seemed from day to day to be on the verge of falling apart. The King was well aware of this situation, and on June 21 summoned his ministers, who needed a strong dose of his own determination, to meet him at Queen's House. At this informal meeting the King invited his ministers to sit in the royal presence. His Majesty spoke for nearly forty minutes and "made a most able speech . . . recommended unanimity and spirit in their several departments, and promised his firm and cordial support. He recapitulated the whole progress of our difficulties ever since the repeal of the Stamp Act, and acknowledged that the change of administration when the Stamp Act was repealed had been a fatal measure."[13] George III made it emphatically clear that he did not propose to parley with the Americans who he was convinced could still be forced to submit.

He wrote Lord North the day after this meeting: "What I said yesterday was the dictates of frequent and severe self examination, I can never depart from it, before I will even hear of any Man's readiness to come into Office I will expect to see it signed under his hand that He is resolved to keep the Empire entire and that no troops shall be consequently withdrawn from thence, nor Independence ever allowed."[14] The King was fully prepared to face the Bourbon powers with courage and equanimity and to prosecute the American war to a victorious conclusion. At this time of grave difficulties both foreign and domestic, George III again showed himself to be a man of stubborn determination.

As they saw their beloved country drifting inexorably toward a calamity, many Britons whose patriotism could not possibly be impugned were increasingly worried. Walpole wrote Sir Horace Mann that he was as impartial as he could be "considering my indignation at the ruin brought upon my country by, both, as worthless and incapable a set of

‡ Were Mulgrave and Kempenfelt reporting on the same fleet? It seems apparent that Mulgrave was telling Sandwich what he knew the First Lord wanted to hear.

men as ever had the front to call themselves politicians. They have hurried us and blundered us into a civil war, a French war, a Spanish war;
America is lost; Jamaica, the West Indian islands, Gibraltar and Port Mahon [Minorca] are scarce to be saved . . . Ireland is in great danger. . . .
Of this country I should have little fear, if men who have conducted
themselves so wretchedly were not still our governors!" He added that
the court, the Tories, and the clergy ("the worst Tories") had "infatuated
the nation." Although he was not yet ready to embrace Opposition, he
affirmed that hourly, daily, and yearly antiadministration spokesmen in
Lords and Commons had "foretold every individual step that has happened." Time had seen every prophecy verified. The nation, he wrote,
faced a terrible predicament. "Prerogative has been whispered into the
nation's ears and taken root. The Tories scruple not to call for it. The
ministers, worthless and incapable wretches, and ill-connected with each
other, and cohering but from common danger, have little or no credit
with their master."[15]

The easy conquest of St. Lucia and the reduction of Georgia raised
spirits in London. Germain promised Clinton reinforcements of 6,000
rank and file and assured him General Grant would soon be returning to
New York from the West Indies. While he awaited the promised troops,
Clinton conferred with Commodore Sir George Collier, R.N., a spirited
officer who had relieved Gambier and was temporarily commander in
chief of the British fleet in American waters.

The general had two projects in mind: the first, to send a raiding
force into Chesapeake Bay to destroy shipping, grain, naval stores, and
tobacco collected there; the second, to seize American forts at Stony
Point, on the west bank of the Hudson about twelve miles south of the
citadel at West Point, and at Verplanck's Point on the east bank. The two
small forts, weakly garrisoned, commanded the important crossing place
at King's Ferry. Control of these complementary positions, where the
river is less than a mile wide, would cover later operations he planned
against the important key to the Hudson Highlands.

The Chesapeake expedition sailed on May 5; five days later Brigadier
General Edward Mathew landed with his assault troops near Portsmouth, Virginia. The defenders of the small fort fled the scene in confusion without taking time to strike the flag. Collier and Mathew then proceeded to carry out planned operations, which they did with destructive
effect: ". . . besides the universal terror and alarm which this armament
spread in its arrival through every part of the country bordering on that
great expanse of water, the loss which the enemy sustained was
prodigious—consisting chiefly of provision magazines, gunpowder, and
naval stores, about 150 vessels of different sizes (several being of force
and richly laden) and a quantity of cannon and ordnance stores, to-

gether with some thousand hogsheads of tobacco. . . ."[16] It seems remarkable that the British could think of no better disposition of these valuable prizes than to consign them to the flames.°°

Collier and Mathew returned from the Chesapeake on May 29. Troops were held aboard, and on the following morning, after General Sir Henry Clinton embarked, the force proceeded upriver on a flowing tide with a following wind. On June 3 Clinton put Major General the Honourable John Vaughan ashore eight miles south of Verplanck's and landed himself on the west bank some three miles south of Stony Point. The defenders wisely departed from this cul-de-sac and the small garrison at Fort La Fayette surrendered to Vaughan. Thus with no difficulty Sir Henry had gained control of positions of great tactical value. But where were the troops he had counted on to enable him to exploit his success? (". . . where, alas, were the promised succors to enable me to prosecute my plan?")

Clinton returned to New York in a pessimistic mood: "Another year's expense of this destructive war was now going to be added to the four which had so unprofitably preceded, without a probability of its producing a single event to better our condition or brighten our prospects."[17] Shortly before sailing up the Hudson he had written Germain to point out the variety of difficulties under which he labored. He was "upon the spot" and competent to assess the situation: "Why then, My Lord, without consulting me will you adopt the ill-digested or interested suggestions of people who cannot be competent judges of the subject, and puzzle me by hinting wishes with which I cannot agree yet am loath to disregard. For God's sake, My Lord, if you wish me to do anything, leave me to myself and let me adapt my effects to the hourly change of circumstances."[18]

The commodore, too, took quill in hand to write a personal letter to Sandwich. He and Clinton were sympathetic: "I am very happy in informing your Lordship that the most perfect confidence and harmony subsists between Sir Henry Clinton and myself. I receive the readiest compliance with every request of mine . . . and flatter myself he has found me particularly attentive to second his exertions for the King's service." He gave his opinion that "this campaign is the last, and that rebellion is at last fairly thrown on its back. Paper money is now worth nothing, credit at an end, resources failing, the rebel Congress no longer possessing the least confidence . . . the distresses of the common people are beyond description, and I rejoice to say the King's affairs have not worn so prosperous an appearance since the rebellion broke out." He predicted that within a "very few weeks" America would give up the "chimera" of independence and sue for peace. ". . . the wisdom and steadiness of the King's Ministers will doubtless prevent the twelve

°° Collier wished to take some of the ships and the most valuable stores to New York, but Mathew insisted that the expedition return there without delay.

headed hydra from doing any more mischief in this century at least.†† This optimistic assessment of British prospects was directly contrary to the tenor of the report Clinton was sending Germain by the same packet.

Although Clinton felt he had not the force in hand to undertake a major operation against Washington, he realized that he could not remain inactive in New York during the campaigning season without incurring severe criticism, and when he returned from his successful foray up the Hudson he began planning for a large-scale punitive raid on Connecticut coastal towns, specifically New Haven, Fairfield, and Norwalk, where privateers that seriously impeded British shipping in Long Island Sound harbored. Clinton had determined to teach these Yankees a lesson, and entrusted the operation to the royal governor of New York, Major General William Tryon. He ordered Tryon to destroy "public stores, privateers, etc." and to do "every other injury he could consistent with humanity." He hoped, too, that the raids would draw Washington from the west bank of the Hudson toward Connecticut, thus creating an opportunity for a descent on his communications and opening the possibility of battle under favorable tactical conditions.

These were reasonable expectations, especially if Major General Grant returned as expected from the West Indies. But as June drew to an end with no sign either of Grant or of the reinforcements earlier promised by Germain, the general withdrew part of the Rhode Island garrison to New York. He assigned Tryon an elite force of 2,600 plus six pieces of artillery. Tryon embarked on July 3, and on the morning of the fifth, Commodore Sir George Collier's small fleet anchored off New Haven. The troops went ashore at West Haven (Brigadier General Garth) and East Haven (Major General Tryon). Garth encountered considerable opposition on his six-mile march; Tryon practically none. The British lay on their arms that night and the next morning destroyed stores, took an armed privateer and half a dozen cannon, but did not burn the town.

Two days later, the Redcoats landed at Fairfield, where militia firing from houses offered scattered resistance. Tryon ordered the town put to the torch and retired to Huntington Bay (Long Island) to rest for two days.‡‡ On July 11 he recrossed the Sound and landed at Norwalk. Here the British met a fairly well organized resistance offered by several hundred militia and 250 Continentals commanded by Brigadier General Samuel Parsons. The Redcoats drove the Americans and plundered and burned the town. Nearly 250 homes, barns, shops, and other buildings, including a church, were destroyed.

If Tryon had attempted, as he told Clinton, to waken "a general terror and despondency," he had not succeeded. On the contrary, his activities aroused general anger and a desire for revenge. The North Carolina

†† Georgia had returned to allegiance to the crown.
‡‡ The town was literally reduced to ashes. Nearly 200 structures, including 100 homes as well as shops, schools, and churches, were destroyed.

delegation to Congress wrote that the raids revealed "the predatory designs of the Enemy and of that inbecility which prevents them from carrying on Operations of greater vigor."[19] James Lovell of the Committee of Foreign Affairs urged Franklin to plan to retaliate "on the coast of England for the burning of our beautiful Fairfield . . . a single privateer might, I think, show there a striking example of the species of war carried on by Britain against America." Henry Laurens compared Tryon "brandishing his torch in Connecticut" to the infamous Duke of Alva.[20] The Marine Committee wrote Franklin that "the Vengeance denounced against these States by the Manifesto of the British Commissioners will be exercised in its fullest extent." The only way to put a stop to wanton plundering, burning, and destruction in America was "to retaliate upon our Enemy by destroying, if possible, some of the most distinguished Cities in Great Britain and the West Indies."[21] James Duane wrote his wife: "We hear, with Horror, of the Devastation committed by Governor Tryon in Connecticut. While it will tarnish the glory of the british nation and render them odious to all Europe; the miserable instruments in this tragedy will be execrated and detested—in a political View it will have an Effect directly contrary to what is intended. Americans can never be worked to submission by Cruelty and Devastation. Their aversion to their Destroyers will become deeper rivetted. . . ."[22]

Although he was distressed by Tryon's raids, Washington realized he could do nothing to impede such operations. Nor did he permit them to distract him from his principal object, which was to ensure the security of the Highlands and to defend West Point. Before Tryon sailed from New York, Washington had established his headquarters near Newburgh, deployed the army to deal with Clinton should he move up the Hudson, and set in motion planning to recapture Stony Point, an operation he entrusted to Brigadier General Anthony Wayne.

Both Washington and Clinton appreciated the difficulties attending an attack on this key position. The British general was not apprehensive, for the natural strength of Stony Point "being near a peninsula at high water and of great height and difficult ascent, seemed to require little more than vigilance to defend it from a *coup de main* which was the only kind of attack the enemy dare engage in." This was precisely the sort of operation Washington and Wayne planned. Both were convinced that a night attack from the land side across the morass could carry the position.

Shortly after midnight on July 16, Wayne's forty-man "forlorn hope," commanded by Lieutenant Colonel Chevalier Louis de Fleury, followed closely by the advanced guard with bayonets fixed, waded the marsh in silence, hacked their way through flimsy abatis, overcame the pickets, and broke into the fort. Surprise was complete; Lieutenant Colonel Henry Johnson had no opportunity to organize his defenses, and after a short fight, surrendered the garrison. The Americans suffered about 100 killed and wounded; British casualties were nearly the same.* Clinton gave the Americans full marks: "The success attending this bold and well combined attempt of the enemy procured very deservedly no small share of reputation to the spirited officer (General Wayne) who conducted it, and was, I must confess, a very great affront to us, the more mortifying since it was unexpected and possibly avoidable."

The Americans demolished the fortifications, set fire to the barracks and storerooms, and withdrew. Four days later British troops reoccupied the site. But the fleeting triumph provided a needed tonic to American morale and gave the press a rare enough opportunity: "Nothing can exceed the spirit and intrepidity of our brave countrymen in storming and carrying the British fortress at Stony Point. . . . No action during the war, performed by the British military has equalled this coup de main. . . . What action has Clinton to boast of, this campaign, that may be compared with this master-piece of soldiership by General Wayne?"†

Washington had not dropped his plans to crush the Mohawk, Onondaga, Cayuga, and Seneca in New York State and to capture their base of support at Fort Niagara on the southeast shore of Lake Ontario. He conceived that vigorous punitive operations would put an end to the depredations of the Iroquois confederacy and its Tory allies, and offered command to Major General Gates. Gates demurred. He was, so he wrote, not in the best of health and was too old to undertake an arduous campaign. Washington then named Major General John Sullivan. Concurrently, Colonel Daniel Brodhead, who had relieved McIntosh, was to set out from Fort Pitt, ravage the Indian settlements in northwest Pennsylvania, and then join Sullivan for the attack on Niagara.

After many delays, Sullivan moved from his advanced base at Tioga at the end of August. On the twenty-ninth, his force of some 2,000 Continentals, reinforced by Brigadier General James Clinton with a column of 1,400 New York militiamen, met Indians and Tories commanded by Chief Joseph Brant and Captain Walter Butler at Newtown, in south-central New York state, a few miles north of the Pennsylvania line. Butler and Brant chose to stand and fight and were decisively beaten. During the next month, Sullivan split his command into half a dozen groups. These moved freely through the Indian country, burned their log houses, laid waste their gardens, orchards, and cornfields, killed warriors (and, when they could, took their scalps), and visited upon the Indians the same terror and destruction they had so often inflicted on settlers. Sullivan did not, however, proceed to reduce Fort Niagara and his failure to do so would be productive of renewed border warfare. And al-

* Wayne's force totaled about 1,200. Clinton reported the British garrison at a strength of 615.

† Congress ordered two medals struck to commemorate this victory. One was struck in honor of General Wayne; the other in honor of De Fleury.

though Brodhead's operations in the Allegheny valley in northwestern Pennsylvania had been as thorough and as brutal as Sullivan's in south-central New York, their effect was equally transitory, for even as the Americans withdrew from the country they had systematically ravaged, the Iroquois began sharpening scalping knives. The Indian warriors had been humiliated, but they were not beaten. Nor were their Tory allies ready to beg peace.

The question of how best to provide for Loyalists who had fled their homes and sought the protection of British arms had for some time received serious consideration in London, and in September 1778, Germain wrote Clinton that the government proposed to provide a secure haven for them in northeastern Maine between the Penobscot and St. Croix rivers. The secretary added that His Majesty intended to constitute this considerable area as a province which would provide Nova Scotia with a secure southern flank and at the same time protect the rich fisheries. And "the obtaining possession of a country abounding with mast timber and naval stores are strong inducements for the adoption of this measure." Penobscot Bay would also provide "a safe and commodious harbor for the King's ships." Clinton directed Brigadier General Francis Mac Lean, commanding in Nova Scotia, to undertake the operation, and on June 26, 1779, Mac Lean landed on the eastern shore of Penobscot Bay near the present town of Castine. The British immediately began felling trees and throwing up parapets for the fort Mac Lean planned.

These activities did not pass unnoticed by the Council of Massachusetts Bay, and Samuel Adams directed the state Navy Board to ready ships for an expedition to evict the British. Three Continental vessels then lay idle in Boston Harbor. These, commanded by Captain Dudley Saltonstall, who flew his flag in frigate *Warren*, were augmented by an assortment of state brigantines, a dozen privateers, and a score of transports. The Council ordered 1,000 militia commanded by Brigadier General Solomon Lovell to be embodied and embark without delay. Although the commander in chief and the gentlemen in Philadelphia were in total ignorance of this project, both Mac Lean and Clinton received full details of preparations from British agents in Boston.

Lovell's nondescript force arrived at Penobscot Bay on July 25, but instead of assaulting Mac Lean's primitive fort at the earliest possible moment, Lovell chose to waste days digging trenches and parallels and otherwise preparing for a classic investment. These ill-considered, useless, and exhausting activities were rudely interrupted on August 12 by the arrival of Commodore Sir George Collier from New York with a landing force of 1,600 Redcoat regulars. Saltonstall and his equally valiant captains fled upriver, beached their ships, set fire to them, and took refuge in the wilderness, where they were soon joined by the quaking Lovell and his disorganized militiamen.

Massachusetts soldiers and sailors whose commanders had refused to face the British soon began fighting among themselves for scarce food. Dozens were hurt in these squabbles; others died of starvation and exposure on the dreary march through the Maine woods to safety. So ended this ill-conceived and ineptly executed fiasco. Congress dismissed Saltonstall from the navy. Major General of Suffolk County militia Lovell and Peleg Wadsworth, his equally feckless second-in-command, should have been brought to trial before a general court-martial and cashiered, but thanks to the influence of Samuel Adams, who in his capacity as a master strategist had planned and promoted this aborted affair, these incompetent cowards escaped the disgrace they so justly merited.

When D'Orvilliers sailed from Brest on June 4, 1779, to rendezvous with the Spanish fleet, he knew that Madrid would soon declare war, and on June 21 she did so. Although Charles III and Floridablanca had no particular interest in the invasion of Britain, participation of the Spanish fleet was the price they had to pay for a French guarantee not to cease hostilities until Gibraltar, the key to the Mediterranean, ceded to England in 1713 by the Treaty of Utrecht, had been returned to Spain.‡ As yet, no detailed plans existed for the Spanish assault on "the Rock," for they believed the defenders could be starved out. On the day Charles III issued his declaration of war, Lieutenant General Don Joaquin de Mendoza sealed off communications between Gibraltar and the mainland, and a Spanish squadron took station to prevent resupply of the Rock by sea.

The Gibraltar garrison, some 5,400 officers and men, commanded by a vigorous, determined, and forbidding general, George Augustus Eliott, made ready to stand a protracted siege. The Rock was reasonably well stocked with food and ammunition, and ministers in Whitehall shared Eliott's conviction that he could hold the position until the navy could bring essential supplies of food and munitions. The immediate concern in London was not Gibraltar but the threat to the British Isles.

Five days after D'Orvilliers left Brest, Hardy sailed from Portsmouth with thirty of the line. His mission was to cover the south coasts of England and Ireland, to pick up a rich homeward-bound West Indian convoy and escort it to safety, and to keep the sea until forced into port by weather or by shortage of water and provisions.** The lords of the Admiralty ordered him to cruise off the Scilly Islands, west of Land's End.

‡ Spain had refused to give a reciprocal guarantee not to lay down arms until Great Britain recognized the independence of the United States. Madrid had no wish to see an independent republic in the Western Hemisphere.

** The convoy brought sugar, fruits, molasses, and rum worth £4 million.

As Hardy's fleet beat its way to the station assigned, D'Orvilliers arrived off Cape Finisterre, where with mounting exasperation and sickly crews, he awaited the arrival of Teniente General Don Luis de Córdoba y Córdoba and his great fleet, delayed at Cádiz to complete fitting-out and provisioning. Admiral d'Orvilliers was worried and had good reason to be. One summer day followed the next with no sign of the Spanish. His sailors were suffering from dysentery and scurvy. Suitable weather for a Channel crossing would soon end. And D'Orvilliers had other problems. He had been hurried out of Brest before his ships were fully provisioned; he had not been given an adequate allowance of wine for his sailors to enjoy their normal liter per day, and was dissatisfied with some of his captains who were not professionally qualified.

Five weeks slid away before De Córdoba appeared on July 23. What measure of relief D'Orvilliers enjoyed was to be momentary, for by a stupid oversight the Spaniards had not been supplied with French signal books. Translation entailed further delay, and not until August 7, nearly nine weeks after D'Orvilliers had sailed from Brest, did the combined fleet with sixty-six ships of the line sight Ushant.†† Spanish crews were afflicted with dysentery, scurvy, and, in most of the ships, a raging epidemic of smallpox.

Hardy now had under command thirty-four of the line and half a dozen frigates. But the vast disparity in both ships and weight of broadside between the British and Bourbon fleets dampened neither the King's spirits nor those of officers with the fleet. His Majesty "sighed" for action; he wrote Sandwich that he found suspense "the most shocking of all situations" and rejoiced when he learned that the fleets of his enemies were approaching: "I trust in the assistance of Divine Providence and the excellent state of the great western fleet, and therefore am quite at ease as to the end of this conflict."[23] Several days later, when the combined fleet had been sighted beating its way toward the English coast, he again wrote Sandwich: "Decision is the joy of my life . . . I cannot but feel happy that now the fleets cannot fail, within very few days, of coming to battle."[24]

That evening (August 16) the Bourbon armada anchored within sight of Plymouth. A landing was momentarily apprehended. Admiral Shuldham reported the townspeople "mightily alarmed, even to the desertion of their houses and professions and retiring into the country." Militiamen and volunteers manned hastily dug entrenchments overlooking the harbor; Shuldham sent three hundred seamen to man the batteries. Captain Paul Ourry, R.N., master of the dockyard, wrote Sandwich he seriously considered setting fire to it before D'Orvilliers did. The First

†† Of these, thirty were French, including flagship *La Bretagne* of 110 guns and *La Ville de Paris* of 100.

Lord thought Ourry was out of his mind, but replied with a calming letter: "I cannot think you in earnest when you talk of burning the dockyard." As Plymouth's panic-stricken citizens deserted their threatened town, Sir Charles Hardy, far to the west, cruised off the Scillies.

Britain was "mightily alarmed" but panic was confined to Plymouth. Elsewhere, citizens of all classes volunteered for the militia and proceeded to designated camps. Within the space of a few weeks, several hundred militia companies were embodied. Wealthy noblemen in England and Scotland raised and equipped battalions and Parliament authorized organization of fencible regiments.‡‡ In Ireland, 40,000 Protestants were in arms. Lords lieutenant of every county bordering on the coast were directed to see that all livestock was driven inland, an order the Duke of Richmond, lord lieutenant of Sussex and leader of Opposition in the House of Lords, refused to obey. The King, properly outraged at "so public and flagrant an instance of disobedience," wrote Lord North urging that the duke be dismissed.* Fortunately, no other lord lieutenant followed Richmond's example. Englishmen in arms were preparing to fight everywhere in defense of their island home, and the Bourbon powers were ceding them the time they needed.

D'Orvilliers had been at sea for ten weeks. His supplies of food and water were dangerously low; his crews more than decimated by dysentery and scurvy. Time was running out. At this critical moment the admiral received new orders directing a radical change in invasion plans. Now, he was not to land on the Isle of Wight, but to the west, on the coast of Cornwall. He was to keep the sea and await further orders and resupply. As D'Orvilliers hastily composed a letter stating his objections to the changes proposed, the weather worsened, and as easterlies built to nearly half-gale force the admiral gave the signal to weigh. For six days the combined fleet ran to the west. The same winds blew Hardy far to the west of the Scillies. For several days the hostile fleets were in distant visual contact. But no guns were fired. As the wind abated, D'Orvilliers bore off to the south, set course for Brest, and on arrival there resigned his command in disgust. Teniente General Luis de Córdoba y Córdoba, with his great ships and their sickly crews, accompanied him. Sir Charles Hardy, fighting the easterlies, gradually beat his way to Plymouth. The invasion threat, aborted by the inexcusable delays, indecision and ineptitude, of both French and Spanish Ministries of Marine, by De Córdoba, and finally by a gale, had passed.

‡‡ Fencible regiments were limited to home service. The Fencibles of 1779 would later become the Territorials.

* Apparently, no action was taken. This episode provides an example both of Lord North's weakness and of the degree to which faction prevailed even during a national crisis. A more confident ministry would have consigned the duke to the Tower.

As British and Bourbon fleets fumbled for one another off the south coast of England, the French expeditionary force commanded by Lieutenant General le Comte de Vaux completed preparation for passage of the Channel. Among those most intimately concerned in final planning for the invasion was Marquis de La Fayette, appointed by De Vaux to be his *aide-maréchal-général des logis*, "a very important and agreeable place." The young marquis had arrived in France five months earlier, had managed to restore himself to the favor of his King, had been received by Marie Antoinette, and had conferred with Vergennes and other ministers on numerous occasions. He had never missed an opportunity to plead for massive French aid to America. He had bombarded the Minister of Finance so assiduously "about that great article, money" that his welcome at the Treasury was somewhat less than cordial. He wrote Washington that money had given him great trouble. "I insisted upon it so much that the Director of Finance looks upon me as a devil. France has met great expences lately; those Spaniards will not give their dollars easily." He could, however, report some small success: "Dr. Franklin has got some money to pay the bills of Congress and I hope I shall determine them to greater sacrifices. Serving America, my dear General, is to my heart an inexpressible happiness."[25]

While he waited at Le Havre to embark for England, La Fayette received a letter from Vergennes asking him for specific suggestions as to how France could best support America. On July 16, 1779, the marquis replied at length. Before leaving America he had discussed this question with Washington and since arriving in France had devoted considerable time to developing several plans, which he now presented to Vergennes. The first of these called for a French expeditionary force to seize Halifax "the store house and bulwark of the British Navy in the new world." This operation would require 4,000 men, 200 dragoons, 100 hussars, and appropriate artillery. "We want officers who can deny themselves, live frugally, abstain from all airs, especially a quick, peremptory manner and who can dispense with for a year the pleasures, society and literature of Paris. Consequently, we ought to take few colonels and courtiers whose habits are in no respect American."[26] The force should sail from France not later than February 1780.

An equally acceptable alternative involved operations in the Chesapeake Bay area in early spring, 1780, seizure of Rhode Island in May, and an attack on Halifax in June or July. Whatever the target selected, he deemed it of first importance to get a body of troops to America. If an advance detachment of 2,000 could be sent to Boston "as early as possible, their presence would restore vigour to the American army and would encourage the Americans to activity." He continued: "The state of America and the new plan the British seem to be adopting, render the expedition more than ever necessary. Devastated coasts, ruined ports, commerce checked, fortified posts whence these missions are made, all seem to call for our assistance both by sea and land." He acknowledged that Americans were "somewhat difficult to deal with, especially by Frenchmen," but would pledge his life that all difficulties would be avoided and the troops cordially received.

Two weeks later he again wrote from Le Havre urging Vergennes to send troops, for "such a detachment would encourage the Americans" to undertake whatever enterprises "circumstances might allow." During August La Fayette was still at Le Havre "divided between uncertainty and impatience, two conditions little calculated to cool my blood." In mid-September, when they all realized there would be no assault over English beaches in 1779, he wrote Vergennes that he had resigned himself "to grieve in silence," but again begged that troops be sent across the Atlantic. In October Comte de Vaux was directed to dismantle the invasion force and order the troops to their permanent stations. The marquis remained at Le Havre. His only wish now was to rejoin Washington, but he was not willing to leave his native land until he had received solid assurances that she would give substantial aid to his adopted one.

The disgrace of the fiasco that terminated the career of Admiral d'Orvilliers was to be retrieved in some measure by the American Captain John Paul Jones, whose ill-assorted squadron sailed from the Groix roadstead near L'Orient on August 14, two days before the Bourbon fleet anchored in sight of the British coast. For six months prior to this time, Jones had been attempting to prevail on De Sartine to provide him with enough ships and men to conduct hit-and-run raids on English and Scottish coastal towns. Both Franklin and La Fayette had given powerful support to the captain's constant addresses to the minister. Finally, in the spring of 1779, Louis XVI and his council had approved the plans and agreed to provide the ships Jones requested. Several "tubs" were offered him; he rejected them; he wanted a fast sailing ship for his flag. Time passed. Jones became fretful and angry. He sometimes thought Franklin was dragging his feet, that John Adams (soon to return to America) was no help, and that Arthur Lee was maliciously conniving against him.

The squadron "Commodore" Jones took to sea consisted of three frigates, a corvette, a cutter, and two privateers. His flagship was a converted East Indiaman, *Le Duc de Duras*. As compliment to Franklin he christened her *Bonhomme Richard*, a name forever to be linked with his own. The officers of this ship were Americans; half the sailors English, Irish, and Scotch. The marines were French. Frigate *Alliance* was commanded by Captain Pierre Landais; frigate *La Pallas* by Captain Nicolas

Cottineau. As Jones had anticipated, the two privateers deserted him shortly after he was well at sea, and cutter *Cerf* returned to L'Orient. Her captain claimed that in the storm of August 26 "the devil himself could not have kept at sea." Jones had.

The little squadron sailed west of Ireland, set a course north toward the Shetlands, picked up several prizes, and on September 7 was off the Orkneys. For several months the Admiralty had kept fairly close track of Jones, but the threat of invasion absorbed everyone in Whitehall as it did every available ship. For the time being this "pirate," as the British chose to describe him, was thus able to operate unmolested. But, North wrote Sandwich, "One of the first things to be done after the departure of the combined fleets will be to send a squadron, or perhaps two, to look for Paul Jones and prevent the mischief he intends against the coasts of Great Britain and Ireland."[27]

At the moment, the "commodore" was having a more serious problem within his own command than any created by the Royal Navy. He had some time earlier discovered that Captain Landais of *Alliance* had no intention of co-operating. The French captain, insubordinate and insolent, announced that he proposed to take no further orders from Jones, who no doubt wished he could dispense with the services of this eccentric, incompetent, and unreliable French officer. But just as there was no way to command his obedience, there was no way to get rid of him.

On September 15 Jones, displaying his customary audacity, entered the Firth of Forth. His intention was to sink what ships were lying in the Firth and to levy a contribution of £100,000 on Leith. He threw a mighty fright into citizens of Dunbar, Edinburgh, Leith, and Kirkcaldy, many of whom packed their families into carriages and their most cherished possessions in carts and departed for the countryside. But adverse winds foiled his projects, and on the evening of September 17 his little squadron cleared the Firth and set course toward the south.

On September 21 Jones was off the Yorkshire coast, steering south toward the Humber. His presence was enough to throw the gentry and merchants in every coastal town from Scarborough to the estuary of the Humber into a panic. Many fled inland with their families; the militia was called out and appeals for help were rushed to the Admiralty. On the following day, contrary winds thwarted his design to enter the Humber. He turned north toward his rendezvous with fame.

Off Flamborough Head he sighted a convoy of forty-four sail escorted by forty-four-gun frigate *Serapis* (Captain Richard Pearson) and sloop of war *Countess of Scarborough* (Captain Thomas Piercy). As *Bonhomme Richard* approached, the convoy made for safety at Scarborough. Jones made for *Serapis*, but could not get within gun range until moonrise. With *Bonhomme Richard* closing, Pearson hailed. Jones replied by striking his British colors and running up the American flag. Less than one hundred feet apart, both fired broadsides.

Now on the starboard quarter of *Serapis* and with his bow in contact with her stern, Jones called away boarders. They were repulsed, and he sheered off. But in moments, the ships were again locked in fiery embrace. At this point, Pearson called: "Have you struck?" Jones replied with the dramatic words: "I have not yet begun to fight." From the tops and yards of each ship a hail of bullets and showers of grenades fell on the other. Both were battered and afire; on each, scores of men lay dead and mortally wounded on blood-drenched decks. And still the battle raged. Meanwhile, Landais in *Alliance* cruised around and discharged three broadsides. He was not aiming at *Serapis*, but at *Bonhomme Richard*, as crewmen on *Richard* later testified. *Richard* was slowly sinking. It was now Pearson's turn to call away boarders. The party was bloodily repulsed. With his mainmast tottering, and in a moment to crash, Pearson struck. Some three hundred officers and men of both ships were killed or wounded in the sanguinary fight. Later, Jones wrote Gouverneur Morris that after his second maneuver, the ships were alongside, "the enemy's stern opposite to our bows and the yards being locked. In that situation the action continued two hours and a half, both ships being on fire for the greater part of the time . . . At last the enemy struck the English flag, but the victory was too dear."[28]

Piercy, in *Countess of Scarborough*, had previously struck to Captain Cottineau of *Pallas*, and all able hands struggled in exhausting and futile efforts to save *Bonhomme Richard*. After forty-eight hours, Jones reluctantly abandoned her; she sank late in the morning of September 25, 1779. With *Serapis* jury-rigged, the squadron sailed for the Texel with five hundred officers and men as prisoners of war. Jones was acclaimed in Holland, as he would shortly be in France.

Jones was not to rest easily in the Texel roadstead. Shortly after he arrived with battered *Serapis*, *Countess of Scarborough*, and his prisoners, Sir Joseph Yorke, His Britannic Majesty's envoy to The Hague, addressed the High and Mighty Lords who sat as the States General of the United Provinces with a "strong and urgent demand for the seizure and restitution of said vessels" and for the immediate release of their crews captured "by the pirate Paul Jones, a Scotsman, a rebellious subject and state criminal." Fortunately, Their High Mightinesses were not disposed to grant Yorke's request, although they did make it clear to Jones that he must depart "with the first fair wind" after necessary repairs had been made and supplies put aboard.

Pearson had lost his ship, but had saved the Baltic convoy. He would eventually return home to be knighted for gallantry, which all participants—including Jones—testified he had exhibited on that memorable night. But it was "Commodore" John Paul Jones, Continental Navy, who off Flamborough Head entered his name in brilliant letters in the annals of naval history.†

While De Córdoba squandered precious time getting his fleet to the agreed rendezvous with the thoroughly frustrated D'Orvilliers, D'Estaing awaited an opportunity to strike at the British in the West Indies. In late June he was reinforced by eleven of the line and five frigates, and now, with twenty-five of the line and twelve frigates at Martinique, he held a clear superiority over Vice-admiral Byron, who commanded the British fleet in West Indian waters. The British admiral had but one frigate for reconnaissance, and that, apparently commanded by a timorous captain, produced nothing but misinformation. As Byron was much engaged refitting, escorting homeward-bound merchant convoys for several hundred miles, and meeting incoming convoys, D'Estaing had opportunity to fall upon poorly defended British islands and took St. Vincent and Grenada with no trouble.

In early July Byron returned from escorting a valuable homeward-bound convoy of more than two hundred sail to learn that Grenada had surrendered and that the French fleet was there. The British admiral sailed immediately and at dawn on July 6 encountered D'Estaing as his ships were leaving harbor. The disjointed battle that followed was bloody but inconclusive. The French admiral, with a decisive superiority, displayed great courage, poor judgment, and worse seamanship. Byron, who held the weather gauge, did not handle his fleet well, and four of his ships of the line were dismasted. Both admirals were anxious to break off the action. D'Estaing, who should have inflicted a decisive defeat on Byron's inferior force, did not even linger to take the British cripples. Byron, an admiral never favored by luck or weather, was soon thereafter relieved by Vice-admiral Hyde Parker. At Cap François D'Estaing busied himself refitting and provisioning for an expedition to recapture Savannah, Georgia, where he hoped to gain the victory that had eluded him since his arrival off the Delaware Capes thirteen months earlier.

Although the French admiral was under orders to leave half his fleet in the West Indies and return home with the remainder, he chose to disregard these instructions, and on the first day of September appeared unexpectedly off the coast of Georgia with twenty of the line, seven frigates, and transports carrying 5,000 troops. The few British ships present could not seriously oppose him; he quickly took frigate *Experiment* and several supply ships.‡ A privateer eluded him and set course for New

---

† When Jones finally arrived in Paris, after assorted troubles in Holland, to be decorated by Louis XVI and to learn that Pearson had been knighted, he observed laconically, "If I meet him again, I'll make a milord of him."

‡ *Experiment* carried £30,000 for payment of the Savannah garrison.

York to carry the news to Clinton. Brigadier General Augustine Prevost, commanding in Savannah, called in outlying detachments and set every able-bodied white and hundreds of slaves to work around the clock strengthening his defenses.

The weather delayed the French, who could not begin disembarking some fourteen miles south of Savannah until September 11. Five days later, D'Estaing drew up his forces before the city and summoned Prevost. The British commander played for time; he was hourly expecting Lieutenant Colonel John Maitland from Port Royal with reinforcements. As drums beat the "parley" and flags passed back and forth between the two headquarters, Maitland arrived by inland waterways with nearly 1,000 regulars, and Prevost, now confident his strengthened garrison could repel an assault, replied that he intended to defend the city "to the last extremity." By this time several detachments of Americans, including Count Casimir Pulaski's legion, had appeared and Major General Benjamin Lincoln came in with 1,250 Continentals. He and D'Estaing immediately fell into an argument as to how best to assault the now well-defended town. The decision, in which Lincoln concurred, was to undertake formal siege operations, and on October 3, French guns opened on the works, but with little effect.

As the days passed, D'Estaing's impatience increased. His squadron, denuded of seamen, gunners, and marines manning heavy cannon landed from the ships, lay in an exposed position, vulnerable to a hurricane as well as to sudden attack by a British fleet. He who had waited too long now decided he could wait no longer, and on October 8, 1779, again with Lincoln's agreement, ordered a general assault for the following day. Before dawn on October 9, French regiments led by D'Estaing assaulted the British redoubt at Spring Hill. Their guides led them into a bog. A thick fog shrouded the field; on the left, Lincoln's Americans mistook the way and came under heavy fire in low-lying ground. The attack collapsed in confusion: "Count D'Estaing, wounded in the arm, encouraged the soldiers to commence another attack" but "half of the officers were killed or wounded, the soldiers uncertain, the columns broken and intermingled without order, to retire was the general idea."[29] Prevost described the assaults as "certainly spirited and obstinately persevered in particularly on the Ebenezer Road [Spring Hill] redoubt. Two stand of colors were actually planted, and several of the assailants killed, upon its parapet." But they were driven off and "retired everywhere, in disorder and with precipitation."[30] The defenders suffered but sixteen killed and thirty-nine wounded; the attackers, nearly one thousand. Count Pulaski died of his wounds; D'Estaing, twice wounded, survived. Some wounded were carried from the field, but "want of linen and of surgeons prevented their wounds being dressed." Only the very slightly wounded were saved. "The rest were abandoned and are dead."[31]

The British made no attempt to interfere with withdrawal of the defeated allied forces. Lincoln, muttering against the French, returned to Charleston; D'Estaing, with eleven of the line, to France. Admiral de Grasse with half a dozen ships and transports carrying the battered French regiments sailed to Martinique. So ended D'Estaing's final attempt to retrieve his reputation in America.** The episode at Savannah, which Sir Henry Clinton described as "the greatest event that has happened the whole war," had wasted allied lives to no purpose and produced a further deterioration in Franco-American relations.

** When he arrived in France, he was retired and given a generous pension.

3

On the Brink of a Precipice

Anne César, Chevalier de la Luzerne, Louis XVI's minister designate to the United States who would relieve the ailing Gérard, landed in Boston, where he received an enthusiastic welcome, and went on to West Point to confer with Washington. One may infer the state of affairs in the American Army from the substance of the conversations as recorded by Colonel Alexander Hamilton. Washington hoped a French squadron could come north, but observed that the campaigning season was nearly over, and that a winter operation against New York or Rhode Island would require reorganization of his magazines and entail "a large increase of expense." Unless definite assurances could be given he could not undertake "to make extensive preparations for cooperating nor pledge himself for doing it effectually." Luzerne could give no such assurances.

Louis XVI's minister arrived in Philadelphia to find adherents of Silas Deane still engaged in vindictive and futile debates with their colleagues who supported Arthur Lee. Elbridge Gerry wrote John Adams he was not yet able to give him a full account of the proceedings of Congress relative to foreign affairs: ". . . the Embarrassments Difficulties and Delays attending this Business, in Consequence of the Disputes between the late Commissioners, have exceeded everything of the Kind, which I have before met with: So far have some of their friends in Congress been influenced in Attachments and Prejudice. . . ."

Congress had finally determined to cease issuing paper, but faced the imminent danger of running out of money. States were laggard in collecting taxes, or when they did collect them were not transmitting their apportioned shares to Philadelphia.* As speculators made fortunes, delegates debated price controls. Some were beginning to ask themselves how the war could possibly be carried on for another two months. The only hope seemed to be to induce Versailles to lend more money, or preferably to give it. Congress instructed Franklin to do what he could and commissioned Henry Laurens to proceed to Holland to negotiate a treaty of commerce and to borrow $10 million at 6 per cent.

For long hours Congress debated other important questions: the Newfoundland fisheries; the future boundaries of the United States; postwar rights to navigation on the Mississippi (which delegates agreed on as a western boundary); arrangements with Spain to use the port of New Orleans; and instructions for John Jay, who had been named minister to the court of Charles III.† But vexing trivialities continued to consume valuable time. Henry Laurens feared the worst. "We are at this moment on the brink of a precipice." As usual, finances were in "an awful state"; he anticipated "convulsions among the people" and mutiny in a "hungry and naked army" perennially short of provisions, lacking equipment, and for months unpaid.[1]

Before La Fayette left America he had asked Chevalier Louis de Fleury to write him occasional confidential reports of the prevailing situation, and before Christmas, 1779, De Fleury sent the marquis "A Summary of the political and military condition in America." The young colonel, an observant and slightly cynical realist, was by no means optimistic: "Four years of war have somewhat worn the springs of patriotism. The mercantile spirit and luxury are gradually stifling the love of independence." He had little respect for the gentlemen assembled in Philadelphia: "As for Congress, in spite of the names of France and England, Country and Liberty, with which they hide their mutual animosity, the secret motives of their intrigues, their cabals, and their everlasting barking, is individual hatred, or that between State and State." But "Independence is the rallying word for all parties." Although the Tories, "passive and despised," were no real threat, inflation was. Finances were "in a very broken down and confused state. Congress has manufactured money like newspapers."

His sketches of conditions in the various colonies were not entirely

---

* States were supposed to remit a total of $15 million per month to Congress.
† This appointment revoked Arthur Lee's commission.

complimentary. In Massachusetts the French were not admired. The Bostonians regarded them "like pedlars, very honest thieves." He described Samuel Adams as "a sensible and intelligent, but indolent man"; Bowdoin as "a double faced hypocrite"; and his rival, the wealthy and popular John Hancock, as "King of the Rabble." Trumbull of Connecticut and Clinton of New York fared better. Fleury judged Trumbull a true "man of the people"; Clinton "an enlightened republican, resolute and incorruptible." The citizens of New Jersey had displayed "heroic constancy." Jersey militiamen needed no urging to take the field; they assembled spontaneously "at the sight of a Redcoat." Pennsylvania was laggard and "infested with Royalists." As for Philadelphia: "Patriotism is non-existent; it has there almost become ridiculous. Fortune is the idol of all ranks; all the wealthy people are cankered at the heart and hunger for peace, which they would accept at any price." Virginia had made "great efforts" in the common cause, but North Carolina was weak. Her sister to the south had "neither strength nor virtue. Charlestown, like all commercial towns, is open to the highest bidder," and would not hold out against a siege.

The army was in fair shape and improving. "Farmers and merchants have become passable officers." Anthony Wayne's brilliant victory at Stony Point had raised morale and restored confidence, but the army stood in need of "food, clothes, arms, money or even still more efficacious aid." America, so he wrote the marquis, was an exhausted but by no means an expiring patient.

Fleury left posterity in no doubt as to his esteem and respect for the commander in chief, whose authority he described as "gentle and paternal. He is perhaps the only man who could have effected a revolution." General Washington stood above party: "the Atlas of America and the god of the Army."[2]

The flag officer Sandwich sent to relieve Commodore Sir George Collier, who had worked so effectively with Clinton, was Mariot Arbuthnot, an aging vice-admiral whose career had been entirely undistinguished. Arbuthnot was nearing the biblical life-span; he was neither vigorous nor decisive, and unlike his predecessor was determined to accept as little responsibility as possible. No sooner had he dropped anchor off Sandy Hook than he began to complain of the inadequacy and poor condition of his force. This complaint was a justifiable one. He had under command at New York two 74's, three 64's, two 50's, two 44-gun frigates, and a dozen assorted smaller ships. None had a full complement and most needed major overhaul.‡ The Americans, he incorrectly reported,

‡ Captain Middleton was having his own problems at the Admiralty, and at about this time wrote Sandwich: "If I was free to declare my opinion, the fleet is terribly managed, and cannot be otherwise while the present system continues. The

had seven frigates of 36 to 40 guns building and "20 gun frigates almost without number in the different ports."

Germain had previously given Clinton authority to withdraw the garrison from Newport at discretion, and the question of evacuation was the first matter of importance the general had to discuss with Arbuthnot. The admiral was in no position to guarantee the safety of the troops on Rhode Island; his small fleet was distinctly inferior to D'Estaing's, and should the French admiral decide to come north and again combine with the Americans to assault the island, the garrison must inevitably surrender. The alternatives seemed simple: The troops must be brought to New York, or left at Newport to be taken at leisure by the Americans and their French allies. The problem was that neither Arbuthnot nor Clinton was willing to accept responsibility for the decision, and for three weeks nothing was done. At one point Arbuthnot, convinced D'Estaing was coming north to attack Halifax, threatened to sail off to defend the base there. Clinton prevailed on him to give up this wild idea, and in late October Major General Pigot and his garrison of 7,000 British and Hessians embarked for New York.**

The occupying troops had not endeared themselves to the citizens of Newport. They had pulled down several hundred houses and barns for firewood, ripped the pews out of churches, gutted the handsome State House and turned it into a stable, taken all the planking from every private wharf in town, and cut down thousands of trees including most fruit trees on the island. These indiscriminate ravages were not entirely malevolent; a vast amount of wood had been required to keep the troops minimally comfortable during two bitter Newport winters.

Prevost's courageous defense of Savannah and departure of D'Estaing's fleet from North American waters permitted Clinton and Arbuthnot to begin planning for a move against Charleston, South Carolina. Clinton had good sources of information. He knew what he needed to know about the condition of the American Army and had no apprehen-

---

cause of every disorder, my Lord, is in the admiralty, and till a reformation is begun there, no good can be expected from any other quarter. For want of proper men to conduct the business at the posts, no expedition is used in refitting the ships. The officers are not kept to their duty. The men are daily deserting in scores, and those who remain are inclined to mutiny." The comptroller's singlehanded campaign to reform Sandwich and the Admiralty had obviously made little or no progress, and the gross inefficiency of which he constantly complained explains why admirals on the West Indies and North American stations were so poorly supported.

** Under the circumstances as known to Clinton and Arbuthnot in late September and early October 1779, this decision, for which both commanders were later to be severely criticized, made sense. Count D'Estaing's fleet was overwhelmingly superior to Arbuthnot's, and had he proceeded to New York rather than Savannah he might, in conjunction with Washington's army, have ended the war. Although Clinton would later attempt to place the blame for the evacuation of Rhode Island on the admiral, the record shows that every senior British officer in New York (including Cornwallis) concurred in this decision.

sion for the safety of New York during his absence. Nor was he worried that Washington would dispatch any substantial body of troops to reinforce the garrison at Charleston. Clinton reviewed his plans for the operation with Cornwallis, who had recently returned from England and would accompany him as second-in-command. Although Sir Henry knew the earl carried in his pocket a dormant commission to succeed him in command, he did not allow this fact to impair their relationship, which was ostensibly cordial.

Clinton did not think much of Arbuthnot's professional competence, but knew he had to rely on the irascible and dogmatic old admiral to get him to the target area, put him ashore, and support his army during the investment he anticipated. Clinton was optimistic: He had "such confidence in the spirit and discipline of the corps and the ability of the officers" that he "did not doubt of success."

Viewed in both the political and military contexts, the decision to mount a major operation against Charleston was to accept a calculated risk. But if Charleston could be taken expeditiously with minimum losses, and strong outposts established at Ninety Six and Camden in South Carolina and Augusta in Georgia, there was reason to hope that the well-affected would rally to the King's standard at those focal points and that South Carolinians would gradually return to their traditional allegiance, as many Georgians had. Seizure of Charleston would put a stop to the extensive trade between that port and French and Spanish Caribbean islands, as well as with the merchants on the small Dutch island of St. Eustatius. Although there was no immediate danger that a French fleet could interfere, and even less that Washington would be able to move substantial reinforcements southward, the operation must be concluded in time to permit Sir Henry to return to New York to commence summer operations.

Political reality dictated that Charleston must be defended, and Congress had entrusted the task of holding the city to Major General Benjamin Lincoln and Commodore Abraham Whipple. Washington's private opinion was that the city could not be held, but he was not consulted, nor did he proffer his advice.

Withdrawal of the Bourbon armada from the south coast of England gave George III opportunity to express his views as to future strategy. His first care, he wrote Sandwich, was the West Indies: "Our Islands must be defended even at the risk of the invasion of this Island; if we lose our Sugar Islands it will be impossible to raise Money to Continue the War . . . We must be ruined if every idea of offensive War is to lye dormant until this Island is thought in a situation to defy attacks if there is the smallest spark of resolution in the Country it must defend itself at home though not a Ship remained for its defense." He ended his letter with this admonitory paragraph:

> If Ministers will take a firm decided part and risk something to Save the Empire I am ready to be the foremost on the Occasion, as my Stake is the deepest; but if nothing but measures of caution are pursued and further Sacrifices are made from a Want of boldness which alone can preserve a state when hard pressed I shall certainly not think myself obliged after a conduct shall have been held so contrary to my opinion to screen them from the violence of an enraged nation.[3]

Several days later His Majesty again wrote the First Lord of the Admiralty to emphasize the importance of protecting the Sugar Islands. He was willing to take risks: "I know nothing advantageous can be obtained without some hazard . . . Perhaps no man in my dominion has a mind more ready to bear up against misfortunes, . . . it is by bold and manly efforts Nations have been preserved. . . ."[4]

Nothing the King could say could possibly prevail upon Lord North to make "bold and manly efforts." The First Minister had but one idea in mind: to get out of office at the earliest possible moment. He was no longer able to deal with the critical problems facing his stumbling and inept administration and wrote his royal master that "in conscience as well as in prudence" he felt himself obliged to request "immediate dismission from his employment, when he can be of no use in averting the evils which impend over this country . . . there is no discipline in the State, in the Army, or the Navy . . . Inevitable ruin must be the consequence of the present system of government." He could no longer carry on the King's business. He did not think it "the duty of a faithful servant to endeavour to preserve & condition a system which must terminate in the ruin of your Majesty & this country." He thought the only solution in the present crisis was a coalition government. He could go on no longer and would retire without honor or emolument. "I am forced to confess that my Spirits & my faculties fail me sensibly & grow worse every day . . . I am really so broken, that I cannot trust my judgement more than my abilities."[5]

His Majesty had neither time nor inclination to attend to these pleas. He was willing to make minor adjustments in the Cabinet, and did so, but his principal concern was to prosecute the war to a victorious conclusion. Accordingly, he called upon Lord Amherst and the Earl of Sandwich to recommend the most effectual means of employing the army and the navy during the winter and spring of 1780. Sandwich responded with "Thoughts Upon Measures to be Taken"; Amherst with "Proposals humbly Offered to the King regarding the Services of the Troops." Both agreed with His Majesty that as the winter climate in North America did not favor extensive operations there, and as the threat of French maritime supremacy imperiled the British Sugar Islands, the principal effort should be made in the Caribbean.

Sandwich described the state of the fleet in the Leeward Islands as "very deplorable" and recommended that reinforcements be sent without delay. A successful operation against Martinique was "the Measure of all others most to be wished," for if Martinique could be taken the other French islands would fall; "the stroke would be so sensibly felt by France that it would probably put an end to the War." Stores of all descriptions, particularly foodstuffs, must be sent to Gibraltar; Minorca should be reinforced. He recommended, too, that action be taken against the Dutch island of St. Eustatius, from which the French could supply their West Indies fleet with provisions and naval stores. The First Lord concluded his "Thoughts" with a summary of current deployment of ships of the line. Of these, forty-two were with Admiral Hardy, sixteen in the Leeward Islands, eight in the East Indies, and five in America. Ten more would be ready for sea prior to February. Sandwich did not wish to take more than a few ships from Hardy's fleet: ". . . this Stock should not be drawn so low as to leave us unable to resist the united efforts of the house of Bourbon in these seas." Amherst, too, thought there were opportunities in the Caribbean and suggested subsidiary operations against New Orleans and Charleston. But he was quite as reluctant to detach any significant number of troops from England for offensive action in the West Indies as Sandwich was to detach ships from the Channel fleet.[6]

The King was more audacious than his senior military advisers. He correctly perceived that the invasion threat had collapsed and was not likely to be renewed. He was eager to take the offensive and was convinced, as was Germain, that a decision must be sought in the Caribbean. Both His Majesty and Lord George appreciated that wasted time is irrecoverably lost and both wanted substantial reinforcement of ships of the line, frigates, and troops sent as soon as possible to the Leeward Islands even at the cost of stripping Hardy's fleet and the army at home.

Now, and for the first time, a coherent strategy had been formulated. The credit belongs to the King. If French maritime power could be irretrievably broken in the Caribbean and their islands wrested from them, the full force of Great Britain's majestic navy and powerful army could be turned against the Americans, the rebellion put down, and the traitors who led it brought to their deserved fate. At a dinner at Lord Weymouth's town house in Arlington Street the King's "Confidential Servants" recommended immediate resupply of Gibraltar, reinforcement of Minorca, and offensive operations in the West Indies. His Majesty approved.

There remained the critical problem of command. This was finally settled by appointment of Vice-admiral Sir George Brydges Rodney as commander in chief, Leeward Islands. Rodney had fled to France from England in 1774 to escape his creditors. From Paris he had sent repeated requests for a sea command, and on one occasion had dispatched Lady Rodney to London to plead his cause with Sandwich. The earl refused to receive her ladyship and replied to her letter that he found it politically impossible to give Rodney an active command until he had discharged his debts to private creditors and to the Exchequer. In the autumn of 1779 the admiral's embarrassing problem was suddenly solved and in a most unusual way: A wealthy French friend, Maréchal de Biron, gave him the money he needed to pay off his debts in Paris and he returned to London. He soon made arrangements to discharge his most pressing obligations.

Rodney had moved in the highest circle of London society. He was not known as a temperate man. Sir William Wraxall, an intimate friend, wrote: "Throughout his life, two Passions, both highly injurious to his repose, the Love of Women and of Play, carried him into many Excesses." Nocturnal adventures in boudoirs and at the gaming tables were not held against him; his superior, the Earl of Sandwich, was noted for similar activities. Although Rodney had distinguished himself in the Seven Years' War, it was suspected that he had sometimes devoted his energies to gathering in prizes to the detriment of the King's affairs. This was, indeed, the basis for opposition to the appointment. But he was politically acceptable and was endowed with qualities of initiative, courage, tactical judgment, and determination so lacking in most of the senior admirals. And he was a superb seaman who had demonstrated his ability to handle a fleet.

His Majesty delivered the customary speech from the throne on November 25, 1779. He did not mention America, but clearly indicated that he and his government proposed to prosecute the war against the rebels and their perfidious French allies with vigor. Parliament responded to the King's call for a renewed effort by authorizing 25,000 seamen and 18,000 marines for the Royal Navy and providing for 35,000 additional troops with five battalions of electoral mercenaries. Supplies approved for the armed forces and generous bounties for services of German hirelings exceeded £21 million.

The proposed reply to the King's speech provoked Opposition to move an amendment beseeching His Majesty to reflect on the happy condition of Great Britain at the time of his accession as compared to the present sad state of his realm, "endangered, impoverished, enfeebled, distracted and dismembered." Only "new counsellors," so the amendment asserted, could "prevent the consummation of public ruin." Affairs in America were not prospering; the performance of the fleet in home waters had been "superlatively wretched." Such were the results of an "in-

sidious and most pernicious system of government" which Opposition
speakers averred had spread its "baleful influence through the army, the
navy and the senate"; had produced "confusion, discord and ruin" in the
country; had brought disgrace on British arms; and had invited the justified contempt, ridicule, and execration of mankind. If not immediately
changed, this pernicious and malignant "system" would destroy the state.
Opposition leaders had a ready cure for these evils: immediate dismissal
of serving ministers and appointment of themselves to positions of power.
This remedy appealed neither to the King nor to his confidential servants.

At Plymouth dockyard, workers and ships' crews were readying four
of the line Rodney would take to the Leeward Islands via Gibraltar. Rear
Admiral Robert Digby with sixteen of the line temporarily withdrawn
from the Channel fleet was placed under his command until Gibraltar
had been resupplied. Digby would then return to England with empty
supply and victualing ships and Rodney would proceed to the West
Indies. Four days after Christmas, 1779, Sir George sailed with this powerful fleet. Three hundred miles south of the English coast he parted
from the transports, supply ships, victualers, and merchantmen bound
for the West Indies.

In his annual "Ode to the New Year" the poet laureate indulged his
fancies with remarkable prescience in a stanza in praise of the Royal
Navy, which during the preceding year had done nothing to deserve
praise poetical:

> Even from the birth of Time,
> 'Twas Heaven's decree
> The Queen of Isles should reign
> Sole Empress of the Sea.

Rodney would shortly confirm the decree of heaven.

On January 8, 1780, he took a Spanish convoy of sixteen supply ships
bound for Cádiz, and captured undamaged a sixty-four-gun ship of the
line and six frigates. A week later off Cape St. Vincent he encountered a
Spanish fleet of eleven of the line and two frigates commanded by
Teniente General Don Juan de Langara. Rodney ran up battle signals at
4 P.M. and put his fleet between the enemy and the Spanish coast.
Shortly after the British opened fire a Spaniard blew up; during the following two hours six others struck. Four escaped; two ran aground. Rodney put prize crews on the four remaining and ordered them to Gibraltar. That most of the British ships were coppered and that Rodney
enjoyed an overwhelming advantage in both number of ships and weight
of broadside does not detract from his victory. A more cautious admiral
would not have dared take the lee gauge, as Rodney had done, nor
would he have continued pursuit along an unchartered and hazardous

coast after nightfall with high seas running and "the weather . . . at times very tempestuous." The victor of Cape St. Vincent entered the Straits of Gibraltar several days later.

Rodney arrived just in time. General Eliott's garrison and the hundreds of civilian men, women, and children on the Rock had subsisted for several months on very short rations. The general set the example; for several weeks he had restricted himself to a ration of four ounces of rice a day, two bowls of pudding, and tea. "The bakers had long been limited to the quantity of bread daily to be issued to the inhabitants and sentries were placed at the wickets where it was delivered, to prevent confusion and riot. The strongest, nevertheless had the advantage, so that numbers of women, children and infirm persons returned to their miserable habitations frequently without tasting, for some days, that chief, and perhaps necessary, support of life."[7] Other food was scarce and exorbitantly priced. Although Eliott issued orders to ration bread and rice, he had taken no effective measures to control issue of other dwindling supplies of food. Had Rodney arrived three or four weeks later, Gibraltar must have been starved into surrender.

With his mission accomplished, Rodney weighed on February 15, 1780. Three days later he detached Digby with the prizes and empty supply ships, directed him to return to England, and with four coppered ships of the line set course for the West Indies. Sandwich wrote him: "I scarcely know how to find words to congratulate you enough upon your late glorious successes, and upon the eminent services you have done your country. . . . I have obtained for you the thanks of both Houses of Parliament . . . [and] am also in hopes that I shall be able to prevail on his Majesty to give you some more substantial proofs of his approbation.†† . . . You have done nobly . . . I perceive you cry out loudly for coppered ships, and I am therefore determined to stop your mouth. You shall have copper enough, and you shall have everything that I can give you. . . ."[8]

As soon as rumors that D'Estaing and Lincoln had failed to take Savannah and that the French fleet had sailed for the West Indies were confirmed, Washington realized there was no longer the slightest possibility of joint action against New York and began moving the main army from "the remote fastnesses" of the upper Hudson to Morristown, New Jersey, where he planned to put the troops in winter quarters. He would station a strong force in the Highlands to ensure the security of West Point, cover the lower Hudson, and post the cavalry and one brigade at Danbury, east of the river. This disposition was dictated by available

†† Sandwich kept this promise. He procured a life pension of £1,000 per annum for the admiral with reversion at his death to Lady Rodney and when she had died, to her heirs.

supplies of beef, flour, and forage. Morristown was deep in the New Jersey farming country; here, he believed, the main army could winter undisturbed by the British with good prospects that its requirements could be at least minimally satisfied.

He reported to Congress that muster rolls showed his total enlisted strength to be 27,099, but "the amount of an Army on paper will greatly exceed its real strength . . . it cannot be supposed that the whole of the Troops borne upon the Muster Rolls, were either in service or really in existence." Enlistments of 10,158 men would expire within six months. As the system of voluntary enlistment stood "on too precarious and uncertain a footing to depend on," he again urged an annual draft for one year as "the only means left us of maintaining the army on a proper and responsible ground."[9] Unless this or a similar system were adopted he could not formulate his plans for operations in 1780 with any degree of certainty.

Washington established his headquarters at Morristown on the first day of December. Already there were portents of a vicious winter; soldiers working from dawn to dusk cutting trees, squaring off logs, and sawing lumber suitable for huts suffered severely. The work, laborious under the best conditions, was made miserable by frost and snow, sleet and slush. Officers and men alike were sleeping without blankets in tattered tents. Added to a critical and continuing shortage of flour, meat, and rum was the constant affliction of driving snow and piercing winter winds. Steuben wrote that the soldiers presented the most shocking picture of misery: ". . . scarce a man having the wherewithal to cover his nakedness and a great number very bad with the itch." Washington faced another problem: Citizens of Morristown and vicinity had refused to accommodate officers in their houses: "I regret that the Inhabitants should be unwilling to give shelter to men who have made and are still making every sacrifice in the service of their Country." He resolved this "perplexing dilemma" by directing Nathanael Greene to inform local magistrates that if they and the townspeople would not co-operate, he should billet officers as he saw fit.

Letters the general received from correspondents in Philadelphia were gloomy. General Schuyler, now a delegate to Congress from New York, wrote him that finances were "exceedingly deranged" and depreciation of the currency "proceding with the most Alarming rapidity, Every department so deeply In debt and no plan adopted which gives the least prospect of remedy to these Evils that I very seriously apprehend the most disagreeable Consequences." Nothing had been done toward the "Intended new arrangement of the Quarter Master General and Commissary General department." Nor was Schuyler optimistic that anything would soon be done. Cyrus Griffin, a delegate from Virginia, wrote that demands for money had overwhelmed the Treasury office: "The different

states must supply those demands, or the period will shortly arrive when
the whole Continent must totter to its foundation." One of the problems,
as Schuyler wrote Governor Clinton, was that there was no member of
Congress "adequate to the important business of finance."

Washington had written Congress of his pressing need for flour. Samuel Huntington, elected president after John Jay's appointment to the
Court of Madrid, was doing what he could and urged the governor of
New Jersey to provide several thousand barrels: "It is needless for me to
mention the fatal consequences that might ensue in this critical conjuncture of affairs should the army now in that State be without bread." Neither Huntington nor anyone else mentioned the word "mutiny," the
ineluctable "fatal consequence" should the army be left to starve in the
snow at Morristown.

In a circular letter to governors of New York, New Jersey, Pennsylvania, Delaware, and Maryland, Washington wrote that the situation of
the army was "beyond description alarming." He had on hand but "three
days bread at a third allowance. . . . Our magazines are absolutely
empty everywhere, and our commissaries entirely destitute of money or
credit to replenish them. We have never experienced a like extremity at
any period of the war." He begged the governors to make "extraordinary
and immediate exertions" for there was "every appearance that the army
will infallibly disband in a fortnight."[10]

Although his spies in New York reported British ships loading men,
horses, supplies, and ordnance for an amphibious move against the
southern states or in the West Indies, the general was skeptical; the activity in New York, he thought, was probably designed to deceive him
and so prepare an opportunity for Clinton to take West Point by a *coup
de main* or to strike suddenly against the army at Morristown. He made
arrangements to summon the New York and New Jersey militia at short
notice. Departure of the British fleet with its convoy of transports and
supply ships the day after Christmas did not immediately allay his fears.

Possibly no general in history—and certainly no American general—
has been so overwhelmed with frustrating administrative paper work as
Washington was at Morristown. He had industrious and reliable secretaries, and he kept them busy with their quills from dawn until midnight.
But save for Nathanael Greene he had no staff officer able to take any of
the burden. Although his shoulders were broad enough to bear it, Washington was compelled to cope with such a volume of "minutious details"
that it had become impossible for him to discharge "the general duties"
of the office of commander in chief. With a degree of fatuity remarkable
even for that assemblage, Congress had arbitrarily abolished all the
army's express riders and had informed the general he would hereafter
be expected to avail himself of the services of a newly established postal

system. Necessity, he calmly replied, required him "to suspend the operation of the Act."

The weather was bitterly cold. General Orders of January 3 gave the parole as "Lapland"; the countersign as "Muscovy" or "Norway." The army was freezing and starving. Soldiers, "at last brought to such a dreadful extremity that no authority or influence of the officers no virtue of patience in the men themselves could any longer restrain them from obeying the dictates of their sufferings," had begun to plunder.[11] Temperatures were holding between 12° and 16° below zero; New York harbor was frozen solid. In the depth of the most ferocious winter in living memory, and faced with an appalling shortage of food, Washington still considered possibilities for offensive action. Perhaps, he thought, an attempt might be made on the British garrison on Staten Island.

Of that terrible winter in Morristown, Major General Baron de Kalb wrote: "It is so cold the ink freezes in my pen, while I am sitting close by the fire. The roads are piled with snow until, at some places, they are elevated twelve feet above their ordinary level." Officers and men were at long last hutted, but "the times are growing worse from hour to hour. The dearth of the necessaries of life is almost incredible, and increases from day to day." For the first time in his life the baron was reduced to shaving himself: "The barber's compensation would consume all my pay."[12] His uniforms were in rags and he was not to have opportunity to visit a tailor in Philadelphia to replenish his tattered wardrobe, for in late February Washington assigned him to the arduous command of outpost positions covering the army. This vicious winter broke in March, and there was some improvement in the food situation. But De' Kalb was not destined to enjoy the delights of spring in New Jersey.

Although the charges preferred against Major General Arnold had arrived at Washington's headquarters in late March 1779, the trial was twice postponed, and not until several days before Christmas was the commander in chief able again to convene a general court-martial for the purpose. This court, with Major General Robert Howe as president, sat at Morristown from December 23 until January 26. The following charges were brought:

> First. That while in the Camp of General Washington at Valley Forge last spring, he gave permission to a Vessel belonging to persons then voluntarily residing in this City, with the enemy, and of disaffected characters to come into a Port of the United States without the knowledge of the authority of the State or of the Commander in Chief tho' then present.
>
> 2nd. In having shut up the Shops and stores on his arrival in the City, so as even to prevent officers of the army from purchas-

ing, while he privately made considerable purchases for his own benefit as is alledged and believed.

3rd. In imposing menial offices upon the sons of Freemen of this State, when called for by the desire of Congress, to perform militia duty, and when remonstrated to hereupon, justifying himself in writing upon the ground of having power so to do. For that when a citizen assumed the character of a soldier, the former was intirely lost in the latter, and that it was the duty of the militia to obey every order of his Aids (not a breach of the laws and constitution) as his (the General's) without judging of the propriety of them.

4th. The appropriating the waggons of this State, when called forth upon a special emergency last autumn, to the transportation of private property and that of Persons who voluntarily remained with the enemy last winter, and were deemed disaffected to the Interests and Independence of America.[13]

John Lawrence, judge advocate general of the Continental Army, managed the prosecution; Arnold conducted his own defense, and the record shows that he did so with great emotion and passion and considerable forensic skill.

The court acquitted Arnold of the second and third charges, but brought in findings of guilty on the first and fourth, and sentenced him to receive a reprimand from the commander in chief. On February 12, 1780, Congress confirmed the sentence. The reprimand appeared in General Orders debated at Morristown on Thursday, April 6, and read:

> The Commander in Chief would have been much happier in an occasion of bestowing commendations on an officer who has rendered such distinguished services to his Country as Major General Arnold; but in the present case a sense of duty and a regard to candor oblige him to declare, that he considers his conduct in the instance of the permit as peculiarly reprehensible, both in a civil and military view, and in the affair of the waggons as "Imprudent and improper."[14]

For eight months prior to his trial Arnold had been deeply engaged in an affair considerably more "reprehensible" and "improper" than issuing unauthorized permits or temporarily appropriating a dozen wagons, property of the state of Pennsylvania.

Debates in Lords and Commons on the reply to the King's speech of November 25 and on amendments offered by Opposition with the usual lack of success had aroused great interest. During early January 1780, "Committees of Correspondence and Association," pledged to support economic and political reform, sprang up in nearly every county in Eng-

land and Wales and in dozens of cities and towns. The House of Commons was engulfed by a torrent of petitions and remonstrances. Supporters of Administration in both Houses attacked the petitions and the
county meetings that had originated them. A noble earl expressed his
hope that the malignant spirit that had given birth to county meetings
would be summarily crushed, and described the petitions in words he
and his colleagues had used some time before when they had attacked
petitions from the Americans as factious, dangerous, and unconstitutional
innovations. In both Lords and Commons "sedition" was a word flung
about with abandon.

The Yorkshire petition, signed by more than 6,000 freeholders in the
county, provided a model for scores of others. In this, Yorkshiremen
cited "the alarming magnitude of the public debt; the present extensive
and undue influence of the crown; the enormous load of burdensome
taxes yearly increasing." Walpole was surprised that the discontent had
first been manifested where least expected: by the country gentlemen,
"who after encouraging the Court to war with America, now, not very
decently, are angry at the expence . . . very serious associations are
forming in many countries." Pensions and sinecures granted by the King
were principal objects of attack and "a protracted battle was fought with
reciprocal animosity." The situation of the ministry was "desperate";
Walpole thought Lord North doomed. The ministry weathered this
storm, but another, and one more serious, was making up.

Parliament assembled after the Easter recess with every indication
that the session would be a memorable one. Petitions lay in stacks on the
table and every post brought a new batch. Opposition leaders, who had
met almost daily during the recess, had prepared a series of motions designed to bring down the government. "The very first," Walpole wrote
Mann, was made by Mr. Dunning and "was a thundering one. The
words were: 'That the influence of the Crown has increased, is increasing, and ought to be diminished.' The walls could not believe their own
ears." Dunning followed with a motion urging minute examination of the
King's Civil List and investigation of public revenues and expenditures.

Thomas Pitt charged Lord North with responsibility for the American
war and stated that the First Minister's policies had rendered "his countrymen and their country despicable." This attack aroused the usually
torpid First Minister and "threw him into a rage against Opposition that
produced a mighty tumult."[15] Walpole thought this succession of blows
would be decisive. Administration was staggering, but the ministry was
still on its feet. Within three weeks, Lord North managed to lure a score
of errant sheep back to the fold.

The French, too, had decided to mount a major maritime effort
in the West Indies in the spring of 1780, but ministers had as yet no

plans to assist the struggling Americans otherwise than with money, arms, ammunition, and clothing. La Fayette, convinced that more substantial aid must be sent if collapse was to be averted, wrote passionately and persuasively to Vergennes. The urgent need was ships and men; a small fleet and a well-equipped corps of 6,000 troops, so the marquis asserted, would prove decisive. Nor did he fail to remind the Foreign Minister on more than one occasion that victory in America was in the best interests of France.

Vergennes replied that the proposals had been discussed by the Cabinet and were receiving serious consideration. The marquis urged Franklin to exert his influence. The doctor was discreet; he was not sure French troops would be welcome in America. He expressed his hope that ships could be spared when convenient "to aid in reducing New York and Rhode Island" and added that he had heard of no intention to send troops. As he had no instructions from Congress to request such aid, he dared not take "any farther Steps than I have done in such a Proposition without Orders."[16]

This tactful check did not diminish La Fayette's endeavors to gain support for the cause of his adopted country. He was now on intimate terms with the King's *chef de cabinet*, Comte de Maurepas, who had earlier intimated that he favored sending ships and troops. In January 1780 the marquis sent Maurepas a lengthy memorandum "In Regard to Sending a Detachment of French Troops to America." After a hasty review of assorted possibilities for co-operation with Washington's army, he stated frankly: "We are losing precious time . . . the armament ought already to have been begun. It is important for it to reach them early in the spring. . . ." He set the composition of the detachment that should be sent, and stated his qualifications to command it.[17] Several days later he wrote Vergennes a similar letter. The minister would not yet make a positive commitment. Millions of livres would be required to finance an expedition of the size La Fayette had proposed. Additionally, Louis XVI had already approved a gift of 6 million livres. Support of his transatlantic ally was draining his Treasury.

In February 1780 the King's ministers accepted La Fayette's plan in principle. A French corps of twelve battalions, each at a strength of five hundred enlisted, and suitably reinforced with artillery and cavalry, would be organized at Brest and placed under command of Lieutenant General Jean-Baptist-Donatien de Vimeur, Comte de Rochambeau, perhaps the most distinguished general in the French Army. Six ships of the line and two frigates commanded by Charles Louis d'Arsac, Chevalier de Ternay, would escort the transports. La Fayette would proceed at once to America by fast frigate to concert plans for the reception of the French.

Vergennes instructed him to inform General Washington, under a bond of secrecy, of the King's intentions; of the size and composition of the force to be expected; that it would serve under his command as an entity; and that if circumstances did not favor an attack on New York, the preferred destination was Rhode Island. He was to inform Washington that the ministry would not propose any specific operations "because these must depend on circumstances and upon the local possibilities; it will be for General Washington and the Council of War to decide on such as may be most useful. All that the King desires is, that the troops whom he is sending to the aid of his allies, the United States, should co-operate effectively to deliver them, once for all, from the yoke and tyranny of the English." After meeting with Washington and discussing the points set forth in his instructions, the marquis was to proceed to Philadelphia to confer with Chevalier de la Luzerne. He was then to present himself to Congress, "but he will have agreed beforehand with the American general as to how far he shall admit Congress into the secret of our movement."[18]

The "secret" of the proposed movement was soon common gossip in the halls of Versailles, at fashionable salons in Paris, and in the army and navy. The idea of crossing the Atlantic to aid a new nation to throw off the chains fastened upon her by the hereditary enemy exerted a compelling influence on young officers of noble families who pressed relatives and friends at court and in the army to exert every influence to gain them appointments to Rochambeau's staff or in one of the six elite regiments—Bourbonnais, Saintonge, Soissonnais, Deux-Ponts, Anhalt, and Nuestrie—scheduled to sail from Brest. The Duc de Lauzun's privately raised "Legion" and an adequate train of field artillery with the heavy cannon and large mortars required for siege operations would accompany the regiments of foot.

The ardor of these young aristocrats can be comprehended only if one recalls that they were living in an age dominated by the thought of Voltaire, Montesquieu, and D'Alembert, whose writings extolled the virtues of liberty.‡‡ Those who sought to join the "crusade" were convinced, as Turgot was, that America was "the hope of mankind . . . it must give the example of political liberty, religious liberty, commercial and industrial liberty. The shelter which it is going to offer to the oppressed will console the earth."

Comte de Rochambeau was fifty-five years of age when he arrived at Brest. He was not possessed of the republican zeal animating so many of his juniors. He was a courageous and competent professional officer who had served for thirty-nine years. The units he had commanded in the Seven Years' War were recognized as being the best trained in the

‡‡ When he heard that General Howe had defeated Washington's army on Long Island, Voltaire wrote D'Alembert: "The troops of Doctor Franklin have been beaten by those of the King of England. Alas! philosophers are being beaten every where. Reason and liberty are unwelcome in this world."

French Army. He was a strict disciplinarian but always attentive to the needs of his soldiers, who responded to his leadership with loyalty and devotion. Louis XVI could not have made a better choice than Rochambeau to command the small army he was sending to America.

On March 14, 1780, La Fayette, wearing the uniform of an American major general, boarded frigate *Hermione* at New Rochelle. His destination was Boston. As *Hermione* slipped silently past the harbor lights into the open sea, the marquis had reason to be a happy young man.

THE TRAITOR
and
THE SPY

45. Major General Benedict Arnold

46. Major John André

47. Louis XVI

48. Comte de Vergennes

49. Caron de Beaumarchais

50. Comte de Rochambeau

51. Vice-admiral Comte de Grasse

52. Vice-admiral Comte d'Estaing

53. "The Able Doctor": This cartoon depicts Lord North pouring tea down the throat of America.

54. "Recruits"

55. "Moore" (Arnold) letter to "Anderson" (André) setting his conditions for selling West Point and its defenders, July 15, 1780. The cipher is on the left; the decipher (clear) is on the right.

Two days since I received a letter without date or Signature, informing me that S. Henry — was obliged to me for the intelligence communicated, and that he placed a full confidence in the Sincerity of my intentions, &c. &c. — On the 13th Instant I addressed a letter to you expressing my Sentiments and expectations, viz, that the following Preliminaries be settled previous to coöperating. — First, that S. Henry secure to me my property, valued at ten thou=sand pounds Sterling, to be paid to me or my Heirs in case of Loss: and, as soon as that ~~happens~~ shall happen, — hundred pounds per annum to be secured to me for life, in lieu of the pay and emoluments I give up, for my Services as they shall deserve. — If I point out a plan of coöperation by which S. H. shall possess himself of West Point, the Garrison, &c. &c. &c. twenty thousand pounds Sterling I think will be a cheap purchase for an object of so much importance. At the same time I request a thousand pounds to be paid my Agent. — I expect a full and explicit answer. — The 20th I set off for West Point. A personal interview with an officer that you can confide in is absolutely necessary to plan matters. In the mean time I shall communicate to our mutual Friend S—y all the intelligence in my power, until I have the pleasure of your answer.

                                    Moore

July 15th

To the line of my letter of the 13th
I did not add seven. —

N.B. the postscript only relates to the manner of composing the Cypher in the letter referred to. —

Watertown Wednesday Morn:
Near 10 OClock.

To all the Friends of American Liberty, be it known that this morning, Before break of Day, a Brigade Consisting of about 1000 or 1200 Men landed at Phip's Farm in Cambridge and March'd to Lexington where they found a Company of our Colony Militia in Arms, upon whom they fired without the least Provocation and killed six, and Wounded four Others, By an Express this Moment from Boston, We find another Brigade are now on their March from Boston supposed to be 1000, The Bearer Mr. Isaac Bissell is Charged to Alarm the Country quite to Connecticut and all Persons are Desired to furnish him with fresh Horses, as they may be needed, I have spoke with several Persons, who have seen the Dead and Wounded Pray let the Delegates from this Colony to Connecticut, see this,

They know

J. Palmer one of
the Committe of S[afe]y

A true Coppy of the ...

56. Palmer letter to "All Friends of Liberty."

57. Benjamin White letter directing defense of Bunker Hill.

In Committee of Safety   Cambridge June 15th 1775
                    Whereas it appears of Importance, to the Safety
of this Colony, that possession of the Hill, called Bunkers hills in Charles
town be Securely kept and defended; and allso some one hill on Dorchester
be likewise Secured. Therefore unanimously Resolved, that it be recommended to the
Council of War, that the Abovementioned Bunkers hill, be maintained, by Sufficient force being posted there, and as the particular
Situation of Dorchester, which is unknown to this Committee, they
advise that the Council of war pursue such Steps respecting
the Same, as to them Shall appear to be, for the Security of this Colony.

                    Benja: White Chairman

4

Something Should Be Hazarded

A month before La Fayette sailed for America, Comte Luc Urbain de Guichen, a competent but cautious admiral, cleared Brest for the West Indies with sixteen sail of the line, four frigates, and eighty-three merchantmen. Aboard his line-of-battle ships were 3,000 elite infantrymen. He came into Fort Royal, Martinique, on March 22. Rodney had arrived in Carlisle Bay in Barbados five days earlier.

An hour after De Guichen dropped his anchors, Marquis François Claude de Bouillé, the royal governor, boarded the flagship and proposed that they immediately undertake an operation against St. Lucia. The admiral agreed and orders were issued accordingly. The fleet, increased by seven of the line based on Fort Royal, sailed to the target area thirty miles south of Martinique. Here the French discovered Rear Admiral Hyde Parker with seventeen of the line, and here they learned that Rodney had arrived in the theater and was at Barbados, but a few days' sail from St. Lucia. The admiral and the governor decided to return to Fort Royal.

Parker immediately dispatched a frigate to inform Rodney of the situation. The commander in chief, suffering from kidney stones, gout in both feet and in his right hand, was resting ashore. He directed that he be carried to his barge and hoisted aboard flagship *Sandwich*. There his private physician, Dr. Gilbert Blane, ordered him to bed in the flag cabin. The ailing admiral, who had spent the trying hours off Cape St. Vincent in bed, had the utmost confidence that Walter Young, his flag captain, would keep him in touch with developments and execute his orders loyally as he had done on that memorable night. This confidence was not misplaced.* Rodney ordered his squadron to weigh at once and anchored at St. Lucia on March 27.

The stage was set, the protagonists in position, one perhaps more eager for decisive action than the other, for while British naval battle doctrine emphasized the importance of closing with the enemy and overwhelming him with broadsides at short range, French doctrine taught that the first duty of an admiral was to preserve his fleet. Aggressive British admirals (as both Howe and Rodney were) would press an enemy to the limits of their own, their captain's, and their ship's capabilities.

Rodney had under command twenty-one of the line, four (those he had brought with him) coppered. Parker's seventeen were in no better than fair condition. Most hulls were foul; some ships needed new masts, yards, and bowsprits; others, suits of new sails and new running gear.† The French ships, on the contrary, were in excellent condition. All had been cleaned and overhauled before leaving Brest. Clean hulls gave De Guichen a considerable advantage in speed and made for easier ship handling. Thus although on paper the fleets were nearly equal the balance, slight as it was, lay with De Guichen. This did not perturb Rodney, who appeared off Fort Royal on April 2. The French remained quietly at anchor. Rodney, unable to lure De Guichen out of the harbor, returned to St. Lucia. Challenge of battle had restored his health and spirits.

The governor and the admiral, having given up the idea of an operation against St. Lucia, now conceived another plan. This was to launch a sudden surprise attack on Barbados, and on April 13 De Guichen stood out of Fort Royal with five frigates and twenty-two of the line carrying 3,000 assault troops. How the French admiral could possibly have concluded he would be able to manage such an operation in the presence of a British fleet under command of such an admiral as Rodney remains a mystery. One of Rodney's coppered 74's on cruising station off the harbor immediately bore the news to St. Lucia: The French fleet was at sea.

---

* When one reads the letters written by Young to his friend Middleton, one is likely to infer that Rodney's victories in 1780 were due entirely to the perspicacity of Captain Young. There is no doubt that Young was able, and Rodney did listen to his advice and often acted in accordance with it. The captain did not live long enough to write his name in British naval history.

† Captain Young blamed Admiral Parker for the sorry condition of his fleet. Properly, the blame should be attributed to Sandwich.

Within hours Rodney cleared St. Lucia, and during late afternoon of April 16 was off Martinique standing north in line of battle ahead. Soon one of his scouting frigates sighted the French. Rodney was determined De Guichen should not escape him, and ordered frigates to watch the enemy column during the night. Shortly after dawn he signaled his intention to attack the French rear division with his whole force, and ordered ships to close to one cable's length (720 feet). At 11 A.M. he made the signal to prepare for battle and fifty minutes later the signal for every ship to "steer for her opposite in the enemy's line" agreeable to the 21st Article of the sacrosanct "Additional Fighting Instructions."

At noon the flagship struck eight bells, the watch was relieved, and grog issued. Surgeons stood by in ships' sick bays; "Powder-monkeys" spread clean sand on the gun decks to prevent gun crews, barefoot and stripped to the waist, from slipping in the bloody gore that would be the immediate result of an enemy broadside. All guns were shotted and manned as they had been since before dawn; slow-burning matches were lit and marine sentries with loaded muskets and bayonets fixed stood by hatchways with orders to shoot any seaman who attempted to desert his gun. During the morning both admirals had made maneuvering signals and at noon both fleets in line ahead were steering south on the starboard tack, the British ships well closed, the French in loose column. Martinique loomed dark green against a clear blue sky.

Within the hour Rodney's dream of a victory that would destroy French maritime power in the Caribbean and would convey the rich French Sugar Islands to Great Britain was to be wrecked, for what took place was not the shattering attack he had planned on the enemy's rear division, but a series of unconcerted actions. For the rear admirals commanding Rodney's van and rear (Hyde Parker and Joshua Rowley) had concluded that the commander in chief's last signal superseded the earlier one to concentrate on De Guichen's rear division. They understood the last signal to mean precisely what "Additional Fighting Instructions" prescribed: that each ship should attack her *numerical* opposite in the enemy line of battle. This was normal British naval battle doctrine, and to fail to adhere to it might well cost a captain his career and possibly his life.

Rodney had conceived an unorthodox plan that violated this doctrine, but that he had every reason to believe would assure the annihilation of the French fleet. His subordinates, bound equally by rigid "Fighting Instructions" and tradition, simply did not comprehend what the admiral had in mind. Parker, then, sailed off in one direction, Rowley in another. Rodney, in *Sandwich,* broke through the French line and the flagship fought unsupported for nearly an hour. Other ship-to-ship engagements were taking place in the expanding battle area and not all favored the British.

586 THE COMMON CAUSE

In late afternoon, De Guichen closed the day by signaling his ships to follow him into Fort Royal Bay. Rodney returned to St. Lucia. More than a thousand officers and men were killed or wounded in this inconclusive action, one made memorable only by Rodney's concept. The opposing admirals had each taken measure of his adversary, and each claimed a victory. Neither had won one on the sea, but Rodney had won the battle of wills. He had subdued De Guichen; he now intended to subdue his subordinates, whose inattention, wavering, and ineptitude had, so he thought, cost him the day.

On April 26 he wrote the First Lord of the Admiralty: "The French Admiral, who appeared to be a brave and gallant officer, had the honor to be nobly supported during the whole action. 'Tis with concern inexpressible, mixt with indignation, that the duty I owe my sovereign and my country obliges me to acquaint Your Lordship that during the action with the French fleet on the 17th instant His Majesty's—the British flag—was not properly supported." He blamed Parker and Rowley for their "inattention" and attributed to them the loss of "that glorious opportunity (perhaps never to be recovered) of terminating the naval contest in these seas."

He was delighted to receive orders to send Hyde Parker home and paved the way for a less than cordial reception at the Admiralty by writing Sandwich that Parker was "a dangerous man with a very bad temper, hostile in the highest degree to the Administration and capable of anything." Rowley fared little better. But he was not a "designing man" as Hyde Parker was—only an incompetent one. Rowley made excuses; Rodney informed him tartly that he expected his subordinates to obey orders immediately, implicitly, and without questions. "I made no hesitation to tell him that his motion without orders had saved the enemy's fleet, and that for the future he must not attempt to do the like; that the painful task of thinking belonged to me, to him *obedience* to signals and orders.‡[1]

Shortly after the encounter off Martinique, De Guichen sailed for France. Rodney had not destroyed the French fleet, but he had temporarily neutralized the threat to the British Sugar Islands. The strategic initiative in the Caribbean now lay with the British.

During the dangerous and tiresome voyage from New York to Charleston, Sir Henry Clinton was in a state of constant anxiety. The

‡ In justice to Rowley and the other officers so severely castigated by their commander in chief, it must be said that Rodney had not made clear to them precisely what his plan was. If he had discussed his scheme of maneuver at St. Lucia, one must agree with the conclusion of Sir John Knox Laughton, editor of the Barham Papers, that the admiral's "power of exposition" must have been "altogether wanting; for it is quite certain that not one man to whom he thus explained his intention had the faintest notion of what Rodney wanted him to do, or how he wanted him to do it." (Barham Papers, Vol. I, Introduction.)

passage was stormy; several troop transports were separated; an ordnance ship carrying all the heavy guns for the siege operation the general anticipated foundered, as did ships carrying four hundred horses. "However, the Admiral's commendably zealous perseverance fortunately proved superior to the malevolence of the wind, and we had the happiness at last to arrive with the greatest part of the transports in Tybee River by the last of January, after a most harassing and tempestuous voyage."** Clinton's plan was to land the army at South Edisto Inlet, march to the south bank of the Ashley River at a point some fifteen miles from Charleston, ferry the troops across the river, move down Charleston Neck (bounded on the south by the Ashley River and on the north by the Cooper), and establish a river-to-river line of investment with both flanks secure. The movement involved tedious marches and a complicated river crossing. Ferrying operations were directed by Captain George K. Elphinstone, R.N., who handled his task so ably that Clinton unbent sufficiently to write him a personal letter expressing his appreciation. Clinton, always cautious and methodical, was not one to hurry matters. The approach to Charleston proceeded on schedule and precisely as he had planned it.

Clinton was fortunate to meet at Charleston an adversary even more cautious than he. Major General Benjamin Lincoln, Continental Army, charged with the defense of the city, was a loyal and courageous soldier who lacked the essential qualities of imagination and initiative. He made no effort to impede Clinton's approach to the Ashley River, nor did he attempt to discover and disrupt the ferrying operations so admirably executed by Captain Elphinstone's sailors. Lincoln sat in Charleston, drank his madeira, and awaited his fate. On Sunday, the first day of April, British fatigue parties commenced breaking ground for a first parallel less than eight hundred yards from his outworks.

The only remaining hope for the garrison was to attempt to flee across the Cooper River. This vanished when Arbuthnot ran by Fort Moultrie with his warships. Commodore Abraham Whipple, commanding the Continental squadron at Charleston, had earlier sent his ships' guns and most of his sailors ashore and had sunk four small frigates to block the Cooper.†† With the city thus closely invested by land and water, the British commanders issued a joint summons to Lincoln. This was promptly rejected. Clinton as promptly opened a second parallel less than four hundred yards from Lincoln's works and subjected them to heavy bombardment. These methodical tactics took time, but also saved

** Clinton had his geography slightly confounded. The fleet anchored off Tybee Island in the Savannah River on January 30, 1780.

†† The commodore's action seems justified; he could have offered no effective resistance to Arbuthnot, and his cannon and gunners would be of some assistance to Lincoln.

lives; Clinton "had not the smallest doubt" he would soon be master of Charleston. He later wrote he had planned his operations so as *to secure the capture of all the rebel corps in Charleston* [which] had been from the first a very principal object with me, as I saw the reduction of the rest of the province in great measure depended on it."

Aside from Lincoln's army, now effectively locked up in Charleston, there were but three small American detachments in South Carolina. One, stationed north of the Cooper near Monck's Corner where there was a supply depot, was commanded by Brigadier General Isaac Huger. Huger was an officer of some combat experience. When only seventeen he had served as a volunteer against the Cherokee. He had been commissioned a lieutenant colonel of militia in 1775, and at Savannah had commanded one of Lincoln's militia divisions. With about four hundred cavalry he was now protecting the supplies at Monck's Corner and the American line of communications to North Carolina. At 3 A.M. on April 14 he was rudely awakened to find Lieutenant Colonel Banastre Tarleton's saber-swinging legion in the middle of his camp. Huger and a few others escaped. Tarleton took a hundred prisoners, several hundred horses, and two dozen wagons loaded with ammunition and assorted supplies. With Huger's small force annihilated, Cornwallis moved across the Cooper River in strength.

No chance remained that Lincoln could cut his way through Clinton's army to safety. He asked for terms and surrendered on May 9. The loss of a city many of whose principal inhabitants were ambivalent in their loyalties was not of critical importance. What was of great importance to the American cause in the south was the loss of Lincoln's army and of arms, equipment, and supplies that could not be replaced for many months.

On April 2, 1780, Washington had put the Maryland Line and the Delaware regiment under immediate marching orders to South Carolina: "Something should be hazarded here . . . for the purpose of giving further succor to the Southern States." Major General de Kalb would command the detachment. Washington anticipated that Charleston would probably fall, but hoped the Continentals he was sending "might assist to check the progress of the enemy and save the Carolinas."[2]

De Kalb hastened to Philadelphia to confer with the Board of War. Although he encountered the usual delays, he managed to arrange for some supplies and a little money. While there, he learned that La Fayette had landed in Boston in late April and was hurrying to Morristown with news of the greatest importance. The baron was not the only person in Philadelphia to speculate on the nature of the secret conversations La Fayette and Washington were said to be holding at head-

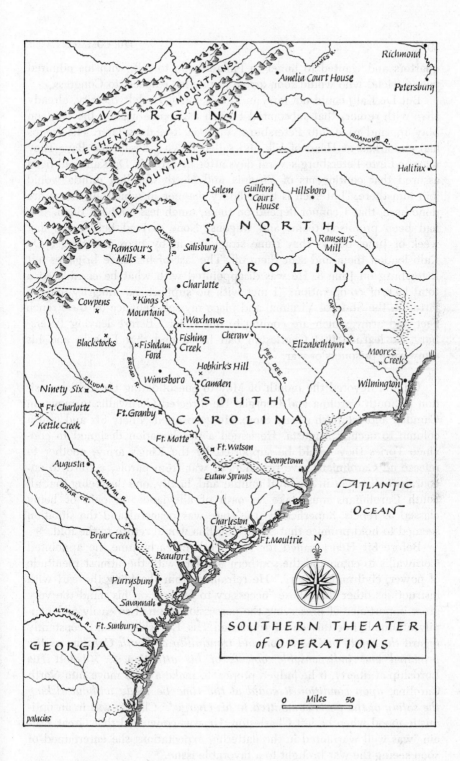

Richmond
Petersburg

JAMES R.
Amelia Court House

VIRGINIA

VIRGINIA MOUNTAINS

ROANOKE R.

ALLEGHENY

Halifax

BLUE RIDGE MOUNTAINS

Salem
Guilford
Court
House
Hillsboro

NORTH

CATAWBA R.

Ramsour's
Mills
Salisbury

CAROLINA

Ramsay's
Mill

Charlotte

CAPE FEAR R.

Cowpens
Kings
Mountain
Waxhaws

Fishing
Creek
Cheraw
Elizabethtown
Moore's
Creek

Blackstocks
Fishdam
Ford
PEE DEE R.

BROAD R.

Winnsboro
Hobkirk's Hill
Camden

Wilmington

Ninety Six
SALUDA R.
SOUTH

Ft. Charlotte
Ft. Granby
CAROLINA

Kettle Creek
Ft. Motte
SANTEE R.
Ft. Watson

Augusta
SAVANNAH R.
Georgetown

Eutaw Springs

BRIAR CR.

ATLANTIC

Briar Creek
Charleston
OCEAN

Beaufort
Ft. Moultrie

N

Purrysburg

Savannah

ALTAMAHA R. Ft. Sunbury

GEORGIA

SOUTHERN THEATER
of OPERATIONS

0   Miles   50

palacios

quarters and wanted to linger in Philadelphia to talk with his admired young friend who would soon arrive to pay his respects to Congress.

But De Kalb could not tarry in Philadelphia. He left the city, already alive with rumors that substantial French assistance was on the way, on May 13, and rode into Petersburg, Virginia, ten days later. His troops had embarked at Head of Elk and sailed down Chesapeake Bay. They marched into Petersburg several days after he arrived. De Kalb had been assured that contingents of Virginia and North Carolina militia would join him there, "but such is the dilatory manner in which all things are done here, that I cannot depend on them, much less wait for them." He had been promised teams and wagons. None arrived before the first week of June, but as they came straggling in by twos and threes, De Kalb loaded them and sent them off. The last of his three brigades left Petersburg on June 8. He was disappointed with what he considered a total lack of co-operation: "I met with no support, no integrity and no virtue in the State of Virginia, and place my sole reliance on the French fleet and army which are coming to our relief." Before leaving Petersburg, he learned that Charleston had fallen and that Lincoln and his army were prisoners of war.

Clinton devoted the month of May to consolidating the British position in South Carolina and Georgia. He directed Cornwallis to move on Camden and establish a base there. He garrisoned Ninety Six and sent a column to occupy Augusta. He issued a proclamation designed to convince Tories they would be supported by the King's army; another to release all Carolinians save prisoners of war from parole; a third to encourage enlistment in the loyal militia; and, finally, one decreeing that all South Carolinians must take an oath of allegiance on pain of being classed as rebels. Superficially, the state was peaceful and the situation seemed to hold promise that South Carolina would return to the fold.

Before Sir Henry sailed for New York in early June, he appointed Cornwallis to command the southern district "with the utmost plenitude of power, civil and military." He refrained from shackling the earl with instructions other than those "necessary to impress on his mind the very great importance of preserving the possession we had so easily and happily attained. For this end I requested His Lordship would constantly regard *the safety of Charleston and tranquility of South Carolina as the principal and indispensable objects of his attention.* . . . I left His Lordship at liberty, if he judged proper, to make a *solid* move into North Carolina, *upon condition it could at the time be made without risking the safety of the posts committed to his charge.*"[3] Clinton was in an optimistic mood when he left Charleston. He was convinced that Great Britain "was well warranted in the flattering expectations she entertained of soon seeing the war brought to a favorable issue."[4]

It is difficult to comprehend precisely why Sir Henry entertained such flattering expectations. He was one of the few senior British generals in America who had little faith in Loyalist support. He was also one of the very few, if not indeed the only one, who had studied geography and topography and who had developed a keen sense of how the sea and the great bays, estuaries, and river systems on the Atlantic seaboard could be used to advantage, both strategically and tactically, by an army supported by a fleet holding maritime supremacy. He understood how factors of time and space could affect operations. And he had frequently expressed his opinion that the rebellion could not be crushed until Washington's army was annihilated.

Why then did he disperse the British Army in America by creation of a "southern district" so distant from New York when he had no assurance the Royal Navy could maintain control of American coastal waters? His experiences had certainly taught him that no such control could be guaranteed. Under these circumstances, how could he expect to give Cornwallis the support the earl would need? Finally, why did he endow Cornwallis, an officer he no longer trusted and a favorite of Lord George Germain, a man he detested, "with the utmost plenitude of power"? Indeed, he went a step further when he at least tacitly agreed that Cornwallis could communicate directly with Germain.

Although Sir Henry had professed to be overjoyed when Cornwallis joined him in New York, the relationship between the two men had progressively and perceptibly deteriorated during the operations leading to the capture of Charleston. The earl was ambitious and courageous. He had proved himself as a division or corps commander. He was considerably younger than Sir Henry, and something of an extrovert. His subordinates admired him as a man and respected him as a soldier. The personality contrast between him and Sir Henry Clinton was readily apparent. If in victory the two generals were unable to establish a bond of sympathetic understanding and to collaborate on terms of mutual trust and confidence, how could they possibly be expected to do so in periods of crisis, especially as they were now to be separated by hundreds of miles of ocean? Clinton recognized that the personal relationship had broken down, but as was his habit would not accept any responsibility for the situation. The fault could not possibly lie with him. It must therefore be solely ascribed to Cornwallis and to members of the earl's staff who, so he had convinced himself, were exercising a malign influence.

Major General Baron de Kalb had been receiving belated reports of British activities in South Carolina, and none had given him any cause for optimism. As he entered North Carolina, he learned that Lieutenant Colonel Banastre Tarleton's mounted legion, composed of a small number of officers and men of the 17th Dragoons and selected Provincials, had pursued, caught, and annihilated the second of three small organized American forces remaining in South Carolina, Colonel Abraham Buford's Virginia Continentals, at Waxhaws on May 29.‡‡

De Kalb had not been long in North Carolina before he discovered that he might expect even less support than had been afforded him in Virginia, for the state took no steps to attend to his wants and could not or would not provide the teams and wagons he requested. Nor would those in authority bestir themselves to provide even a morsel of food for his half-starved troops. Days of abominably hot and humid weather broken by thunderstorms and torrential rains compounded his supply difficulties. He had no recourse but to order foragers to strip the countryside, a system not conducive to increasing his popularity. The governor paid no attention to his urgent solicitations, nor did Major General Richard Caswell, an inept braggart who commanded the North Carolina militia, join him with provisions as he had been ordered to do. De Kalb and his exhausted army might as well have been operating in hostile country.

On July 13 De Kalb received a letter from Major General Horatio Gates. In this missive the hero of Saratoga announced that Congress had named him to command the army in the south. Congress had not requested a recommendation from Washington and the commander in chief had not offered one. Gates had accepted, and hastened from his plantation in Virginia to Hillsboro, North Carolina, where he was conferring with Governor Nash and the Executive Council. De Kalb replied with a realistic report of his situation: "I have struggled with a good many difficulties for provisions ever since I arrived in this State." Troops had not eaten bread for days; no flour was to be had "and no disposition made for any . . . no assistance from the legislative or executive power; and the greatest unwillingness in the people to part with anything."[5] He was happy to welcome an officer whose name and reputation would be of sufficient weight to ensure the support the army so desperately needed.

Gates arrived at De Kalb's headquarters on July 25, assumed command of the Southern Department, and announced that he proposed to take up the march on Camden on the twenty-seventh. All his senior officers protested this decision and had reason for doing so. Gates had never commanded an army, not even an army as small as this one, in a moving campaign. He was now in a dynamic situation. His first obvious duty was to rest and refresh his undernourished and exhausted army. But

‡‡ Here it was that Tarleton, not entirely deservedly, came by the sobriquet "Bloody." After Waxhaws, the Americans always referred to him as "Bloody Tarleton." Legend had it that he personally sabered a young American officer who was holding up a white handkerchief in token of surrender, and that some of his troops wantonly cut down others who had appealed for quarter. This brutality evoked its own reprisal: to Americans, "Tarleton's Quarter" meant "No Quarter."

Gates, ambitious to add to the laurels of Saratoga, was impatient. He did not even inspect the troops, nor did he make the slightest attempt to discover how many rank and file were fit for duty, how well they were clothed, fed, trained, and equipped, or what arrangements had been made to supply their wants. He "estimated" he had 7,000 men fit for duty and was amazed to learn from his adjutant general, Colonel Otho Williams, that he had but 3,025 and that of these some 1,600 were militiamen from North Carolina and Virginia.

The route Gates selected for his march appeared to be the most direct, but in terms of terrain to be negotiated was the worst conceivable. Every senior officer attempted to persuade the general, whose vanity was equaled only by his dogmatic arrogance, to consider a somewhat longer but more advantageous approach. Gates refused to discuss the matter. Apparently he thought his reputation sufficient to frighten Lieutenant Colonel Lord Rawdon out of Camden. And so the march began: "The land traversed was poor and desolate, hardly reclaimed from its natural condition and rather worse even than the gloomy descriptions which had been made of it. The first rude efforts at civilization and culture which appeared here and there, had been either abandoned by their owners or plundered by their neighbors. All men had fled this wilderness. . . . In consequence, the distress and misery of the troops increased from day to day."[6] Officers and men alike were living on a diet of green corn, freshly killed stringy beef, and half-ripened peaches, and subsisted for days without salt, bread, or rum. For drink there was only brackish water scooped from sluggish streams. The overburdened soldiers, afflicted with chronic diarrhea, scurvy, and covered with ticks, staggered along the sandy roads. The searing sun beat upon them.

Gates, heretofore blinded by dreams of glory soon to be his, was now faced with reality, and wrote Governor Abner Nash begging him to exert his authority to send forward supplies of flour and rum. Nash, a slippery politician, made the usual promises. Actually, he had no intention of providing more than token assistance to another "Yankee" who had been imposed on North Carolina and whose locusts were eating up its substance. Neither the governor nor the Executive Council, comfortably situated at Hillsboro, paid any attention to his urgent pleas. Gates had to push on to Camden, and on August 15, when less than fifteen miles from his objective, issued orders for a night march.

Lord Rawdon, not sufficiently frightened to withdraw from Camden, had kept Cornwallis informed of Gates's approach. The earl left Charleston with his staff and a troop of dragoons and joined Rawdon. Cornwallis had good current information and lost little time making his decision. He would march at night and take Gates by surprise. "Thus, by a singular coincidence, both these armies marched against each other at the same time, each ignorant of the designs of the other. The night was sultry and the air as oppressively hot as in the daytime. The sky was clear and bright with stars. The sound of footsteps was stifled by the deep sand."[7]

Gates had made an egregious blunder in ordering his debilitated army to make a night march. He compounded this by sending Lieutenant Colonel Armand's mounted legion forward as advance guard. Shortly after midnight on August 16, Armand's troopers collided with Redcoats marching as vanguard of Cornwallis' small army. After an exchange of shots in the dark the troopers turned their horses and fled to the rear. This produced considerable confusion in the American column, but calm was restored when it became apparent that darkness prevented the British from improving their initial advantage.

Dawn found the two little armies deployed face to face on a narrow front astride a sandy road in a thin pine forest flanked by swamps.* The Americans were in no physical condition to fight. Enervating heat, scarcity of decent food, and a tiring night march had exhausted them, and on this particular morning practically every man in the army was suffering from gastroenteritis induced by eating half-baked bread and drinking several gills of molasses in lieu of the rum they had not tasted for weeks.

Gates had formed his militia on the left and his Continentals under De Kalb on the right; Cornwallis disposed his regulars under Lieutenant Colonel Webster on the right, the provincial troops under Lord Rawdon on the left, and held Tarleton's legion in reserve. Thus, British regulars were facing American militia, and here battle was joined. "The right wing of the British under Webster advanced in closed ranks with such noise, hurrahs and impetuosity upon the militia that they were thrown into confusion and seized by a panic." Colonel Williams, who witnessed the debacle on the American left, wrote that the Virginia militiamen "threw down their *loaded* arms and fled in the utmost consternation. The unworthy example of the Virginians was almost instantly followed by the North Carolinians." The entire weight of Cornwallis' small army now fell on the Continentals, who fought with great gallantry, but could not hold out against the steel. Major General de Kalb, mortally wounded, was captured. Some escaped by hiding in the swamps; some fled north toward Rugeley's Mills. To his credit, Gates made a vigorous attempt to stop the panic-stricken men who had no thought but to put as much distance as possible between themselves and Redcoat bayonets. Many were felled by the sabers of Tarleton's fierce legionnaires. Gates and a handful of mounted officers and troops escaped. The disgraced general scarcely drew rein until he arrived at Hillsboro.

Charles Stedman, a provincial officer serving under Cornwallis, surveyed the field and the road the fleeing Americans had taken in their precipitate retreat, and wrote: "The road for some miles was strewed with

* Numerical strengths were about equal.

the wounded and killed, who had been overtaken by the legion in their pursuit. The number of dead horses, broken waggons, and baggage scattered on the road, formed a perfect scene of horror and confusion: arms, knapsacks and accoutrements found were innumerable, such was the terror and dismay of the Americans." A final reckoning of American casualties showed 1,000 killed and wounded and an equal number taken prisoner.

Two days after the disaster suffered by American arms at Camden, another, the last in a series that began with Lincoln's surrender, overtook Colonel Thomas Sumter at Fishing Creek, North Carolina. Here the partisan leader had camped for the night, and here Banastre Tarleton, after a driving pursuit, caught up to him. Sumter was unaware that Tarleton was following him and had failed to take even the most elementary precautions. Tarleton charged into the camp where men were bathing in the river and others were cooking and eating supper. Their horses, on a picket line, were unsaddled.

Tarleton appeared so unexpectedly and so suddenly that there was no possibility of organized resistance. The colonel emerged half-clothed from under a wagon where he was enjoying a siesta, to a scene of confusion. He quickly found a bridled horse, leaped on it, and escaped. He left his coat, hat, sword, and pistols to the British. Tarleton's casualties totaled 16; his Green Dragoons killed 150 Americans, captured 300, and released 100 British prisoners. The victory justifiably added to Tarleton's growing reputation, as it diminished Sumter's.

News of Gates's defeat and the destruction of Sumter's force reached Washington's headquarters on September 6 and evoked dismay and anger. Hamilton wrote James Duane: "Was there ever an instance of a general running away as Gates has done from his whole army? And was there ever so precipitous a flight? One hundred and eighty miles in three days and a half! It does admirable credit to the activity of a man at his time of life. . . . But what will be done by Congress? Will he be changed or not? If he is changed, for God's sake overcome prejudice, and send Greene. . . . I stake my reputation on the events give him but fair play."[8]

Loss of men, arms, and equipment suffered at Charleston and in Tarleton's crushing victories over Huger, Buford, and Sumter was compensated to a degree by the safe arrival of Admiral de Ternay's squadron and convoy at Newport on July 11. Rochambeau had been forced to leave two of his regiments and all the Duc de Lauzun's cavalry horses at Brest, but had promised that men, animals, and other equipment would follow in a second echelon. Residents of Newport had not expected the French, and not until the following evening were there any signs of a civic welcome: "The Bell rang at Newpt; till after Midnight &

the evening of 12th Newpt illuminated, the Whigs put 13 Lights in the Windows, the Tories or doubtfuls, 4 or 6. The Quakers did not choose their Lights should shine before men, & their Windows were broken."[9]

Although the French were not aware of the fact, they were lucky to reach Newport, for had the Earl of Sandwich been less dilatory in dispatching Rear-admiral Thomas Graves with six of the line and a frigate to New York to reinforce Arbuthnot, the British, who correctly guessed the French destination to be Rhode Island, might well have intercepted De Ternay and brought him to battle. Graves arrived off Sandy Hook three days after De Ternay anchored.†

Arbuthnot's scouting cruisers had lost De Ternay after he passed the Chesapeake Capes and ten days elapsed before Clinton received reports that the French had landed at Newport and were working at top speed to restore the defensive positions Pigot's troops had not dismantled. Both De Ternay and Rochambeau anticipated an attack, and had the British admiral been almost anyone but Arbuthnot their expectations would probably have been realized.

Even such a master as Voltaire could scarcely have done justice to the command fiasco that now took place. Arbuthnot had stationed himself and his fleet off the eastern end of Long Island; couriers rode to and from New York; sloops traveled back and forth on the Sound; Clinton and his troops embarked and then disembarked; Arbuthnot agreed with Sir Henry's plans and then disagreed; he was ready, he was not ready. Clinton rode from New York in his chariot to the eastern tip of Long Island to confer with the vascillating admiral. He arrived to discover that Arbuthnot had departed. Not a sail was to be seen, nor had the admiral left any message. The general climbed into his chariot, and as it lumbered slowly back toward New York, frustration fed his anger.

Clinton had given up on Arbuthnot, and when he arrived at his headquarters wrote a friend in England: "Is your Lord Sandwich, who, to my knowledge, has long since considered the American War as Secondary, forever to send out Gambiers and Arbuthnots? if so, I intreat that I may return." With a competent admiral "all might have been expected from this Campaign, but from this old Gentleman, nothing can: he forgets from hour to hour—he thinks aloud—he will not answer any of my letters." Sir Henry admitted the admiral's heart might be in the right place, "but his head is gone."[10]

The "old Gentleman" was by no means the only object of Clinton's

---

† The Admiralty made little effort to anticipate events. Had Sandwich detached Graves a week or ten days earlier, the reinforcement would have arrived in time to intercept De Ternay. There was of course then no certainty that the French were going to Rhode Island, or even to America. They might have been going to reinforce their Spanish allies at Gibraltar, or to the French West Indies. British intelligence agents had not provided the Admiralty with precise information, but there was substantial evidence that De Ternay's destination was North America.

wrath. Lord George Germain, although not as accessible as Arbuthnot, provided another target. To him, Sir Henry reported he could hold what he had, but "I tremble for Canada." And "Why that number of troops in the West Indies. If superior at sea, you need them not, if inferior, of no avail." He continued: "For God's sake, send us Money, Men and Provisions or expect nothing but Complaints. Send out another admiral, or let me go home. . . . My wish is to retire from a Situation the most irksome that ever Man was placed in." Victualing ships expected for a month had not arrived and the June packet had been captured. "Look to your Canada next year, look to South Carolina, look to this place. Reinforce us, OR . . ."

Shortly after the French arrived, La Fayette wrote Vergennes to assure him that Rochambeau and Washington would reach a sympathetic understanding. The French general could not fail to be pleased with Washington's "uprightness, his delicacy, with that noble and frank politeness which characterises him." Since his return to America the marquis had found little else to encourage his habitual optimism.

Since mid-May, when he had been welcomed in Philadelphia as a hero, conferred with Luzerne, and received by Congress, the financial situation had steadily deteriorated; Congress had neither specie nor paper; the military chest was empty.‡ Washington hoarded the few guineas he had to pay his spies; he had not enough to pay express riders; "officers and men of the American army do not possess a shilling"; the army had "neither bread nor any other source of nourishment." Washington, described by La Fayette as "the tutelary genius of America," was making unremitting efforts to bring the army to a strength of 15,000 regulars. The marquis did not attempt to explain how 15,000 men were to be adequately paid, fed, clothed, sheltered, and equipped when 5,000 could not be. Although Washington's "grand object" was to take New York, he realized it could not be attained without maritime superiority, and La Fayette urged Vergennes to act speedily to establish in American waters "that empire of the sea without which nothing can be done."[11]

This was not an optimistic letter, but there was no cause for optimism. Exchange speculators, contractors, and merchants were making fortunes while Congress dallied and an unpaid army hovered from day to day on the brink of starvation, a fate averted only by the zeal of Quartermaster General Nathanael Greene. After a brief visit to Philadelphia, Greene wrote a friend: "The local policy of all the States is directly opposed to the great national plan; and if they continue to persevere in it,

‡ The rapid depreciation of Continental paper began in January 1779 when the average exchange rate was eight dollars Continental for one in silver. By July, the rate was nineteen to one; by October, thirty to one; at Christmas, forty to one. By July 1780, paper stood at sixty for one.

God knows what the consequences will be. There is a terrible falling off in public virtue since the commencement of the present contest. The loss of morale and the want of public spirit leave us almost like a rope of sand. . . . Luxury and dissipation are very prevalent. These are the common offspring of sudden riches." He had found luxury and ostentation "very predominant" in Boston but in these respects Bostonians could no more compare with Philadelphians "than an infant babe to a full grown man. I dined at one table where there were an hundred and sixty dishes; and at several others not far behind. The growing avarice and a declining currency are poor materials to build an independence upon."

The decline in public virtue was not confined to Boston and Philadelphia. On August 26, 1780, Greene, who had taken a large foraging party into Bergen County, New Jersey, wrote Washington: "There has been committed some of the most horrid acts of plunder by some of the Pennsylvania line that has disgraced the American Arms during the War. The instances of plunder and violence is equal to any thing committed by the Hessians. . . . It is absolutely necessary to give a check to the licentious spirit which increases amazingly. The impudence of the Soldiers is intolerable." He recommended that at least "one of these fellows" be executed, and added, "If your Excellency will give permission I will have one hung up this afternoon where the army are to march by."[12] He asked for authority to hang a deserter at the same time. Washington read this letter "with extreme pain and anxiety" and directed Greene to inflict the "prompt punishment" proposed. As the army marched by, two corpses swayed in the wind.

The question of whether the army could be relied upon as a fighting instrument troubled all senior officers. Money, food, clothes, shoes, and discipline were not the only problems. A major and apparently insoluable one was the constant change of personnel. Men who had been drafted for three months, six months, or a year left camp as their time expired; the militiamen drafted to replace them arrived inadequately equipped and with no training. Major General Baron von Steuben and his deputies did what they could in the short time available to inculcate fundamentals of discipline, to instill a modicum of morale, and to transform recruits and reluctant militiamen into passable soldiers.

Although Washington and Rochambeau shared the desire for a meeting, both were engaged in affairs that commanded their daily attention. Washington was busy with a "Committee of Conference," whose members, endowed by Congress with power to act for it and so expedite preparations for the coming campaign, had recently arrived at his headquarters in New Jersey. Rochambeau's time and energies were consumed in perfecting the defenses of Newport. Until the generals could meet personally, confidential communications would have to be entrusted to liaison officers. The officer Washington selected to represent his views in these delicate negotiations was La Fayette. Doubtless it appeared to him that the marquis was eminently well qualified to conduct such important secret conversations. But actually this was an unhappy choice.

La Fayette was a major general in the Continental Army; in the French Army he was no more than a captain, and a reserve captain at that. In the eyes of officers serving under Rochambeau, the marquis was a young, ambitious, bumptious "volunteer general" with little professional experience. Happily Rochambeau took a less prejudiced view, and after perusing one of La Fayette's letters in which the marquis urged an attack on New York without waiting for the French to establish essential naval superiority if only temporarily, he wrote, referring to himself as "old papa Rochambeau":

> Permit an old father, my dear Marquis to reply to you as to a son who is very dear to him. You know me quite well enough to realize that I do not need to be spurred into action, and furthermore, that at my age, once I have taken all the military and political factors into account and have reached a decision, under the hard compulsion of circumstances, nothing can make me change that decision unless it be a direct order from my superior officer. Such is not the case here. On the contrary, I am delighted that General Washington's dispatches indicate that my ideas are substantially in accord with his. . . . Rest assured of my very real friendship for you. . . .

He knew La Fayette was spirited and courageous but reminded him that the quality most wanted in the council chamber was "sober judgement."[13]

The conference between the French and American commanders was arranged for September 20, 1780, in Hartford, Connecticut. Washington brought with him Generals Knox and La Fayette, Colonels de Gouvion (chief of engineers) and Alexander Hamilton, and several junior aides. Rochambeau arrived with Admiral de Ternay, two aides (Colonels Count Axel de Fersen and Mathieu Dumas), and his son, Vicomte de Rochambeau.

The atmosphere was friendly and dinners convivial. Rochambeau and Washington immediately established a cordial relationship that was to grow into a firm friendship. The French officers found Washington to be all they had expected. Fersen thought him "a man illustrious, if not unique in our century. His handsome and majestic, but at the same time mild and open countenance, perfectly reflects his moral qualities; he looks the hero. He is very cold; speaks little but is courteous and frank. A shade of sadness overshadows his countenance, which is not unbecoming and gives him an interesting air." Dumas was greatly impressed with

Washington's bearing, demeanor, and conversation, and Comte Louis Philippe de Ségur wrote: "His exterior almost told his story. Simplicity, grandeur, dignity, calm, kindness, firmness shone in his physiognomy as well as in his character. He was of a noble and high stature, his expression was gentle and kindly, his smile pleasing, his manners simple without familiarity. . . . All in him announces the hero of a republic."[14]

Before they met in Hartford, Washington had written Rochambeau his hope that the allies would "be able to combine some plan of future operations . . . as the affairs of this country absolutely require activity." He realized that any plan could only "turn up possibilities," and an attack on New York was not within the realm of "possibilities" until the French could establish naval superiority. This now seemed a remote prospect, for Rodney had arrived in New York harbor on September 14 with ten of the line. Washington and Rochambeau thus "decided on passing the whole winter in passive observation, always holding themselves ready to profit by the most favorable circumstances." Washington would employ his energies "in putting the American Army in good condition for the opening of the campaign" and General Rochambeau, who was expecting the arrival of his second division, would prepare himself to aid his American allies "with vigor."[15]

The conference between Washington and Rochambeau was not the only one scheduled for Wednesday, September 20, 1780. Another was to be held aboard British sloop of war *Vulture*, anchored in the Hudson about ten miles north of Dobbs Ferry. There a senior American officer, believed by Clinton to be Major General Benedict Arnold, but known to him only as "Gustavus," was to meet with Sir Henry's acting adjutant general, Major John André, and there final arrangements were to be made for the betrayal of West Point and its 3,000 defenders to the British at an agreed price of two guineas per man.

This meeting was planned to culminate a long clandestine correspondence between Major General Benedict Arnold, commanding West Point and American outposts on both sides of the Hudson as far south as King's Ferry, and Major John André, deputy adjutant general of the British Army, who was in charge of Clinton's secret operations. Arnold had successively used "Monk," "Moore," and "Gustavus" as pseudonyms; André, plain "John Anderson." As neither man was certain of the identity of his correspondent, a personal meeting was essential.

André, clad in immaculate regimentals, boarded *Vulture* during late afternoon on September 20. There was some confusion in his mind as to whether "Gustavus" would come to the sloop or would send a boat to convey him to a secluded meeting place ashore. He spent a sleepless night awaiting the boat, but none came. He decided to wait through

Thursday. His companion, Beverly Robinson, a prominent Hudson Valley Tory who had fled to New York and been commissioned a colonel in a provincial regiment, agreed that this was the best course to adopt.

There is some doubt as to precisely how much Robinson knew of the nature and extent of the conspiracy.** He was a friend of Arnold's, who was then making Robinson's handsome house his headquarters. He and Arnold had recently exchanged several letters relating to Robinson's property, and Arnold had been informed that he would be aboard *Vulture* with "Anderson." Robinson provided a convenient cover for the plotters.

Toward midnight, a boat pulled alongside *Vulture*, and Joshua Hett Smith, one of Arnold's neighbors with whom the general was intimate, and to whom he had given a pass and a letter to Robinson, identified himself. He was ordered aboard and sent to the captain's cabin, where refreshments were served. André soon entered, was introduced as "Mr. Anderson," and announced that he wished to depart at once for the rendezvous.

When the boat beached on the west side of the Hudson at a point known as the Long Clove, Smith disembarked, climbed the bank, and disappeared into the forest. There, "hid among the firs," he found his friend, Major General Benedict Arnold. He returned to the boat and guided "Mr. Anderson" to the meeting place. Arnold told him to go back to the beach and await orders. First light came, but there was no sign of "Mr. Anderson." Smith was becoming nervous and clambered up the bank, interrupted the conversation being conducted in low tones, and observed that it was time to return to the sloop. All then scrambled back to the narrow shingle and Smith aroused the boatmen.

There now occurred a contretemps, for the oarsmen, pleading fatigue and the danger of a trip to the sloop in daylight, adamantly refused to return to *Vulture*. The solution the conspirators then reached was for André to mount the horse ridden to the rendezvous by Arnold's Negro servant, and to proceed with Arnold to Smith's house, some four miles away, and within the American lines. This upset André, for to enter the American lines was distinctly contrary to Sir Henry Clinton's instructions.

As dawn broke on September 22 the pair arrived at Smith's house. Shortly thereafter, Smith himself appeared. Breakfast was interrupted by the sound of cannon fire. Looking from a window, the visitors saw to their dismay that two small cannon, emplaced in a redoubt on Gallows Point, were firing on *Vulture*, then aground on a mud bank. A rising tide

** It was later stated that only Clinton, Rodney, Knyphausen, and André were fully aware of the details. Smith would later testify he thought "Mr. Anderson" a spy in Arnold's pay and he believed he was serving the cause by putting him ashore to confer with the general.

freed the sloop, and with a favoring wind she dropped downstream. André, so Smith was later to testify, was obviously "annoyed." The three sat down to finish their meal, after which Arnold and André retired to an upstairs bedroom to settle details of the "attack" during which West Point would be surrendered.

Arnold had made elaborate plans to weaken the defenses of the citadel at critical points. He had removed a link from the heavy iron chain placed from bank to bank of the Hudson to impede passage of ships. He had depleted the garrison by sending off several large parties to cut firewood. He had prepared elaborate plans indicating routes of access to the fort. These plans he gave André, together with a detailed strength report. André folded the papers and placed them between his stockings and the soles of his boots. After providing "Anderson" and Smith with passes required to see them safely through the American outpost line, Arnold, confident that all details (including the reward for his perfidy) had been settled, departed. He left secure in the understanding that Smith would convey André to *Vulture* that night.

It shortly developed that Smith had no intention of spending another chilly night in a rowboat on the Hudson. He suffered from a constant ague, or so he told "Mr. Anderson." Clinton's deputy adjutant general would have to proceed overland. André had no choice but to submit to this, and on Friday afternoon Smith, his Negro groom, and Major André set off in the direction of New York. André was wearing a beaver hat and one of Smith's coats. In assuming this disguise, he was for the second time directly disobeying Sir Henry Clinton's explicit orders, but, again, he had no choice. At twilight the three travelers crossed the Hudson at King's Ferry, and turned south toward Tarrytown. At about 9 P.M. they were stopped by an American patrol. The captain examined their passes and waved them on, but cautioned them that as the road to Tarrytown was infested with bands of plunderers known as "Cow-boys" and "Skinners," they would be wise to stop for the night.†† Smith knew a Tory in the vicinity and there they found a bed they were forced to share. The groom was accommodated in the stable.

Shortly after dawn on Saturday, the three again set off. They were now riding in the so-called "Neutral Ground" between the American and British outpost lines. A country woman, who the night before had been robbed by a band of marauders, provided each of them with a generous bowl of porridge. Here Smith turned back to ride to Arnold's headquarters, where he expected to dine that night. André would dine with his messmates in New York. They would all toast his ingenuity and courage. He—the man responsible for winning over one of the two most re-

†† "Cow-boys" professed to be patriotic Whigs; "Skinners" alleged that they were Loyalists. Both gangs devoted themselves to terrorizing and robbing the inhabitants of the area.

spected major generals in the American Army, and for gaining West Point—would certainly be promoted and probably knighted.

Such thoughts, if he entertained them, were rudely dispelled when a man with a musket emerged from the shrubbery lining the road and seized the horse's bridle. Two other armed men now appeared. The leader of the trio, Isaac Van Vert, ordered André to dismount.‡‡ At this moment, all André needed to do to ensure his safe return to the British lines was to produce his pass. He did not. Instead, he asked the men where they belonged. "To below," they replied, meaning, André thought, New York. "And so do I," André said, adding that he was a British officer on urgent business and could not be detained. Van Vert and his friends realized they had a valuable captive. André now showed Arnold's pass, to which Van Vert paid no attention.

André then tried to bribe his captors to release him. This confirmed their opinion that they held a man of some importance. They ordered him into the bushes and told him to strip. They found the incriminating papers, in Arnold's handwriting, and decided to deliver "Mr. Anderson" to Lieutenant Colonel John Jameson, Continental Army, commanding the outpost at North Castle.

Jameson was in a quandary. Here was a "Mr. Anderson" with a pass from Arnold, carrying suspicious material. Jameson, an officer not noted for his acumen, now proceeded to botch the situation. He sent a messenger to Arnold to inform him that he was holding a "Mr. Anderson" who held a pass signed by him and had started him under guard to headquarters at Robinson's. He sent another courier with the confiscated papers to Danbury, with instructions to deliver them to General Washington, who was returning from his conference with Rochambeau via Danbury and West Point to headquarters in New Jersey.*

A new actor now appeared on the stage. This was Major Benjamin Tallmadge, Washington's most effective intelligence officer, who ran the American agent network in New York. Jameson described the papers found on "Anderson," and Tallmadge immediately concluded that "Anderson" was someone other than he purported to be, and that he was acting in a suspicious and possibly treasonable collusion with Arnold. He sent a courier with peremptory orders to bring "Anderson" back to North Castle and to intercept the man carrying the note to Arnold, and another to recall the rider carrying the papers to Washington. The first succeeded only in catching up with "Anderson" and his guards, and toward evening on Saturday, September 23, the little group returned to North Castle.

‡‡ It is said that the three "Cow-boys" were playing cards under the shade of an aged oak.

* Apparently, Jameson had no very clear idea about the paper found in "Anderson's" boots. He thought "Anderson" had been given them possibly by someone who had stolen them from Arnold.

On Sunday morning the prisoner was removed to more secure quarters at Lower Salem, where he was informed that the secreted papers found on him had been sent to Washington. He thereupon asked for pen and paper and wrote a letter to the commander in chief, telling him that "the person in your possession is Major John André, Adjutant General of the British army."† At about this time, the courier who had set off to Danbury returned to North Castle. He had been unable to find Washington, who had changed his route. Nor had the dispatch rider sent with the note to Arnold yet reached Robinson's house.

Thus Arnold spent Sunday night unaware that André had been caught and had revealed his identity. The traitor was happy to have Peggy, his secret collaborator, with him, and was no doubt made even happier as he and his wife discussed what they would do with the £6,000 he expected to receive as a reward for "surrendering" West Point. Clinton had no idea where André was, but did know he had not returned to the sloop as scheduled. He and Rodney were fully prepared for a dash up the Hudson within twenty-four hours of André's return. A select body of troops stood on the alert ready to embark at a moment's notice.

Greene, who commanded the army at Tappan during Washington's absence, was perplexed. All reports from New York indicated that Clinton was planning to move, but the objective was held as such a close secret that spies could only guess at it. Would Rodney join Arbuthnot, and with Clinton's army descend on the French at Newport? Was the destination Virginia, as some agents speculated? Or were the British going to Wilmington, North Carolina? Greene could only conjecture. He passed what information he received to the president of Congress.

Colonel Beverly Robinson, anxiously awaiting André aboard *Vulture*, was no less perturbed than was his commanding general in New York. André rested under heavy guard at New Salem. Washington sought his repose near Fishkill. He expected to meet Arnold on Monday, breakfast with him, inspect the fortifications at West Point, and later dine at Robinson's.

On Monday morning at about eight o'clock, Colonel Alexander Hamilton and another aide arrived at Robinson's house. Arnold greeted them and invited them to breakfast. Washington, Hamilton told him, would be arriving with La Fayette and Knox within the hour. While the three were chatting at table, a militia officer handed Arnold a letter from Colonel Jameson. This was Jameson's report that "Anderson" was in custody and that certain papers he was carrying had been forwarded by courier to Washington. Arnold excused himself, went upstairs to the bed-

† André was not yet a major, nor was he "Adjutant General of the British Army." He was a captain, acting major, awaiting confirmation of his promotion, and was deputy adjutant general.

room, bade Peggy farewell, returned, announced that he had been summoned to West Point on an emergency, mounted his horse, and galloped to the landing. There he boarded his barge and was rowed to the British sloop. As Arnold stepped into his barge, Washington arrived at Robinson's house with La Fayette and Knox. Washington evinced no particular surprise when he was told that Arnold had departed on an emergency visit to West Point and observed only that he would see him there.

Washington had no sooner left Robinson's to cross the river than Peggy Arnold fell into a hysterical fit. She sent for Colonel Richard Varick, Arnold's senior aide, and told him tearfully that the general had "gone forever." Varick described her as frantic with grief, her hair and dress disheveled, and "in an utter frenzy." All attempts to calm her were futile; her incoherent ravings distressed the young aide, who summoned the doctor stationed at headquarters. The doctor thought Peggy had lost her mind, and would die.‡

When Washington returned from West Point, the courier who had been chasing him for two days was waiting. The commander in chief looked over the papers. He ordered Hamilton to ride at all speed to Verplanck's Point and arrest Arnold if he could catch him. There was no chance of this; Arnold was safe aboard *Vulture*, from where he sent a letter to Verplanck's. In this, he attempted to justify his treason, stated that Mrs. Arnold was innocent of any wrongdoing, and appealed to Washington's "humanity" to afford her protection and to permit her to return to Philadelphia.

Washington had seen the lady at her request and was convinced she was innocent of complicity in the plot. Hamilton, too, had seen Mrs. Arnold, and he too was certain she was innocent.** This business took up a great part of Sunday afternoon and not until after dinner at 4 P.M. did Washington begin dictating a stream of orders to secure the safety of West Point. He ordered the commanders of the posts at King's Ferry to be changed, and directed Greene to march to the ferry at once with one division and to place the remainder of the army under an alert to march to West Point at a moment's notice. On Monday morning Greene had issued a General Order announcing that TREASON OF THE BLACKEST DYE had been discovered. On that day, André was brought under heavy guard to Robinson's house and then sent to West Point, the citadel he had expected to enter in triumph.

On Friday, September 29, André, who had been transferred to Tappan, was brought to trial before a board of inquiry of which Major General Nathanael Greene was president. Washington's letter convening the

‡ She was not too far gone to remember to destroy letters that had passed between her husband and herself before her recent arrival at the Robinson house.
** Peggy Arnold was permitted to proceed to Philadelphia. She was later banished from the city and sent to join her husband in New York.

board was read, as was André's letter of September 24 to the commander in chief. André admitted that he had landed from *Vulture* at night; that he had been within the American lines; that he had assumed a disguise and was under an assumed name; and that he had carried the incriminating documents produced for the board's inspection by John Lawrence, judge advocate general, concealed between his stockings and the inner soles of his boots. He stated that he had not come ashore under a flag, as letters from Clinton, Arnold, and Robertson falsely alleged.

The deliberations were brief. The evidence was irrefutable; there were no mitigating circumstances. The verdict, signed by each of the six major generals and eight brigadiers who sat as André's judges, found: "First, that he came on shore from the Vulture sloop-of-war in the night of the 21st of September, instant, on an interview with General Arnold, in a private and secret manner. Secondly, that he changed his dress within our lines, and under a feigned name and disguised habit, passed our works at Stony and Verplank's Points, in the evening of the 22nd of September, instant, and was taken the morning of the 23rd of September, at Tarrytown, in a disguised habit, being then on his way to New York; and when taken he had in his possession several papers which contained intelligence for the enemy. The Board having maturely considered these facts, do also report to his excellency General Washington, that Major André, adjutant-general to the British army, ought to be considered as a spy from the enemy, and that agreeably to the law and usage of nations it is their opinion he ought to suffer death." The commander in chief approved the verdict and sentence and directed that the execution take place on October 1 at 5 P.M.[16]

Clinton, who realized that André's life was at stake, did all he could to persuade Washington that the spy was not really a spy. His efforts were of no avail. The case against his deputy adjutant general was too damning, too conclusive, to be argued.

Dr. James Thacher, a senior surgeon in the Continental Army, who was present at Tappan at the time, and who knew personally most of the men who sat in judgment on André, wrote of him: "During the trial of this unfortunate officer, he conducted [himself] with unexampled magnanimity and dignity of character. He very freely and candidly confessed all the circumstances relative to himself, and carefully avoided every expression that might have a tendency to implicate any other person. So firm and dignified was he in his manners, and so honorable in all his proceedings on this most trying occasion, that he excited universal interest in his favor. He requested only to die the death of a soldier and not on the gibbet."[17]

But André was a convicted spy, and after a respite of one day, was hanged as a spy on October 2. He marched with a firm step to the scene, mounted the wagon on which the black coffin rested, adjusted the noose to his neck, and asked Colonel Alexander Scammel, adjutant general of the army, to bear witness that he was meeting his fate "like a brave man." He replaced the handkerchief over his eyes; the executioner whipped the horses; and this courageous man suffered "but a momentary pang."

A great concourse of spectators witnessed André's death. So well had he comported himself during his arrest and as he faced his last moments on earth that his fate aroused much sympathy. "The spot was consecrated by the tears of thousands."

Washington wrote several days later:

> In no instance since the commencement of the war has the interposition of Providence appeared more remarkably conspicuous than in the rescue of the post and garrison at West Point. How far Arnold meant to involve me in the catastrophe of this place, does not appear by any indubitable evidence, and I am rather inclined to think he did not wish to hazard the more important object, by attempting to combine two events, the lesser of which might have marred the greater. A combination of extraordinary circumstances, and unaccountable deprivation of presence of mind in a man of the first abilities, and the virtue of three militiamen, threw the adjutant-general of the British forces, with full proof of Arnold's intention, into our hands, and but for the egregious folly or the bewildered conception of Lieutenant-Colonel Jamison, who seemed lost in astonishment, and not to have known what he was doing, I should undoubtedly have gotten Arnold. Andre has met his fate, and with that fortitude which was to be expected from an accomplished man and a gallant officer; but I mistake if Arnold is suffering at this time the torments of a mental hell. He wants feeling. From some traits of his character which have lately come to my knowledge, he seems to have been so hacknied in crime, so lost to all sense of honor and shame, that while his faculties still enable him to continue his sordid pursuits, there will be no time for remorse.[18]

⁊ 5

To Spirit Up the People

The steady diet of bad news from the Carolinas changed for the better in October when Congress learned that on the seventh of the month a heterogeneous "army" of 900 Carolinians, Virginians, and "Over Mountain Men" from eastern Tennessee and Kentucky, most armed with rifles and led by Colonels William Campbell, John Sevier, and Isaac Shelby, had surrounded and annihilated Major Patrick Ferguson's 1,400 provincials and Tories at Kings Mountain in western North Carolina. Ferguson, the only British soldier present, was killed, his force destroyed, and 700 prisoners with 1,400 stand of arms taken. Of those captured, 24 were tried on the field by an impromptu general court-martial on the charge of treason. Nine, found guilty, were promptly strung up. These summary executions of Americans by Americans, described by Cornwallis as "most cruel murders," carried a grim message to Loyalists in the Carolinas.

Cornwallis had moved into Charlotte, North Carolina, on September 26 and was resting his small army preparatory to operations to subdue that state. He was unjustly blamed for not having sent assistance to Ferguson. The major had not asked for help. Indeed, he had stated earlier that his command was competent to deal with any force the Americans could raise. When he finally realized that his situation was precarious, he sent off two mounted messengers asking for aid. Both were captured and hanged.

Although in New York Ferguson's defeat was publicly dismissed as a "small check," it was a reverse of sufficient gravity to force Cornwallis to make an immediate and radical alteration to his plans. Charles Stedman, who was with the army in Charlotte when the news arrived at head-quarters, wrote later: "The total loss of so considerable a detachment, from the operations of which so much was expected, put a stop, for the present, to the farther progress of the commander in chief, and obliged him to fall back into South Carolina, for the protection of its western borders against the incursions of a horde of mountaineers, whose appearance was as unexpected as their success was fatal to the prosecution of the intended expedition."[1]

Cornwallis abandoned Charlotte in mid-October and fell back to the vicinity of Winnsboro, South Carolina. The march soon became an ordeal. "In this retreat the King's troops suffered much . . . the soldiers had no tents; it rained for several days without intermission; the roads were over their shoes in water and mud. . . . At night [the army] encamped in the woods in a most unhealthy climate, for many days without rum. . . . The water that the army drank was frequently as thick as puddle."[2] As De Kalb's Americans had done earlier, the Redcoats were subsisting on Indian corn.* Cornwallis, who was ill, fared no better than his men.

The earl, suffering from a "severe fever" and unable to write, arrived at Winnsboro on October 29. There the disagreeable task of reporting the withdrawal to South Carolina was discharged by Lieutenant Colonel Lord Rawdon, who informed Sir Henry Clinton that Ferguson's defeat had so "dispirited" the Loyalists that none would now come forward. Further, the "long fatigue" of the troops "made it seriously requisite to give some refreshment to the army." At Winnsboro, Cornwallis could protect his garrisons at Ninety Six and Camden while he awaited a reinforcement of 1,500 commanded by Major General Alexander Leslie.†

But even with this significant addition, he could not hope to subdue the proliferating partisan bands that had gained many adherents after Kings Mountain, an event that on the one hand had mightily discouraged Loyalists and on the other fanned "the dying embers of resistance." Sumter, "The Carolina Game-cock," was back in the field with a

---

* Stedman reports that the militia with the British used a bayonet to punch holes in canteens, used these as graters, and so rasped dried corn on the cob to make corn meal, which when mixed with water could be used to make a mush or corn-cakes. Cornwallis ate both products and recommended them to the army. This is reminiscent of Burgoyne's order on the subject of pancakes.

† Clinton had sent Leslie to Virginia and placed him under command of Cornwallis. While he was at Charlotte, the earl ordered Leslie to embark his troops at Portsmouth, proceed to Charleston, and join him.

numerous following, as was Colonel Francis Marion, who had sought a temporary haven in Virginia after the debacle at Camden. Marion, soon to be known by British and Americans as "the Swamp Fox," was operating with a heterogeneous collection of boys and older men, including a dozen Negroes. ". . . the northeast parts of the province were infested by the depredations of an enterprising partizan of the name of Marion. This man, previous to the defeat of General Gates, had been active in stirring up the inhabitants upon Black River to revolt; but after that event had thought it prudent for some time to retire out of the province. He had now again returned, and, traversing the country between the rivers Pedee and Santee, without opposition, was so successful in firing up rebellion, that the whole of that district was upon the eve of a revolt."[3] Cornwallis sent Tarleton after Marion, who retired into the swamps. Tarleton with his frustrated legionnaires and their exhausted horses returned to Winnsboro. For the first time, Banastre Tarleton had found an enemy able to outmarch and outwit him.

While Marion was leading Tarleton on the first of many unprofitable "fox hunts," Sumter was busy in the northwestern part of the state, where "he was indefatigable in firing up [the inhabitants] to take up arms; and the reputation he had already acquired, with his peculiar talent for enterprise, in a short time procured him a number of followers."[4] With "the Fox" hidden deep in the swamps and out of his reach, Tarleton turned his attention to Sumter, and at his hands, at Blackstocks on November 20, the dashing young cavalry leader, who claimed a victory, was "roughly handled." The American loss was severe; Sumter was seriously wounded, and "after conveying him to a place of safety" his followers dispersed. They dispersed not to return to their small plantations and farms, but to join other partisan leaders.

Cornwallis was not intellectually prepared to cope with a guerrilla war. On December 3, 1780, he wrote Sir Henry Clinton that Colonel Marion had "so wrought on the minds of the people, partly by the terror of his threats and cruelty of his punishments, and partly by the promise of plunder, that there was scarcely an inhabitant between the Santee and Pedee, that was not in arms against us."[5] Cornwallis was unable to comprehend that the men who took arms in their hands, suffered almost intolerable deprivation and hardship, and risked their lives against the British could possibly be motivated by any ideas other than self-preservation or hope of material reward. He was fully confident that his own ability and the loyalty, devotion, and courage of the officers and men he led were more than adequate to defeat any ragtag American army in an orthodox battle situation.

But now no American field army challenged him. The partisan bands, impalpable enemies, drifted with the wind, always threatening to cut his tenuous communications, to ambush his supply and evacuation columns, to strike suddenly and viciously at his outlying posts. They were here one day, there another, and gone to ground the next. They were familiar with the terrain; they knew the short cuts and the bypaths. They could make their way through forbidding swamps inaccessible to the British infantry. They traveled light and usually at night with several days' supply of parched corn, salt, and dried beef in small wallets. And they could take advantage of the inestimable benefit of timely and accurate information, not only of British moves, but frequently of British plans. Cornwallis, on the contrary, complained that the Loyalists were "so timid or so stupid" that he could get no intelligence. Thus, he had not the vaguest notion of when or where to expect the next blow. Apparently it did not occur to the noble earl that the partisans had information because the great majority of the men and women in the countryside supported them. Marion had indeed "wrought on the minds of the people."

With Leslie's reinforcements on the way, Cornwallis felt able to plan to return to North Carolina. His first objective was Hillsboro. In that part of the state, he was told, hundreds of Loyalists only awaited the presence of a Redcoat army to openly declare their allegiance. For this expedition the earl assembled a well-equipped and compact striking force of about 2,500 rank and file, dragoons and artillery. He was not at all satisfied with the quality of the troops Clinton had sent him, and wrote Sir Henry that with the exception of the guards and the Hessian regiment of Bose they were "exceedingly bad."‡ Whatever the quality may have been, it was not a factor of sufficient importance to deter Cornwallis from undertaking the campaign he projected.

On October 14, the commander in chief wrote Major General Nathanael Greene that Congress had directed him to order a court of inquiry on the conduct of Major General Gates, and "As Congress have been pleased to leave the Officer to command [in the Southern Department] to my choice, it is my wish to appoint You; and from the pressing situation of affairs in that quarter . . . that You should arrive there, as soon as circumstances will possibly admit."⁶ Greene, who was then commanding West Point, accepted immediately, and a few days later proceeded to Washington's headquarters to receive his instructions.**

These reflected the confidence Washington reposed in the man he had selected: "Uninformed as I am of the enemy's force in that quarter, of our own, or of the resources which it will be in our power to command

‡ A list of the units composing this small army suggests that the converse was true. Sir Henry Clinton thought so, and later wrote that Cornwallis might "have had a foreboding of the train of evils which were to attend his subsequent operations and wished in time to prepare this plausible excuse" (Willcox, *Clinton Narrative*, p. 232). Quite the contrary, for the earl was inclined to be as optimistic as he frequently was impetuous.

** Greene had resigned his commission as quartermaster general and returned to the line of the army.

for carrying on the war, I can give you no particular instructions, but must leave you to govern yourself intirely according to your own prudence and judgement and the circumstances in which you find yourself." He was aware that Greene would encounter "embarrassments of a singular and complicated nature," but relied on his "abilities and exertions for everything your means will be able to effect." He assigned Major General Baron von Steuben to the Southern Department: ". . . his talents, knowledge of service, zeal and activity will make him very useful to you in all respects and particularly in the formation and regulation of the raw troops, which will principally compose the Southern Army." He had put Major Henry Lee's cavalry under marching orders for the south. Further than this, he could promise nothing, and sent Greene off to his new command with warm wishes for his "success, reputation, health and happiness."[7]

En route to the south, Greene stopped in Philadelphia where he spent frustrating days conferring with members of Congress and the Board of War respecting supplies of money; medicines; arms and munitions; shoes and clothing; tentage and other camp equipment; tools, artificers, and wagons; and tack for Major Lee's horses. For, he wrote, there was not "the least probability" the southern states could supply these essential items in adequate amounts. He soon discovered that there was not the least probability he could depend on Congress to satisfy his most elementary needs. Congress could promise him a small sum of money, but had no arms, no wagons, no powder, no clothes, and no ready cash to purchase anything. Greene appealed to the Executive Council of Pennsylvania and was promised 1,500 stand of arms, some clothing, and one hundred wagons. At his request, Congress appointed Major Henry Lee, the cavalry commander soon to acquire the sobriquet of "Light-Horse Harry," a lieutenant colonel in the Continental Army.

While he was dealing with these problems, Greene found time to read reports of the battle of Camden and of the situation of the army. From these, he correctly concluded that he was inheriting the demoralized, disorganized, and ill-equipped remnants of an army "rather a Shadow than a Substance, and has only an imaginary Existence." He wrote Washington that all he could hope to do at first was to create a small "flying Army to consist of about eight hundred horse and one thousand Infantry." He would use this, with help from the militia, "to confine the enemy in their limits and render it difficult for them to subsist in the interior country." Until he could raise, equip, and train a force large enough to meet Cornwallis in the field he would "make the most of a kind of partisan war."[8]

Greene arrived in Richmond, Virginia, on November 16, 1780, to find the city in a state of total confusion. The government had no money, no credit, and no prospect of getting either. During the trip from Philadelphia, Greene had written Governors Rodney of Delaware and Lee of Maryland asking for their assistance in forwarding supplies. In Richmond he turned to Jefferson. The governor responded by calling up 3,500 militia. Of this number, only half responded and those who had done so began to desert "in shoals" the moment they discovered the state had no money to pay them, no arms to put in their hands, no clothing to put on their backs, no shoes to put on their feet, and no blankets to cover them at night. Governor Jefferson, who was not particularly interested in sending Virginians to fight in North and South Carolina, managed to collect thirty wagons with teams and reluctant teamsters.

From Richmond, Greene wrote letters to Washington, the president of Congress, the Board of War, Brigadier General Timothy Pickering (who had succeeded him as quartermaster general), and to others who might be able to bring influence to bear to improve the distressing supply situation. To one powerful friend he wrote that clothing must be provided even if that meant drawing on France for funds. On November 20 he wrote Colonel Timothy Matlack: "It may [be] disagreeable to draw on France, but it is better to do this, than to let the Army go to Ruin. The Distress and Suffering of the Troops of the Southern Army on Account of Provision is sufficient to render the Service so disagreeable as to make it impossible to keep Men in the Field, but when they are starved with Cold as well as Hunger the whole Army must become Deserters or Patients in the Hospitals."[9] Before he left Richmond on November 21, he directed Steuben to assume command in Virginia, and wrote Washington: "I cannot contemplate my own situation without the greatest degree of anxiety. I . . . have to prosecute a war in a country in the best state attended with almost insurmountable difficulties, but doubly so now from the state of our finances and the loss of public credit. How I shall be able to support myself under these embarrassments, God only knows."[10]

On the afternoon of December 2, Greene rode into Charlotte and formally relieved Gates. The bedraggled Southern Army, which numbered fewer than 700 Continentals who had escaped from Camden and about 1,000 equally tattered and ill-shod militia, passed in review. The two generals and their aides dined together. The next morning Gates departed, en route to deserved oblivion.

In early November, Major General Marquis François Jean de Chastellux, who had obtained Rochambeau's permission to visit Washington's headquarters and to proceed to Philadelphia to confer with Luzerne and members of Congress, departed from Newport. Chastellux was something more than a major general in the French Army. He was a member of the Academy and a distinguished intellectual. En route, he was entertained at West Point by Major General William Heath, who had taken command there when Greene was ordered to the Southern Department. Here he learned the details of Arnold's treason. He was deeply impressed with West Point and the majestic Hudson, not alone by the imposing and forbidding grandeur of the site, but also because there it was that "the liberty of America had been bartered in the market place and sold."

On November 23 the marquis arrived at La Fayette's headquarters where he inspected the light infantry. The troops were well dressed, perfectly accoutered, and moved with verve and precision. Chastellux drank several glasses of claret with his young friend, complimented him on the spirit of the officers and the excellence of the troops, and with him rode on to Washington's headquarters. He was late for the four o'clock dinner, but found Washington still at table with Generals Wayne, Howe, and Knox and Colonel Hamilton. Washington was drinking madeira and cracking nuts. The commander in chief greeted the visitor hospitably and ordered a dinner prepared.

Chastellux, in the midst of strangers, was made one of the party: "A few glasses of claret and Madeira hastened aquaintance, and I soon found myself quite at ease, near to the greatest and best of all men." He discovered Washington to be neither grave and withdrawn nor familiar; "the sentiments he inspired in everyone had the same origin, a profound esteem for his virtues and a high opinion of his talents." Several days and several pleasant dinners later, he wrote that Washington had appeared to him as a man "Brave but without temerity; generous without prodigality, noble without pride, virtuous without severity. . . . Soldiers, Magistrates, People, all loved and admired him; all spoke of him with affection and veneration."[11]

At the first of these intimate dinners he had conversed with Knox, "a man of spirit, well-educated, sincere and loyal . . . it is impossible to know him without esteeming him." Later, he met Major General William Alexander, Lord Stirling, who, so he wrote, was accused of loving food and drink in a manner suitable in a lord but more than was suitable in a general. He thought Stirling "a courageous man, but without capacity."[12]

Chastellux arrived in Philadelphia on December 1, 1780, and went at once to the residence of the minister, where he was to be entertained during his stay. Luzerne introduced him to the notables, including Joseph Reed; Charles Thomson, secretary of the Congress; Thomas Paine; and Samuel Adams. He found Adams having a dish of tea, served to him by a comely young lady of sixteen. The marquis informed Adams that "No one in Europe was ignorant that he had been a principal author of the present revolution." This compliment was all that was needed to persuade Adams to talk. Chastellux was enchanted as Adams, speaking clearly, precisely, and with warmth, related his part in the events that led to the independence of the former British colonies.[13] The marquis left Philadelphia on December 16 to return by a circuitous route to Newport.

The trip had confirmed his faith in the character of his royal master's American allies.

Admiral Rodney, who had spent two months in New York, was ready to leave. Although he had accomplished nothing during his stay in North American waters, he was fortunate not to have lingered in the islands, for on October 10 and 11 "a most terrible hurricane . . . expended its violence upon the southern islands . . . sweeping all that chain of islands quite to Dominica" and making "horrid devastation among the shipping. . . . It is said there is scarce a building to be seen on any of those islands." Dozens of British ships were driven ashore; others foundered at sea. Many were totally or partially dismasted; others lost their sails, running gear, and boats and were saved only by heaving all their guns and ammunition over the side. "How thankful we should be to providence that our fleet, under Sir George Rodney, were out of these seas. . . . The accounts from Barbados are terrible."††[14]

Rodney and Clinton had established a sympathetic relationship. A common bond was their shared contempt for Admiral Arbuthnot, who remained in the vicinity of Gardiner's Bay watching De Ternay's small fleet. From there, he had dispatched carping letters to Rodney as well as several to Sandwich, in which he was immoderately critical of his senior, who was enjoying the limited amenities offered in the metropolis while he pitched and tossed in the wintry seas off the eastern tip of Long Island. Rodney replied to these letters with studied politeness. Nor did he officially complain of Arbuthnot's insolent and irritating behavior.

Rodney's flag captain was less reserved, and wrote Captain Middleton, comptroller at the Admiralty, that Arbuthnot and his venal secretary, one Mr. Green, had acquired conspicuous notoriety for their corrupt and avaricious behavior. According to Captain Young, Green lost no opportunity "to rob and distress." Young provided Middleton with a catalogue of Green's assorted villanies and observed that "with the rapacity of this man of the navy, and others such as this fellow is, and those in the army of the same kidney, how can it be supposed that a minister and a nation can support a war? Sir, it is not possible."[15] Just how much Clinton and Rodney knew of what was going on to the disgrace of the British Army and Navy is problematical, but there is no record that either the admiral or the King's indolent general in America took any action.

On November 13, 1780, Rodney embarked in *Sandwich*. He wrote Clinton a note which ended: "God bless you and send me from this cold

†† For a brilliant description of this disaster, see *Bermuda Historical Quarterly*, Vol. XXXI, No. 1 (Spring 1974), in which appears a letter from Lieutenant Benjamin Archer, R.N., then first lieutenant in H.M.S. *Phoenix*, a forty-four gun frigate. Two ships of the line, six frigates including *Phoenix*, and three smaller ships were lost. Thanks to the efforts of Archer, most of the crew of *Phoenix* survived.

country and from such men as Arbuthnot." Three days later he sailed for St. Lucia and the sunshine. He had not yet heard of the great hurricane and the appalling damage it had done the navy in the West Indies.

For some time Clinton had been "fully sensible of the great advantages likely to arise from our possessing a naval station in the lower district [of Virginia] and [from] the pursuing my original plan of striking at the enemy's depots at Petersburg and Richmond."[16] For this purpose he had sent Leslie to Virginia. But Cornwallis had called Leslie to Charleston, and Clinton now decided to send Brigadier General in America Benedict Arnold with a force of 1,800 to establish a secure base at Portsmouth and to destroy supplies being collected along the James River for further shipment to the American Army in North Carolina. He had selected Arnold for this task, so he wrote, "by the very high estimation in which he was held among the enemy for active intrepidity . . . and for a persuasion that he would exert himself to the utmost to establish an equal fame with us in this first essay of his capacity."[17] Arnold sailed from Sandy Hook on December 20 and arrived in the Chesapeake ten days later.

As Sir William Wraxall surveyed the scene in Great Britain on New Year's Day, 1781, he saw nothing to persuade him that his country would again attain the wealth, power, and majesty she had enjoyed under William Pitt:

> The empire under Lord North's administration was shaken and convulsed in almost every quarter. Domestic faction pervaded all the departments of Government, infected the navy and manifested itself in every debate of either House of Parliament. The English were discontented, the Scots were sullen, and the Irish had become clamorous for political as well as commercial emancipation. A Ministry, the members of which body did not always act in union, and still prosecuting a hopeless contest with America . . . inspired no public confidence in the success of their future measures. National credit began to droop under the expenses of a war carried on across the Atlantic at an immense distance, while the commerce of the country suffered at least in an equal degree from the depredations of the enemy.[18]

The King had not regained the popularity he had steadily lost since his accession twenty years earlier. His support in Parliament had eroded significantly. Once again there was much talk of a malign "secret influence," now alleged to be exerted by Charles Jenkinson, at one time the Earl of Bute's private secretary. Jenkinson had served in the Treasury under Lord North and had recently taken Barrington's place as Secretary at War. He enjoyed the confidence of the King, often saw him privately, and corresponded with him.

His Majesty's ministers, at variance with one another and distrusted where they were not detested, were under continual attack in the House of Commons. The American war hung like a dark cloud over both Houses of Parliament and obtruded itself directly or indirectly in nearly every debate. Fox lost no opportunity to assail Lord North: "The noble Lord would never have been invited to accept his present office except under the condition of promising to execute the measures *chalked out* to him in respect to America. He would not have been suffered to remain in office if he had declined to carry on the war with the Colonies. His acquiesance in and submission to those weak as well as wicked measures, in madly beginning and more madly persevering in that accursed war *is the price of his place*."[19] Nor did Opposition spare North's colleagues; Germain and Sandwich were always readily available targets.

The steady stream of complaints against Arbuthnot that flowed from General Clinton's quill created further dissension in a Cabinet which Wraxall had observed rarely acted in union, but as pressure for the admiral's removal grew, Sandwich was forced to give in. In mid-October 1780 he wrote Arbuthnot that as it was apparent he and Clinton could not serve together, the Cabinet thought it advisable to employ the admiral elsewhere "in a command at least equally honourable and advantageous."‡‡ The First Lord's idea was to order Arbuthnot to Jamaica to relieve Sir Peter Parker. He wrote Parker that Clinton and Arbuthnot were "under such violent animosities against each other that the very important service entrusted to them, and on which the fate of this kingdom very probably depends, cannot go on under their joint command."[20] Germain had long since lost confidence in Clinton, who, he said, was acting "more from caprice than from common sense." The command situation in America, never satisfactory since the departure of Admiral Viscount Howe two and a half years earlier, was now in a worse muddle than ever.

The European scene was equally depressing. Of the continental powers, only Portugal, bound to Great Britain by treaty, could be considered friendly. The others were avowed or secret enemies. But "in the midst of so universal a dejection the King remained altogether unmoved. Neither defeats, nor difficulties, nor the number of his foreign enemies nor domestic opposition unhinged his mind or shook his resolution. . . . he never vacillated nor showed for a single moment any disposition to dismiss his ministers."[21]

‡‡ "Advantageous" meant "financially advantageous," in terms of prize money. All British admirals were interested in posts where they could be assured of a good return in prize money.

Perhaps a more imaginative and less obstinate ruler than George III might have reconciled himself and his policies to the inevitable loss of the American colonies; might have recognized their independence and sought to balance the ledger by deploying land and naval forces bogged down in an apparently endless and exceedingly expensive continental war, to drive France and Spain from the Caribbean, New Orleans, and the Floridas. This policy would have found support in the nation, in the press, in disparate parliamentary factions, and in the armed forces. British feelings toward the Americans may have been ambivalent, but toward the Roman Catholic Bourbon powers were not. Englishmen in all walks of life hated France and despised Spain, and would have endorsed and supported a policy designed to bring Great Britain's full powers to bear on land and sea against the distant possessions of these hereditary enemies.

Here again the strategic question was posed. Had the moment come to relinquish an objective deemed by almost everyone save the King, Germain, Sandwich, and their sycophantic advisers to be unobtainable, and to concentrate on vulnerable targets in seas the navy could command? Again, there is little evidence that the question was faced, for His Majesty made it emphatically clear that he was determined, at any cost, to suppress the rebellion and to bring the Americans to a proper acknowledgment of dutiful subordination. None of his ministers dared disagree or to suggest that circumstances demanded a more objective appreciation of a war situation now further complicated by the imminent outbreak of hostilities with Holland.

At noon on January 3, 1781, Major Benjamin Fishbourne, ADC to Brigadier General Anthony Wayne, rode into Washington's headquarters at New Windsor, New York (about six miles north of West Point), with a personal and confidential letter addressed to the commander in chief. In this communication, Wayne reported that "a most general and unhappy mutiny in the Pennsya [Pennsylvania] line" had occurred at 9 P.M. on New Year's Day.* ". . . a great proportion of the troops, with some Artillery are marching towards Phila., every exertion has been made by the officers to divide them in their Determination to revolt." He had ordered the New Jersey brigade to move "lest the Enemy should take advantage of this Alarming Crisis." The mutineers had killed one captain and mortally wounded another.[22] Wayne did not report that he had taken position in front of the mutinous regiments to exhort the men, or that when his attempt to recall them to their duty proved of no avail he had faced them with his pistols cocked.† At this, the men "instantly

---

* Major General Arthur St. Clair commanded the Pennsylvania troops. Wayne commanded the brigade that had mutinied.

† No doubt apocryphal. Another story has it that he bared his breast and asked his men either to return to their duty or to shoot him. They did neither.

presented their bayonets to his breast" and one of their leaders said: "We respect and love you, often you have led us into the field of battle . . . if you fire your pistols, or attempt to enforce your commands we shall put you instantly to death."[23] Wayne holstered his pistols but stood his ground. He again addressed the men with no effect.

The leaders stated their grievances. Hundreds of soldiers who had enlisted three years earlier had served their time but had not been discharged as specified in their contracts; none of them had been paid for more than a year; all were shoeless, in rags, and on the verge of starvation. Their purpose, so their spokesman asserted, was simply to get justice. They would not forsake the cause. They proposed to march on Philadelphia, and once there, peacefully to appeal to Congress for a redress of grievances. Wayne decided he and his senior colonels should accompany them, and en route again attempt to persuade them to return to their duty.

In his reply to Wayne's report Washington urged him to attempt to dissuade the defectors from crossing the Delaware, or if they insisted on marching toward Philadelphia, to urge them to stop at Germantown, where negotiations could be undertaken. He cautioned Wayne that "any attempt to reduce them by force will either drive them to the Enemy, or dissipate them in such a manner that they will never be recovered."[24]

Clinton learned of the mutiny on January 3, alerted a picked force to march into New Jersey, and dispatched two emissaries to the mutineers with promises to satisfy all claims for arrears of pay in "hard money" and to assure those who came over that they would not be forced to serve against their fellow countrymen. The mutinous Pennsylvanians listened to these proposals, rejected them, arrested the men who had brought them, and turned them over to General Wayne.‡

Washington had made immediate preparations to move, but before troops from West Point took the road, he learned that Joseph Reed, president of the Executive Council of Pennsylvania, was negotiating with the mutineers and expected to reach a settlement satisfactory to them and to the committee of Congress nervously awaiting results of the protracted conversations being held first at Princeton and later at Trenton. Reed agreed to meet the principal demands: immediate honorable discharge of those who swore they had enlisted for three years and whose time had expired; arrears of pay to be met as soon as possible; and provision made for a clothing allowance. Scores of individual controversies arose over the question of length of enlistment. Officers called to testify usually alleged that men who swore under oath that they had enlisted for three years had enlisted for the duration, and were perjuring themselves. Those una-

‡ Clinton's emissaries were tried by general court-martial as spies, convicted, and hanged.

voidable confrontations increased tensions between the men and their officers. But finally all points were settled, and 1,250 infantrymen with 67 artillerymen went home to their wives and sweethearts. Their departure left the Pennsylvania Line with about 1,150 rank and file.

Washington did not challenge the terms of settlement, but was displeased that the affair had been taken out of the hands of the army. He felt strongly that discipline in the army was exclusively within his jurisdiction and decided that should another mutiny occur (and he was apprehensive one would) he would not give the civil authority opportunity to intervene. Within three weeks his apprehensions were justified. On January 20 two hundred of the New Jersey Line in winter quarters at Pompton refused to obey their officers. Washington, determined that this latest example should be settled immediately, ordered Major General Robert Howe to march "with orders to compel the mutineers to unconditional submission," and requested the civil authority not "to interpose with any terms of conciliation." He wrote Rochambeau: "It appears to me essential that this spirit should be suppressed by force and by an exemplary punishment of the principal instigators of the defection."[25] Howe marched from West Point on January 23, and at dawn four days later deployed his troops within musket shot of the huts occupied by the mutineers. He ordered cannon placed to command their huts and called on the men to come out unarmed. They did so. Snow was falling gently as the sun rose.

Dr. James Thacher witnessed the scene:

> General Howe ordered that three of the ring-leaders should be selected as victims for condign punishment. These unfortunate culprits were tried on the spot, Colonel Sprout being president of the court-martial, standing on the snow, and they were sentenced to be immediately shot. Twelve of the most guilty mutineers were next selected to be their executioners. . . . the first that suffered was a sergeant and an old offender. . . . The second criminal was, by the first fire, sent into eternity in an instant.[26]

The third man was pardoned, as were all others who had taken part.

Washington wrote he had "reason to believe the mutinous disposition of the troops" was "completely subdued" and had been "succeeded by a genuine penitence. But having punished guilt and supported authority it now becomes proper to do justice." For this purpose, he appointed three commissioners to inquire into grievances. The principal one (as with the Pennsylvanians) was that of men who alleged they had enlisted for three years and had been held over their time. To those who could support their claim, justice was done. They were paid off and honorably discharged. Washington was confident there would be no more such "daring and atrocious" departures from the duty soldiers "owed to their Country, to their Officers to their Oaths and to themselves."[27]

A few days in Charlotte sufficed to convince Greene that this was no suitable base for his small army. The area had been picked clean of grain, flour, and beef, and the army, at a paper strength of 2,457 enlisted, was living on a hand-to-mouth basis.** He directed Colonel Thaddeus Kosciusko to survey the west bank of the Pee Dee River for a suitable base site, and in December 20, 1780, he left Charlotte to establish his headquarters at Cheraw, close to the river, 10 miles from the North-South Carolina line and about 120 miles east of Winnsboro. General Greene had already developed his strategy. He realized that the strength, equipment, and physical condition of his soldiers were such that for some time he could not face Cornwallis in the field. The earl's well-appointed army, lying at Winnsboro, was numerically twice as strong as his, was well disciplined and hardened to the rigors of campaigning. But Greene did not propose to allow his army to sit idly at a "camp of repose," and on December 16, while still at Charlotte, issued orders to Brigadier General Daniel Morgan to march with 320 light infantry, 200 Virginia militia, and Colonel William Washington's light horse to an area west of the Catawba River. There Morgan would be joined by militia under command of Major General William Davidson.

Greene directed Morgan to employ his force in the area west of the Catawba either offensively or defensively, as his "prudence and judgement" might direct. Morgan's mission was to "spirit up the people" in that part of the state, "to annoy the enemy in that quarter," and "to collect the provision and forage out of their way." Should Cornwallis move toward the Pee Dee in an attempt to force Greene to give battle, Morgan was to operate on his flanks and rear and join Greene if ordered to do so. Greene had marched out of Charlotte with 1,110 enlisted men, half Continentals. Morgan set out for the Catawba early on December 21.

Greene was aware that in dividing his army he was taking a bold risk, but believed that in so doing he was making the most of his inferior force. "For," he wrote Washington, "it compells my adversary to divide his . . . he cannot leave Morgan behind him to come at me, or his posts of Ninety-six and Augusta would be exposed. And he cannot chase Morgan far, or prosecute his views upon Virginia while I am here."[28] Greene believed his strategy would create doubts and uncertainty in the mind of the enemy commander in chief, who, lacking the information Greene and Morgan enjoyed, would be groping in the dark, inclined to act impul-

** "The first returns were not cheering. His whole army consisted of 2,307 men; 1482 of whom were present and fit for duty; 547 were absent on command; and 128 were detached on extra service. These, with 90 cavalry and 60 artillery, completed the roll of the Southern Army. Of these, 949 only were Continentals."

sively, and would hazard detached elements that might be met under favorable circumstances.

Cornwallis, awaiting the arrival of Major General Leslie at Winnsboro, was faced with a variety of difficulties, and in early January wrote Clinton that "the constant incursion of refugees, North Carolinians, Back Mountain men, and the perpetual risings in different parts of this province, the invariable successes of all those parties against our militia, keep the whole country in continual alarm, and render the assistance of regular troops everywhere necessary."[29] He was, however, determined to strike north with the major part of the army and carry the war into Virginia. As he took this decision he received information that Morgan was moving toward the British position at Ninety Six, and ordered Lieutenant Colonel Banastre Tarleton to deal with this threat and to push Morgan to the limit.

Morgan soon had news that Tarleton was coming after him. He was in a vulnerable position; he had to move and move fast. He did. But so, too, did Tarleton, and by January 16 he was hot on Morgan's heels. The Broad River, which Morgan had hoped to put between himself and the British, was ten long miles to the north, and he decided he had to take a stand. He chose to do so on favorable rising ground at a site known as "Hannah's Cowpens." Broad River lay five miles to his rear. Morgan had never read the ancient Chinese strategist Sun Tzu, who centuries earlier had advised that in a critical situation—and Morgan was in one—a general should deploy his troops in "Death Ground": ground from which there was no possibility of escape and there was no choice but to fight to the death. This was the ground Morgan selected.††

Morgan deployed his troops with great skill. In his forward line, where trees afforded good concealment and cover, he posted militia riflemen chosen for their ability as marksmen. He instructed them to allow the enemy to approach to killing range before firing. Each man was to fire twice. Primary targets were officers and sergeants. They were then to retire up the hill and join a second line manned by three hundred South Carolinians commanded by Colonel Andrew Pickens, esteemed by Morgan as "a valuable, discreet and attentive officer [who has] the confidence of the militia." Here again each man was to fire two well-

---

†† Morgan was later to be severely criticized for his selection of the ground and for the manner of deployment. He replied: "I would not have had a swamp in the view of my militia on any consideration; they would have made for it, and nothing could have detained them from it. And as to covering my wings, I knew my adversary, and was perfectly sure I should have nothing but down-right fighting. As to retreat it was the very thing I wished to cut off all hope of. I would have thanked Tarleton had he surrounded me with his cavalry. It would have been better than placing my own men in the rear to shoot down those who broke from the ranks. When men are forced to fight they will sell their lives dearly; and I knew that the dread of Tarleton's cavalry would give due weight to the protection of my bayonets, and keep my troops from breaking. . . . Had I crossed the river, one half of the militia would immediately have abandoned me."

aimed shots. All were then to retire around the left (east) flank of Major John Eager Howard's Maryland Continentals and the picked Georgia and Virginia militiamen who held the main battle position just below the crest of the hill. He held Colonel Washington's eighty dragoons and fifty mounted Georgians armed with sabers in reserve just behind the hill. When dawn broke on January 17, Morgan's little army of 970 men was in position.‡‡ The men had rested easily and breakfasted well; they were ready to receive the British.

As the sun rose, Tarleton's advance guard pushed forward to make contact, and without pausing for a thorough reconnaissance or to refresh men and horses after a four-hour march in darkness, he directed his infantry "to disencumber themselves of everything except their arms and ammunition" and issued orders for deployment. "The animation of the officers and the alacrity of the soldiers afforded the most promising assurances of success." As the British advanced, Morgan's militia marksmen delivered two well-directed "fires," as they had been ordered, before they retired. The Redcoats, although falling into some disorder, managed to advance. "The fire on both sides was well supported and produced much slaughter." The Continentals held steady, and for several minutes the battle hung in the balance. The Redcoats rushed forward, but unexpected fire from the Americans who suddenly came about as they were falling back stopped the British. Another volley threw them into confusion.

Washington's cavalry now swept around the east side of the hill, unsheathed sabers flashing, and bore down on the British right as Howard's Continentals advanced with fixed bayonets glistening in the morning sun. Burgoyne had written four years earlier that the bayonet in the hands of the valiant would prove irresistible. So it proved at Cowpens, and at Cowpens the Americans had the bayonets. The British broke; "a general flight ensued." Tarleton and his officers attempted to rally the men, but "neither promises nor threats could gain their attention; they surrendered or dispersed . . . all attempts to restore order . . . proved fruitless."[30] Each side suffered about two hundred battle casualties. The Americans took six hundred prisoners, two brass cannon, one hundred cavalry mounts, and the colors of the 7th Regiment.

Tarleton had been soundly whipped, and as defeated commanders are wont to do in such humiliating circumstances, looked for someone on whom to place the blame. His troops had failed him as had Cornwallis, who, so Tarleton charged, had not moved forward with his accustomed celerity: "It would be mortifying to describe the advantages that might have resulted from his lordship's arrival at the concerted point, or to expatiate upon the calamities which were produced by this event."[31]

‡‡ 290 Continentals, 80 cavalry, and 600 militia.

With Zeal and Bayonets Only

Morgan, certain that reports of Tarleton's defeat would reach Cornwallis at Turkey Creek before sunset, wasted no time contemplating the scene of his triumph and passed the army with his prisoners across the Broad River. Before dawn on the following morning he was leading his weary troops toward the forks of the Catawba.

As Morgan marched, Tarleton rode into Turkey Creek with fourteen officers and fifty troopers and Cornwallis learned the worst.* At Cowpens, Tarleton had lost something more than the prestige and reputation he so valued; his legion had been put to flight and he had lost all the light troops, who lay dead or mortally wounded on the field of battle, or would shortly be hustled north by Colonel William Washington's cavalry to prisoner-of-war camps in Virginia.

Cornwallis was not one to meditate on ill fortune. He composed a factual report to Sir Henry Clinton and issued orders to the army, joined on that day by Major General Leslie with about 1,500 regulars, to be prepared to march the next morning in pursuit of Morgan, catch him, bring him to battle, defeat and scatter his forces, and release the British

---

* About two hundred mounted members of the legion, who had fled from Cowpens, straggled into Turkey Creek during the night.

prisoners. The earl had no reliable information on which to base his plans; he had to guess where Morgan was and in which direction he might be heading. He guessed Morgan would seek refuge to the west in the Blue Ridge Mountains, and on January 19 marched from Turkey Creek toward Cowpens. He guessed wrong, and not until January 21, when he reached Buffalo Creek, northeast of Cowpens, did he receive certain information that Morgan was marching not west toward the mountains but north and east toward the Catawba River.

Six days later the earl was at Ramsour's Mills on the west branch (south fork) of the Catawba. Here, "as the loss of [the] light troops could only be remedied by the activity of the whole corps," he decided to burn all superfluous baggage, including tents, and all his wagons except those loaded with medical supplies, salt, and ammunition, and four reserved for transportation of sick and wounded. Officers retained a bare minimum of personal baggage. On the afternoon of January 27, troops received a double ration of rum. There would be no more. Cornwallis ordered casks of rum stoved and all spirits and wine, including his personal stock, destroyed. Men were issued an extra pair of soles for their shoes and a two-day supply of corn meal. And thus, as General Charles O'Hara wrote, "without baggage, necessaries or provisions of any sort for officer or soldier, in the most barren, inhospitable, unhealthy part of North America, opposed to the most savage, inveterate, perfidious, cruel enemy, with zeal and bayonets only, it was resolved to follow Greene's army to the end of the world."[1]

On the following morning the army marched toward the Catawba, and on January 29 reached the west bank of the river. Morgan was on the east side. Rain was falling; the river in spate; the British could find no boats, and all fords above the forks were guarded by either Davidson's militia "or the gang of plunderers usually under the command of General Sumpter."† In the eleven days since leaving Turkey Creek, Cornwallis had covered only fifty miles. He had spent one day waiting for Leslie and two more in destroying impedimenta. The army, on the road for eight days, had averaged little better than six miles a day. Had the earl acted with his usual celerity, he could have been over the river before it rose. Now he could do nothing but wait for the rain to stop and the water to subside. By January 31 the river was falling rapidly and he decided to attempt a crossing on the following day.

Greene made good use of the time Cornwallis wasted. After directing Huger to break camp, march to Salisbury, and await him there, he left Cheraw with an aide, a sergeant, and three dragoons, and rode 130 miles in three days to join Morgan on the Catawba. Greene had no illusions. He knew Cornwallis would cross when the river fell and that his force was superior to the Americans, both in numbers and in quality. He directed

† Sumter had not yet recovered from the serious wound suffered at Blackstocks.

Morgan to march at once to Salisbury, meet Huger, and go north toward Hillsboro. Morgan, in constant pain from a rheumatic fever, left the Catawba on January 30. Two days later Cornwallis forded the river and took up the pursuit.‡

The earl arrived at the south bank of the Yadkin River, north of Salisbury, on the evening of February 3 to learn that Morgan had crossed the night before. Rain was falling; the Yadkin in flood; no boats or "flats" were to be found. Cornwallis had shaken off the mood of indecision so uncharacteristic of him, and moved rapidly to the forks, about twenty miles north of Salisbury. This detour cost him two precious days. He correctly concluded the Americans were making for the Dan River on the border of North Carolina and Virginia, and was "in great hope" that Greene would not escape. He arrived on the south bank of the Dan to find Greene safe on the north side, the river in full flood, and no boats.

"Nothing," Cornwallis wrote Germain, "could exceed the patience and alacrity of the officers and soldiers under every species of hardship and fatigue in endeavouring to overtake him. But our intelligence on this occasion was exceedingly defective, which, with heavy rains, bad roads, and the passage of many deep creeks and bridges destroyed by the enemy's light troops, rendered all our exertions vain."[2] He fell back on Hillsboro by easy marches, erected the King's standard and by proclamation invited "all faithful and loyal subjects" to repair to it and to stand forth and take an active part in restoring royal government. Very few answered the call. Cornwallis described Loyalist behavior as "dastardly and pusillanimous."

During the last three days of the 230-mile retreat from the Catawba to the Dan, Greene's soldiers, many shoeless and with feet bloodied, marched at a rate of about 27 miles per day, no mean achievement for troops well shod, well clothed, and decently fed. Under the circumstances the march was a memorable one. "Light-Horse Harry" Lee wrote: "Happily for these States, a soldier of consummate talents guided the destinies of the South." And Tarleton testified that Greene's "every measure . . . was judiciously designed and vigorously executed."**

On New Year's Eve, 1780, Governor Jefferson received information that a fleet of twenty-seven sail had passed Old Point Comfort and entered the James River estuary. He notified Baron von Steuben, but took no action to verify the report. In fact, he did not believe it. Steuben did, and ordered stores at depots he had organized at Chesterfield Court House and Petersburg, south of Richmond, to be moved. Not until forty-eight hours had passed could Von Steuben prevail on Jefferson to ask the

‡ Morgan soon thereafter retired from the army for reasons of health.
** At the time, this retreat was properly recognized as a masterpiece by Washington, Jefferson, and the Congress.

Council to call out the militia. By this time the fleet carrying Brigadier General Benedict Arnold and his troops was beyond Jamestown; on Thursday, January 4, he landed at Westover, and at noon the following day was in Richmond. He had met no opposition. He sent Lieutenant Colonel John Simcoe with his Queen's Rangers to Westham (or West Haven), a few miles above the falls of the James, to destroy the small arsenal there. Simcoe was not opposed. The British spent Friday morning looting Richmond, putting the torch to public buildings and warehouses, and retired to Westover unmolested.

Militia, too late to be of any conceivable use, now began straggling into Richmond. Most arrived without arms, powder, shoes, or blankets, and many were nearly naked. Baron von Steuben, in command of the state's so-called "troops," looked them over, and as he had but few muskets and no clothes to issue, sent many of them home. He wrote Washington: "It is impossible to describe the situation I am in; nothing can be got from the state." Had Jefferson heeded the baron's earlier advice, Arnold's progress might have been impeded and his devastations limited. Arnold embarked at Westover on January 10 and was at Portsmouth on the nineteenth. Here he took up the position General Leslie had occupied before sailing to join Cornwallis.

From the British point of view Arnold's foray into Tidewater was a huge success; from the American, a disaster. Arnold and Simcoe had not only terrified the inhabitants but destroyed twenty-six cannon, three hundred barrels of powder, and a great quantity of grain. Warehouses with several thousand hogsheads of tobacco destined for shipment to France and valued at above £1 million went up in dense clouds of smoke.

Washington was distressed to learn of Arnold's depredations in his native state, but his concern was primarily with British ability to penetrate the Chesapeake Bay area at will, destroy supplies laboriously collected for the Southern Army, and so alarm the citizens that the government would be unable to enlist Continentals or draft militia to send to the southward. He wrote Rochambeau that Virginia was extremely vulnerable to such predatory expeditions, "nor is there any remedy against them but a naval superiority."

Shortly before Arnold descended on Virginia, Congress learned that Henry Laurens, minister-designate to Holland, had been captured on the high seas en route to Amsterdam and was being held in the Tower of London on the charge of high treason. Laurens had disposed of his papers by throwing them overboard, but an agile British sailor equipped with a boat hook had retrieved a bag containing Laurens's instructions and the draft of a proposed treaty between the United States and Holland. Relations between Great Britain and the United Provinces had been steadily deteriorating; this affair brought them to breaking point,

and in late December the Court of St. James's issued Letters of Marque
and Reprisal against the States-General of the United Provinces of
Holland and seized scores of Dutch ships then in British ports. The
Dutch replied with similar measures. Although neither side declared
war, a state of war existed.

As both Sweden and Denmark had with Holland adhered to the Declaration of Armed Neutrality earlier promulgated by Empress Catherine,
the break with the Dutch could conceivably lead to a hostile coalition of
North Atlantic maritime powers. In a memorandum he prepared for the
King's "Confidential Servants," Sandwich wrote that England was "on the
point of being at war with the whole world," and that her finances were
so exhausted "that every new campaign plunges a dagger deep into her
vitals." Something had to be done, and done quickly, to avert a danger
that might prove mortal.

On January 19, 1781, His Majesty summoned his ministers to an
emergency Cabinet Council at Queen's House. Recent alarming news
from St. Petersburg indicated that the Empress was seriously considering
entering the war on the side of the Bourbon powers but had hinted to
the British ambassador that she could change her mind if Great Britain
would cede Minorca to Russia.†† Members of the Cabinet were "clearly
of opinion that the Empress's friendship [would] be very cheaply
purchased" with the cession of the island.[3] In return for Minorca, which
would provide the Russians a fleet base in the Mediterranean, the
ministers expected Catherine to "secretly engage to take part in the war
unless the Belligerent Powers agreed to make Peace upon the footing of
the Treaty of Paris." If she would perform such a service and join England in a "perpetual Defensive Alliance," her reward would be the island.

Sandwich, who spoke for his colleagues, stated bluntly that should
Russia declare against Great Britain "we shall then, literally speaking be
in actual war with the whole world: Russia, Denmark, Sweden, Holland,
France, Spain and the rebellious colonies of America will be in open
hostilities with us." Among nations on the Continent no friend was "able
or willing to step forth" in support of the British cause. Most, indeed,
were "very powerful and eager enemies." Should Catherine enter the war
on the side of France and Spain, England would lose everything: ". . .
the Powers united against us will dismember our State and make such
partition among them as they shall think fit." An alliance with Russia,
bought at bargain price, would save the empire and secure for England
"such a peace as we can with honour and safety accept. Our colonies,"
the earl continued, "will return to their obedience, and this country as
before, enjoy an exclusive trade with them."[4] The King, who had earlier
announced his opposition to any such scheme, was persuaded to recon-

†† Minorca was then besieged by a large army commanded by the Duc de
Crillon.

sider, and directed the Secretary of State for the Northern Department to proceed with negotiations.‡‡

At the same time, measures were taken to chastise the Dutch for their repeated attempts to aid France and their insolent support of the American rebels, and Sandwich dispatched urgent orders to Rodney, who had resumed his command in the Leeward Islands, to seize the island of St. Eustatius and all Dutch shipping he could find in Caribbean waters. For years, St. Eustatius had been much more than an irritant to Great Britain. The flourishing little island was the entrepôt of the Caribbean. Warehouses belonging to English, Dutch, and French firms lined her waterfront. At any time dozens of ships were discharging and loading at her quays. All the tobacco, rice, salt fish, and lumber in her bulging stores was of American origin. Many articles from Europe and West Indian islands awaiting shipment were destined for merchants in Baltimore, Boston, Providence, Philadelphia, Havana, Guadeloupe, and Martinique. There was now an opportunity to excise this commercial cancer, and with considerable profit. Rodney immediately proceeded to do so.

From day to day Congress and the country sank deeper into the financial swamp. Continental paper had dropped to 100 for 1. James Varnum, recently elected a delegate from Rhode Island, had little hope that anything decisive would be accomplished. "The want of a fixed Consideration," he wrote, "frustrates almost every Measure, and the dull inergetic Mode of Prodecure, resulting from the long habit of insipid Formality render our Effort too feeble and dilatory to effect the greatest Objects."[5] Certainly the "greatest" object was money, and in hope that more could be wrung from France, Congress named Colonel John Laurens special envoy to Versailles, charged with negotiating another loan, and directed him to confer with Washington before he sailed.

The commander in chief welcomed his former aide to his headquarters at Windsor, entertained him with customary hospitality, and presented a grim assessment of the current situation and the country's future prospects. He thought a point of crisis had been reached. "Immediate and efficacious succours from abroad" were indispensably necessary to support the struggle. The people in general had lost confidence, and regarded the impressment of supplies for the army as "burthensome and oppressive." The system had "excited serious discontents, and, in some places, alarming symptoms of opposition." The army had suffered from a series of "calamitous distresses"; the patience of the troops was "nearly exhausted; their discontents matured to an extremity which has recently had very disagreeable consequences."

With an "immediate [and] ample" supply of money, the allies could

‡‡ Happily for the cause of American liberty and independence, Catherine decided Minorca was not worth a war.

make "a decided effort" in 1781 to secure America's liberty and independence; without such aid "we may make a feeble and expiring effort
the next campaign; in all probability the period to our opposition." But
money was not the only requisite to success in 1781. Of equal importance
was "a constant naval superiority on these coasts." Command of North
Atlantic waters would reduce the British to a static defense and confer
upon the allies the initiative the enemy had for so long enjoyed. The es-
sentials, then, were money and maritime supremacy.

Washington assured Laurens that although many people were
displeased with "the feeble and oppressive mode of conducting the war,"
a large majority detested the British and were "firmly attached" to the
object of independence. The country had the moral and material resources for "great and continued exertions," but with a system that
promoted "the progress of disgust," these could not be called forth.[6]

Lack of money was not the only impediment to mobilization of latent
resources. An equally important one was the lack of a supreme executive
authority. Congress could debate, resolve, recommend, urge, and exhort
from dawn to dusk, but had no power to enforce its calls to the states for
men, money, or supplies. Some state executives, notably Livingston of
New Jersey, Clinton of New York, Trumbull of Connecticut, and Reed of
Pennsylvania, were vigorous war governors and were usually willing to
subordinate parochial interests to the greater good. Others set rights of
states ahead of the national interest. Many men in public life, including
Washington, felt strongly that confederation, so ably but ineffectually
urged by John Adams six years earlier, would be but a first step in solution of the problem. Washington wrote Livingston that there could be no
radical cure for the evils that beset the nation "till Congress is vested by
the several States with full and ample powers to enact Laws for general
purposes and till the Executive business is placed in the hands of able
Men and responsible characters."[7]

Confederation was nearing reality as Jefferson persuaded the Virginia
Legislature to cede 60 million acres she claimed beyond the Ohio River
to a federal government. With this cession made, Maryland agreed to
confederate. James Duane wrote Washington: "The day is at length arrived when dangers and distresses have opened the Eyes of the People
and they perceive the Want of a common head to draw forth in some
Just proportion the Resources of the several Branches of the federal
Union. They perceive that the deliberate power exercised by States indi-
vidually over the Acts of Congress must terminate in the common Ruin;
and the Legislatures, however reluctantly, must resign a portion of their
Authority to the national Representative. . . ."[8]

Washington was pleased that confederation had been achieved and
that the generosity of his own beloved state had made union possible. He
did not anticipate any substantial results. And he had a more immediate

problem than speculation as to the future. He did not propose to allow Arnold to roam around Virginia burning and plundering and ordered that a detachment of 1,200 light troops be organized.* He exhorted regimental commanders to select their best officers and men for assignment, and asked for "well made men from five feet six to five feet ten inches stature." But these companies had to be formed, clothed, equipped, and drilled and it was a long way from New Windsor and army camps in New Jersey to the scene of action in Virginia. In the meantime, something must be done to stop Arnold's depredations, and Rochambeau appealed to Chevalier Des Touches to send a small force to the Chesapeake to attack and destroy British ships there and so immobilize him.

This project was favored in early February by a violent storm which lashed the coast from New York eastward and dispersed Arbuthnot's fleet blockading Newport. One ship of the line was lost and two others badly damaged. Des Touches took advantage of the opportunity to send Captain le Gardeur de Tilly with one of the line and two frigates to the Chesapeake. This flotilla arrived without mishap, entered the bay, surveyed the scene, accomplished little, and returned safely to Newport, picking up a British frigate (forty-four-gun *Romulus*) and several sloops en route. Washington had reposed no hope in such faint measures. His idea had been for Des Touches to sail with his entire fleet and a landing force including artillery, and attack Arnold. A visit to Rochambeau seemed imperative.

Washington wanted action, not gestures, in Virginia. He started 1,200 light infantry moving toward Head of Elk, and issued instructions to La Fayette, chosen to command these elite troops. He was thus in effect forcing Des Touches and Rochambeau to co-operate more effectively with each other and with him in joint operations in the Chesapeake area. He wrote Rochambeau: "The capture of Arnold and his detachment will be an event particularly agreeable to this Country; a great relief to the Southern States and of important utility in our future operations."⁹ He instructed La Fayette to co-operate with the French amphibious force and with Baron von Steuben, and directed him "to do no act whatever with Arnold that directly or by implication may screen him from the punishment due to his treason and desertion, which if he should fall into your hands, you will execute in the most summary way."¹⁰

He was still not sure the French would co-operate and wrote La Fayette, who had followed the light troops to Philadelphia, not to embark at Head of Elk until he had received "certain advices that our friends are below." Several days after dispatching this letter, he received positive assurances from Rochambeau that he and Des Touches had discussed his proposals, agreed with them, and were preparing an expe-

* Each company to consist of one captain, two subalterns, four sergeants, one fifer, one drummer, and twenty-five rank and file.

dition to sail to Chesapeake Bay at the earliest possible moment. At last, after a dozen letters, several misunderstandings, and considerable delay, his plans to trap and destroy Arnold's force, capture the traitor, and string him up were in motion. On March 2, 1781, he set out for Newport.

He arrived there on March 6 and was welcomed with formal honors by Des Touches. Rochambeau and all his senior officers met him at Long Wharf when he landed after his visit to the flagship. Ships of Des Touches's squadron, which Washington had hoped were on their way to Virginia, again fired salutes. As the procession moved slowly toward the State House between ranks of French soldiers, the ships' guns continued to thunder. A spectator wrote: "The firing from the French ships that lined the harbor was tremendous; it was one continued roar." That night the fleet illuminated with hundreds of lanterns suspended from the yards, and every window in Newport showed candles. Dinners, tea parties, suppers, and balls enlivened the social scene. At a ball given on the night of his arrival, Washington chose Miss Margaret Champlin, "radiant with the charms of beauty and of culture," to be his partner in the "stately minuet" that was first on the program.

Chevalier Des Touches and his officers missed most of the festivities. His fleet, consisting of seven of the line and three frigates with 1,200 grenadiers and light infantry embarked, sailed for the Chesapeake on March 8. Two days later Arbuthnot, cruising east of Long Island, had news of the French and set course for Cape Henry. Washington wrote La Fayette cautioning him to be circumspect and to remain at Head of Elk until he had confirmed that ships of war entering the great bay were indeed French. He reported developments to the president of Congress, and added: "A meeting of the two fleets seems unavoidable, and perhaps the issue of a contest between them was never more interesting."

The British in New York entertained great hopes that Arbuthnot would catch and defeat Des Touches before the French entered the Chesapeake. Frederick Mackenzie thought the engagement might well prove decisive; if Arbuthnot could best them, "it will in a great measure determine the fate of America, and end the Rebellion, or at least prevent any further exertions of consequence on the part of the Rebels." Most officers in New York had very little faith in Arbuthnot, and if he was beaten, the situation for both Arnold and Cornwallis would be critical. "But," Mackenzie wrote, "we must beat them—our all in a manner is left at stake at present." He was not optimistic: "Our fleet has done nothing brilliant yet during the war."

At daybreak on March 16 a British frigate sighted the French about forty miles northeast of Cape Henry. Arbuthnot, whose ships were coppered, had passed the French during the preceding night. The British admiral immediately made the signal for line of battle and ordered his eight ships, then in extended line, to close. He had an advantage of eighty guns in broadside batteries and his ships were faster sailers than were the French.

At two o'clock in the afternoon, after much maneuvering in high winds and increasingly rough seas, the vans of both fleets opened fire. Arbuthnot did not push the center to support of his van, nor did he make the signal for close action. Des Touches, taking advantage of this indecision, attacked the British van with his entire fleet and crippled all three British ships. Now the way into the Chesapeake was open. Arbuthnot could not pursue. But Des Touches did not enter the bay. He abandoned his mission and returned to Newport, claiming a victory. A hollow victory it was.

Washington arrived at his New Windsor headquarters on March 20. He was sanguine that all had gone well in the Chesapeake. His spirits were not dampened by news that Clinton had sent reinforcements under Major General William Phillips to Virginia. And he learned, too, that contrary to his orders, La Fayette had embarked at Head of Elk, dropped down the bay, and was in Annapolis.

Major General Nathanel Greene had no idea of lingering on the north side of the Dan. His intention was to re-enter North Carolina as soon as recruits sent him by Baron von Steuben could be assimilated and the militia be brought to a minimum standard of order and discipline, a task that anyone save Greene would have regarded as insuperable. Even before Cornwallis arrived at Hillsboro, Greene ordered Colonel Pickens and Light-Horse Harry Lee to cross the river, get to the south of Hillsboro, interrupt the earl's communications, encourage the militia, and suppress the Tories. He directed them to be active, to forward information, and, as Lee testified, impressed upon them "in fervid terms . . . the necessity of unceasing vigilance and the most cautious circumspection."

A few days later, Pickens and Lee stumbled on opportunity. A Loyalist colonel, one Pyles, had collected three hundred Tories, all armed and well mounted, and was leading them to Hillsboro to join Cornwallis. Pyles mistook Lee's cavalrymen for Tarleton's, and just as Lee called on him to surrender, a Tory noticed that several of Lee's horsemen were wearing green twigs—a Whig emblem—in their caps. He fired. Lee's troopers drew their sabers: "In a few moments ninety of the three hundred [Tories] lay dead, and the survivors with their leader were nearly all wounded. Scattering through the country in wild affright, and bearing with them the proofs of their disaster, they carried terror into every Tory dwelling, and warmed with a sudden glow the waning hopes of the Whigs." For Cornwallis, this disastrous slaughter ended all hopes of Loyalist aid in North Carolina.

On February 23 Greene crossed the Dan and re-entered North Carolina. Although he had not yet received all the reinforcements promised by

634   THE COMMON CAUSE

Virginia, he was determined to press Cornwallis. This bold decision was
characteristic. His intent was to hold the initiative in his hands and to
give battle when and where he chose. Intelligence was the key, and he
spared no effort to obtain information as he maneuvered his small army
from day to day. Detachments commanded by Pickens, Lee, and Otho
Williams, the able and daring young colonel who had been adjutant general to the disgraced Gates, hovered threateningly around Cornwallis,
fell upon his foragers and patrols, captured his scouts, strung up his
Tory informants, and denied him information of Greene's movements.
Greene's design was to keep the earl in a state of anxious perplexity until
he could create a favorable situation for battle. He succeeded. Cornwallis was totally bewildered. Here, as in the harrowing retreat from the
Catawba to the Dan, Greene exhibited qualities that mark him as a
master strategist.

On March 10 he wrote Jefferson that he had been practicing by
finesse what he dared not attempt by force. He knew the people were
awaiting a general action, "but be the consequences of censure what it
may, nothing shall hurry me into a measure that is not suggested by prudence or connects not with the interest of the southern department."[11]
On the day he wrote this letter, 400 Continentals arrived, as did more
militia from North Carolina and Virginia. His army stood at a strength of
4,234 infantry and 161 cavalry; of these, 1,490 were experienced Continentals.

Each passing day aggravated Cornwallis' supply difficulties and made
it increasingly necessary for him to bring Greene as soon as possible to a
decisive action. But for days on end the American had deceived and out-
maneuvered him. When the battle both anticipated was fought, it would
be on Greene's terms, not his. And Greene held a decided psychological
advantage, for the earl needed a victory. A drawn battle would be no
help to the British cause in North Carolina. Destruction of Greene's army
had to be his aim. Greene's was more limited: to inflict as many casualties as possible on the earl's small army. But he did not intend to put his
own to the hazard of a destructive defeat; that would in all probability
put an end to his hopes of recovering the Carolinas. Greene had studied
the terrain at Guilford Court House when the army stopped there during
the retreat to the Dan, and Daniel Morgan had no doubt pointed out the
similarity of the ground to that at Cowpens. On the afternoon of March
14, 1781, Greene marched from High Rock Ford to Guilford, surveyed
the scene as Cornwallis would see it, and decided to stand.

Greene followed Morgan's battle plan and arrayed his troops on
gently rising ground in three lines. In the first he placed selected North
Carolina militia marksmen, many armed with rifles; in the second, three
hundred yards to the rear, and in the midst of a wood, the Virginians. Finally, in a third line, he posted Virginia and Maryland Continentals, with

Washington's cavalry on the right and Lee's "legion" on the left. As Morgan had done at Cowpens, he asked no more of the militia in the first two lines than that they concentrate their fire on officers and sergeants and deliver two or three well-aimed shots before they retired. He was well aware the militia would not stay around when the steel approached. British musketry, often high and usually ineffective, did not unduly perturb marksmen hidden by trees and behind rail fences. What did was the sight of ordered Redcoats closing upon them with bayonets fixed.

Troops deployed to positions he had selected, cooked a meager supper, and slept. Greene supped, but did not sleep. He personally inspected each position, and at each he talked to the officers and men posted to defend it. No member of the Southern Army would be able to claim that he had not understood the general's battle plans. Greene's confidence was infectious. The morning of March 15 dawned cold and clear. The men broke their fast, checked their ammunition, and waited for Cornwallis.

During early evening of March 14, scouts brought information to Cornwallis, encamped between the forks of Deep River twelve miles from Guilford Court House, that Greene had been reinforced by drafts from Virginia and was taking up a defensive position on rising ground in the vicinity of the Court House.† This was the sort of information Cornwallis accepted with anticipation; at daybreak on the fifteenth he broke camp and started north with 1,900 regulars and three guns. Tarleton's cavalry in the advance guard made contact before noon. Cornwallis deployed in woods, in a line, with Leslie commanding his right, Webster his left, and guards, grenadiers, guards' light infantry, and Jägers in support. He surveyed the ground carefully and decided to attack the American left where the fields were relatively clear of trees.

The action began at 1:30 P.M. when three British cannon opened on the American center and the infantry advanced, covered by smoke which blew from the south toward the American position. The North Carolina militia in the first line waited long enough to see the Redcoats approaching "with firm countenance and regular tread, and arms that flashed and gleamed in the slanting sun" and immediately fled in terror. "In the madness of fear" they threw down their loaded muskets, cartridge boxes, canteens, and anything else that would impede their escape. Officers and sergeants attempted vainly to stop the torrent, but "all was useless; terror had overmastered them; and dashing madly [to the rear] they were quickly beyond the sound of remonstrance and threat."[12]

The flight of the North Carolinians did not dismay the Virginians in the second line three hundred yards to the rear, who held their fire until the British came within killing range. As their aimed shots tore the Red-

† The scouts reported Greene's strength to be between 9,000 and 10,000.

coat ranks, the gaps were filled from the supports and the British pressed on. The American right crumbled, but not in chaotic flight. The Virginians on the left stood firm.

Lieutenant Colonel Webster's wing now appeared in the cleared ground around the Court House and engaged the 1st Regiment of Maryland Continentals manning the final position. The Marylanders poured a deadly fire on the Redcoats, then charged with the bayonet. The British broke, but the Virginians on the left, assailed by O'Hara's fresh support troops, could not hold; the British advanced on the 2nd Maryland. They did not stand their ground, but the situation was retrieved by the 1st Maryland. All was now in confusion; a fresh brigade thrown in by either general would have secured a decisive victory, but both Greene and Cornwallis had committed everything. Neither had that fresh brigade.

The British, pressed hard, were giving ground slowly when Cornwallis arrived on the scene and ordered his guns to open fire. General O'Hara, who was nearby and seriously wounded, objected. The story is that he exclaimed, "It is destroying our own men," and that Cornwallis replied, "I see it, but it is a necessary evil we must endure to avert impending destruction."[13] The fierce cannonade served its purpose. Both commanders ordered action to be broken off and retirement to begin. The battle of Guilford Court House was over.

In his report to Germain, Cornwallis claimed "a signal victory." He had forced Greene to withdraw from the field and had taken four guns. But he had suffered heavy casualties, and his army was in no condition to pursue the Americans.‡ Two days after the battle he wrote: "Our troops were excessively fatigued by an action which lasted an hour and a half, and our wounded, dispersed over an extensive space of country, required immediate attention. The care of our wounded and the total want of provisions in an exhausted country, made it equally impossible for me to follow the blow the next day."[14] Stedman, who was present, assessed the situation correctly when he wrote: "In this battle the British troops obtained a victory most honourable and glorious to themselves, but in its consequences of no real advantage to the cause in which they were engaged. . . . A victory achieved under such disadvantages of numbers and ground . . . placed the bravery and the discipline of the troops beyond all praise, but the expence at which it was obtained rendered it of no utility."[15]

During the forty-eight hours after the battle, Cornwallis studied reports of casualties. Some of his best officers had been killed; others, including Brigadier General O'Hara, severely wounded.** His regiments

‡ His "Morning State" on March 15 showed 286 officers and noncommissioned officers and 1,638 rank and file, for a total of 1,924. The battle cost him 532 casualties: 93 killed, 413 wounded, and 26 missing.
** O'Hara's younger brother was killed.

had been shot to pieces by Greene's riflemen. He decided to leave the seriously wounded men under a flag with medical attendants at a Quaker meeting house in the vicinity and gain Cross Keys on the Cape Fear River where he hoped to be supplied by boat from Wilmington, North Carolina. For two days neither officers nor men had eaten bread, and prospects that they would soon enjoy an ample ration were slim indeed, for no supplies of grain or flour could be had. He had burned all his tents; the officers had no wine; the troops no rum, an article conceived by British and American soldiers to be as indispensable as bread. Cavalry horses were starving; Tarleton's legion could not contend with the well-mounted troopers commanded by William Washington and Light-Horse Harry Lee.

A few days after Cornwallis started his retreat to the coast, Greene was on his trail. The earl, intent on saving what was left of his army, set such a fast pace that (in Clinton's words) Greene "wisely determined to give over the pursuit." Partisans hung on Cornwallis' flanks, harried his foragers and prevented them from drawing on the countryside, "and, by keeping possession of the steep banks on each side Cape Fear River, made it impossible to navigate boats from Wilmington."[16] Cornwallis had no alternative but to move to Wilmington. The army arrived there on April 7.

Three days later, he wrote Clinton: "I am as yet totally in the dark as to the intended operations of the summer," and expressed his wish to see "the seat of war" transferred to the Chesapeake Bay area, "even (if necessary) at the expense of abandoning New York. Until Virginia is in a manner subdued our hold on the Carolinas must be difficult, if not precarious."††[17]

†† In an "impartial review" of Cornwallis' operations in the Carolinas, Clinton later wrote: "His Lordship withdrew from South Carolina the chief means of its security and defense, in direct disobedience of the orders left him by his Commander in Chief; and . . . after forcing the passage of several great rivers, fighting a bloody battle, and running eight hundred and twenty miles over almost every part of the invaded province at the expense of above three thousand men he accomplished no other purpose but the having exposed, by an unnecessary retreat to Wilmington, the two valuable colonies behind him to be overrun and conquered by that very army which he boasts to have completely routed but a week or two before."

✠ 7

A Perilous Adventure

During the winter and early spring of 1781 serious cracks made their appearance in the presumably solid alliance of France and Spain. Great Britain had earlier sent Richard Cumberland, one of Lord George Germain's secretaries, to Madrid to conduct secret negotiations for a separate peace. Cumberland was accompanied by an Irish Roman Catholic priest, Thomas Hussey, who had been chaplain to the Spanish embassy in London and who had persuaded the British Cabinet he could secure Floridablanca's agreement to accede to terms that did not involve cession of Gibraltar. As regaining the Rock had been Spain's principal reason for entering the war, it is difficult to comprehend why George III and his ministers conceived that these unaccredited emissaries could entice Spain to withdraw from it without recovering the "pile of stones" that towered over Algeciras and guarded the entrance to the Mediterranean.

One of Cumberland's unofficial proposals was that Spain divorce herself from any general settlement of the war and encourage Great Britain to enter into a period of truce with her former colonies on the foundation of *uti possidetis*. This would allow each participant, at suspension of hostilities, to hold what he had until negotiations had been concluded, an arrangement blatantly favorable to Great Britain, whose army at the time held New York, Niagara, Penobscot (in present Maine), Detroit, Wilmington, N.C., Charleston, S.C., and Georgia. These secret conversations dragged on with no result other than to alarm Vergennes, who directed his ambassador in Madrid to make strenuous verbal objections to a mediation on this basis, which would put the Americans, to whom France was bound by solemn engagement, at the mercy of Great Britain.

In March the Foreign Minister had summoned Franklin to Versailles to inform him that Empress Catherine of Russia and Emperor Joseph II of Austria had offered to mediate, but that Louis XVI had refused to accept their good offices without concurrence of his transatlantic ally. Franklin replied that he would inform Congress of this development. Vergennes was not averse to mediation. He had little faith in the ability of Washington's army, reliably reported to be at the point of disintegrating, to conduct anything more than desultory and insignificant operations. America, sustained only by French loans and gifts, was dragging France toward inexorable bankruptcy. The country could afford to make just one more effort. Should that fail to bring a decision, the only course for France was mediation.

At that time, French ministers seemed no more able than were their contemporaries in Whitehall to decide on a strategic focus. The mercantile community, with financial interest in the cane fields and sugar mills of Martinique and Guadeloupe, demanded that the major effort be made in the Caribbean to protect investments and to acquire Great Britain's rich Sugar Islands. Merchants and traders had derived no advantage whatever from the court's entanglement with the United States and thought further aid to America equivalent to throwing money into the Seine. The Dutch had entered the war and were crying for a fleet to be sent to the East Indies. The Cabinet had committed a large fleet to support a Spanish army commanded by the Duc de Crillon for the reduction of Minorca. From the other side of the Atlantic, Luzerne, Rochambeau, and La Fayette continued to send pleas for ships and money. These conflicting pressures produced dissensions in the French Cabinet and compromises in allocation of forces that were dispersed when they should have been concentrated.

Great Britain enjoyed one great advantage over her enemies, for she did not (as France did) have to concert strategy with a feckless and unreliable ally. Twice she had attempted to get help from Catherine of Russia; twice the Empress had refused. British resources were strained to the limit. Security of the homeland and protection of incoming and outgoing trade required the Royal Navy to cover the south coast and Channel approaches. Armies in New York, Canada, the West Indies, and the

Carolinas had to be supported; positions in India held; Gibraltar periodically supplied; Minorca defended. Horace Walpole was even more pessimistic than usual. In his opinion the King would persist stubbornly in the American war: "Our foolhardiness is past all credibility—the nation is besotted."[1] Lord North was again begging to be relieved of his responsibilities and informed his royal master that "the decline in his health, his spirits & his understanding" made him every day more anxious "to retire from the hurry of business and the bustle of the world." The King replied that he, too, found his task an unpleasant one, "but both of us are in tramels and it is our duty to continue."[2]

On April 12 Vice-admiral George Darby with twenty-nine of the line and seventy transports and supply ships arrived off Cádiz. His mission was to relieve Gibraltar. He sent four of the line and his convoy through the straits to resupply the Rock and while the ships were unloading cruised in clear sight of the Spanish fleet huddled in the harbor of Cádiz. The Spaniards, who had made no effort to break up the convoy, were even less inclined to challenge a British battle fleet cleared for action, and remained safely in the harbor. Sir Horace Mann described the conduct of the timorous Spanish admiral and his impotent fleet as "disgraceful."

Stocks rose a few points when it was learned that Darby had accomplished his mission, but promptly fell when news arrived that a small French fleet had intercepted the convoy laden with loot Rodney had taken at St. Eustatius, and had carried off ships and cargo valued at a million sterling. Some viewed this event as the appropriate reward of Rodney's indiscriminate avarice.

And unpleasant news came to London from the United Provinces of Holland. On April 19, as if to celebrate the events at Lexington and Concord six years previously, "Their High Mightinesses" recognized the independence of the United States of America. John Adams, minister plenipotentiary, had labored assiduously with tongue and pen, and the burghers of Amsterdam had finally succumbed to his persuasive powers. Treaties of amity and commerce were to be negotiated and a generous loan was promised.* Adams was entitled to feel, as he did, that his unremitting and frequently frustrated efforts had finally been rewarded.

Washington spent the last week of March at New Windsor "in a most critical and disagreeable state of suspence" as he awaited news from Virginia. Finally, on the thirtieth, he received a letter from Chevalier Des Touches giving him details of the naval engagement off Cape Henry. He had been so exasperated with failure to get the expedition to Virginia under way as promptly as he wished that he had allowed himself to

---

* The loan promised was not granted until 1782.

write half a dozen indiscreet letters on the subject, and the report from the French naval commander was not one designed to restore his equanimity.†

The British position in Virginia had been saved not by the performance of their admirals but by a French *chef d'escadre*, who, with his enemy crippled and a decisive victory within his grasp, chose to leave control of the battle area to a damaged fleet he could have demolished the following morning, and to seek the safety of Narragansett Bay. In so doing, Des Touches was following the pernicious French naval battle doctrine that prescribed that "one should risk much to defend one's own positions and very little to attack those of the enemy."[3] Preservation of the French position at Newport was indeed important, and was a factor he had to take into account, but had he destroyed Arbuthnot's fleet, he would have removed that threat. One can scarcely imagine Howe, Rodney, Barrington, or Hood not waiting until the morrow to make victory complete. Washington surely had tongue in check when after reading the account Des Touches sent to New Windsor he wrote the *chef d'escadre* a polite letter of congratulation. He knew that Des Touches had forfeited a great opportunity. But he could say nothing of that.

He had learned that a detachment of about 2,100 under Major General William Phillips (who with Riedesel had been exchanged for Benjamin Lincoln) had sailed from New York and had correctly concluded that its destination was Virginia. In early April he wrote: "Every day convinces me that the Enemy are determined to bend their force against the Southern states and that we must support them powerfully from this Quarter or they may be lost." He was doing what he could to restore the situation there, or at least hold it in equilibrium, and directed Brigadier General Anthony Wayne to hasten reorganization and equipment of the Pennsylvania Line which he had ordered to join the Southern Army. He also directed La Fayette to move south and report to Greene.

He revealed his state of mind at this time in a letter to John Laurens. In this candid summary of the situation he assured Laurens that every day brought "additional proof" of the impossibility of carrying on the war without "timely and powerful aid." The desperate picture was one he had limned many times: "We cannot transport provisions because we cannot pay the Teamsters; Our troops are approaching fast to nakedness and . . . we have nothing to cloath them with . . . our Hospitals are

---

† The British captured the mail in which one of these letters had been sent, and promptly published it in Rivington's New York *Gazette*. This created a most embarrassing situation for Washington, who had to explain his uncomplimentary reflections on the competence of the French commanders. He chose not to disavow his expressed opinions with an outright lie, but suggested to Rochambeau that a part of the letter was probably a forgery. The letter as published by Rivington appeared precisely as he had written it.

without medicines and our Sick without Nutriment . . . all our public works are at a stand and the Artificers disbanding. . . ."

He again emphasized the necessity for money. Without it, the Pennsylvania Line could not be equipped to march to the south, nor could La Fayette carry out his orders to join Greene: "How either can march without money or credit is more than I can tell." But even if money were to be supplied, the French must keep "a superior Fleet always in these seas . . . the ruin of the enemy's schemes would then be certain." There was no need to "run into the detail, when it may be declared in a word that we are at the end of our tether, and that now or never our deliverance must come."[4]

Thanks to the ingenuity and courage of Commodore James Nicholson, Continental Navy, the two British sloops blocking Annapolis had withdrawn, and La Fayette had managed to embark his small force and return in safety to Head of Elk. He arrived there on April 8 and was awaiting orders. Washington learned of this move three days later, and immediately wrote the marquis to communicate with Greene and to take his directions "as to marching forward to join him, or remaining there to keep a watch upon the motions of Phillips, should he have formed a junction with Arnold at Portsmouth." Even a "watch" on Phillips was more than La Fayette could possibly manage. He was practically immobilized by lack of clothing and shoes.

Two days before Washington sent La Fayette these instructions, Cornwallis learned that Phillips had joined Arnold at Portsmouth, and wrote him: "Now, my dear friend, what is our plan? Without one, we cannot succeed, and I assure you I am quite tired of marching about the country in quest of adventures." Obviously, as Sir Henry Clinton seemed to have no plans, or at least had none that suited the earl, he and Phillips would have to formulate them. As he had earlier suggested to Clinton, he wanted the seat of war moved to Virginia, even if that meant abandonment of New York. The war, he wrote, could not be won by a defensive strategy "mixed with desultory expeditions." If this was Clinton's plan, the British might just as well "stick to our salt pork at New York, sending now and then a detachment to steal tobacco, &s."[5]

After the battle off Cape Henry on March 16, Arbuthnot had anchored in Lynnhaven Roads to repair his damaged ships. He returned to New York on April 10, and was greeted with a noticeable lack of enthusiasm. Letters received in New York before he arrived were "full of complaints." General opinion was that the admiral had wasted three weeks at Lynnhaven, where he had done nothing. His critics, and he had many, agreed that he had conducted the battle badly. Mackenzie talked to officers who returned with the fleet; some thought he should be brought before a general court-martial; others, that he deserved to be summarily hanged. "Great dissensions" prevailed. "The Admirals Arbuthnot and Graves do not speak and the fleet is divided into parties." With such rancor "nothing great can be expected."[6]

On April 2, the greater part of Greene's militia, having served their allotted time, left for home. Again his army was reduced to a skeleton. He wrote Washington that he could expect little help from either Virginia or Maryland "nor is there a man raised in North Carolina, or the least prospect of it." In this "critical and distressing situation" he had determined "to carry the War into South Carolina."[7] In a report to the president of Congress he wrote that at Guilford Court House, Cornwallis had "met with defeat in victory," but that he had not been able to press the pursuit because the militia was disbanding. Whigs and Tories in North Carolina were destroying each other; "blood and slaughter" prevailed among them; "their inveteracy must, if it continue, depopulate the country." He outlined his plans to Sumter and Marion, directed Sumter to collect militia and provisions and if possible to reduce "all their little outposts" before he arrived with the army in the vicinity of Camden, where he hoped to encounter Lord Rawdon, now in command in South Carolina. On April 6 he set out on a march of 130 miles to Camden.

Greene hoped to surprise Rawdon, whose garrison amounted to about nine hundred, including men recuperating from illness and wounds. This small force, which consisted for the most part of Americans enlisted in provincial regiments, was augmented by a few local Tories. The population of the country through which Greene marched was hostile. He found it difficult to get provisions and impossible to get information; his every movement was reported to Rawdon, who hastened to improve his already strong fortifications. On April 19, Greene arrived within sight of Camden, reconnoitered the terrain and the defensive works, and decided he could not take the place by assault. He fell back about a mile and took position on Hobkirk's Hill in hope of enticing Rawdon to come out and give battle. He deployed on what he described as "a very advantageous piece of ground" covered by a pine forest.

His formation deviated from that he had adopted at Guilford. Here, he put light infantry sharpshooters out with his pickets to impede the enemy, his Maryland and Virginia Continentals in a first line, the militia in a second, and Washington's cavalry troop, reduced to fifty-six men, on the left of the militia.‡ On the morning of April 25, provisions (less the rum) arrived together with his three small field pieces. At about ten o'clock, after the men had breakfasted, sporadic firing was heard. All was in readiness to receive Rawdon.** A road up which the British would

‡ Greene's "army" at Hobkirk's Hill consisted of 1,174 Continentals, 254 North Carolina militia, 56 troopers, and 40 artillerymen—a total of 1,524 rank and file.

** It was later asserted that Greene was surprised. This was not so. The defense had been carefully planned and defenders were in their assigned positions when firing was first heard to the front.

probably advance bisected the American position. The Virginians were on the right, the Marylanders on the left, and behind them the three field pieces. But Greene had made one inexcusable error. He had failed to hold out a reserve and had thus deprived himself of ability to restore a situation or to exploit an advantage.

Rawdon did not make the same mistake. He advanced on a relatively narrow front and held nearly half his small force in reserve. Greene now took another questionable decision. He ordered a double envelopment. Even with the best of troops, with perfect timing and co-ordination, and with suitable terrain for maneuver this tactic can be dangerous. Here it was disastrous, for the American center, which he thought would hold, collapsed. Colonel Washington, ordered to sweep around Rawdon's flank to strike the British line in the rear, got himself and his troops deeply entangled "in a mixed multitude" of "doctors, surgeons, quartermasters, commissaries, wagon masters, waiters, and all the loose trumpery of an army"[8] and did not attempt to execute his mission until it was too late to affect the issue.

Greene kept his composure and managed to extricate his damaged army, his field pieces, and his wagons. He fell back three miles, reorganized, rested, and prepared to receive the attack he anticipated. But Rawdon, too, had been hurt, and retired in good order to the safety of Camden. Greene blamed his defeat on Colonel Gunby, who had withdrawn the 1st Maryland slightly in an attempt to pull it together after a momentary panic, and ordered Gunby before a court of inquiry. The court found that Gunby's order to retire was "extremely improper and unmilitary; and in all probability the only cause why we did not obtain a complete victory."†† This was small solace to Greene, who wrote that he was "almost frantic with vexation" at the disappointment of his hopes. "Fortune has not been much our friend."[9]

During the first week of May "old" Continental paper plunged from a rate of 175 for 1 to a calamitous 600, then 800, and finally to a disastrous 900 for 1. The "old" paper, "prostrate," no longer had currency and the "new" (which Congress began emitting in the spring of 1780) was also falling. In a letter to Governor Jefferson the Virginia delegates wrote of "commotions" in Philadelphia: "What this Convulsion will end in is difficult to surmise, in the mean time we are in infinite distress." Sailors armed with clubs paraded in the streets. "The Beer houses demand hard for a Pot of Drink." Speculators seized the opportunity to ship bales of "old" paper from Philadelphia to New England where the rate of exchange had not as yet dropped as drastically. Their "horrible doings," from which they reaped a rich harvest, quickly put a stop to circulation

†† Not so. Greene had made the tactical errors that led to loss of the battle.

of "old" paper in Boston. But there was a glimmer of hope. Robert Morris had been appointed to superintend the finances of the United States: "Great matters are expected from this gentleman's abilities. The finances of no country were at any time more deranged or more in want of wisdom. . . ."

Many members of Congress did not take their duties as seriously as they should have. Often as many as five or six states were unrepresented and it was frequently impossible "to make a Congress." For a time in May, no delegates from any state east of New Jersey attended Congress. Those present found the cost of living unbearable and wanted to return to their homes. In letters, they described the country's condition as wretched and deplorable; Congress was at "its wits End—everything at a stand." The only hope was speedy arrival of a French army and fleet.[10]

At his headquarters in New Windsor, Washington found himself amid "innumerable sollicitudes and embarrassments." Not the least of these were, as usual, money and food; there was "not a farthing in the Military Chest." Available specie, remitted by the states for payment of their line regiments, could not be diverted to any other purpose. The financial situation was so bad that La Fayette had pledged his personal credit to merchants of Baltimore for a loan of £2,000 to buy linen for shirts and overalls, shoes, "and a few hats." Washington wrote that while he was not able to express the "pleasing sensations" he experienced from La Fayette's "unparalleled and repeated instances of generosity and zeal," they would endear his name to the country and serve as "an everlasting monument" to his attachment to the cause of America.

No other circumstance induced "pleasing sensations" in the breast of the commander in chief, who was "Distressed beyond expression, at the present situation and future prospects of the Army, with regard to provisions" and was convinced that "unless an immediate and regular supply" could be obtained "the most dangerous consequences" were to be expected. He was determined, so he wrote, "to make one great effort more, on the subject" and was sending Major General Heath to the New England states, where Heath had wide personal influence, "to represent our distresses for meat in their true Colours."[11] As he wrote this letter to the president of Congress, the commissionary officer reported that the army's magazines held not one single barrel of salt beef and but thirty-one barrels of flour.

Washington was not sure Heath's personal pleas would be any more effective than his own frequent applications had been, but he was certain that "if there is not a very great and sudden change of measures, it will be next to impossible to keep the Army together." In committing to Heath "a *Negotiation*: on the success of which, the very existence of the Army depends," Washington charged him with arranging for "an immediate supply of Beef Cattle"; for transportation of salt provisions and·

with co-operation of the New England states, for establishing "a *regular, systematic, effectual Plan* for feeding the Army through the Campaign."[12]

He felt strongly that the eastern states had not responded to his many prior requests as they should have done, and his "Circular" of May 10 reflected this. He had, he stated, written of his continual embarrassments "not merely once or twice" but had "reiterated them over and over again." His pleas had made but little impression. What was the situation? "From the Post of Saratoga to that of Dobbs Ferry inclusive, I believe there is not . . . at this moment one day's supply of Meat on hand." He followed with one of his rare ultimata: "I intreat that this representation may be received in the serious light it is meant and deserves, or that I may stand exculpated from the dread consequences which must otherwise inevitably follow in a short time."[13]

Washington's correspondence during April and May 1781 reveals the never-ending demands that bore upon him with immediacy every day, from every direction and on every subject. Shortage of lead at one place, of powder at another, of clothing here, of shoes there, and of provisions everywhere. All received his careful attention. Much needed to be done before the American Army would be ready to take the field for what he fervently hoped might be the decisive campaign.

On March 22 Admiral Count de Grasse cleared Brest for the West Indies with a cumbersome convoy of 150 merchantmen.‡‡ Five weeks later, on April 28, he passed through the strait between Martinique and St. Lucia and set course for Fort Royal. He now learned that Rear Admiral Sir Samuel Hood was lying off the harbor with seventeen sail and that four French ships of the line had taken refuge under the guns of the fortress. When one of Hood's cruising frigates reported that De Grasse had passed the southern tip of Martinique and was steering north, the British admiral abandoned his blocking position, set a southerly course, and made signals to form line of battle and clear for action. Rear Admiral Sir Samuel Hood was prepared to fight for mastery of the Caribbean.

The French admiral, cautious and concerned for the safety of his convoy, was not equally eager. Numerical odds were greatly in his favor, for when Hood left his position off Fort Royal the four French ships he had locked in the harbor ran out, eluded British cruisers, and joined De Grasse. This accession gave the French a preponderance of twenty-four of the line to Hood's seventeen. But De Grasse made no use of his overwhelming strength, and during the last two days of April devoted his energies to shepherding the convoy. The fleets indulged in desultory and wasteful exchanges at long range, but Hood could not entice the French to close. With such marked inferiority, he would fight only on his terms.

‡‡ François Joseph Paul, Marquis de Grasse-Tilly, Comte de Grasse, commander of the Order of St. Louis, then the most distinguished officer in the French Navy.

These were unacceptable to De Grasse, who anchored in Fort Royal harbor on May 6.

On the same day, Colonel Vicomte de Rochambeau, the French general's son and one of his aides, who had sailed for France after the Hartford conference to carry his father's request for ships, men, and money, returned to Boston in frigate *Concorde*. His companion during the voyage was Vice-admiral Louis Comte de Barras St. Laurent, sent to take command of the French fleet based in Narragansett Bay.* The vicomte brought Louis XVI's promise of a gift of 6 million livres and news of other aid on the way. Six hundred fighting men, in convoy escorted by frigate *Sagittaire*, would soon arrive in Boston. These six hundred constituted but one tenth of the strength of Rochambeau's second division, effectively sealed up in Brest by British cruisers. And the dispatches carried by the vicomte made it clear that these troops were all the general could expect. This decision, so Vergennes wrote, had full concurrence of his new Ministers of War and Marine, Marshal the Marquis de Ségur and Marquis de Castries.† Rochambeau's disappointment in learning that his second division would not join him was alleviated to a degree by a letter from the Marquis de Castries informing him that Admiral de Grasse was en route to the West Indies with a powerful fleet and could operate at his discretion in North American waters to establish the maritime supremacy essential if offensive operations of consequence were to be undertaken.

Rochambeau immediately wrote Washington proposing a meeting to discuss plans for joint operations during the summer of 1781. In his reply, Washington suggested Wethersfield, Connecticut, as a convenient site, and set Monday, May 21, as the date. Generals Knox and du Portail accompanied him. Rochambeau arrived with Major General the Marquis de Chastellux, but as Admiral Arbuthnot was lying off the entrance to the bay, De Barras thought it his duty to remain in Newport.

Both generals had given much thought to employment of the combined armies during the summer of 1781, and both rejected as "impracticable" the proposition that French troops in Newport be moved by sea to the Chesapeake Bay area. Alternatively, the French could march "as soon as possible to the North River" and there join Washington's army. Finally, Rochambeau asked Washington's opinion as to what operations the combined force should undertake "in event of a French naval rein-

---

* Admiral de Ternay died in Newport on December 15, 1780, and was buried in the Trinity Church cemetery. Until De Barras arrived in May 1781 the French fleet was commanded by Chef d'Escadre Charles René Dominique Gochet, Chevalier Des Touches.

† The eighty-year-old Comte de Maurepas, although nominally *chef du cabinet*, had withdrawn from active political life in December 1780, and Vergennes, acting as Louis XVI's chief minister, brought De Ségur and De Castries into the Cabinet to replace Montbarey and De Sartine, neither of whom any longer enjoyed his confidence.

forcement from the West Indies."‡ To this, Washington replied that as
the British garrison at New York had been much reduced by repeated
detachments to the south, he thought it advisable for the combined force
to move down the Hudson "to the vicinity of New York to be ready to
take advantage of any opportunity which the weakness of the enemy
may afford. Should the West India Fleet arrive upon the Coast; the force
thus combined may either proceed in the operation against New Yk. or
may be directed against the enemy in some other quarter, as circumstances shall dictate."[14]

At this time, Washington was opposed to moving overland into Virginia. He thought the season too advanced, the march too long, and
transportation too difficult and too expensive, and concluded his remarks
with the statement that these considerations, with others known to
Rochambeau, pointed out "the preference which an operation against
New York seems to have, in present circumstances, to attempt sending a
force to the Southward."

Washington estimated Clinton's garrison in and around New York at
a strength of 7,500, and informed Rochambeau that his own returns
showed 8,250 Continentals, "almost the whole of them raw men, but
under good officers."** He believed that if the states responded to his urgent requests to bring their lines to established strengths, he could muster 10,250 rank and file for an attack on New York. This number, with
5,000 French, would give the allies a superiority of two to one. Although
the commander in chief had his heart set on New York, he was not
averse to operations elsewhere if "circumstances" were favorable. Such
"circumstances" could be assured only by the arrival of Admiral de
Grasse off the coast of North America.

Clinton had a variety of plans. One was to mount an attack on West
Point; another to seize what he called "Delaware Neck," the piece of
land lying between Delaware and Chesapeake bays, presumably as a
base for operations in Virginia or possibly against Philadelphia. He wrote
Arnold asking for advice and suggestions on the West Point scheme. Arnold had not been at West Point for eight months, and in his reply tactfully discouraged the idea. Clinton, floundering again, was indecisive and
unable to formulate a coherent strategy. By sending first Leslie, then Arnold, then Phillips to Virginia, he had reduced his strength at New York
by about 5,700 rank and file and condemned himself to a frustrating defensive.

An operation to occupy Delaware Neck did not recommend itself to
Cornwallis, and a week after he wrote Phillips he sent off a letter to Ger-

‡ Rochambeau arrived at Wethersfield with five "Propositions" to which he
requested responses. The three described above bore directly on combined strategy
for 1781.

** Paper strength. Washington had fewer than 5,000 rank and file present fit for
duty.

main recounting the problems he had encountered in North Carolina. The Loyalists had not responded. Experience had shown him "that their numbers are not so great as had been represented, and that their friendship was only passive." The terrain of North Carolina made it impossible for the army to operate "in the heart of the country" for extended periods. His opinion was that "a serious attempt upon Virginia would be the most solid plan, because successful operations might not only be attended with important consequences there, but would tend to the security of South Carolina and ultimately to the submission of North Carolina."[15] In another letter to Germain, written about a week later, he again summarized the situation in North and South Carolina and made it clear that he did not propose to commit the small army under his command to the hazards of operations in the interior of either state. Nor did he have any intention of lingering in Wilmington to await transports to evacuate him by sea, an alternative he described as "ruinous and disgraceful to Britain." He had no fear for Charleston and had "resolved to take advantage of General Greene's having left the back of Virginia open and march immediately into that province to attempt a junction with General Phillips."[16]

Cornwallis left Wilmington on April 25. The editor of the *Annual Register* for 1781 would later write that the earl had formed "the bold and vigorous resolution of marching to Virginia, and endeavouring a junction with General Phillips. This measure, in a situation which afforded only a choice of difficulties and dangers was undoubtedly the best that could have been adopted; but yet it was a resolution of such a nature as could have been only conceived or entertained by an enterprizing and determined mind. It was indeed a perilous adventure. The distance was great, the means of subsistence uncertain, and the difficulties and hazards were sufficient to appall the boldest."[17]

But Cornwallis could not avoid glancing back toward Camden. As he lingered south of the Roanoke, he sent Tarleton forward to reconnoiter routes to Petersburg and to establish secure and speedy communication with Phillips. On May 12 he learned that Rawdon had defeated Greene at Hobkirk's Hill. That afternoon he turned his eyes toward Virginia and the following morning led his small army across the river.

The earl arrived at Petersburg on May 20, 1781, to find that Phillips had died a few days earlier and that Arnold was in command. Phillips had been in Virginia for about seven weeks, had conducted some raids, destroyed a considerable amount of property, and kept the state in a ferment. He had not, however, done anything about locating a suitable site for a naval base in the Chesapeake area as Clinton had instructed him to do. Cornwallis inherited this mission. Although he had not been to Portsmouth, he was assured by officers familiar with the place, including Ar-

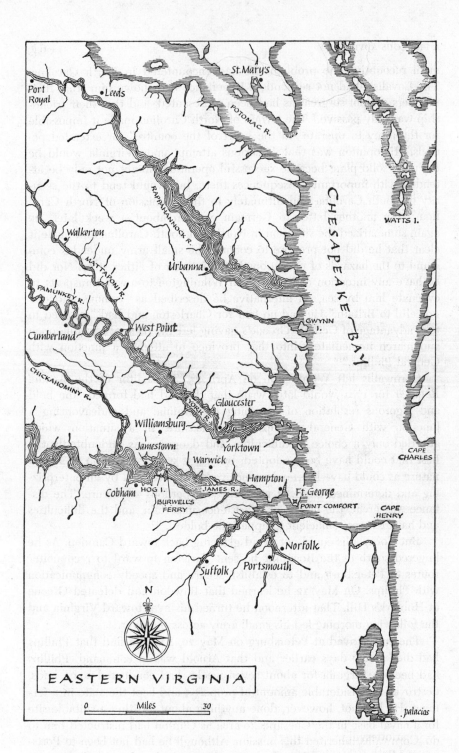

Port
Royal

Leeds

St.Mary's

POTOMAC R.

WATTS I.

RAPPAHANNOCK R.

Walkerton

MATTAPONI R.

Urbanna

PAMUNKEY R.

GWYNN I.

Cumberland

West Point

CHESAPEAKE BAY

CHICKAHOMINY R.

YORK R.

Gloucester

Williamsburg

Jamestown

Yorktown

Warwick

CAPE
CHARLES

Cobham

HOG I.

JAMES R.

BURWELL'S
FERRY

Hampton

Ft.George

POINT COMFORT

CAPE
HENRY

Norfolk

Suffolk

Portsmouth

N

EASTERN VIRGINIA

0   Miles   30

palacias

nold, that it would not do, as it was difficult to defend, "remarkably unhealthy," and the channel not deep enough for ships of the line. With the reliable O'Hara as second-in-command, he had no further use for Arnold, and ordered him to return to New York.

By May 26, Cornwallis had formulated plans for the immediate future. He had received a reinforcement of 2,000 and now commanded a respectable army of nearly 7,000 rank and file. On that day he wrote Clinton from Westover, north of the James, that his intent was to "dislodge La Fayette from Richmond," to destroy magazines and stores, and then move down to Williamsburg, on the neck of land between the York and the James, and to reconnoiter that area for the naval base Clinton was so anxious to establish. There he would await orders for further operations. Reports he had received indicated that Yorktown, with a complementary post at Gloucester on the north of the York River, would be a satisfactory site for a "place of arms" and the naval base.

He repeated his conviction that "if offensive war is intended," Virginia appeared to be "the only province in which it can be carried on, and in which there is a stake." But "a considerable army" would be necessary. Experience in the Carolinas had taught him that "wherever the King's troops are, they should be in respectable force"; he had "too often observed that when a storm threatens, our friends disappear."[18]

After dispatching this letter, the earl moved north to Hanover Court House. His threat was sufficient to cause La Fayette, whose small army could not stand against Cornwallis, to leave Richmond. Members of the Virginia Legislature forsook their threatened capital for Charlottesville. Now the earl learned that Baron von Steuben with about five hundred men, many without bayonets and cartouche boxes, was at Point of Fork where the Rivanna and Fluvanna join west of Richmond to form the James. Here the baron had assembled the few supplies he had managed to get. Cornwallis sent Lieutenant Colonel John Simcoe, probably the finest battalion commander in the British Army, with his Queen's Rangers to deal with Von Steuben and destroy the magazines.

The baron's ragged force was in no condition to challenge the aggressive Simcoe and his battle-tested Rangers. Many men were ill; many deserted. When a handful arrived, an equal number departed. He had given up any hope of seeing a Virginia Line established and wrote Greene that his efforts to find cavalry mounts to send to the south met with countless obstacles. Nor could he get draft horses and wagons. "In general, all the preparations for the protection of the State against the enemy continued as inefficient as ever. All the departments were in disorder, which increased to the highest degree when the Executive and Legislature, at the approach of Cornwallis, moved hurriedly from Richmond to Charlottesville."[19] The baron had but one thought, which was to join Greene with the Continentals he had. His battalion, as yet untrained and undisciplined, was serving no useful purpose in Virginia, and there was not the slightest prospect his situation would improve. Indeed, it was steadily deteriorating. He was no longer popular with the governor, the State Council, or the Legislature. His quartermaster could purchase nothing by certificate, and wrote the baron that private trade had broken down, that he could get no leather for shoes, and that he had no money.

But a more immediate problem than preparing to march to the Carolinas occupied von Steuben. This was to save the stores collected with such difficulty at Point of Fork. With much labor, these were transported to the south bank of the Fluvanna. But Simcoe was not to be denied. His Rangers rafted across the river and captured a considerable supply of powder, 2,500 muskets, sixty hogsheads of rum and brandy, "a thirteen inch mortar, five brass eight inch howitzers, and four long brass nine pounders, mounted afterward at Yorktown: all French pieces, and in excellent order."[20] Loss of these stores did not increase the baron's popularity, but he had no choice other than to abandon them. Politicians in Charlottesville conveniently forgot his repeated requests to the state to move the stores west toward the mountains where they would be safe, and were loud in their unwarranted censures.

While Simcoe was thus profitably engaged, Tarleton, ordered by Cornwallis to "disturb" the Legislature, rode into Charlottesville on June 4. The gentlemen, happily for them, had some warning and most managed to hide or get out of town. Jefferson escaped from Monticello only a few minutes before the green-coated legionnaires arrived to arrest him. Tarleton proceeded to destroy stores and rejoined Cornwallis, who started on a leisurely march toward Williamsburg.

La Fayette, recently joined by Anthony Wayne's Pennsylvania Line, followed Cornwallis at a respectful distance. But the earl was not interested in chasing "the Boy," as he called the marquis, over the state of Virginia. Tarleton's cavalry kept touch with La Fayette, who, with an inferior force, displayed exemplary caution.†† Cornwallis would attend to "the Boy" on a suitable occasion. At this time he wished to see Clinton's dispatches he expected to find at Williamsburg, where he arrived on June 27.

In the first of these, Sir Henry directed the earl to locate a suitable base for line-of-battle ships, and suggested Old Point Comfort. Accompanied by some engineers and naval officers, Cornwallis proceeded on the reconnaissance Clinton had ordered. After examining the area, the experts rejected it. The earl concurred, and on his return to Williamsburg wrote Sir Henry that he and his advisers favored Yorktown and Gloucester on the York River, and that he proposed to move the army there immediately.

†† Several historians have asserted that La Fayette forced Cornwallis to "retreat" to Williamsburg.

From this point on, relations between Cornwallis and his chief deteriorated steadily from bad to worse. Clinton had no firm idea what he wanted to do and seemed content to sit idly in New York devising assorted plans, none of which materialized. And he spent hours ruminating on the insubordination of Cornwallis who without orders had committed his army to Virginia and had spent a month rambling to no purpose.

✄ 8

At the Eve of Great Events

When Cornwallis marched north, he passed command of His Majesty's forces in South Carolina to Lieutenant Colonel Lord Rawdon, whose victory at Hobkirk's Hill elicited the earl's praise but had not improved the British situation. Greene, Marion, Pickens, Lee, and Sumter were all active. Each passing day made Rawdon's position more vulnerable, and on May 9 he decided to evacuate Camden. He pulled down the town jail, set fire to several houses, wrecked the flour mill, left sixty seriously wounded officers and men to the mercy of the inhabitants, and marched out of the ruins the next morning.

One after another, British posts fell. On May 24 Greene was able to write that since Hobkirk's Hill the Americans had taken fifty British officers and eight hundred rank and file. Greene estimated that one third of the enlisted captured were deserters from the American Army.

At this time the British held only two interior posts, Augusta and Ninety Six. Greene turned his attention to Ninety Six, commanded by Lieutenant Colonel John Cruger. The garrison of some nine hundred consisted of about five hundred Tories, many from New York, and several Provincial units. Greene reached Ninety Six on May 22. On the same day Pickens invested Augusta. Ninety Six was strongly fortified, and skillfully, courageously, and tenaciously defended. Greene could make no impression on the fortifications and none on the morale of Cruger and his garrison.

On June 8 Lieutenant Colonel Light-Horse Harry Lee arrived with his legion from Augusta, where the garrison had capitulated three days earlier. With this reinforcement, a decision seemed inevitable. Greene knew he had very little time, for he had learned that Rawdon with a strong column of regulars was marching to raise the siege. He had previously ordered Sumter to delay Rawdon; Sumter chose to pursue his own schemes. With Rawdon hurrying forward by forced marches, there remained but one last chance to take Ninety Six, and that by a sudden and carefully prepared assault. At noon on June 18 the assault was launched. Cruger was ready and the attackers were beaten back. Much blood was shed in a short hour of fighting when Greene, realizing that further efforts were hopeless, called off the attack. At daybreak the following morning, with Rawdon closing rapidly, the army retreated with its wounded. Greene moved north and crossed the Saluda River.

Here he found time to write several letters in which he was justifiably critical of Sumter, who had paid no attention to his orders. To Marion, he said: "I am surprised that people should be so averse to joining in some general plan of operations. It will be impossible to carry on the war to advantage, or even to attempt to hold the Country, unless our force can be directed to a point, and as to flying parties here and there they are of no consequence in the great events of War."[1] Here Greene made his position clear: Unco-ordinated partisan action was futile. Indiscriminate rampaging would not defeat the enemy, conciliate the terrorized inhabitants, or recover the country. To be effective, all efforts must be combined, directed, and controlled in accordance with a specific plan of operations. The general had obviously had his fill of the "Carolina Gamecock."

In this letter, Greene was not depreciating the potential of partisan war as an effectual adjunct to orthodox operations. When he took command in the Southern Department, he wrote Washington that he intended to conduct "a kind of partisan war." The political situation, the character of the people, primitive communications, and the nature of the terrain in the Carolinas combined to favor guerrilla operations. But these had to be co-ordinated with strategic and tactical plans formulated by the commander of the department. Marion and Pickens understood this. Sumter either did not or was too individualistic or too avid to enhance his own reputation, to accept a subordinate role.

Greene retired farther north to a camp "of rest and repose in a healthy area known then as the "High Hills of the Santee." He urged

Governor Rutledge to establish civil government as soon as possible, "as it is important to have the minds of the people formed to the habits of civil rather than military authority." South Carolinians, ravaged and plundered alike by marauding bands of Whigs and Tories, were destitute. Bridges had been broken, mills wrecked, homes burned, stock stolen. The fabric of an entire society outside the guarded limits of Charleston had been ripped to pieces. Colonel Wade Hampton wrote Greene that many country people, reduced to starvation, had "combined in committing robberies, the most base and inhuman that ever disgraced mankind." He had "secured all of those wretches who could be found." But many escaped with their loot to North Carolina and Virginia.

During early June, Rochambeau made final preparations to leave Newport and march to join Washington, who was then encamped near New York in the area known as White Plains. By evening of June 12, the entire army with field artillery, ammunition, baggage, and camp equipment had arrived at Providence, Rhode Island.* Here Rochambeau learned that the six hundred reinforcements he had been expecting were safe in Boston and would join him. The convoy, shepherded across the Atlantic by frigate *Sagittaire*, brought two batteries of light artillery, needed supplies, and several heavy iron "military chests" containing money for Rochambeau as well as some portion of the 6 million livres King Louis had sent as a gift.†

A week later, the first of four divisions, each of a regiment with a proportion of the artillery and baggage, set out on the long march to the Hudson. The flamboyant Duc de Lauzun rode with his legion in the vanguard. The second, third, and fourth divisions followed on successive days. French engineers had mapped the route with their usual meticulous care, but were not able to do anything to improve the roads. One diarist who marched with the first division described them as "very poor," "very bad," "very difficult," and "frightful." But the same diarist, Comte de Clermont-Crèvecour, a lieutenant in the Royal Artillery, grew rhapsodic when the division arrived in Connecticut, which he thought beautiful and "the most fertile province in America. The beef is exceptionally good. The poultry and game are exquisite." The people, healthy, amiable, and cordial, labored for themselves: "The sweat of their brow is not expended on satisfying the extravagant desires of the rich and luxury loving." The division rested two days at Hartford. The regimental band played in the evenings and the officers danced with the "charming young ladies."[2]

---

* A garrison of six hundred men, many ill or convalescing, was left at Newport with the siege artillery.

† Approximately two thirds of the gift was used by Franklin to pay outstanding debts.

The remainder of the trip was not to be so idyllic, for the French were now approaching the Hudson, and the march was in territory both British and American armies had fought over and which irregulars of both sides had ravaged. On July 6 they encamped between the Bronx and Sawmill rivers, with the right wing resting on the American left. Two days later Washington reviewed the two armies, and after the ceremony Clermont-Crèvecour visited the camp of the American Army, then consisting of about 4,000 men. The young count was struck "not by the army's smart appearance, but by its destitution: the men were without uniforms and covered with rags; most of them were barefoot. They were of all sizes, down to children who could not have been over fourteen. There were many negroes, mulattos, etc. Only their artillerymen were wearing uniforms."[3] On the night of July 21, contingents of the allied armies marched toward the Hudson and deployed on the heights overlooking King's Bridge.

Clinton was agitated and embarrassed. Rumors that Admiral de Grasse was on his way north from the West Indies and that he would no doubt join in an attack on New York were circulating. Frederick Mackenzie thought the reduction of New York "an operation of such difficulty, that the Enemy will not attempt it, unless they are very certain of a very decided superiority at Sea, during its continuance."[4] Washington had no intention of doing anything more at this time than making a reconnaissance in force, and after he and Rochambeau had surveyed the British positions, the allied troops withdrew to their camps.

Admiral de Grasse cleared Fort Royal for St. Domingue with a convoy of two hundred sail on July 5. There he found frigate *Concorde* awaiting him with dispatches from Luzerne, Washington, Rochambeau, and De Barras. And aboard *Concorde* were thirty American pilots familiar with the waters of New York and the Chesapeake. In their letters, the minister and the three commanders outlined the perilous situation in the southern states and begged the admiral's aid. He acted immediately. From M. de Lillancourt, governor of St. Domingue, he borrowed three regiments commanded by Marquis de Saint Simon. He needed money, too, and as De Lillancourt had none to give, he sent a letter by fast frigate to the Spanish governor of Havana begging the equivalent of 1.2 million livres. The money was raised by popular subscription within forty-eight hours.

All was in readiness—ships watered and provisioned, American pilots assigned, troops aboard, the money on the way. On August 5 De Grasse cleared St. Domingue with twenty-eight sail of the line. His destination was Chesapeake Bay. A few days before the French admiral sailed, Rodney, who for some time had been suffering from a variety of ailments,

passed command of the British fleet in the West Indies to Sir Samuel
Hood, and left for England to recover his shattered health.‡

On August 14, 1781, a courier carrying urgent dispatches from Count
de Barras rode into Washington's headquarters. Frigate *Concorde*, sent
by De Grasse from Cap Français, had arrived in Newport with letters
from the French admiral. In these, De Grasse announced his intention to
sail for Chesapeake Bay on August 3 with twenty-five of the line and
3,200 troops, and urged that everything be "in the most perfect readiness" to commence operations at the moment of his arrival as "particular
engagements with the Spaniards" required him to be in the West Indies
by the middle of October. Washington's diary entry for August 14 reads
in part:

> Matters having now come to a crisis and a decisive plan to be
> determined on, I was obliged from the shortness of Count de
> Grasses promised stay on this Coast, the apparent disinclination in
> their Naval Officers to force the harbour of New York and the fee-
> ble compliance of the States to my requisition for Men, hitherto,
> and little prospect of greater exertion in the future, to give up all
> idea of attacking New York; and instead thereof to remove the
> French Troops and a detachment from the American Army to the
> Head of Elk to be transported to Virginia for the purpose of co-
> operating with the force from the West Indies against the Troops
> in that State.[5]

On August 19 the armies set out on their "slow and disagreeable march"
to Head of Elk.

A month earlier, Rear Admiral Thomas Graves had received orders
from Sandwich to intercept a French convoy carrying arms, ammunition,
and clothing to Boston. After cruising off the fog-bound coast of Cape
Cod for nearly three weeks with no result, he returned to Sandy Hook on
August 16. During his absence, a dispatch from Rodney arrived in New
York and was forwarded by sloop. The sloop was captured by an American privateer in Long Island Sound. In this letter, Rodney advised
Graves that De Grasse with "a part" of his fleet might come north, promised he would watch the French carefully, and assured Graves that the
squadron in America would be reinforced "should the enemy bend their
force that way." A brig carrying a second letter, this from Hood, was
captured off the mouth of Delaware Bay. In this letter Hood wrote that
Rodney had ordered him to New York with fourteen of the line. Graves
read a copy of the first letter when he anchored off the Hook after his fu-

‡ In private letters, Hood expressed the opinion that Rodney's bodily illness had
affected his powers of judgment, and if his peculiar behavior off Tobago, much criticized by Hood and several captains, is a valid criterion, Hood's diagnosis was probably correct.

tile cruise in the fog. He of course never saw the second, which would have alerted him that a confrontation was in the making.

Both he and Clinton discounted rumors that the French were coming north. And even if De Grasse did send a squadron, both were certain Rodney would soon be along to remove the threat. On August 26 a frigate sent by Hood, then off the Chesapeake, arrived in New York harbor. The admiral had paused to look into the bay. He had found it empty. Forty-eight hours later, he anchored off the bar at New York and set off in his barge to find Graves conferring with Clinton on Long Island. These two had just learned that De Barras had left Newport on August 25 for parts unknown and were planning an expedition to Narragansett Bay.** Until Hood's unexpected arrival, neither the general nor the admiral had given any thought to the variety of possibilities signaled by the sudden departure of De Barras.

Hood had. He surmised that De Barras was steering for the Chesapeake and a probable junction with De Grasse, and urged Graves, who was his senior, to provision his ships and get them out of New York harbor. Graves demurred and suggested Hood bring his fleet across the bar. Hood made it clear that he did not wish to do so: "In his opinion, every day—every hour—was precious. Finally he prevailed, and on August 31 Graves joined him with five of the line, assumed chief command, and with nineteen of the line and one fifty-gun ship set course for Cape Henry.

Clinton thought this an appropriate time to employ some of the troops he had proposed to use against Newport to "annoy the enemy's coasts" and to "cause a diversion somewhere," and several days after the fleet sailed, Arnold with a force of about 1,700 embarked for a raid on New London, "a remarkable place for privateers." Clinton ordered him to burn stores and shipping. He did not order him to burn a large part of the town, which Arnold did after a very hot fight with the garrison at Fort Griswold. This predator had gained considerable experience during his destructive career in Virginia, and his statement that the conflagration was caused by sparks flying from burning warehouses seemed scarcely credible. There were no thatched-roof cottages in New London. Clinton had lost the last shred of his diminished control over events, and his talk about "annoying" the coast and creating "a diversion somewhere" reveals his frustration. There was no place in the rapidly developing drama for petty diversions.

Although the fleet commanded by Graves was not in the best condition for sustained action, both he and Hood deemed the force adequate to deal with any French fleet they might encounter. Both shared Rodney's belief that De Grasse would send but "a part" of his fleet north.

** Count de Barras sailed with eight of the line, four frigates, and sixteen supply ships carrying siege artillery, heavy mortars, ammunition, and army equipment.

Neither dreamed the French admiral would dare strip the West Indies of every French ship of the line. Their estimate was that he might bring as many as twelve, or at most fourteen. With the eight of De Barras, he would have a total of twenty-two. In Hood's mind, it would be a sad day for the British Navy when nineteen of His Majesty's ships could not cope with twenty-two French.

The van of the American Army crossed the Hudson at King's Ferry on August 20, and by evening of the following day the entire army, under tactical command of Major General Benjamin Lincoln, camped on the Jersey shore. During the next four days the French crossed. Washington's principal concern now was to arrange the march of the armies so as to induce Clinton to believe that the destination was Sandy Hook for an attack on Staten Island. Washington's deception plan was designed not only to deceive the British but to mislead everyone in the allied armies except the few senior officers who shared the secret. So successful were his measures that one officer wrote "our own army, no less than the Enemy, are completely deceived." Rumors flew; conjectures multiplied. Dr. James Thacher was skeptical. Although the reduction of New York would be a "decisive stroke," the city was "well fortified both by land and water, and garrisoned by the best troops of Great Britain." The doctor, basing his opinion on "doubtful conjecture," concluded that the purpose of the marching and maneuvering, the survey of a large area for encampment of the two armies, and the construction of bake ovens were part of a plan to cover Washington's true intentions. Thacher was sufficiently well acquainted with the commander in chief to write that he "resolves and matures his great plans under an impenetrable veil of secrecy."[8]

Thanks to a confidential letter intercepted earlier, in which Washington had stated that his objective was to be New York, Clinton did not indulge in doubtful conjectures. He was certain Washington proposed to mount an attack on Manhattan Island. Had he not said as much in confidential correspondence, and did not reports from British agents, who watched the activities on the Jersey side of the Hudson, confirm the intent? Here Clinton fell headlong into the trap that awaits commanders who confuse intentions with capabilities. But others in New York, including Frederick Mackenzie, did not share the general's complacency. Mackenzie's opinion was that should De Grasse come north, he would "endeavor to go into Chesapeake. In this case their design is the destruction of Lord Cornwallis' Army." Mackenzie made this diary entry on August 21. By the following evening he was "strongly of the opinion that the design of the Enemy is against Lord Cornwallis."

A few days later, Dr. Thacher wrote in his journal:

The great secret respecting our late preparations and movements can now be explained. It was a judiciously concerted strategem calculated to menace and alarm Sir Henry Clinton for the safety of the garrison of New York, and induce him to recall a part of his troops from Virginia, for his own defence; or, perhaps, keeping an eye on the city, to attempt its capture, provided that by the arrival of a French fleet, favorable circumstances should present. The deception has proved completely successfull; a part of Cornwallis' troops are reported to have returned to New York.†† His Excellency General Washington, having succeeded in a masterly piece of generalship, has now the satisfaction of leaving his adversary to ruminate on his own mortifying situation, and to anticipate the perilous fate which awaits his friend, Lord Cornwallis, in a different quarter.[7]

If as early as August 22 Frederick Mackenzie, on the staff of Clinton's adjutant general, had made a calculated estimate that Cornwallis was the probable target of the allied armies, one may ask why Sir Henry had not arrived at a similar conclusion. The answer would seem to be that he was so obsessed with New York (as Washington had been) that he had automatically eliminated consideration of the only other possible objective, and by the time he got around to accepting it, the French and Americans were marching through western New Jersey, and it was too late.

That a powerful French fleet was on the way north and that its operations combined with those of the allied armies would probably be in the southern theater was no longer a secret in Philadelphia. John Mathews of South Carolina, who derived his information "from the most authentic source," wrote Nathanael Greene to prepare himself for this "critical conjuncture." Six and a half weary years had passed since Massachusetts minutemen died on a distant village green, but at last Mathews could write: "The prospect brightens, my friend! and opens to us the most flattering view of the end of all our toils, that I have yet seen." He thought the year 1781 would be "the grand Epocha" of America's glory: ". . . when her arms will acquire the highest renown, and raise her into consequence among the nations of the earth."[8]

Washington, Rochambeau, and their staffs rode into Philadelphia on September 1, and on the three days following, the American and French armies marched through the city. The French, with their clean uniforms, their marching discipline, and their bands, passed in review before delegates to Congress, who were suitably impressed.

On August 23 Greene's army of 2,000 marched from its "camp of rest

†† Clinton had issued orders to Cornwallis to send some troops back to New York. Several days after the earl received them, Clinton revoked them.

and repose" toward Eutaw Springs on the south bank of the Santee about fifty miles northwest of Charleston, where the British Army, commanded now by Lieutenant Colonel John Stuart, was encamped. Stuart was not an officer of Rawdon's caliber, nor had he any experience in independent command. His army of about 1,600 consisted of a backbone of regulars fleshed out with Cruger's Provincials and Tories, who had given such a good account of themselves at Ninety Six.

For the first time, Greene had been able to put together a force not formidable in numbers but of a quality superior to any he had yet commanded. Marion and Pickens had joined; he had Lee's legion as well as two cavalry detachments commanded by Wade Hampton and William Washington for scouting and security of the column. Four understrength battalions of tried and proven Continentals from Maryland and Virginia provided a reliable nucleus. Greene had reason to be confident.

Nature had provided Stuart with most advantageous terrain and he made the most of it. His right was protected by Eutaw Creek. The steep banks and heavy brushwood lining the creek made access from that side practically impossible. To the front, an extensive open space formerly cultivated and bordered by trees provided his cannoneers a clear field of fire. To his rear, a two-story brick house gave his sharpshooters, posted on the second floor and in the attic, a point of vantage. His left was protected to some degree by a ravine. This would be an extremely difficult position to assault.

During early morning of September 8, Greene moved cautiously through thick woods, with here and there a cultivated field. In one of these his cavalry discovered a British "rooting party" of one hundred men gathering yams. All were taken. This was an auspicious beginning to a confused battle which swung first toward the Americans, then toward the British. The brick house was the key. The British held it tenaciously and Greene's six-pounders made no impression on its stout walls. Other Americans pressed forward into the British encampment where they gulped down rum retreating Redcoats had left behind. With victory in sight, Greene lost control of the battle. The British position was restored in a counterattack led by Major John Majoribanks.

Greene collected the drunks, pulled his disorganized army together, and retired. Official figures gave American losses at 139 killed, 375 wounded, and 8 missing, a total of 522 or about one quarter of Greene's force.‡‡ Stuart gave his losses as 693.* Both armies were severely crippled in what has been described as the bloodiest battle of the entire war. Stuart fell back toward Charleston. Greene followed cautiously and

‡‡ Figures do not tally. Other sources put Greene's losses much higher than those he reported.
* Again discrepancies appear. A more likely figure is in the neighborhood of 800. This would include the yam "rooters" and about 300 taken during the battle.

camped twenty miles west of the city. He had not won a battle, but he had won victory in the south. After Eutaw Springs, the British were confined to Charleston, Wilmington, and Savannah.

On the day Graves left New York, De Grasse made his landfall and anchored in Lynnhaven Roads. Here he was greeted by Washington's chief of engineers, Brigadier General du Portail, who brought letters from Washington and Rochambeau, and emphasized the critical need to reinforce La Fayette. Admiral de Grasse had come north to co-operate, not to quibble. Plans to disembark Saint Simon's three regiments were promptly made and speedily executed. This operation required all the boats in the fleet, and drafts of one hundred sailors from each ship. By noon the next day, Saint Simon and his troops were on their way to the James to a rendezvous with La Fayette. The boats were towed by three ships De Grasse detached for the purpose.

News that a great fleet had arrived and that La Fayette was being reinforced was sped to Baltimore, where dispatch riders waited to carry the tidings north. One of the horsemen found Washington at Chester on September 5. The commander in chief had chosen to accompany his army rather than descend the Delaware by boat as Rochambeau had elected to do. As the French general and his staff approached Chester, they discerned on the bank a figure wildly waving a hat in one hand and a handkerchief in the other. This strange figure occasionally leaped into the air as he beckoned the sloop to the beach. As they approached the shore, the French recognized Washington, evidently in a transport of joy. Washington embraced Rochambeau and showed him the dispatches from Du Portail and De Grasse. The grand concentration by land and sea would soon be effected, and Cornwallis locked in his positions at Yorktown and Gloucester.

Three factors might upset these optimistic calculations. The first was Cornwallis. British sloops had reported a large French fleet in the bay. That much Cornwallis knew. He knew also that La Fayette had been reinforced. What he did not know was that a combined allied army was marching south and that De Grasse had promised to hasten the movement by sending vessels to the head of the bay to transport troops. The chance that the earl might attempt to overcome La Fayette had to be accepted. A final question had to do with De Barras, who had left Newport on August 25 and promptly disappeared. The third consideration was the British fleet.

On September 2 Graves and Hood had been sighted off the coast steering south. Thomas McKean presumed they were headed for the Chesapeake and wrote Arthur Lee: "In all probability we shall soon hear of a Sea Engagement. We are at the Eve of great events. May God grant them to be prosperous to us, and that they may terminate in securing to us, peace, liberty, and safety."[9]

The British fleet, running before the wind, passed eighteen miles east of Cape Henry at 10 A.M. on September 5. A cruiser had sighted the French fleet half an hour earlier, a report verified at 11 A.M. when Graves, who had previously made the signal to clear for action, now signaled for line of battle ahead at "two cables length asunder" (1,440 feet). From the leading ship of the van to the last ship in the rear his fleet was stretched out over five miles of ocean. But with the favoring wind, Graves could close his formation quickly. He held the advantage of wind and position, and had sea room.

Tactically, De Grasse was at a great disadvantage. Not only was he lacking one hundred men from each ship, but he was at anchor and unprepared for battle. He had not taken the precaution to send several fast frigates north to scout, and when the enemy first appeared he judged the ships were those of his colleague De Barras. He was soon disillusioned, and made signals for the fleet to stand out of the bay when the ebb tide started to run.

One after another, the French ships made sail, cut cables, and maneuvered to clear Cape Henry and the dangerous shoals—"the Middle Ground"—only three miles to the north. The French could do no better than straggle out, but their captains were accomplished seamen and a degree of order was soon restored. Still, two hours after cutting cables a full two thirds of the French fleet was struggling to negotiate Cape Henry. A British naval historian has put the situation succinctly: "Graves was in a position almost beyond the wildest dreams of a sea-commander. His whole fleet was running down before the wind, and his enemy was before him, working slowly out of harbor. He had only to fall on their van with full force and the day was his." But Graves did not order close action, and the fleeting opportunity passed.

His official "Account of the proceedings of the fleet under the Command of Rear Admiral Graves in an action with the French fleet off Cape Henry on the 5th of September, 1781" indicates clearly that he was so completely absorbed in arranging his fleet in the perfect formation prescribed in "Fighting Instructions" that he had little time to devote to thinking of falling on the French van. Not until 3:46 P.M. did he make the signal for close action. Firing ceased at 6:30 when the Battle of the Capes became history. Hood's rear division never engaged.[10] Again the problem seemed to be signals both incorrectly displayed by Graves in flagship *London* and misinterpreted by his captains.

How did Hood, an energetic and aggressive admiral, see it? "The French," so he wrote Sandwich, "began to come out in line [of battle] ahead, but by no means regular and connected, which afforded the British fleet a most glorious opportunity for making a close attack to advantage, but it was not embraced."[11] And in his more detailed account, he wrote: "Yesterday the British fleet had a rich and most delightful harvest of glory presented to it, but omitted to gather it in more instances than one."[12] Graves had failed on September 5, "that truly unfortunate day," and in Hood's opinion made no effort in the days that followed to retrieve the situation. On September 9, with both fleets still off the capes, Hood urged Graves to get the British fleet into the bay. "It appeared to me," he wrote Sandwich, "of the utmost importance to keep the French out, and if they did get in, they should first beat us." When Graves summoned him to a Council of War held aboard *London*, he again stated his opinion "fully and clearly" that the fleet "should get into the Chesapeake to the succor of Lord Cornwallis, if possible."[13]

Neither fleet had suffered great damage. The English lost one of the line. The French lost none, though some were hulled repeatedly. Hood wrote there was nothing to be done but to return to New York, "much lamented as this alternative was." Had Rodney led the fleet to the coast of America, he, not Graves, would have been in command and the "5th of this month would have proved a most glorious day for England."

At the time, no one save Hood seemed to comprehend what this "partial engagement" (as Washington described the action of September 5) portended. But in strategic terms the French victory on that day was quite as decisive as it would have been had De Grasse sent half the British fleet to the bottom. The French admiral held to one objective before him: to deny Chesapeake Bay to the British, and so to prevent the succor of Cornwallis. He had succeeded.†

Washington spent two days at Head of Elk, where, having no officer competent to deal with the "great deficiency of transports," he wrote many letters "to Gentn of Influence on the Eastern Shore [of Maryland] beseeching them to exert themselves in drawing forth every kind of Vessel" which would answer for this purpose. "Nothing my Dear Sir!" he wrote Brigadier General Cadwalader, a man of considerable influence, "is of more importance at the present Moment toward fordwarg the Troops under my Command at this Place, than the Means of transportation on the Bay. And I may say to you, Sir! That our Views are so much dependent on the rapidity of our movements, that I wish to be helped forward with all the celerity that is possible."[14]

He dispatched a courier to Robert Morris urging him to send forward specie for one month's pay "on the Wings of speed," and in General Orders called upon "the gallant Officers" and "brave and faithful soldiers" he had the honor to command to "exert their utmost abilities in the

† Admiral de Barras had stayed well out of sight of land and had slipped into the bay undetected by either French or British. In addition to the heavy artillery and baggage, he brought with him 1,500 barrels of salt provisions.

cause of their Country." The soldiers were habituated to such exhortations, but not to having in their pockets a full month's pay in specie. The money they received at Head of Elk was probably the first "hard" most of them had ever seen.

Washington left Head of Elk on the morning of September 8 and arrived at the Fountain Inn in Baltimore that afternoon. He was physically in Baltimore, but his spirit was already at Mount Vernon. The general had left his plantation on the Potomac in the spring of 1775 and had not seen it since. Mount Vernon exercised a powerful emotional influence on this man so many of the contemporaries thought devoid of emotion. He arrived at his "seat" on September 9 and allowed himself three nights there. On one, he gave a splendid banquet for Rochambeau. Then he was off to Fredericksburg, and two days later was greeted in Williamsburg by La Fayette, whose troops were encamped near the College of William and Mary. The Marquis de Saint Simon welcomed him with twenty-one guns, and La Fayette with kisses.

The commander in chief had not been more than a short day in Williamsburg before he was again face to face with the perennial shortages of food and clothing. Flour was urgently needed; one third of the Virginia Line, "almost totally destitute of clothing," was unfit for service. Knox, ordinarily so provident, belatedly discovered that he was short of ammunition, which could be procured only by the Board of War. The problems that had afflicted Washington since the day he took command of the army at Cambridge were still with him. He brigaded the Continental Army and worked closely with Rochambeau on plans for the twelve-mile march to Yorktown, for deployment there, for investment of the British garrison across the York River at Gloucester, and for employment of the artillery.

Washington had no time now for ceremonies and banquets, and September 17 set off in *Queen Charlotte*, a fast sailing sloop the French had taken, to visit De Grasse on his three-decked flagship, *Ville de Paris*. The run to Lynnhaven was delightful. The party, which included Rochambeau, Chastellux, Knox, Jonathan Trumbull, Jr., and Colonel Tench Tilghman, arrived at noon, boarded the great ship, and received honors. The visitors were escorted to the admiral's cabin, where the allied commanders got to business.

The principal point to be settled was how long De Grasse could stay in the bay. After some discussion, the admiral agreed to stay until the first day of November, but expressed his desire to leave on October 15 if operations progressed satisfactorily. He explained that he had irrevocable commitments to the Spaniards in the West Indies and would have to embark Saint Simon's three regiments before he sailed. He agreed to expedite movement of troops waiting for transport at Head of Elk and

Baltimore, but his fleet would not be available to support operations against Charleston or Savannah.

This was not a bad bargain, and at sunset, after an elegant collation, Washington's party embarked in *Queen Charlotte*. The downward voyage had been one of four or five pleasant hours, but the trip back against contrary winds required four days. The party, exhausted by ceaseless buffeting and drenched with salt water, arrived at Williamsburg in late afternoon of September 22.

Washington had scarcely time to change clothes and have a late dinner before he turned to a stack of mail accumulated during his absence. The most important item, a letter that demanded immediate attention, reported Rear Admiral Digby's arrival in New York with eleven of the line. He forwarded this to Count de Grasse immediately. The following day he received a letter from the admiral which caused him the most "painful anxiety," for the course of action the admiral proposed to adopt would infallibly place the entire operation in grave jeopardy.

In his lengthy communication, De Grasse stated that Digby's arrival had altered the situation and he felt he must take most of his fleet outside the capes to cruise in the offing, where he would have sea room and could intercept the British should they make another attempt to relieve Cornwallis. He added that once at sea he could not be certain he could re-enter the bay. He closed with a real bombshell. He thought he might "set out for New York," where he could possibly "do more for the common cause, than by remaining here, an idle spectator," and requested Washington to discuss the proposals with Rochambeau and to favor him with their opinions.[15]

The French admiral had lost sight of his mission. For should his fleet be blown out to sea, suffer damage to masts, sails, and rigging, and perhaps be dispersed by violent winds and heavy weather, the British might slip in, destroy the few ships the admiral proposed to leave to cover the mouths of the York and the James, relieve Cornwallis, who might then attack the allied army. His foolhardy suggestions, if adopted, could wreck everything.

Washington and Rochambeau consulted and drew up a letter expressing their decided objections. They urged "perseverance in the plan already agreed upon" and assured De Grasse that "the enterprise against York, under the protection of your Ships, is as certain as any military operation can be rendered by a decisive superiority of Strength and means that is in fact reducible to calculation and that the surrender of the British garrison must necessarily go a great way toward terminating the war, and securing the invaluable objects of it to the Allies." The allied commanders provided an analysis of the various possibilities which abandonment of the mission might produce and again urged De Grasse not to allow himself to be diverted, but to persevere.[16]

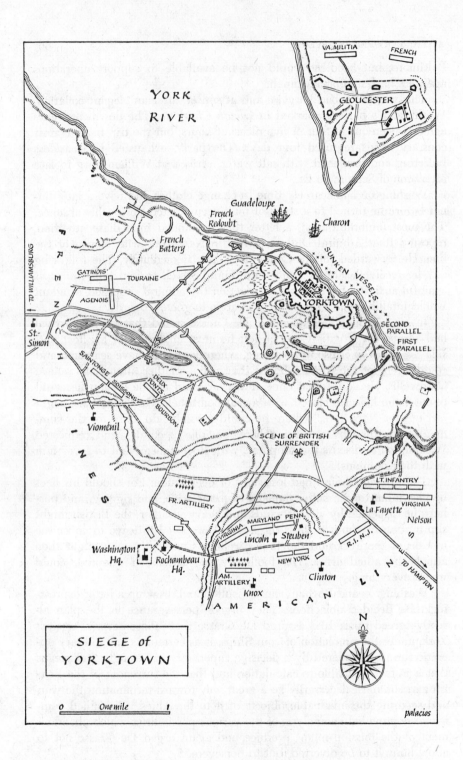

YORK
RIVER

VA. MILITIA   FRENCH

GLOUCESTER

Guadeloupe

French
Redoubt   Charon

French
Battery   SUNKEN VESSELS

GATINOIS   TOURAINE

AGENOIS   YORKTOWN

St-
Simon   SECOND
                                     PARALLEL
                                     FIRST
SAINTONGE   PARALLEL
SOISSONS
DEUX
PONTS
BOURBON

Vioménil

SCENE OF BRITISH
SURRENDER

LT. INFANTRY

FR. ARTILLERY   VIRGINIA
                                        La Fayette
                            VIRGINIA   Nelson
                    MARYLAND PENN
                    Lincoln Steuben
Washington   R.I. N.J.
Hq.   Rochambeau   TO HAMPTON
         Hq.   NEW YORK
                  AM.   Clinton
                  ARTILLERY
                    Knox
            A M E R I C A N   L I N

TO WILLIAMSBURG

F
R
E
Z
H
L
I
N
E
S

N

SIEGE of
YORKTOWN

0   One mile   1

palacios

This letter, signed by Washington, was entrusted to La Fayette, who hastened to the flagship, to discover that De Grasse had summoned a Council of War, and after due deliberation had taken the decision to remain. In a letter the marquis carried back to Williamsburg, De Grasse stated that the plans he had suggested, "while the most brilliant and glorious," did not "appear to fulfill the aims we had in view." Possibly a late confirmed report that Digby had brought only three of the line to New York brought him to reconsider. Washington and Rochambeau, relieved of anxiety, could pick up their planning at the point the admiral's letter had interrupted it.

Now everything moved rapidly. By September 27 all the troops had arrived at Williamsburg and encamped, and shortly after dawn on the twenty-eighth "having with some difficulty obtained horses and Waggons sufficient to move our field artillery, Intrenching Tools, and such other articles as were indespensably necessary, we commenced our March for the Investiture of the Enemy at York."‡[17]

In late afternoon, troops marched to the ground assigned them, Americans on the right, French on the left, "about Cannon shot" from the enemy's outer works. The line was the shape of a rough crescent with the left horn resting on the York River and the right on a branch of Wormeley's Creek, which flowed into the York. "The line being formed, all the Troops, Officers and Men, lay upon their arms during the night."

The day after the Battle of Cape Henry, Sir Henry Clinton wrote Cornwallis that he was planning to come to Virginia "as soon as possible with all the force that can be spared from hence, which is about 4000 men. They are already embarked and will proceed the instant I receive information from the Admiral that we may venture. . . ." The sloop carrying this message eluded French cruisers stationed at the entrance to the bay and at the mouth of York River.

Cornwallis replied on September 16. He was able to inform Sir Henry that Washington had arrived at La Fayette's headquarters two days previously, that several ships of the line, frigates, and transports were at Head of Elk and Baltimore, and that frigates lay off the mouth of the York. He could attack, he wrote, but as he expected relief he did not think himself justified "in putting the fate of the war on so desperate an attempt." He said he had provisions for six weeks, and closed with: "I am of opinion that you can do me no effectual service but by coming directly to this place." On the following morning he wrote a postscript: "I am just informed that since the Rhode Island squadron had joined, they have thirty-six sail of the line. This place is in no state of defense. If you cannot relieve me very soon, you must be prepared to hear the worst."[18]

‡ At the same time, the troops designated to invest the British garrison at Gloucester moved to their positions.

In the meantime, Clinton had heard from Graves. The admiral reported "a pretty sharp brush" with the French van and "part of their center." He described the enemy force as so overpowering that they were "absolute masters" of the bay. "Things," he said, were in a "ticklish state." He promised co-operation, "for we must either stand or fall together." Clinton's response to this bad news was to call another Council of War. Indeed, until the fleet returned to New York he could do nothing. At this conference, he asked his general officers whether he should attempt to reinforce Cornwallis or await "more favorable accounts" from Graves. Rear Admiral Digby was expected at any hour. His arrival would afford "a more certain prospect of success." Cornwallis was amply supplied and could hold out for thirty days. The council resolved unanimously that prudence dictated delaying action until Graves returned and Digby arrived.

Clinton received the earl's letter of September 16 with its postscript written the following day a week later, and immediately summoned a Council of War for the next morning. At this meeting, attended by all general and flag officers, the decision was taken to make every effort to relieve Cornwallis. Rear Admiral Digby had just arrived with three of the line to assume command in North American waters. The British fleet now consisted of twenty-six sail of the line, scarcely a match for the thirty-six commanded by De Grasse. But the situation was critical. The five general officers voted unanimously that the risk must be accepted. Certainly one, and possibly two, of the flag officers did not concur, but the decision had been taken, and Clinton wrote: "There is every reason to hope we start from hence the 5th October." When Cornwallis received this letter, he reported to Clinton that he had "ventured these last two days to look General Washington's whole force in the face." He was planning to withdraw from his outer works, and had "no doubt" that if relief came within "any reasonable time," the British would still be in firm possession of York and Gloucester.[19]

Washington and Rochambeau devoted September 28 to reconnaissance, adjusting their positions, and conferring. Nothing serious could be attempted until the heavy siege artillery and mortars brought from Newport by De Barras could be put ashore, moved from the banks of the James, and emplaced. And artillery could inflict no extensive damage on the British before their outer works were reduced. Washington had under command troops ample for the purpose: 8,000 French, about 5,000 Continentals, ill-disciplined and poorly equipped and 1,000 militia, and thus enjoyed the superiority of two to one deemed necessary for the successful conduct of an orthodox siege operation. The outer works were not impressive; nor did Cornwallis have the man power to defend them. Washington awakened on the morning of the last day of September to hear the pleasing news that during the night Cornwallis had evacuated his outer lines.

The first five days of October were spent in positioning the artillery and preparing fascines and gabions essential in siege operations. During the night of October 5/6, American and French fatigue parties, working as quietly as possible, began opening trenches. Washington was pleased with the progress, and on October 6 wrote in his diary: "Before Morning the Trenches were in such forewardness as to cover the men from the enemys fire. The work was executed with so much secrecy and dispatch that the enemy were, I believe, totally ignorant of our labor till the light of the Morning discovered it to them. Our loss . . . was extremely inconsiderable. . . ."[20]

The classic pattern was beginning to take shape under the watchful supervision of French experts, Du Portail, and Baron von Steuben. The three succeeding days were devoted to opening parallels. Finally, at "3 o'clock P.M." on October 9, French artillery opened. Two hours later an American battery of six 18- and 24-pounders and another of four mortars and two howitzers were in position. "His Excellency General Washington put the match to the first gun, and a furious discharge of cannon and mortars immediately followed, and Earl Cornwallis has received his first salutation."[21]

New batteries were put in position each day, and from the tenth through the fifteenth of October French and American batteries kept up "a tremendous and incessant" bombardment of the British positions. Hot shot was thrown into the town and directed at a British frigate (Charon) and three transports. All burned to the water's edge. Dr. Thacher enjoyed "a fine view of this splendid conflagration . . . all around was thunder and lightning from our numerous cannon and mortars, and in the darkness of night, presented one of the most sublime and magnificent spectacles which can be imagined."[22]

During darkness, and covered by heavy fire from the artillery, working parties pushed forward a zigzag trench to within three hundred yards of the British left, where two strong redoubts barred the way to an assault on that flank of the enemy's final battle position. At the end of this communication trench an epaulement, a Y-shaped "shoulder" (or embankment), was constructed to protect the assembly of two storming parties. At the same time, other working parties constructed redoubts for cannon and guns were moved forward. Washington could not account for the earl's behavior, and on October 12 wrote the governor of Maryland, Thomas Sim Lee, "We last night advanced our second parallel within 300 yards of the Enemy's Works, without the least annoyance from them. Lord Cornwallis' conduct has hitherto been passive beyond conception; he either has not the means of defence, or he intends to reserve himself until we approach very near him. A few days must determine whether he will or will not give us much trouble."[23]

At dusk on October 14 the storming parties moved forward. The Americans, to assault the right redoubt (as seen from the American lines), were led by Colonel Alexander Hamilton[**]; the French by Major General Baron de Vioménil. After brief but heavy fighting at close quarters, both redoubts were taken with relatively few casualties.[††] Washington described the attack as "emulous and praiseworthy. Few cases have exhibited stronger proofs of Intrepidity, coolness and firmness than are shown upon this occasion." On the night of October 16 the British made an ineffectual sortie, spiked a few guns, and withdrew.

At ten the next morning a Redcoat drummer, accompanied by an officer with a white flag, appeared on the British parapet. All firing ceased. The drummer beat a parley. Cornwallis proposed a cessation of hostilities for twenty-four hours. Washington replied:

> Camp before York, October 17, 1781
> My Lord: I have had the Honor of receiving Your Lordship's Letter of this Date.
> An Ardent Desire to spare the further Effusion of Blood, will readily incline me to listen to such Terms for the Surrender of your Posts and Garrisons of York and Gloucester, as are admissible.
> I wish previously to the Meeting of Commissioners, that your Lordship's proposals in writing, may be sent to the American lines: for which Purpose, a Suspension of Hostilities during two Hours from the Delivery of this Letter will be granted. I have the Honor etc. [24]

Cornwallis replied within the stated time. His proposals for surrender of the garrisons of York and Gloucester were for the most part approved and on the following morning, Washington sent this letter:

To CHARLES, EARL CORNWALLIS

> Head Quarters before York, October 18, 1781.
> My Lord: To avoid unnecessary Discussions and Delays, I shall at Once, in Answer to your Lordships Letter of Yesterday, declare the general Bases upon which a Definitive Treaty and Capitulation must take place. The Garrisons of York and Gloucester, including the Seamen, as you propose, will be received Prisoners of War. The Condition annexed, of sending the British and German Troops to the parts of Europe to which they respectively be-

---

[**] La Fayette in nominal command. Hamilton led the assault.

[††] Washington's diary gives casualty figures "from the Investiture to the assault of the Redoubts Inclusive" as 88 Americans and 186 French.

long, is inadmissible. Instead of this, they will be marched to such parts of the Country as can most conveniently provide for their Subsistence; and the Benevolent Treatment of Prisoners, which is invariably observed by the Americans, will be extended to them. The same Honors will be granted to the Surrendering Army as were granted to the Garrison of Charles Town. The Shipping and Boats in the two Harbours with all their Guns, Stores, Tackling, Furniture and Apparel, shall be delivered in their present State to an Officer of the Navy, appointed to take possession of them.

The Artillery, Arms, Accoutrements, Military Chest and Public Stores of every Denomination, shall be delivered unimpaired to the Heads of Departments, to which they respectively belong.

The Officers will be indulged in retaining their Side Arms, and the Officers and Soldiers may preserve their Baggage and Effects, with this Reserve, that Property taken in the Country will be reclaimed.

With Regard to the Individuals in civil Capacities, whose Interests Your Lordship wishes may be attended to, until they are more particularly described, nothing definitive can be settled.

I have to add, that I expect the Sick and Wounded will be supplied with their own Hospital Stores, and be attended by British Surgeons, particularly charged with the Care of them.

Your Lordship will be pleased to signify your Determination either to accept or reject the Proposals now offered, in the Course of Two Hours from the Delivery of this Letter, that Commissioners may be appointed to digest the Articles of Capitulation, or a Renewal of Hostilities may take place. I have the Honor etc.[25]

Cornwallis acceded to the terms; the appointed commissioners met; details of the surrender and the ceremony were discussed and settled. British and German troops would march out of Yorktown at 2 P.M. on October 19 with colors cased, arms shouldered, and bands playing a slow march.

At 1 P.M. French and American troops took position on both sides of the road. Washington with his staff, Lincoln, Knox, Von Steuben, La Fayette, Du Portail; then Rochambeau with his staff, Baron de Vioménil, Chastellux, Saint Simon, and De Barras (who represented De Grasse), rode slowly to the head of the lines of silent troops, halted, turned their horses, and waited.

In a few moments they heard the sound of distant drums beating "a slow and solemn step." The drumming stopped. A British band picked up the tempo with a "melancholy" air.

At the head of the column rode not the noble earl for whom the thousands were anxiously waiting, but his deputy, Brigadier General Charles O'Hara, the handsome fighting Irish general who had commanded the Guards Brigade in the Carolinas and was representing his "indisposed" commander in chief. He approached Rochambeau and reined in. The French general nodded toward Washington. Washington, always courteous, indicated that Major General Benjamin Lincoln, who had surrendered to Clinton at Charleston, should receive the sword. O'Hara bared his head and tendered the earl's sword. Lincoln accepted it and returned it. O'Hara wheeled his horse and rode with his staff slowly back toward Yorktown. The British and German troops laid down their arms.

Six and a half years earlier, several hundred Redcoats had marched confidently from Boston to disperse rebels at Lexington. From the field at Yorktown 7,000 would march to prisoner-of-war camps.

Six weeks later, Horace Walpole wrote Sir Horace Mann: "Long ago I told you, that you and I might not live to see an end of the American war—It is very near its end indeed now—its consequences are far from a conclusion. In some respects they are commencing a new date which will reach far beyond *us*."[26]

NOTES

BOOK I

Chapter 1

1. Waldegrave, James, Second Earl, *Memoirs from 1754 to 1758*, pp. 7–9.
2. John Carswell and Lewis Arnold Dralle, eds., *The Political Journal of George Bubb Dodington*, p. 244.
3. Waldegrave, p. 63.
4. Ibid., p. 16.
5. Carswell and Dralle, p. 244.
6. L. H. Butterfield et al., eds., *Diary and Autobiography of John Adams*, Vol. I, p. 201.
7. Edmund Burke, *Works*, 4th ed., Vol. I, p. 450.
8. L. H. Butterfield, Vol. I, pp. 168–69.

Chapter 2

1. L. H. Butterfield, Vol. III, p. 275.
2. Ibid., p. 276.
3. *The North Briton*, No. 1, Saturday, June 5, 1762. Collections, American Antiquarian Society, Worcester, Mass.
4. Ibid., No. 45, Saturday, April 23, 1763.

Chapter 3

1. Albert Henry Smyth, *The Writings of Benjamin Franklin*, Vol. IV, pp. 71–72.
2. Ibid., pp. 212–13.
3. The Honourable Sir John Fortescue, ed., *The Correspondence of King George the Third from 1760–1783*, Vol. I, p. 168.

4. Bonamy Dobrée, ed., *The Letters of Philip Dormer Stanhope, 4th Earl of Chesterfield*, Vol. VI, p. 2696.
5. Ibid., pp. 2712–14.
6. *The Examination of Doctor Benjamin Franklin before an August Assembly relating to the Repeal of the Stamp Act . . .* , Rare Book Room, Bowdoin College.

Chapter 4

1. Dobrée, *Chesterfield*, Vol. VI, p. 2752.
2. *Annual Register*, 1769, pp. 64–65.
3. Fortescue, *Correspondence*, Vol. I, p. 480.
4. This and following quotations from Dickinson's *Letters* are as published in the Boston *Gazette*. Collections, American Antiquarian Society, Worcester, Mass.
5. Mercy Otis Warren, *History of the Rise, Progress and Termination of the American Revolution*, Vol. I, p. 65.
6. Clarence E. Carter, *The Correspondence of General Thomas Gage*, Vol. I, p. 197.
7. Ibid., p. 205.
8. Ibid., p. 206.
9. W. S. Lewis, ed., *Horace Walpole's Correspondence with Sir Horace Mann*, Vol. VII, p. 86.
10. Ibid., p. 106.
11. Junius, *Letters*, p. 11.
12. Ibid., p. 176.
13. L. H. Butterfield, pp. 349–50.

Chapter 5

1. Carter, Vol I, pp. 248–51.
2. L. H. Butterfield, Vol. III, p. 292.
3. Harry Alonzo Cushing, ed., *The Writings of Samuel Adams*, Vol. II, p. 321.
4. L. H. Butterfield, Vol. II, pp. 58–59.
5. Ibid., p. 59.
6. Cushing, Vol. II, pp. 339–42, 346–48.
7. Ibid., pp. 348–74.
8. Ibid., Vol III, pp. 1–2.
9. Lawrence Shaw Mayo, ed., *The History of the Colony and Province of Massachusetts Bay*, by Thomas Hutchinson, Vol. III, pp. 282–83.
10. Cushing, Vol. II, pp. 428–30.
11. Cushing, Vol. III, pp. 20–21.
12. Ibid., pp. 25–28.
13. Ibid., p. 41.
14. Ibid., p. 44.
15. Ibid., p. 48.

16. Smyth, Vol. VI, p. 57.
17. Cushing, Vol. II, pp. 67–69.
18. Ibid., p. 70.
19. Arlene Kleeb, *The Boston Tea Party, Catalyst for Revolution*, p. 10.
20. Ibid., p. 28.
21. L. H. Butterfield, Vol. II, pp. 85–86.

BOOK II

Chapter 1

1. William Temple Franklin, *Memoirs of the Life and Writings of Benjamin Franklin*, App. 7.
2. Ibid.
3. W. Bodham Donne, ed., *The Correspondence of King George the Third with Lord North from 1768 to 1783*, Vol. I.
4. Ibid., Letter 209 and note.
5. Peter Force, *American Archives*, Fourth Series, Vol. I, p. 32.
6. *Annual Register*, 1774, p. 99.
7. Ibid., p. 60.
8. Ibid., pp. 61, 63.
9. Force, Fourth Series, Vol. I, p. 38.
10. Ibid., pp. 35–50.
11. Ibid., pp. 51–56.
12. Ibid., pp. 81–82.
13. Ibid., pp. 83–90.
14. Ibid., p. 114.
15. Ibid., pp. 111–18.
16. A. Francis Steuart, ed., *The Last Journals of Horace Walpole During the Reign of King George III*, Vol. I, p. 369.
17. Force, Fourth Series, Vol. I, pp. 167–70.
18. J. Rogers Hollingsworth and Bell I. Wiley, eds., *American Democracy: A Documentary Record*, Vol. I, p. 86.
19. Cushing, Vol. III, p. 88.
20. Ibid., p. 93.
21. Ibid., pp. 107–8.
22. Sir N. William Wraxall, *Historical Memoirs of My Own Time*, Vol. I, pp. 113–14.
23. Henri Doniol, *Histoire de la Participation de la France . . .* , Vol. I, p. 27.

Chapter 2

1. Merrill Jensen, ed., *English Historical Documents*, Vol. IX, pp. 785–89.
2. Force, Fourth Series, Vol. I, pp. 332–33.

3. Carter, Vol. I, p. 355.
4. Royal R. Hinman, *A Historical Collection . . .* , p. 162.
5. Jensen, Vol. IX, pp. 860–63.
6. Aubrey C. Land, ed., *Letters from America by William Eddis*, pp. 87–88.
7. Julian P. Boyd, ed., *The Papers of Thomas Jefferson*, Vol. I, pp. 105–7.
8. Ibid., pp. 107–9.
9. Worthington Chauncey Ford, ed., *Journals of the Continental Congress*, Vol. I, pp. 15–16.
10. Captain William C. Evelyn, *Memoirs and Letters from North America*, p. 27.
11. Ibid., p. 29.
12. Carter, Vol. I, pp. 367–68.
13. Force, Fourth Series, Vol. I, pp. 289–95.
14. Ibid., p. 336.
15. Cushing, Vol. III, p. 128.
16. Force, Fourth Series, Vol. I, pp. 489–92.
17. Cushing, Vol. III, p. 149.
18. John C. Fitzpatrick, *The Writings of George Washington*, Vol. III, pp. 227–34.
19. Force, Fourth Series, Vol. I, pp. 598–602.
20. Ibid.

Chapter 3

1. Donne, Vol. I, Letter 240.
2. Peter Orlando Hutchinson, ed., *The Diary and Letters of His Excellency Thomas Hutchinson, Esq.*, pp. 159–78.
3. Donne, Vol. I, Letter 246.
4. Franklin, pp. 225–26.
5. Steuart, Vol. I, p. 396.
6. Ibid., p. 398.
7. W. S. Lewis, *Correspondence with Mann*, Vol. VIII, p. 67.
8. Steuart, Vol. I, p. 431.
9. Franklin, pp. 220–21.
10. James Truslow Adams, *Revolutionary New England, 1691–1776*, p. 406.
11. Edmund C. Burnett, ed., *Letters of the Members of the Continental Congress*, Vol. I, Letter 1.
12. Ibid., Letter 5.
13. Ibid., Letter 30.
14. L. H. Butterfield, Vol. II, pp. 117–21.
15. Force, Fourth Series, Vol. 1, pp. 900–4.
16. Ibid.
17. Burnett, Vol. I, Letter 74.
18. Ibid., Letter 85.
19. Charles Francis Adams, ed., *Letters of Mrs. Adams*, Vol. I, pp. 25–29.
20. Force, Fourth Series, Vol. I, pp. 935–38.
21. Carter, Vol. I, p. 374.

22. Ibid.
23. Ibid., p. 380.
24. Ibid., Vol. II, p. 656.
25. Evelyn, p. 34.
26. Ibid., p. 43.
27. Ibid., p. 35.
28. Carter, Vol. II, pp. 658–59.
29. Fortescue, *Correspondence*, Vol. III, Letters 1556, 1557, 1563.
30. Force, Fourth Series, Vol. I, pp. 461–67.
31. Carter, Vol. II, p. 79.
32. *Remembrancer, or Impartial Repository of Public Events*, Vol. I, pp. 9–10.

Chapter 4

1. Carter, Vol. I, p. 390.
2. Evelyn, p. 56.
3. Ibid., p. 47.
4. Force, Fourth Series, Vol. I, pp. 1323–43.
5. Evelyn, pp. 50–51.
6. *Remembrancer*, Vol I, p. 11.
7. Allen French, "General Haldimand in Boston 1774–1775," *Massachusetts Historical Society Proceedings*, Vol. LXVI.
8. Force, Fourth Series, Vol. I, p. 1344.
9. Franklin, p. 249.
10. Force, Fourth Series, Vol. I, pp. 1489–1504.
11. Franklin, p. 257.
12. Peter Orlando Hutchinson, pp. 363–64.
13. Franklin, p. 249.
14. Force, Fourth Series, Vol. I, pp. 1503–4.
15. Ibid., pp. 1503–14.
16. Ibid., p. 1502.
17. Donne, Vol. I, Letter 270.
18. Wraxall, Vol. II, p. 131.
19. Force, Fourth Series, Vol. I, p. 1681.
20. *Remembrancer*, Vol. I, p. 31.

Chapter 5

1. G. R. Barnes and J. H. Owen, eds., *The Private Papers of John, Earl of Sandwich*, Vol. I, p. 57.
2. Ibid., p. 59.
3. Frank Moore, ed., *Diary of the American Revolution from Newspapers and Original Documents*, Vol. I, p. 14.
4. Ibid., pp. 7–9.
5. Allen French, ed., *Diary of Frederick Mackenzie*, Vol. I, p. 10.

6. Barnes and Owen, Vol. I, p. 61.

7. Ibid., p. 63.

8. Carter, Vol. II, pp. 179–83.

9. Donne, Vol. I, Letter 279.

10. Ibid., Letter 283.

11. Edmund Burke, *Speeches and Letters on American Affairs*, p. 88.

12. Ibid., p. 141.

13. Force, Fourth Series, Vol. I, pp. 1781–94.

14. W. S. Lewis, *Correspondence with Mann*, Vol. VIII, pp. 85–86.

15. William Wirt, *Sketch of the Life and Character of Patrick Henry*, pp. 121–23.

16. Public Record Office, State Papers Domestic, 37/11.

17. French, *Mackenzie*, pp. 55–56.

18. Ibid., p. 71.

19. Carter, Vol. I, pp. 396–97.

20. Ibid., Vol. II, pp. 673–74.

21. French, *Mackenzie*, p. 74.

22. Elizabeth Merritt, "The Lexington Alarm," *Maryland Historical Magazine*, Vol. XLI.

23. *Remembrancer*, Vol. I, p. 33.

24. Steuart, Vol. I, p. 491.

25. Ibid.

BOOK III

Chapter 1

1. Donne, Vol. I, Letter 290.

2. Carter, Vol. II, p. 684.

3. Public Record Office, State Papers Domestic, 37/11.

4. Ibid.

5. Burnett, Vol. I, Letter 161.

6. Fitzpatrick, *Writings of George Washington*, Vol. III, pp. 293–97.

7. Burnett, Vol. I, Letter 181.

8. W. S. Lewis, *Correspondence with Mann*, Vol. VIII, pp. 128–29.

9. Henry Steele Commager and Richard B. Morris, *The Spirit of 'Seventy-six*, Vol. I, p. 134.

10. Fortescue, *Correspondence*, Vol. III, pp. 220–24.

11. Edward Barrington de Fonblanque, *Political and Military Episodes in the Latter Half of the Eighteenth Century*, p. 147.

12. Fortescue, *Correspondence*, Vol. III, pp. 224–27.

13. Carter, Vol. I, p. 407.

14. Ibid., Vol. II, p. 686.
15. Ibid., Vol. I, p. 408.
16. W. S. Lewis, *Correspondence with Mann*, Vol. VIII, pp. 119–20.
17. Moore, Vol. I, p. 102.
18. Fitzpatrick, *Writings of George Washington*, Vol. III, pp. 329–31.
19. Ibid., pp. 371, 374.
20. Ibid., p. 423.
21. Ibid., p. 452.
22. Burnett, Vol. I, Letter 167.
23. Fitzpatrick, *Writings of George Washington*, Vol. III, pp. 359–60.

Chapter 2

1. Carter, Vol. I, p. 408.
2. Evelyn, pp. 63–64.
3. Ibid., p. 64.
4. Ibid., p. 65.
5. Carter, Vol. I, pp. 408–9.
6. Land, pp. 113–15.
7. Burnett, Vol. I, Letter 206.
8. Boyd, Vol. I, p. 217.
9. David C. Douglas, ed., *English Historical Documents*, Vol. IX, pp. 847–50.
10. Burnett, Vol. I, Letter 212.
11. Ibid., Letter 242.
12. Fitzpatrick, *Writings of George Washington*, Vol. III, p. 395.
13. Ibid., p. 440.
14. Ibid., p. 454.
15. Ibid., p. 512.
16. Ibid., p. 438.
17. Carter, Vol. I, pp. 413–14.
18. De Fonblanque, pp. 181, 195.
19. Fortescue, *Correspondence*, Vol. III, Letter 1693.
20. Barnes and Owen, Vol. I, pp. 72–73.
21. Fortescue, *Correspondence*, Vol. III, Letter 1683.
22. Lord Mahon, *History of England from the Peace of Utrecht to the Peace of Versailles*, Vol. VI, p. 102.
23. Fortescue, *Correspondence*, Vol. III, Letter 1697.
24. Jensen, pp. 850–51.
25. William Bell Clark and William James Morgan, eds., *Naval Documents of the American Revolution*, Vol. II, pp. 670–71.
26. *Annual Register*, 1775, p. 13.
27. Fortescue, *Correspondence*, Vol. III, Letter 1687.
28. W. S. Lewis, *Correspondence with Mann*, Vol. VIII, p. 129.

Chapter 3

1. Benjamin F. Stevens, ed., *General Sir William Howe's Orderly Book at Charlestown, Boston and Halifax June 17, 1775 to 1776, 26 May.*
2. Douglas, Vol. IX, pp. 851–52.
3. *Annual Register*, 1776, pp. 55–57.
4. Ibid., pp. 66–68.
5. Steuart, Vol. II, p. 3.
6. Alan Valentine, *Lord George Germain*, p. 45.
7. Donne, Vol. I, Letter 312.
8. Ibid., Letters 316, 317.
9. Barnes and Owen, Vol. I, p. 75.
10. Eric Robson, ed., *Letters from America, 1775 to 1780*, p. 17.
11. Ibid., p. 19.
12. Donne, Vol. I, Letter 322.

Chapter 4

1. Burnett, Vol. I, Letter 328.
2. Ibid., Letter 327.
3. *Annual Register*, 1776, pp. 2–3.
4. Ibid.
5. Fitzpatrick, *Writings of George Washington*, Vol. III, p. 492.
6. Justin H. Smith, *Arnold's March from Cambridge to Quebec. Together with a Reprint of Arnold's Journal*, pp. 74–78.
7. Ibid., p. 104.
8. Ibid., *Arnold's Journal*, p. 468.
9. William Willis, ed., *Collections*, Maine Historical Society, 1st Series, Vol. I, p. 469.
10. Ibid., pp. 471–72.
11. Ibid., pp. 476–77.
12. Barnes and Owen, Vol. I, pp. 83–84.
13. Willis, Vol. I, pp. 487–89, 494.
14. Ibid., p. 498.

Chapter 5

1. De Fonblanque, p. 208.
2. Ibid., p. 209.
3. Stevens, *Orderly Book*, pp. 304–5.
4. Barnes and Owen, Vol. I, pp. 82 ff.
5. Ibid., p. 86.
6. Benjamin F. Stevens, *B. F. Stevens's Facsimiles of Manuscripts in European Archives Relating to America*, No. 1310 of December 26, 1775.
7. Doniol, Vol. I, pp. 240–49.
8. Steuart, Vol. II, pp. 1–2.
9. Ibid., pp. 3–4.

10. Ibid., p. 2.
11. Fitzpatrick, *Writings of George Washington,* Vol. IV, p. 194.
12. Ibid., p. 208.
13. Ibid., p. 221, note 8.
14. Ibid., p. 241.
15. Ibid., p. 222.
16. Ibid., p. 195, note 87.
17. Burnett, Vol. I, Letters 532, 534, 535.
18. Force, Fourth Series, Vol. 1, pp. 59–63.
19. Major General William Heath, *Memoirs of General Heath During the American War,* pp. 32–33.
20. Ibid., p. 36.

BOOK IV

Chapter 1

1. Fitzpatrick, *Writings of George Washington,* Vol. IV, p. 207.
2. Ibid., pp. 409–10.
3. Ibid., p. 404.
4. Ibid., pp. 424, 430–31.
5. Ibid., pp. 454–55.
6. Donne, Vol. II, Letter 346 and note.
7. Stevens, *Facsimiles,* Vol. XIII, No. 1328 of April 26, 1776.
8. Ibid.
9. Silas Deane, *Papers,* Vol. I, pp. 100–15.
10. Stevens, *Facsimiles,* Vol. XIII, Nos. 1315, 1316 of March 12, 1776.
11. W. S. Lewis, *Correspondence with Mann,* Vol. VIII, p. 185.
12. Barnes and Owen, Vol. I, pp. 209–11.
13. James Phinney Baxter, ed., *The British Invasion from the North,* p. 119.
14. Ibid.
15. Fitzpatrick, *Writings of George Washington,* Vol. V, p. 79.
16. Burnett, Vol. I, Letter 718.
17. Commager and Morris, Vol. I, p. 221.
18. *Annual Register,* 1776, p. 12.
19. Robson, *Letters from America, 1775–1780,* p. 23.
20. Ibid., p. 29.
21. Barnes and Owen, Vol. I, p. 44.
22. C. H. Firth, *Naval Songs and Ballads,* pp. 246–47.

Chapter 2

1. Burnett, Vol. I, Letter 660.
2. Ibid., Letter 681.

3. Sir George O. Trevelyan, *The American Revolution*, Vol. I, p. 49.
4. Burnett, Vol. I, Letter 632.
5. Boyd, Vol. I, p. 309.
6. Burnett, Vol. I, Letter 690.
7. Ibid., Letter 706.
8. Ibid., Letter 750.
9. Ibid., Letter 751.
10. Ibid., Letter 755.
11. Ibid., note 1.
12. Paul L. Ford, ed., *The Works of Thomas Jefferson*, Vol. XII, p. 409.
13. Burnett, Vol. II, Letter 3.
14. Ibid., Letter 4.
15. Ibid., Letter 12.
16. Ibid., Letter 17.
17. Edward H. Tatum, Jr., ed., *The American Journal of Ambrose Serle*, pp. 30–31.
18. Ibid.
19. Ibid., p. 33.

Chapter 3

1. Fitzpatrick, *Writings of George Washington*, Vol. V, pp. 19–20.
2. Tatum, pp. 73–74.
3. Force, Fifth Series, pp. 1259–60.
4. Commager and Morris, Vol. I, p. 445.
5. Tatum, p. 84.
6. Ibid., pp. 86–87.
7. The Honourable Sir John Fortescue, *A History of the British Army*, Vol. VIII, p. 185.
8. Force, Fifth Series, pp. 182–83.
9. French, *Mackenzie*, Vol. I, Pt. II, p. 37.
10. Burnett, Vol. II, Letter 97.
11. Ibid., Letter 107.
12. Ibid., p. 69n.
13. Franklin, pp. 296–99.
14. Fitzpatrick, *Writings of George Washington*, Vol. VI, p. 28.
15. Steuart, Vol. II, p. 57.
16. Commager and Morris, Vol. I, p. 467.
17. Fitzpatrick, *Writings of George Washington*, Vol. VI, p. 58.
18. Ibid., pp. 106–16.
19. Burnett, Vol. II, p. 61.
20. Ibid., pp. 98–100.
21. Ibid., p. 102.
22. Thomas Jones, *History of New York during the Revolutionary War*, Vol. I, p. 136.
23. Ibid., p. 140.

Chapter 4

1. Steuart, Vol. II, p. 69.
2. Ibid., p. 80.
3. Ibid., p. 73.
4. Barnes and Owen, Vol. I, p. 184.
5. Fitzpatrick, *Writings of George Washington*, Vol. V, p. 89.
6. Barnes and Owen, Vol. I, pp. 185–91.
7. Ibid., p. 178.
8. French, *Mackenzie*, pp. 74–75.
9. Ibid., p. 89.
10. Ibid., pp. 64–68.
11. Fitzpatrick, *Writings of George Washington*, Vol. VI, p. 39.
12. Ibid., pp. 115–16.
13. Ibid., p. 138.
14. Ibid., pp. 244–45.
15. French, *Mackenzie*, p. 105.
16. Ibid., pp. 110–11.
17. Moore, Vol. I, pp. 262–63.
18. French, *Mackenzie*, p. 27.
19. Burnett, Vol. II, Letter 244.
20. Ibid., Letter 246.
21. Deane, Vol. I, pp. 324–25.
22. Ibid., pp. 338–39.
23. Ibid., p. 358.
24. Steuart, Vol. II, p. 89.
25. W. S. Lewis, *Correspondence with Mann*, Vol. VIII, p. 269, note 6.
26. Stevens, *Facsimiles*, Vol. III, No. 235.
27. W. S. Lewis and Warren Hunting Smith, eds., *Horace Walpole's Correspondence with Madame du Deffand*, Vol. IV, pp. 385–86.
28. Stevens, *Facsimiles*, Vol. VIII, Nos. 239, 241, of early 1777.

Chapter 5

1. Stevens, *Orderly Book*.
2. Sir William Howe, *Narrative*, p. 8.
3. Fitzpatrick, *Writings of George Washington*, Vol. VI, p. 426, note 68.
4. Ibid., pp. 441–44.
5. Ibid., pp. 467–71.
6. Moore, Vol. I, p. 367.
7. Tatum, pp. 163–67.
8. Ibid.
9. Howe, pp. 6–7.
10. Ibid., p. 6.
11. Moore, Vol. I, p. 357.
12. Howe, p. 9.
13. Fitzpatrick, *Writings of George Washington*, Vol. VI, pp. 461–62, note 26.
14. Ibid., pp. 460–61.

15. Ibid., Vol. VII, pp. 3–4.
16. Ibid., pp. 290–93.
17. Ibid., p. 44.
18. Burnett, Vol. II, Letter 332.
19. Ibid., Letter 340.
20. Ibid., Letter 344.
21. Ibid., Letter 365.
22. Fitzpatrick, *Writings of George Washington*, Vol. VII, pp. 221–24.
23. Ibid., p. 234.
24. Burnett, Vol. II, Letter 404.
25. Ibid., Letter 387.
26. Moore, Vol. I, pp. 400–1.
27. W. S. Lewis, *Correspondence with Mann*, Vol. VIII, p. 287.
28. Stevens, *Facsimiles*, Vol. VII, No. 149 of spring 1777.
29. Ibid., Vol. II, No. 154 of May 7, 1777.

BOOK V

Chapter 1

1. Fortescue, *Correspondence*, Vol. III, Letter 1938.
2. Ibid.
3. Howe, pp. 4–10.
4. John Burgoyne, *A State of the Expedition from Canada*, App. 3, pp. ii–vii.
5. Ibid.
6. Howe, p. 11.
7. Ibid., p. 12.
8. George Bancroft, *History of the American Revolution*, Vol. V, p. 147.
9. De Fonblanque, p. 229.
10. Fortescue, *History of the British Army*, Vol. III, p. 208.

Chapter 2

1. Thomas B. Furcron, "Mt. Independence 1776–1777," *Bulletin*, Fort Ticonderoga Museum, Vol. IX, No. 4, p. 232.
2. Eleanor M. Murray, "The Medical Department of the Revolution," *Bulletin*, Fort Ticonderoga Museum, Vol. VIII, No. 3, pp. 95–96.
3. Burgoyne, *State of the Expedition*, App. 5, p. xi.
4. De Fonblanque, p. 236.
5. William L. Stone, trans., *Letters and Journals relating to the War of the American Revolution by Mrs. General Riedesel*, p. 94.
6. James M. Hadden, *A Journal Kept in Canada and Upon Burgoyne's Campaign in 1776 and 1777*, p. 55.

7. Ibid., pp. 12–13.
8. "Journal of Carleton and Burgoyne's Campaigns," *Bulletin*, Fort Ticonderoga Museum, Vol. XI, No. 6, p. 309.
9. Thomas S. Hughes, *History of England from the Accession of George III . . .* , Vol. II, p. 323.
10. William L. Stone, trans., *Memoirs and Letters and Journals of Major General Riedesel*, Vol. I, p. 111.

Chapter 3

1. Hadden, p. 95.
2. Baxter, *British Invasion from the North*, pp. 224–28.
3. Mahon, Vol. VI, p. 259.
4. Hadden, App. 7, pp. 433–34.
5. R. Lamb, *An Original and Authentic Journal of Occurrences During the Late American War From Its Commencement to the Year 1783*, p. 144.
6. "Journal of Carleton and Burgoyne's Campaigns."
7. Major John André, *Journal*, pp. 27–28.
8. Ibid., p. 28.
9. Tatum, pp. 236–38.
10. Moore, Vol. I, pp. 464–65.
11. Ibid.
12. Burnett, Vol. II, Letter 551.
13. William B. Willcox, ed., *The American Rebellion*, p. 64.
14. De Fonblanque, p. 258.
15. "Journal of Carleton and Burgoyne's Campaigns," pp. 328–29.
16. Commager and Morris, Vol. I, p. 571.
17. De Fonblanque, p. 227.
18. Ibid., pp. 280–81.
19. Baxter, *British Invasion from the North*, p. 242.
20. Barnes and Owen, Vol. I, pp. 221–50.
21. Steuart, Vol. II, p. 128.
22. Tatum, p. 241.
23. Burnett, Vol. II, Letter 567.
24. Fitzpatrick, *Writings of George Washington*, Vol. VIII, p. 499.
25. Burnett, Vol. II, Letter 579.
26. Ibid., Letter 569.
27. Ibid., Letter 586.

Chapter 4

1. W. L. Stone, *General Riedesel*, p. 127.
2. Hadden, pp. 111–17.
3. Ibid., p. 133.
4. "Journal of Carleton and Burgoyne's Campaigns," p. 331.

5. Ibid., p. 332.
6. Ibid., p. 334.
7. W. L. Stone, *General Riedesel*, p. 131.
8. Hadden, pp. 128–29.
9. W. L. Stone, *General Riedesel*, p. 133.
10. De Fonblanque, pp. 275–85.
11. Burgoyne, *Order Book*.
12. Lamb, p. 254.
13. Fortescue, *History of the British Army*, Vol. III, p. 231.
14. De Fonblanque, p. 276.
15. Baxter, *British Invasion from the North*, p. 245.
16. Burgoyne, *State of the Expedition*, pp. 50–51.
17. Burnett, Vol. II, Letter 615.
18. Fitzpatrick, *Writings of George Washington*, Vol. IX, pp. 2–3.
19. Ibid., p. 16.
20. Ibid., p. 20.
21. Ibid., p. 28.
22. Ibid., p. 57.
23. Ibid., pp. 76–78.
24. Ibid., p. 115.
25. Tatum, pp. 245–46.
26. Ibid., p. 246.
27. Ibid., p. 249.
28. S. Sydney Bradford, ed., "A British Officer's Revolutionary War Journal," *Maryland Historical Magazine*, Vol. LVI, No. 2.
29. Burnett, Vol. II, Letter 642.
30. Friedrich Kapp, *The Life of John Kalb . . .* , p. 127.
31. André, pp. 49–50.
32. Steuart, Vol. II, p. 132.

Chapter 5

1. *Bulletin*, Fort Ticonderoga Museum, Vol. VI (1942), p. 155.
2. W. L. Stone, *General Riedesel*, Vol. I, p. 149.
3. Ibid., p. 151.
4. Lamb, p. 161.
5. General James Wilkinson, *Memoirs of My Own Times*, pp. 245–46.
6. Ibid., p. 254.
7. Ibid., p. 256.
8. S. Sydney Bradford, ed., "Lord Francis Napier's Journal of the Burgoyne Campaign," *Maryland Historical Magazine*, Vol. LVII, No. 4.
9. W. L. Stone, *General Riedesel*, Vol. I, pp. 157–58.
10. W. L. Stone, *Letters and Journals by Mrs. General Riedesel*, p. 101.
11. Wilkinson, p. 273.
12. W. L. Stone, *Letters and Journals by Mrs. General Riedesel*, p. 127.
13. Burgoyne, *State of the Expedition*, p. 56.
14. Bradford, "Francis Napier's Journal," pp. 324–25.

15. *Bulletin,* Fort Ticonderoga Museum, Vol. IX, No. 2, p. 107.
16. Barnes and Owen, Vol. I, p. 307.
17. Burnett, Vol. I, Letter 729.
18. Hadden, p. 311.
19. Ibid., pp. 314–15.
20. Charles Stedman, *The History of the Origin, Progress and Termination of the American War,* Vol. II, p. 2.

BOOK VI

Chapter 1

1. Burnett, Vol. II, Letter 627.
2. Stirke, *The Narrative of Lieut Gen William Howe . . . ,* pp. 172–73.
3. Donne, Vol. II, Letter 409.
4. Ibid., Letter 411.
5. Stevens, *Facsimiles,* Vol. III, No. 262 of September 8, 1777.
6. Ibid., No. 256 of June 6, 1777.
7. Ibid., No. 277 of October 21, 1777.
8. Donne, Vol. II, Letter 410.
9. Ibid., Letter 412.
10. W. S. Lewis, *Correspondence with Mann,* Vol. VIII, pp. 355–56.
11. Hughes, Vol. II, p. 155.
12. Ibid.
13. John Adolphus, *History of England from the Accession to the Decease of King George III,* Vol. II, p. 485.
14. Ibid., p. 486.
15. Ibid., p. 488.
16. Donne, Vol. II, Letter 419.
17. Ibid.
18. Ibid., pp. 93–94.
19. Samuel Eliot Morison, *John Paul Jones, a Sailor's Biography,* p. 114.
20. Ibid., p. 115.
21. Ibid., pp. 122–26.
22. Barnes and Owen, Vol. I, pp. 314–15.
23. Ibid., pp. 327–35.
24. Fortescue, *Correspondence,* Vol. IV, Letter 123.
25. Barnes and Owen, Vol. I, pp. 314–15.
26. Robert Morton, *Diary. The Pennsylvania Magazine,* Vol. I, pp. 7–8.
27. Ibid., p. 23.
28. Ibid.
29. Tatum, p. 264.
30. Ibid., pp. 265–66.
31. Morton, pp. 31–32.

32. Ibid., pp. 34–35.
33. Ibid., p. 5.
34. Smyth, Vol. VII, pp. 68–72.
35. Franklin, p. 314.

Chapter 2

1. Kapp, *Kalb*, p. 137.
2. Ibid., pp. 141–44.
3. Fitzpatrick, *Writings of George Washington*, Vol. X, pp. 192–93.
4. Ibid., pp. 194–95.
5. Ibid., p. 196.
6. Ibid., p. 255.
7. Ibid., p. 310.
8. North Callahan, *Henry Knox, General Washington's General*, p. 134.
9. Kapp, *Kalb*, p. 134.
10. Ibid., p. 140.
11. Burnett, Vol. III, Letter 22.
12. Ibid.
13. Ibid., Letter 27.
14. Fitzpatrick, *Writings of George Washington*, Vol. X, p. 356.
15. Ibid., pp. 362–403.
16. Ibid., pp. 410–11.
17. Ibid., pp. 437–41.
18. Donne, Vol. II, Letter 436.
19. Ibid., Letter 439.
20. Ibid., pp. 123–24.
21. Ibid., Letter 444.
22. W. S. Lewis, *Correspondence with Mann*, Vol. VIII, p. 350.

Chapter 3

1. Donne, Vol. II, Letter 466.
2. Barnes and Owen, Vol. I, pp. 349–52.
3. Donne, Vol. II, Letter 444.
4. Stevens, *Facsimiles*, Vol. IV, No. 344 of January 1778.
5. Ibid., No. 345 of January 1778.
6. Donne, Vol. II, Letter 450.
7. Cited by Mahon, Vol. I, p. 328.
8. W. S. Lewis, *Correspondence with Mann*, Vol. VIII, p. 355.
9. Donne, Vol. II, Letter 457.
10. Willcox, p. 84.
11. Donne, Vol. II, Letter 463.
12. Barnes and Owen, Vol. I, p. 524.
13. William Laird Clowes, ed., *The Royal Navy: A History from the Earliest Times to the Present*, Vol. I, p. 396.
14. Fitzpatrick, *Writings of George Washington*, Vol. X, p. 222.

15. Worthington Chauncey Ford, ed., *Journals of the Continental Congress,* Vol. X, pp. 213–15.
16. Fitzpatrick, *Writings of George Washington,* Vol. X, pp. 236–37.
17. Burnett, Vol. III, Letter 92.
18. Fitzpatrick, *Writings of George Washington,* Vol. XI, pp. 8–10.
19. Ibid., pp. 117–18.
20. Ibid., pp. 185–94.

Chapter 4

1. Fortescue, *Correspondence,* Vol. IV, No. 2241.
2. Ibid., No. 2242.
3. Ibid., No. 2251.
4. John W. Jordan, "Some Account of James Hutton's Visit to Franklin in France," *The Pennsylvania Magazine,* Vol. XXXII, pp. 229–30.
5. Barnes and Owen, Vol. II, pp. 30–31.
6. Fortescue, *Correspondence,* Vol. IV, No. 2312.
7. Smyth, Vol. VII, pp. 129–32.
8. Mrs. Reginald de Koven, *The Life and Letters of John Paul Jones,* Vol. I, p. 276.
9. Ibid., pp. 278–79.
10. Ibid., pp. 283–84.
11. Ibid.
12. Ibid., p. 287.
13. W. S. Lewis, *Correspondence with Mann,* Vol. VIII, p. 377.
14. Augustus C. Buell, *Paul Jones, Founder of the American Navy,* Vol. I, p. 134.
15. Fortescue, *Correspondence,* Vol. IV, No. 2316.
16. Barnes and Owen, Vol. II, pp. 36–37.
17. Burnett, Vol. III, Letter 191.
18. Ibid., Letter 195.
19. Fitzpatrick, *Writings of George Washington,* Vol. XI, pp. 284–93.
20. Ibid.
21. Ibid., p. 295.
22. Ibid., p. 335.
23. Worthington Chauncey Ford, Vol. X, p. 375.
24. Ibid., pp. 378–79.
25. Ibid.
26. Fitzpatrick, *Writings of George Washington,* Vol. XI, p. 295.
27. Ibid., p. 335.
28. Burnett, Vol. III, Letter 248 and note 3, p. 215.
29. Ibid., Letter 250.
30. Ibid., Letter 252.
31. Ibid., Letter 255.
32. Fitzpatrick, *Writings of George Washington,* Vol. XI, pp. 354–56.
33. Moore, Vol. II, pp. 49–52.
34. Ibid.

35. Ibid.
36. Kapp, *Kalb*, pp. 158–59.
37. Fitzpatrick, *Writings of George Washington*, Vol. XI, pp. 363–66.
38. Elias Boudinot, "Exchange of Major General Charles Lee," *The Pennsylvania Magazine*, Vol. XI, pp. 26–34.
39. Fitzpatrick, *Writings of George Washington*, Vol. XI, pp. 401–8.
40. Willcox, p. 85.

Chapter 5

1. Steuart, Vol. II, p. 179.
2. Ibid.
3. Ibid., pp. 179–80.
4. Fortescue, *Correspondence*, Vol. IV, pp. 144–45.
5. Ibid.
6. Ibid., pp. 163–68.
7. Ibid., pp. 174–76.
8. Barnes and Owen, Vol. II, pp. 88–93.
9. Ibid., pp. 99–100.
10. Ibid., pp. 92, 95.
11. Ibid., p. 96.
12. Ibid., p. 98.
13. Ibid., pp. 98–99.
14. W. S. Lewis, *Correspondence with Mann*, Vol. VIII, pp. 390–91.
15. Ibid., pp. 386–88.
16. Burnett, Vol. III, Letter 343.
17. Ibid., Letter 346.
18. Ibid., Letters 348–60.
19. Stevens, *Facsimiles*, No. 499 of June 15, 1778.
20. Ibid., No. 500 of June 18, 1778.
21. Ibid.
22. Fitzpatrick, *Writings of George Washington*, Vol. XI, p. 495.
23. Ibid., p. 479.
24. Ibid., p. 483.
25. Ibid., Vol. XII, pp. 77–78.
26. Callahan, p. 143.
27. Fitzpatrick, *Writings of George Washington*, Vol. XII, pp. 112–15.
28. Stedman, Vol. II, Clinton Marginalia, p. 15.
29. Fitzpatrick, *Writings of George Washington*, Vol. XII, p. 117 and note 20.
30. Ibid., pp. 117–18.
31. Ibid., pp. 119–20 and note 24, p. 119.
32. Ibid., p. 122.
33. Ibid., p. 120n.
34. Ibid., p. 128.
35. Stedman, Vol. II, Clinton Marginalia, p. 17.
36. Benson J. Lossing, *The Pictorial Field Book of the Revolution*, Vol. II, p. 355.
37. Fitzpatrick, *Writings of George Washington*, Vol. XII, pp. 132–33.

BOOK VII

Chapter 1

1. Francis Wharton, ed., *The Revolutionary Diplomatic Correspondence of the United States*, Vol. II, pp. 640–42; p. 644.
2. A. T. Mahan, *The Major Operations of the Navies in the War of American Independence*, p. 68.
3. Barnes and Owen, Vol. II, p. 123.
4. Ibid., p. 126.
5. Ibid., p. 128.
6. W. S. Lewis, *Correspondence with Mann*, Vol. VIII, p. 399.
7. Charlemagne Tower, *The Marquis de La Fayette in the American Revolution*, Vol. I, pp. 464–65.
8. Moore, Vol. II, p. 93.
9. Fitzpatrick, *Writings of George Washington*, Vol. XII, pp. 364–65.
10. Ibid., pp. 366–67.
11. Ibid., p. 368n.
12. Ibid., p. 369.
13. Stevens, *Facsimiles*, Vol. V, No. 519 of September 6, 1778.
14. Ibid., Vol. XIII, No. 1975 of October 10, 1778.
15. Willcox, p. 104.
16. Stevens, *Facsimiles*, Vol. V, No. 529 of September 25, 1778.
17. Willcox, p. 106.
18. Burnett, Vol. III, Letter 407.
19. Worthington Chauncey Ford, Vol. IV, p. 282.
20. Burnett, Vol. III, Letter 524.
21. Wharton, Vol. II, p. 659.
22. Ibid., p. 677.
23. Ibid., p. 678.
24. Fortescue, *Correspondence*, Vol. IV, p. 208.
25. Barnes and Owen, Vol. II, pp. 179–83.
26. Fortescue, *Correspondence*, Vol. IV, pp. 214–17.
27. W. S. Lewis, *Correspondence with Mann*, Vol. VIII, p. 412.
28. Fitzpatrick, *Writings of George Washington*, Vol. XIII, pp. 223–25.
29. Ibid., p. 226.
30. Ibid., p. 230.
31. Ibid., pp. 254–57.
32. Barnes, Vol. II, pp. 317–25.

Chapter 2

1. Fitzpatrick, *Writings of George Washington*, Vol. XIII, pp. 485–91.
2. Burnett, Vol. IV, Letter 53.
3. Ibid., Vol. III, Letter 616.
4. Ibid., Vol. IV, Letter 88.
5. Steuart, Vol. II, p. 234.
6. Ibid., p. 236.

7. Barnes and Owen, Vol. II, p. 255.

8. Samuel Flagg Bemis, *The Diplomacy of the American Revolution,* p. 79.

9. Sir John Knox Laughton, ed., *Letters and Papers of Charles, Lord Barham,* Vol. II, pp. 2–6.

10. Ibid., Vol. I, pp. 293–95.

11. Barnes and Owen, Vol. II, p. 255.

12. Ibid., Vol. III, p. 20.

13. Ibid., p. 25.

14. Fortescue, *Correspondence,* Vol. IV, p. 370.

15. W. S. Lewis, *Correspondence with Mann,* Vol. VIII, pp. 490–92.

16. Willcox, p. 123.

17. Ibid., p. 127.

18. Ibid., pp. 407–8.

19. Burnett, Vol. IV, Letter 414.

20. Ibid., Letter 419.

21. Ibid., Letter 426.

22. Ibid., Letter 433.

23. Barnes and Owen, Vol. III, p. 49.

24. Ibid., p. 61.

25. Tower, Vol. II, p. 74.

26. Stevens, *Facsimiles,* Vol. XVII, No. 1609 of July 18, 1779.

27. Barnes and Owen, Vol. III, p. 97.

28. Wharton, Vol. III, p. 376.

29. Stevens, *Facsimiles,* Vol. XXIII, No. 2010 of September 1 to October 18, 1779.

30. Willcox, pp. 232–34.

31. Stevens, *Facsimiles,* Vol. XXIII, No. 2010.

Chapter 3

1. Burnett, Vol. IV, Letter 575.

2. Stevens, *Facsimiles,* Vol. XVII, No. 1616 of November 16, 1779.

3. Fortescue, *Correspondence,* Vol. IV, pp. 433–34.

4. Ibid., pp. 434–35.

5. Ibid., p. 443.

6. Ibid., pp. 436–42, 445–48.

7. John Drinkwater, *History of the Late Siege of Gibraltar,* pp. 76–77.

8. Barnes and Owen, Vol. III, pp. 206–7.

9. Fitzpatrick, *Writings of George Washington,* Vol. XVII, p. 126.

10. Ibid., pp. 273–74.

11. Ibid., p. 366.

12. Kapp, *Kalb,* pp. 182–83.

13. Fitzpatrick, *Writings of George Washington,* Vol. XVIII, p. 223.

14. Ibid., p. 225.

15. W. S. Lewis, *Correspondence with Mann,* Vol. X, pp. 34–36.

16. Smyth, Vol. VII, p. 380.

17. Tower, Vol. II, App. E, pp. 499–500.

18. Ibid., pp. 95–98.

Chapter 4

1. Barnes and Owen, Vol. III, pp. 216–17.
2. Fitzpatrick, *Writings of George Washington*, Vol. XVIII, p. 204.
3. Willcox, p. 186.
4. Ibid., p. 188.
5. Kapp, *Kalb*, pp. 204–5.
6. Ibid., p. 211.
7. Ibid., p. 226.
8. G. W. Greene, Vol. II, p. 366.
9. Franklin B. Dexter, ed., *The Literary Diary of Ezra Stiles*, Vol. II, p. 454.
10. Stevens, *Facsimiles*, Vol. X, No. 1043 of August 14, 1780.
11. Ibid., Vol. XVII, No. 1626 of July 19, 1780.
12. Nathanael Greene, *Papers*, Library of Congress, Washington, D.C.
13. Quoted by Arnold Whitridge, *Rochambeau: America's Neglected Founding Father*, p. 98.
14. Edwin Martin Stone, *Our French Allies in the Great War of the American Revolution*, p. 284.
15. James Thacher, M.D., *Military Journal during the American Revolutionary War*, p. 224.
16. Ibid., p. 225.
17. Ibid., p. 232.
18. Fitzpatrick, *Writings of George Washington*.

Chapter 5

1. Stedman, Vol. II, pp. 217–18.
2. Ibid., pp. 224–25.
3. Ibid., pp. 226–27.
4. Ibid., p. 227.
5. Lieutenant Colonel Banastre Tarleton, *A History of the Campaigns of 1780 and 1781 . . .* , p. 200.
6. Fitzpatrick, *Writings of George Washington*, Vol. XX, pp. 181–82.
7. Ibid., pp. 238–40.
8. Nathanael Greene, *Papers*.
9. Ibid.
10. Ibid.
11. M. le Marquis de Chastellux, *Voyages*, Vol. I, p. 87.
12. Ibid., pp. 100, 119.
13. Ibid., pp. 182–83.
14. Laughton, Vol. II, pp. 104–6.
15. Ibid., Vol. I, p. 83.
16. Willcox, p. 234.
17. Ibid., pp. 236–37.
18. Wraxall, Vol. I, pp. 277–78.
19. Ibid., p. 417.
20. Barnes and Owen, Vol. III, pp. 253–59.
21. Wraxall, Vol. I. pp. 359–60.
22. Fitzpatrick, *Writings of George Washington*, Vol. XXI, pp. 55–56 and note.

23. Thacher, p. 247.
24. Fitzpatrick, *Writings of George Washington*, Vol. XXI, p. 57.
25. Ibid., p. 137.
26. Thacher, pp. 251–53.
27. Fitzpatrick, *Writings of George Washington*, Vol. XXI, p. 158.
28. G. W. Greene, Vol. III, p. 131.
29. Charles Ross, *Correspondence of Charles, First Marquis Cornwallis*, Vol. I, pp. 81–82.
30. Tarleton, pp. 215–18.
31. Ibid., p. 220.

Chapter 6

1. Franklin and Mary Wickwire, *Cornwallis, The American Adventure*, pp. 277–78.
2. Ross, Vol. I, p. 519.
3. Barnes and Owen, Vol. IV, p. 24.
4. Ibid., p. 25.
5. Burnett, Vol. V, Letter 587.
6. Fitzpatrick, *Writings of George Washington*, Vol. XXI, pp. 105–10.
7. Ibid., p. 164.
8. Burnett, Vol. V, Letter 627.
9. Fitzpatrick, *Writings of George Washington*, Vol. XXI, p. 231.
10. Ibid., pp. 253–56.
11. G. W. Greene, Vol. III, p. 188.
12. Ibid., p. 198.
13. Ibid., p. 201.
14. Ross, Vol. I, App. 7, p. 522.
15. Stedman, pp. 343–44.
16. Ross, Vol. I, p. 87.
17. Ibid., pp. 87–88.

Chapter 7

1. W. S. Lewis, *Correspondence with Mann*, Vol. IX, p. 139.
2. Fortescue, *Correspondence*, Vol. V, pp. 207–9.
3. Captain W. M. James, *The British Navy in Adversity*, pp. 274–75.
4. Fitzpatrick, *Writings of George Washington*, Vol. XXI, pp. 436–40.
5. Ross, Vol. I, pp. 88–89.
6. French, *Mackenzie*, Vol. I, p. 508.
7. G. W. Greene, Vol. III, pp. 213–14.
8. William Johnson, *Sketches of the Life and Correspondence of Nathanael Greene*, Vol. II, p. 83.
9. Ibid., p. 87.
10. Burnett, Vol. VI, Assorted Letters, May 1781.
11. Fitzpatrick, *Writings of George Washington*, Vol. XXII, pp. 58–59.

12. Ibid., p. 64.
13. Ibid., pp. 68–69.
14. Ibid., pp. 105–7.
15. Ross, Vol. I, pp. 90–91.
16. Ibid., pp. 94–95.
17. *Annual Register,* 1781, p. 89.
18. Ross, Vol. I, pp. 101–2.
19. Kapp, *Steuben,* p. 433.
20. Ibid., p. 447.

Chapter 8

1. G. W. Greene, Vol. III, p. 320.
2. Howard C. Rice, Jr., and Anne S. K. Brown, trans. and eds., *The American Campaigns of Rochambeau's Army,* Vol. I, pp. 28–29.
3. Ibid., pp. 32–33.
4. French, *Mackenzie,* Vol. II, p. 565.
5. Fitzpatrick, *Diaries of George Washington,* Vol. II, p. 254.
6. Thacher, p. 269.
7. Ibid., p. 270.
8. Burnett, Vol. VI, Letter 273.
9. Ibid., Letter 291.
10. Barnes, Vol. IV, pp. 181–86.
11. Ibid., pp. 186–87.
12. Ibid., p. 189.
13. Ibid., p. 188.
14. Fitzpatrick, *Writings of George Washington,* Vol. XXIII, pp. 102–3.
15. *Correspondence of General Washington and Comte de Grasse 1781, August 17–November 4.*
16. Ibid., pp. 48–51.
17. Fitzpatrick, *Diaries of George Washington,* Vol. II, pp. 261–62.
18. Ross, Vol. I, p. 120.
19. Ibid., pp. 121–22.
20. Fitzpatrick, *Diaries of George Washington,* Vol. II, p. 263.
21. Thacher, p. 283.
22. Ibid.
23. Fitzpatrick, *Writings of George Washington,* Vol. XXIII, pp. 209–10.
24. Ibid., pp. 236–37.
25. Ibid., pp. 237–38.
26. W. S. Lewis, *Correspondence with Mann,* Vol. IX, p. 213.

SELECTED BIBLIOGRAPHY

Abernethy, Thomas Perkins. *Western Lands and the American Revolution.* New York: Russell and Russell, 1959.

Acomb, Evelyn N., ed. *The Revolutionary Journal of Baron Ludwig von Closen, 1780–1783.* Chapel Hill: The University of North Carolina Press, 1958.

Adams, Charles Francis, ed. *Letters of Mrs. Adams.* Boston: Charles C. Little and James Brown, 1840.

Adams, James Truslow. *Revolutionary New England, 1691–1776.* Boston: The Atlantic Monthly Press, 1923.

Adolphus, John. *The History of England from the Accession to the Decease of King George III.* 6 vols. London: John Lee, 1841.

Alden, John R. *A History of the American Revolution.* New York: Alfred A. Knopf, 1969.

——. *General Gage in America.* Baton Rouge, La.: Louisiana State University Press, 1948.

——. *The War of the Revolution.* Edited by Christopher Ward. New York: The Macmillan Company, 1952.

Allen, William. *Account of Arnold's Expedition.* Portland, Me.: Collections of the Maine Historical Society, Vol. I, 1865.

André, Major John. *Journal. Operations of the British Army under Lieutenant Generals Sir William Howe and Sir Henry Clinton. June 1777 to November 1778.* Tarrytown, N.Y.: William Abbot, 1930.

Andrews, Charles M. *The Colonial Period of American History.* New Haven and London: Yale University Press, 1964.

Annual Register, or a View of the History, Politics and Literature for the Year. London, 1760–82.

Appleton, Nathaniel. *A Thanksgiving SERMON on the total Repeal of the STAMP ACT.* Boston: Edes and Gill, 1766.

Arnold, Benedict. *Letters.* Portland, Me.: Collections of the Maine Historical Society, Vol. I, 1865.

Ayling, Stanley. *George the Third.* London: Collins, 1972.

Bailyn, Bernard. *The Ideological Origins of the American Revolution.* Cambridge, Mass.: The Belknap Press of Harvard University Press, 1967.

——. *The Ordeal of Thomas Hutchinson.* Cambridge, Mass.: The Belknap Press of Harvard University Press, 1965.

——, ed. *Pamphlets of the American Revolution.* Cambridge, Mass.: The Belknap Press of Harvard University Press, 1974.

Bancroft, George. *History of the American Revolution.* London: Richard Bentley, 1852.

Bargar, B. D. *Lord Dartmouth and the American Revolution.* Columbia, S.C.: The University of South Carolina Press, 1965.

Barnes, G. R., and Owen, J. H., eds. *The Private Papers of John, Earl of Sandwich, First Lord of the Admiralty, 1771–1782.* Vol. I. London: The Navy Records Society, 1932.

Barton, John A. "The Battle of Valcour Island." *History Today,* Vol. IX, No. 12 (December 1957).

Baxter, James Phinney, ed. *Documentary History of the State of Maine.* Collections of the Maine Historical Society, 2nd Series, Vol. XIV. Portland, Me.: Lefavor-Tower, 1910.

——, ed. *The British Invasion from the North. The Campaigns of Generals Carleton and Burgoyne from Canada, 1776–1777, With the Journals of Lieut William Digby of the 53d, or Shropshire Regiment of Foot.* Albany: Joel Munsell's Sons, 1887.

Beatson, Robert. *Naval and Military Memoirs of Great Britain from 1727 to 1783.* 6 vols. London: Longman, Hurst, Reese, Moore, 1804.

Becker, Carl L. *The Declaration of Independence: A Study in the History of Political Ideas.* New York: Harcourt, Brace & Company, 1922.

——. *The Eve of Revolution.* New Haven: Yale University Press, 1918.

Beer, George Louis. *British Colonial Policy 1754–1765.* New York: The Macmillan Company, 1922.

Beloff, Max, ed. *The Debate on the American Revolution.* London: Nicholas Kaye, 1949.

Bemis, Samuel Flagg. *The Diplomacy of the American Revolution.* New York and London: D. Appleton-Century Company, Inc., 1935.

Bill, Alfred Hoyt. *Valley Forge: The Making of an Army.* New York: Harper, 1952.

Billias, George A., ed. *George Washington's Opponents.* New York: William Morrow and Company, Inc., 1969.

Bird, Harrison. *March to Saratoga: General Burgoyne and the American Campaign, 1777.* New York: Oxford University Press, 1963.

——. *Navies in the Mountains: The Battles on the Waters of Lake Champlain and Lake George 1609–1814.* New York: Oxford University Press, 1962.

Boatner, Mark M., III, Colonel, U.S.A. *Encyclopedia of the American Revolution.* New York: McKay Company, Inc., 1969.

Bowler, R. Arthur. *Logistics and the Failure of the British Army in America.* Princeton, N.J.: Princeton University Press, 1975.

Boyd, Julian P. "Silas Deane: Death by a Kindly Teacher of Treason." *William and Mary Quarterly,* Williamsburg, Va.: The Institute of Early American History and Culture. 3rd Series, Vol. XVI (April, July, October 1959).

——, ed. *The Papers of Thomas Jefferson.* 19 vols. Princeton, N.J.: Princeton University Press, 1950–74.

Bradford, S. Sydney, ed. "A British Officer's Revolutionary War Journal 1776–1778." *Maryland Historical Magazine,* Vol. LVI, No. 2 (June 1961).

——. "Lord Francis Napier's Journal of the Burgoyne Campaign." *Maryland Historical Magazine,* Vol. LVII, No. 4 (December 1962).

Bridenbaugh, Carl. *Vexed and Troubled Englishmen 1590–1642.* Oxford: The Clarendon Press, 1968.

——. *Mitre and Sceptre; Transatlantic Faiths, Ideas, Personalities, and Politics, 1689–1775.* New York: Oxford University Press, 1962.

——. *Cities in Revolt; Urban Life in America, 1743–1776.* New York: Alfred A. Knopf, 1955.

Brooke, John. *King George III.* London: Constable, 1972.

Brown, Peter. *The Chathamites.* London: Macmillan, 1967.

Brown, Wallace. *The Good Americans: The Loyalists in the American Revolution.* New York: William Morrow and Company, Inc., 1969.

Buell, Augustus C. *Paul Jones: Founder of the American Navy.* New York: Charles Scribner's Sons, 1900.

Burgoyne, Lieutenant General John. *A State of the Expedition from Canada as Laid before the House of Commons with a Collection of Authentic Documents, etc. etc.* London: Printed for J. Almon, 1780.

——. *Official report to Lord George Germain respecting the capture of Ticonderoga.* Dated Skenesboro, N.Y., July, 1777. PRO. C.O. 42/36. fol. 343.

——. *Order Book.* Collection Captain Tagdh Maglinchey.

Burke, Edmund. *Speeches and Letters on American Affairs.* London: J. M. Dent & Sons, 1908. Reprint, 1961.

Burnett, Edmund C., ed. *Letters of Members of the Continental Congress.* 8 vols. Washington, D.C.: The Carnegie Institute of Washington, 1921–1936.

Butterfield, H. *George III, Lord North, and the People, 1779–80.* London: G. Bell and Sons, Ltd., 1949.

——. *George III and the Historians.* London: Collins, St. James Place, 1957.

——. *The Whig Interpretation of History.* London: G. Bell and Sons, Ltd., 1959.

Butterfield, L. H.; Falser, Leonard C.; and Garrett, Wendell D., eds. *Diary and Autobiography of John Adams.* 4 vols. Cambridge: The Belknap Press of Harvard University Press, 1961.

Callahan, North. *Henry Knox, General Washington's General.* New York: Rinehart, 1958.

Carswell, John, and Dralle, J. A., eds. *The Political Journal of George Bubb Dodington.* Oxford: The Clarendon Press, 1965.

Carter, Clarence E., ed. *The Correspondence of General Thomas Gage with the Secretaries of State and with the War Office and the Treasury, 1763–1775.* New Haven: Yale University Press, 1933.

Chastellux, le Marquis de. *Voyages de M. le Marquis de Chastellux dans l'Amérique Septentrionale*. Paris: Chez Prault, Imprimeur du Roi, 1786.

Chidsey, Donald Barr. *The Loyalists: The Story of Those Americans who Fought Against Independence*. New York: Crown Publishers, Inc., 1973.

Clark, Dora Mae. *British Opinion and the American Revolution*. New Haven: Yale University Press, 1930.

Clark, George L. *Silas Deane: A Connecticut Leader in the American Revolution*. New York and London: G. P. Putnam's Sons, 1913.

Clark, William Bell, and Morgan, William James, eds. *Naval Documents of the American Revolution*. 5 vols. Washington, D.C.: U. S. Government Printing Office, 1964–74.

Clowes, William Laird. *The Royal Navy: A History from the Earliest Times to the Present*. London: Sampson, Low, Marston and Company, Ltd., 1898.

Colby, C. B. *Revolutionary War Weapons*. New York: Coward McCann, 1963.

Collins, Varnum L., ed. *A Brief Narrative of the Ravages of the British and the Hessians at Princeton in 1776–77*. Princeton, N.J. The University Library, 1906.

Commager, Henry Steele, ed. *Documents of American History*. New York: Appleton-Century-Crofts, 1949.

Commager, Henry Steele, and Morris, Richard B. *The Spirit of 'Seventy-six*. New York: Bobbs-Merrill, 1958.

Copeland, Thomas W., ed. *The Correspondence of Edmund Burke*. Chicago: The University of Chicago Press, 1958.

Correspondence of General Washington and Comte de Grasse 1781, August 17–November 4. Senate Document No. 211. 71st Cong., 2nd Sess. Washington, D.C.: U. S. Government Printing Office, 1931.

Corwin, Edward S. "The French Objective in the American Revolution." *The American Historical Review*, Vol. XXI (October 1915).

Coupland, R. *The American Revolution and the British Empire*. New York: Russell and Russell, 1965.

Cranston, Maurice. *John Locke*. London: Longmans, Green and Company, 1957.

Curtis, Edward E. *The Organization of the British Army in the American Revolution*. New Haven: Yale University Press, 1926.

Cushing, Harry Alonzo, ed. *The Writings of Samuel Adams*. 4 vols. New York: G. P. Putnam's Sons, 1908.

Davis, Burke. *The Campaign that Won America: The Story of Yorktown*. New York: The Dial Press, 1970.

Deane, Silas. *Papers*. 5 vols. New York: Collections, New-York Historical Society, 1886–90.

De Fonblanque, Edward Barrington. *Political and Military Episodes in the Latter Half of the Eighteenth Century, Derived from the Life and Correspondence of John Burgoyne*. London: Macmillan, 1876.

De Koven, Mrs. Reginald. *The Life and Letters of John Paul Jones*. New York: Charles Scribner's Sons, 1913.

Dexter, Franklin B., ed. *The Literary Diary of Ezra Stiles, D.D., L.L.D.* New York: Charles Scribner's Sons, 1901.

Dickinson, John. *Letters from a Farmer in Pennsylvania as Published in the*

Boston Gazette. Worcester, Mass.: Collections, American Antiquarian Society.

Dobrée, Bonamy, ed. *The Letters of King George III.* London: Cassell, 1935.

——. *The Letters of Philip Dormer Stanhope, 4th Earl of Chesterfield.* New York: Viking, 1932.

Doniol, Henri. *Histoire de la Participation de la France à l'Établissement des États-Unis d'Amérique.* Vol. I. Paris: Imprimerie Nationale, 1886.

Donne, W. Bodham, ed. *The Correspondence of King George the Third with Lord North from 1768 to 1783.* London: John Murray, 1867.

Donoughue, Bernard. *British Politics and the American Revolution.* London: Macmillan and Company, Ltd., 1964.

Douglas, David C., ed. *English Historical Documents.* Vol. IX. *American Colonial Documents to 1776.* Edited by Merrill Jensen. London: Eyre and Spottiswoode, 1955.

Drinkwater, John. *History of the Late Siege of Gibraltar.* Dublin, 1783.

Evans, Elizabeth. *Weathering the Storm: Women of the American Revolution.* New York: Charles Scribner's Sons, 1975.

Evelyn, Captain William C. *Memoirs and Letters from North America.* London, 1879.

Examination of Doctor Benjamin Franklin, etc. Bowdoin College Special Collections. Philadelphia: Hall and Tellers, 1766.

Executive Council of the State of Pennsylvania. Resolutions relating to the oppressive conduct of Mayor General Benedict Arnold during his command in Philadelphia. Dated February 3ᵈ, 1779 and published by order of the Supreme Executive Authority. Printed by Francis Bailey, Philadelphia, Pennsylvania.

Firth, C. H. *Naval Songs and Ballads.* London: For the Navy Records Society, 1908.

Fiske, John. *The American Revolution.* 2 vols. Boston: Houghton Mifflin Company, 1901.

Fitzpatrick, John C., ed. *The Writings of George Washington.* 39 vols. Washington, D.C.: U. S. Government Printing Office, 1931–44.

——, ed. *The Diaries of George Washington 1748–1785.* 4 vols. New York: Houghton Mifflin Company, 1925.

Flexner, James Thomas. *George Washington.* 4 vols. Boston: Little, Brown and Company, 1965–72.

——. *Washington: The Indispensable Man.* Boston: Little, Brown and Company, 1974.

Force, Peter. *American Archives. Fourth Series Containing A Documentary History of The English Colonies in North America from The King's Message to Parliament of March 7, 1774 to the Declaration of Independence by the United States.* Washington, December 1837. *Fifth Series from July 4, 1776 to 1783.*

Ford, Paul L., ed. *The Writings of Thomas Jefferson.* 10 vols. New York: G. P. Putnam's Sons, 1892–99.

Ford, Worthington Chauncey, ed. See *Journals of the Continental Congress.*

Fortescue, the Honourable Sir John, ed. *The Correspondence of King George the Third from 1760 to 1783.* London: Macmillan, 1928.

——. *A History of the British Army*. Vol. III. London: Macmillan and Company, Ltd., 1902.

Franklin, William Temple. *Memoirs of the Life and Writings of Benjamin Franklin, LL.D., F.R.S. etc., Minister Plenipotentiary from the United States of America at the Court of France, and for the Treaty of Peace and Independence with Great Britain*, etc. etc. London: Henry Colburn, 1818.

Freeman, Douglas Southall. *George Washington: A Biography*. 7 vols. New York: Charles Scribner's Sons, 1948–57.

French, Allen. "The British Expedition to Concord in 1775." *The Journal of the American Military History Foundation*. Washington, 1937.

——. *The Taking of Ticonderoga in 1775: The British Story*. Cambridge, Mass., 1928.

——. *General Gage's Informer*. Ann Arbor: The University of Michigan Press, 1932.

——. "General Haldimand in Boston 1774–1775." *Massachusetts Historical Society Proceedings*, Vol. LXVI (1942), pp. 80–95.

——, ed. *Diary of Frederick Mackenzie, Giving a Daily Narrative of His Military Servvice as an Officer of the Regiment of Royal Welch Fusiliers During the years 1775–1781 in Massachussetts, Rhode Island and New York*. Cambridge, Mass.: Harvard University Press, 1930.

——, ed. *The First Year of the American Revolution*. Boston: Houghton Mifflin Company, 1934.

Frothingham, Richard, Jr. *History of the Siege of Boston and of the Battles of Lexington, Concord and Bunker Hill*. Boston: Charles C. Little and James Brown, 1849.

Furcron, Thomas B. "Mt. Independence 1776–1777." *Bulletin*, Fort Ticonderoga Museum, Vol. IX, No. 4 (1954).

Galloway, Joseph. *Letters to a Nobleman on the Conduct of the War in the Middle Colonies*. London: J. Wilkie, 1779.

Gottschalk, Louis. *Lafayette Joins the American Army*. Chicago: The University of Chicago Press, 1937.

Greene, George Washington. *The Life of Nathanael Greene*. New York: Hurd and Houghton, 1871.

Gruber, Ira D. *The Howe Brothers and the American Revolution*. New York: Atheneum, 1972.

Guttridge, G. H. *English Whiggism and the American Revolution*. Berkeley: The University of California Press, 1966.

Hadden, Lieutenant James M. *A Journal Kept in Canada and Upon Burgoyne's Campaign in 1776 and 1777*, with Explanatory Chapter and Notes by Horatio Rogers. Albany: Joel Munsell's Sons, 1884.

Hammersley, Colonel Sydney E. *The Lake Champlain Naval Battles of 1776–1814*. Waterford, N.Y., 1959.

Heath, Major General William. *Memoirs of General Heath During the American War*. Boston: Thomas and Andress, 1789.

Henry, John Joseph. *Account of Arnold's Campaign Against Quebec*. Albany: Joel Munsell, 1877.

Higginbotham, Don. *The American War of Independence. Military Attitudes,*

Policies, and Practices, 1763–1789. New York: The Macmillan Company, 1971.

Hinman, Royal R., ed. *A Historical Collection from Official Records, Files, etc., of the Part Sustained by Connecticut During the War of the Revolution.* Hartford: E. Gleason, 1842.

Hobhouse, Christopher. *Fox.* London: Constable and Company, Ltd., 1934.

Hollingsworth, J. Rogers, and Wiley, Bell I., eds. *American Democracy: A Documentary Record.* Vol. I: 1620–1865. New York: Thomas Y. Crowell Company, 1961.

Howe, Lieutenant General Sir William. *The Narrative of Lieut Gen Sir William Howe in a Committee of the Whole House of Commons on the 29th of April, 1779 Relative to His Conduct during His Late Command of the King's Troops in North America: To which are added Some Observations Upon a Pamphlet entitled Letters to a Nobleman.* London: Almon and Debret, 1780.

Huddleston, F. J. *Gentleman Johnny Burgoyne.* New York: Garden City Publishing Company, Inc., 1927.

Hughes, Thomas S. *History of England from the Accession of George III in 1760 to the Accession of Queen Victoria in 1837.* 7 vols. London: George Bellis, 1855.

Hutchinson, Peter Orlando, ed. *The Diary and Letters of His Excellency Thomas Hutchinson, Esq., Captain General and Governor-in-Chief of His Late Majesty's Province of Massachusetts Bay in North America.* London: Sampson, Low, Marston, Searle and Rivington, 1883.

Hutchinson, Thomas. *The History of the Province of Massachusetts Bay from 1749 to 1774, Comprising a Detailed Narrative of the Origin and Early Sources of the American Revolution.* London: John Murray, 1828.

Jackman, Sydney, ed. *With Burgoyne from Quebec. An Account of the Life at Quebec and of the Famous Battles at Saratoga. First Published as Volume One of Travels Through The Interior Parts of North America.* By Thomas Anburey. Toronto: Macmillan of Canada, 1963.

James, Captain W. M. *The British Navy in Adversity: A Study of the War of American Independence.* New York: Russell and Russell, 1970.

Jameson, J. Franklin. *The American Revolution Considered as a Social Movement.* Princeton, 1926.

Jenyns, Soame. *The Works of Soames Jenyn, Esq.* Dublin, 1971.

Johnson, William. *Sketches of the Life and Correspondence of Nathanael Greene.* 2 vols. Charleston, 1822. Reprint: New York: De Capo Press, 1973.

Jones, Thomas. *History of New York during the Revolutionary War.* New York: New-York Historical Society, 1879.

"Journal of Carleton and Burgoyne's Campaigns, A." Anon. *Bulletin,* Fort Ticonderoga Museum, Vol. XI, Nos. 5 and 6 (1965).

Journals of the Continental Congress. Vols. I–XV edited by Worthington Chauncey Ford. Washington, D.C.: U. S. Government Printing Office, 1904–9. Vols. XVI–XXVII edited by Gaillard Hunt. Washington, D.C.: U. S. Government Printing Office, 1910–28.

Judd, Gerrit P., IV. *Horace Walpole's Memoirs.* London: Vision Press, 1959.

Junius. *Letters*. London, 1810.

Kapp, Friedrich. *The Life of John Kalb, Major-General in the Revolutionary Army*. New York: Holt and Company, 1884.

———. *The Life of Frederick William von Steuben, Major-General in the Revolutionary Army*. New York: Macon Brothers, 1859.

Keppel, George Thomas, Earl of Albermarle. *Memoirs of the Marquis of Rockingham and his Contemporaries*. London: Richard Bentley, 1852.

Kingsford, William. *The History of Canada*. Toronto: Rowsell and Hutchinson, 1892.

Kleeb, Arlene. *The Boston Tea Party, Catalyst for Revolution*. Ann Arbor, Mich.: William L. Clements Library, 1973.

Knollenberg, Bernhard. *Origin of the American Revolution 1759–1766*. New York: The Macmillan Company, 1960.

Knox, William. *Knox Papers*. Ann Arbor, Mich.: William L. Clements Library.

Lacour-Gayet, G. *Le Marine Militaire de la France sous le Regne de Louis XVI*. Paris: Librairie Spécial pour l'Histoire de la France, 1905.

Lamb, R. *An Original and Authentic Journal of Occurrences During the Late American War From Its Commencement to the Year 1783*. Dublin: Wilkinson and Courtney, 1809.

Land, Aubrey C., ed. *Letters from America by William Eddis*. Cambridge, Mass.: Harvard University Press, 1969.

Larrabee, Harold A. *Decision at the Chesapeake*. London: William Kimber, 1965.

Laughton, Sir John Knox, ed. *Letters and Papers of Charles, Lord Barham*. 3 vols. London: The Navy Records Society, 1910.

Lecky, William E. H. *A History of England in the Eighteenth Century*. London: Longmans, Green and Company, 1882.

Lewis, Charles Lee. *Admiral de Grasse and American Independence*. Annapolis, Md.: United States Naval Institute, 1945.

Lewis, W. S., ed. *Horace Walpole's Correspondence with Sir Horace Mann*. New Haven: Yale University Press, 1967.

Lewis, W. S., and Smith, Warren Hunting, eds. *Horace Walpole's Correspondence with Madame du Deffand*. 6 vols. New Haven: Yale University Press, 1939.

Lossing, Benson J. *The Pictorial Field Book of the Revolution*. New York: Harper and Brothers, 1852.

———. *Seventeen Hundred and Seventy Six, or the War of Independence. pendence*. New York: Edward Walker, 1848.

Luzader, John F. *The Construction and Military History of Fort Stanwix*. Division of History, U. S. Department of the Interior, Washington, D.C., 1969.

Mackesy, Piers, *The War for America, 1775–1783*. London: Longmans, Green and Company, Ltd., 1964.

Maclay, Edgar Stanton. *A History of American Privateers*. Freeport, N.Y.: Books for Libraries Press, 1970.

Mahan, A. T. *The Major Operations of the Navies in the War of American Independence*. London: Sampson, Low, Marston and Company, Ltd., 1913.

———. *The Influence of Sea Power Upon History*. London: Sampson, Low, Marston and Company, Ltd., 1918.

Mahon, Lord. *History of England from the Peace of Utrecht to the Peace of Versailles, 1713–1783.* 7 vols. London: John Murray, 1858.

Manuscript Journal of a British Officer, 1776–1777. Special Collections, United States Military Academy, West Point, N.Y.

Mayo, Lawrence Shaw, ed. *The History of the Colony and Providence of Massachusetts Bay,* by Thomas Hutchinson. Cambridge, Mass.: Harvard University Press, 1936.

Merritt, Elizabeth. "The Lexington Alarm, April 19, 1775." *Maryland Historical Magazine,* Vol. XLI, No. 2 June 1946.

Miller, John C. *Sam Adams: Pioneer in Propaganda.* Stanford, Calif.; Stanford University Press, 1960.

Moore, Frank, ed. *Diary of the American Revolution from Newspapers and Original Documents.* New York: Charles Scribner, 1860.

Morison, Rear Admiral Samuel Eliot. *John Paul Jones, a Sailor's Biography.* Boston: Little, Brown, 1959.

Morton, Robert. *Diary. The Pennsylvania Magazine,* Vol. 1 (1877). Philadelphia: The Historical Society of Pennsylvania.

Murray, Eleanor M. "The Medical Department of the Revolution." *Bulletin,* Fort Ticonderoga Museum, Vol. VIII, No. 3 (1949).

Namier, L. B. *The Structure of Politics at the Accession of George III.* London: Macmillan and Company, Ltd., 1929.

Namier, Sir Lewis. *England in the Age of the American Revolution.* New York: St. Martin's Press, 1961.

Napier, Lord Francis. "Journal of the Burgoyne Campaign." *Maryland Historical Magazine,* Vol. LVII, No. 4 (December 1963).

Narrative of Lieut Gen Sir William Howe in a Committe of the Whole House of Commons on the 29th of April, 1779 Relative to His Conduct during His Late Command of the King's Troops in North America: To which are added some Observations Upon a Pamphlet entitled Letters to a Nobleman. London: Almon and Debret, 1780.

Nelson, William H. *The American Tory.* Oxford, 1961.

Nevins, Allan. *The American States During and After the Revolution 1775–1789.* New York: The Macmillan Company, 1924.

Olsen, Alison G., and Brown, Richard Maxwell. *Anglo-American Political Relations.* New Brunswick. N.J.: Rutgers University Press, 1970.

Paine, Thomas. *Political Works.* New York: Peter Eckler, 1891.

Palmer, John McCauley. *General von Steuben.* New Haven: Yale University Press, 1937.

Parrington, Vernon Lewis. *Main Currents in American Thought.* Vol. I, 1620–1800. *The Colonial Mind.* New York: Harcourt, Brace & Company, 1927.

Pemberton, W. Baring. *Lord North.* London: Longmans, Green and Company, 1938.

Plumb, J. H. *The First Four Georges.* London: B. T. Batsford, Ltd., 1961.

Pole, J. R., ed. *The Revolution in America 1754–1788.* London: Macmillan and Company, Ltd., 1970.

Quarles, Benjamin. *The Negro in the American Revolution.* New York: W. W. Norton and Company, Inc., 1973.

Ramsey, David. *The History of the American Revolution,* London, 1791.

Reed, John F. *Campaign to Valley Forge: July 1, 1777–December 19, 1777.* Philadelphia: University of Pennsylvania Press, 1965.

Remembrancer, or Impartial Repository of Public Events. London: Printed for J. Almon.

Rice, Howard C., Jr., and Brown, Anne S. K., trans. and eds. *The American Campaigns of Rochambeau's Army: 1780, 1781, 1782, 1783.* Princeton: Princeton University Press; and Providence: Brown University Press, 1972.

Riling, Joseph R. *Baron von Steuben and His Regulations.* Philadelphia: Ray Riling Arms Books Company, 1966.

Robson, Eric, ed. *Letters from America, 1775–1780: Being the Letters of a Scots officer, Sir James Murray, to His Home During the War of American Independence.* Manchester: Manchester University Press, 1951.

——. "Lord North." *History Today,* Vol. II, No. 8 (August 1952).

——. "Prelude to Independence. The American Colonies in the Eighteenth Century." *History Today,* Vol. IX, No. 2 (February 1954).

——. "The War of American Independence Reconsidered." *History Today,* Vol. II, No. 2 (May 1952).

——. "The Expedition to the Southern Colonies 1775–1776." *The English Historical Review,* 1951.

Rodney, Vice-admiral Sir George Brydges. *Letter Books.* 2 vols. New York: The New-York Historical Society, 1932.

Rosengarten, J. G., trans. *The American Allied Troops in the North American War of Independence.* Baltimore: Genealogical Publishing Company, 1969.

Ross, Charles. *Correspondence of Charles, First Marquis Cornwallis.* London: John Murray, 1859.

Rude, George. *Wilkes and Liberty.* Oxford: The Clarendon Press, 1962.

Russell, Jack. *Gibraltar Besieged 1779–1783.* London: Heinemann, 1965.

Saratoga: U. S. National Park Service. *Historical Handbook Series No. 4.*

Sargent, Winthrop. *The Life of Major John André.* New York: D. Appleton and Company, 1871.

Schlesinger, Arthur M. *The Birth of the Nation.* New York: Alfred A. Knopf, 1969.

Scull, G. D., ed. *Memoirs and Letters of Captain W. Glanville Evelyn of the 4th Regiment (King's Pawn) from North America, 1774–1776.* Oxford: James Parker, 1879.

Sedgwick, Romney, ed. *Some Materials Towards Memoirs of the Reign of King George III.* John, Lord Harvey. London: Eyre and Spottiswoode, 1931.

Shy, John. *Toward Lexington. The Role of the British Army in the Coming of the American Revolution.* Princeton, N.J.: Princeton University Press, 1965.

Siege of Quebec. Literary and Historical Society. Quebec: The Morning Chronicle Office, 1876.

Smith, Justin H. *Arnold's March from Cambridge to Quebec. A Critical Study. Together with a Reprint of Arnold's Journal.* New York and London: G. P. Putnam's Sons, 1903.

Smyth, Albert Henry, ed. *The Writings of Benjamin Franklin*. New York: The Macmillan Company, 1902.

Stedman, Charles. *The History of the Origin, Progress and Termination of the American War*. London, 1794.

Stephenson, Nathaniel W., and Dunn, Waldo H. *George Washington*. New York: Oxford University Press, 1940.

Steuart, A. Francis, ed. *The Last Journals of Horace Walpole During the Reign of King George III*. 2 vols. London: The Bodley Head, 1910.

Stevens, Benjamin F. ed., *General Sir William Howe's Orderly Book at Charlestown, Boston and Halifax June 17, 1775 to 1776, 26 May*. London: B. F. Stevens and Brown, 1890.

——. *B. F. Stevens's Facsimiles of Manuscripts in European Archives Relating to America, 1773–1783*. London: Maltby and Sons, 1889–95.

——. *Clinton-Cornwallis Controversy*. London, 1888.

Stone, Edwin Martin. *Our French Allies in the Great War of the American Revolution*. Providence: Providence Press, 1884.

——, ed. *The Invasion of Canada in 1775 including the Journal of Captain Simeon Thayer*. Providence: Knowles, Anthony and Co., 1867.

Stone, William L., trans. *Journal of Captain Pausch, Chief of the Hanau Artillery During the Burgoyne Campaign*. Albany: Joel Munsell's Sons, 1886.

——, trans. *Letters and Journals relating to the War of the American Revolution by Mrs. General Riedesel*. Albany: Joel Munsell's Sons, 1867.

——, trans. *Memoirs and Letters and Journals of Major General Riedesel*. 2 vols. Albany: Joel Munsell's Sons, 1868.

Stuart-Wortley, the Honorable Mrs. E., ed. *A Prime Minister and His Son*. New York: E. P. Dutton, 1925.

Sutherland, Stella. *Population Distribution in Colonial America*. New York, 1936.

Syrett, David. *Shipping and the American War 1775–83: A Study of British Transport Organization*. London: The Athlone Press, 1970.

Tarleton, Lieutenant Colonel Banastre. *A History of the Campaigns of 1780 and 1781 in the Southern Provinces of North America*. London, 1787.

Tatum, Edward H., Jr., ed. *The American Journal of Ambrose Serle*. San Marino, Calif.: The Huntington Library, 1940.

Thacher, James, M.D. *Military Journal during the American Revolutionary War from 1775–1783*. Hartford, Conn., 1854.

Tower, Charlemagne, Jr. *The Marquis de La Fayette in the American Revolution*. Philadelphia: J. B. Lippincott Company, 1895.

Trevelyan, Sir George Otto, Bart. *The American Revolution*. London: Longmans, Green and Company, 1903.

——. *George the Third and Charles Fox*. New York: Longmans, Green and Company, 1914.

Valentine, Alan. *Lord Stirling*. New York: Oxford University Press, 1969.

——. *Lord George Germain*. Oxford: The Clarendon Press, 1962.

Van Doren, Carl, ed. *Benjamin Franklin's Autobiographical Writings*. New York: The Viking Press, 1945.

——. *The Secret History of the American Revolution*. New York: The Viking Press, 1968.

————. *Mutiny in January*. New York: The Viking Press, 1943.

Van Tyne, Claude H. *The Founding of the American Republic*. Vol. I. *The Causes of the War of Independence*. Boston: Houghton Mifflin Company, 1922.

————. "Influence which Determined the French Government to make the Treaty with America, 1778." *American Historical Review*, Vol. XX (April 1916).

————. "French Aid Before the Alliance of 1778." *American Historical Review*, Vol. XXXI.

Waldegrave, James, Second Earl. *Memoirs from 1754 to 1758*. London: John Murray, 1821.

Warren, Mercy Otis. *History of the Rise, Progress and Termination of the American Revolution*. Boston: Manning and Loring, 1805.

Watson, J. Steven. *The Reign of George III*. Oxford: The Clarendon Press, 1960.

Wharton, Francis, ed. *The Revolutionary Diplomatic Correspondence of the United States*. 6 vols. Washington, D.C.: U. S. Government Printing Office, 1889.

Whitridge, Arnold. *Rochambeau: America's Neglected Founding Father*. New York: Collier Books, 1974.

Wickwire, Franklin and Mary. *Cornwallis, The American Adventure*. Boston: Houghton Mifflin Company, 1970.

Wilkes, John. *The North Briton*. Nos. 1 and 45. Worcester, Mass.: Collections, American Antiquarian Society.

Wilkinson, General James. *Memoirs of My Own Times*. Philadelphia: Abraham Small, 1816.

Willcox, William B., ed. *The American Rebellion. Sir Henry Clinton's Narrative of his Campaigns 1775–1782*. New Haven: Yale University Press, 1954.

Willis, William, ed. *Collections of the Maine Historical Society*, 1st Series, Vol. I. Portland: Bailey and Noyes, 1865.

Wirt, William. *Sketch of the Life and Character of Patrick Henry*. Philadelphia, 1817.

Wraxall, Sir N. William, Bart. *Historical Memoirs of My Own Time*. 3rd ed. 2 vols. London, 1818.

Wright, Louis B. *The Cultural Life of the American Colonies 1607–1763*. London: Hamish Hamilton, 1957.

Yerxa, Donald A. "The Burning of Falmouth, 1775: A Case Study in British Imperial Pacification." *Maine Historical Quarterly*, Vol. XIV, No. 3 (Winter 1975).

Zobel, Hiller B. *The Boston Massacre*. New York: W. W. Norton and Company, 1970.

INDEX

Abenaki Indians, 213, 376
Abercrombie, Maj. Gen. James, 177, 295
Acland, Lady Harriet, 282
Acland, Maj. John, 282, 376, 377
Acts of Navigation, 31, 151
Acts of Trade, 14–15, 16, 79
Adams, Abigail, 132, 133–34, 137, 181, 182, 187–88, 210, 291
Adams, John, 10–12, 32, 45, 60, 65, 69, 72, 73, 78, 80–83, 86, 98, 126, 151, 159, 180–82, 187–88, 209–10, 214–15, 239, 263, 265, 283–84, 310, 315, 352, 353, 355, 393–94, 416–17, 436, 439, 630, 640: Declaration of Independence, 287, 289–90, 291, 293–94; election of (1770), 75; First Continental Congress, 188–19, 131–38; on George III, 7; "Oration" notes (1772), 77; in Paris, 483, 490, 526, 527, 559, 565–66; political astuteness of, 210; Preston case, 75; snubbed by Dickinson, 210; on Washington, 401–2; on Writs of Assistance, 14, 15–16
Adams, Samuel, 11, 32, 51, 57, 98, 108–9, 114, 122, 123, 126, 151, 159, 170, 204, 239, 265–66, 344, 400, 439, 503, 526, 527, 554, 555, 567, 614; agitation for separation from England, 70, 72–73, 75–86; First Continental Congress, 118–19, 129–30, 132, 134, 136, 143; political astuteness of, 77; Sons of Liberty membership, 82; Stamp Act and, 35, 38–39, 40, 41, 45–46; Townshend Acts and, 54, 55, 58, 59, 60, 63, 64–65, 68
Administration of Justice Act, 102
Aiguillon, Duc d', 110
Alabama, 29
Albany, N.Y., 191, 284, 286, 296, 324, 366, 410, 460, 533; British campaign (1777) and, 363, 367, 369, 371, 372, 379, 389, 395, 400, 403, 411, 418, 424, 431
Alden, Col. Ichabod, 533
Alembert, Jean Le Rond d', 581
Alexander, Lady Kitty, 494
Alexander, Brig. Gen. William. See Stirling, Lord
Alexandria, Va., 117
Algonquin Indians, 376
Allen, Andrew, 344–45, 448
Allen, Col. Ethan, 177–78, 208, 237, 239
Allen, William, 344–45, 448
Allentown, Pa., 506
Alliance (frigate), 559–61
Almacks, 90
Almodóvar, Marquis, 544
Alva, Duke of, 552
Amboise, Chevalier d', 220

Amélie (ship), 337
American Revolution, 175–674; beginning of, 157–71; decision for, 127–42; events leading to, 3–171; southern theater of operations (1780–81), 586–97, 608–13, 614, 616, 621–27, 631–37, 640–53, 654–56; in the west (trans-Appalachia), 510–12. See also British Army; Continental Army; Hessians; names of battles
Amherst, Gen. Sir Jeffrey, 28, 177, 195, 218, 469, 570–71
Amity and Commerce, Treaty of, 471–72
Amphitrite (ship), 337
Anburey, Thomas, 378
André, Maj. John, 241, 437, 542, 600–7; trial and execution of, 605–7
Annapolis, Md., 39, 116–17, 182, 207, 208
Annual Register, The, 220, 251, 284
Anomine (frigate), 397
Apollo (ship), 375
Appleton, Rev. Nathaniel, 45, 144
Apsley, Baron, 76
Aquidneck Island, 516, 517, 519
Aranda, Count Pedro d', 472
Aranjuez, Treaty of (1779), 545
Arbuthnot, Vice-adm. Mariot, 567–68, 569, 587, 596, 597, 604, 615, 616, 617, 631, 632–33, 642–43, 647
Archer, Lt. Benjamin, 615
Armand, Lt. Col., 594
Armstrong, John, 494–95
Arnold, Benedict, 177–78, 243, 354–55, 358, 456, 460; army appointment of, 178, 393; campaign of 1777 and, 393, 399, 408, 410, 421–23, 426; Canada expedition, 208, 242–51, 280, 284, 423; Council of War (May 1778), 494–95; court-martial of, 577–78; financial dealings of, 541; Freeman's Farm battle, 422; at Lake Champlain, 213–14, 322–24; marriage of, 542; New London raid, 659; Philadelphia command, 505, 540–42; promoted to major general, 359; treason of, 600–7, 614; Valcour Bay defeat, 323, 324, 381; in Virginia, 616, 627, 631, 632, 642, 648, 659
Arnold, Mrs. Benedict, 541, 542, 604, 605
Arnold Expedition Historical Society, 245
Articles of Confederation, 309, 525–26
Assunpink Creek, 341
Attucks, Crispus, 71
Auditor, 19
Augusta (ship), 449
Augusta, Dowager Princess of Wales, 4, 6, 17, 33
Augusta, Ga., 535–36, 569, 590, 621, 654, 655

PHOTO CREDITS